D1229883

Index of American Periodical Verse: 1972

by

Sander W. Zulauf

and

Irwin H. Weiser

The Scarecrow Press, Inc.
Metuchen, N.J. 1974

Library of Congress Catalog Card No. 73-3060

ISBN 0-8108-0698-3

CONTENTS

PREFACE

This second Index of American Periodical Verse lists the poetry published in 163 periodicals in the United States in 1972. It is designed in three parts. The main, or central, part alphabetically lists poets and translators in serial number order. Individual poems are listed alphabetically under the name of the poet. Each entry begins with the title or first line of the poem; the name of the translator or translated poet if the poem is a translation; the symbol of the periodical containing the poem; the volume and number in parentheses [(2:1) signifies volume 2, number 1]; the date of the issue; and finally the page on which the poem appears (if the pages were numbered).

A key to the periodical symbols appears at the front of the Index, along with editorial addresses and subscription information so that the reader can subscribe, order a sample copy or back issue, or submit manuscripts.

The index of titles (or first lines) of poems completes the work; each title is followed by the entry number of the poet, under which the published poem can be located.

Once again a wide variety of publications has been indexed. Several periodicals included in 1971 have been dropped and new periodicals have been added, with an increase of nearly 400 poet entries. We wish to thank the editors of the magazines indexed here who had poetic faith, willingly suspended their disbelief, and generously supplied us with their publications.

Bloomington, Indiana — S. W. Z.
July 23, 1973 — I. H. W.

ABBREVIATIONS

arr.	-	arranged
Back:	-	back-issue copy price
(indiv.)	-	price for individuals
(inst.)	-	price for institutions
(lib.)	-	price for libraries
Sing:	-	single copy price
(stud.)	-	price for students
Subs:	-	subscriptions (address or price)
tr.	-	translation
(19)	-	number 19
(7:2)	-	volume 7, number 2
U	-	University
w.	-	with

Months:

Ja	-	January
F	-	February
Mr	-	March
Ap	-	April
My	-	May
Je	-	June
Jl	-	July
Ag	-	August
S	-	September
O	-	October
N	-	November
D	-	December

Seasons:

Aut, Fall	-	Autumn
Wint	-	Winter
Spr	-	Spring
Sum	-	Summer

PERIODICALS INDEXED

AAUP
AAUP BULLETIN
Lawrence S. Poston, III, ed.
Dept. of English
U of Nebraska
Lincoln, Neb. 68508
Subs:
Suite 500
One Dupont Circle, N. W.
Washington, D. C. 20036
(58:1-4)
Subs: $10/yr
Sing: $3

AbGR
THE ABOVE GROUND REVIEW
George Roland Wood, ed.
Box 337
Arden, N. C. 28704
(3:1)
Subs: $2.90/yr
Sing: $1

AmerR
THE AMERICAN REVIEW
Richard Howard, poetry ed.
666 Fifth Avenue
New York, N. Y. 10019
Subs: Dept. AR-1
Bantam Books, Inc.
666 Fifth Avenue
New York, N. Y. 10019
(14-15)
Subs: $5.95/yr
Sing: $1.95

AmerS
THE AMERICAN SCHOLAR
Hiram Haydn, ed.
1811 Q St., N. W.
Washington, D. C. 20009
(41:1-4)
Subs: $5/yr
Sing: $1.75

Antaeus
ANTAEUS
Daniel Halpern, ed.
G. P. O. Box 3121
New York, N. Y. 10001
(5-7)
Subs: $8/yr
Sing: $2

AntR
ANTIOCH REVIEW
Laurence Grauman, Jr., ed.
Box 148
Yellow Springs, Ohio 45387
(31:4) (32:1/2)
Subs: $6/yr
Sing: $1.75

Aphra
APHRA
Box 273 Village Sta.
New York, N. Y. 10014
(3:1-4)
Subs: $4.50/yr
Sing: $1.25

Apple
APPLE
David Curry, ed.
Box 2271
Springfield, Ill. 62705
(7)
Subs: $4
Sing: $1

AriD
ARION'S DOLPHIN
Stratis Haviaras, ed.
Box 313
Cambridge, Mass. 02138
(1:2-5)
Subs: $4
Sing: $1

ArizQ
ARIZONA QUARTERLY
Albert F. Gegenheimer, ed.
U of Arizona
Tucson, Ariz. 85721
(28:1-4)
Subs: $2/yr
Sing: $ .50

AS
ARTS IN SOCIETY
Edward Kamarck, ed.
U of Wisconsin--Extension
610 Langdon St.
Madison, Wis. 53703
(9:1-3)
Subs: $5.50/yr
Sing: $2

Atl
THE ATLANTIC
8 Arlington St.
Boston, Mass. 02116
Subs: Subscription Dept.
125 Garden St.
Marion, Ohio 43302
(229:1-6) (230:1-6)
Subs: $10.50
Sing: $1

BabyJ
BABY JOHN
RFD 3
Gorham, Maine 04038
(5)
Subs: $3/4
Sing: $ .50

BallSUF
BALL STATE UNIVERSITY FORUM
Ball State U
Muncie, Ind. 47306
(13:1-4)
Subs: $5/yr
Sing: $1.50

BelPoJ
THE BELOIT POETRY JOURNAL
Box 2
Beloit, Wis. 53511
(22:3-4) (23:1-2)
Subs: $3
Sing: $ .75

BerksR
BERKSHIRE REVIEW
Thompson Physical Laboratory
Williams College
Williamstown, Mass. 01267
(8:1-2)
Subs: $1
Sing: $ .50

BeyB
BEYOND BAROQUE
George Drury Smith, ed.
Bayrock Press
1639 W. Washington Blvd.
Venice, Calif. 90291
(2:2) (3:1)
Subs: $3.50/2
Sing: $1.95

Books
BOOKS ABROAD
U of Oklahoma
1000 Asp Ave. Room 214
Norman, Okla. 73069
(46:1-4)
Subs: $15/yr (lib.)
$ 8/yr (indiv.)
Sing: $ 2.50

BosUJ
BOSTON UNIVERSITY JOURNAL
Box 357
Boston U Sta.
Boston, Mass. 02215
(20:1-3)
Subs: $5.50/yr
Sing: $1.95

Broad
BROADSIDE SERIES
Dudley Randall, ed.
Broadside Press
12651 Old Mill Place
Detroit, Mich. 48238
(55-62; 65; 66)
Subs: ltd. eds.--prices on request
Sing: $ .50

Cafe
CAFE SOLO
Glenna Luschei, ed.
The Solo Press
1209 Drake Circle

San Luis Obispo, Calif. 93401
(4)
Subs: $2.50
Sing: $1.50

CalQ
CALIFORNIA QUARTERLY
Alan Wald, ed.
100 Sproul Hall
U of California
Davis, Calif. 95616
(2-3)
Subs: $5
Sing: $1.50

CarlMis
CARLETON MISCELLANY
Carleton College
Northfield, Minn. 55057
(12:1-2)
Subs: $3
Sing: $1.50

CarolQ
CAROLINA QUARTERLY
Rosanne Coggeshall, poetry ed.
Box 1117
Chapel Hill, N.C. 27514
(24:1-3)
Subs: $4/yr

CEACritic
CEA CRITIC
Earle Labor, ed.
Centenary College of Louisiana
Box 4188
Shreveport, La. 71104
Subs: Donald R. Swanson
Wright State U
Dayton, Ohio 45431
(34:2-4) (35:1)
Subs: $8/yr

ChiR
CHICAGO REVIEW
U of Chicago
5757 S. Drexel Ave.
Chicago, Ill. 60637
(23:3-4) (24:1-2)
Subs: $5/yr
Sing: $1.50

ChiTM
CHICAGO TRIBUNE MAGAZINE
Marcia Lee Masters, ed.
"Today's Poets"
435 N. Michigan Ave.
Chicago, Ill. 60611

ChrC
THE CHRISTIAN CENTURY
Alan Geyer, ed.
407 S. Dearborn St.
Chicago, Ill. 60605
(89:1-47)
Subs: $12/yr
Sing: $ .40

Cim
CIMARRON REVIEW
Oklahoma State U
Stillwater, Okla. 74074
(18-21)
Subs: $6
Sing: $2
Back: $1

ColEng
COLLEGE ENGLISH
Richard Ohmann, ed.
Wesleyan U
Middletown, Conn. 06457
Subs: Nat'l Council of Teachers of English
1111 Kenyon Road
Urbana, Ill. 61801
(33:4-8) (34:1-3)
Subs: $12/yr
Sing: $1.50

ColQ
THE COLORADO QUARTERLY
Paul J. Carter, ed.
Hellems 134
U of Colorado
Boulder, Colorado 80302
(20:3-4) (21:1-2)
Subs: $4/yr
Sing: $1

ColumF
THE COLUMBIA FORUM
612 West 114th St.
New York, N.Y. 10025

Subs: Alumni Records Center
632 West 125th St.
New York, N. Y. 10027
(1:2-4)
Subs: $6.50/yr
Sing: $1.75
Back: $3

Comm
COMMONWEAL
James O'Gara, ed.
232 Madison Ave.
New York, N. Y. 10016
(95:14-22) (96:1-21) (97:1-12)
Subs: $12/yr
Sing: $ .40

ConcPo
CONCERNING POETRY
Dept. of English
Western Washington State College
Bellingham, Wash. 98225
(5:1-2)
Subs: $3/yr
Sing: $1.50

Confr
CONFRONTATION
Martin Tucker, ed.
English Dept.
The Brooklyn Center, Long Island U
Brooklyn, N. Y. 11201
(5)
Sing: $ .50

Conrad
CONRADIANA
Box 4229
Texas Tech U
Lubbock, Texas 79409
(3:2-3) (4:1)
Subs: $4/yr
Sing: $2

Cord
CORDUROY
406 Highland Ave.
Newark, N.J. 07104
(1:3-4)
Subs: $2.50/3
Sing: $1

Cosmo
COSMOPOLITAN
224 West 57th St.
New York, N. Y. 10019
Subs: 250 W. 55th St.
New York, N. Y. 10019
(172:1-6) (173:1-6)
Subs: $9/yr
Sing: $1

DenQuart
DENVER QUARTERLY
Burton Feldman, ed.
U of Denver
Denver, Colorado 80210
(6:4) (7:1-3)
Subs: $4/yr
Sing: $1.25

Drag
DRAGONFLY
Duane Ackerson, ed.
Box 147
Idaho State U
Pocatello, Idaho 83201
(3:1-4)
Subs: $3.50/4
Sing: $1

EngJ
ENGLISH JOURNAL
Richard S. Alm, ed.
College of Education
U of Hawaii
1776 University Ave.
Honolulu, Hawaii 96822
Subs: Nat'l Council of Teachers of English
1111 Kenyon Road
Urbana, Ill. 61801
(61:1-9)
Subs: $12
Sing: $1.50

Epoch
EPOCH
Gary French, poetry ed.
245 Goldwin Smith Hall
Cornell U
Ithaca, N. Y. 14850
(21:2/3) (22:1)
Subs: $3/yr
Sing: $1

Epos
EPOS
Evelyn Thorne, ed.
Rollins College
Crescent City, Fla. 32012
(23:3-4) (24:1)
Subs: $3/yr
Sing: $1

Esq
ESQUIRE
Rachel Crespin, poetry ed.
488 Madison Ave.
New York, N.Y. 10022
Subs: Subscription Dept.
Portland Place
Boulder, Colo. 80302
(77:1-6) (78:1-6)
Subs: $10/yr
Sing: $1

Etc.
ETC.
Elizabeth Bartlett, poetry ed.
Constitución 14
Cuauhtomec, Colima, Mexico
Subs: Internat'l Soc. for General Semantics
Box 2469
San Francisco, Calif. 94126
(29:1-4)
Subs: $6/yr
Sing: $1.50

EverR
EVERGREEN REVIEW
Barney Rosset, ed.
53 E. 11th St.
New York, N.Y. 10003
(16:95)
Subs: $5/yr
Sing: $1.50

ExpR
THE EXPATRIATE REVIEW
Box D
Staten Island, N.Y. 10301
(2-3)
Subs: $2.50/2
Sing: $1.25

Field
FIELD
David Young, ed.
Rice Hall
Oberlin College
Oberlin, Ohio 44074
(6-7)
Subs: $3/yr
Sing: $1.50

Focus
FOCUS/MIDWEST
Charles L. Klotzer, ed.
Box 3086
St. Louis, Mo. 63130
(8:56) (9:57)
Subs: $4/yr
Sing: $ .85

Folio
FOLIO
Adele Sophie de la Barre, ed.
Box 3-1111
Birmingham, Ala. 35222
(8:1-2)
Subs: $3/2
Sing: $1.70

FourQt
FOUR QUARTERS
La Salle College
Philadelphia, Pa. 19141
(21:2-4)
Subs: $2
Sing: $ .50

FreeL
FREE LANCE
6005 Grand Ave.
Cleveland, Ohio 44104
(15:1/2)
Subs: $2/2
Sing: $1

GeoR
THE GEORGIA REVIEW
U of Georgia
Athens, Ga. 30601
(25:1-4)
Subs: $3/yr
Sing: $1

Granite
GRANITE
George M. Young, Jr., ed.
Box 774
Hanover, N.H. 03755
(2)
Subs: $5/3
Sing: $2

GreenR
THE GREENFIELD REVIEW
Joseph Bruchac, III, ed.
Greenfield Center, N.Y. 12833
(2:2-3)
Subs: $4/4
Sing: $1

HangL
HANGING LOOSE
301 Hicks St.
Brooklyn, N.Y. 11201
(16-18)
Subs: $3.50/yr
Sing: $1

Harp
HARPER'S
2 Park Ave.
New York, N.Y. 10016
Subs: 381 W. Center St.
Marion, Ohio 43302
(244:1460-1465) (245:1466-1471)
Subs: $8.50
Sing: $1

Hiero
HIEROPHANT
Thomas Kerrigan, ed.
3017 Willow Glen Rd.
Los Angeles, Calif. 90046
(7)
Ceased publication

HiramPoR
HIRAM POETRY REVIEW
Hale Chatfield, ed.
Box 162
Hiram, Ohio 44234
(12-13)
Subs: $2/yr
Sing: $1

HolCrit
THE HOLLINS CRITIC
John Reese Moore, ed.
Box 9538
Hollins College, Va. 24020
(9:1-4)
Subs: $2/yr
Back: $ .45

Horizon
HORIZON
Charles L. Mee, Jr., ed.
1221 Ave. of the Americas
New York, N.Y. 10020
Subs: 379 W. Center St.
Marion, Ohio 43302
(14:1-4)
Subs: $20/yr
Sing: $6

Hudson
THE HUDSON REVIEW
Frederick Morgan, ed.
65 E. 55th St.
New York, N.Y. 10022
(25:1-4)
Subs: $7/yr
Sing: $2

Humanist
HUMANIST
Paul Kurtz, ed.
SUNY at Buffalo
4244 Ridge Lea Rd.
Amherst, N.Y. 14226
Subs: 923 Kensington Ave.
Buffalo, N.Y. 14215
(32:1-6)
Subs: $6/yr
Sing: $1

Indian
THE INDIAN HISTORIAN
1451 Masonic Ave.
San Francisco, Calif. 94117
(5:1-4)
Subs: $6/yr
Sing: $1.40

Iowa
IOWA REVIEW
Merle E. Brown, ed.

EPB 453
U of Iowa
Iowa City, Iowa 52240
Subs: Dept. of Publications
U of Iowa
Iowa City, Iowa 52240
(3:1-4)
Subs: $6/yr
Sing: $1.50

Iron
IRONWOOD
Michael Cuddihy, ed.
Box 49023
Tucson, Ariz. 85717
(1-2)
Subs: $3/yr
Sing: $2

Isthmus
ISTHMUS
J. Rutherford Williams, ed.
2514 Milvia St.
Berkeley, Calif. 94704
(1)
Subs: $4/yr
Sing: $2

JnlOBP
THE JOURNAL OF BLACK POETRY
Jon Goncalves, ed.
922-B Haight St.
San Francisco, Calif. 94117
(2:16)
Subs: $5/yr
Sing: $1.25

JnlOPC
JOURNAL OF POPULAR CULTURE
University Hall
Bowling Green U
Bowling Green, Ohio 43403
(5:4) (6:1-3)
Subs: $10/yr
$ 5/yr (stud.)
Sing: $ 3

KanQ
KANSAS QUARTERLY
Harold Schneider,
W.R. Moses, eds.
Dept. of English
Kansas State U
Manhattan, Kansas 66502
(4:1-4)
Subs: $7.50/yr
Sing: $2

Kayak
KAYAK
George Hitchcock, ed.
3965 Bonny Doon Rd.
Santa Cruz, Calif. 95060
(28-30)
Subs: $3/4
Sing: $1

LadHJ
LADIES' HOME JOURNAL
641 Lexington Ave.
New York, N.Y. 10022
(89:1-12)
Subs: $5.94/yr
Sing: $ .50

Lilla
LILLABULERO
Russell Banks
William Matthews, poetry ed.
Krums Corners Rd.
R.D. 3
Ithaca, N.Y. 14850
Subs: Lillabulero Press
Northwood Narrows, N.H. 03261
(12)
Prices on request

LitR
THE LITERARY REVIEW
Charles Angoff, ed.
Fairleigh Dickinson U
Rutherford, N.J. 07070
Subs: Circulation Office
Rutherford, N.J. 07070
(15:3-4) (16:1-2)
Subs: $7/yr
Sing: $2

Literature
LITERATURE EAST & WEST
Roy E. Telle, ed.
Box 8107 University Sta.
Austin, Texas 78712

(15:3)
Subs: $8/vol.
Sing: $2

LittleM
THE LITTLE MAGAZINE
David G. Hartwell, ed.
Box 207 Cathedral Sta.
New York, N. Y. 10025
(6:1-2/3)
Subs: $4/yr
Sing: $1

Madem
MADEMOISELLE
420 Lexington Ave.
New York, N. Y. 10017
Subs: Box 5204
Boulder, Colo. 80302
(74:3-6) (75:1-6) (76:1-2)
Subs: $7/yr
Sing: $ .75

Madrona
MADRONA
J. K. Osborne,
V. Zambaris, eds.
502 12th Ave. E.
Seattle, Wash. 98102
(1:1-4)
Subs: $5/yr
Back: $10/vol. 1, bd.

Magazine
MAGAZINE
Kirby Congdon, ed.
Interim Books
Box 35
New York, N. Y. 10014
(5)
Subs: irregular
Sing: $10/vol. 5

Mark
MARK TWAIN JOURNAL
Cyril Clemens, ed.
Kirkwood, Mo. 63122
(16:2-3)
Subs: $3
Sing: $1

MassR
THE MASSACHUSETTS REVIEW
Jules Chametzky,
Robert Tucker, eds.
Memorial Hall
U of Massachusetts
Amherst, Mass. 01002
(13:1/2-4)
Subs: $7/yr
Sing: $2

Meas
MEASURE
Howard McCord, ed.
Dept. of English
Bowling Green State U
Bowling Green, Ohio 43403
(1-4)
Subs: $3/yr
Sing: $1.50

MedR
THE MEDITERRANEAN REVIEW
Robert De Maria,
Ellen Hope Meyer, eds.
Orient, New York 11957
(2:2-4)
Subs: $5/yr
Sing: $1.50

MichQR
MICHIGAN QUARTERLY REVIEW
Radcliffe Squires, ed.
3032 Rackham Bldg.
U of Michigan
Ann Arbor, Mich. 48104
(11:1-4)
Subs: $6/yr
Sing: $1.50
Back: $2

MidwQ
THE MIDWEST QUARTERLY
Rebecca Patterson, ed.
Michael Heffernan, poetry ed.
Kansas State College
of Pittsburg
Pittsburg, Kan. 66762
(12:2-4) (13:1)
Subs: $2.50/yr
Sing: $1

MinnR
THE MINNESOTA REVIEW
Roger Mitchell, ed.
Box 5416
Milwaukee, Wis.
53211
(2-3)
Subs: $2.50/yr
Sing: $1.50

ModernO
MODERN OCCASIONS
Philip Rahv, ed.
Sydeman Hall
Box 2073
Brandeis U
Waltham, Mass. 02154
(2:1-2)
Subs: $7/yr
Sing: $1.95

ModernPS
MODERN POETRY STUDIES
147 Capen Blvd.
Buffalo, N.Y. 14226
(2:6) (3:1-4)
Subs: $6/yr
Sing: $2

Mund
MUNDUS ARTIUM
Rainer Schulte, ed.
English Dept.
Ohio U
Athens, Ohio 45701
(5:1/2-3)
Subs: $6/yr
Sing: $3.50

Nat
THE NATION
Grace Schulman, poetry ed.
333 Sixth Ave.
New York, N.Y. 10014
(214:1-26) (215:1-20)
Subs: $15/yr
Sing: $ .50
Back: $ .50

NegroHB
NEGRO HISTORY BULLETIN
J. Rupert Picott, ed.
1407 14th St., N.W.
Washington, D.C. 20005
(35:1-8)
Subs: $3.50/yr
Sing: $1

New:ACP
NEW: American and Canadian Poetry
John Gill, ed.
Crossing Press
RD 3
Trumansburg, N.Y. 14886
(18-19)
Subs: $2.75/yr
Sing: $1
Back: $3

NewL
NEW LETTERS
David Ray, ed.
U of Missouri--Kansas City
Kansas City, Mo. 64110
(38:3-4) (39:1-2)
Subs: $6
Sing: $1.50

NewRena
THE NEW RENAISSANCE
Louise T. Reynolds, ed.
Olivera Sajkovic, poetry ed.
9 Heath Rd.
Arlington, Mass. 02174
(6)
Subs: $5.50/yr
Sing: $1.50
Back: $1.60

NewRep
NEW REPUBLIC
Reed Whittemore, lit. ed.
1244 19th St., N.W.
Washington, D.C. 20036
Subs: Subscription Dept.
381 W. Center St.
Marion, Ohio 43302
(166:1/2-26) (167:1-24/25)
Subs: $15/yr
Sing: $ .50

NewWR
NEW WORLD REVIEW
Jessica Smith, ed.
Suite 308

156 Fifth Ave.
New York, N.Y. 10010
(40:1-4)
Subs: $4/yr
Sing: $1.25

NewYQ
NEW YORK QUARTERLY
William Packard, ed.
Room 603
Columbia University Club
4 West 43rd St.
New York, N.Y. 10036
(9-12)
Subs: $7/yr
Sing: $2
Back: $2

NewYRB
NEW YORK REVIEW OF BOOKS
Robert B. Silvers,
Barbara Epstein, eds.
250 W. 57th St.
New York, N.Y. 10019
Subs: Box 1162,
Ansonia Sta.
New York, N.Y. 10023
(17:12) (18:1-12) (19:1-10)
Subs: $10/yr
Sing: $.60

NYT
THE NEW YORK TIMES
Thomas Lask, poetry ed.
229 W. 43rd St.
New York, N.Y. 10036

NewYorker
THE NEW YORKER
Howard Moss, poetry ed.
25 W. 43rd St.
New York, N.Y. 10036
(47:46-53) (48:1-45)
Subs: $15/yr
Sing: $.50

NoAmR
NORTH AMERICAN REVIEW
Robley Wilson, Jr., ed.
Peter Cooley, poetry ed.
U of Northern Iowa
1222 W. 27th St.
Cedar Falls, Iowa 50613
(257:1-4)
Subs: $6/yr
Sing: $1.50

NoCaFo
NORTH CAROLINA FOLKLORE
Leonidas Betts, Guy Owen, eds.
Dept. of English
North Carolina State U
Raleigh, N.C. 27607
Subs: Box 5308
Raleigh, N.C. 27607
(20:1-4)
Subs: $2/yr
$1/yr (stud.)

Northeast
NORTHEAST
John Judson, ed.
1310 Shorewood Drive
LaCrosse, Wis. 54601
Aut-Wint 71-72; Sum 72
Subs: $6/yr
Sing: $1.50

NowestR
NORTHWEST REVIEW
John Haislip, ed.
U of Oregon
Eugene, Oregon 97403
(12:2-3)
Subs: $4/yr
Sing: $1.50

OhioR
OHIO REVIEW
Wayne Dodd, ed.
Stanley Plumly, poetry ed.
Ellis Hall
Ohio University
Athens, Ohio 45701
(13:2-3) (14:1)
Subs: $5/yr
Sing: $2

Pan
PANACHE
R.B. Frank
Box 89
Princeton, N.J. 08540
D.R. Lenson, poetry ed.
91 Sugarloaf St.
South Deerfield, Mass. 01373

(9)
Sing: $1

ParisR
THE PARIS REVIEW
Tom Clark, poetry ed.
45-39 171 Place
Flushing, N. Y. 11358
(53-55)
Subs: $4/4
Sing: $1.25

PartR
PARTISAN REVIEW
William Phillips, ed.
Rutgers U
New Brunswick, N. J. 08903
(39:1-4)
Subs: $5.50/yr
Sing: $1.50

Peb
PEBBLE
Greg Kuzma, ed.
118 S. Boswell Ave.
Crete, Neb. 68333
(6-9)
Subs: $4/4
Sing: $1
Back: $2

Perspec
PERSPECTIVE
Austin Warren, advisory ed.
Washington U
Box 1122
St. Louis, Mo. 63130
(17:1)
Subs: $4/yr
Sing: $1

Phoenix
PHOENIX
James Cooney, ed.
Morning Star Press
RFD
Haydenville, Mass. 01039
(3:4)
Subs: $8/yr
Sing: $2.50

Phy
PHYLON
John D. Reid, ed.
Atlanta U
Atlanta, Ga. 30314
(33:1-4)
Subs: $4.50/yr
Sing: $1.50

Playb
PLAYBOY
Playboy Bldg.
919 N. Michigan Ave.
Chicago, Ill. 60611
(19:1-12)
Subs: $10/yr
Sing: varies

Poem
POEM
Robert L. Welker, ed.
Box 1247, West Sta.
Huntsville, Ala. 35807
(14-16)
Subs: $3.50/yr

PoetC
POET AND CRITIC
Richard Gustafson, ed.
210 Pearson Hall
Iowa State U
Ames, Iowa 50010
Subs: Iowa State U Press
Press Bldg.
Ames, Iowa 50010
(7:1)
Subs: $3/yr
Sing: $1

PoetL
POET LORE
John Williams Andrews, ed.
Box 688
Westport, Conn. 06880
(67:1-4)
Subs: $8/yr
Sing: $2
Back: $3

Poetry
POETRY
Daryl Hine, ed.

1228 N. Dearborn Pkwy
Chicago, Ill. 60610
(119:4-6) (120:1-6) (121:1-3)
Subs: $12/yr
Sing: $1.25

PoetryNW
POETRY NORTHWEST
David Wagoner, ed.
Parrington Hall
U of Washington
Seattle, Wash. 98195
(13:1-4)
Subs: $4.50/yr
Sing: $1.25

PraS
PRAIRIE SCHOONER
Bernice Slote, ed.
Nebraska Hall
U of Nebraska
901 N. 17th St.
Lincoln, Neb. 68508
(46:1-4)
Subs: $4.50/yr
Sing: $1.50

QRL
QUARTERLY REVIEW OF LITERATURE
T. Weiss, Renée Weiss, eds.
26 Haslet Ave.
Princeton, N.J. 08540
(18:1/2)
Subs: $5
Sing: $2.50

Qt
QUARTET
Richard H. Costa, ed.
Joseph Colin Murphey, poetry ed.
1119 Neal Pickett Dr.
College Station, Texas 77840
(5:37-39/40)
Subs: $4/yr
Sing: $1

Ramp
RAMPARTS
Noah's Ark, Inc.
2054 University Ave.
Berkeley, Calif. 94704
(10:7-12) (11:1-6)
Subs: $9.50/yr
Sing: $1

Rend
RENDEZVOUS
Idaho State U
Campus P.O. Box 267
Pocatello, Idaho 83201
(7:1-2)
Subs: $2.50/yr
Sing: $1.50

RoadAR
ROAD APPLE REVIEW
Brian Salchert, ed.
334 Linden
Fond du Lac, Wisc. 54935
(3:4) (4:1-3)
Subs: $3/4
Sing: varies

RusLT
RUSSIAN LITERATURE TRI-QUARTERLY
Carl and Ellendea Proffer, eds.
Ardis Publishers
615 Watersedge Dr.
Ann Arbor, Mich. 48105
(2-4)
Subs: $19/yr (inst.)
$15/yr (indiv.)
$12/yr (stud.)
Sing: varies

St. AR
ST. ANDREWS REVIEW
Charles W. Joyner, ed.
Jeffrey T. Gross, poetry ed.
St. Andrews Presbyterian College
Laurinburg, N.C. 28352
(1:4) (2:1)
Subs: $3.50/yr
Sing: $2

Salm
SALMAGUNDI
Robert Boyers, ed.
Skidmore College
Saratoga Springs, N.Y. 12866
(18-20)
Subs: $6/yr.
Sing: $1.50
Back: $2.50

SaltCR
THE NEW SALT CREEK READER
Ted Kooser, ed.
Windflower Press
1720 1/2 C St.
Lincoln, Neb. 68502
(5:1)
Subs: $3.50/4
Sing: $1

SatireN
SATIRE NEWSLETTER
Richard Frost, poetry ed.
SUNY College
Oneonta, N.Y. 13280
(9:2)
Subs: $3/yr
Sing: $1.50

SatEP
THE SATURDAY EVENING POST
Beurt SerVaas, ed.
1100 Waterway Blvd.
Indianapolis, Ind. 46202
(244:1-3)
Subs: $6/yr
Sing: $1

SatR
SATURDAY REVIEW OF THE ARTS
(Ceased publication; merged to form Saturday Review/World.)

SenR
SENECA REVIEW
James Crenner, Ira Sadoff, eds.
Box 115
Hobart and William Smith Colleges
Geneva, N.Y. 14456
(3:1)
Subs: $2/yr
Sing: $1.25

SewanR
SEWANEE REVIEW
Andrew Lytle, ed.
U of the South
Sewanee, Tenn. 37375
(80:1-4)
Subs: $7/yr
Sing: $2
Back: $3

Shen
SHENANDOAH
James Boatwright, ed.
Dabney Stuart, poetry ed.
Washington and Lee U
Box 722
Lexington, Va. 24450
(23:2-4) (24:1)
Subs: $4/yr
Sing: $1.25

Sky
SKYWRITING
Martin Grossman,
Scott Walker, eds.
2917 Madison Box 5408
Eugene, Oregon 97405
(1:2)
Subs: $3/3
Sing: $1.25

SoCaR
SOUTH CAROLINA REVIEW
Alfred S. Reid, ed.
Dept. of English
Box 28661
Furman U
Greenville, S.C. 29613
(4:2) (5:1)
Subs: $2/yr
Sing: $1

SoDakR
SOUTH DAKOTA REVIEW
John R. Milton, ed.
U of South Dakota
Box 1111 University Exchange
Vermillion, S.D. 57069
(10:1-4)
Subs: $4/yr
Sing: $1.25

SouthernHR
SOUTHERN HUMANITIES REVIEW
Norman A. Brittin,
Eugene Current-Garcia, eds.
9088 Haley Center

Auburn U
Auburn, Ala. 36830
(6:1-4)
Subs: $4/yr
Sing: $1.25

SouthernPR
SOUTHERN POETRY REVIEW
Guy Owen, ed.
English Dept.
North Carolina State U
Raleigh, N.C. 27607
(12:2) (Special Issue) (13:11)
Subs: $3/yr
Sing: $1.50

SouthernR
SOUTHERN REVIEW
Donald E. Stanford,
Lewis P. Simpson, eds.
Drawer D
University Sta.
Baton Rouge, La. 70803
(8:1-4)
Subs: $5/yr
Sing: $1.50

SouthwR
SOUTHWEST REVIEW
Margaret L. Hartley, ed.
Southern Methodist U
Dallas, Texas 75222
(57:1-4)
Subs: $4/yr
Sing: $1

Spec
SPECTRUM
Sam Hamill, ed.
Box 14800
U of California
Santa Barbara, Calif. 93106
(14:1/2)
Subs: $2.50/yr
Sing: $1.50

Stand
STAND
Edward Brunner,
Robert Ober, Amer. eds.
409 Ronalds St.
Iowa City, Iowa 52240
(13:2-4) (14:1)
Subs: $3.50/yr
Sing: $ .95

StoneD
STONE DRUM
Joseph Colin Murphey
Box 2234
Sam Houston Sta.
Huntsville, Texas 77340
(1:1)
Subs: $3/yr
Sing: $1.50

TexQ
TEXAS QUARTERLY
Harry Ransom, ed.
Box 7517 University Sta.
Austin, Texas 78712
(15:1-4)
Subs: $4/yr
Sing: $1.50

Thought
THOUGHT
Joseph E. O'Neill, S.J., ed.
441 E. Fordham Rd.
Bronx, N.Y. 10458
(47:184-187)
Subs: $8/yr
Sing: $2.25

TransR
TRANSATLANTIC REVIEW
J.F. McCrindle, ed.
B.S. Johnson, poetry ed.
Box 3348 Grand Central Sta.
New York, N.Y. 10017
(41) (42/43)
Subs: $3/yr
Sing: $1

TriQ
TRIQUARTERLY
Charles Newman, ed.
University Hall 101
Northwestern U
Evanston, Ill. 60201
(23/24)
Subs: $7/yr
Sing: varies

UnicornJ
UNICORN JOURNAL
Teo Savory, ed.
Box 3307
Greensboro, N.C. 27402
(4)
Sing: $2
Back: $2

UTR
UT REVIEW
Duane Locke, ed.
U of Tampa
Tampa, Fla. 33606
(1:1-4)
Subs: $2.50/yr
Sing: $ .75

UnmOx
UNMUZZLED OX
Michael André, ed.
Box 374
Planetarium Sta.
New York, N.Y. 10024
(1:1-4)
Subs: $4/yr
Sing: $1

VilV
THE VILLAGE VOICE
80 University Place
New York, N.Y. 10003

VirQR
VIRGINIA QUARTERLY REVIEW
Charlotte Kohler, ed.
One W. Range
Charlottesville, Va. 22903
(48:1-4)
Subs: $5/yr
Sing: $1.50

WestHR
WESTERN HUMANITIES REVIEW
Jack Garlington, ed.
U of Utah
Salt Lake City, Utah 84112
(26:1-4)
Subs: $4/yr
Sing: $1

WestR
WESTERN REVIEW
Lewis A. Richards, ed.
Roger Murray, poetry ed.
Western New Mexico U
Silver City, N.M. 88061
(9:1-2) (10:1)
Ceased publication with (10:1).

Wind
WIND
Quentin R. Howard, ed.
RFD 1 Box 810
Pikeville, Ky. 41501
(2:5-6)
Subs: $3.50/yr
Sing: $1.25

WindO
THE WINDLESS ORCHARD
Robert Novak, ed.
Purdue U
Fort Wayne, Ind. 46805
(9-12)
Subs: $3.75/yr
Sing: $1

Works
WORKS
John Hopper, ed.
AMS Press, Inc.
56 E. 13th St.
New York, N.Y. 10003
(3:2-3/4)
Subs: $5/yr
Sing: $1.50

World
WORLD
Norman Cousins, ed.
488 Madison Ave.
New York, N.Y. 10022
(1:1-13)
Subs: $12/yr
Sing: $ .60
Back: $1

WorldO
WORLD ORDER
2011 Yale Sta.
New Haven, Conn. 06520
(6:2-4) (7-1)

Subs: 415 Linden Ave.
Wilmette, Ill. 60091
Subs: $4.50/yr
Sing: $1.25

WormR
WORMWOOD REVIEW
Marvin Malone, ed.
Box 8840
Stockton, Calif. 95204
(45-48)
Subs: $5.50/yr (inst.)
$3.50/yr (indiv.)
Sing: $1.50

YaleLit
THE YALE LIT
Box 243-A Yale Sta.
New Haven, Conn. 06520
(141:1-4/5)
Subs: $9/yr
Sing: $2

YaleR
THE YALE REVIEW
J.E. Palmer, ed.
399 Temple St.
New Haven, Conn. 06520
(61:3-4) (62:1-2)
Subs: $6/yr
Sing: $1.75

Zahir
ZAHIR
Diane Kruchkow, ed.
English Dept.
Hamilton-Smith
Durham, N.H. 03824
(1:4/5)
Subs: $2/yr
Sing: $1.50

INDEX OF POETS

01 AARNES, William
"Play Dead." PoetryNW (13:4) Wint 72-73, p. 19.

02 AARON, Jonathan
"Finding the Prone Landscape." NewYorker (48:35) 21 O 72, p. 40.

03 ABATZOPOULOU, Frangiski
from Reading: (I, II, VII, IX) (tr. by Stavros Deligiorgis). AriD (1:4/5) Sum-Aut 72, p. 13.

04 ABBOTT, Keith
"Red Lettuce." Madrona (1:3) My 72, p. 34.

05 ABDALLAH ibn Al-mu tazz
"Seven Poems" (tr. by Andras Hamori). Literature (15:3) 72, p. 495.

06 ABEL, Robert
"Fenner's Chickens." MidwQ (13:2) Wint 72, p. 133.

07 ABHAU, Elliot
"Res ipsa loquitur." AmerS (41:2) Spr 72, p. 274.

08 ABSE, Dannie
"The Bereaved." Poetry (120:3) Je 72, p. 158.
"Explanation of a News Item." Poetry (120:3) Je 72, p. 159.
"Forgotten." Poetry (120:3) Je 72, p. 160.
"An Old Commitment." Poetry (120:3) Je 72, p. 161.

09 ACKERMAN, Diane
"Anchor of Veins." Epoch (22:1) Fall 72, p. 39.
"Organism." Epoch (22:1) Fall 72, p. 38.
"Streetcar Named Proxima Centauri." Epoch (22:1) Fall 72, p. 39.

10 ACKERSON, Cathy
"First Day of Spring, 1972: Blister." Drag (3:2) Sum 72, p. 52.

11 ACKERSON, Duane
"Aunt Jean." SaltCR (5:1) Wint 72.

"Dark Marathon." Peb (7) Aut 71.
Four Poems. Peb (6) Sum 71.
"The Glass Blower." Sky (1:2) 72, p. 8.
"Great Uncle Wright's Fourth of July Family Bash." Drag (3:2) Sum 72, p. 54.
"How It Got Here." GreenR (2:2) 72, p. 9.
"In light of the latest news" (tr. of Carlos Drummond De Andrade, w. Ricardo Sternberg). Drag (3:1) Spr 72, p. 82.
"Literary Politics" (to Manuel Bandeira) (tr. of Carlos Drummond De Andrade, w. Ricardo da Silveira Lobo Sternberg). Mund (5:3) 72, p. 59.
"The Minus Touch." Peb (9) Wint 72.
"Moonlight in Any City..." (tr. of Carlos Drummond De Andrade, w. Ricardo da Silveira Lobo Sternberg). Mund (5:3) 72, p. 59.
"News Porm" (tr. of Carlos Drummond De Andrade, w. Ricardo Sternberg). Drag (3:1) Spr 72, p. 84.
"Night Piece." Meas (2) 72.
"Old Movie Blues." Cafe (4) Fall 72, p. 13.
"Our Time" (to Osvaldo Alves) (tr. of Carlos Drummond De Andrade, w. Ricardo da Silveira Lobo Sternberg). Mund (5:3) 72, p. 57.
"Poem of Seven Facets" (tr. of Carlos Drummond De Andrade, w. Ricardo Sternberg). Drag (3:1) Spr 72, p. 83.
"Poems." Drag (3:3/4) Fall-Wint 72, pp. 49-70 (special issue).
"Stop the Family Tree, I Want to Get Off." SaltCR (5:1) Wint 72.
"Sunset." Peb (6) Sum 71.
"The Survivor" (tr. of Carlos Drummond De Andrade, w. Ricardo Sternberg). Drag (3:1) Spr 72, p. 81.
"Ten Second Tragedies." Drag (3:1) Spr 72, p. 59.
"Two Poems In Praise of Coffee." GreenR (2:2) 72, p. 8.
"Umbrella." Peb (6) Sum 71.
"The Unlucky Rabbits" (for Peter Wild). LittleM (6:1) Spr 72, p. 9.

12 ACKLEY, Randall
"For the Captain." Conrad (4:1) 72, p. 71.
"Sea Troll Song No. 9." SouthernPR (13:1) Aut 72, p. 9.
"Troll Song for a Cossack" (for Wasyl Klym). SouthernPR (13:1) Aut 72, p. 28.
"Trolls-3." St. AR (1:4) Spr-Sum 72, p. 28.
"Trolls-2." St. AR (2:1) Aut-Wint 72, p. 19.

13 ADAIR, V. H.
"Grasmere Journal (May 14-June 7, 1800)." SouthernHR (6:3) Sum 72, p. 256.
"O Western Wind." SouthernHR (6:2) Spr 72, p. 196.
"The Sound of Progress." SouthernHR (6:2) Spr 72, p. 196.

"Staff Notes from the Mental Hospital: Case X." BallSUF (13:2) Spr 72, p. 45.

14 ADAM, Helen
"Counting out Rhyme." Magazine (5) part 4, 72.
"No Green Wave." NewYQ (10) Spr 72, p. 49.
"A Tale Best Forgotten." NewYQ (12) Aut 72, p. 52.
"The Triumphs of True Love." NewYQ (11) Sum 72, p. 62.

15 ADAMS, Kaywynne
"Funeral Chairs." Northeast Aut-Wint 71-72, p. 22.

16 ADAMS, R. B.
"The Parts Roster." NewYQ (12) Aut 72, p. 69.

17 ADAMS, Sam
"Gwbert: Mackerel Fishing." TransR (42/43) Spr-Sum 72, p. 67.

18 ADAMS, Terence M.
"Early Riser." FourQt (21:2) Ja 72, p. 35.

19 ADCOCK, Betty
"After Love." SouthernPR (13:1) Aut 72, p. 29.
"Eight Poems. SouthernPR (12:Special Issue) 72, p. 3.
"Looking for Cures." NoCaFo (20:4) N 72, p. 173.

20 ADDICKS, Mentor
"Two Herons Feeding." SoDakR (10:3) Aut 72, p. 11.

21 ADEN, Carlin
"Nato the Barber." SatireN (9:2) Spr 72, p. 167.

22 ADLER, Carol
"Haiku: we must live these days." Cim (18) Ja 72, inside front cover.

23 ADONIS
"Hunger" (tr. by Samuel Hazo). Books (46:2) Spr 72, p. 251.
"Stone" (tr. by M. B. Alwan). Books (46:2) Spr 72, p. 251.

24 AGNIHORTRI, V. K.
"Untitled Poem." Meas (3) 72, p. 1.

25 AHMAD, Aijaz
"Ghazal XXXIV" (tr. of Mirza Ghalib). Madem (74:3) Ja 72, p. 50.

26 AI
"Abortion." Iron (1) Spr 72, p. 49.
"The Cripple." Iron (2) Fall 72, p. 7.
"Cuba, 1962." Iron (2) Fall 72, p. 8.

"Why Can't I Leave You." Iron (1) Spr 72, p. 47.
"The Widow." Iron (1) Spr 72, p. 50.
"Woman." Iron (1) Spr 72, p. 48.
"Young Farm Woman Alone." Iron (2) Fall 72, p. 6.

27 AIKEN, William
"Getting It All Together." HiramPoR (12) Spr-Sum 72, p. 7.

28 AJAY, Stephen
"Autumn Equinox." NewYQ (9) Wint 72, p. 72.
"The Fist, the Sun, the Palm." PoetryNW (13:4) Wint 72-73, p. 43.
"Summer Eclipse." NewYQ (10) Spr 72, p. 67.
"A Winter Mind." NewYQ (10) Spr 72, p. 68.

29 AKHMATOVA, Anna
"Don't Repeat" (tr. by John M. Gogol). Wind (2:5) Sum 72, p. 26.
"Eighty-eight poems by Anna Akhmátova" (tr. by Eugene M. Kayden). ColQ (20:3) Wint 72, p. 396.
"The Four Seasons" (tr. by John M. Gogol). Wind (2:5) Sum 72, p. 26.
"How Can You Look at the Neva" (tr. by Stanley Kunitz and Max Hayward). Antaeus (6) Sum 72, p. 115.
"I Am Not One of Those Who Left the Land" (tr. by Stanley Kunitz and Max Hayward). Antaeus (6) Sum 72, p. 116.
"Leningrad" (tr. by John M. Gogol). Wind (2:5) Sum 72, p. 26.
"Pushkin" (tr. by Stanley Kunitz and Max Hayward). Antaeus (6) Sum 72, p. 114.
"Requiem" (tr. by Herbert Marshall). RusLT (2) Wint 72, p. 201.
"The Return to the Summer Palace" (tr. by Stanley Kunitz). AriD (1:2) Wint 72, p. 24.
"Seven poems by Anna Akhmátova" (tr. by Eugene M. Kayden). ColQ (20:4) Spr 72, p. 530.
"There Remain" (tr. by John M. Gogol). Wind (2:5) Sum 72, p. 26.
"This Cruel Age Has Deflected Me" (tr. by Stanley Kunitz and Max Hayward). Antaeus (6) Sum 72, p. 117.
"Voronezh" (tr. by Stanley Kunitz). AriD (1:2) Wint 72, p. 23.
"When in the Throes of Suicide" (tr. by Stanley Kunitz). AriD (1:2) Wint 72, p. 22.
from The White Flock (tr. by Stanley Burnshaw). MassR (13:3) Sum 72, p. 326.

30 AKIN, Katy
"Canjuani-February." HangL (16) Wint 71-72, p. 61.

31 AKSAL, Sabahattin Kudret
"Embellishments" (tr. by Murat Nemet-Nejat). LitR (15:4) Sum 72, p. 435.

32 ALBERS, Gary E.
"The Breaking Up of New Ground." Spec (14:1/2) My 72, p. 5.

33 ALBERT, Rosemary
"Spring Morning in Haarlem." Wind (2:5) Sum 72, p. 50.

34 ALBERTI, Rafael
"Buster Keaton Looks in the Woods For His Love Who Is a Real Cow" (tr. by Mark Strand). Antaeus (7) Aut 72, p. 153.
"Charlie's Sad Date" (tr. by Mark Strand). Antaeus (7) Aut 72, p. 149.
"Harold Lloyd, Student" (tr. by Mark Strand). Antaeus (7) Aut 72, p. 151.
"The Moldy Angel" (tr. by Mark Strand). Peb (6) Sum 71.
"On the Day of His Death By an Armed Hand" (tr. by Mark Strand). Antaeus (7) Aut 72, p. 155.
"Song of the Angel Without Luck" (tr. by Mark Strand). Peb (6) Sum 71.

35 ALBURY, Joan
"Date." Kayak (28) 72, p. 10.

36 ALDAN, Daisy
"Glaciers." Poetry (120:1) Ap 72, p. 19.
"The Little Mermaid." Poetry (120:1) Ap 72, p. 20.
"Mutilated Fire." Poetry (120:1) Ap 72, p. 19.
"Rocks: Easter." NewYQ (12) Aut 72, p. 53.
"Stones: Avesbury." Poetry (120:1) Ap 72, p. 18.
"Tears Fall in My Heart" (tr. of Paul Verlaine). NewYQ (10) Spr 72, p. 92.

37 ALDRICH, Michael
"Because I Thought That" (tr. of Tarapada Ray, w. the poet). Meas (3) 72, p. 76.
"Car Going Far (A Long Distance Car)" (tr. of Shokti Chattopadhyay, w. Tarapada Ray). Meas (3) 72, p. 11.
"Five Poems of Dharma and Kama" (tr. of Shankar Chattopadhyay, w. Shri Chatterjee). Meas (3) 72, p. 9.
"Kush-Kush" (tr. of Tarapada Ray, w. the poet). Meas (3) 72, p. 75.

38 ALEIXANDRE, Vicente
"Cautious Dampness" (tr. by Robert Lima). PoetL (67:3) Aut 72, p. 227.
"Idea." Mund (5:1/2) 72, p. 122.
"La Muerte o Antesala de Consulta." Mund (5:1/2) 72, p. 124.
"Nakedness" (tr. by Robert Lima). PoetL (67:3) Aut 72, p. 227.
"Reposo." Mund (5:1/2) 72, p. 120.

39 ALEXANDER, Charlotte
"Angus Observed." PraS (46:1) Spr 72, p. 49.
"Girl on Trapeze." PoetL (67:3) Aut 72, p. 218.
"Where's Charlie?" PoetL (67:3) Aut 72, p. 258.

40 ALEXANDER, Floyce
"Night Latch Blues" (for Paula). Drag (3:1) Spr 72, p. 61.
"Odi, Amo" (after Catullus). Drag (3:1) Spr 72, p. 60.

41 ALEXANDER, J.
"Fenway." Confr (5) Wint-Spr 72, p. 86.

42 ALEXANDER, William
from Un Lavoro Difficile: "In Consequence" (tr. of Roberto Sanesi). MedR (2:4) Sum 72, p. 86.
"Park Hotel" (tr. of Roberto Sanesi). MichQR (11:4) Aut 72, p. 276.
from Viaggio Verso il Nord: "Journey Toward the North" (tr. of Roberto Sanesi). MedR (2:4) Sum 72, p. 84.
from Viaggio Verso il Nord: "Vaucluse" (tr. of Roberto Sanesi). MedR (2:4) Sum 72, p. 83.

43 ALEXANDROU, Ares
"Bion" (tr. by Thanasis Maskaleris). AriD (1:4/5) Sum-Aut 72, p. 15.
"The Clouds" (tr. by Stratis Haviaras). AriD (1:4/5) Sum-Aut 72, p. 17.
"Into the Rocks" (tr. by Thanasis Maskaleris). AriD (1:4/5) Sum-Aut 72, p. 17.
"Return" (tr. by Stratis Haviaras). AriD (1:4/5) Sum-Aut 72, p. 16.

44 ALFRED, William
"Orare John Berryman." NewYRB (18:4) 9 Mr 72, p. 8.

45 ALLARDT, Linda
"Bush." PoetryNW (13:3) Aut 72, p. 37.
"Cleaning the Well." Folio (8:2) Fall 72, p. 16.
"In Your Common Cup." Folio (8:2) Fall 72, p. 31.
"Masquerade." Folio (8:1) Spr 72, p. 24.

46 ALLDRED, Pauline
"A Trip." NewRena (6) My 72, p. 63.

47 ALLEN, Dick
"The Odd Poem." NewYQ (12) Aut 72, p. 77.

48 ALLEN, Robert
"Hawk." NYT 21 Ag 72, p. 30.
"Hawk." NYT 22 Ag 72, p. 42.
"Mole." NYT 20 S 72, p. 46.
"Pulling Strings." Epoch (21:2) Wint 71, p. 176.

49 ALLEN, Sara Van Alstyne
"Slow Journey into the Past." SouthwR (57:3) Sum 72, p. 208.
"This Continent." ChiTM 27 Ag 72, p. 16.
"Two Nuns On a City Bus." Comm (96:7) 21 Ap 72, p. 163.

50 ALLISON, Byron
"Southern Flute." Isthmus (1) Spr 72, p. 84.

51 ALLMAN, John
"Last Attempts." Epos (23:4) Sum 72, p. 14.
"A Sunday Off." Hiero (7) Ap 72.
"Widow." SouthernPR (12:2) Spr 72, p. 38.

52 ALMON, Bert
"The Mutilation." Meas (2) 72.
"The Sisters." WestR (9:1) Spr 72, p. 79.
"The Stress Report." BelPoJ (23:2) Wint 72-73, p. 2.

53 ALOFF, Mindy
"The Invaders from Nod." HangL (16) Wint 71-72, p. 3.

54 ALONSO, Dámaso
"¿Como Era?" Mund (5:1/2) 72, p. 118.
"Sueño de las Dos Ciervas." Mund (5:1/2) 72, p. 116.

55 ALOTTA, Robert I.
"Class Report." Folio (8:1) Spr 72, p. 40.
"Dreams." Epoch (21:2) Wint 71, p. 171.
"Seagull." PoetL (67:1) Spr 72, p. 64.
"You IX." Wind (2:6) Aut 72, p. 24.

56 ALTA
"Poem: i could not love you more." Aphra (3:2) Spr 72, p. 21.

57 ALTANY, Alan
"The Browning of Autumn." SoDakR (10:3) Aut 72, p. 65.
"Clouds, Ground, and Imaginary Mountains." SoDakR (10:3) Aut 72, p. 65.
"The Earth's Feel." SoDakR (10:3) Aut 72, p. 65.
"End of April." WindO (11) Aut 72, p. 37.
"The Radical Night." Epos (23:4) Sum 72, p. 10.

58 ALTOLAGUIRRE, Manuel
"Go" (tr. by Robert Lima). PoetL (67:3) Aut 72, p. 228.

59 ALWAN, Ameen
"Alex." Nat (214:23) 5 Je 72, p. 739.
"Barbara." MinnR (3) Aut 72, p. 70.
"The End of August." Nat (215:4) 21 Ag 72, p. 120.
"Garlic." MinnR (3) Aut 72, p. 71.
"I Translate Rain." Nat (215:4) 21 Ag 72, p. 120.

"July." Epoch (22:1) Fall 72, p. 74.
"Mailbox." Nat (215:4) 21 Ag 72, p. 120.
"The Main Library at U.C.L.A." MinnR (3) Aut 72, p. 71.
"A Picture of This/A Shot of That" (tr. of Carlos Castro Saavedra). MinnR (3) Aut 72, p. 75.
"Riches." MinnR (3) Aut 72, p. 70.
"Three Women." MinnR (3) Aut 72, p. 72.

60 ALWAN, M. Bakir
"I Wish You ..." (tr. of Buland al-Haydarī). Books (46:2) Spr 72, p. 249.
"Interrogation" (tr. of Nizar Qabbani). ConcPo (5:2) Fall 72, p. 37.
"Silence and the Wind" (tr. of Salah Abd as-Sabur). Books (46:2) Spr 72, p. 248.
"Stone" (tr. of Adonis). Books (46:2) Spr 72, p. 251.
"The Wall" (tr. of Abd al-Wahhāb al-Bayāti). Books (46:2) Spr 72, p. 249.

61 ALYN, Marc
"Burning Coal" (tr. by Robert Holkeboer). Books (46:3) Sum 72, p. 425.
"Daybreak" (tr. by Robert Holkeboer). Books (46:3) Sum 72, p. 425.

62 AMABILE, George
"Adultery." UnmOx (1:3) Sum 72, p. 56.
"The Adventures of Birdman." BeyB (2:2) 72, p. 51.
"The Eclipse (for Vic & Gerry Cowie)." ModernPS (3:4) 72, p. 171.
from "Generation Gap (to my father, 1895-1961)." New: ACP (19) Aut 72, p. 36.

63 AMES, Bernice
"Consider the Country Flower." Shen (24:1) Aut 72, p. 64.
"I Am." Zahir (1:4/5) 72, p. 61.
"Of Motion and Circle." Wind (2:6) Aut 72, p. 23.
"Prodigal." SouthernPR (12:2) Spr 72, p. 37.
"A Rise of Light." MidwQ (14:1) Aut 72, p. 40.
"White Oleander." ChiTM 2 Jl 72, p. 2.

64 AMICHAI, Yehuda
"End of Summer Evening in Motsa" (tr. by Harold Schimmel). Humanist (32:1) Ja-F 72, p. 32.

65 AMINI, Johari M. (Jewel Latimore)
"A Hip Tale in the Death Style." Broad (59) My 72.

66 AMMONS, A. R.
"Certainty." NewL (39:2) Wint 72, p. 75.
"Currencies." NYT 27 S 72, p. 46.
"Fall Creek." Epoch (21:3) Spr 72, p. 235.
"Model." NewL (39:2) Wint 72, p. 76.

"Rectitude." Epoch (21:3) Spr 72, p. 235.
"Self-Projection." NewL (39:2) Wint 72, p. 76.
"Spring Tornado." NewL (39:2) Wint 72, p. 75.

67 AMOROSI, Ray
"August Afternoons." Iowa (3:3) Sum 72, p. 12.
"Capuccini." MidwQ (14:1) Aut 72, p. 79.
"Catching the First Line." NewL (38:4) Sum 72, p. 25.
"Chopping for the A-Frame." Iowa (3:3) Sum 72, p. 10.
"The Feast." Iowa (3:3) Sum 72, p. 11.
"Guadellajo Blesses Borgia." CarolQ (24:1) Wint 72, p. 23.
"In the Borgia Apartments." NewL (38:4) Sum 72, p. 26.
"Instructions For a Hypochondriac." CarolQ (24:1) Wint 72, p. 23.
"Lovers." NewL (38:4) Sum 72, p. 27.
"Pilgrims." Iowa (3:3) Sum 72, p. 12.
"Reprieved." Iowa (3:3) Sum 72, p. 11.
"Vampire." Iowa (3:3) Sum 72, p. 10.

68 ANAGNOSTAKIS, Manolis
"Each Morning" (tr. by Athan Anagnostopoulos). AriD (1: 4/5 Sum-Aut 72, p. 21.
"Epilogue" (tr. by Athan Anagnostopoulos). AriD (1:4/5) Sum-Aut 72, p. 20.
"Epitaph" (tr. by Athan Anagnostopoulos). AriD (1:4/5) Sum-Aut 72, p. 20.
"Haris 1944" (tr. by Athan Anagnostopoulos). AriD (1:4/5) Sum-Aut 72, p. 19.
"Landscape" (tr. by Athan Anagnostopoulos). AriD (1:4/5) Sum-Aut 72, p. 21.
"Rhythmic Pacing" (tr. by Stratis Haviaras). AriD (1:4/5) Sum-Aut 72, p. 20.
"The Shipwreck" (tr. by Athan Anagnostopoulos). AriD (1: 4/5) Sum-Aut 72, p. 18.

69 ANAGNOSTOPOULOS, Athan
"Dangerous Age" (tr. of Nikos Alexis Aslanoglou) AriD (1: 4/5) Sum-Aut 72, p. 22.
"Each Morning" (tr. of Manolis Anagnostakis). AriD (1:4/5) Sum-Aut 72, p. 21.
"The Embattled Christ" (tr. of Th. D. Frangopoulos). AriD (1:4/5) Sum-Aut 72, p. 40.
"Epilogue" (tr. of Manolis Anagnostakis). AriD (1:4/5) Sum-Aut 72, p. 20.
"Epitaph" (tr. of Manolis Anagnostakis). AriD (1:4/5) Sum-Aut 72, p. 20.
"Freedom 1945" (tr. of Dimitris Papaditsas). AriD (1:4/5) Sum-Aut 72, p. 83.
"Give Me a Place to Stand" (tr. of Nikos Zoumboulakis). AriD (1:4/5) Sum-Aut 72, p. 123.
"Haris 1944" (tr. of Manolis Anagnostakis). AriD (1:4/5) Sum-Aut 72, p. 19.
"The House 2" (tr. of Loukas Theodora Kopoulos). AriD

(1:4/5) Sum-Aut 72, p. 108.
"Landscape" (tr. of Manolis Anagnostakis). AriD (1:4/5) Sum-Aut 72, p. 21.
"Like a Worn Out Shoe" (tr. of Loukas Theodora Kopoulos). AriD (1:4/5) Sum-Aut 72, p. 107.
"Litochorion Station" (tr. of Nikos Alexis Aslanoglou). AriD (1:4/5) Sum-Aut 72, p. 23.
"The Night and the Barracks" (tr. of Loukas Theodora Kopoulos). AriD (1:4/5) Sum-Aut 72, p. 106.
"On Patmos" (tr. of Dimitris Papaditsas). AriD (1:4/5) Sum-Aut 72, p. 84.
"The Passionate Relics" (tr. of Dimitris Papaditsas). AriD (1:4/5) Sum-Aut 72, p. 84.
"Prelude" (tr. of George Thaniel). AriD (1:4/5) Sum-Aut 72, p. 103.
"Root" (tr. of Nikos Zoumboulakis). AriD (1:4/5) Sum-Aut 72, p. 124.
"The Shipwreck" (tr. of Manolis Anagnostakis). AriD (1:4/5) Sum-Aut 72, p. 18.
"The Slug" (tr. of Loukas Theodora Kopoulos). AriD (1:4/5) Sum-Aut 72, p. 107.
from Twenty-Four Executions: "The Third," "The Eleventh," "The Eighteenth." (tr. of George Kaftantzis). AriD (1:4/5) Sum-Aut 72, p. 50.
"Unknown Words" (tr. of Nikos Zoumboulakis). AriD (1:4/5) Sum-Aut 72, p. 122.
"Until the Fall" (tr. of Th. D. Frangopoulos). AriD (1:4/5) Sum-Aut 72, p. 41.
"With Soft Voice" (tr. of Dimitris Papaditsas). AriD (1:4/5) Sum-Aut 72, p. 86.
"0-24" (tr. of Teos Salapassidis). AriD (1:4/5) Sum-Aut 72, p. 94.

70 ANDAY, Melih Cevdet
"Copper Age" (tr. by Talat Sait Halman). LitR (15:4) Sum 72, p. 494.

71 ANDERSEN, Astrid Hjertenaes
"Gustav Vigeland's Woman and Reptile" (tr. by F. H. König). NoAmR (257:1) Spr 72, p. 61.
"The Poet Recites His Own Poem" (tr. by F. H.. König). NoAmR (257:1) Spr 72, p. 61.

72 ANDERSEN, Sally S.
"Raccoon." BallSUF (13:4) Aut 72, p. 74.

73 ANDERSON, C. M.
"Black Studies." KanQ (4:1) Wint 71-72, p. 44.

74 ANDERSON, Elliott
Three Poems (tr. of Tomaz Salamun). NewL (38:4) Sum 72, p. 108.

75 ANDERSON, Forrest
"Encounters." Folio (8:1) Spr 72, p. 7.

76 ANDERSON, Jack
"After the Human." Peb (6) Sum 71.
"Behind My Back." PraS (46:2) Sum 72, p. 105.
"Bodies." Peb (9) Wint 72.
"Disquiet of a Room." Peb (6) Sum 71.
"The Evil." Stand (13:4) 72, p. 64.
"Feelings." PraS (46:2) Sum 72, p. 106.
"A Garden of Situations." Poetry (120:2) My 72, p. 80.
"The Last Poems." PraS (46:1) Sum 72, p. 107.
"Mulatto." KanQ (4:1) Wint 71-72, p. 45.
"A Poet's Guide to the Subway." Poetry (120:2) My 72, p. 78.
"A Providence." MinnR (3) Aut 72, p. 111.

77 ANDERSON, Jon
"John Clare." Field (7) Fall 72, p. 37.

78 ANDERSON, Sally
"At Ruth's Place in Vermont." Folio (8:1) Spr 72, p. 37.
"Christmas Song." Folio (8:1) Spr 72, p. 16.

79 ANDERSSON, Dan
"A Swedish Tribute to Huck Finn" (tr. by Frances Brown Price, w. Marianne Fosselius). Mark (16:2) Sum 72, p. 20.

80 ANDRADE, Jorge Carrera
"Columna en Memoria de las Hojas." Mund (5:3) 72, p. 68.
"Domingo." Mund (5:3) 72, p. 64.
"Vida del Grillo." Mund (5:3) 72, p. 66.

81 ANDRE, Michael
"Bowling" (for F. G.). UnmOx (1:4) Aut 72.
"Cunts Sewed Cheap." UnmOx (1:1) N 71, p. 64.
"I Met This Man." UnmOx (1:1) N 71, p. 2.
"No Poem." LittleM (6:2/3) Sum-Aut 72, p. 87.
"Trials of Eustace." UnmOx (1:3) Sum 72, p. 13.

82 ANDRE, Theresa Kathleen
"(disquiet)." SouthernR (8:4) Aut 72, p. 911.
"On City Park Pool." SouthernR (8:4) Aut 72, p. 909.
"Street Poems." SouthernR (8:4) Aut 72, p. 910.

83 ANDREA, Marianne
"Twilight." Comm (96:8) 28 Ap 72, p. 190.

84 ANDREWS, Bruce
"Bananas are an example." ParisR (53) Wint 72, p. 162.

85 ANDREWS, Jenné R.
"Albuquerque, Midsummer." Apple (7) Aut 72, p. 24.
"Anything's Uses." Apple (7) Aut 72, p. 28.
"Falling Back." Apple (7) Aut 72, p. 29.
"Message to a Dying Man." Apple (7) Aut 72, p. 26.
"An Order of Winter." Apple (7) Aut 72, p. 25.
"A Sweet Fear of June." LittleM (6:1) Spr 72, p. 10.
"Waking to Birds or Branches on the Window." Peb (9) Wint 72.
"Wild Geese Going North." Apple (7) Aut 72, p. 27.
"Words from Storms and Geese in the Morning." Apple (7) Aut 72, p. 30.

86 ANDREWS, Miriam
"Brattleboro Retreat." PoetL (67:2) Sum 72, p. 133.
"For a Spanish Madonna." PoetL (67:2) Sum 72, p. 136.
"Jewels at Nag's Head." PoetL (67:2) Sum 72, p. 135.
"Lines From a Book of Hours." ChiTM 19 N 72, p. 10.

87 ANGOFF, Charles
"At the Tomb of Herzi, Jerusalem." NYT 25 F 72, p. 38.
"Before Dante's Tomb in the Church of Santa Croce, Florence." LitR (15:3) Spr 72, p. 380.
"Before the Tomb of Galileo in the Church of Santa Croce, Florence." LitR (15:3) Spr 72, p. 381.
"The Colosseum at Midnight." LitR (16:1) Aut 72, p. 91.
"Every Woman." ChiTM 10 S 72, p. 10.
"Florence, Italy." LitR (15:3) Spr 72, p. 379.
"God Blessed Me." ChrC (89:44) 6 D 72, p. 1244.
"The Keats-Shelley Memorial in Rome." LitR (16:1) Aut 72, p. 90.
"Rome." LitR (16:1) Aut 72, p. 89.
"The Things I Revere." ChiTM 13 F 72, p. 16.

88 ANNENSKY, Innokénty
"Before the Funeral" (tr. by Dale Plank). RusLT (4) Aut 72, p. 50.
"I Am at the Bottom" (tr. by Raisa Scriabine and Harvey Feinberg). RusLT (4) Aut 72, p. 49.
"It Happened at Vallen Koski" (tr. by Raisa Scriabine and Harvey Feinberg). RusLT (4) Aut 72, p. 48.
"July" (tr. by Rodney L. Patterson). RusLT (4) Aut 72, p. 50.
"Thirteen poems by Innokénty Annensky" (tr. by Eugene M. Kayden). ColQ (20:3) Wint 72, p. 387.
"Waiting at the Station" (tr. by Raisa Scriabine and Harvey Feinberg). RusLT (4) Aut 72, p. 47.

89 ANONYMOUS
"A Charme Agaynst a Misconcepcyon." PoetC (7:1) 72, p. 17.
"elective perplexities." VilV 2 N 72, p. 10.
"Greek Diary." UnicornJ (4) 72, p. 13.

"In the Season When the Earth" (tr. by Giuliana Mutti). MassR (13:1/2) Wint-Spr 72, p. 104.
"Thoughts of a Male Chauvinist Pig at the Demonstration." SouthernPR (13:1) Aut 72, p. 48.

90 ANTHONY, David
"Imago." JnlOBP (2:16) Sum 72, p. 54.

91 ANTHONY, George
"Letter." CarlMis (12:1) Fall-Wint 71-72, p. 123.

92 APOLLINAIRE, Guillaume
"Marizibill" (tr. by Joan Larkin). SouthernPR (13:1) Aut 72, p. 42.
"There Is" (tr. by Michael Benedikt). Iron (2) Fall 72, p. 57.

93 APPLEMAN, Philip
"The Girl Who Hated Threes." ChiTM 23 Ap 72, p. 12.
"Kicking Sea Urchins." LitR (16:1) Aut 72, p. 104.
"Last Will and Testament." ColEng (33:5) F 72, p. 582.
"Love Song." NYT 15 Mr 72, p. 46.
"On the Beagle." ColEng (33:5) F 72, p. 580.
"Saturday, In Color." NYT 1 Jl 72, p. 20.
"This Christmas at Dingley Dell." ChiTM 17 D 72, p. 16.

94 APPLEWHITE, James
"Driving Through the Country America That Is Vanishing." Esq (78:6) D 72, p. 298.
"Sun on Morrow Mountain." SouthernPR (13:1) Aut 72, p. 4.

95 ARDAYNE, Julia Collins
"Full Circle." LadHJ (89:6) Je 72, p. 116.

96 ARIDJIS, Homero
"On the Outside You Are Sleeping and On the Inside You Dream" (tr. by Douglas Lawder and Katherine Grimes). Drag (3:2) Sum 72, p. 47.
"Sometimes One Touches a Body" (tr. by Douglas Lawder and Katherine Grimes). Drag (3:2) Spr 72, p. 48.

97 ARNDT, Walter
"Autumn" (tr. of Alexander Pushkin). RusLT (3) Spr 72, p. 32.
"The Dream" (tr. of Mikhail Lermontov). RusLT (3) Spr 72, p. 58.
"Grapes" (tr. of Alexander Pushkin). RusLT (3) Spr 72, p. 35.
"Huddled hamlets, scanty granges" (tr. of Fyodor Tyutchev). RusLT (3) Spr 72, p. 65.
"I loved you--and my love, I think, was stronger" (tr. of Alexander Pushkin). RusLT (3) Spr 72, p. 36.
"Silentium" (tr. of Fyodor Tyutchev). RusLT (3) Spr 72, p. 65.

"Thanksgiving" (tr. by Mikhail Lermontov). RusLT (3) Spr 72, p. 60.
"We parted--your medallion, though" (tr. of Mikhail Lermontov). RusLT (3) Spr 72, p. 60.
"Wherefore" (tr. of Mikhail Lermontov). RusLT (3) Spr 72, p. 60.
"You're the kind that always loses" (tr. of Alexander Pushkin). RusLT (3) Spr 72, p. 35.

98 ARNETT, Carroll
"Papa D." Peb (7) Aut 71.
"Plain Man." Peb (7) Aut 71.
"Sex." Cafe (4) Fall 72, p. 30.

99 ARNOLD, Kenneth
"Colloquy in a Different Language About a Different Time." Perspec (17:1) Sum 72, p. 60.
"Necktie." Drag (3:1) Spr 72, p. 5.
"Stew." Drag (3:1) Spr 72, p. 6.

100 ARNSTEIN, Felix G.
"November." Cord (1:4) 72, p. 29.

101 ARP, Jean
"I Want to Salute Crudely" (tr. by Joachim Neugroschel). DenQuart (6:4) Wint 72, p. 31.
"The Inconceivable That Resounds" (tr. by Joachim Neugroschel). DenQuart (6:4) Wint 72, p. 29.
"O Mezzanine" (tr. by Joachim Neugroschel). DenQuart (6:4) Wint 72, p. 30.
"What Is That?" (tr. by Joachim Neugroschel). DenQuart (6:4) Wint 72, p. 32.

102 ARRURRUZ, Sebastian
"Copla" (tr. by Geoffrey Hill). Stand (14:1) 72, p. 4.

103 ARTHUR, Lew
"Stone Age." Pan (9) 72, p. 51.
"Yes Again." Pan (9) 72, p. 50.

104 ARYANPUR, M.
"The Wind-Up Doll" (tr. of Forūgh Farrokhzād). Books (46:2) Spr 72, p. 248.

105 ASAF, Ozdemir
from "The Corners of the Round" (tr. by Yildiz Moran). LitR (15:4) Sum 72, p. 452.

106 ASCHER, Rhoda Gaye
"Harlem Day." JnlOBP (2:16) Sum 72, p. 17.

107 ASHBERRY, John
"Voyage in the Blue." NewYorker (48:39) 18 N 72, p. 60.

108 ASHLEY, Franklin B.
"Before June." Granite (2) Wint 71-72, p. 77.

109 ASHLEY, Nova Trimble
"Decently to Dust." KanQ (4:3) Sum 72, p. 95.

110 ASLANOGLOU, Nikos Alexis
"Dangerous Age" (tr. by Athan Anagnostopoulos). AriD (1:4/5) Sum-Aut 72, p. 22.
"Litochorion Station" (tr. by Athan Anagnostopoulos). AriD (1:4/5) Sum-Aut 72, p. 23.

111 ATCHITY, Kenneth John
"A Card Laid." Folio (8:1) Spr 72, p. 17.
"On Leaving California." Folio (8:2) Fall 72, p. 34.

112 ATHAS, Daphne
"I Remain Permanent." SouthernPR (13:1) Aut 72, p. 12.
"The Snivelling Gravy Boat to Its Owner." SouthernPR (13:1) Aut 72, p. 12.

113 ATKINS, Russell
"Exteriors, Interiors." Works (3:3/4) Wint 72-73, p. 32.

114 ATWOOD, Calvin
"Good Friday Spell." SouthernPR (13:1) Aut 72, p. 34.

115 ATWOOD, Margaret
"I Knew What I Wanted." UnmOx (1:4) Aut 72.
"Last Prayer." UnmOx (1:3) Sum 72, p. 57.
"Tricks with Mirrors." Aphra (3:4) Fall 72, p. 16.
"yes at first you." Madem (75:3) Jl 72, p. 180.
"your back is rough all." Madem (75:3) Jl 72, p. 180.

116 AUBERT, Alvin
"Black Aesthetic." GreenR (2:2) 72, p. 3.
"De Profundus." JnlOBP (2:16) Sum 72, p. 44.
"Matador." GreenR (2:2) 72, p. 4.
"Passages." GreenR (2:2) 72, p. 5.
"Testament." GreenR (2:2) 72, p. 4.

117 AUDEN, W. H.
"In the silent river of evening" (tr. of Par Lagerkvist, w. Leif Sjöberg). Shen (23:4) Sum 72, p. 76.
"The Insects" (tr. of Harry Martinson, w. Leif Sjöberg). MichQR (11:4) Aut 72, p. 284.
from "Li Kan Speaks Beneath the Tree" (tr. of Harry Martinson, w. Leif Sjöberg). DenQuart (7:3) Aut 72, p. 14.
"Loneliness." Atl (230:3) S 72, p. 88.
"Ode to the Diencephalon." NewYRB (19:9) 30 N 72, p. 10.
"Poem: Everywhere, in all the heavens you will find his footprints" (tr. of Par Lagerkvist, w. Leif Sjöberg).

WestHR (26:4) Aut 72, p. 350.
"Poem: O who can ever praise enough." Poetry (121:1) O 72, p. 1.
"Pseudo-questions." Atl (230:3) S 72, p. 88.
"The Rain" (tr. of Erik Lindegren, w. Leif Sjöberg). MichQR (11:4) Aut 72, p. 282.
"A Shock." NewYorker (48:4) 18 Mr 72, p. 40.
"Short One to the Cuckoo." Atl (230:2) Ag 72, p. 55.
"Stark Bewölkt" (for Stella Musulin). Atl (230:3) S 72, p. 89.
"The Suit K" (tr. of Erik Lindegren, w. Leif Sjöberg). MichQR (11:4) Aut 72, p. 283.
"Talking to myself." NewYorker (48:18) 24 Je 72, p. 32.

118 AURTHUR, Timothy
"To Bayard Ruskin." HangL (18) Fall 72, p. 3.

119 AUSTER, Paul
"Spokes." Poetry (119:6) Mr 72, p. 311.

120 AUSTIN, Edgar
"Hashi." Folio (8:1) Spr 72, p. 19.

121 AXELROD, David B.
"For Richard." WestHR (26:2) Spr 72, p. 154.
"March 1st and I Forgot My Jacket." YaleLit (141:2) 71, p. 8.
"Meprobamate." WestHR (26:2) Spr 72, p. 155.
"Sad Song." YaleLit (141:2) 71, p. 8.

122 AXINN, Donald
"Down on the Beach." NewYQ (11) Sum 72, p. 84.

123 BACHE, Kay E.
"Crossing." Folio (8:2) Fall 72, p. 19.
"October." Folio (8:2) Fall 72, p. 8.

124 BAGG, Robert
"Epidaurus." Poetry (120:1) Ap 72, p. 40.

125 BAGG, Terry R.
"Ballad for the Dead Narcissus." Poetry (119:5) F 72, p. 254.
"Reflections Approximately Divine." Poetry (119:5) F 72, p. 256.
"Small Homeric Overture." Poetry (119:5) F 72, p. 257.

126 BAGRYANA, Elisaveta
"No One Has Replaced You." LitR (16:2) Wint 72-73, p. 172.
"Poetry." LitR (16:2) Wint 72-73, p. 170.

127 BAIL, Jay
"Caught." UTR (1:4) 72, p. 25.
"This Life Will End Fruitful." UTR (1:3) 72, p. 18.

128 BAILES, Dale Alan
"The Trick." St. AR (1:4) Spr-Sum 72, p. 34.

129 BAILEY, Alice Morrey
"Deluded." LadHJ (89:9) S 72, p. 92.

130 BAILEY, Don
"Mary: Nov. 7/71." NewYQ (11) Sum 72, p. 83.

131 BAIN, Read
"To Jesse Stuart." ArizQ (28:3) Aut 72, p. 196.

132 BAKAITIS, Vytautas
"Double-Time Ballad." Works (3:2) Wint-Spr 72, p. 4.

133 BAKALIS, John
"He Was Like a Gull Lost Between Heaven & Earth." Kayak (30) D 72, p. 58.
"Love and the Human Echo." Kayak (30) D 72, p. 60.
"A Serious Note on Redemption." Kayak (30) D 72, p. 59.

134 BAKER, Carol
"The Canadian Rockies: A Log (for Dan)." Kayak (28) 72, p. 5.

135 BAKER, Charlie
"This Poem Is for Pablo Cassals." St. AR (1:4) Spr-Sum 72, p. 70.
"You." St. AR (2:1) Aut-Wint 72, p. 17.

136 BAKER, J. P.
"Down Cellar." SouthernPR (12:2) Spr 72, p. 8.

137 BAKKEN, Dick
"For Pranati in the Street" (tr. of Shaileswar Ghosh). Meas (3) 72, p. 30.
"I Am Hungry" (tr. of Shaileswar Ghosh). Meas (3) 72, p. 31.

138 BALAZS, Mary
"Prayer for a Child." Folio (8:1) Spr 72, p. 39.

139 BALDERSTON, Jean
"Salem, Salem!" NewYQ (11) Sum 72, p. 77.

140 BALDWIN, Jim
"The Lodger" (for Mrs. Knight). SouthernR (8:1) Wint 72, p. 164.
"No Sun." SouthernR (8:1) Wint 72, p. 165.

141 BALL, Hugo
"Sun" (tr. by Reinhold Johannes Kaebitzsch). WormR (48) 72, p. 118.

142 BALL, William
"Coal Smoke." PoetL (67:1) Spr 72, p. 61.
"The Kite." PoetL (67:1) Spr 72, p. 63.
"New Hampshire March." PoetL (67:1) Spr 72, p. 61.
"Obsequies." PoetL (67:1) Spr 72, p. 62.
"On Eastern Point." PoetL (67:1) Spr 72, p. 62.

143 BALLARD, Charles G.
"As Long As Rivers Flow." Indian (5:3) Fall 72, p. 24.
"Grandma Fire." Indian (5:3) Fall 72, p. 25.
"Old Fighter." Indian (5:3) Fall 72, p. 24.
"Out On the Plains." Indian (5:3) Fall 72, p. 24.
"Sand Creek." Indian (5:3) Fall 72, p. 25.

144 BALLINGER, Franchot
"Epistle (to Bob Foskett)." KanQ (4:1) Wint 71-72, p. 108.

145 BALLO, Guido
from L'Albero Poeta: "Someone Doesn't Want to Live in the Clouds" (tr. by Richard Burns). MedR (2:4) Sum 72, p. 87.
from Giano Indeciso: "Hupkucha (to Philip Martin)." MedR (2:4) Sum 72, p. 87.
from 7 Magnetico: "Roots." MedR (2:4) Sum 72, p. 87.

146 BALLOWE, James
"The Monster in the Prado: Desnuda y Vestida." KanQ (4:1) Wint 71-72, p. 81.

147 BALMONT, Konstantin
"I Came into This World" (tr. by Leonard Opalov). PoetL (67:1) Sum 72, p. 31.
Seventeen Poems (tr. by Rodney L. Patterson). RusLT (4) Aut 72, p. 51.

148 BALOIAN, James
"Robert Mezey." LittleM (6:2/3) Sum-Aut 72, p. 67.

149 BANGS, Carol Jane
"Re-entry." ConcPo (5:2) Spr 72, p. 72.

150 BANKS, Russell
"Journey." Cafe (4) Fall 72, p. 31.
"On the Birth of a Daughter." Cafe (4) Fall 72, p. 31.
"Stasis." Cafe (4) Fall 72, p. 31.

151 BARAS, Alexandros
"The Cleopatra, the Semiramis, and the Theodora" (tr. by Yannis Goumas). Mund (5:3) 72, p. 70.

"Insomnia" (tr. by Yannis Goumas). Mund (5:3) 72, p. 72.

152 BARATYNSKY, Evgeny
Nine Poems (tr. by Jamie Fuller). RusLT (3) Spr 72, p. 46.

153 BARBA, Sharon
"Terry, at Twenty-eight." CarlMis (12:2) Spr-Sum 72, p. 54.

154 BARBER, Cynthia Coggan
"The Casual Transplantation." PoetL (67:3) Aut 72, p. 247.

155 BARBOUR, George
"Hunt." Wind (2:5) Sum 72, p. 33.

156 BARD, William E.
"Bristlecone Pines." PoetL (67:1) Spr 72, p. 58.
"Horses." PoetL (67:1) Spr 72, p. 58.
"Nishi." PoetL (67:1) Spr 72, p. 59.
"The Singing of Whales." PoetL (67:1) Spr 72, p. 19.
"Song for an Old Cowhand." PoetL (67:4) Wint 72, p. 320.
"The Whippoorwill's Nest." PoetL (67:1) Spr 72, p. 58.

157 BARE, Colleen Stanley
"Telephone Talk." SatEP (244:1) Spr 72, p. 102.

158 BARFIELD, Steve
"Baptism from a Dynamited Beaver Dam." UTR (1:1) 72, p. 13.
"Duente." PoetL (67:4) Wint 72, p. 333.
"Ode to the Buzzard." UTR (1:3) 72, p. 29.
"Teach Me To Sing." PoetL (67:4) Wint 72, p. 332.

159 BARKER, Dan A.
"The Walls Echoes Hold (A poem in four voices for the prisoners in Atascadero State Mental Hospital in California, from a visit there)." NowestR (12:3) Aut 72, p. 70.

160 BARKER, Eric
"In a Dark House." Kayak (28) 72, p. 15.

161 BARKS, Coleman
"A Five Hour Drive" (for my parents). GeoR (26:2) Sum 72, p. 221.
"The Last Rebirth." GeoR (26:2) Sum 72, p. 223.
"Sunbath in May" (for my mother). GeoR (26:2) Sum 72, p. 219.
"The Water Table" (for my father). GeoR (26:2) Sum 72, p. 217.

162 BARLOW, George
"Flowers at the Jackson Funeral Home" (Daddy? Sugar-daddy? You really dead?). Broad (66) D 72.

163 BARNES, Jim
"John Berryman: Last Dream Song." PoetryNW (13:3) Aut 72, p. 27.

164 BARNES, Keith
"Because It Is Bitter." Madem (75:5) S 72, p. 87.

165 BARNSTONE, Aliki
"The Sun Made Life." NYT 3 My 72, p. 46.

166 BARNSTONE, Willis
"Delphi" (tr. of André Reszler). Mund (5:3) 72, p. 15.
"The Long March" (tr. of Mao Tse-Tung). NYT 19 F 72, p. 31.
"Winter Clouds" (tr. of Mao Tse-Tung). NYT 19 F 72, p. 31.
"Snow" (tr. of Mao Tse-Tung, w. Ko Ching-Po). NewRep (167:12) 30 S 72, p. 30.

167 BAROLINI, Helen
"The Moon Above Rome." MedR (2:2) Wint 72, p. 66.
"On Celebrating the Night of Apollo 11, July 16, 1969." MedR (2:2) Wint 72, p. 66.
"Rosatti's." MedR (2:2) Wint 72, p. 65.

168 BARRAX, Gerald W.
"America." SouthernPR (12: Special Issue) 72, p. 10.
"Big Bang." PoetryNW (13:4) Wint 72-73, p. 31.
"For Malcolm: After Mecca." SouthernPR (12: Special Issue) 72, p. 12.
"I Called Them Trees." SouthernPR (12: Special Issue) 72, p. 8.
"In This Sign." Works (3:3/4) Wint 72-73, p. 11.
"Moby Christ." SouthernPR (12: Special Issue) 72, p. 7.
"There Was a Song." SouthernPR (12: Special Issue) 72, p. 8.

169 BARRETT, Mark
"I'm writing a poem." WindO (11) Aut 72, p. 9.

170 BARROWS, Roy F.
"Bad Days on Welton Street." Folio (8:2) Fall 72, p. 20.
"The Body of the Smith." Confr (5) Wint-Spr 72, p. 59.

171 BARRY, James B.
"jurassic Mayflies." WestR (9:2) Wint 72, p. 21.

172 BARRY, Jan
"The Longest War." NYT 31 Mr 72, p. 29.

173 BARSNESS, John
"Legerdemain." Wind (2:6) Aut 72, p. 29.

174 BARTLETT, Elizabeth
"Color Questions." Etc. (29:2) Je 72, Inside Front Cover.

175 BARTLETT, Stephen
"After the Solipsist Died." Etc. (29:4) D 72, Inside Front Cover.

176 BARTON, David
"John Ruskin Inspects the Class." AriD (1:2) Wint 72, p. 32.

177 BARTON, Frances
"Current Complaint." SatEP (244:3) Aut 72, p. 88.

178 BARZE, Marguerite Enlow
"At Hippie Beach." PoetL (67:1) Spr 72, p. 49.
"Blue-Streak Blues." PoetL (67:1) Spr 72, p. 49.
"Not Quite Sixteen." PoetL (67:1) Spr 72, p. 48.
"Realist." PoetL (67:1) Spr 72, p. 54.

179 BASAK, Subimal
"Poem V on Imitating Myself." Meas (3) 72, p. 5.
"The Trick." Meas (3) 72, p. 4.

180 BAŞARAN, M.
"I've Registered for Germany" (tr. by Nermin Menemencioglu). LitR (15:4) Sum 72, p. 483.

181 BASHEV, Vladimir
"Grief." LitR (16:2) Wint 72-73, p. 165.

182 BASKFIELD, Jerry
"Eighteen with Silver Star." AbGR (3:1) Spr-Sum 72, p. 19.
"7-16-69, The Lunatic Race While Cronkite Weeps For Joy." AbGR (3:1) Spr-Sum 72, p. 20.

183 BASS, Madeline
"Newark (i)." NewYQ (11) Sum 72, p. 87.
"Observations: love in the city & so forth." HangL (17) Sum 72, p. 7.
"A Proverb." Confr (5) Wint-Spr 72, p. 101.

184 BASTIAN, Richard
"Small Things Pain Throughout Their Size." ChrC (89:33) 20 S 72, p. 912.

185 BATCHELOR, Ruth
"Boy Meets Girl." VilV 9 Mr 72, p. 79.
"Cock-a-Doodle-Do." VilV 20 Ap 72, p. 82.

"Elvis." VilV 8 Je 72, p. 51.
"Paranoia (Or would I sell my soul for a song?)" VilV 16 Mr 72, p. 76.
"Props." VilV 24 Ag 72, p. 50.
"The Sale." VilV 25 My 72, p. 6.

186 BATES, Elizabeth B.
"Incantation." PoetL (67:2) Sum 72, p. 171.

187 BATES, Grif
"Writing Behind the Garage." Esq (77:4) Ap 72, p. 84.

188 BATES, Scott
"The Heartwarming Saga of Peyote Bean the Provincial Plant Who Went to College and Made Good." NewRep (167:9) 9 S 72, p. 28.

189 Ba THAUNG, Linda Durkee
"Teacher." EngJ (61:3) Mr 72, p. 357.
"To My Second Period Class." EngJ (61:2) F 72, p. 209.

190 BATKI, John
"An Altercation Rectified." Iowa (3:4) Fall 72, p. 24.
"Bellow, Tower" (tr. of Attila Jozsef). SenR (3:1) My 72, p. 17.
"Descent." Esq (77:4) Ap 72, p. 14.
"Frost" (tr. of Attila Jozsef). SenR (3:1) My 72, p. 21.
"I Did Not Know" (tr. of Attila Jozsef). SenR (3:1) My 72, p. 18.
"The Mad Shoemaker." AmerS (41:3) Sum 72, p. 390.
"Medallions 1" (tr. of Attila Jozsef). SenR (3:1) My 72, p. 19.
"Medallions 3" (tr. of Attila Jozsef). SenR (3:1) My 72, p. 20.
"A Transparent Lion" (tr. of Attila Jozsef). SenR (3:1) My 72, p. 16.

191 BATY, Robert
"The Loneliness of Lying Down." UTR (1:1) 72, p. 18.
"The Visit." UTR (1:2) 72, p. 19.

192 BAUDELAIRE, Charles
"Beatrice" (tr. by William Doreski). PoetL (67:1) Spr 72, p. 42.

193 BAUER, Marion Dane
"The Intersection." KanQ (4:1) Wint 71-72, p. 125.

194 BAUER, Michael
"Poem: Well it's about my face." AriD (1:2) Wint 72, p. 20.

195 BAUMANN, Susan L.
"Dried Butterflies." BelPoJ (22:3) Spr 72, p. 37.

196 BAXTER, Charles
"The Creation of Weather." MinnR (3) Aut 72, p. 42.
"The Indian in His Car." PraS (46:4) Wint 72-73, p. 352.
"Indians: A Position Paper." PraS (46:4) Wint 72-73, p. 354.
"Indians and Beasts." PraS (46:4) Wint 72-73, p. 353.
"An Indian Speaks." PraS (46:4) Wint 72-73, p. 354.
"Ma Tells about Indians." PraS (46:4) Wint 72-73, p. 352.

197 al-BAYATI, Abd al-Wahhāb
"The Wall" (tr. by M. B. Alwan). Books (46:2) Spr 72, p. 249.

198 BAYES, Ronald
"A November Waka (for Yukio Mishima)." St.AR (1:4) Spr-Sum 72, p. 12.

199 BEACHAM, Hans
"From a Window Turning." TexQ (15:2) Sum 72, p. 25.
"Loving." TexQ (15:2) Sum 72, p. 24.
"Water Wind." TexQ (15:2) Sum 72, p. 26.
"When Three Are One." TexQ (15:2) Sum 72, p. 24.
"Without Permission." TexQ (15:2) Sum 72, p. 25.

200 BEAIRD, Alice Boyd
"Is That You, Son?" LadHJ (89:2) F 72, p. 126b.

201 BEARDSLEY, Jene E.
"Nearing the End of January." ChrC (89:4) 26 Ja 72, p. 90.

202 BEAUDRY, Glenn
"Details of Marching Men." WestR (10:1) Spr 73, p. 73.

203 BEAUSOLEIL, Beau
"Poem from the Bank." NewYQ (12) Aut 72, p. 64.

204 BEIER, Ulli
"Folk Songs from Papua" (edited by Ulli Beier, tr. by Allan Natachee and Don Laycock). UnicornJ (4) 72, p. 85.

205 BELASIK, Paul
"Once in a While." Epoch (22:1) Fall 72, p. 46.

206 BELDEN
"Greetings." Folio (8:2) Fall 72, p. 34.
"Recollections of a Jungian Lover." Folio (8:1) Spr 72, p. 25.

207 BELITT, Ben
"Aware of the Word's Brevity" (tr. of Enrique Huaco). Mund (5:1/2) 72, p. 31.
"Block Island: 1971." VirQR (48:4) Aut 72, p. 532.

"V: Manual Metaphysics" (tr. of Pablo Neruda). VirQR (48:2) Spr 72, p. 192.
"The Size of a Man" (tr. of Enrique Huaco). Mund (5:1/2) 72, p. 29.
"Time's Skin" (tr. of Enrique Huaco). Mund (5:1/2) 72, p. 25.

208 BELL, Charles G.
Ten Poems. QRL (18:1/2) 72, p. 18.

209 BELL, Marvin
"Residue of Song." Stand (13:4) 72, p. 33.

210 BELL, Richard
"I Eat a Pear." StoneD (1:1) Spr 72, p. 12.

211 BELLMAN, Samuel I.
"Am Lit Symmetrics (3) Melville." CEACritic (34:4) My 72, p. 19.
"Am Lit Symmetrics (2) Hawthorne." CEACritic (34:2) Ja 72, p. 37.
"Eng Lit Symmetrics (1) John Keats." CEACritic (34:3) Mr 72, p. 34.
"Whitman's Learned Astronomer (To Himself)." SatireN (9:2) Spr 72, p. 163.

212 BELY, Andrei
"To Friends" (tr. by Rodney L. Patterson). RusLT (4) Aut 72, p. 61.

213 BENCKENSTEIN, Pat
"(To Name You)." HiramPoR (13) Fall-Wint 72, p. 20.

214 BENEDIKT, Michael
"Balloon-Cream." Iron (1) Spr 72, p. 72.
"Café Life." Drag (3:1) Spr 72, p. 10.
"Café Life II." Drag (3:1) Spr 72, p. 11.
"Clyde's Style." Madrona (1:1) Je 71, p. 4.
"The Discussion." Iowa (3:2) Spr 72, p. 25.
"Flower-Market Quay" (tr. of Pierre Reverdy). Drag (3:1) Spr 72, p. 79.
"A Further Revelation." Peb (7) Aut 71.
"Hello" (tr. of Benjamin Péret). Kayak (29) S 72, p. 27.
"The Moralist of Bananas." Field (6) Spr 72, p. 32.
"Poems." Drag (3:3/4) Fall-Wint 72, pp. 22-47 (special issue).
"Purity." Drag (3:1) Spr 72, p. 13.
"Radiant Reason." Field (6) Spr 72, p. 33.
"The Snowman." Peb (7) Aut 71.
"Some Words, Which Until Now, Had Remained Mysteriously Forbidding to Me" (tr. of Paul Eluard). Kayak (30) D 72, p. 26.
"There Is" (tr. of Guillaume Apollinaire). Iron (2) Fall 72, p. 57.

"Twinkling of an Eye" (tr. of Benjamin Péret). Kayak (29) S 72, p. 26.
"Where Are You" (tr. of Benjamin Péret). Field (6) Spr 72, p. 77.
"The Wing of Poetry." Drag (3:1) Spr 72, p. 12.

215 BENNETT, Benjamin K.
"Ahab Laughs." QRL (18:1/2) 72, p. 25.
"Our Usefulness." QRL (18:1/2) 72, p. 25.
"Paradox." QRL (18:1/2) 72, p. 25.
"Socrates." QRL (18:1/2) 72, p. 24.

216 BENNETT, John
"Aunt Ruth." WormR (48) 72, p. 144.
"The Awakening." ChiTM 19 Mr 72, p. 14.
"Cheyenne Friend." WormR (48) 72, p. 146.
"Fingernails in Spring." WormR (48) 72, p. 143.
"A Forest of Cameras Submerging." MinnR (3) Aut 72, p. 104.
"The Giant Cups." MinnR (3) Aut 72, p. 102.
"I Do Protest." WormR (48) 72, p. 146.
"Insomniac Sleep." MinnR (3) Aut 72, p. 103.
"It Is Spring." MinnR (3) Aut 72, p. 102.
"Margie & Arlene." WormR (48) 72, p. 146.
"Now wildmen are as tame as hens." Cord (1:4) 72, p. 18.
"School Days." Cord (1:4) 72, p. 18.
"Sodden Burning." MinnR (3) Aut 72, p. 103.
"To All Who Would Know" (a primer for Mel Lyman). WormR (48) 72, p. 145.
"Uncle Eddy." WormR (48) 72, p. 143.

217 BENNETT, Paul
"Saul His Thousands." Poem (15) Jl 72, p. 31.

218 BENNING, Guy R.
"Cindy." Wind (2:5) Sum 72, p. 41.
"Description." Wind (2:6) Aut 72, p. 24.

219 BENSON, John W.
"Black is a stone." UTR (1:4) 72, p. 12.
"The decaying boy engulfed the ice-berg." UTR (1:4) 72, p. 13.

220 BENTLEY, Nelson
"Sam Abelson." Madrona (1:3) My 72, p. 21.

221 BERG, Stephen
"Don't Forget." Poetry (121:2) N 72, p. 83.
"First Cold." Poetry (121:2) N 72, p. 81.
"In the Middle of Life." Poetry (121:2) N 72, p. 81.

222 BERGE, Carol
"Andropoulis at the Concert." Meas (1) 71.

"'In Our Terribleness'" (a LeRoi Jones title). Iowa (3:4) Fall 72, p. 23.
"The London Jew." Meas (1) 71.
"Nature Lecture." PartR (39:3) Sum 72, p. 380.

223 BERGER, Bruce
"Arizona Dreaming." SoDakR (10:1) Spr 72, p. 44.
"Basic Blue." Comm (96:14) 16 Je 72, p. 336.
"Electric Silence" (for Su Lum). ColQ (20:4) Spr 72, p. 515.
"The Enemy." SoDakR (10:1) Spr 72, p. 44.
"Non-Apology." ColQ (20:4) Spr 72, p. 515.
"Point of Music." Comm (95:15) 14 Ja 72, p. 347.
"Reaching Rider Canyon." WestR (10:1) Spr 72, p. 60.
"Valediction." AriD (1:3) Spr 72, p. 40.

224 BERGER-RIOFF, Suzanne
"Trout." NewYorker (48:15) 3 Je 72, p. 101.

225 BERK, Ilhan
"'Neither Did I See Such Loves nor Such Partings'" (tr. by Murat Nemet-Nejat). LitR (15:4) Sum 72, p. 439.

226 BERMAN, Elaine
"Triad for my Sister." Spec (14:1/2) My 72, p. 9.

227 BERMAN, John
"The Altar." LitR (16:1) Aut 72, p. 84.

228 BERNER, Robert Leslie
"Aquatic Park, San Francisco (for Marvin Glass)." Phoenix (3:4) Aut 72, p. 95.
"Seagull." Folio (8:1) Spr 72, p. 20.
"Song." Folio (8:1) Spr 72, p. 13.
"Song for Ceci." Phoenix (3:4) Aut 72, p. 98.

229 BERRIGAN, Daniel
"Some Poems from Underground: 1970." UnmOx (1:4) Aut 72.

230 BERRIGAN, Ted
"Coda: Three Sonnets for Tom Clark." ParisR (53) Wint 72, p. 166.
"Lady." StoneD (1:1) Spr 72, p. 10.
"Three Sonnets for Tom Clark." ParisR (53) Wint 72, p. 163.
"Words for Joanne Kyger." Iowa (3:4) Fall 72, p. 19.

231 BERRY, D. C.
"Annette." Shen (23:3) Spr 72, p. 82.
"Drinking with a Dead Bear." SouthernR (8:4) Aut 72, p. 906.
"If You Smile at This." WindO (10) Sum 72, p. 42.

"Michaelangelo." SouthernR (8:4) Aut 72, p. 905.
"Out of My Forehead." Confr (5) Wint-Spr 72, p. 32.
"Poem: I stepped." St. AR (1:4) Spr-Sum 72, p. 8.

232 BERRY, Jan
"The Longest War." HangL (18) Fall 72, p. 36.

233 BERRY, Wendell
"The Cruel Plumage." Apple (7) Aut 72, p. 14.
"The Gathering." Nat (214:5) 31 Ja 72, p. 151.
"Inland Passages." Apple (7) Aut 72, p. 12.
"Leaving Home." Hudson (25:2) Sum 72, p. 261.
"Poem for J." OhioR (14:1) Aut 72, p. 21.
"The Porch in the Evening." Iron (1) Spr 72, p. 63.
"Song." Kayak (29) S 72, p. 5.
"The Strangers." Hudson (25:2) Sum 72, p. 260.
"Testament." Kayak (29) S 72, p. 3.
"To William Butler Yeats." Kayak (29) S 72, p. 6.

234 BERRYMAN, John
"Beethoven Triumphant." NewYRB (18:6) 6 Ap 72, p. 4.
"Fare Well." Poetry (121:1) O 72, p. 2.
"King David Dances." NewYorker (47:53) 19 F 72, p. 42.

235 BERTOLINO, James
"Amongst Buttons." Meas (1) 71.
"The Dangerous Immaculate." Iron (2) Fall 72, p. 64.
"From the New Window." Poetry (120:3) Je 72, p. 148.
"A Hammer" (tr. of Eugène Guillevic). Drag (3:1) Spr 72, p. 78.
"Of Permanence." Cafe (4) Fall 72, p. 11.
"Prostrate Charisma." Iron (2) Fall 72, p. 65.
"Relentless." MinnR (3) Aut 72, p. 105.
"Spring Roads." Drag (3:1) Spr 72, p. 66.

236 BETHEL, Gar
"A Barbed Wire Fence." GeoR (26:1) Spr 72, p. 93.
"The Candle." Cim (19) Ap 72, p. 52.
"The Cold, Winter 1949." WindO (12) Wint 72-73, p. 29.
"Eating More." WindO (9) Spr 72, p. 23.
"Gigging Frogs in Kansas." KanQ (4:1) Wint 71-72, p. 34.
"Homage to Bogart." ColQ (21:1) Sum 72, p. 80.

237 BETOCCHI, Carlo
"With My Brother at Settignano, 1959" (tr. by I. L. Salomon). MichQR (11:4) Aut 72, p. 275.

238 BETTS, Leonidas
"Love" (Children's rhyme from Harnett County, North Carolina). NoCaFo (20:2) Ag 72, p. 144.

239 BEUM, Robert
"Interim." Thought (47:185) Sum 72, p. 280.

"On a Painting of Gethsemane." Poetry (120:3) Je 72, p. 137.
"A Psalm for Summer." Comm (96:20) 8 S 72, p. 482.

240 BEVER, Bernard
"Body naked." WormR (47) 72, p. 75.
"50¢ poem." WormR (47) 72, p. 76.
"Wilderness Poem #1a." Zahir (1:4/5) 72, p. 71.
"Wind over the hill rounding." WormR (47) 72, p. 76.

241 BEVERAGE, Mary
"The Abortion." ChiTM 19 N 72, p. 8.

242 BEYER, William
"The Climb." Wind (2:6) Aut 72, p. 28.
"A Matter of Doubt." Folio (8:1) Spr 72, p. 17.
"Silent Journey." Zahir (1:4/5) 72, p. 77.

243 BHASKARAN, M. P.
"Suddenly I Saw Him." Meas (3) 72, p. 6.

244 BHATTACHARYA, Arun
"Childhood: A Dedication." Meas (3) 72, p. 7.

245 BIASOTTI, Ray
"The Coca-Cola Girl." NewYQ (12) Aut 72, p. 78.

246 BICHSEL, Peter
"Grammatik Emer Abreise." Field (6) Spr 72, p. 34.

247 BIDERMAN, Sol
"The Falls of the Sparrows." ColQ (21:1) Sum 72, p. 68.

248 BIERMAN, Larry
"anyway, Papa Joe." Cim (19) Ap 72, p. 52.
"I Wonder Why." WindO (11) Aut 72, p. 36.
Seven Haiku. WindO (10) Sum 72, p. 1.

249 BILLIPP, Betty
"Hors d'oeuvres." SatEP (244:3) Aut 72, p. 88.

250 BINSFELD, Edmund L.
"Recall." ChrC (89:34) 27 S 72, p. 951.

251 BIRNEY, Earle
"the marriage." HangL (17) Sum 72, p. 8.
"museum of man." HangL (17) Sum 72, p. 8.

252 BIRSEL, Salâh
"Un Ballade contre les amours" (tr. by Ahmet O. Evin). LitR (15:4) Sum 72, p. 427.

253 BISHOP, Elizabeth
"A Miracle for Breakfast." Poetry (121:1) O 72, p. 3.

"The Moose." NewYorker (48:21) 15 Jl 72, p. 27.
"Night City." NewYorker (48:30) 16 S 72, p. 122.
"Poem: About the size of an old-style dollar bill." NewYorker (48:38) 11 N 72, p. 46.

254 BISHOP, Gordon
"But Let These Words Not Fail." HangL (18) Fall 72, p. 4.

255 BISSONETTE, David
"Let Me Ride." Confr (5) Wint-Spr 72, p. 81.
"Painting of Man." Esq (77:4) Ap 72, p. 212.

256 BIXLER, James P.
"The Car Preacher's Son Talking at a Rotary Club Luncheon Meeting at Twelve O'clock Noon in the Viking Room of Mason's Resturant." WormR (48) 72, p. 109.
"Death of God." ExpR (2) Wint-Spr 72, p. 37.
"London Times." ExpR (3) Fall-Wint 72/73, p. 11.
"Nancy Hooper." ExpR (3) Fall-Wint 72/73, p. 10.
"Stopping Off for a Drink." WormR (48) 72, p. 111.
"To the Divorcee." Poem (14) Mr 72, p. 6.

257 BLACK, Charles
"The East Wind." SouthwR (57:1) Wint 72, p. 15.
"The Letter." BosUJ (20:3) Aut 72, p. 43.
"My Daughter Asks Relief from Monotony of Response." BelPoJ (22:3) Spr 72, p. 16.
"My Daughter Is Too Smart For Me Anymore." ArizQ (28:2) Sum 72, p. 173.

258 BLACK, David
"Intermezzo." Pan (9) 72, p. 14.
"Psyche." Pan (9) 72, p. 15.

259 BLACK, Isaac J.
"Brooklyn Bridges Falling Down." JnlOBP (2:16) Sum 72, p. 15.

260 BLACK, John
"Freshman." WestR (9:2) Wint 72, p. 78.

261 BLACKWELL, Will H.
"Habit." Epos (23:4) Sum 72, p. 15.

262 BLAKE, George
"March 16, 1968." KanQ (4:3) Sum 72, p. 26.

263 BLANCO, Andres Eloy
"The Boa" (tr. by Seth Wade). Drag (3:1) Spr 72, p. 77.

264 BLAZEK, Douglas
"Armchair Affidavit." Poetry (119:6) Mr 72, p. 318.
"Bells & Bursting." Poetry (119:6) Mr 72, p. 315.

"The Bridal Body." UnmOx (1:1) N 71, p. 16.
"excursion into total access." Meas (2) 72.
"For Those Who Walk Back & Forth Across the Bridge (for T. L. Kryss)." Meas (2) 72.
"Fusing Sperm to Eternity." BabyJ (5) N 72, p. 9.
"Girders of a New Chemistry." ExpR (3) Fall-Wint 72/73, p. 4.
"In the Wheel of Her Palm." MinnR (3) Aut 72, p. 36.
"Loneliness." New:ACP (19) Aut 72, p. 29.
"The Long Table." Iron (2) Fall 72, p. 17.
"Nor Travels Nor Loves Anymore." Poetry (119:6) Mr 72, p. 316.
"A Personal Ecology." Poetry (119:6) Mr 72, p. 315.
"A Portable Moment in Our Lives" (for Alta). UnmOx (1:1) N 71, p. 14.
"Slaughter Mesh." BabyJ (5) N 72, p. 8.
"A Soft Brevity." BabyJ (5) N 72, p. 8.
"Thanksgiving Birthday Song." BabyJ (5) N 72, p. 8.
"There Is." Poetry (119:6) Mr 72, p. 317.
"Things Decay/Reason Argues." Meas (2) 72.
"To Be, But Be More." Iron (2) Fall 72, p. 16.

265 BLESSING, Richard
"The Dead." Poem (15) Jl 72, p. 27.
"Flatness." JnlOPC (6:3) Spr 72, p. 621.
"Last House." PoetryNW (13:2) Sum 72, p. 32.
"Love Poem." PoetryNW (13:2) Sum 72, p. 31.
"The Mailbox." Poem (15) Jl 72, p. 28.
"Recurring Dream." HiramPoR (13) Fall-Wint 72, p. 5.
"September: Looking East." Poem (14) Mr 72, p. 2.
"To My Father (I)." SouthernR (8:2) Spr 72, p. 426.
"To My Father (II)." SouthernR (8:2) Spr 72, p. 427.

266 BLISH, James
"Grand Pause." PraS (46:2) Sum 72, p. 149.

267 BLISS, Alice
"Courtroom." SouthernHR (6:2) Spr 72, p. 154.

268 BLOK, Alexander
"For Anna Akhmatova" (tr. by Barbara Heldt Monter). RusLT (4) Aut 72, p. 19.
"From sunset she appeared" (tr. by Gary Kern). RusLT (4) Aut 72, p. 20.
"How burdensome to walk among the people" (tr. by Gary Kern). RusLT (4) Aut 72, p. 19.
"I pass away this life of mine" (tr. by Gary Kern). RusLT (4) Aut 72, p. 18.
"Nightingale Garden" (tr. by Rodney L. Patterson). RusLT (4) Aut 72, p. 9.
"Seven poems by Alexander Blok" (tr. by Eugene M. Kayden). ColQ (20:3) Wint 72, p. 443.
"Today I don't want to remember what happened yesterday" (tr. by Barbara Heldt Monter). RusLT (4) Aut 72, p. 18.

269 BLOMFIELD, Adelaide
"Moonlight." HiramPoR (13) Fall-Wint 72, p. 21.

270 BLOOM, Edward
"Aubade for an Editor." AAUP (58:4) D 72, p. 383.

271 BLOOM, Robert
"In the Quiet of the Trees." ChiTM 9 Ja 72, p. 12.

272 BLUM, Margaret
"Primavera Revisited." CEA Critic (34:3) Mr 72, p. 32.

273 BLY, Robert
"The Age of the Great Symphonies" (tr. of Rolf Jacobsen). Madrona (1:1) Je 71, p. 19.
"'Clouds Torn Open'" (tr. of Antonio Machado). MichQR (11:4) Aut 72, p. 279.
"Country Roads" (tr. of Rolf Jacobsen). Madrona (1:1) Je 71, p. 32.
"Dance of Death" (tr. of Federico Garcia Lorca). NewL (38:4) Sum 72, p. 6.
"The Dead Seal Near McClure's Beach." Stand (13:4) 72, p. 19.
"Death" (for Isidoro de Blas) (tr. of Federico Garcia Lorca). NewL (38:4) Sum 72, p. 9.
"Evening in Skane" (tr. of Rainer Maria Rilke). Madrona (1:2) N 71, p. 12.
"Ghazal of the Terrifying Presence" (tr. of Federico Garcia Lorca). NewL (38:4) Sum 72, p. 10.
"The Name" (tr. of Tomas Tranströmer). Books (46:1) Wint 72, p. 48.
"Night Farmyard." StoneD (1:1) Spr 72, p. 15.
"On a Farm." NYT 28 Ap 72, p. 41.
"On a Moonlit Road in the North Woods." StoneD (1:1) Spr 72, p. 14.
"The Open Window" (tr. of Tomas Tranströmer). Books (46:1) Wint 72, p. 48.
"Orchard Grass." StoneD (1:1) Spr 72, p. 15.
"Pilgrim Fish Heads." Stand (13:4) 72, p. 18.
"Poem Adapted from the Chinese." UnmOx (1:1) F 72, p. 28.
"Pulling the Boat Up Among Lake Reeds." Kayak (28) 72, p. 54.
from The Shadow Poem: "Someone is asleep in the back of my house." NewYQ (11) Sum 72, p. 44.
"Sonata and Destructions" (tr. of Pablo Neruda). AbGR (3:1) Spr-Sum 72, p. 1.
"Thinking of Tedious Ways Eight." UnmOx (1:1) F 72, p. 29.
"Throw Yourself Like Seed" (tr. of Unamuno). MichQR (11:4) Aut 72, p. 280.
"Time To Be ..." OhioR (13:3) Spr 72, p. 17.
"A Walk." UTR (1:1) 72, p. 3.
"Windy Day." UTR (1:2) 72, p. 3.

"Writing Again." OhioR (14:1) Aut 72, p. 41.
"Written at Island Lake." OhioR (13:3) Spr 72, p. 18.

274 BOBROWSKI, Johannes
"Russian Song" (tr. by Nicholas Kolumban). Folio (8:1) Spr 72, p. 24.

275 BODE, Carl
"The Message." ChiTM 1 O 72, p. 17.
"Troglodyte." CarlMis (12:1) Fall-Wint 71-72, p. 76.

276 BOEHM, Ann
"Fingernagelgross" (tr. of Hilde Domin). Field (6) Spr 72, p. 16.

277 BOGEN, Karen I.
"a metamorphosis." Humanist (32:2) Mr-Ap 72, p. 35.

278 BOGGS, Lawrence
"Near Gilroy, California." New:ACP (19) Aut 72, p. 22.

279 BOGGS, Mildred W.
"This Rent Receipt." Wind (2:6) Aut 72, p. 25.

280 BOGIN, George
"Arterio Sclerosis." ColumF (1:2) Spr 72, p. 16.
"Cape Cod." ColumF (1:2) Spr 72, p. 16.
"Dispatch." ColumF (1:3) Sum 72, p. 23.
"How to Write a Poem (and Make a Film)." ColumF (1:4) Fall 72, p. 26.
"Nineteen." ColumF (1:2) Spr 72, p. 18.

281 BOHM, Robert
from The Ox Poems: "Almost." MassR (13:4) Aut 72, p. 677.
from The Ox Poems: "Both Gone." MassR (13:4) Aut 72, p. 677.
from The Ox Poems: "The Ox." MassR (13:4) Aut 72, p. 676.
from The Ox Poems: "The Oxherd Gets to Know the Ox." MassR (13:4) Aut 72, p. 676.
from The Ox Poems: "Without Thought." MassR (13:4) Aut 72, p. 677.

282 BOIES, J. J.
"The Lost Domain #3 (Golf Courses)." BallSUF (13:4) Aut 72, p. 79.

283 BOLLS, Imogene L.
"Glencoe Place." KanQ (4:1) Wint 71-72, p. 42.

284 BONAZZI, Robert
"Ballet Rehearsal at the Opera by Degas." Folio (8:1) Spr 72, p. 29.

"Beethoven Walks in the Forest." Folio (8:1) Spr 72, p. 28.
"The Blue Death Wish." MinnR (2) Spr 72, p. 120.
"Bly's Minnesota." MinnR (2) Spr 72, cover.
"Dan's Dream." MinnR (2) Spr 72, p. 117.
"My Image." SaltCR (5:1) Wint 72.
"The Ivory Table." MinnR (2) Spr 72, p. 118.
"Marginal Notes from a Text on Method Acting." MinnR (2) Spr 72, p. 117.
"Odalisque by Ingres, 1814." Folio (8:1) Spr 72, p. 28.
"Seagull over Prospect Park." RoadAR (3:4) Wint 71-72, p. 13.

285 BOND, Harold
"The Air Forest." AriD (1:3) Spr 72, p. 20.
"The Way It Happens to You." Shen (23:4) Sum 72, p. 77.

286 BONFIM, Paulo
"Wind Song." ArizQ (28:1) Spr 72, p. 60.

287 BONNER, Robert
"Requiem for Negro History Week." NegroHB (35:3) Mr 72, p. 67.

288 BONOS, V. N.
from Outerearth: "Fledglings and the speeches of prophecy" (tr. by Stavros Deligiorgis). AriD (1:4/5) Sum-Aut 72, p. 25.
from Outerearth: "The mother done in and the dead scornful" (tr. by Stavros Deligiorgis). AriD (1:4/5) Sum-Aut 72, p. 24.

289 BOO, Maureen H.
"Fog Road." St. AR (2:1) Aut-Wint 72, p. 19.

290 BOOKER, F. C.
"'The Planets' by Gustave Holst" (for my muse). LittleM (6:1) Spr 72, p. 32.
"A Post Card to a Friend from 'Nemesis' by Orehym Dog." LittleM (6:1) Spr 72, p. 33.
"Song of the Leviathan from 'Nemesis' by Orehym Dog" (for her). LittleM (6:1) Spr 72, p. 31.

291 BOOTH, Philip
"Another Man's Wife." Peb (9) Wint 72.
"Big Mouth." Shen (24:1) Aut 72, p. 49.
"Gurney Norman, Kentucky Coal Field Orphan, Is Gurney Stronger Than History, or What?" Field (7) Fall 72, p. 73.
"Household." AmerS (41:3) Sum 72, p. 391.
"I Pass on the Road, See Myself in a Country Graveyard" (for Walker R. Hall 1901-1970). Field (7) Fall 72, p. 72.
"Impotence." Esq (77:6) Je 72, p. 71.

"Self-Portrait." Harp (245:1467) Ag 72, p. 69.
"Strata." Kayak (29) S 72, p. 57.
"Ways." Field (7) Fall 72, p. 69.

292 BORCHERT, Wolfgang
"Aranka." SoDakR (10:1) Spr 72, p. 74.
"At the Window." SoDakR (10:1) Spr 72, p. 74.
"The Wind and the Rose." SoDakR (10:1) Spr 72, p. 74.

293 BORDEN, Maureen
"Kitehood." Etc. (29:1) Mr 72, Inside Front Cover.

294 BORENSTEIN, Emily
"The Zero Place." Epos (23:4) Sum 72, p. 16.

295 BORGES, Jorge Luis
"Dos Milongas." WestHR (26:4) Aut 72, p. 330.
"Fragment" (tr. by Brewster Ghiselin). MichQR (11:4) Aut 72, p. 281.
"John 1:14" (tr. by Norman Thomas DiGiovanni). NewYorker (47:52) 12 F 72, p. 38.
"Montevideo" (tr. by Norman Thomas DiGiovanni). NewYorker (48:3) 11 Mr 72, p. 34.
"The Watcher" (tr. by Norman Thomas DiGiovanni). NewYorker (48:1) 26 F 72, p. 42.

296 BORLASE, Christina
"Sam." Peb (7) Aut 71.

297 BORMANN, Manfred
"After One O' Clock at Night" (tr. of Omer Faruk Toprak). LitR (15:4) Sum 72, p. 414.

298 BOSE, Shishir Kumar
"The Man is a Wreck of Marijuana." Meas (3) 72, p. 8.

299 BOSWELL, C. Barkley Jr.
"April Departure." ColQ (21:1) Sum 72, p. 88.

300 BOSWORTH, Donald N.
"Veiled Vision." EngJ (61:7) O 72, p. 1014.

301 BOTTOMS, David Jr.
"I Have Not Met a Season." Wind (2:6) Aut 72, p. 53.

302 BOTTOSTO, Rando
"Blood." Zahir (1:4/5) 72, p. 34.
"By Nature Without." Zahir (1:4/5) 72, p. 34.
"Dracula Piano Debussy's Quick Soul." Zahir (1:4/5) 72, p. 35.
"Rain." UTR (1:2) 72, p. 34.
"The River Horse." Zahir (1:4/5) 72, p. 34.
"Tomato at Seashore." PoetL (67:4) Wint 72, p. 334.

303 BOURGO, David Del
"To a Greek Friend." Epos (23:4) Sum 72, p. 20.

304 BOURNE, Louis M.
"Death or the Doctor's Waiting Room" (tr. of Vicente Aleixandre). Mund (5:1/2) 72, p. 125.
"Idea" (tr. of Vicente Aleixandre). Mund (5:1/2) 72, p. 123.
"Repose" (tr. of Vicente Aleixandre). Mund (5:1/2) 72, p. 121.

305 BOWDEN, James H.
"Early Sunday Morning (after a painting by Edward Hopper)." KanQ (4:3) Sum 72, p. 58.
"Easter In Jeffersonville." ChrC (89:13) 29 Mr 72, p. 369.
"Had Silicon Been a Gas." KanQ (4:3) Sum 72, p. 58.
"John Calvin Watches a Football Game." St. AR (1:4) Spr-Sum 72, p. 38.
"King Kong Died for Your Sins." ChrC (89:3) 19 Ja 72, p. 62.
"Plan de Paris a Vol d'Oiseau." PraS (46:1) Spr 72, p. 48.

306 BOWEN, James K.
"Donne's Room." CEACritic (34:2) Ja 72, p. 25.
"Frost." CEACritic (34:4) My 72, p. 12.
"New Winter." WestHR (9:1) Spr 72, p. 81.

307 BOWEN, Robert T.
"Just for the Record." FreeL (15:1/2) 71-72, p. 49.
"Just for the Record." JnlOBP (2:16) Sum 72, p. 64.

308 BOWERS, Larry Neal
"Arlington, 1969." Drag (3:2) Sum 72, p. 41.
"Horses." WindO (9) Spr 72, p. 31.
"Hunting Squirrel in October." Wind (2:6) Aut 72, p. 14.
"Memorial." WindO (9) Spr 72, p. 32.
"Midnight." Epos (23:3) Spr 72, p. 28.

309 BOWERS, Sara Bartlett
"For My Wrists, on Departure." SouthernPR (13:1) Aut 72, p. 30.
"Poem: When Laura lets down her hair." SouthernPR (12:2) Spr 72, p. 4.

310 BOWIE, Robert
"Elements and Unnamed Elements." WindO (11) Aut 72, p. 31.
"A Stream Flows Out of My Eyes." WindO (11) Aut 72, p. 32.

311 BOWLING, Sam
"Bellows." Cafe (4) Fall 72, p. 30.

312 BOWMAN, Geoff
"Daimonji Hill." Madrona (1:4) S 72, p. 44.
"Eikando." Madrona (1:4) S 72, p. 43.
"For David Owens." Madrona (1:4) S 72, p. 49.
"Letter from Lake Erie." Madrona (1:4) S 72, p. 45.
"Rhizones." Madrona (1:4) S 72, p. 50.
"Three Border Pieces." Madrona (1:4) S 72, p. 52.
"Yodo Valley, Osaka Plain." Madrona (1:3) My 72, p. 6.

313 BOWMAN, Peggy
"Foliage of War." NewYQ (10) Spr 72, p. 73.

314 BOXER, David
"Embassy." St. AR (2:1) Aut-Wint 72, p. 30.

315 BOXER, Ray
"Depths." SouthwR (57:1) Wint 72, p. 65.
"Kingdoms." UTR (1:2) 72, p. 33.

316 BOYD, Melba J.
"1965" (dedicated to all my Brothers and Sisters of southwest Detroit, who did and did not survive). Broad (66) D 72.

317 BOYD, Sue Abbott
"On Becoming Very Weary." Zahir (1:4/5) 72, p. 74.

318 BOYD, Verlaine
"Most Tried--Some Succeeded." Northeast Sum 72, p. 16.
"Stone." RoadAR (3:4) Wint 71-72, p. 41.

319 BOYLE, Kay
"For an Historian, Following an Operation on His Eyes (for Roger Burlingame)." Mark (16:3) Wint 72, p. 25.

320 BOZANIC, Nick, Jr.
"At the Orchard." Pan (9) 72, p. 60.

321 BRACKER, Jon
"At Thirty-Six." SaltCR (5:1) Wint 72.
"Seventh and Wabash at a Quarter to Five." Qt (5:39/40) Sum-Aut 72, p. 58.

322 BRADBURY, Ray
"Remembrance." LadHJ (89:9) S 72, p. 84.
"This Time of Kites." ChiTM 10 S 72, p. 10.

323 BRADLEY, Audrey H.
"To an Unsung Poet." SouthernPR (13:1) Aut 72, p. 17.

324 BRADLEY, Sam
"Be As Dear To Me As I Am To Myself." Poetry (120:3) Je 72, p. 146.

"Beginner." Poem (14) Mr 72, p. 60.
"Cain on the Eve." Poetry (120:3) Je 72, p. 147.
"December 31: Watch Night." ChrC (89:47) 27 D 72, p. 1317.
"Distinctions." Poem (14) Mr 72, p. 61.
"He Comes from the Sea, to Take a Beachhead." ArizQ (28:3) Aut 72, p. 256.
"Hoyden from Nazareth." ChrC (89:46) 20 D 72, p. 1293.
"I Sniff Outside the Circle of Your Fire." LittleM (6:2/3) Sum-Aut 72, p. 99.
"Pushing the Dark Around a Little." KanQ (4:1) Wint 71-72, p. 10.
"Reverting, Reconverting." SoCaR (5:1) D 72, p. 42.
"Sojourner and Sire." KanQ (4:1) Wint 71-72, p. 10.
"Thrall of Three." St. AR (1:4) Spr-Sum 72, p. 34.
"The Way Forward May Be the Way Back." SouthernPR (12:2) Spr 72, p. 51.

325 BRAINARD, Franklin
"Because My Horses Wait." Cafe (4) Fall 72, p. 10.
from Diary August 1, 1970 (For William O. Douglas):
"III." HiramPoR (12) Spr-Sum 72, p. 8.
"The Stove Leaks Light." MidwQ (13:4) Sum 72, p. 349.
"Waiting." Cafe (4) Fall 72, p. 10.

326 BRANCACCIO, Patrick
"Invite." AAUP (58:4) D 72, p. 418.

327 BRAND, Sister Helena, SNJM
"Germination." SewanR (80:2) Spr 72, p. 261.

328 BRANDTS, Bob
"Advice to Young Poets." Spec (14:1/2) My 72, p. 16.

329 BRANSON, Branley Allan
"Apartment Complex." FreeL (15:1/2) 71-72, p. 52.
"Child Lost in the Smokies." LitR (16:1) Aut 72, p. 86.
"Winter Work at a Wildlife Refuge." KanQ (4:1) Wint 71-72, p. 35.

330 BRASHEAR, Sherry
"Poster: 'The Romantics' Last Stronghold in Utah.'" Wind (2:6) Aut 72, p. 17.

331 BRASIER, Virginia
"Grandchild." ChiTM 24 D 72, p. 5.

332 BRAUN, Richard Emil
"The Gift." ModernPS (3:1) 72, p. 25.

333 BRAUTIGAN, Richard
"Autobiography (Polish It Like a Piece of Silver)." Esq (78:3) S 72, p. 50.

334 BRAXTON, Joanne M.
"Ujamaa Sun Lines." JnlOBP (2:16) Sum 72, p. 19.

335 BRAYMER, Nan
"The Burning Steppe" (tr. of Berdynazar Khudainazarov, w. Matthew Kahan). NewWR (40:4) Aut 72, p. 13.
"The Coming of the Flowers" (tr. of Uigun, w. Bernard Koten). NewWR (40:4) Aut 72, p. 133.
"Invitation to Kirghizstan" (tr. of Kurbanychbek Malikov, w. Bernard Koten). NewWR (40:4) Aut 72, p. 24.
"Love of Country" (tr. of Mara Greeazanie, w. Matthew Kahan). NewWR (40:4) Aut 72, p. 83.
"Maples in Bloom" (tr. of Yan Sudrabkali, w. Matthew Kahan). NewWR (40:4) Aut 72, p. 84.
"My Land" (tr. of Eduardo Miezelaitis, w. Bernard Koten). NewWR (40:4) Aut 72, p. 114.
"Song About Our Stones" (tr. of Silva Kaputikian, w. Bernard Koten). NewWR (40:4) Aut 72, p. 64.

336 BREDENBERG, Jeff
"Che Guevara." SouthernPR (12: Special Issue) 72, p. 46.

337 BREWER, Kenneth
"The Classroom." HangL (16) Wint 71-72, p. 5.
"The Stairway." PoetryNW (13:1) Spr 72, p. 17.
"Taking Turns." RoadAR (3:4) Wint 71-72, p. 5.
"The Visitor." HangL (16) Wint 71-72, p. 4.
"Young Woman." Drag (3:1) Spr 72, p. 54.

338 BREWSTER, Elizabeth
"Seasonal." New:ACP (18) Ap 72, p. 18.

339 BRICUTH, John
"The Knowledge of Connaturality." PraS (46:3) Aut 72, p. 223.

340 BRIGGS, A. D.
"The Godyssey" (tr. of Alexander Pushkin). RusLT (3) Spr 72, p. 17.

341 BRIGGS, John
"Lucid Prodigy in Snow (for Joe LaRocca)." NewYQ (11) Sum 72, p. 81.

342 BRIGGS, Lea
"So That I Can Forgive My Absence." ChiTM 2 Jl 72, p. 2.

343 BRIGHAM, Besmilr
from Blue Fields of Malinche: "Their Long Walk, Peregrino." MinnR (2) Spr 72, p. 60.
"The Child." SouthernR (8:4) Aut 72, p. 891.
"The Face of Baudelaire." SouthernR (8:4) Aut 72, p. 885.

"The Figures' Math." SouthernR (8:4) Aut 72, p. 896.
"The Gate of Fire." SouthernR (8:4) Aut 72, p. 886.
"Hearn at Grand Anse." SouthernR (8:4) Aut 72, p. 883.
"In My Father's Lying Fallow Field." Apple (7) Aut 72, p. 10.
"To the Unwritten Poems of Young Joy." SouthernR (8:4) Aut 72, p. 888.
from The Valley of San Miguel: "Cemetery in New Mexico." MinnR (2) Spr 72, p. 57.

344 BRIGHT, Albert D.
"The Bride's Song." LitR (16:1) Aut 72, p. 33.
"Sounds." LitR (16:1) Aut 72, p. 32.

345 BRILLIANT, Alan
"Folder." UnicornJ (4) 72, p. 56.
"The Lost Atlantis." UnicornJ (4) 72, p. 58.
"They Write Me." UnicornJ (4) 72, p. 54.
"To a Poet Friend." UnicornJ (4) 72, p. 57.
"Words." UnicornJ (4) 72, p. 55.

346 BRITT, Alan
"The Day Folds Into." Epoch (21:2) Wint 71, p. 147.
"lizard." UTR (1:3) 72, p. 30.
"one thought puts the antlers." UTR (1:1) 72, p. 9.
"Upon Hearing a Halloween Parade, as I Awaken from Sleep." UTR (1:2) 72, p. 11.
"Vallejo." UTR (1:4) 72, p. 19.
"A Yellow Flower." PoetL (67:4) Wint 72, p. 334.

347 BRIXIUS, Robert
"Parler et lise." BeyB (2:2) 72, p. 45.

348 BROCK, Edwin
"Collage." NewYorker (48:20) 8 Jl 72, p. 28.
"Ghosts Dying." Nat (215:7) 18 S 72, p. 214.

349 BROCK, Randall
"carve your." BabyJ (5) N 72, p. 23.
"jump & spin." BabyJ (5) N 72, p. 23.
"up the road." BabyJ (5) N 72, p. 23.
"with every." BabyJ (5) N 72, p. 23.

350 BROCK, Van K.
"The Daydream." SouthernR (8:4) Aut 72, p. 917.
"The Evidence." GeoR (26:1) Spr 72, p. 91.
"In the Zebra." PraS (46:2) Sum 72, p. 160.
"King." SouthernPR (13:1) Aut 72, p. 3.
"Littoral." NoAmR (257:4) Wint 72, p. 46.

351 BRODEY, Jim
"No Time in Homestead" (w. Jan Herman). UnmOx (1:3) Sum 72, p. 38.

"Poem: Back at San Francisco Greyhound, leaning." ParisR (55) Aut 72, p. 71.
"Unemployed Tunes." ParisR (55) Aut 72, p. 70.

352 BRODSKY, Joseph
"Conversation with an Angel" (tr. by Harvey Feinberg and H. W. Tjalsma). New:ACP (18) Ap 72, p. 22.
"Einemalten Architekten in Rom" (tr. by George L. Kline). Antaeus (6) Sum 72, p. 109.
"Evening" (tr. by George L. Kline). Antaeus (6) Sum 72, p. 106.
"Exhaustion now is a more frequent guest" (tr. by George L. Kline). Antaeus (6) Sum 72, p. 105.
"In villages God does not live only" (tr. by George L. Kline). Antaeus (6) Sum 72, p. 102.
"Nature Morte" (tr. by George L. Kline). SatR (55:33) 12 Ag 72, p. 45.
"Post aetatem nostram." RusLT (2) Wint 72, p. 443.
"Razgovor s nebozhitelem." RusLT (2) Wint 72, p. 437.
"Refusing to catalogue all of one's woes" (tr. by George L. Kline). Antaeus (6) Sum 72, p. 107.
"Sonnet" (tr. by George L. Kline). Antaeus (6) Sum 72, p. 100.
"Spring Season of Muddy Roads" (tr. by George L. Kline). Antaeus (6) Sum 72, p. 103.
"You're coming home again" (tr. by George L. Kline). Antaeus (6) Sum 72, p. 101.

353 BRODWIN, Stanley
"Inscription in a Gift Copy of The Adventures of Huckleberry Finn." Mark (16:2) Sum 72, p. 21.

354 BROKAW, Cary
"You in a sudden gust." Spec (14:1/2) My 72, p. 17.

355 BROMIGE, David
"A Blessing." Spec (14:1/2) My 72, p. 19.
"Outside." Spec (14:1/2) My 72, p. 18.

356 BROOK, Donna
"Chanting to Loosen My Grip." MinnR (3) Aut 72, p. 40.
"If the Razzle Dazzle Limps..." MinnR (3) Aut 72, p. 41.
"On the Death of George Jackson." Kayak (29) S 72, p. 10.

357 BROOKHOUSE, Christopher
"Daniel Berrigan, Poet and Priest freed from federal prison." CarolQ (24:2) Spr 72, p. 73.
"Fragments at the turn of the year." SouthernR (8:2) Spr 72, p. 424.
"Mobile." CarolQ (24:2) Spr 72, p. 72.

358 BROOKS, Gwendolyn
"Aurora." Broad (65) N 72.

359 BROSMAN, Catherine Savage
"Ash Lawn." SouthernR (8:3) Sum 72, p. 600.
"Space Traveler." Shen (23:2) Wint 72, p. 19.

360 BROSSARD, Iris
"Riddle: She boils stones for soup." Antaeus (7) Aut 72, p. 31.

361 BROTT, Ruth
"Cemetery." AriD (1:2) Wint 72, p. 41.
"Morning." AriD (1:2) Wint 72, p. 40.

362 BROUGHTON, T. Alan
"Ballad of the Falling Angel." Epoch (22:1) Fall 72, p. 83.
"Becalmed." Northeast Sum 72, p. 7.
"The Day We Found a Monster on the Beach." LittleM (6:2/3) Sum-Aut 72, p. 117.
Eight Poems. Poem (14) Mr 72, p. 11.
"Evening at Taos." Northeast Sum 72, p. 5.
"The Eyes He Wears." PraS (46:2) Sum 72, p. 159.
"First Christmas." PraS (46:3) Aut 72, p. 256.
"Green Beer." Epoch (22:1) Fall 72, p. 82.
"Homage to Keats." BelPoJ (22:3) Spr 72, p. 8.
"In the Face of Descent." BelPoJ (22:3) Spr 72, p. 12.
"Meditation of a Wife." Epoch (22:1) Fall 72, p. 84.
"Music Teacher." Wind (2:6) Aut 72, p. 43.
"Night Drive." Epoch (22:1) Fall 72, p. 82.
"Old father." Northeast Sum 72, p. 8.
"Poised." Cim (20) Jl 72, p. 37.
"Spring Comes In." Northeast Sum 72, p. 10.
"Sunday Afternoon." PraS (46:2) Sum 72, p. 158.
"Ties." Confr (5) Wint-Spr 72, p. 88.
"Transmutations." FourQt (21:3) Mr 72, p. 33.
"War Again." Comm (96:9) 5 My 72, p. 211.
"What's In It?" LittleM (6:2/3) Sum-Aut 72, p. 120.

363 BROWN, Bruce Bennett
"Lunch Before Plane Time" (for Melissa Randolph). Wind (2:6) Aut 72, p. 21.
"Nocturne" (for Sylvia Trent Auxier). Wind (2:5) Sum 72, p. 3.

364 BROWN, Clarence
"Armed with the sight of the fine wasps" (tr. of Osip Mandelstam, w. W. S. Merwin). Hudson (25:1) Spr 72, p. 73.
"Five Poems" (tr. of Osip Mandelstam, w. W. S. Merwin). Antaeus (6) Sum 72, p. 92.
Fourteen Poems (tr. of Osip Mandelstam, w. W. S. Merwin). QRL (18:1/2) 72, p. 7.
"I am alone staring into the eye of the ice" (tr. of Osip Mandelstam, w. W. S. Merwin). NewYRB (17:12/18:1) 27 Ja 72, p. 35.
"Insomnia. Homer. Taut Sails" (tr. of Osip Mandelstam,

w. W. S. Merwin). Hudson (25:1) Spr 72, p. 71.
"Oh the horizon steals my breath and takes it nowhere" (tr. of Osip Mandelstam, w. W. S. Merwin). NewYRB (17:12/18:1) 27 Ja 72, p. 35.
"Tristia" (tr. of Osip Mandelstam, w. W. S. Merwin). Hudson (25:1) Spr 72, p. 71.
"We shall meet again, in Petersburg" (tr. of Osip Mandelstam, w. W. S. Merwin). Hudson (25:1) Spr 72, p. 72.
"What can we do with the plains' beaten weight?" (tr. of Osip Mandelstam, w. W. S. Merwin). NewYRB (17:12/18:1) 27 Ja 72, p. 35.

365 BROWN, Harry
"Poem: The word love comes easy young." Conrad (3:2) 71-72, p. 81.

366 BROWN, Sharon Lee
"End of the Year Sale." KanQ (4:1) Wint 71-72, p. 31.

367 BROWNE, Michael Dennis
"The Driving Lesson." Iron (1) Spr 72, p. 64.
"Hallowe'en 1970." SenR (3:1) My 72, p. 62.
"Inspiration Point." SenR (3:1) My 72, p. 64.
"Pebble." SenR (3:1) My 72, p. 65.
"Poem with Repeated Phrase." Kayak (29) S 72, p. 7.

368 BROWNSTEIN, Michael
"Baby Blue Eyes." UnmOx (1:3) Sum 72, p. 25.
"Darwin." UnmOx (1:3) Sum 72, p. 24.
"Garden Talk." UnmOx (1:3) Sum 72, p. 22.
"Have You Found Your Roller Coaster Yet?" UnmOx (1:3) Sum 72, p. 23.

369 BRUCHAC, Joseph
"August Night." RoadAR (3:4) Wint 71-72, p. 11.
"Crayfish." Cafe (4) Fall 72, p. 33.
"Directions." NewL (39:2) Wint 72, p. 138.
"Falling Star." RoadAR (3:4) Wint 71-72, p. 11.
"Notes on the Defense Economy." NewL (39:2) Wint 72, p. 139.
"The Police" (tr. of Pablo Neruda, w. Liliana Goldin). SenR (3:1) My 72, p. 22.
"The Roots of Mountains." OhioR Wint 72, p. 84.
"The Second Time Around." Peb (6) Sum 71.
"The Ship." NewL (39:2) Wint 72, p. 140.
"Skinning Out the Last Deer." Meas (2) 72.
"Surprise Party." New:ACP (19) Aut 72, p. 19.
"Two Poems Written in the Tin and Lint Bar." Shen (23:2) Wint 72, p. 51.
"Written in a Hammock in Ghana" (for Rajat). NewL (39:2) Wint 72, p. 139.

370 BRUNA, Raúl
"Public Man" (tr. by Edward Oliphant). RoadAR (4:1) Spr

72, p. 12.

371 BRUNN, Donald
"Palomino Blue." PoetryNW (13:2) Sum 72, p. 30.
"Urban Renewal." PoetryNW (13:2) Sum 72, p. 31.

372 BRUSH, Thomas
"Burglars at Noon." PoetryNW (13:4) Wint 72-73, p. 45.
"The Dreams of Gerard De Nerval." Shen (24:1) Aut 72, p. 63.
"Drowning" (in memory of H. C. who died December 1, 1969). PraS (46:1) Spr 72, p. 62.
"Let Us Be Superficial." PoetryNW (13:2) Sum 72, p. 25.
"Moonrise." PoetryNW (13:4) Wint 72-73, p. 46.
"Nightsong." PoetryNW (13:4) Wint 72-73, p. 45.
"On the Road." PoetryNW (13:4) Wint 72-73, p. 46.
"The War in the Lucky Dollar Tavern." Shen (24:1) Aut 72, p. 62.

373 BRUTUS, Dennis
from Poems From Algiers: "A wrong-headed bunch we may be." GreenR (2:3) 72, p. 11.

374 BUCHMAN, Marion
"Riderless Horse." ChiTM 13 Ag 72, p. 61.

375 BUCKELS, Elizabeth
"Pine." PoetC (7:1) 72, p. 29.

376 BUCKNER, Sally
"Camel." SouthernPR (12: Special Issue) 72, p. 38.
"Oratorio for Autumn." ChrC (89:39) 1 N 72, p. 1095.

377 BUELL, Frederick
"Ballad." Epoch (21:3) Spr 72, p. 278.
"Canoeing." Epoch (21:3) Spr 72, p. 281.
"Swamp Hours." Epoch (21:3) Spr 72, p. 276.

378 BUGGS, George
"For the Children." Phy (33:1) Spr 72, p. 78.

379 BUKOWSKI, Charles
"Beefrice." Cord (1:3) 72, p. 8.
"The Best Love Poem I Can Write at the Moment." Madrona (1:2) N 71, p. 16.
"The Brainless Eyes." LittleM (6:2/3) Sum-Aut 72, p. 25.
"Bullshit Pain." LittleM (6:1) Spr 72, p. 14.
"Coffee and Babies." Peb (9) Wint 72.
"A Day at the Oak Tree Meet." Peb (9) Wint 72.
"The Death of an Idiot." NewYQ (12) Aut 72, p. 46.
"5 Dollars." NewYQ (12) Aut 72, p. 49.
"Goodyear." UnmOx (1:2) F 72, p. 42.
"He Wrote in Lonely Blood." NewYQ (10) Spr 72, p. 44.
"I met this woman." WormR (47) 72, p. 103.

"The Last Poetry Reading." WormR (48) 72, p. 135.
"Law." NewYQ (10) Spr 72, p. 46.
"Looking at the Cat's Balls." NewYQ (12) Aut 72, p. 44.
"My Friend, Andre." NewYQ (12) Aut 72, p. 48.
"My Literary Fly." NewYQ (9) Wint 72, p. 50.
from Outcast Six: "Heat." Magazine (5) part 8, 72, p. 17.
"the painter." WormR (47) 72, p. 104.
"The People, No." LittleM (6:1) Spr 72, p. 15.
"Poem: When the violets roar at the sun." UnmOx (1:1) N 71, p. 16.
"Poetry, You Whore..." WormR (46) 72, p. 63.
"The Smoking Car." WormR (46) 72, p. 63.
"Style." NewYQ (9) Wint 72, p. 49.
"The Sun, the Bushes, the Hell of it." LittleM (6:2/3) Sum-Aut 72, p. 26.
"3:16 and One Half ..." UnmOx (1:4) Aut 72.
"Tragedy Is My Bacon." UnmOx (1:1) N 71, p. 17.

380 BULLIS, Jerald
"The Doe." Epoch (22:1) Fall 72, p. 51.
"An Outing." BelPoJ (23:2) Wint 72-73, p. 21.
"Winter Apples." BelPoJ (23:2) Wint 72-73, p. 18.
"Woodland Interior." Epoch (22:1) Fall 72, p. 50.

381 BULLOCK, Michael
"Crime." Mund (5:1/2) 72, p. 104.
"Poem on Two Levels." Mund (5:1/2) 72, p. 104.
"The Rope." Mund (5:1/2) 72, p. 105.

382 BULSECO, Donna
"The Waiter." Spec (14:1/2) My 72, p. 22.

383 BURFORD, William
"Prometheus" (tr. of Simone Weil). Phoenix (3:4) Aut 72, p. 92.
"The Swimmers: Munich 1972." Nat (215:17) 27 N 72, p. 534.

384 BURKARD, Michael
"Inventions of the Dead." NoAmR (257:4) Wint 72, p. 28.
"Taking Notes on the Black." NoAmR (257:3) Aut 72, p. 46.

385 BURKE, Clifford
"Choices." Isthmus (1) Spr 72, p. 1.

386 BURKE, Paul
"Balance." Poem (14) Mr 72, p. 35.
"Learn." Poem (14) Mr 72, p. 36.
"Realization." Poem (14) Mr 72, p. 34.
"Shadows." Poem (14) Mr 72, p. 33.

387 BURKHARD, Michael
"Exit." CarolQ (24:3) Fall 72, p. 83.
"Torrid" (for Norman). CarolQ (24:3) Fall 72, p. 82.

388 BURLINGAME, Randall Sanford
"The Balloon." Meas (2) 72.
"Dusk." Meas (2) 72.

388A BURLINGAME, Robert
"Pollution." SouthwR (57:2) Spr 72, p. 123.

389 BURMEISTER, Magdalene
"Pilgrim, What of the Night?" KanQ (4:3) Sum 72, p. 60.

390 BURNHAM, Geoffrey
"A Red Room in Provence." ExpR (3) Fall-Wint 72/73, p. 15.

391 BURNHAM, Richard
"Mr. Flavella." WindO (11) Aut 72, p. 35.

392 BURNS, Gerald
"From Boccherini's Minuet." SouthwR (57:3) Sum 72, p. 213.

393 BURNS, Richard
from L'Albero Poeta: "Someone Doesn't Want to Live in the Clouds" (tr. of Guido Ballo). MedR (2:4) Sum 72, p. 87.

394 BURNS, Robert Grant
"Windy Point." NewYorker (48:31) 23 S 72, p. 78.

395 BURNS, Stanley
"Wrestler." Folio (8:1) Spr 72, p. 10.

396 BURNSHAW, Stanley
"Me Destierro..." (tr. of Miguel de Unamuno). MassR (13:3) Sum 72, p. 327.
"Retour des Martinets" (tr. of André Spire). MassR (13:3) Sum 72, p. 325.
from The White Flock (tr. of Anna Akhmatova). MassR (13:3) Sum 72, p. 326.

397 BURROWS, E. G.
"Gulliver." SenR (3:1) My 72, p. 58.
"Order of Beasts." SenR (3:1) My 72, p. 57.

398 BUTCHER, Grace
"Death Song for the King of Beasts." AbGR (3:1) Spr-Sum 72, p. 9.
"Mood, Beyond Weeping." AbGR (3:1) Spr-Sum 72, p. 10.
"Ode to Dead Snakes and Love." AbGR (3:1) Spr-Sum 72, p. 7.
"Resurrection." AbGR (3:1) Spr-Sum 72, p. 11.

"When You Are Gone." AbGR (3:1) Spr-Sum 72, p. 8.

399 BUTLER, Jack
"Subplot." NewYorker (48:29) 9 S 72, p. 40.

400 BUTLER, Jone
"The Calculus." SoCaR (4:2) Je 72, p. 47.

401 BUTLER, M. G.
"Poem: As summer's smell rots in the garden." AriD (1:2) Wint 72, p. 29.
"Sophocles." AriD (1:2) Wint 72, p. 28.

402 BUTLER, Terry
"Are." CarlMis (12:1) Fall-Wint 71-72, p. 82.

403 BUTMAN, John
"Fingers Are." Nat (215:3) 7 Ag 72, p. 88.

404 BUTRICK, L. H.
"Julia At Twelve O'Clock." Comm (96:2) 17 Mr 72, p. 39.

405 BUTSCHER, Edward
"Aunt Caroline's Metamorphoses." Confr (5) Wint-Spr 72, p. 72.
"By Land and Sea." BelPoJ (23:1) Fall 72, p. 4.
"Our Lady of Bedlam." BelPoJ (23:1) Fall 72, p. 2.
"Songs of Experience." LittleM (6:1) Spr 72, p. 42.
"Winter: An Appreciation." LittleM (6:1) Spr 72, p. 44.

406 BUTTACI, St. John
"Metaphor." EngJ (61:2) F 72, p. 288.

407 BYRD, Bobby
"Afternoon Chores" (for Mrs. Werner, while she was away). Cafe (4) Fall 72, inside front cover.
"Coverings." SouthernPR (13:1) Aut 72, p. 23.
"I Too Remember Waves." Epos (23:3) Spr 72, p. 16.

408 CABALQUINTO, Luis
"Standing By a Window." GreenR (2:2) 72, p. 6.

409 CAGE, John
"Re and Not Re Fuller and Mao." AS (9:2) Sum-Fall 72, p. 270.

410 CAIN, John
"A Poem for the Grass." NewL (38:3) Spr 72, p. 79.
"A Poem Written in the Morning or All That Is Heard Goes By Like the Glaciers." NewL (38:3) Spr 72, p. 80.
"The Room." NewL (38:3) Spr 72, p. 78.

411 CALLENBACH, Carl
"To Mr. Clean, Ph. D." EngJ (61:3) Mr 72, p. 412.

412 CAMERON, Charles
"rumour." TransR (41) Wint-Spr 72, p. 106.

413 CAMP, Roger
"The Spectator." MidwQ (13:4) Sum 72, p. 363.
"Ten and Texan." MidwQ (13:4) Sum 72, p. 435.

414 CAMPBELL, C. Smith
"First Freeze, 1933 (or hog killin' time)." SoCaR (4:2) Je 72, p. 36.

415 CAMPBELL, Cory Wade
"Growing." SouthernR (8:1) Wint 72, p. 182.
"Late October." SouthernR (8:1) Wint 72, p. 181.
"A Quiet Descends." SouthernR (8:1) Wint 72, p. 182.

416 CAMPBELL, Donald
Excerpts from "Exotic Erotic Love Poems." Cord (1:3) 72, p. 25.

417 CAMPBELL, Douglas
"The Birth." UTR (1:4) 72, p. 26.

418 CAMPOS, Luis
"Rainy Sun Day." New:ACP (18) Ap 72, p. 11.
"Underdonkey." New:ACP (18) Ap 72, p. 12.

419 CANADA, Stephen
"Black See Girls." ParisR (55) Aut 72, p. 127.
"We Believe Like Wildfire." ParisR (55) Aut 72, p. 128.

420 CANADA, Wanda R.
"Oconee V." SouthernPR (12: Special Issue) 72, p. 51.

421 CANAN, Janine
"Atonement" (tr. of Else Lasker-Schueler). Isthmus (1) Spr 72, p. 72.
from Hebrew Ballads: "Abel" (tr. of Else Lasker-Schueler). CalQ (2) Sum 72, p. 61.
from Hebrew Ballads: "Esther" (tr. of Else Lasker-Schueler). CalQ (2) Sum 72, p. 61.
from Hebrew Ballads: "Moses and Joshua" (tr. of Else Lasker-Schueler). CalQ (2) Sum 72, p. 63.
"Jacob" (tr. of Else Lasker-Schueler). Isthmus (1) Spr 72, p. 70.
"Montano." Isthmus (1) Spr 72, frontispiece.
"Pharoh and Joseph" (tr. of Else Lasker-Schueler). Isthmus (1) Spr 72, p. 69.
"Saul" (tr. of Else Lasker-Schueler). Isthmus (1) Spr 72, p. 71.

422 CANDELARIA, Frederick
"Cardiac." Meas (2) 72.
"Plaza de Toros." Madrona (1:1) Je 71, p. 14.

423 CANE, Melville
"A Kind of Sound." AmerS (41:3) Sum 72, p. 352.

424 CANFIELD, Douglas
"Big Bad Bill." ColEng (33:8) My 72, p. 890.

425 CANNON, Maureen
"Father of the Bride." LadHJ (89:4) Ap 72, p. 201.
"Still Life: Winter." LadHJ (89:1) Ja 72, p. 146.
"Two." LadHJ (89:9) S 72, p. 150.
"Valentine." LadHJ (89:2) F 72, p. 81.

426 CANNON, Melissa
"Southern Lyric." Wind (2:5) Sum 72, p. 42.
"There and Back" (for Evelyn). Poem (16) N 72, p. 11.

427 CANSEVER, Edip
"The Bedouin" (tr. by Nermin Menemencioglu). LitR (15:4) Sum 72, p. 482.

428 CANTAROVICI, Jaime
"There Must Be a Way In." AAUP (58:3) S 72, p. 292.

429 CANTY, Emma
"A Tribute to Black Poets." JnlOBP (2:16) Sum 72, p. 20.

430 CANZONERI, Robert
"Back to Columbus." SouthernR (8:1) Wint 72, p. 169.

431 CAPLIN, Loren Paul
"Charlie's Eye." ParisR (55) Aut 72, p. 148.

432 CARDENAL, Ernesto
"Mayapán" (tr. by Robert Stock). Works (3:3/4) Wint 72-73, p. 82.

433 CARDONA-HINE, Alvaro
"Driving in the Mountains." UTR (1:2) 72, p. 27.

434 CARDOZO, Nancy
"In the Mirror." Madem (75:2) Je 72, p. 86.
"The Sleeping Porch." Madem (75:2) Je 72, p. 86.
"Transformations." Madem (75:2) Je 72, p. 86.

435 CARLIN, Richard
"child's fantasy." HangL (17) Sum 72, p. 65.
"Psychiatrist." HangL (18) Fall 72, p. 60.

436 CARLISLE, Thomas John
"All One Body We." ChiTM 6 F 72, p. 12.

"Conviction." ChrC (89:6) 9 F 72, p. 161.
"In Answer to Yours of That Instant." ChrC (89:3) 19 Ja 72, p. 63.
"Jesus Laughed." ChrC (89:12) 22 Mr 72, p. 335.

437 CARLSON, Burton L.
"Poem to Diety." ChrC (89:41) 15 N 72, p. 1144.
"Saltwater Fishing." SouthwR (57:4) Aut 72, p. 302.

438 CARMI, T.
"The Stranger" (tr. by Stephen Mitchell). Humanist (32:1) Ja-F 72, p. 33.

439 CAROUTCH, Yvonne
"Temporary Landscapes" (tr. by Raymond Federman). Pan (9) 72, p. 13.

440 CARPENTER, John R.
"Apollo and Marsyas." PoetryNW (13:4) Wint 72-73, p. 27.
"The Colonel." PoetryNW (13:4) Wint 72-73, p. 28.
"The Meeting." Poetry (120:1) Ap 72, p. 25.
"Orange Scarves (SAC)." QRL (18:1/2) 72, p. 29.
"The Poet and His Desk Drawer (for Zbigniew Herbert)." QRL (18:1/2) 72, p. 28.
"Rust." QRL (18:1/2) 72, p. 26.
"The Sand Forest." Poetry (120:1) Ap 72, p. 25.
"Three Poinsettia Poems." QRL (18:1/2) 72, p. 27.
"The Trolleycar." Poetry (120:1) Ap 72, p. 26.

441 CARPENTER, Pete
"Angela Be Strong." JnlOBP (2:16) Sum 72, p. 46.
"Last Will and Testament." JnlOBP (2:16) Sum 72, p. 47.

442 CARR, John
"Spenser in Ireland, March, 1595." HolCrit (9:2) Je 72, p. 9.

443 CARRIER, Constance
"Lascaux." ConcPo (5:1) Spr 72, p. 67.
"A Lost Village." ChiTM 2 Ap 72, p. 9.

444 CARRIER, Warren
"The Chase" (for Bill Stafford). SenR (3:1) My 72, p. 54.
"Deaf to Death." Shen (23:4) Sum 72, p. 40.
"Windigo." SenR (3:1) My 72, p. 53.

445 CARRIGAN, Andrew
"Another Cure for Boredom." Sky (1:1) 71.
"Both Ways on a One Way Bridge." Sky (1:1) 71.
"Dead Elms or Oaks." Sky (1:2) 72, p. 12.
"Rustlin." Field (6) Spr 72, p. 84.
"This Place." Sky (1:2) 72, p. 11.

446 CARRITHERS, Dennis C.
"Parting--A Reply--Adieu." EngJ (61:9) D 72, p. 1333.

447 CARROLL, Wallace
"A Christmas Carol." NYT 23 D 72, p. 25.

448 CARRUTH, Hayden
"Abandoned Ranch, Big Bend." PartR (39:1) Wint 72, p. 59.
"A Dedication in Sorry Times." QRL (18:1/2) 72, p. 37.
"The Insomniac Sleeps Well For Once And." QRL (18:1/2) 72, p. 34.
"On Being Asked to Write a Poem Against the War in Vietnam." Kayak (30) D 72, p. 68.
"Senior Citizen." QRL (18:1/2) 72, p. 31.
"The Song." QRL (18:1/2) 72, p. 30.
"Twilight Comes" (after Wang Wei). Antaeus (5) Spr 72, p. 53.
"The Ushers." QRL (18:1/2) 72, p. 35.

449 CARSON, Gerald
"Breakfast with the New York Times, City Edition." VilV 11 My 72, p. 76.

450 CARTER, Dyeatra
"Space." JnlOBP (2:16) Sum 72, p. 32.
"Words." JnlOBP (2:16) Sum 72, p. 31.

451 CARTER, Joseph
"Sudden Pheasant." SouthernHR (6:4) Aut 72, p. 392.

452 CARTER, Karl W.
"In Apology for All Black Women." Broad (58) Ap 72.
"The Old Woman." Broad (58) Ap 72.
"Song." Broad (58) Ap 72.

453 CARTER, Lee M.
"Of Dense Bodies and Opaque Surfaces." GeoR (26:3) Fall 72, p. 371.
"Verses in Protest Against the Alphabet." GeoR (26:3) Fall 72, p. 372.

454 CARTER, Lillie Mae
"Contrasts." NegroHB (35:8) D 72, p. 181.
"Who." NegroHB (35:7) N 72, p. 159.

455 CARTER, Nancy
"I Do Not See Her Often." Folio (8:1) Spr 72, p. 17.
"In All This Training." Folio (8:2) Fall 72, p. 40.
"The Mad Garden Waits." BabyJ (5) N 72, p. 28.

456 CARVER, Raymond
"In a Greek Orthodox Church near Daphne." SoDakR (10:4)

Wint 72-73, p. 88.
"Prosser." Kayak (28) 72, p. 62.
"Sudden Rain." MidwQ (14:1) Aut 72, p. 63.
"This Word Love." PoetC (7:1) 72, p. 2.
"Two Worlds." MidwQ (14:1) Aut 72, p. 63.

457 CASE, Dick
"From Crab Bay--With Love." PoetryNW (13:3) Aut 72, p. 19.

458 CASEY, Michael
"A Bummer." NYT 31 Mr 72, p. 29.
"Forget About It." SaltCR (5:1) Wint 72.
"Nguyen Hoc." LittleM (6:1) Spr 72, p. 17.

459 CASHMAN, David
"Abel Hill Cemetery, Martha's Vineyard." WindO (10) Sum 72, p. 17.
"For My Sister." WindO (10) Sum 72, p. 17.

460 CASSITY, Turner
"City of the Angels." Poetry (120:5) Ag 72, p. 282.
"Music of the Co-Prosperity Spheres." SouthernR (8:2) Spr 72, p. 408.

461 CAUDRON, Cordell
"Flower Lady." FourQt (21:2) Ja 72, p. 23.

462 CAULK, C.
"Clumsy Lover." KanQ (4:3) Sum 72, p. 56.
"Haiku: Birch." KanQ (4:3) Sum 72, p. 39.
"Haiku: Spiders." KanQ (4:3) Sum 72, p. 9.
"Haiku: Starlings." KanQ (4:3) Sum 72, p. 55.

463 CAVAFY, C. P.
"Antony's Ending" (tr. by Edmund Keeley and Philip Sherrard). Antaeus (6) Sum 72, p. 39.
"Body, Remember..." (tr. by Edmund Keeley and Philip Sherrard). Nat (215:15) 13 N 72, p. 469.
"Dareios" (tr. by Edmund Keeley and Philip Sherrard). Antaeus (6) Sum 72, p. 42.
"The Distress of Selefkidis" (tr. by Edmund Keeley and Philip Sherrard). Antaeus (6) Sum 72, p. 40.
"The Enemies" (tr. by Rae Dalven). Poetry (120:5) Ag 72, p. 259.
"An Exiled Byzantine Nobleman Who Composes Verses" (tr. by Edmund Keeley and Philip Sherrard). Antaeus (6) Sum 72, p. 44.
"Exiles" (tr. by Edmund Keeley and Philip Sherrard). NewYorker (48:17) 17 Je 72, p. 31.
"The Footsteps" (tr. by Edmund Keeley and Philip Sherrard). Poetry (120:5) Ag 72, p. 266.
"For Ammonis, Who Died at 29, in 610" (tr. by Edmund

Keeley and Philip Sherrard). QRL (18:1/2) 72, p. 42.

"From the School of the Renowned Philosopher" (tr. by Edmund Keeley and Philip Sherrard). NewYorker (48:17) 17 Je 72, p. 31.

"Half an Hour" (tr. by Edmund Keeley and Philip Sherrard). NewYorker (48:17) 17 Je 72, p. 31.

"The Ides of March" (tr. by Edmund Keeley and Philip Sherrard). Poetry (120:5) Ag 72, p. 266.

"In a Large Greek Colony, 200 B.C." (tr. by Edmund Keeley and Philip Sherrard). NewYRB (18:11) 15 Je 72, p. 13.

"Ionic" (tr. by Edmund Keeley and Philip Sherrard). Antaeus (6) Sum 72, p. 47.

"Ithaka" (tr. by Edmund Keeley and Philip Sherrard). QRL (18:1/2) 72, p. 40.

"Julian and the Antiochians" (tr. by Edmund Keeley and Philip Sherrard). NewL (38:3) Spr 72, p. 76.

"King Demetrius" (tr. by Rob Swigart). Antaeus (7) Aut 72, p. 145.

"The Mimiambi of Herodas" (tr. by Rae Dalven). Poetry (120:5) Ag 72, p. 258.

"Myris: Alexandria, A.D. 340" (tr. by Edmund Keeley and Philip Sherrard). Antaeus (6) Sum 72, p. 45.

"Nero's Respite" (tr. by Edmund Keeley and Philip Sherrard). QRL (18:1/2) 72, p. 42.

"Nero's Term" (tr. by Rob Swigart). Antaeus (7) Aut 72, p. 144.

"On the Outskirts of Antioch" (tr. by Edmund Keeley and Philip Sherrard). NewL (38:3) Spr 72, p. 77.

"One of Their Gods" (tr. by Edmund Keeley and Philip Sherrard). QRL (18:1/2) 72, p. 41.

"Orophernes" (tr. by Rob Swigart). Antaeus (7) Aut 72, p. 147.

"The Pawn" (tr. by Rae Dalven). Poetry (120:5) Ag 72, p. 257.

"Philhellene" (tr. by Edmund Keeley and Philip Sherrard). Antaeus (6) Sum 72, p. 41.

"A Prince from Western Libya" (tr. by Edmund Keeley and Philip Sherrard). NewYRB (18:11) 15 Je 72, p. 13.

"The Retinue of Dionysus" (tr. by Rob Swigart). Antaeus (7) Aut 72, p. 146.

"The Satrapy" (tr. by Edmund Keeley and Philip Sherrard). Nat (215:15) 13 N 72, p. 469.

"Theodotos" (tr. by Edmund Keeley and Philip Sherrard). Poetry (120:5) Ag 72, p. 267.

"Thermopylae" (tr. by Edmund Keeley and Philip Sherrard). QRL (18:1/2) 72, p. 39.

"To Have Taken the Trouble" (tr. by Edmund Keeley and Philip Sherrard). NewYorker (48:17) 17 Je 72, p. 31.

"Very Seldom" (tr. by Edmund Keeley and Philip Sherrard). QRL (18:1/2) 72, p. 43.

"Waiting for the Barbarians" (tr. by Edmund Keeley and Philip Sherrard). QRL (18:1/2) 72, p. 38.

464 CELAN, Paul
"Afternoon with a Circus and Citadel" (tr. by Michael Hamburger). QRL (18:1/2) 72, p. 45.
"Alchemical" (tr. by Michael Hamburger). QRL (18:1/2) 72, p. 47.
"Crowned Out..." (tr. by Michael Hamburger). QRL (18:1/2) 72, p. 44.
"Dumb Autumn Smells" (tr. by Michael Hamburger). QRL (18:1/2) 72, p. 48.
"From Darkness to Darkness" (tr. by Michael Hamburger). Nat (215:6) 11 S 72, p. 182.
"In the Daytime" (tr. by Michael Hamburger). QRL (18:1/2) 72, p. 48.
"Leap-Centuries" (tr. by Michael Hamburger). QRL (18:1/2) 72, p. 46.
"Plashes the Fountain" (tr. by Michael Hamburger). QRL (18:1/2) 72, p. 49.
"Tenebrae" (tr. by Michael Hamburger). Nat (215:6) 11 S 72, p. 182.
"To My Right" (tr. by Michael Hamburger). Nat (215:6) 11 S 72, p. 182.

465 CENDRARS, Blaise
"Homage to Guillaume Apollinaire" (tr. by Peter Hoida). Stand (13:2) 72, p. 56.

466 CERDA, Hernán Lavín
"The Hand of God" (tr. by Edward Oliphant). RoadAR (4:1) Spr 72, p. 35.
"Neurotic Art" (tr. by Edward Oliphant). RoadAR (4:1) Spr 72, p. 34.

467 CERNUDA, Luis
"I'm Tired" (tr. by Robert Lima). PoetL (67:3) Aut 72, p. 228.

468 CERVANTES, James V.
"The L. C. Smith." Madrona (1:2) N 71, p. 31.
"The Lady Poet." Madrona (1:2) N 71, p. 31.

469 CERVO, Nathan
"The Poor Man." HolCrit (9:3) O 72, p. 5.

470 CESA, Margaret
"Love Note." Northeast Aut-Wint 71-72, p. 21.
"Reunion." Northeast Aut-Wint 71-72, p. 21.

471 CHAFFIN, Lillie D.
"Ended: Boon Begging." SouthernPR (13:1) Aut 72, p. 30.
"For a Virtuous Maiden Grown Older." Wind (2:6) Aut 72, p. 22.
"Planting Time." Northeast Aut-Wint 71-72, p. 48.
"Propositions." Northeast Aut-Wint 71-72, p. 48.

472 CHAKRABATY, Jagdish
"Criminal, As I Am" (tr. of Debi Ray, w. the poet). Meas (3) 72, p. 67.

473 CHAMBERLAND, Paul
from "The Bill-Poster Howls" (tr. by Fred Cogswell). New:ACP (18) Ap 72, p. 29.
"Everyday Wife" (tr. by Fred Cogswell). New:ACP (18) Ap 72, p. 30.

474 CHANDRA, G. S. Sharat
"Hurray for the Chief Minister." Nat (215:13) 30 O 72, p. 412.
"Once or Twice." Iowa (3:2) Spr 72, p. 9.
"Prophecy: Stone." Meas (2) 72.
"Questions." Nat (215:12) 23 O 72, p. 382.
"Sighting a Bar." Cafe (4) Fall 72, p. 42.

475 CH'ANG Chien
"At Anchor, Sunfall" (tr. by David Gordon). Literature (15:3) 72, p. 486.

476 CHANG Chün
"Yo Yang, An Evening" (tr. by David Gordon). Literature (15:3) 72, p. 435.

477 CHANG, Diana
"Second Nature." NewYQ (11) Sum 72, p. 59.

478 CHANG Tse-Tuan
"Colophon for Ch'ing-Ming Shang-Ho T'u (The Spring Festival on the River)" (tr. by John Peck, w. Roderick Whitfield). QRL (18:1/2) 72, p. 194.

479 CHAPIN, Katherine Garrison
"Country of Summer." NewRep (167:5) 5-12 Ag 72, p. 27.

480 CHARTERS, Samuel
"From a Swedish Notebook." ModernPS (2:6) 72, p. 273.

481 CHASIN, Helen
"June." Poetry (120:3) Je 72, p. 133.
"Perspective." Poetry (120:3) Je 72, p. 134.

482 CHATAIN, Robert
"Attica." NewYQ (12) Aut 72, p. 75.

483 CHATILLON, Pierre
"On a Schoolboy's Drowning" (tr. by Fred Cogswell). New:ACP (18) Ap 72, p. 32.

484 CHATTERJEE, Shri
"Five Poems of Dharma and Kama" (tr. of Shankar

Chattopadhyay, w. Michael Aldrich). Meas (3) 72, p. 9.
"Seven Lines" (tr. of Jibanananda Das). Meas (3) 72, p. 19.

485 CHATTOPADHYAY, Shankar
"Five Poems of Dharma and Kama" (tr. by Shri Chatterjee and Michael Aldrich). Meas (3) 72, p. 9.

486 CHATTOPADHYAY, Shokti
"Car Going Far (A Long Distance Car)" (tr. by Tarapada Ray and Michael Aldrich). Meas (3) 72, p. 11.

487 CHAUDURI, Sukanta
"Anger." Meas (3) 72, p. 12.

488 CHAVES, Jonathan
"Going to Hsieh's Lake by Boat" (tr. of Yang Wan-li). Madem (75:6) O 72, p. 136.
"Poems of Yang Wan-li" (tr. of Yang Wan-li). Hudson (25:3) Aut 72, p. 403.

489 CHENGGES, Larry Steven
"Suppose That a Voice Began It." LittleM (6:2/3) Sum-Aut 72, p. 122.
"Top Stone." WindO (9) Spr 72, p. 4.

490 CHESTER, Laura
"A Distance on Cleopatra." Meas (2) 72.
"Hibernating in an Old Lost Neighborhood." Meas (2) 72.
"Obelisk." Aphra (3:2) Spr 72, p. 35.
"Over the Startled Earth." Meas (2) 72.

491 CHEYFITZ, Eric
"The Otter's Song to Us." Esq (77:3) Mr 72, p. 6.

492 CHEYNEY-COKER, Syl
"Absurdity." GreenR (2:3) 72, p. 37.
"Environne." GreenR (2:3) 72, p. 35.
"Horoscope." GreenR (2:3) 72, p. 34.
"Hydropathy." GreenR (2:3) 72, p. 32.
"Lotus Eater." GreenR (2:3) 72, p. 36.

493 CHICHESTER, Tanyna
"The Call." NegroHB (35:4) Ap 72, p. 86.

494 CH'IEN Ku
"Colophon for Lan-T'ing Hsiu-Hsi (The Gathering at the Orchid Pavilion)" (tr. by John Peck). QRL (18:1/2) 72, p. 196.

495 CHILDERS, Joanne
"The Trash Pile." SewanR (80:4) Aut 72, p. 610.

496 CHILDRESS, William
"Epitome." PoetL (67:1) Spr 72, p. 38.
"The Giant Frog." PoetL (67:1) Spr 72, p. 38.
"The Graves of the Orphan Children." Peb (9) Wint 72.
"The Hearses (for E. V. Griffith)." Peb (9) Wint 72.
"Her Anniversary." ChiTM 2 Ja 72, p. 4.
"Storm." ChiTM 24 S 72, p. 8.

497 CHILTON, Margaret
"The Estranged Friends Consider Their Predicament." PoetL (67:1) Spr 72, p. 55.
"Nest Building in a Northern Climate." PoetL (67:1) Spr 72, p. 55.

498 CHIOLES, John
"Against Woodwaxen" (tr. of George Seferis). Atl (229:5) My 72, p. 58.

499 CHIPASULA, Frank
"Whitecat and Blackmouse." JnlOBP (2:16) Sum 72, p. 88.

500 CHIPLIS, James
Three Haiku. Qt (5:39/40) Sum-Aut 72, p. 58.

501 CHIRI, Ruwa
"A Poem to Baba Before the Essence of His Being." JnlOBP (2:16) Sum 72, p. 68.

502 CHISHOLM, Scott
"Anniversary." Qt (5:39/40) Sum-Aut 72, p. 61.

503 CHOPRA, Ashok
"The Sinker." Meas (3) 72, p. 13.

504 CHOUDHURY, Malay Roy
"Stark Electric Jesus." Meas (3) 72, p. 14.
"Two Excerpts from Jakham." Meas (3) 72, p. 16.

505 CHRISTENSEN, Bonniejean
"Against the Grain." ColEng (33:4) Ja 72, p. 486.

506 CHRISTENSEN, Nadia
"So and So Many Larks" (tr. of Per Højholt, w. Alexander Taylor). WormR (48) 72, p. 122.

507 CHRISTIAN, Marcus
"Men on Horseback." NegroHB (35:8) D 72, p. 181.
"Revolt in the South." NegroHB (35:3) Mr 72, p. 67.

508 CHRISTIANOPOULOS, Dinos
"The Bruise" (tr. by George Thaniel). AriD (1:4/5) Sum-Aut 72, p. 27.
"Love in the Field" (tr. by George Thaniel). AriD (1:4/5)

Sum-Aut 72, p. 27.
"On the Road to Damascus" (tr. by George Thaniel). AriD (1:4/5) Sum-Aut 72, p. 27.
"The Sea" (tr. by George Thaniel). AriD (1:4/5) Sum-Aut 72, p. 26.
"Verses of St. Agnes For St. Sebastian" (tr. by George Thaniel). AriD (1:4/5) Sum-Aut 72, p. 28.

509 CHRISTMAN, Bernice Bunn
"Doves." Comm (97:10) 8 D 72, p. 225.

510 CHRISTMAS, R. A.
"Rodney the Raper." WestHR (26:2) Spr 72, p. 153.

511 CHRISTODOULOU, Dimitris
"Cavocolones" (tr. by Stavros Deligiorgis). AriD (1:4/5) Sum-Aut 72, p. 29.

512 CHU Shu-Chen
"Playing All a Summer's Day by the Lake (to the Tune 'Clear Bright Joy')" (tr. by Kenneth Rexroth and Ling Chung). Kayak (30) D 72, p. 18.
"Plum Blossoms" (tr. by Kenneth Rexroth, w. Ling Chung). Kayak (30) D 72, p. 20.
"Spring Joy" (tr. by Ling Chung and Kenneth Rexroth). NewL (38:4) Sum 72, p. 39.
"Spring Night (to the Tune 'Panning Gold')" (tr. by Kenneth Rexroth and Ling Chung). Kayak (30) D 72, p. 19.

513 CHUNG, Ling
"The Autumn Brook" (tr. of Hsueh T'ao, w. Kenneth Rexroth). UnmOx (1:4) Aut 72.
"For the Courtesan Ch'ing Lin, To the Tune 'The Love of the Immortals'" (tr. of Wu Tsao, w. Kenneth Rexroth). NewYQ (12) Aut 72, p. 43.
"An Old Poem to Yuan Chen" (tr. of Hsueh T'ao, w. Kenneth Rexroth). UnmOx (1:4) Aut 72.
"Playing All a Summer's Day by the Lake (to the Tune 'Clear Bright Joy')" (tr. of Chu Shu-chen, w. Kenneth Rexroth). Kayak (30) D 72, p. 18.
"Plum Blossoms" (tr. of Chu Shu-chen, w. Kenneth Rexroth). Kayak (30) D 72, p. 20.
"Spring Night (to the Tune 'Panning Gold')" (tr. of Chu Shu-chen, w. Kenneth Rexroth). Kayak (30) D 72, p. 19.

514 CHUPA, James
"Boiled Aquarium Summer." Drag (3:1) Spr 72, p. 74.
"Hey, Take That Deer Form." Drag (3:1) Spr 72, p. 73.
"Poetry, 1884-1933." Drag (3:1) Spr 72, p. 74.

515 CHUTE, Robert M.
"Prognosis." Epos (23:4) Sum 72, p. 22.

516 CIARDI, John
"Children's Corner." World (1:10) 7 N 72, p. 12.

517 CIESZYNAKI, Wladyslaw
"Rebus." Northeast Aut-Wint 71-72, p. 43.

518 ÇINARLI, Mehmet
"They" (tr. by Talat Sait Halman). LitR (15:4) Sum 72, p. 403.

519 CIORAN, Samuel D.
"Dearest friend, do you not see" (tr. of Vladimir Solovyov). RusLT (4) Aut 72, p. 30.

520 CLAIRE, William F.
"By their sounds ye shall know them." AmerS (41:2) Spr 72, p. 192.

521 CLAMURRO, William
"Five Poems from Vietnam." Pan (9) 72, p. 40.

522 CLARK, Gordon
"The Voucher and the Eggle." Zahir (1:4/5) 72, p. 27.

523 CLARK, Janet G.
"Krate for Housewives." Folio (8:2) Fall 72, p. 21.

524 CLARK, John
"Grand Achievement" (Amerikan Style). JnlOBP (2:16) Sum 72, p. 30.

525 CLARK, Larry V.
"Poems to Piraye" (tr. of Nâzim Hikmet). LitR (15:4) Sum 72, p. 440.

526 CLARK, Naomi
"Late Spring, Sur Coast." ColQ (21:1) Sum 72, p. 79.

527 CLARK, S. T.
"of." SewanR (80:2) Spr 72, p. 289.
"Prelude" (To: Six Figures and Their Dimensions). SewanR (80:4) Aut 72, p. 607.

528 CLARK, Tom
"The Door to the Forest." ParisR (54) Sum 72, p. 32.
"On Venus." ParisR (54) Sum 72, p. 30.
"Water." ParisR (54) Sum 72, p. 31.

529 CLARKE, Evelyn
"Gonna Free Him." Broad (57) Mr 72.

530 CLARKE, Reed
"Santa Cruz." PoetryNW (13:2) Sum 72, p. 20.

531 CLARKE, Sebastian
"I Put a Spell On You" (for Nina Simone). JnlOBP (2:16) Sum 72, p. 23.

532 CLAUDEL, Alice Moser
"Near Grand Isle, Louisiana." Poem (14) Mr 72, p. 1.
"The Old Library." ColEng (33:5) F 72, p. 584.
"The Tree (New Orleans)." Qt (5:39/40) Sum-Aut 72, p. 16.

533 CLAUSEN, Jan
"i am not a field-goal kicker." HangL (16) Wint 71-72, p. 6.

534 CLIFTON, Charles
"Stained Hotels." Meas (2) 72.

535 CLIFTON, Lucille
"Lately." Madem (74:6) Ap 72, p. 124.
"Turning." MassR (13:1/2) Wint-Spr 72, p. 105.
"Walking Through Walls." MassR (13:1/2) Wint-Spr 72, p. 105.

536 CLINE, Jerene
"Rites." ChiTM 13 F 72, p. 12.

537 CLINTON, D.
"'Land Sakes Alive! They're Opening Pop's Heart!'" LittleM (6:2/3) Sum-Aut 72, p. 29.
"Reading More New American Literary Anthologies." LittleM (6:2/3) Sum-Aut 72, p. 29.

538 CLOTHIER, Peter
from Presences: Six Poems. Northeast Aut-Wint 71-72, p. 39.

539 CLOUTIER, David
"The Fish-ribbed Are the Night." Iron (2) Fall 72, p. 15.
"There Is a Light That Fails in My Mouth." Iron (2) Fall 72, p. 14.

540 COAKLEY, William Leo
"The Secrets of His House." ChiTM 15 O 72, p. 8.

541 CODRESCU, Andrei
"Ars Poetica." Isthmus (1) Spr 72, p. 54.
"Early Fix." Iron (1) Spr 72, p. 51.
"Jewess." CalQ (3) Aut 72, p. 36.
"Mad Rumors." CalQ (3) Aut 72, p. 37.
"My Angelico." CalQ (3) Aut 72, p. 35.
"New Dawn: 25th Street." CalQ (3) Spr 72, p. 36.
Nine Poems. Isthmus (1) Spr 72, p. 55.
"Saturn." CalQ (3) Aut 72, p. 36.

"The Second Coming." Iron (1) Spr 72, p. 52.

542 COFFIN, Patricia
"Sleep." PoetL (67:1) Spr 72, p. 36.
"Stained Grass Cathedral." Pan (9) 72, p. 25.

543 COGGESHALL, Rosanne
"Hitchhiker." Epoch (21:2) Wint 71, p. 160.

544 COGSWELL, Fred
from "The Bill-Poster Howls" (tr. of Paul Chamberland). New:ACP (18) Ap 72, p. 29.
"Dead Leaves and Embers" (tr. of Gaston Miron). New:ACP (18) Ap 72, p. 33.
"Everyday Wife" (tr. of Paul Chamberland). New:ACP (18) Ap 72, p. 30.
"Human Effort" (tr. of Roland Giguere). New:ACP (18) Ap 72, p. 31.
"On a Schoolboy's Drowning" (tr. of Pierre Chatillon). New:ACP (18) Ap 72, p. 32.

545 COHEN, Aaron E.
"Night City." NewRena (6) My 72, p. 47.

546 COHEN, Janis
"Like a Lady." Northeast Aut-Wint 71-72, p. 50.
"Short Life It Is." Northeast Aut-Wint 71-72, p. 50.

547 COHEN, Joseph
"The Poor Sit." Epos (23:4) Sum 72, p. 28.

548 COHEN, Keith
"The Pueblo Deal." Pan (9) 72, p. 8.

549 COHEN, Marcia
"The Spice of Love." LadHJ (89:7) Jl 72, p. 151.

550 COHEN, Marty
"Reading the Chāndogya Upanishad, 1970." HangL (16) Wint 71-72, p. 7.

551 COHEN, Marvin
"An Interexistential Exchange." NewRena (6) My 72, p. 59.

552 COHEN, Richard
"Still Life: River Without Banks" (for Marc Chagall). SouthernPR (13:1) Aut 72, p. 39.

553 COLBY, Joan
"America By Moonlight." Etc. (29:4) D 72, p. 344.
"Birthday Poem for Benjamin." WindO (9) Spr 72, p. 15.
"The Day Breaks." BabyJ (5) N 72, p. 5.
"Deja Vu." WindO (9) Spr 72, p. 13.

"Eleven Poems." Magazine (5) part 5, 72.
"Getting Home." PoetL (67:3) Aut 72, p. 244.
"Going to Bed." WindO (9) Spr 72, p. 14.
"Going to Sleep and Other Journeys." Epos (23:3) Spr 72, p. 11.
"Insomniac Heatscape." WindO (11) Aut 72, p. 4.
"Lament for Your Absence." WindO (12) Wint 72-73, p. 7.
"Missing Code." Etc. (29:2) Je 72, p. 154.
"The Night of Glass Breaking." ColEng (33:5) F 72, p. 587.
"Poem for My Birthday." WindO (9) Spr 72, p. 15.
"Prairie Dwellers." PoetL (67:3) Aut 72, p. 245.
"Requiem." BabyJ (5) N 72, p. 6.
"Waking In a Pseudo Teepee On Highway 5." Epos (23:4) Sum 72, p. 11.

554 COLCHIE, Thomas
"To a Hotel Scheduled for Demolition" (tr. of Carlos Drummond De Andrade). Hudson (25:2) Sum 72, p. 186.

555 COLE, James
"Barbershop." NYT 12 Ap 72, p. 44.

556 COLEMAN, Elliott
"Holy Communion." NewL (38:4) Sum 72, p. 103.
"Late Words." NewL (38:4) Sum 72, p. 103.
"Maskless Halloween Pulse." NewL (38:4) Sum 72, p. 102.
"Missive to Rigg Kennedy." NewL (38:4) Sum 72, p. 101.
"Profile in the Sunlight of March." NewL (38:4) Sum 72, p. 104.
"Reading Anaïs Nin: Volume Four." Cafe (4) Fall 72, p. 42.

557 COLEMAN, Horace
"Everything That Rises." NewL (39:1) Aut 72, p. 90.
"my name is martin." JnlOBP (2:16) Sum 72, p. 87.
"Prospectus." JnlOPC (6:3) Spr 72, p. 622.

558 COLEMAN, Mary Ann
"Thirty." Poem (15) Jl 72, p. 38.

559 COLES, Christie Lund
"Casual Meeting." LadHJ (89:3) Mr 72, p. 138.

560 COLLINS, C. C.
"Down South, North America." JnlOBP (2:16) Sum 72, p. 79.

561 COLLINS, Christopher
"Escargot for the Big Fella." NewYQ (11) Sum 72, p. 67.

562 COLLINS, Martha
"Homecoming." SouthernR (8:2) Spr 72, p. 398.

"On the Care and Feeding of Living Things." NewYQ (9) Wint 72, p. 78.
"We Are Not Trees." SouthernR (8:2) Spr 72, p. 401.

563 COLSTON, Glenn M.
"Dulcinea's Lament." SouthernPR (12: Special Issue) 72, p. 47.

564 COLVIN, Frances
"The Fire Fighter." CalQ (2) Sum 72, p. 30.
"The Great Divide." FourQt (21:3) Mr 72, p. 30.

565 COMAS, Beatrice H.
"The Care and Feeding of Words." EngJ (61:5) My 72, p. 701.
"TV Dinner." SatEP (244:1) Spr 72, p. 103.

566 COMER, John
"Three Prison Poems." Poetry (120:2) My 72, p. 76.

567 CONDIT, David L.
"give me some gentle." Cord (1:3) 72, p. 20. Reprinted with corrections Cord (1:4) 72, p. 38.
"On the Corner of White Street." Cord (1:3) 72, p. 22.
"Sickness at the Seed-Station." Cord (1:3) 72, p. 21.

568 CONFORD, David
"Adult Education." SouthernPR (12:2) Spr 72, p. 38.
"Feeding the Fire." MedR (2:2) Wint 72, p. 69.
"The Picturebook of Flies." MedR (2:2) Wint 72, p. 69.

569 CONGDON, Kirby
"Conch." Magazine (5) part 8, 72, p. 18.
"To the Summer House." NYT 27 Jl 72, p. 30.

570 CONLEY, Zubena
"For All My Black Children." JnlOBP (2:16) Sum 72, p. 17.

571 CONNELL, Evan S., Jr.
"Points for a Compass Rose." Kayak (30) D 72, p. 38.

572 CONNELLAN, Leo
"The Moon Now Flushed." NewYQ (11) Sum 72, p. 68.
"On the Eve of My Becoming a Father." ChiTM 6 F 72, p. 12.
"A Witness." ChiTM 18 Je 72, p. 5.

573 CONOVER, Roger
"Carrowkeel" (w. John Unterecker). UnmOx (1:4) Aut 72.

574 CONRAN, Anthony
"Lineage." TransR (42/43) Spr-Sum 72, p. 69.

575 CONTOSKI, Victor
"Clock." Epoch (21:3) Spr 72, p. 291.
"Four Blessings." Madrona (1:1) Je 71, p. 33.
"The Gallic Wars: Book IX." Peb (7) Aut 71.
"Silences." Epoch (21:3) Spr 72, p. 291.

576 COOLEY, Peter
"Approaching." CarlMis (12:1) Fall-Wint 71-72, p. 88.
"Chicago." Cim (21) O 72, p. 10.
"For Anne." KanQ (4:1) Wint 71-72, p. 85.
"Foreshortening Dark." AmerR (14) 72, p. 180.
"How to Run the World, Be Loved, Rich, Self-Sacrificing, Honored and a Prophet In Your Own Country." ConcPo (5:1) Spr 72, p. 26.
"The Last of the Crusades." YaleR (62:1) Aut 72, p. 77.
"The Listening Chamber." YaleR (62:1) Aut 72, p. 76.
"Picking the Apples." HolCrit (9:4) D 72, p. 11.
"Pilings" (for Yvonne). Cim (21) O 72, p. 11.

577 COOLIDGE, Clark
"Bound In." UnmOx (1:3) Sum 72, p. 33.
"Date Bars." UnmOx (1:1) N 71, p. 49.
"Ply." UnmOx (1:3) Sum 72, p. 34.
"Thermal Poise." UnmOx (1:1) N 71, p. 50.

578 COOPER, Robert
"Everything Died Today." ChrC (89:28) 2 Ag 72, p. 792.

579 COOPERMAN, Stanley
"Homage to Sammler." Mund (5:3) 72, p. 75.
"Political Poem." Nat (214:7) 14 F 72, p. 220.
"The Relic." UnmOx (1:3) Sum 72, p. 55.

580 COOVER, Robert
"Debris." Pan (9) 72, p. 7.

581 CORBIERE, Tristan
"Toad" (tr. by William Doreski). PoetL (67:1) Spr 72, p. 42.

582 CORCORAN, Patricia
"Blueberry/cream." PoetL (67:2) Sum 72, p. 173.

583 CORDIS, Sister Maria, RSM
"Covenant." SewanR (80:2) Spr 72, p. 261.

584 CORLESS, Roger
"America is not New York City." AbGR (3:1) Spr-Sum 72, p. 61.
"Sick." AbGR (3:1) Spr-Sum 72, p. 60.

585 CORMAN, Cid
"Notes from Kyoto." Madrona (1:4) S 72, p. 10.

"Six Poems." Madrona (1:4) S 72, p. 4.
"Three Poems." UnmOx (1:4) Aut 72.

586 CORN, Alfred
"Letter from Mme De Sevigne to Her Daughter: the End of Summer." Poem (14) Mr 72, p. 59.
"Marie-Claire's Spring." SatR (55:29) 15 Jl 72, p. 39.
"Spring, an Old Man, a Mirror." Poem (14) Mr 72, p. 57.
"Vocation." Poem (14) Mr 72, p. 58.

587 CORN, Rokhl
"The Fiddler" (tr. by Leonard Opalov). PoetL (67:1) Spr 72, p. 34.

588 CORNFORD, Adam
"Remains." Antaeus (6) Sum 72, p. 27.

589 CORNING, Howard McKinley
"Darkness, Not to Know." NowestR (12:2) Spr 72, p. 43.
"Gulls Far Inland." ChiTM 9 Jl 72, p. 4.

590 CORNISH, Sam
"close the doors after dark." Works (3:3/4) Wint 72-73, p. 35.
"Ohio After the Shootings at Kent & Jackson State." AriD (1:2) Wint 72, p. 5.
"Poem: the president is a man of the people." AriD (1:2) Wint 72, p. 5.
"the president is a man of the people." Works (3:3/4) Wint 72-73, p. 35.

591 CORRIGAN, Michael
"The Hunter." WindO (12) Wint 72-73, p. 34.
"The Monument of General Conant Speaks on Behalf of the Inquisition." WindO (12) Wint 72-73, p. 31.
"Small Town Boy." WindO (12) Wint 72-73, p. 35.
"The Struggle." WindO (12) Wint 72-73, p. 34.

592 CORRIGAN, Sylvia R.
"Tiamat's Retort." Aphra (3:1) Wint 71-72, p. 46.

593 CORTEZ, Jayne
"The Rising." Works (3:3/4) Wint 72-73, p. 33.
"Solo." Works (3:3/4) Wint 72-73, p. 34.

594 CORTINEZ, Carlos
"Middle Age" (tr. by Edward Oliphant). RoadAR (4:1) Spr 72, p. 32.

595 COSTANZO, Gerald
"At Irony's Picnic." Kayak (30) D 72, p. 25.
"Building." KanQ (4:3) Sum 72, p. 97.

from The Complete Handbook of Ways of Getting Rich with a Medicine Show: (9-14). WormR (48) 72, p. 112.
"The Death Team." PraS (46:4) Wint 72-73, p. 342.
"Everything You Own." Spec (14:1/2) My 72, p. 24.
"Fear." Spec (14:1/2) My 72, p. 24.
"Pastoral." MidwQ (14:1) Aut 72, p. 64.
"Revenge." SouthernPR (13:1) Aut 72, p. 10.
"Saints." New:ACP (19) Aut 72, p. 41.

596 COSTELLO, John V.
"Nursery Rhyme." Folio (8:2) Fall 72, p. 28.

597 COSTLEY, Bill
"New England of Ice." AriD (1:3) Spr 72, p. 15.

598 COUSENS, Mildred
"Rescue at Noonday." ChiTM 16 Ap 72, p. 21.

599 COX, Carol
"From the Direction of the State Mental Institution." Epoch (21:3) Spr 72, p. 287.
"How Soon the Cities Will Merge." Epoch (21:3) Spr 72, p. 286.
"A Young Boy Tattoos Himself." Epoch (21:3) Spr 72, p. 286.

600 COX, Edward
"Harvard Graduate Speaking to His Troops." SewanR (80:4) Aut 72, p. 626.

601 COX, Naomi
"On Receiving the News." Poetry (119:6) Mr 72, p. 325.

602 COXE, Louis
"New Year's Eve." SouthernPR (13:1) Aut 72, p. 42.

603 CRABBE, John K.
"The Rest Is Silence." EngJ (61:3) Mr 73, p. 450.

604 CRANE, Hart
"At Melville's Tomb." Poetry (121:1) O 72, p. 5.
Ten Unpublished Poems. Antaeus (5) Spr 72, p. 18.

605 CRAWFORD, Jack Jr.
"Sally." Perspec (17:1) Sum 72, p. 64.

606 CRAWFORD, John
"Shadow Man." UnmOx (1:4) Aut 72.

607 CRAWFORD, Michael
"Invective Against the Anti-Metaphorites." Comm (95:14) 7 Ja 72, p. 331.

608 CRAWFORD, Tom
"Birds." Iron (1) Spr 72, p. 67.

609 CREAGH, Patrick
from La Belta: "In a Foolish History of Vampires" (tr. of Andrea Zanzotto). MedR (2:4) Sum 72, p. 96.
from IX Ecloghe: "Through the New Window" (tr. of Andrea Zanzotto). MedR (2:4) Sum 72, p. 95.

610 CREEDON, Michael
"He Wants Her To Like." Spec (14:1/2) My 72, p. 25.

611 CREELEY, Robert
"Change" (for Ted). StoneD (1:1) Spr 72, p. 31.
"Here." StoneD (1:1) Spr 72, p. 31.
"Sunset." StoneD (1:1) Spr 72, p. 31.

612 CREMONA, John
"Afternoon in Xaghra." FreeL (15:1/2) 71-72, p. 8.

613 CREW, Louie
"To Canterbury, March 1971." ChrC (89:13) 29 Mr 72, p. 353.

614 CREWS, Judson
"Classic in the deamoned service." Zahir (1:4/5) 72, p. 48.
"Eyes that." Zahir (1:4/5) 72, p. 49.
"I wanted even." Zahir (1:4/5) 72, p. 49.
"If I Thought." BabyJ (5) N 72, p. 16.
"If It Is Neat." Cafe (4) Fall 72, p. 15.
"Is this." Zahir (1:4/5) 72, p. 49.
"Less." Cord (1:4) 72, p. 7.
"Pagan." UnmOx (1:4) Aut 72.
"Realm." BabyJ (5) N 72, p. 16.
"The Special Canopy, Star Dreamed." SoDakR (10:4) Wint 72-73, p. 5.

615 CRINER, Calvin
"Of Summer and Snow." SouthernPR (12: Special Issue) 72, p. 42.

616 CROSBY, Philip B.
"Woman in the Window." KanQ (4:3) Sum 72, p. 136.

617 CROSS, Frank A., Jr.
"The Fifty Gunner." NYT 31 Mr 72, p. 29.

618 CROWE, Steve
"Preparing a Stone." CarolQ (24:3) Fall 72, p. 47.

619 CRUM, Gail
"Ragged Children." PoetL (67:4) Wint 72, p. 337.

620 CRUSZ, Rienzi
"Kamala." PoetL (67:3) Aut 72, p. 230.
"the scrawlers." Confr (5) Wint-Spr 72, p. 84.

621 CULROSS, Michael G.
"Bird/Ends." Iowa (3:4) Fall 72, p. 21.
"Bird/In Love." Iowa (3:4) Fall 72, p. 21.
"Bird/Talk." Iowa (3:4) Fall 72, p. 21.
"Reading Poetry in Wisconsin" (for Stephen Dobyns). Drag (3:2) Sum 72, p. 35.

622 CULVER, Marjorie
"Monday." KanQ (4:1) Wint 71-72, p. 124.

623 CUMALI, Necati
"Ill-Fated Youth" (tr. by Nermin Menemencioglu). LitR (15:4) Sum 72, p. 464.

624 CUMMING, Patricia
"Return." Shen (23:2) Wint 72, p. 24.

625 cummings, e. e.
"Christmas Tree." NYT 23 D 72, p. 25.
"Seven Poems (I)." Poetry (121:1) O 72, p. 6.

626 CUNNINGHAM, Constance
"View from the Horizontal." Cosmo (173:2) Ag 72, p. 44.

627 CURLEY, Daniel
"A Cup of Good Quality but No Distinction, c. 1918." KanQ (4:3) Sum 72, p. 91.
"Let Me Out of Your Dream." KanQ (4:3) Sum 72, p. 93.
"Lines Composed On or About the Albany Bridge." ModernPS (3:4) 72, p. 173.
"The Real Truth about the Peasant Osip." KanQ (4:1) Wint 71-72, p. 8.
"The Sleepwalker." KanQ (4:3) Sum 72, p. 90.

628 CURRIER, John
"Nightrider." Folio (8:1) Spr 72, p. 26.
"Swinging Beef." RoadAR (3:4) Wint 71-72, p. 16.

629 CURRIER, John C., Jr.
"Two Lines to Carol." HolCrit (9:2) O 72, p. 12.

630 CURRY, David
"A Man." SaltCR (5:1) Wint 72.
"Pictures at an Exhibition (after Mussorgsky, after Ravel)." Meas (1) 71.
"Signature." Cafe (4) Fall 72, p. 21.

631 CURRY, Neil
"God Remembers His First Tree" (tr. of Jules Superveille).

Stand (13:2) 72, p. 57.

632 CURRY, Peggy Simson
"By Lower Prairie Dog Creek." ChiTM 19 N 72, p. 12.

633 CUSON, Tom
"Waking in the Night." Isthmus (1) Spr 72, p. 63.
"Weathervane." Isthmus (1) Spr 72, p. 64.

634 CUTLER, Bruce
"Older Than Happiness." PraS (46:2) Sum 72, p. 152.
"There Is Prose in Kansas." SaltCR (5:1) Wint 72.

635 CUTTLER, Eric
"The Spider." PoetL (67:3) Aut 72, p. 240.

636 DACEY, Philip
from The Book of Stones. SoDakR (10:3) Aut 72, p. 72.
"The Card-Player (for Stephen Dunn)." New:ACP (19) Aut 72, p. 35.
"Chain Letter." Shen (23:4) Sum 72, p. 44.
"Cottonwood Poem." SoDakR (10:3) Aut 72, p. 94.
"The Fish in the Attic." PoetC (7:1) 72, p. 22.
"The Five Stones." Cord (1:3) 72, p. 23.
"God Considers How to Make Men Procreate." Drag (3:1) Spr 72, p. 44.
"'His Whole Life Was a Missed Opportunity.'" MidwQ (13:2) Wint 72, p. 134.
"How I Escaped from the Labyrinth." Drag (3:1) Spr 72, p. 45.
"How To Write a Poem." CarolQ (24:1) Wint 72, p. 60.
"In a Game of Telling Secrets, an Adult Confesses He Loves to Play with Toy Trucks." GeoR (26:4) Wint 72, p. 506.
"Kitchen Gothic." NewYQ (11) Sum 72, p. 82.
"Learning to Swim in Middle Age." SouthernPR (12:2) Spr 72, p. 7.
"Levitation." SaltCR (5:1) Wint 72.
"The New Beasts." KanQ (4:3) Sum 72, p. 71.
"Nocturne." KanQ (4:1) Wint 71-72, p. 114.
"The Other Woman." Esq (77:3) Mr 72, p. 14.
"Steps Animals Take." CarolQ (24:1) Wint 72, p. 61.
"The Story Teller." KanQ (4:3) Sum 72, p. 70.
"The Unfinished Sculptures of Michelangelo." Cord (1:3) 72, p. 24.
"Water." Esq (77:6) Je 72, p. 233.
"The Way It Happens." PoetryNW (13:4) Wint 72-73, p. 29.
"A Wife Speaks." PraS (46:2) Sum 72, p. 144.
"The Women." CalQ (3) Aut 72, p. 49.

637 DAGLARCA, Fazil Hüsnü
from Birds of God: Thirty Quatrains (tr. by Talat Sait Halman). LitR (15:4) Sum 72, p. 511.

Four poems (tr. by Talat S. Halman). Books (46:2) Spr 72, p. 252.

638 DAHLEN, Beverly
"Black Train." Isthmus (1) Spr 72, p. 2.
"Hospital." Isthmus (1) Spr 72, p. 3.

639 DAIGAKU, Guchi
"Loneliness" (tr. by Graeme Wilson). DenQuart (7:3) Aut 72, p. 48.

640 DALCHEV, Atanas
"Back Yards." LitR (16:2) Wint 72-73, p. 168.
"The Cuckoo." LitR (16:2) Wint 72-73, p. 167.
"Silence." LitR (16:2) Wint 72-73, p. 166.

641 DALTON, Dorothy
"The Air Is Heavy with Waiting." SouthernPR (12:2) Spr 72, p. 44.

642 DALTON, Eleanor
"To a Student of Poetry." EngJ (61:9) D 72, p. 1314.

643 DALVEN, Rae
"The Enemies" (tr. of C. P. Cavafy). Poetry (120:5) Ag 72, p. 260.
"Free Dodecanese" (tr. of Angelos Sikelianus). Poetry (120:5) Ag 72, p. 261.
"Injustice" (tr. of Yannis Ritsos). Poetry (120:5) Ag 72, p. 260.
"The Mimiambi of Herodas" (tr. of C. P. Cavafy). Poetry (120:5) Ag 72, p. 258.
"The Pawn" (tr. of C. P. Cavafy). Poetry (120:5) Ag 72, p. 257.
"Security" (tr. of Yannis Ritsos). Poetry (120:5) Ag 72, p. 261.
"Supper" (tr. of Angelos Sikelianus). Poetry (120:5) Ag 72, p. 263.
"Who Knows in Other Stars" (tr. of Kostes Palamas). Poetry (120:5) Ag 72, p. 264.
"Without Position" (tr. of Yannis Ritsos). Poetry (120:5) Ag 72, p. 260.

644 DAMAR, Arif
"That's Blood There ..." (tr. by Talat Sait Halman). LitR (15:4) Sum 72, p. 457.

645 DAMASKOS, James
"Amulet" (tr. of Leonidas Zenakos). AriD (1:4/5) Sum-Aut 72, p. 118.
"Anunciation" (tr. of Leonidas Zenakos). AriD (1:4/5) Sum-Aut 72, p. 121.
"Dirge" (tr. of Eleni Vakalo). AriD (1:4/5) Sum-Aut 72,

p. 110.
"Eternal" (tr. of Leonidas Zenakos). AriD (1:4/5) Sum-Aut 72, p. 121.
"Karaghiozes" (tr. of Panos K. Thassitis). AriD (1:4/5) Sum-Aut 72, p. 105.
"Return from War" (tr. of Socrates Kapsaskis). AriD (1:4/5) Sum-Aut 72, p. 55.
"Servants" (tr. of Panos K. Thassitis). AriD (1:4/5) Sum-Aut 72, p. 104.
"Song of the Hanged" (tr. of Eleni Vakalo). AriD (1:4/5) Sum-Aut 72, p. 109.

646 DAMYANOV, Damyan
"Woman." LitR (16:2) Wint 72-73, p. 215.

647 DANA, Robert
"The Drunkard." QRL (18:1/2) 72, p. 53.
"The Joy Tree." QRL (18:1/2) 72, p. 50.
"Picking It Up." QRL (18:1/2) 72, p. 51.
"The Stone Garden." QRL (18:1/2) 72, p. 54.
"Vision and Transformation." NewYorker (48:28) 2 S 72, p. 62.

648 DANIEL, David
"Optical Illusion." ExpR (3) Fall-Wint 72/73, p. 41.

649 DANIEL, John
"Mushrooms." Kayak (30) D 72, p. 12.
"Skull to Hamlet." Kayak (30) D 72, p. 14.

650 DANIELS, R. Bruce
"Six Lines for the Would-Be Poet." EngJ (61:4) Ap 72, p. 614.

651 DANKLEFF, Richard
"Bee in His Bonnet." PoetryNW (13:1) Spr 72, p. 18.
"Coyote Hunt." PoetryNW (13:1) Spr 72, p. 18.
"Exchange in the Night." PoetryNW (13:4) Wint 72-73, p. 24.
"How He Lived." PoetryNW (13:4) Wint 72-73, p. 24.
"Insomnia." PoetryNW (13:4) Wint 72-73, p. 23.
"Lines to Starlings." ColEng (33:4) Ja 72, p. 479.

652 D'ANNUNZIO, Gabrielle
"Grasinda" (tr. by Leonard Orr). Wind (2:6) Aut 72, p. 19.

653 DARR, Ann
"Looking for Origins." NYT 8 Ag 72, p. 32.
"Poetry Workshop." NYT 25 Ag 72, p. 32.

654 DARUWALLA, N. K.
"Fire-Hymn." Meas (3) 72, p. 18.

"The Leper at the Taj." Meas (3) 72, p. 18.

655 DAS, Jibanananda
"Purgatorio" (tr. by Samir Raichowdhry). Meas (3) 72, p. 19.
"Seven Lines" (tr. by Shri Chatterjee). Meas (3) 72, p. 19.

656 DAS, Kamala
"Convicts." Meas (3) 72, p. 23.
"The Descendants." Meas (3) 72, p. 22.
"The Flag." Meas (3) 72, p. 20.
"An Introduction." Meas (3) 72, p. 21.

657 D'AURIA, Gemma
"ceiling low now over the dark plain." MinnR (3) Aut 72, p. 23.
"For Museum Files." MinnR (3) Aut 72, p. 22.

658 DAVID, Dale
"A Game for Children." RoadAR (3:4) Wint 71-72, p. 22.

659 DAVIDSON, Gustav
"Mandala." ChiTM 2 Ap 72, p. 9.

660 DAVIDSON, Richard B.
"Branches in Front of the Moon." ColQ (20:3) Wint 72, p. 320.

661 DAVIE, Donald
"Ireland of the Bombers." Humanist (32:4) Jl-Ag 72, p. 42.
"Of Graces." Antaeus (5) Spr 72, p. 107.

662 DAVIES, Phillips G.
"Resolution and Independence; Or the State of Modern Poetry." PoetC (7:1) 72, p. 28.

663 DAVIES, Piers
"City on an Isthmus." PoetL (67:2) Sum 72, p. 177.

664 DAVIES, Robert A.
"In Review: Kozinsky's Painted Bird." NowestR (12:2) Spr 72, p. 31.
"Night Scenes." St. AR (1:4) Spr-Sum 72, p. 54.

665 DAVIS, Clifford
"The First Time Around." EngJ (61:6) S 72, p. 912.

666 DAVIS, Earle
from I Dream of Democracy: An American Epic: from "Canto One" and "Canto Two." KanQ (4:1) Wint 71-72, p. 86.

667 DAVIS, Glover
"Columns." Poetry (120:6) S 72, p. 345.
"Mouths." Poetry (121:3) D 72, p. 144.
"The Orphan." Poetry (121:3) D 72, p. 143.

668 DAVIS, Henry
"Rebecca 1947-1970." JnlOBP (2:16) Sum 72, p. 86.

669 DAVIS, Lloyd
"Bob Hosey is Dead." Peb (9) Wint 72.
"Fishing the Lower Jackson." Peb (6) Sum 71.
"Panic." Peb (6) Sum 71.

670 DAVIS, William Virgil
"Back and Forth." HiramPoR (12) Spr-Sum 72, p. 10.
"The Birthplace." WormR (46) 72, p. 40.
"Cows Labor Heavily." Focus (8:56) 72, p. 36.
"Dream Poem IV." MichQR (11:2) Spr 72, p. 117.
"Driving Alone in Winter." MassR (13:4) Aut 72, p. 708.
"Early April in Connecticut." WindO (10) Sum 72, p. 46.
"Etching." WindO (10) Sum 72, p. 46.
"Following the Stones." Nat (215:16) 20 N 72, p. 506.
"Girl Behind Glass." MidwQ (13:2) Wint 72, p. 199.
"Hard Sell." WormR (46) 72, p. 40.
"The Hunt." PraS (46:2) Sum 72, p. 109.
"The Hunt." Shen (23:4) Sum 72, p. 26.
"A Husband Speaks to His Wife on Their Fiftieth Anniversary." Zahir (1:4/5) 72, p. 75.
"I Inherited His Hands." WormR (46) 72, p. 40.
"If Women are Always Birds." Peb (6) Sum 71.
"Let Us Call It a Wednesday." MichQR (11:2) Spr 72, p. 116.
"The Marriage." Peb (6) Sum 71.
"November." HiramPoR (12) Spr-Sum 72, p. 9.
"Prairie Schooners." PraS (46:2) Sum 72, p. 110.
"Remember." Peb (6) Sum 71.
"The Robber Bees." Zahir (1:4/5) 72, p. 75.
"Sermon." St. AR (1:4) Spr-Sum 72, p. 60.
"Spring." ChrC (89:14) 5 Ap 72, p. 385.
"String Quartet." Focus (8:56) 72, p. 36.
"The Wolf." PraS (46:2) Sum 72, p. 108.
"The Woman in the Tree." Focus (8:56) 72, p. 36.

671 DAVISON, Peter
"The Heroine." AmerR (14) 72, p. 199.

672 DAVYDOV, Denis
"Dance" (tr. by Lauren Leighton). RusLT (3) Spr 72, p. 57.
"Song of an Old Hussar" (tr. by Lauren Leighton). RusLT (3) Spr 72, p. 55.
"Those Evening Bells" (tr. by Lauren Leighton). RusLT (3) Spr 72, p. 56.

"To a Pious Charmer" (tr. by Lauren Leighton). RusLT (3) Spr 72, p. 53.

673 DAWSON, Leven
"Receptacles." ArizQ (28:4) Wint 72, p. 325.

674 DAY, David J.
"Three Gargoyles." NYT 10 Ag 72, p. 34.
"When Two or Three are Gathered Together." NYT 28 Je 72, p. 44.

675 DEAGON, Ann
"Afternoon of a Sphinx." SouthernHR (6:2) Spr 72, p. 132.
"The Car Half Under." Poem (14) Mr 72, p. 7.
"Id and the Seminar." AAUP (58:4) D 72, p. 393.
"Lesson For Today." AAUP (58:4) D 72, p. 393.
"Once Upon a Greek." WestHR (26:1) Wint 72, p. 16.
"Poet in Residence." AAUP (58:4) D 72, p. 393.
"Prof. Rapunzel." AAUP (58:4) D 72, p. 393.
"Reflection." SouthernHR (6:2) Spr 72, p. 133.
"Roommates." Poem (14) Mr 72, p. 9.
"The Sibyl's Bath." BelPoJ (23:2) Wint 72-73, p. 3.
"Social Security." HiramPoR (12) Spr-Sum 72, p. 11.
"Uncle Bill." PoetL (67:4) Wint 72, p. 371.
"Under Vesuvius." Epos (23:3) Spr 72, p. 18.
"Vigil on Market Street." SouthernPR (12:2) Spr 72, p. 30.

676 De ANDRADE, Carlos Drummond
"Igreja." TexQ (15:4) Wint 72, p. 111.
"In light of the latest news" (tr. by Ricardo Sternberg and Duane Ackerson). Drag (3:1) Spr 72, p. 82.
"Luar em Qualquer Cidade." Mund (5:3) 72, p. 58.
"News Poem" (tr. by Ricardo Sternberg and Duane Ackerson). Drag (3:1) Spr 72, p. 84.
"Nosso Tempo" (a Osvaldo Alves). Mund (5:3) 72, p. 56.
"Palavras No Mar." TexQ (15:4) Wint 72, p. 109.
"Poem of Seven Facets" (tr. by Ricardo Sternberg and Duane Ackerson). Drag (3:1) Spr 72, p. 83.
"Politica Literária" (a Manuel Bandeira). Mund (5:3) 72, p. 58.
"The Survivor" (tr. by Ricardo Sternberg and Duane Ackerson). Drag (3:1) Spr 72, p. 81.
"To a Hotel Scheduled for Demolition" (tr. by Thomas Colchie). Hudson (25:2) Sum 72, p. 186.

677 De BOLT, William Walter
"Corners." KanQ (4:1) Wint 71-72, p. 83.
"Petals of Belief." ChrC (89:13) 29 Mr 72, p. 359.
"Prejudiced Man." ChrC (89:12) 22 Mr 72, p. 330.

678 De BURGOS, Julia
"To Julia de Burgos" (tr. by Grace Schulman). Nat (215:10) 9 O 72, p. 314.

679 DECAVALLES, Andonis
"A Greek Trireme" (tr. by Stavros Deligiorgis). AriD (1:4/5) Sum-Aut 72, p. 33.
"Oceanides." AriD (1:4/5) Sum-Aut 72, p. 34.
"Recording." AriD (1:4/5) Sum-Aut 72, p. 35.
"Trickles and the Drummer." AriD (1:4/5) Sum-Aut 72, p. 35.

680 De CHAZEAU, Eunice
"August, Moon of the Mad Dog." KanQ (4:1) Wint 71-72, p. 98.

681 DECKER, Beverly
"In Time." YaleLit (141:1) 71, p. 20.

682 DeCOSTA, Fredericka
"Something of Mine." GreenR (2:2) 72, p. 7.

683 DeFORD, Miriam Allen
"Essence." PoetL (67:2) Sum 72, p. 132.
"Love Song for This Age." PoetL (67:2) Sum 72, p. 131.
"Wakened at Midnight." PoetL (67:2) Sum 72, p. 131.

684 DeFORD, Sara
"High Wire Act." HiramPoR (13) Fall-Wint 72, p. 9.

685 DeFREES, Madeline
"In the District." St. AR (1:4) Spr-Sum 72, p. 39.
"Reply to an Irremovable Pastor Twenty Years Too Late." NowestR (12:3) Aut 72, p. 56.
"Still Life with Lumbosacral Support." PoetryNW (13:4) Wint 72-73, p. 40.

686 DeGRUSON, Gene
"Highly Sophisticated Swedes." KanQ (4:1) Wint 71-72, p. 45.
"Metaphor Through My Screen Door." KanQ (4:3) Sum 72, p. 30.
"Theresa." KanQ (4:3) Sum 72, p. 30.

687 DEISLER, Guillermo
"Notice of Terminal Illness" (tr. by Edward Oliphant). RoadAR (4:1) Spr 72, p. 53.
"The Story I Never Found" (tr. by Edward Oliphant). RoadAR (4:1) Spr 72, p. 54.

688 DEKIN,. Timothy
"Melancholy." SouthernR (8:1) Wint 72, p. 175.
"A Sunday Afternoon." Spec (14:1/2) My 72, p. 26.

689 DeLAURENTIS, Louise Budde
"Encompassing." Wind (2:6) Aut 72, p. 26.
"Graveside Pastoral." Poem (16) N 72, p. 15.

"Moonscape." Folio (8:1) Spr 72, p. 35.
"Vertigo." Epoch (21:2) Wint 71, p. 156.

690 DELAVAN, Holly
"Irises." New:ACP (19) Aut 72, p. 37.

691 Del BOURGO, David
"The Language." Epos (24:1) Fall 72, p. 22.

692 DELIGIORGIS, Stavros
from Anatomy: (4, 8, 9) (tr. of Yannas Thallas). AriD (1:4/5) Sum-Aut 72, p. 99.
"Cavocolones" (tr. of Dimitris Christodoulou). AriD (1:4/5) Sum-Aut 72, p. 29.
"Episode" (tr. of Nikos Karachalios). AriD (1:4/5) Sum-Aut 72, p. 60.
"Era" (tr. of Ektor Kaknavatos). AriD (1:4/5) Sum-Aut 72, p. 52.
"From Known Languages." AriD (1:3) Spr 72, p. 28.
"The Last Moment" (tr. of Nikos Karachalios). AriD (1:4/5) Sum-Aut 72, p. 58.
"A Greek Trireme" (tr. of Andonis Decavalles). AriD (1:4/5) Sum-Aut 72, p. 33.
"How Far to Death" (tr. of Rovyos Manthoulis). AriD (1:4/5) Sum-Aut 72, p. 80.
"Mannikins" (tr. of Matthaios Moundes). AriD (1:4/5) Sum-Aut 72, p. 81.
from Outerearth: "Fledglings and the speeches of prophecy" (tr. of V. N. Bonos). AriD (1:4/5) Sum-Aut 72, p. 25.
from Outerearth: "The mother done in and the dead scornful" (tr. of V. N. Bonos). AriD (1:4/5) Spr-Aut 72, p. 24.
"Prophetic" (tr. of Nikos Deligiorgis). AriD (1:4/5) Sum-Aut 72, p. 58.
from Reading: (I, II, VII, IX) (tr. of Frangiski Abatzopoulou). AriD (1:4/5) Sum-Aut 72, p. 13.
"Runaway" (tr. of Matthaio Moundes). AriD (1:4/5) Sum-Aut 72, p. 82.
"Terminal" (tr. of Matthaios Moundes). AriD (1:4/5) Sum-Aut 72, p. 82.

693 DeLONGCHAMPS, Joanne
"Letter from Lake Manyara." NYT 7 My 72, sec. 4, p. 14.
"Sub--Prefix. 1. Under, Beneath, Below; as in." Perspec (17:1) Sum 72, p. 48.
"Waterside." NYT 19 Ja 72, p. 36.
"When Grandparents Dance." PoetL (67:1) Spr 72, p. 60.

694 DELP, Michael
"Thinking of Janet in 1966." RoadAR (3:4) Wint 71-72, p. 37.

695 De MARIA, Robert
"Homo Sapiens." MedR (2:3) Spr 72, p. 87.

"P. O. P." MedR (2:3) Spr 72, p. 87.

696 De MELO NETO, João Cabral
"As Estaçoes." Mund (5:1/2) 72, p. 40.
"The Hound Without Plumes" (to Joaquim Cardozo) (tr. by Robert Stock). Works (3:2) Wint-Spr 72, p. 4.
"Noturno." Mund (5:1/2) 72, p. 42.

697 DEMETRE, Diane
"Smiles." WindO (11) Aut 72, p. 13.

698 DEMOREST, Steve
"Giraffe." NewYQ (12) Aut 72, p. 85.

699 DeMUNBRUN, Roland
"Kenneth Patchen Passes." NewYQ (11) Sum 72, p. 40.

700 DENNIS, Carl
"Exercises at a Good Resort." ModernPS (3:1) 72, p. 28.
"The Forgetful Traveller." SoDakR (10:1) Spr 72, p. 3.
"A Middle-Aged Movie Maker." Salm (18) Wint 72, p. 106.
"Readers." Epoch (22:1) Fall 72, p. 40.
"Settling Down." ModernPS (3:1) 72, p. 28.
"The Song of the Mad Troll." ModernPS (3:1) 72, p. 30.
"A Winter Visit." NewRep (167:10) 16 S 72, p. 23.

701 De OCA, Marco Antonio Montes
"A Nivel del Mar." Mund (5:3) 72, p. 60.
"Luz en Ristre." Mund (5:3) 72, p. 62.

702 De PALCHI, Alfredo
from Il Mio Male: (4, 5, 11, 14, 16, 19, 21, 27) (45. by Sonia Raiziss). MedR (2:4) Sum 72, p. 89.
from Origine: (1) (tr. by I. L. Salomon). MedR (2:4) Sum 72, p. 88.

703 DEPTA, Victor M.
"The Creek" (37). Cord (1:4) 72, p. 5.
"Holding you is the same as holding the moon." OhioR (14:1) Aut 72, p. 42.
"Selene." Shen (23:4) Sum 72, p. 43.
"The Swing Shift at Purina Foods." SouthernPR (12:2) Spr 72, p. 53.

704 De RACHEWILTZ, Sizzo
"Cuma" (tr. of Mario Luzi). St. AR (2:1) Aut-Wint 72, p. 54.
"Nature" (tr. of Mario Luzi). St. AR (1:4) Spr-Sum 72, p. 26.
"Night Laves the Mind" (tr. of Mario Luzi). St. AR (2:1) Aut-Wint 72, p. 54.
"The Moment's Immensity" (tr. of Mario Luzi). St. AR (1:4) Spr-Sum 72, p. 26.

705 Der HOVANESSIAN, Diana
"Antique (Doll Room, Jeanette, Louisiana)." NYT 21 Jl 72, p. 30.

706 DERMEN, Judith De Ponceau
"My Graveyard." AmerS (41:4) Aut 72, p. 628.

707 DeROCHE, Joseph
"Once More that Irrepressible Oh!" NewYQ (12) Aut 72, p. 66.

708 DERRICOTTE, Toinette
"Trees." NewYQ (12) Aut 72, p. 90.

709 DESCH, Robert P.
"Dietrich Bonhoeffer." ChrC (89:38) 25 O 72, p. 1066.

710 DESKINS, David
"Galileo Granny and the Quilt." Folio (8:2) Fall 72, p. 32.

711 DESNOS, Robert
"Time of the Dungeons" (tr. by William Kulik and Carole Frankel). Madem (76:2) D 72, p. 104.
"You Take the First Street" (tr. by Raymond Federman). Pan (9) 72, p. 10.

712 DESRUISSEAUX, Paul
"No Faint Glow." WestHR (26:4) Aut 72, p. 367.

713 De STEFANO, Eugene
"Berryman, at the Bridge." ChiTM 5 Mr 72, p. 14.

714 DESY, P. M.
"T. S. Eliot Has a Dream." Epoch (22:1) Fall 72, p. 79.

715 DESY, Peter
"Regrowth." OhioR (13:3) Spr 72, p. 26.

716 DEUTSCH, Joel
"Another Change of Address." Cord (1:4) 72, p. 33.
"Donut Madonna." Cord (1:4) 72, p. 31.
"Dry Dock" (for Karen). Sky (1:1) 71.
"Experiment." Zahir (1:4/5) 72, p. 51.
"Family Album" (for Forrest Duncan). Cord (1:4) 72, p. 37.
"Famous Gangsters #18." Sky (1:1) 71.
"Grandma." Cord (1:4) 72, p. 32.
"Lenin's Letters from Siberia." WormR (47) 72, p. 80.
"Marty Robbins and a Matte Print Memory of You." WormR (47) 72, p. 80.
"Monster Mash." Cord (1:4) 72, p. 35.
"Not Even a Postcard." Cord (1:4) 72, p. 36.
"Reunion." BabyJ (5) N 72, p. 12.

"Spider." Cord (1:4) 72, p. 34.

717 DEUTSCHMAN, Deborah
"Rain." NewYorker (48:12) 13 My 72, p. 38.

718 DE VITA, Gloria
"Chantsong: The Two Women" (for Doris Lessing). CalQ (3) Aut 72, p. 54.

719 De VITO, E. B.
"Episode." Poem (16) N 72, p. 50.
"Leader." Poem (16) N 72, p. 51.
"New Son." ChiTM 5 N 72, p. 15.

720 DEVLIN, Arthur L.
"Combat." LitR (16:1) Aut 72, p. 34.
"Request." LitR (16:1) Aut 72, p. 34.

721 De VOTI, William
"Carnage." Nat (215:4) 21 Ag 72, p. 125.

722 De VRIES, Carrow
"One morning I went out to plow the back four." WindO (11) Aut 72, p. 16.

723 DEWEY, Al
"The Abortion." NewYQ (9) Wint 72, p. 63.
"After Receiving Bad News." HangL (16) Wint 71-72, p. 9.
"At the Drive-In: 'John Wayne vs. God.'" NewYQ (9) Wint 72, p. 63.
"Cross Hairs." Cafe (4) Fall 72, p. 34.
"First Winters." RoadAR (3:4) Wint 71-72, p. 12.
"The Ideal Hitchhiker." HangL (16) Wint 71-72, p. 8.
"In Cold Blood Country." KanQ (4:2) Spr 72, p. 92.

724 De YOUNG, Robert J.
"Driving Home Behind Another Car." HiramPoR (12) Spr-Sum 72, p. 12.
"Travelling Man." HiramPoR (12) Spr-Sum 72, p. 13.
"View from a Mountain." SouthernHR (6:3) Sum 72, p. 283.

725 DHAR, Krishna
"One More Unfortunate." Meas (3) 72, p. 24.

726 DIAMONDSTONE, Judi
"Grace--While You Sleep." Isthmus (1) Spr 72, p. 49.
"In Pursuit of Perfection, Dream Image Projection." Isthmus (1) Spr 72, p. 47.

727 DIBBLE, Brian
"Lausanne." ChiTM 9 Ja 72, p. 12.
"My Clothes." Qt (5:39/40) Sum-Aut 72, p. 37.

728 DIBBLE, Ellen
"Calling the Babysitter." MassR (13:1/2) Wint-Spr 72, p. 290.
"Depression." MassR (13:1/2) Wint-Spr 72, p. 290.

729 DICKER, Harold
"Running Cat." Pan (9) 72, p. 61.

730 DICKEY, James
"Of Holy War." Poetry (121:1) O 72, p. 7.
"The Rain Guitar." NewYorker (47:47) 8 Ja 72, p. 36.

731 DICKEY, William
"Alone I Care For Myself." Poetry (120:4) Jl 72, p. 222.
"At Bablockhythe." Iowa (3:1) Wint 72, p. 9.
"Clayton & the Ducks." ChiTM 13 F 72, p. 16.
"The Death of Mr. Thrale." Poetry (120:4) Jl 72, p. 223.
"The Face." Iowa (3:1) Wint 72, p. 8.
"Happiness." Iowa (3:1) Wint 72, p. 8.
"Here's Mars." Poetry (120:4) Jl 72, p. 221.
"One Ree-Deep (No Charge)." Iowa (3:1) Wint 72, p. 7.
"The Poet's Farewell to His Teeth." Poetry (120:4) Jl 72, p. 220.
"To the Collector of Taxes, City and County of San Francisco." ChiTM 30 Ap 72, p. 14.
"When You See Me." SaltCR (5:1) Wint 72.

732 DICKSON, John
"The Egg." PoetL (67:3) Aut 72, p. 239.
"Peace." PoetL (67:3) Aut 72, p. 239.
"Stained Glass Window." PoetL (67:3) Aut 72, p. 238.

733 Di EMIDIO, Monica
"He is the Doctor's son." Zahir (1:4/5) 72, p. 61.

734 DIGBY, John
"The Ageing of Our Dark Masters." QRL (18:1/2) 72, p. 60.
"A Few Lines for Rene Magritte." QRL (18:1/2) 72, p. 56.
"The Misery of the Perpetual Scholars." QRL (18:1/2) 72, p. 57.
"Return of Saturday." QRL (18:1/2) 72, p. 59.
"The Silence Treats Us as Equals." QRL (18:1/2) 72, p. 58.

735 Di GIOVANNI, Norman Thomas
"John 1:14" (tr. of Jorge Luis Borges). NewYorker (47:52) 12 F 72, p. 38.
"Montevideo" (tr. of Jorge Luis Borges). NewYorker (48:3) 11 Mr 72, p. 34.
"Two Milongas" (tr. of Jorge Luis Borges). WestHR (26:4) Aut 72, p. 331.
"The Watcher" (tr. of Jorge Luis Borges). NewYorker

(48:1) 26 F 72, p. 42.

736 DILDY, Rodney G.
"... And Now a Word From Our Sponsor." JnlOBP (2:16) Sum 72, p. 22.

737 Di LEONARDO, Micaela
"Homage to Michaux." Spec (14:1/2) My 72, p. 59.

738 DILLARD, Annie
"Eleanor at the Office." NewYQ (9) Wint 72, p. 80.

739 DILLARD, Nancy Hollis
"Growth." ChrC (89:2) 12 Ja 72, p. 41.

740 DILLARD, R. H. W.
"March Again." AmerS (41:4) Aut 72, p. 585.

741 Di MAURO, Dorothy
"We sit opposite on the bus." Wind (2:5) Sum 72, p. 44.

742 DIMITROVA, Blaga
"At St. Cyril's Grave." LitR (16:2) Wint 72-73, p. 234.
"The Old Man and the World." LitR (16:2) Wint 72-73, p. 233.
"Rehabilitation." LitR (16:2) Wint 72-73, p. 234.

743 DINER, Steven
"Blue Books." MinnR (2) Spr 72, p. 121.

744 DIOMEDE, Matthew
"Dreams." Phy (33:4) Wint 72, p. 388.

745 DiPALMA, Raymond
"Back in His Pocket." LittleM (6:1) Spr 72, p. 18.
"Chocolates & Wine." Meas (2) 72.
"The Circle." LittleM (6:2/3) Sum-Aut 72, p. 72.
"Scales." LittleM (6:2/3) Sum-Aut 72, p. 70.
"Some Words" (for Darrell). GreenR (2:2) 72, p. 32.
"Two Twisted Wires Spinning." Meas (2) 72.

746 DiPASQUALE, Emanuel
"In This New England." NewYQ (9) Wint 72, p. 52.
"Letter from the Greek Islands." Poem (16) N 72, p. 20.
"My Uncle Emanuel." SouthernPR (12:2) Spr 72, p. 19.
"Poem: In Spring in Washington Square Park." Nat (214:6) 7 F 72, p. 184.
"Reality." Nat (214:9) 28 F 72, p. 285.
"Storms." Nat (214:9) 28 F 72, p. 285.
"Upon the Birth of my Son." NYT 8 O 72, p. 14.

747 di PRIMA, Diane
"Prayer to the Ancestors, at Easter." Isthmus (1) Spr 72, p. 15.

748 Di PRISCO, Joseph
"The Dumb Page." PoetryNW (13:3) Aut 72, p. 33.

749 DISCH, Tom
"Apollo 14." Poetry (119:5) F 72, p. 275.
"The Clouds." Poetry (119:5) F 72, p. 272.
"The Mandarin." LittleR (6:2/3) Sum-Aut 72, p. 8.
"The Prisoners of War." Poetry (120:6) S 72, p. 332.
"The Vegetables." Poetry (119:5) F 72, p. 275.
"The Vowels of Another Language." Poetry (119:5) F 72, p. 274.

750 DISTLER, Bette
"the death of Lottie Shapiro." LitR (16:1) Aut 72, p. 130.

751 DITSKY, John
"A. M. D. G." SouthernHR (6:4) Aut 72, p. 322.
"At the Buffet." New:ACP (19) Aut 72, p. 27.
"Brazilian Impressions" (for Joyce Carol Oates). ColEng (33:7) Ap 72, p. 808.
"Faith Like Sweet Contagion." Poem (15) Jl 72, p. 58.
"Here We Are in a Jesus Time." SouthernHR (6:4) Aut 72, p. 324.
"Just a Shape To Fill a Lack." SouthernHR (6:4) Aut 72, p. 326.
"K. 527." SouthernHR (6:4) Aut 72, p. 320.
"Leminade 5¢." ColEng (33:7) Ap 72, p. 809.
"Montage." TexQ (15:4) Wint 72, p. 54.
"Our Lady's Child." New:ACP (19) Aut 72, p. 26.
"Quanto?" TexQ (15:4) Wint 72, p. 53.
"Vessels." Poem (15) Jl 72, p. 57.
"Wasting Away." Poem (15) Jl 72, p. 59.
"With Some Teeth In It." BabyJ (5) N 72, p. 29.

752 DIXON, Alan
"First Images." Nat (214:14) 3 Ap 72, p. 440.

753 DOAN, Michael
"For Some Ultra-Mod Sisters." JnlOBP (2:16) Sum 72, p. 84.

754 DOANE, Jenny Lynn
"The Outside." StoneD (1:1) Spr 72, p. 12.

755 DOBBS, Jeannine
"First Meeting." WormR (47) 72, p. 76.
"Uncle Bill." WormR (47) 72, p. 77.
"Up the Periscope." SouthernPR (12:2) Spr 72, p. 55.

756 DOBYNS, Stephen
"Clouds." Poetry (119:6) Mr 72, p. 337.
"Getting Away From It All." PoetryNW (13:3) Aut 72, p. 28.

757 DODD, Wayne
"Certain Evidence." NowestR (12:3) Aut 72, p. 51.
"Driving Through Shane Country." Spec (14:1/2) My 72, p. 27.
"Looking, Late at Night." Shen (23:4) Sum 72, p. 23.
"Miss America Pageant, 1971." Spec (14:1/2) My 72, p. 28.
"My Son's Hand." Shen (23:4) Sum 72, p. 24.
"Of His Life." Shen (23:4) Sum 72, p. 22.
"To the City: 1938." PoetryNW (13:1) Spr 72, p. 28.

758 DODSON, Pat
"Darkness." SewanR (80:2) Spr 72, p. 286.

759 DOELL
"That Winter." New:ACP (19) Aut 72, p. 34.

760 DOLCI, Danilo
"Poems from Il Limone Lunare" (tr. by Brian Swann and Ruth Feldman). MedR (2:4) Sum 72, p. 39.

761 DOMIN, Hilde
"Bulletin." Field (6) Spr 72, p. 17.
"Distances" (tr. by Domin and Tudor Morris). DenQuart (6:4) Wint 72, p. 4.
"Fingernagelgross" (tr. by Ann Boehm). Field (6) Spr 72, p. 16.
"I Want You" (tr. by Domin and Tudor Morris). DenQuart (6:4) Wint 72, p. 1.
"Many" (tr. by David Young). Field (6) Spr 72, p. 19.
"Traveling Light." Field (6) Spr 72, p. 18.
"Unicorn" (tr. by Domin and Tudor Morris). DenQuart (6:4) Wint 72, p. 3.

762 DONAHUE, Jack
"The Year of Change." Wind (2:5) Sum 72, p. 4.

763 DONNELLY, Dorothy
"Flowerfall." Comm (96:17) 28 Jl 72, p. 406.
"To Begin With." ChrC (89:43) 29 N 72, p. 1210.

764 DONOVAN, Laurence
"Where I Stood." Epos (24:1) Fall 72, p. 14.

765 DONZELLA, D. W.
"Stonehenge." Poetry (119:6) Mr 72, p. 333.

766 DOOLEY, Dennis
"Eating Alone, Spring 1970 (for Jean)." Peb (9) Wint 72.

767 DOR, Moshe
"Horses." SoDakR (10:1) Spr 72, p. 16.
"A Journey." SoDakR (10:1) Spr 72, p. 16.

"Notes for an Armenian Biography." SoDakR (10:1) Spr 72, p. 16.
"Poem." SoDakR (10:1) Spr 72, p. 16.
"Time is Measured." SoDakR (10:1) Spr 72, p. 16.

768 DORBIN, Sandy
"Around Her Leg She Wore." WormR (47) 72, p. 70.
"Babysitter." WormR (47) 72, p. 71.
"The Collector." WormR (47) 72, p. 73.
"L'Enfance d'un chef." WormR (47) 72, p. 72.
"Go Tell It on the Mountain" (for Dave Londo). Cord (1:4) 72, p. 22.

769 DORESKI, William
"At Baudelaire's Tomb" (tr. of Stephen Mallarmé). PoetL (67:1) Spr 72, p. 43.
"Beatrice" (tr. of Charles Baudelaire). PoetL (67:1) Spr 72, p. 42.
"High School Whore in a Field of Rutabagas and Lettuce." Epoch (22:1) Fall 72, p. 42.
"Marine" (tr. of Arthur Rimbaud). PoetL (67:1) Spr 72, p. 43.
"A Piece of Steel." Epoch (22:1) Fall 72, p. 43.
"Prose" (Pour des Esseintes) (tr. of Stephen Mallarmé). PoetL (67:1) Spr 72, p. 44.
"The Saint" (tr. of Stephen Mallarmé). PoetL (67:1) Spr 72, p. 46.
"Toad" (tr. of Tristan Corbiere). PoetL (67:1) Spr 72, p. 42.
"The Walden Dark." Epoch (22:1) Fall 72, p. 44.
"What cloth soaking up time's salve" (tr. of Stephen Mallarmé). PoetL (67:1) Spr 72, p. 44.

770 DORMAN, Sonya
"Cannibals." LittleM (6:2/3) Sum-Aut 72, p. 65.
"Family Poem." PoetryNW (13:4) Wint 72-73, p. 18.
"Final Dispositions." UTR (1:4) 72, p. 22.
"Five Dialogues." UnicornJ (4) 72, p. 49.
"Mother Salt." Iron (2) Fall 72, p. 54.
"The Mysterious Dr. Morning." PoetryNW (13:4) Wint 72-73, p. 16.
"Stretching Fence on Our Anniversary." PoetryNW (13:4) Wint 72-73, p. 17.

771 DORN, Edward
"Idling with Observation & Song." Iowa (3:4) Fall 72, p. 13.
"The Poet Lets His Tongue Hang Down." ParisR (55) Aut 72, p. 67.

772 DORRIEN, Tom
"Bear Hunting" (for Peter). Shen (24:1) Aut 72, p. 33.
"Into a Drowse of Arms Fired." PoetryNW (13:4) Wint

72-73, p. 33.
"Love Poem." Comm (95:14) 7 Ja 72, p. 326.
"Mirrors." Shen (24:1) Aut 72, p. 34.

773 DOSTAL, Cyril A.
"Cabbages" (Hard Edged Poem #2). FreeL (15:1/2) 71-72, p. 71.
"Donkey Tale" (Hard Edged Poem #3). FreeL (15:1/2) 71-72, p. 70.
"The Fashion Model." FreeL (15:1/2) 71-72, p. 69.

774 DOUGLASS, Suzanne
"BRRRRR." LadHJ (89:10) O 72, p. 104.

775 DOUKARIS, Dimitris
"The Crippled Dog" (tr. by Ruth Whitman). AriD (1:4/5) Sum-Aut 72, p. 38.
"Krypteia" (tr. by Ruth Whitman). AriD (1:4/5) Sum-Aut 72, p. 38.
"Photographs" (tr. by Ruth Whitman). AriD (1:4/5) Sum-Aut 72, p. 36.

776 DOUSKEY, Franz
"A Careful Vigil." Nat (214:15) 10 Ap 72, p. 470.
"Minoration." WestR (10:1) Spr 73, p. 2. [Final issue.]
"The Sheriff." Nat (214:19) 8 My 72, p. 597.

777 DOUTINE, Heike
"Addicted" (tr. by Gisele Frohlinde-Meyer). Zahir (1:4/5) 72, p. 16.
Eight Poems (tr. by Gisele Frohlinde-Meyer). PoetL (67:2) Sum 72, p. 155.
"Escaped" (tr. by Gisele Frohlinde-Meyer). Zahir (1:4/5) 72, p. 17.

778 DOVAISWAMY, T. K.
"The Bitch." Meas (3) 72, p. 25.

779 DOWD, Romayne
"Iron Wings." EngJ (61:8) N 72, p. 1198.
"The Road Not Taken" (Apologies to Frost). EngJ (61:3) Mr 72, p. 371.

780 DOWNING, Scarff
"Reflections on Watching the Film The War Game or Here's to You, Mr. Vonnegut." EngJ (61:8) N 72, p. 1231.

781 DOWTY, Leonhard
"MMMMmmmmm." LadHJ (89:6) Je 72, p. 102.

782 DOXEY, W. S.
"Being Counted." BabyJ (5) N 72, p. 13.
"Conversion of Energy." Zahir (1:4/5) 72, p. 60.

"Cool." SouthernHR (6:4) Aut 72, p. 367.
"Kittens." SouthernHR (6:4) Aut 72, p. 366.
"Self Portraits." SouthernHR (6:4) Aut 72, p. 366.

783 DOYLE, James
"Encounter." WestR (9:2) Wint 72, p. 20.
"Funeral." CalQ (3) Aut 72, p. 51.
"The Instruments." SouthernHR (6:3) Sum 72, p. 285.
"Landscapes." OhioR (13:3) Spr 72, p. 81.

784 DOZIER, Brent
"th' green bow at th' back of her dress." Folio (8:1) Spr 72, p. 31.

785 DRAKE, Albert
"1939 Mercury." St. AR (2:1) Aut-Wint 72, p. 33.
"Oregon." Drag (3:1) Spr 72, p. 34.

786 DRAPIN, Lois
"Weep Not. She is Not Dead, But Sleepeth." NYT 25 Jl 72, p. 32.

787 DRAVES, Cornelia
"Snow." NewYQ (9) Wint 72, p. 79.

788 DRESSEL, Jon
"Perspectives of a Honky in the New Saint Louis." PraS (46:1) Spr 72, p. 20.

789 DREWRY, Carleton
"Stillborn." SouthwR (57:1) Wint 72, p. 40.

790 DRISCOLL, Jack
"Another Scanlon." Meas (2) 72.
"Middle of the Day." Sky (1:2) 72, p. 10.
"Searching for Love." Shen (24:1) Aut 72, p. 70.

791 DRIZ, Shike
"Sew Me a Green Old Age" (tr. by Leonard Opalov). PoetL (67:1) Spr 72, p. 35.

792 DRUIT, Greg O.
"Rhymes." BeyB (2:2) 72, p. 73.

793 DRUSKA, John
"On Her Fourth Birthday." Comm (97:4) 27 O 72, p. 88.

794 DUBERSTEIN, Helen
"My Brother Incestuously." Confr (5) Wint-Spr 72, p. 63.
"Settling Accounts." BeyB (2:2) 72, p. 57.
"Women Over Forty, Forget It!" Confr (5) Wint-Spr 72, p. 62.

795 DUBIE, Norman
"Little Frederick's Song." QRL (18:1/2) 72, p. 61.

796 DUBIE, William
"The Older Days." Zahir (1:4/5) 72, p. 66.
"There Will Be No Sojourns." Zahir (1:4/5) 72, p. 67.
"The Weekly High School Dance." Zahir (1:4/5) 72, p. 69.

797 DUDIS, Ellen Kirvin
"Lily Morning." Poetry (119:6) Mr 72, p. 314.

798 DUFAULT, Peter Kane
"At Vera Frost's Pony Farm." NewYorker (47:46) 1 Ja 72, p. 28.

799 DUFF, Lyndon
"For My Father." PoetL (67:3) Aut 72, p. 260.
"Mary." PoetL (67:3) Aut 72, p. 222.

800 DUFFEY, Richard
"An American Dreaming." ChrC (89:14) 5 Ap 72, p. 393.

801 DUFFIN, John H.
"Beetlewolf." EngJ (61:5) My 72, p. 652.

802 DuFRESNE, E. R.
"Shooting Stars." PoetL (67:2) Sum 72, p. 165.

803 DUGAN, Alan
"Aside." Poetry (121:1) O 72, p. 8.
"Stentor and Mourning." Poetry (120:6) S 72, p. 355.

804 DUHAMEL, Vaughn L.
"Instant Theater (to Will Stubbs)." KanQ (4:2) Spr 72, p. 30.
"Polarization Conversation." Zahir (1:4/5) 72, p. 54.
"savage mind." St.AR (2:1) Aut-Wint 72, p. 42.

805 DUKE, Ruth H.
"The Brink." EngJ (61:7) O 72, p. 1009.

806 DUKES, Norman
"The Bed Charges Along Its Rails of Blue Honey." Kayak (29) S 72, p. 23.
"Message from a Woman Gone Mad." Kayak (29) S 72, p. 23.

807 DUNANN, Louella
"Hot Line." SatEP (244:3) Aut 72, p. 88.

808 DUNCAN, Marty
"The past turns around in a parking lot." WindO (11) Aut 72, p. 34.

"the world is a dormitory." WindO (11) Aut 72, p. 34.

809 DUNETZ, Lora
"The Deer." PoetL (67:1) Spr 72, p. 21.
"I Wandered into a Wood." PoetL (67:1) Spr 72, p. 21.
"Ice Storm in New England." PoetL (67:1) Spr 72, p. 20.
"Resignation." GeoR (26:4) Wint 72, p. 507.
"Sleeper in the Vale" (tr. of Arthur Rimbaud). PoetL (67:1) Spr 72, p. 20.

810 DUNN, Douglas
"A Faber Melancholy" (for P. L. and I. H.). Antaeus (6) Sum 72, p. 72.

811 DUNN, Phyllis
"World Literature Without Footnotes." EngJ (61:9) D 72, p. 1369.

812 DUNN, Robert
"I have asked for apples." Folio (8:2) Fall 72, p. 29.
"Song of the First Cook." Folio (8:2) Fall 72, p. 42.

813 DUNN, Stephen
"Among Blackberries." Peb (9) Wint 72.
"California, This Is Minnesota Speaking." NewRep (167:22) 9 D 72, p. 31.
"Carrying On." Shen (24:1) Aut 72, p. 45.
"Going Through the Moon." Iowa (3:2) Spr 72, p. 10.
"How to Be Happy: Another Memo to Myself." PoetryNW (13:4) Wint 72-73, p. 21.
"Lakes: the Ocean Speaking." PoetryNW (13:4) Wint 72-73, p. 22.
"Looking for a Rest Area." Antaeus (5) Spr 72, p. 93.
"Men in Winter." Poetry (119:4) Ja 72, p. 220.
"Nights of Sirius." NewYorker (47:51) 5 F 72, p. 82.
"Notes from a Writer's Conference." SoDakR (10:3) Aut 72, p. 80.
"On Psyching the Skyjackers." NewRep (166:13) 25 Mr 72, p. 20.
"A Poem for Atheists." Shen (24:1) Aut 72, p. 44.
"Small Town: America." AntR (32:1/2) Spr-Sum 72, p. 55.
"Small Town: Sonnet." NoAmR (257:4) Wint 72, p. 63.
"Small Town: The Cycle." Kayak (29) S 72, p. 41.

814 DUNSTER, Mark
"Flight." NYT 21 Ap 72, p. 38.

815 DuPLESSIS, Rachel Blau
"In her hands." HangL (16) Wint 71-72, p. 10.
"Travel by train, the trees are money." HangL (16) Wint 71-72, p. 10.

816 DURHAM, John
"In the Manner of Gregory Corso." AriD (1:2) Wint 72, p. 43.

817 DURHAM, Susan
"To Sappho." SouthernPR (13:1) Aut 72, p. 47.

818 DURRELL, Lawrence
"Hey, Mister, There's a Bulge in Your Computer." Playb (19:12) D 72, p. 219.
"Spring Song." Playb (19:12) D 72, p. 219.

819 DUSENBERY, Robert
"Huck Finn." Mark (16:3) Wint 72, p. 14.

820 DYBEK, Stuart
"1533." WestHR (26:4) Aut 72, p. 348.

821 DYER, Dan
"Bearing January's Pale Candle." WindO (10) Sum 72, p. 15.
"Poem: The wound was nothing." WindO (10) Sum 72, p. 15.
"The Quilt." WindO (10) Sum 72, p. 14.
from Tales of the Snow. WindO (10) Sum 72, p. 15.

822 EATON, Anne
"The Civic Banquet." NYT 22 S 72, p. 42.

823 EATON, Charles Edward
"The Aquarium." SoCaR (4:2) Je 72, p. 4.
"Birth of the Ox." HolCrit (9:2) Je 72, p. 11.
"The Cannibal." HiramPoR (13) Fall-Wint 72, p. 6.
"The Carcass." ConcPo (5:2) Fall 72, p. 71.
"The Cuckold." SouthernHR (6:4) Aut 72, p. 318.
"The Factory." Qt (5:37) Wint 72, p. 13.
"Harpoon." ColEng (33:5) F 72, p. 578.
"The Man in the Green Chair." PoetryNW (13:2) Sum 72, p. 9.
"Memoirs of a Dandy." QRL (18:1/2) 72, p. 62.
"The Pearl Diver." KanQ (4:1) Wint 71-72, p. 9.
"Portrait of an Artist." St. AR (1:4) Spr-Sum 72, p. 59.
"Red Neck." Poem (14) Mr 72, p. 55.
"The Rendezvous." NewL (38:4) Sum 72, p. 105.
"The Scout in Summer." SouthernPR (12:2) Spr 72, p. 27.
"The Senile Rooster." SatireN (9:2) Spr 72, p. 157.
"The Stickpin." MidwQ (13:3) Spr 72, p. 318.
"Water Polo." Shen (23:3) Spr 72, p. 32.
"The Wisteria Sailor." Poem (14) Mr 72, p. 56.

824 EBBERTS, Ruth N.
"August Morning." KanQ (4:3) Sum 72, p. 107.
"My Uncle Harry's Bed." KanQ (4:3) Sum 72, p. 106.

"Ritual." KanQ (4:3) Sum 72, p. 106.

825 EBERHARD, Edward
"Korinna." SouthernPR (13:1) Aut 72, p. 14.

826 EBERHART, Richard
"Broken Wing Theory." Atl (230:2) Ag 72, p. 73.
"Emblem." NewYorker (48:42) 9 D 72, p. 47.
"Evening Bird Song." ConcPo (5:2) Fall 72, p. 10.
"Going to Maine." ChiTM 10 D 72, p. 8.
"Lenses." VirQR (48:2) Spr 72, p. 214.
"Meaningless Poem." ConcPo (5:2) Fall 72, p. 11.
"Order." ConcPo (5:2) Fall 72, p. 9.
"Plain Song Talk." Poetry (121:2) N 72, p. 80.
"Vermont Idyll." Poetry (121:2) N 72, p. 79.
"You Think They Are Permanent But They Pass." NewRep (167:1) 1 Jl 72, p. 22.
"The Young and the Old." Nat (214:25) 19 Je 72, p. 793.

827 ECKMAN, Frederick
"On Being Loved." NewL (38:4) Sum 72, p. 99.
"Regina Coeli." NewL (38:4) Sum 72, p. 100.

828 ECONOMOU, George
from Glossary: (II, III) (tr. of Leonidas Zenakos, w. Stratis Haviaras). AriD (1:4/5) Sum-Aut 72, p. 119.
from Poems for Self Therapy: (1.). AriD (1:2) Wint 72, p. 8.
from Poems for Self-Therapy: (6.). AriD (1:2) Wint 72, p. 9.

829 EDELMAN, Prewitt
"Dame Edith Serves Tea, 1939." CarolQ (24:1) Wint 72, p. 78.

830 EDGERTON, David
"Acid Blessing." NewYQ (10) Spr 72, p. 53.

831 EDIGER, Peter J.
"An American Trilogy." ChrC (89:37) 18 O 72, p. 1034.
"November 7, 1972." ChrC (89:42) 22 N 72, p. 1176.

832 EDKINS, Anthony
"Snapshots." NewYQ (11) Sum 72, p. 66.

833 EDSON, Russell
"The Blinking Owl." Peb (6) Sum 71.
"Children." Drag (3:1) Spr 72, p. 63.
"The Epic." Drag (3:1) Spr 72, p. 62.
"Eskimo Story." Esq (78:6) D 72, p. 32.
"The Floor." Peb (6) Sum 71.
"The Modern Hunter." Field (7) Fall 72, p. 50.
"The Nearsighted Rich Man." Field (7) Fall 72, p. 46.

"Oatmeal." New:ACP (18) Ap 72, p. 5.
"An Old Man's Son." Field (7) Fall 72, p. 46.
"One Wonders." Field (7) Fall 72, p. 47.
"Out of Whack." Field (7) Fall 72, p. 48.
"Poems." Drag (3:3/4) Fall-Wint 72, pp. 3-18 (special issue).
"The Royal Affliction." New:ACP (18) Ap 72, p. 4.

834 EDWARDS, Dan
Three Haiku. WindO (10) Sum 72, p. 35.

835 EDWARDS, Eric
"Oarmeal." BosUJ (20:1/2) 72, p. 78.

836 EDWARDS, Margaret
"From the Reader." ArizQ (28:4) Wint 72, p. 338.

837 EGGERS, Angela W.
"Hands." SouthernPR (12:2) Spr 72, p. 6.

838 EHRENSTEIN, Albert
"Eternal Sleep" (tr. by Reinhold Johannes Kaebitzsch). UTR (1:4) 72, p. 9.

839 EIBEL, Deborah
"A Clown in History." LitR (15:3) Spr 72, p. 356.
"Freethinkers." LitR (15:3) Spr 72, p. 358.
"The Kabbalist." LitR (15:3) Spr 72, p. 357.
"Kol Nidrei Night." LitR (15:3) Spr 72, p. 360.
"Of Children Who Keep Journals." LitR (15:3) Spr 72, p. 359.

840 EICH, Günter
"Erwerb." Field (6) Spr 72, p. 54.

841 EICHHORN, Douglas
"Marriage Song." GreenR (2:2) 72, p. 33.

842 EIDENIER, Elon G.
"No Crystal Can Divine." Epos (23:4) Sum 72, p. 8.

843 EISELEY, Loren
"The Cardinals." LadHJ (89:1) N 72, p. 26.

844 EISENSTEIN, Sam
"Ad." JnlOPC (6:3) Spr 72, p. 620.
"A Dream of Glorious Astronauts." JnlOPC (6:3) Spr 73, p. 528.
"Michael." JnlOPC (6:3) Spr 72, p. 528.

845 EISIMINGER, Skip
"For Edellyn." SouthernPR (13:1) Aut 72, p. 52.

846 EKELOF, Gunnar
"Byzantium" (tr. by David McDuff). Stand (13:4) 72, p. 31.
"Heard in a dream ..." (tr. by David McDuff). Stand (13:4) 72, p. 29.
"The Hypnagogue" (tr. by David McDuff). Stand (13:4) 72, p. 32.
"Someone said:" (tr. by David McDuff). Stand (13:4) 72, p. 30.

847 ELDER, Karl
"Items." ChiR (23:4 & 24:1) 72, p. 91.
"a printer knows a." WindO (10) Sum 72, p. 3.

848 ELLIOTT, Harley
from Animals That Stand in Dreams: "Lizards." HangL (18) Fall 72, p. 10.
from Animals That Stand in Dreams: "Skunk Heaven." HiramPoR (12) Spr-Sum 72, p. 14.
from Animals That Stand in Dreams: "The Deer." HangL (18) Fall 72, p. 11.
from Animals That Stand in Dreams: "Wolf." Northeast Sum 72, p. 4.
"The Children." MinnR (3) Aut 72, p. 98.
"The Citizen Game." HangL (16) Wint 71-72, p. 13.
"Custer Like a Painting in the Greasy Grass." ExpR (3) Fall-Wint 72-73, p. 32.
"Found Logic Poems." HangL (18) Fall 72, p. 9.
"Half Asleep Near the Three Rivers." New:ACP (18) Ap 72, p. 3.
"He Spoke in Numbers." HangL (16) Wint 71-72, p. 11.
"Landscape Workers." ExpR (3) Fall-Wint 72-73, p. 31.
"Leaving New York." HangL (17) Sum 72, p. 9.
"Night Flight." Epos (23:4) Sum 72, p. 27.
"Night Song." MinnR (3) Aut 72, p. 96.
"Numbers." ExpR (3) Fall-Wint 72-73, p. 30.
"The Occulist Justifies Being Hit By a Car." HangL (18) Fall 72, p. 8.
"Outside Abilene." MinnR (3) Aut 72, p. 97.
"A Photograph of My Grandparents on Their Wedding Day." HangL (18) Fall 72, p. 7.
"Pictures of Women." Northeast Sum 72, p. 3.
"A Poem for Those Who Die Enroute." HangL (18) Fall 72, p. 6.
"Saturday Night in Mora." Cord (1:4) 72, p. 12.
"The Science Lesson." New:ACP (18) Ap 72, p. 2.
"Subway Song." Cord (1:4) 72, p. 13.
"There Is a White Girl in the Jungle." LittleM (6:2/3) Sum-Aut 72, p. 48.
"To a Man Who Has Described the Universe." HangL (17) Sum 72, p. 10.

849 ELLIOTT, William D.
"Laboratory: Biology." SoCaR (4:2) Je 72, p. 46.

"Paul Bunyan State: Bemidji." MinnR (2) Spr 72, cover.
"St Croix." MidwQ (13:4) Sum 72, p. 436.
"The Show Begins." Wind (2:5) Sum 72, p. 28.
"View from the Third Street Cafe." MidwQ (13:4) Sum 72, p. 408.

850 ELLIS, Grover
"Muffy and Me." SouthernPR (12:2) Spr 72, p. 17.

851 ELLIS, R. J.
"America." PoetL (67:3) Aut 72, p. 246.

852 ELLIS, Randolph
from "Madam." CarolQ (24:1) Wint 72, p. 43.

853 ELLISON, Jerome
"Socrates on Horror." SouthwR (57:3) Sum 72, p. 233.

854 ELLISON, Jessie T.
"Child at Family Dinner" (American Gothic). Epos (24:1) Fall 72, p. 21.
"Clitumnis Springs." WindO (12) Wint 72-73, p. 27.

855 ELLMAN, Dennis
"May Day, 1970." SouthernR (8:2) Spr 72, p. 417.
"Party." SouthernR (8:2) Spr 72, p. 419.
"Shadow." SouthernR (8:2) Spr 72, p. 416.
"To Awaken in the Dark." SouthernR (8:2) Spr 72, p. 418.

856 ELLWOOD, Robert S., Jr.
"St. Bruno at Prayer." SewanR (80:4) Aut 72, p. 609.
"St. Francis at Prayer." SewanR (80:4) Aut 72, p. 609.

857 ELOGLU, Metin
"The Address of Turkey" (tr. by Murat Nemet-Nejat). LitR (15:4) Sum 72, p. 404.

858 ELON, Florence
"Possession." LittleM (6:2/3) Sum-Aut 72, p. 47.

859 ELSON, Virginia
"Maenad." Folio (8:1) Spr 72, p. 23.
"Sonnet for Emily Dickinson." Epos (23:3) Spr 72, p. 13.
"Stonecutter outside Notre Dame." SouthwR (57:4) Aut 72, p. 283.

860 ELUARD, Paul
"Inside the Cylinder of Tribulations" (tr. by Richard Weisman). SenR (3:1) My 72, p. 13.
"Nil" (tr. by Richard Weisman). SenR (3:1) My 72, p. 14.
"Some Words, Which Until Now, Had Remained Mysteriously Forbidding To Me" (tr. by Michael Benedikt). Kayak (30) D 72, p. 26.

"The Unequalled" (tr. by Richard Weisman). SenR (3:1) My 72, p. 15.

861 EMAN, Gabriel Jiménez
"The Fabulists" (tr. of Orlando Flores Menessini). WormR (48) 72, p. 117.
"Quebec" (tr. of Victor Valera Mora). WormR (48) 72, p. 117.
"Together, I and Me." WormR (48) 72, p. 116.

862 EMANS, Elaine V.
"The Excuse." WormR (46) 72, p. 41.
"Exhortation." PoetL (67:3) Aut 72, p. 267.
"Mouse in the Morning." PoetL (67:3) Aut 72, p. 267.
"The Plantsitters." WormR (46) 72, p. 41.
"A Snake in the Hands." PoetL (67:3) Aut 72, p. 268.

863 EMERSON, Gloria
"Slayers of the Children." Indian (5:1) Spr 72, p. 18.

864 EMMONS, Dick
"Going Concern." SatEP (244:1) Spr 72, p. 102.
"The Strange Case of the Bulky Billfold." SatEP (244:2) Sum 72, p. 103.

865 ENDERS, Pat
"Dreams of Desire As Joy." St. AR (1:4) Spr-Sum 72, p. 60.
"Reality as Joy." St. AR (2:1) Aut-Wint 72, p. 59.

866 ENGELS, John
"The Bed." Antaeus (7) Aut 72, p. 59.
"The Broken Hose." Antaeus (7) Aut 72, p. 60.
"Night Storm." Antaeus (7) Aut 72, p. 57.
"Terribilis est locusiste." Antaeus (7) Aut 72, p. 54.

867 ENGLE, Paul
"Seven Poems" (tr. of Mao Tse-Tung, w. Nieh Hua-Ling). Playb (19:4) Ap 72, p. 163.

868 ENGONOPOULOS, Nikos
"Early in the Morning" (tr. by Yannis Goumas). Mund (5:3) 72, p. 55.
"Morning Song" (tr. by Yannis Goumas). Mund (5:3) 72, p. 52.
"News of the Death of the Spanish Poet Federico García Lorca on August 19, 1936, in a Ditch at Camino de la Fuente" (tr. by Yannis Goumas). Mund (5:3) 72, p. 54.
"Sinbad the Sailor" (tr. by Yannis Goumas). Mund (5:3) 72, p. 48.

869 ENGSTROM, Richard
"People live." PoetC (7:1) 72, p. 27.

870 ENRICO, Harold
"Some Lines from Dante's Al Poco Giorno." Madrona (1:2) N 71, p. 6.
"Vertigo." Madrona (1:3) My 72, p. 14.

871 ENSLIN, Theodore
"Excuse Me." UnmOx (1:3) Sum 72, p. 16.
"Looking." Antaeus (6) Sum 72, p. 26.
"A Paper For H. McC." Isthmus (1) Spr 72, p. 82.
"The View from Old City." Meas (1) 71.
"The View from the Intervale." Meas (1) 71.
"Where the Clouds Opened." UnmOx (1:3) Sum 72, p. 15.

872 ENZENSBERGER, Hans Magnus
"To a Man in the Tramway" (tr. by Dan Latimer). MichQR (11:4) Aut 72, p. 277.

873 EOYANG, Eugene
"Tune: 'As in a Dream'" (tr. of Li Ch'ing-chao). Madem (75:6) O 72, p. 136.

874 EPP, Robert
"Autumn" (tr. of Kaoru Maruyama). HiramPoR (13) Fall-Wint 72, p. 7.
"Camping Grounds" (tr. of Yuji Kinoshita). PoetL (67:4) Wint 72, p. 351.
"Commuter" (tr. of Yuji Kinoshita). PoetL (67:4) Wint 72, p. 352.
"Dirge" (tr. of Kaoru Maruyama). PoetL (67:4) Wint 72, p. 353.
"Harbor Festival" (tr. of Yuji Kinoshita). PoetL (67:4) Wint 72, p. 353.
"Light's Path." HiramPoR (13) 72, p. 8.
"Night Journey" (tr. of Kaoru Maruyama). PoetL (67:4) Wint 72, p. 353.
"The Poetry of Kaoru Maruyama" (tr. of Kaoru Maruyama). BelPoJ (22:4) Sum 72 (Entire issue).

875 EPSTEIN, Daniel Mark
"L'Esprit." ModernO (2:2) Spr 72, p. 231.
"Lady in Her Bath." Nat (214: 17) 24 Ap 72, p. 538.
"Letter Concerning the Yellow Fever." PoetL (67:3) Aut 72, p. 270.
"Miss Ellie's 78th Spring Party." NewYorker (48:9) 22 Ap 72, p. 44.
"The Secret." Nat (214: 10) 6 Mr 72, p. 316.
"To My Grandmother" (dead at 76). Folio (8:2) Fall 72, p. 33.

876 ERIKSSON, Edward
"Lilith." PoetL (67:2) Sum 72, p. 149.
"Old World Autumn." PoetL (67:2) Sum 72, p. 150.
"Symphony on Hurricane Night." PoetL (67:2) Sum 72,

p. 151.
"Winter." PoetL (67:2) Sum 72, p. 151.

877 ESHLEMAN, Clayton
"The Bridge at the Mayan Pass." Madrona (1:1) Je 71, p. 15.
"Credo." Nat (214:10) 6 Mr 72, p. 317.

878 ESKOW, John
"Aspects of Eddie: 1972." HangL (18) Fall 72, p. 12.
"Brazil in Brooklyn." Nat (214:26) 26 Je 72, p. 826.
"Children's Songs." HangL (18) Fall 72, p. 13.
"Dreaming of the Crawl." HangL (18) Fall 72, p. 13.
"Night in Orange County." Nat (215:4) 21 Ag 72, p. 122.
"On Reading That Wealthy South Vietnamese Pay Great Sums to American Doctors for Cosmetic Surgery." Kayak (29) S 72, p. 31.

879 ESPELAND, Pam
"Sleeping in the Middle of a Field: Autumn, Minnesota." CarlMis (12:1) Fall-Wint 71-72, p. 90.

880 ESPY, Willard R.
"Suffix the Little Prefixes To Come Unto Me (Comparatively Speaking)." Harp (245: 1471) D 72, p. 68.

881 ETEVE, Huguette Huber
"The Theater of Ill Repute." MedR (2:3) Spr 72, p. 95.
"Le Theatre Malfame." MedR (2:3) Spr 72, p. 94.

882 ETHEREDGE, Cuyler
"For Ralph (1953-1971)." BallSUF (13:3) Sum 72, p. 65.

883 ETTER, Dave
"Angel." ChiTM 17 D 72, p. 16.
"At the Home for Unwed Mothers." Drag (3:1) Spr 72, p. 3.
"Elwood Hickey." ChiTM 26 Mr 72, p. 12.
"Factory Worker." Shen (23:2) Wint 72, p. 53.
"Lovers' Quarrel." NoAmR (257:2) Sum 72, p. 45.
"The One-Legged House Painter." Drag (3:1) Spr 72, p. 4.
"Two Days Out of Three Churches." Peb (6) Sum 71.
"Wilson and Wilson's Daughter." Peb (6) Sum 71.

884 EVANS, David Allan
"The Cattle Ghosts." PoetryNW (13:3) Aut 72, p. 25.
"The Citizens' Complaint." NYT 13 Jl 72, p. 34.
"Deer on Cars." PoetryNW (13:3) Aut 72, p. 24.
"Ford Pickup." PraS (46:4) Wint 72-73, p. 318.
"Fifteen Years Later." Esq (78:1) Jl 72, p. 44.
"Old Man Driving in a Blizzard." PraS (46:4) Wint 72-73, p. 318.
"Some Lines After the Razing of the Sioux City Armour's Plant." NYT 10 S 72, sec. 4, p. 16.

885 EVANS, James
"In Memoriam." WormR (48) 72, p. 123.
"Living Around Other People." WindO (11) Aut 72, p. 40.
"Sexy Trickster." WormR (48) 72, p. 123.
"Touching you, Baby." WindO (11) Aut 72, p. 40.
"under a mat of juniper." WormR (48) 72, p. 122.
"a very humorous man." WormR (48) 72, p. 122.

886 EVANS, John C.
"Hail Storm." ChiTM 12 N 72, p. 28.
"The Home Place." FourQt (21:3) Mr 73, p. 31.

887 EVANS, William R.
"The Tree Cutter." SouthernPR (12:2) Spr 72, p. 16.

888 EVERHARD, Jim
"The Way She Moves." Epos (23:3) Spr 72, p. 24.

889 EVERHARDT, Jim
"The Silence of Angels" (for Evelyn Thorne). Folio (8:1) Spr 72, p. 7.

890 EVERWINE, Peter
"The Coat." NewYorker (48:31) 23 S 72, p. 42.
"Drinking Cold Water." NewYorker (48:38) 11 N 72, p. 42.

891 EVIN, Ahmet O.
"Un Ballade contre les amours" (tr. of Salâh Birsel). LitR (15:4) Sum 72, p. 427.
"Shortcoming" (tr. of Cahit Irgat). LitR (15:4) Sum 72, p. 426.

892 EWING, Annemarie
"Absent Thee From Utility Awhile." Folio (8:2) Fall 72, p. 23.
"Advice to the Old, Whatever Their Age." Folio (8:2) Fall 72, p. 23.
"Air for French Horn and Fife." Folio (8:2) Fall 72, p. 31.

893 EZEKIEL, Nissim
"Very Indian Poem in Indian English (for Glorya Hale)." Meas (3) 72, p. 26.

894 FABER, RobertOh
"Security." NewYQ (11) Sum 72, p. 60.

895 FAGIN, Larry
"Poems (1970)." ParisR (53) Wint 72, p. 167.

896 FAGLES, Robert
"The German and the Jew." Pan (9) 72, p. 58.
"Nietzsche." Pan (9) 72, p. 57.

"Orestes" (for George Seferis). YaleR (62:1) Aut 72, p. 79.
"Writing It Out." Pan (9) 72, p. 56.

897 FAHY, Christopher
"My Three-Year-Old Is Ill." Qt (5:39/40) Sum-Aut 72, p. 31.

898 FAIN, Gordon L.
"Manitoba." SouthernR (8:1) Wint 72, p. 174.

899 FANDEL, John
"Come Holy Ghost." Comm (95:19) 11 F 72, p. 446.
"Doubling." Thought (47:186) Aut 72, p. 447.
"Refrain." Thought (47:186) Aut 72, p. 448.
"The Tree Hive." Thought (47:186) Aut 72, p. 447.

900 FANNING, Patrick
"Jack O'lantern and Butch His Bride." WestR (9:2) Wint 72, p. 33.
"Treasure." WestR (9:1) Spr 72, p. 55.

901 FARAGO, Alan
"A Bad Dog." Epoch (21:3) Spr 72, p. 273.

902 FARBER, Norma
"Death and Life of the 109." PoetryNW (13:1) Spr 72, p. 31.
"Hey Diddle Abraham." ChrC (89:3) 19 Ja 72, p. 57.
"The Latest Survival Equipment." SatireN (9:2) Spr 72, p. 153.
"Looking at the Coelacanth." SatireN (9:2) Spr 72, p. 151.
"On the Way to Praise." Wind (2:6) Aut 72, p. 11.
"Out of This Stony Rubbish." AriD (1:2) Wint 72, p. 25.
"Since There's No Help ..." SatireN (9:2) Spr 72, p. 152.
"Theory of Flight." PoetryNW (13:1) Spr 72, p. 31.
"A Third Party." Wind (2:6) Aut 72, p. 11.
"Usual News." ChrC (89:1) 5 Ja 72, p. 6.

903 FARINELLA, Salvatore
"Bare." WindO (11) Aut 72, p. 29.
"Full Moon Depression." AriD (1:2) Wint 72, p. 42.
Hunger. RoadAR (4:3) Aut 72. (Entire issue).
"Paper." ExpR (3) Fall-Wint 72/73, p. 39.

904 FARLEY, Grant
"Defining Government." Spec (14:1/2) My 72, p. 37.

905 FARRANT, Elizabeth
"Illusions of Reflected Light." PoetL (67:1) Spr 72, p. 53.
"Ophelia." PoetL (67:1) Spr 72, p. 54.
"Where the Long Path Ends." PoetL (67:1) Spr 72, p. 53.

906 FARROKHZAD, Forūgh
"The Wind-Up Doll" (tr. by M. Aryan pur). Books (46:2) Spr 72, p. 248.

907 FARZAN, Massud
"The Sound of Water's Footsteps" (tr. of Sohrab Sepehri). Mund (5:1/2) 72, p. 13.

908 FAZIO, Damon
"perhaps we are." UTR (1:2) 72, p. 36.
"A Poem for Duane Locke." (1:1) 72, p. 15.

909 FEDERMAN, Raymond
"The Candle" (tr. of Francis Ponge). Pan (9) 72, p. 11.
"Central Park" (tr. of Jacques Temple). Pan (9) 72, p. 12.
"Justine" (tr. of Jacques Temple). Pan (9) 72, p. 12.
"The Pleasures of the Door" (tr. of Francis Ponge). Pan (9) 72, p. 11.
"Ravignan Street" (tr. of Max Jacob). Pan (9) 72, p. 10.
"Temporary Landscapes" (tr. of Yvonne Caroutch). Pan (9) 72, p. 13.
"You Take the First Street" (tr. of Robert Desnos). Pan (9) 72, p. 10.

910 FEENEY, Mary
"In a book dating from the time of Buffon" (tr. of Jean Follain, w. William Matthews). Drag (3:2) Sum 72, p. 42.
"Indian Poem." Cafe (4) Fall 72, p. 24.
"My Vacuum Cleaner Speaks of Inner Space." GreenR (2:2) 72, p. 24.
"Prose poems of Jean Follain" (tr. of Jean Follain, w. William Matthews). Iron (1) Spr 72, pp. 23-28.
"Rush Chant." GreenR (2:2) 72, p. 25.
"Silver." Cafe (4) Fall 72, p. 24.

911 FEHSENFELD, Struven
"Hagia Sophia" (tr. of Osip Mandelstam). RusLT (2) Wint 72, p. 189.
"I came upon a lake, a house constructed fresh" (tr. of Osip Mandelstam). RusLT (2) Wint 72, p. 192.
"The idol lolls alone inside the mountain's bowels" (tr. of Osip Mandelstam). RusLT (2) Wint 72, p. 191.
"Notre Dame" (tr. of Osip Mandelstam). RusLT (2) Wint 72, p. 190.

912 FEIGENBAUM, Robert
"Two Paintings by Van Gogh." CalQ (2) Sum 72, p. 27.

913 FEIGON, Lee
"An Officer's Tartar Horse" (tr. of Tu Fu). Focus (8:56) 72, p. 36.

"The Return" (tr. of Tu Fu, w. Mark Perlberg). Atl (229:4) Ap 72, p. 103.

914 FEINBERG, Harvey
"Conversation with an Angel" (tr. of Joseph Brodsky, w. H. W. Tjalsma). New:ACP (18) Ap 72, p. 22.
"I Am at the Bottom" (tr. of Innokenty Annensky, w. Raisa Scriabine). RusLT (4) Aut 72, p. 49.
"It Happened at Vallen Koski" (tr. of Innokenty Annensky, w. Raisa Scriabine). RusLT (4) Aut 72, p. 48.
"Lullaby." New:ACP (18) Ap 72, p. 34.
"Waiting at the Station" (tr. of Innokenty Annensky, w. Raisa Scriabine). RusLT (4) Aut 72, p. 47.

915 FEIRSTEIN, Frederick
"Edge." QRL (18:1/2) 72, p. 65.
"Rage." QRL (18:1/2) 72, p. 65.
"Walking Away." QRL (18:1/2) 72, p. 64.

916 FELDMAN, Alan
"Contact Sheet." Pan (9) 72, p. 38.
"Our Early Courtships." Pan (9) 72, p. 36.
"Plea." ColEng (33:5) F 72, p. 588.

917 FELDMAN, Irving
"Birthday." ColumF (1:2) Spr 72, p. 39.
"From the Balcony." Nat (214:11) 13 Mr 72, p. 347.
"The Jumping Children." MichQR (11:1) Wint 72, p. 6.
"These." MichQR (11:1) Wint 72, p. 8.
"When the Lion Dies." MichQR (11:1) Wint 72, p. 8.

918 FELDMAN, Ruth
"Death of a Child." PraS (46:1) Spr 72, p. 75.
"Delos." PraS (46:1) Spr 72, p. 73.
from Dentro la Sostanza: "The Garden of Europe" (tr. of Nelo Risi, w. Brian Swann). MedR (2:4) Sum 72, p. 99.
from Mediterranea: "Mediterranean" (tr. of Umberto Saba, w. Brian Swann). MedR (2:4) Sum 72, p. 99.
"Mykonos." PraS (46:1) Spr 72, p. 74.
"Poems from Il Limone Lunare" (tr. of Danilo Dolci, w. Brian Swann). MedR (2:4) Sum 72, p. 39.
"Sirocco" (tr. of Lucio Piccolo, w. Brian Swann). MedR (2:2) Wint 72, p. 57.
"The Soul and Sleights of Hand" (tr. of Lucio Piccolo, w. Brian Swann). Antaeus (5) Spr 72, p. 25.
from Gli Strumenti Umani: "Saba" (tr. of Vittorio Sereni, w. Brian Swann). MedR (2:4) Sum 72, p. 81.
"The Sundial" (tr. of Lucio Piccolo, w. Brian Swann). Antaeus (5) Spr 72, p. 23.
"The Three Figures" (tr. of Lucio Piccolo, w. Brian Swann). Antaeus (5) Spr 72, p. 26.
"Truce." PraS (46:1) Spr 72, p. 75.

from Gli Uccelli Indomitabili: "Scherzo" (tr. of Alberto Lattuada, w. Brian Swann). MedR (2:4) Sum 72, p. 100.
"We live by pauses; don't let deep searching" (tr. of Lucio Piccolo, w. Brian Swann). MedR (2:2) Wint 72, p. 58.

919 FELLENBERG, William Y.
"Buenos Dias, New Jersey." Cord (1:4) 72, p. 20.

920 FELLOWES, Peter
"The Child Between." Shen (23:3) Spr 72, p. 39.
"Leaving the World." Hiero (7) Ap 72.
"Self-Assessment." Hiero (7) Ap 72.
"What Got Through." Shen (23:3) Spr 72, p. 38.

921 FENTON, Elizabeth
"Polar Bear." HangL (17) Sum 72, p. 13.

922 FERLINGHETTI, Lawrence
"An Elegy on the Death of Kenneth Patchen." VilV 9 Mr 72, p. 21.

923 FERRALL, Russell
"Wetback's Return." PoetL (67:3) Aut 72, p. 243.

924 FERSEN, Nicholas
"An Ironical Elegy Born in Those Most Distressing Moments When ... One Cannot Write" (tr. of Andrei Voznesensky, w. William Jay Smith). NewRep (167:19) 18 N 72, p. 31.

925 FESSENDEN, Anne
"Holocaust at U.S. Steel." MassR (13:4) Aut 72, p. 540.

926 FET, Afanasi
"Fantasy and other poems" (tr. by Eugene M. Kayden). ColQ (20:4) Spr 72, p. 563.
"Twenty-seven poems by Afanasi Fet" (tr. by Eugene M. Kayden). ColQ (21:1) Sum 72, p. 90.

927 FIDDLE, Tom
"Fiddledown." UnmOx (1:2) F 72, p. 40.
"Fiddle's Works and Days." UnmOx (1:2) F 72, p. 41.

928 FIELD, Matt
"City Poet." FourQt (21:2) Ja 72, p. 6.
"The Poet As Put-on." Folio (8:1) Spr 72, p. 40.
"Pound Wise." CEACritic (35:1) N 71, p. 42.

929 FIELDS, Julia
"Totems." SouthernPR (12: Special Issue) 72, p. 55.

930 FIFER, Kenneth
"The Fisherman (for B.)." MichQR (11:3) Sum 72, p. 176.

931 FIGGINS, Ross
"Two Haiku." WindO (9) Spr 72, p. 6.

932 FIGUEROA, José-Angel
"X Pressing Feelin." Broad (66) D 72.

933 FIKE, Francis
"Cape Hatteras." SouthernR (8:1) Wint 72, p. 157.
"Lazarus." SouthernR (8:1) Wint 72, p. 158.
"Separation." SouthernR (8:1) Wint 72, p. 158.
"Una Guitarra Mexicana." SouthernR (8:1) Wint 72, p. 160.

934 FILIATREAU, John
"Jefferson County Jail." MassR (13:4) Aut 72, p. 563.

935 FINALE, Frank
"The Grandmother." Zahir (1:4/5) 72, p. 24.
"Seascape." Poem (16) N 72, p. 14.

936 FINCKE, Gary
"Bar." Zahir (1:4/5) 72, p. 44.
"Father/Daughter." Zahir (1:4/5) 72, p. 42.

937 FINCO, John
"The Globe." WindO (10) Sum 72, p. 19.

938 FINKEL, Donald
"Riddle: What hangs in the sky." Antaeus (7) Aut 72, p. 25.

939 FINLEY, Mike
"A Continuing Interest in Roget." Kayak (30) D 72, p. 65.
"5 Ways To Make Morning Come." PraS (46:4) Wint 72-73, p. 339.

940 FINN, Seamus
"Beach Gal." Qt (5:38) Spr 72, p. 11.
"It Came In One Day." Qt (5:38) Spr 72, p. 11.
"We Are Yo Fee." ExpR (2) Wint-Spr 72, p. 33.

941 FINNELL, Marjorie
"Waiting." NewYQ (10) Spr 72, p. 74.

942 FIORINI, John E., Jr.
"Everything I Always Wanted to Know about English**But Was Afraid To Ask." EngJ (61:7) O 72, p. 999.

943 FIRER, Susan
"Lost Nights." ChiTM 8 O 72, p. 8.

944 FISHBEIN, Susan
"Amputee." LittleM (6:2/3) Sum-Aut 72, p. 85.

945 FISHER, Dale
"The Saga of a Salmon." SatEP (244:2) Sum 72.

946 FISHER, David
"The Man from Asturias." Granite (2) Wint 71-72, p. 81.
"The Retarded Class at F.A.O. Schwarz's Celebrates Christmas." Granite (2) Wint 71-72, p. 83.
"Shearon's Grill." Granite (2) Wint 71-72, p. 82.
"Two Milks." Granite (2) Wint 71-72, p. 80.

947 FISHER, Grant
"(For Josie." Isthmus (1) Spr 72, p. 18.

948 FISHER, Roy
"Occasional Poem: January 7th 1972." Stand (13:2) 72, p. 4.
"One World." Stand (13:2) 72, p. 4.

949 FISHER, William
"holiday" (for john berryman). EngJ (61:4) Ap 72, p. 554.

950 FISHMAN, Charles
"How to Thank (for Frances Silver)." NYT 11 Ag 72, p. 28.
"The Monsters." Epoch (21:2) Wint 71, p. 162.

951 FITZ GERALD, Barbara
"Odysseus." Epoch (21:2) Wint 71, p. 172.

952 FITZGERALD, Nancy
"descent." Spec (14:1/2) My 72, p. 38.

953 FIXEL, Lawrence
"The Lecture." Sky (1:2) 72, p. 19.

954 FLAHERTY, Doug
"Cerberus." NoAmR (257:3) Aut 72, p. 63.
"Child in the Womb." Northeast Sum 72, p. 29.
"Home Before Dark." NewYorker (48:6) 1 Ap 72, p. 68.

955 FLANAGAN, Robert
"On My Own Two Feet." PoetryNW (13:4) Wint 72-73, p. 44.
"Once My Father." NYT 15 Jl 72, p. 22.
"Rerun." KanQ (4:2) Spr 72, p. 59.
"Whitman's Song." PoetryNW (13:4) Wint 72-73, p. 44.

956 FLANNER, Hildegarde
"Arrived." ChiTM 21 My 72, p. 22.

957 FLAUMENHAFT, A. S.
"Suggestion." EngJ (61:7) O 72, p. 1032.

958 FLAVIN, Jack
"The Birds at Dawn." NewRena (6) My 72.

959 FLENNIKEN, Nancy
"Storms of Flying Ponies." StoneD (1:1) Spr 72, p. 37.

960 FLINT, Roland
"Heads of the Children." PoetryNW (13:3) Aut 72, p. 36.

961 FLORA, Lari Kathleen
"Leona." PoetL (67:3) Aut 72, p. 221.

962 FLUDAS, John
from Etudes: "If winter flings down snow unstintingly" (tr. of Loukas Kousoulas, w. Stuart Silverman). AriD (1:4/5) Sum-Aut 72, p. 78.
"Horses Riding Astride the People" (tr. of George Gavalas, w. Stuart Silverman). AriD (1:4/5) Sum-Aut 72, p. 43.
"On the Edge of a Bridge" (tr. of Nikos Vranas, w. Stuart Silverman). AriD (1:4/5) Sum-Aut 72, p. 116.

963 FLUME, Sheila
"Country Woman." PoetL (67:3) Aut 72, p. 222.

964 FOGLE, Richard Harter
"With Epithets of Wayward Love." CEACritic (34:3) Mr 72, p. 24.

965 FOLKINS, Carolyn
"Keeper of the Future." WindO (10) Sum 72, p. 47.

966 FOLLAIN, Jean
"Les Accidents." Mund (5:1/2) 72, p. 132.
"A common man is walking" (tr. by William Matthews and Mary Feeney). Apple (7) Aut 72, p. 9.
"A crossroads" (tr. by William Matthews and Mary Feeney). Apple (7) Aut 72, p. 7.
"L'Histoire." Mund (5:1/2) 72, p. 132.
"Houses contain so many, many objects" (tr. by William Matthews and Mary Feeney). Apple (7) Aut 72, p. 8.
"In a book dating from the time of Buffon" (tr. by William Matthews and Mary Feeney). Drag (3:2) Sum 72, p. 42.
"It happens" (tr. by William Matthews and Mary Feeney). Apple (7) Aut 72, p. 5.
"Prose poems of Jean Follain" (tr. by William Matthews and Mary Feeney). Iron (1) Spr 72, pp. 23-28.
"Store windows start to light up" (tr. by William Matthews and Mary Feeney). Apple (7) Aut 72, p. 6.

967 FONTAINE, Will
"Another Nightmare." Zahir (1:4/5) 72, p. 12.
"I Confess." Zahir (1:4/5) 72, p. 14.
"The Man with the Beard." Zahir (1:4/5) 72, p. 15.

"An Old Grave Digger." Zahir (1:4/5) 72, p. 13.
"A Poet Has To Be." Zahir (1:4/5) 72, p. 14.

968 FONTE, Anita
"John Cicero." Epoch (21:2) Wint 71, p. 169.
"Verisimilitude." Epoch (21:2) Wint 71, p. 169.

969 FORBES, Calvin
"For You." AmerS (41:3) Sum 72, p. 408.

970 FORD, Gena
"In the Japanese Garden." St. AR (1:4) Spr-Sum 72, p. 25.

971 FORD, William
"Lains's Lament." KanQ (4:1) Wint 71-72, p. 44.
"Visit to the Home." KanQ (4:3) Sum 72, p. 72.
"Yesterday." KanQ (4:3) Sum 72, p. 72.

972 FORSH, Jerry
"We'll Dance, We'll Sing, Our Own Way." Broad (61) Jl 72.

973 FORSTER, Armand
"My Father's Room." Perspec (17:1) Sum 72, p. 62.
"Wheeling Into Summer." Perspec (17:1) Sum 72, p. 32.

974 FOSS, Phillip, Jr.
"Changing Pasture." WestR (9:2) Wint 72, p. 21.
"The Pawnee Grasslands." Esq (78:6) D 72, p. 294.

975 FOSSELIUS, Marianne
"A Swedish Tribute to Huck Finn" (tr. of Dan Andersson, w. Frances Brown Price). Mark (16:2) Sum 72, p. 20.

976 FOSTER, John L.
"The Memphis Ferry." ChiR (23:3) Wint 72, p. 94.
"The Narrow Road Through the Deep West." Poetry (120:5) Ag 72, p. 277.

977 FOWLER, Gene
"Credo." Etc. (29:3) S 72, p. 318.

978 FOWLER, Mark
"Engine." CarlMis (12:2) Spr-Sum 72, p. 56.

979 FOX, Hugh
"Anniversary." NewYQ (10) Spr 72, p. 58.
"Future (Nearsight)." UTR (1:1) 72, p. 24.
"Guilt." SouthernPR (12:2) Spr 72, p. 34.
"Image." WormR (47) 72, p. 100.
from Journal on the Edge of Autumn: "I want winter now." Folio (8:2) Fall 72, p. 8.
"Revolutionary Landscape" (an excerpt). Folio (8:2) Fall

72, p. 10.
"Utopia." WormR (47) 72, p. 100.

980 FOX, Robert R.
"Everywhere Something Is Breaking." RoadAR (3:4) Wint 71-72, p. 23.

981 FOX, Siv Cedering
"Morning." Antaeus (6) Sum 72, p. 131.
"Pomegranates." NewYQ (9) Wint 72, p. 65.
"River and Light." Antaeus (6) Sum 72, p. 132.
"Zoological Gardens." Antaeus (6) Sum 72, p. 129.

982 FOX, William L.
"free enterprise." Drag (3:2) Sum 72, p. 40.

983 FRAGIACOMO, Livio
"I Have Lost Nothing" (tr. of Salvatore Quasimodo). SenR (3:1) My 72, p. 26.

984 FRAME, James A.
"Writing as a Neurological Disorder." EngJ (61:7) O 72, p. 984.

985 FRAMPTON, Richard
"Legally Separate Reasons." KanQ (4:3) Sum 72, p. 110.
"Memory Exercise." KanQ (4:1) Wint 71-72, p. 80.
"Musings." KanQ (4:3) Sum 72, p. 109.

986 FRANCIS, David
"Cokito Ergo Sum." NewYQ (10) Spr 72, p. 59.

987 FRANCIS, Robert
"Dog-Day Night." Harp (245:1469) O 72, p. 133.
"New England Mind." Harp (245:1469) O 72, p. 133.

988 FRANGOPOULOS, Th. D.
"The Embattled Christ" (tr. by Athan Anagnostopoulos). AriD (1:4/5) Sum-Aut 72, p. 40.
from The Plans for a Journey: "The poet is born mute" (tr. by Stratis Haviaras). AriD (1:4/5) Sum-Aut 72, p. 39.
"Until the Fall" (tr. by Athan Anagnostopoulos). AriD (1:4/5) Sum-Aut 72, p. 41.

989 FRANK, Rosalie
"Creator." Pan (9) 72, p. 20.
"The Garden." Pan (9) 72, p. 20.
"The Tangible Dark." Pan (9) 72, p. 21.

990 FRANKE, Christopher
"Ars Mortis." FreeL (15:1/2) 71-72, p. 6.

991 FRANKEL, Carole
"Time of the Dungeons" (tr. of Robert Desnos, w. William Kulik). Madem (76:2) D 72, p. 104.

992 FRANKLYN, A. Fredric
"Hanging Stone Connection." NewYQ (10) Spr 72, p. 39.

993 FRANKS, Steve
"Lying on the couch." WindO (9) Spr 72, p. 8.
"When it's very dark." WindO (9) Spr 72, p. 8.

994 FRANZEN, Byron
"Grandfather." SoDakR (10:3) Aut 72, p. 75.

995 FRASER, Kathleen
"Day and Night." Kayak (28) 72, p. 56.
"Now." PoetryNW (13:2) Sum 72, p. 34.
"Sunday, With Others." Kayak (28) 72, p. 58.
"Yellow--for Stephen's Palette." Kayak (28) 72, p. 58.

996 FRAZEE, Clara Mann
"Cinquain: The Artist." WindO (10) Sum 72, p. 43.
"Fraka: The Artist." WindO (10) Sum 72, p. 43.
"Seven Dirty Glasses in the Sink." WindO (11) Aut 72, p. 16.

997 FRAZIER, Steven
"Pictures at Nashport, Ohio." Peb (9) Wint 72.

998 FREED, Ray
"Six." UnmOx (1:1) N 71, p. 49.

999 FREEDMAN, William
"The Gift." Poem (16) N 72, p. 17.
"Janis." Poem (16) N 72, p. 16.
"Last Willed Testament of the Self-Murdered Man." Northeast Aut-Wint 71-72, p. 46.
"An Old Man's Hands." Poem (16) N 72, p. 18.
"Seaside Hanging." Northeast Aut-Wint 71-72, p. 47.
"To Psyche." FreeL (15:1/2) 71-72, p. 76.

1000 FREEMAN, A. D.
"Marvelous." ChiTM 31 D 72, p. 5.

1001 FREEMAN, Jean Todd
"Only Mothers Know." LadHJ (89:3) Mr 72, p. 38.

1002 FRIEBERT, Stuart
"Dogs are supposed to be walked on a leash" (tr. of Erica Pedretti). Field (7) Fall 72, p. 39.
"Family in a Yard." Apple (7) Aut 72, p. 16.
"Fool's Poem. April (for Jean and Bob)." MidwQ (13:3) Spr 72, p. 246.

"Gain" (tr. of Günter Eich). Field (6) Spr 72, p. 55.
"German Summer 1971" (tr. of Karl Krolow). Field (6) Spr 72, p. 81.
"Grammar of a Departure" (tr. of Peter Bichsel). Field (6) Spr 72, p. 35.
"Here" (tr. of Erica Pedretti). Field (7) Fall 72, p. 40.
"Higher Ground." Epoch (22:1) Fall 72, p. 70.
"How Long?" BeyB (2:2) 72, p. 40.
"In Zurich." GeoR (26:4) Wint 72, p. 509.
"Just One More." Shen (23:4) Sum 72, p. 71.
"Long Enough." Esq (78:6) D 72, p. 90.
"No, That Can't Be" (tr. of Erica Pedretti). Field (7) Fall 72, p. 38.
"Side Trip." Madrona (1:3) My 72, p. 19.
"Starting to Wait." NewL (39:2) Wint 72, p. 112.
"Then What" (tr. of Rolf-Rafael Schröer). Field (7) Fall 72, p. 75.
"Through the Fence." BeyB (2:2) 72, p. 41.
"Toward the End." Qt (5:38) Spr 72, p. 9.

1003 FRIED, Elliot
"The Man with the Electric Heart." WindO (12) Wint 72-73, p. 5.
"Motorcycle Roadrace--Riverside." WindO (12) Wint 72-73, p. 6.
"They All Want To Be Bukowski." WindO (11) Aut 72, p. 7.

1004 FRIEND, Robert
"The Wedding." ChiTM 13 Ag 72, p. 61.

1005 FRITZ, Martha
"Between You and Sleep." Poetry (119:4) Ja 72, p. 190.
"January Thaw." Poetry (119:4) Ja 72, p. 189.
"The Visitor." Poetry (119:4) Ja 72, p. 190.

1006 FROEHLICH, John F.
"The Lumber Yard." BallSUF (13:4) Aut 72, p. 61.

1007 FROHLINDE-MEYER, Gisele
"Addicted" (tr. of Heike Doutine). Zahir (1:4/5) 72, p. 16.
Eight Poems (tr. of Heike Doutine). PoetL (67:2) Sum 72, p. 155.
"Escaped" (tr. of Heike Doutine). Zahir (1:4/5) 72, p. 17.

1008 FRUMKIN, Gene
"Cloning: First Person for Anyone." Nat (214:24) 12 Je 72, p. 759.
"Hypnos Waking Knocks at the Door." Cafe (4) Fall 72, p. 23.
"The Moth." Cafe (4) Fall 72, p. 22.

"The Nature of My Sexual Problem." Meas (1) 71.
"Still Life With Pear And Old Man." Meas (1) 71.

1009 FUCHS, Paul
"Work, the Day-to-dayness of It All." HangL (16) Wint 71-72, p. 14.

1010 FUENTES, Miguel Morales
"A Tale for Cami" (tr. by Edward Oliphant). RoadAR (4:1) Spr 72, p. 55.

1011 FULLER, Chester
"Sunday in December 1970" (for Larry Owen). HangL (16) Wint 71-72, p. 22.

1012 FULLER, Jamie
"About What, Night Wind, Do You Cry?" (tr. of Fyodor Tyutchev). RusLT (3) Spr 72, p. 63.
"Autumn Evening" (tr. of Fyodor Tyutchev). RusLT (3) Spr 72, p. 63.
"The bond between your soul and mine was quite" (tr. of Marina Tsvetaeva). RusLT (2) Wint 72, p. 214.
"Day and Night" (tr. of Fyodor Tyutchev). RusLT (3) Spr 72, p. 64.
"Dream on the Sea" (tr. of Fyodor Tyutchev). RusLT (3) Spr 72, p. 61.
"The House" (tr. of Marina Tsvetaeva). RusLT (2) Wint 72, p. 215.
"I--a spotless page beneath your pen" (tr. of Marina Tsvetaeva). RusLT (2) Wint 72, p. 214.
"Just like the hour of the Moon" (tr. of Marina Tsvetaeva). RusLT (2) Wint 72, p. 216.
"A Little House in Kolomna" (tr. of Alexander Pushkin). RusLT (3) Spr 72, p. 1.
Nine Poems (tr. of Evgeny Baratynsky). RusLT (3) Spr 72, p. 46.
"Winter Evening" (tr. of Boris Pasternak). RusLT (2) Wint 72, p. 221.

1013 FULLER, R. Buckminster
"Evolutionary 1972-1975 Aboard Space Vehicle Earth." World (1:4) 15 Ag 72, p. 33.
"Humanity's Common Wealth." World (1:8) 10 O 72, p. 42.
"Go In To Go Out." World (1:2) 18 Jl 72, p. 27.
"No Race--No Class." World (1:3) 1 Ag 72, p. 42.
"Poem: To enduringly endearing Indira" (to Prime Minister Indira Ghandi). World (1:9) 24 O 72, p. 42.

1014 FULTON, Robin
"Each Particle Has the Whole Universe for Its Field of Activity" (tr. of Osten Sjöstrand). DenQuart (7:3) Aut 72, p. 19.

from In Memoriam Antonius Block. MinnR (2) Spr 72, p. 8.
"In the Beginning" (tr. of Osten Sjöstrand). DenQuart (7:3) Aut 72, p. 20.
"It Doesn't Get Written" (tr. of Andrei Voznesensky). Stand (13:2) 72, p. 49.
from A Northern Habitat: (4, 6, 7, 8). Stand (14:1) 72, p. 8.
"Thoughts Before a Papal Galley" (tr. of Osten Sjöstrand). DenQuart (7:3) Aut 72, p. 17.
from Time and Water (1952): Fifteen Poems (tr. of Steinn Steinarr, w. Hermann Palsson). MinnR (3) Aut 72, p. 63.

1015 FUQUA, Nancy
"Evensong." SouthernPR (13:1) Aut 72, p. 20.

1016 FURTADO, Raul
"Phlox." ChiTM 27 Ag 72, p. 16.

1017 GAFFORD, Charlotte
"From My Scarf Drawer." Iowa (3:4) Fall 72, p. 22.
"Poem: Brandy & Water an all right aperitif." Iowa (3:4) Fall 72, p. 22.

1018 GAGE, Ruben
"Dialogue Six." NegroHB (35:6) O 72, p. 133.

1019 GALAZ, Alicia
"Far North" (tr. by Edward Oliphant). RoadAR (4:1) Spr 72, p. 52.
"From the Rescuable Corners" (tr. by Edward Oliphant). RoadAR (4:1) Spr 72, p. 52.
"Julian" (tr. by Edward Oliphant). RoadAR (4:1) Spr 72, p. 51.

1020 GALBRAITH, Georgie Starbuck
"The Cold, Hard Facts." SatEP (244:2) Sum 72, p. 102.
"Maternal Diet." SatEP (244:1) Spr 72, p. 102.

1021 GALE, Vi
"On the Little North Fork." PoetryNW (13:1) Spr 72, p. 20.

1022 GALLAGHER, Tess
"Skies." Madrona (1:2) N 71, p. 4.

1023 GALLER, David
"Envoi for a Poem." UnmOx (1:2) F 72, p. 45.
"The Page." UnmOx (1:2) F 72, p. 45.
"A Phoenix." Nat (215:11) 16 O 72, p. 347.
"The Poem." UnmOx (1:2) F 72, p. 44.
"Questions." Poetry (120:5) Ag 72, p. 271.

1024 GALLO, Philip
"Bestiary One." Qt (5:37) Wint 72, p. 29.
"Bestiary Two." Qt (5:37) Wint 72, p. 29.

1025 GALLUP, Dick
"Watching the Xmas trees." VilV 14 D 72, p. 25.

1026 GALVIN, Brendan
"Assembling a Street." PoetryNW (13:3) Aut 72, p. 11.
"The Dream House." Epoch (21:2) Wint 71, p. 170.
"The Man With a Hole Through His Chest (Eskimo Wood-Carving)." PoetryNW (13:3) Aut 72, p. 9.
"The Snow." NowestR (12:2) Spr 72, p. 66.
"Thunder Storm, Cape Saint Vincent." ConcPo (5:1) Spr 72, p. 48.
"Towards a Native American Opera." PoetryNW (13:3) Aut 72, p. 10.

1027 GALVIN, Martin
"Earthworks Memoranda." Poem (16) N 72, p. 32.
"Highway Man." FourQt (21:3) Mr 73, p. 32.
"A Little Family Quarrel." SouthernPR (12:2) Spr 72, p. 35.
"Reasons for Cages." Poem (16) N 72, p. 31.
"Smalltown Satyr." Wind (2:5) Sum 72, p. 38.
"Weekending in America." Folio (8:2) Fall 72, p. 32.

1028 GAMZATOV, Rasul
Three Poems (tr. by Louis Zellikoff). NewWR (40:4) Aut 72, p. 151.

1029 GANGOPADHYAY, Sunil
"Cool Age." Meas (3) 72, p. 28.

1030 GARBARINI, Steve
"The Personal Touch." Epoch (22:1) Fall 72, p. 37.

1031 GARCIA LORCA, Federico
"Dance of Death" (tr. by Robert Bly). NewL (38:4) Sum 72, p. 6.
"Death" (for Isidoro de Blas) (tr. by Robert Bly). NewL (38:4) Sum 72, p. 9.
"Ghazal of the Terrifying Presence" (tr. by Robert Bly). NewL (38:4) Sum 72, p. 10.
"If My Hands Could Only Depetal" (tr. by Robert Lima). PoetL (67:3) Aut 72, p. 226.
"The Moon Appears" (tr. by Robert Lima). PoetL (67:3) Aut 72, p. 226.
"Sorpresa." NewRena (6) My 72, p. 42.

1032 GARDNER, John
"Cards." AbGR (3:1) Spr-Sum 72, p. 49.
"Chicken Story." AbGR (3:1) Spr-Sum 72, p. 50.

"Little Lads." AbGR (3:1) Spr-Sum 72, p. 48.
"Ugliness Gets." AbGR (3:1) Spr-Sum 72, p. 51.

1033 GARITANO, Rita
"In Suburbia." Drag (3:1) Spr 72, p. 28.

1034 GARLICK, Raymond
"Public Gallery." TransR (42/43) Spr-Sum 72, p. 71.

1035 GARMHAUSEN, J.
"Anarchy." Folio (8:2) Fall 72, p. 24.
"Argument on Behalf of the Thing in the Jar." Folio (8:2) Fall 72, p. 29.
"A Dark Picture." Peb (9) Wint 72.
from Drawings: "#27 study: old age." Zahir (1:4/5) 72, p. 58.
"An Eclipse in the Andes." SouthernPR (12:2) Spr 72, p. 6.
"The Fall." Iron (2) Fall 72, p. 43.
"Morphology." Epoch (21:3) Spr 72, p. 294.
from Ohio Nights: "VIII. Cutter." HiramPoR (12) Spr-Sum 72, p. 15.
from Ohio Nights: "IX. The Wake." HiramPoR (12) Spr-Sum 72, p. 16.
from Ohio Nights: "X. Following Day." HiramPoR (12) Spr-Sum 72, p. 17.
"Thanksgiving Day." Peb (9) Wint 72.

1036 GARRETT, Charlotte W.
"The End Is Here." SouthernR (8:2) Spr 72, p. 390.
"Migrations." SouthernHR (6:2) Spr 72, p. 158.
"Poem from Here." SouthernPR (12:2) Spr 72, p. 15.
"Spring Disappeared." SouthernR (8:2) Spr 72, p. 391.

1037 GARRIGUE, Jean
"Arrival at the Final Station." MichQR (11:4) Aut 72, p. 290.
"Elegy." MedR (2:3) Spr 72, p. 86.
"For Such a Bird He Had No Convenient Cage." Nat (215:9) 2 O 72, p. 283.
"The Gift of Summer." SouthernR (8:2) Spr 72, p. 378.
"Lead in the Water." Poetry (120:6) S 72, p. 341.
"Moondial." SouthernR (8:3) Sum 72, p. 594.
"On Actors Scribbling Letters Very Quickly in Crucial Scenes." NewYorker (47:46) 1 Ja 72, p. 58.
"Requiem." MichQR (11:4) Aut 72, p. 292.
"Studies for an Actress." QRL (18:1/2) 72, p. 66.
"Tide at Gloucester." NewYorker (48:28) 2 S 72, p. 24.
"The War Has Just Begun Soliloquy." YaleR (61:4) Sum 72, p. 544.
"Why the Heart Has Dreams is Why the Mind Goes Mad (after seeing The Seagull once again)." Poetry (119:5) F 72, p. 284.

1038 GARRINGER, Jeff
"Ambiguous Love Poem." WindO (10) Sum 72, p. 10.
"Family." WindO (10) Sum 72, p. 12.
"i awake to sounds in the next room." WindO (10) Sum 72, p. 11.
"The Lady of Bixler Lake." BabyJ (5) N 72, p. 12.
"Snow Storm." WindO (10) Sum 72, p. 10.
"we make love in an old house." WindO (10) Sum 72, p. 11.

1039 GARRISON, Joseph
"Adam Again." St. AR (1:4) Spr-Sum 72, p. 70.

1040 GARY, Claudia Lee
"the answer to where." HangL (18) Fall 72, p. 14.

1041 GATHMAN, Diane
"Three Digressions." WindO (9) Spr 72, p. 18.

1042 GAUSE, Melanie
"The Wait Is Over." SoCaR (5:1) D 72, p. 4.

1043 GAVALAS, George
"Horses Riding Astride the People" (tr. by John Fludas and Stuart Silverman). AriD (1:4/5) Sum-Aut 72, p. 43.

1044 GAVENDA, Walt
"Eco Right." SatEP (244:1) Spr 72, p. 103.

1045 GAWDIAK, Natalie
"Teaching Freshman English in the Spring." EngJ (61:4) Ap 72, p. 590.

1046 GAY, Reginald
"Haunting distant boat whistle." Magazine (5) part 8, 72, p. 20.

1047 GEETING, Corinne
"Dumb Memory Drum." SatEP (244:3) Aut 72, p. 88.

1048 GEHA, Joseph
"Shakespeare Exam." NewYQ (12) Aut 72, p. 65.

1049 GEHMAN, Helen M.
"The Drifter." PoetL (67:4) Wint 72, p. 355.

1050 GELLER, Stephen
"Scenes from the Slaughterhouse." Granite (2) Wint 71-72, p. 68.

1051 GENEREUX, George
"Fantasia" (tr. of Nikolai Ogarev). RusLT (3) Spr 72,

p. 67.
"Her doorway! Firmly did I pull the bell" (tr. of Nikolai Ogarev). RusLT (3) Spr 72, p. 66.

1052 GEORGAKAS, Dan
"At the Barracks" (tr. of Yannis Ritsos, w. Eleni Paidoussi). ChiTM 6 Ag 72, p. 7.

1053 GEORGE, Emery E.
"I Can Understand." LitR (16:1) Aut 72, p. 35.
"Italian Sonnets" (tr. of Vyacheslav Ivanov). RusLT (4) Aut 72, p. 39.
"Winter Sonnets" (tr. of Vyacheslav Ivanov). RusLT (4) Aut 72, p. 31.

1054 GERAUD, Saint
"Poem: A strange occurance happened in Cthulhu City, Michigan today. For." UnmOx (1:4) Aut 72.
"Winter in Amherst Mass." UnmOx (1:4) Aut 72.

1055 GERBER, Dan
"Death and the Pineapple." NewL (38:4) Sum 72, p. 27.
"The Last of a Species." Peb (6) Sum 71.
"Self-Portrait." PartR (39:3) Sum 72, p. 378.
"Sources." OhioR (14:1) Aut 72, p. 86.

1056 GERBER, Lewis
"The Blind Are Foxes with Darkened Eyes." PoetL (67:2) Sum 72, p. 144.
"Ecstatic." PoetL (67:2) Sum 72, p. 130.
"Old Man." MichQR (11:2) Spr 72, p. 118.
"Summer Images." PoetL (67:2) Sum 72, p. 148.
"Watching." SoDakR (10:4) Wint 72-73, p. 87.

1057 GERNES, Sonia
"The Bats." PoetryNW (13:1) Spr 72, p. 15.
"California: The Season of Advent." Madrona (1:3) My 72, p. 11.
"The Commencement." SewanR (80:2) Spr 72, p. 262.
"Departure." SoDakR (10:4) Wint 72-73, p. 85.
"Exits." SoDakR (10:4) Wint 72-73, p. 85.
"The River Muse." PoetryNW (13:1) Spr 72, p. 15.
"Storm at Bird Island." Madrona (1:3) My 72, p. 13.

1058 GERRY, David
"New England Rain." Magazine (5) part 8, p. 21.
"my apple's turning brown." Magazine (5) part 8, 72, p. 22.

1059 GERSHGOREN, Sid
"All the Dead Animals." CalQ (2) Sum 72, p. 29.
"Pastoral." CalQ (2) Sum 72, p. 28.
"situations." UTR (1:2) 72, p. 21.

1060 GERSHON, Karen
"Note to Stella." NYT 6 D 72, p. 46.

1061 GERTEINY, Elizabeth
"Medieval Love Songs" (tr.). PoetL (67:4) Wint 72, p. 359.

1062 GESNER, Carol
"To John Milton." Qt (5:39/40) Sum-Aut 72, p. 38.
"Untitled: Distinguish implications to the night." Wind (2:5) Sum 72, p. 33.

1063 GETSI, Lucia
"Anif" (tr. of Georg Trakl). Mund (5:3) 72, p. 29.
"Metamorphosis of Evil" (tr. of Georg Trakl). Mund (5:3) 72, p. 25.
"Radiance" (tr. of Georg Trakl). Mund (5:3) 72, p. 31.

1064 GEYER, Alan
"Mercy for an Editor." ChrC (89:14) 5 Ap 72, p. 386.

1065 GHALIB, Mirza
"Ghazal XXXIV" (trs. by Aijaz Ahmad, Adrienne Rich, and William Stafford). Madem (74:3) Ja 72, p. 50.

1066 GHISELIN, Brewster
"Fragment" (tr. of Jorge Luis Borges). MichQR (11:4) Aut 72, p. 281.
"This Is Vietnam." Poetry (120:6) S 72, p. 320.

1067 GHOSH, Shaileswar
"For Pranati in the Street" (tr. by Dick Bakken). Meas (3) 72, p. 30.
"I Am Hungry" (tr. by Dick Bakken). Meas (3) 72, p. 31.

1068 GIACOMELLI, Eloah F.
"Nocturne" (tr. of João Cabral de Melo Neto). Mund (5:1/2) 72, p. 43.
"The Seasons" (tr. of João Cabral de Melo Neto). Mund (5:1/2) 72, p. 41.

1069 GIANNINI, David
"Because I Am Prosperous." QRL (18:1/2) 72, p. 73.
"By Balance Words Bargaining." QRL (18:1/2) 72, p. 73.
"Poem in Two." QRL (18:1/2) 72, p. 74.
"Who Love." QRL (18:1/2) 72, p. 74.

1070 GIBB, Robert
"Fiction pour le Bain." PraS (46:1) Spr 72, p. 60.
"Nightwalk." Esq (78:4) O 72, p. 92.

1071 GIBSON, Douglas
"A Biography." NYT 6 Jl 72, p. 36.

1072 GIBSON, Margaret
"Leaving." SouthernR (8:1) Wint 72, p. 177.
"Miss Sally Explains about Monument Avenue." SouthernPR (13:1) Aut 72, p. 5.
"The Nun Who Died in the Maternity Ward: Last Testament." SouthernR (8:1) Wint 72, p. 179.
"Reprise." SouthernR (8:1) Wint 72, p. 176.

1073 GIBSON, Morgan
"saws whine, hammers." Meas (2) 72.
"starlight snowing leaves." Meas (2) 72.
"Three for the First Americans and for Gary Snyder." AS (9:1) Spr-Sum 72, p. 145.

1074 GIBSON, Priscilla
"Frayings." MassR (13:1/2) Wint-Spr 72, p. 155.

1075 GIFFORD, Barry
"Coyote Tantra: 139, 140." Meas (1) 71.
"My Father." CalQ (3) Aut 72, p. 53.

1076 GIGGANS, Patricia
"vietnam is a crypt." Aphra (3:3) Sum 72, p. 33.
"What do you know of me." Aphra (3:3) Sum 72, p. 32.

1077 GIGUERE, Roland
"Human Effort" (tr. by Fred Cogswell). New:ACP (18) Ap 72, p. 31.

1078 GILBERT, Celia
"Language Is the Survival of the Race." Kayak (29) S 72, p. 54.
"Life & Death in Fat City." Kayak (29) S 72, p. 55.
"Virgo." Kayak (29) S 72, p. 56.
"Whales Sing." Kayak (29) S 72, p. 53.

1079 GILBERT, Sandra M.
"Doing Laundry." SenR (3:1) My 72, p. 38.
"Mafioso." SenR (3:1) My 72, p. 39.
"The Suits." Poetry (119:5) F 72, p. 271.

1080 GILBERT, Virginia
"Leaving, the Sepulchre City." BelPoJ (23:1) Fall 72, p. 32.

1081 GILBOA, Amir
"I Have Travelled All Day" (tr. by A. C. Jacobs). Books (46:2) Spr 72, p. 250.
"Song of Red and Blue" (tr. by Stephen Mitchell). Humanist (32:1) Ja-F 72, p. 33.

1082 GILDNER, Gary
"Around the Horn." Field (7) Fall 72, p. 51.

"The Closet." PoetryNW (13:3) Aut 72, p. 43.
"Final Exam." Nat (214:18) 1 My 72, p. 571.
"How to Buy an Old Farm in the Woods." Qt (5:39/40) Sum-Aut 72, p. 15.
"Kneeling in the Snow." SaltCR (5:1) Wint 72.
"My Neighbor." AmerR (15) 72, p. 229.
"Passion Play." Field (6) Spr 72, p. 26.
"The Physical Exam." NoAmR (257:2) Sum 72, p. 29.
"Prayer." AmerR (15) 72, p. 230.
"The Proposition to Go Rich." NoAmR (257:4) Wint 72, p. 37.
"Song of the Runaway Girl." Nat (214:16) 17 Ap 72, p. 502.
"They Have Turned the Church Where I Ate God." PoetryNW (13:3) Aut 72, p. 41.

1083 GILL, Brendan
"Wicklow." NewYorker (48:29) 9 S 72, p. 35.

1084 GILL, John
"Dick's Trumpet Solo." HangL (18) Fall 72, p. 15.
"11/8/70." Northeast Aut-Wint 71-72, p. 17.
"Long Time No." Northeast Aut-Wint 71-72, p. 16.

1085 GILLEY, Leonard
"Breaking." LitR (16:1) Aut 72, p. 83.
"College President." AAUP (58:1) Mr 72, p. 30.
"The Detective in the Department Store." Zahir (1:4/5) 72, p. 33.
"Fox." NYT 8 N 72, p. 46.
"Nine Bells." AAUP (58:1) Mr 72, p. 30.
"A Ram of a Lad." AAUP (58:1) Mr 72, p. 30.

1086 GILLON, Adam
"I Sit at the Edge of the Street" (tr. of Nathan Zach). Books (46:2) Spr 72, p. 249.

1087 GILLPATRICK, Margaret J.
"Among the Ruins." Wind (2:6) Aut 72, p. 19.

1088 GILMORE, Haydn
"Ghostly Fire." ChrC (89:41) 15 N 72, p. 1150.

1089 GILMORE, Louis
"Toward Nirvana." Poetry (119:5) F 72, p. 265.
"Toward Parnassus." Poetry (119:5) F 72, p. 263.
"Toward Tahiti." Poetry (119:5) F 72, p. 264.
"Toward the North Pole." Poetry (119:5) F 72, p. 265.
"Toward Utopia." Poetry (119:5) F 72, p. 263.
"Toward Zion." Poetry (119:5) F 72, p. 264.

1090 GILSON, Saul
"The Consultation." NewRena (6) My 72, p. 62.

1091 GINSBERG, Allen
"Christmas Blues." UnmOx (1:4) Aut 72.
"Elegy for Neal Cassidy." ParisR (53) Wint 72, p. 76.
"An Open Window on Chicago." ParisR (54) Sum 72, p. 27.

1092 GINSBERG, Louis
"Art." St. AR (1:4) Spr-Sum 72, p. 38.
"Emily Dickinson." NewYQ (12) Aut 72, p. 55.
"Spring Morning." ChiTM 16 Ap 72, p. 21.

1093 GIORNO, John
"Guru Rinpoche." ParisR (55) Aut 72, p. 158.
"I got." UnmOx (1:4) Aut 72.
"Poem: If one/If one." UnmOx (1:3) Sum 72, p. 29.
"'We told.'" UnmOx (1:4) Aut 72.

1094 GIOSEFFI, Daniela
"Buildings." NewL (38:3) Spr 72, p. 63.
"A Desire to Fly and Lock Fingers." Nat (214:16) 17 Ap 72, p. 510.
"The House." ExpR (3) Fall-Wint 72/73, p. 27.
"The Sun Was a Trumpet Then." MinnR (2) Spr 72, p. 112.
"Warm Keys." NewYQ (10) Spr 72, p. 55.

1095 GIOVANNI, Nikki
"Poem for Flora." TransR (41) Wint-Spr 72, p. 57.
"A Poem Too Late for You." TransR (41) Wint-Spr 72, p. 55.

1096 GITIN, David
"Related to the Sea" (homage to John Martin). Isthmus (1) Spr 72, p. 9.
"Spirit Bliss!" Isthmus (1) Spr 72, p. 9.

1097 GITLIN, Todd
"Homage to Paul Goodman." NewYRB (19:3) 31 Ag 72, p. 17.
"The McGovern Campaign." VilV 26 O 72, p. 16.
"Nixon." VilV 16 N 72, p. 87.

1098 GJELSNESS, Barent
"Arrival." Kayak (28) 72, p. 46.
"Cat Dreaming." MinnR (3) Aut 72, p. 25.
"Dream of a Meeting." Kayak (28) 72, p. 45.
"Erotic Song." Kayak (28) 72, p. 46.
"5 a.m." Kayak (28) 72, p. 46.
"Inscape." MinnR (3) Aut 72, p. 25.
"Learning." MinnR (3) Aut 72, p. 25.
"Near Miller Peak." MinnR (3) Aut 72, p. 24.
"Song." MinnR (3) Aut 72, p. 24.
"Song for Stephanie." Kayak (28) 72, p. 44.

"Song of Apples." Kayak (28) 72, p. 44.
"Thanks." Kayak (28) 72, p. 45.

1099 GLASER, Elton
"Footloose Among the Impediments." Madrona (1:3) My 72, p. 3.
"Hunting Song of the Kayak-Paddler." Iowa (3:4) Fall 72, p. 12.
"Survival and Song." Madrona (1:3) My 72, p. 38.
"Tracking the Beast." LittleM (6:1) Spr 72, p. 53.
"The World Is Flush with Saviors." SoCaR (5:1) D 72, p. 2.

1100 GLASER, Joe
"Belmont County, Ohio." SouthernPR (13:1) Aut 72, p. 7.

1101 GLASS, Malcolm
"Firstborn." SouthernHR (6:2) Spr 72, p. 176.
"In the Garden." Zahir (1:4/5) 72, p. 68.
"Ladies' Luncheon." WindO (11) Aut 72, p. 15.
"On Reading John's Poems." Epos (23:3) Spr 72, p. 21.
"Sacre Coeur." KanQ (4:1) Wint 71-72, p. 78.
"Sailing (for Carlos)." KanQ (4:1) Wint 71-72, p. 79.
"The Sitting." SouthernPR (13:1) Aut 72, p. 22.
"The Sonnet." EngJ (61:2) F 72, p. 264.
"The Stripper." Poem (16) N 72, p. 45.
"Tremor." FreeL (15:1/2) 71-72, p. 5.

1102 GLASS, Terrence
"When I Have Fears That I May Cease To Be Abnormal." Epos (23:4) Sum 72, p. 12.

1103 GLATSTEIN, Jacob
"The Little Tree" (tr. by Ruth Whitman). Nat (215:13) 30 O 72, p. 411.

1104 GLAZE, Andrew
"Big Top." Folio (8:2) Fall 72, p. 7.
"A Choice." NewYQ (12) Aut 72, p. 54.
"Combat." Folio (8:2) Fall 72, p. 6.
"I Want to Have Been the Shaman." Folio (8:1) Spr 72, p. 4.
"I Want to Turn to the South: 1914" (tr. of Pablo Neruda). Atl (229:4) Ap 72, p. 46.
"Island." BosUJ (20:3) Aut 72, p. 29.
"Making Country." Folio (8:2) Fall 72, p. 4.
"Mankind Needs to Believe in Something." Folio (8:2) Fall 72, p. 5.
"Me." Folio (8:2) Fall 72, p. 5.
"Of Wars and the Rumours of Wars." Folio (8:2) Fall 72, p. 3.

1105 GLEASON, Marian
"Scholastic Setting." EngJ (61:1) Ja 72, p. 51.

1106 GLEN, Emilie
"Barefoot in the Grass." Zahir (1:4/5) 72, p. 27.
"Big Black." Antaeus (6) Sum 72, p. 139.
"Broken Cup." Folio (8:2) Fall 72, p. 31.
"Bugs." Zahir (1:4/5) 72, p. 26.
"Conducive." Zahir (1:4/5) 72, p. 28.
"Ding Pinkula." LitR (16:1) Aut 72, p. 139.
"Doorstep." BabyJ (5) N 72, p. 29.
"Evening Meal." FreeL (15:1/2) 71-72, p. 94.
"Familiar." Wind (2:5) Sum 72, p. 37.
"Furnished Room To Let." PoetL (67:1) Spr 72, p. 51.
"Girls from Fifty-Ninth Street." Zahir (1:4/5) 72, p. 28.
"High and Dry." Zahir (1:4/5) 72, p. 27.
"Inside Outside In." NewYQ (9) Wint 72, p. 74.
"Large Economy." Qt (5:39/40) Sum-Aut 72, p. 4.
"Minute Minute." Folio (8:1) Spr 72, p. 29.
"Naked Round." Nat (214:21) 22 My 72, p. 666.
"Not So Very Neighborly." FreeL (15:1/2) 71-72, p. 95.
"Run." ExpR (3) Fall-Wint 72/73, p. 9.
"Smell of Spain." PoetL (67:1) Spr 72, p. 51.
"Write to Me." Folio (8:1) Spr 72, p. 14.

1107 GLICKEN, Daniel
"The Day of Five Sunsets." Humanist (32:2) Mr-Ap 72, p. 35.

1108 GLUCK, Louise
"All Hallows." NewYorker (48:36) 28 O 72, p. 44.

1109 GOBA, Ronald J.
"Recess." EngJ (61:6) S 72, p. 830.
"The Token Pupil." ColEng (33:7) Ap 72, p. 813.

1110 GOEDICKE, Patricia
"Between the Sheets." ExpR (3) Fall-Wint 72/73, p. 13.
"Census." Perspec (17:1) Sum 72, p. 59.
"The Embrace." Perspec (17:1) Sum 72, p. 58.
"Escalator." AmerR (15) 72, p. 208.
"The Great Depression." Nat (215:20) 18 D 72, p. 632.
"The Mountains." RoadAR (3:4) Wint 71-72, p. 31.
"Sprinkle Me, Just." ExpR (3) Fall-Wint 72/73, p. 13.
"Walking On Water." Iowa (3:1) Wint 72, p. 15.

1111 GOGOL, John M.
"Don't Repeat" (tr. of Anna Akhmatova). Wind (2:5) Sum 72, p. 26.
"The Four Seasons" (tr. of Anna Akhmatova). Wind (2:5) Sum 72, p. 26.
"Leningrad" (tr. of Anna Akhmatova). Wind (2:5) Sum 72, p. 26.
"There Remain" (tr. of Anna Akhmatova). Wind (2:5) Sum 72, p. 26.

1112 GOLD, Edward
"Indefinition." Etc. (29:2) Je 72, p. 168.
"Labanotation." Etc. (29:2) Je 72, p. 214.

1113 GOLD, Larry
"To Paul Eluard." Wind (2:6) Aut 72, p. 28.

1114 GOLD, Lloyd
"After the Falls." Folio (8:2) Fall 72, p. 39.
"Amputation." Folio (8:1) Spr 72, p. 22.
"grammar school in july." ExpR (3) Fall-Wint 72-73, p. 39.

1115 GOLDBARTH, Albert
"Against the Odor." PoetryNW (13:2) Sum 72, p. 7.
"Ambush Going Home." Confr (5) Wint-Spr 72, p. 48.
"Beast Song." NewL (39:1) Aut 72, p. 102.
"Body Mechanics." Sky (1:1) 71.
"Bones." WindO (10) Sum 72, p. 41.
"The Castle Bard Sings of Seeking." BallSUF (13:3) Sum 72, p. 69.
"Claiming Ground." AntR (31:4) Wint 71-72, p. 516.
"The Concept of Voice In Fiction." Epoch (21:3) Spr 72, p. 301.
"The Concept of Voice in Fiction." Epoch (22:1) Fall 72, p. 73.
"The Cover of My Book." Shen (23:2) Wint 72, p. 22.
"Cryogenics." Salm (18) Wint 72, p. 96.
"Dialogue." DenQuart (7:1) Spr 72, p. 63.
"Dialogue: William Harvey and Joan of Arc." MinnR (3) Aut 72, p. 46.
"Excerpts from the Book of Positions" (A Wedding Poem for Wayne). Sky (1:2) 72, p. 13.
"The Expedition to the Edge of the World." MassR (13:4) Aut 72, p. 636.
"Fairy Tale." Epoch (22:1) Fall 72, p. 72.
"Field." OhioR (13:2) Wint 72, p. 85.
"The First Amendment to the Constitution of the United States." PoetryNW (13:2) Sum 72, p. 4.
"The First Law of Thermodynamics." LittleM (6:1) Spr 72, p. 56.
"For Norman Morrison." WindO (10) Sum 72, p. 40.
"For We Are Happy." Qt (5:39/40) Sum-Aut 72, p. 37.
"Horizons." HangL (16) Wint 71-72, p. 25.
"Hospital." BelPoJ (23:2) Wint 72-73, p. 34.
"How to Read a Poem." ConcPo (5:1) Spr 72, p. 70.
"How to Survive in Wilderness." LitR (16:1) Aut 72, p. 102.
"Letter Back to Oregon." NowestR (12:2) Spr 72, p. 5.
"Linda's." KanQ (4:1) Wint 71-72, p. 47.
"Lining Up." MassR (13:4) Aut 72, p. 633.
"Menu." KanQ (4:1) Wint 71-72, p. 47.
"Money Changing." LittleM (6:2/3) Sum-Aut 72, p. 94.

"Nebula Dynamics" (for Linda). Sky (1:1) 71.
"Parallel Lines." Sky (1:2) 72, p. 16.
"Poem: Linda, when I write of your name." PoetryNW (13:2) Sum 72, p. 5.
"A Poem About Death." Northeast Sum 72, p. 34.
"Return." MassR (13:4) Aut 72, p. 635.
"Return Post." Folio (8:1) Spr 72, p. 11.
"The Sense of Hearing." St. AR (2:1) Aut-Wint 72, p. 42.
"the smell that squats, a dog." WindO (10) Sum 72, p. 40.
"Song for Pure Direction." PoetryNW (13:2) Sum 72, p. 6.
"Straddling the Banks." Nat (215:7) 18 S 72, p. 221.
"Things I've Put In This Poem." PoetryNW (13:2) Sum 72, p. 3.
"A Tour of the Midwest." NoAmR (257:4) Wint 72, p. 64.
from Translations from the American Savior Predictions: "If you dream of holocaust-fire." HangL (16) Wint 71-72, p. 23.
"Unearthed." Salm (18) Wint 72, p. 97.
"Water Ways." SouthernPR (13:1) Aut 72, p. 43.
"Weighting." Epos (23:3) Spr 72, p. 7.
"Wind Against Face" (a song). Drag (3:1) Spr 72, p. 7.
"Witch Trial, Transcript." MinnR (3) Aut 72, p. 43.
"The Wonder of Clothes." Confr (5) Wint-Spr 72, p. 48.
"... The World's Greatest Illusion." Sky (1:1) 71.

1116 GOLDBERG, Ben
"Eddy Boy." HangL (18) Fall 72, p. 16.

1117 GOLDHOR, Harriet
"once you held me so hard and." Aphra (3:2) Spr 72, p. 32.
"once you said your." Aphra (3:2) Spr 72, p. 31.

1118 GOLDIN, David Bruce
"Karl Marx in California." St. AR (1:4) Spr-Sum 72, p. 54.

1119 GOLDIN, Liliana
"The Police" (tr. of Pablo Neruda, w. Joseph Bruchac). SenR (3:1) My 72, p. 22.

1120 GOLDMAN, Lloyd
"The Back of the House." NYT 14 F 72, p. 28.
"The Killer." PraS (46:2) Sum 72, p. 151.

1121 GOLDMAN, Michael
"Answering Questions." AmerR (15) 72, p. 175.

1122 GOLDSMITH, Sheilah
"Sylvia Moves Slow Like Her Coat." JnlOBP (2:16) Sum 72, p. 45.

1123 GOLDSTEIN, Janet M.
"Anti-Romantic." EngJ (61:3) Mr 72, p. 404.
"Homage to Conrad." EngJ (61:4) Ap 72, p. 487.

1124 GOLDSTEIN, Laurence
"Found Poem." NewYQ (9) Wint 72, p. 79.

1125 GOLL, Iwan
"Forest" (tr. by Reinhold Johannes Kaebitzsch). UTR (1:1) 72, p. 31.

1126 GOODENOUGH, J. B.
"Birthday." NYT 1 S 72, p. 26.
"Death and Scientist." NYT 27 Mr 72, p. 34.

1127 GOODMAN, Christina P.
"Autumn in the Hills." Wind (2:6) Aut 72, p. 22.

1128 GOODMAN, Miriam
"Frontal Assault." LittleM (6:2/3) Sum-Aut 72, p. 96.
"Take a Light." LittleM (6:2/3) Sum-Aut 72, p. 96.

1129 GOODMAN, Paul
from La Gaya Scienza: "Aging." NewYRB (19:2) 10 Ag 72, p. 32.
from La Gaya Scienza: "Sick." NewYRB (19:2) 10 Ag 72, p. 32.

1130 GOODMAN, Ryah Tumarkin
"Morning Talk: Jamaica." Granite (2) Wint 71-72, p. 84.

1131 GOODREAU, William
"Jean Baptiste Chardin." NYT 16 Ja 72, sec. 4, p. 14.
"To a Prophet" (for Flannery O'Connor). CarlMis (12:2) Spr-Sum 72, p. 116.

1132 GORDON, Ambrose, Jr.
"End of Phase." TexQ (15:3) Aut 72, p. 100.
"Hamlet." TexQ (15:3) Aut 72, p. 103.
"Over the Hedge." TexQ (15:3) Aut 72, p. 101.
"The Stance of Trees." TexQ (15:3) Aut 72, p. 104.
"Thoughts on the First Warm Day." TexQ (15:3) Aut 72, p. 102.

1133 GORDON, David
"At Anchor, Sunfall" (tr. of Ch'ang Chien). Literature (15:3) 72, p. 486.
"A Frontier Song" (tr. of Li Po). Northeast Aut-Wint 71-72, p. 55.
"Li, on His Way to Chang Chou." (tr. of Ku Chih). Literature (15:3) 72, p. 485.
"The Mounds, Early Spring Lifting" (tr. of Liu Tsung-

yüan). Literature (15:3) 72, p. 486.
"On Jo Yeh Stream" (tr. of Ts'ui Hao). Literature (15:3) 72, p. 487.
"Plum Flowers Are" (tr. of Wang Ch'i). Northeast Aut-Wint 71-72, p. 3.
"Yo Yang, An Evening" (tr. of Chang Chün). Literature (15:3) 72, p. 485.

1134 GORDON, Melvin
"A Salute to Vector Geometry." MichQR (11:3) Sum 72, p. 172.

1135 GORDON, Sarah
"Offered Here for the First Time: The Unpublished Journal of Sylvia Plath." GeoR (26:3) Fall 72, p. 378.

1136 GOREN, Judith
"Of Three or Four in a Room." Northeast Aut-Wint 71-72, p. 20.
"Soon." Northeast Aut-Wint 71-72, p. 20.

1137 GORKY, Maxim
"The March of Man" (tr. by Eugene M. Kayden). ColQ (20:4) Spr 72, p. 579.
"Songs of Heroic Madness" (tr. by Eugene M. Kayden). ColQ (21:1) Sum 72, p. 106.

1138 GORMAN, Katherine
"Encounter at the Cocktail Hour." Folio (8:2) Spr 72, p. 21.

1139 GOROSTIZA, José
"Adán." Mund (5:3) 72, p. 10.
"Del Poema Frustrado." Mund (5:3) 72, p. 6.
"Espejo No." Mund (5:3) 72, p. 12.

1140 GOTTFRIED, Herbert
"Ohio and the B&O." Shen (23:4) Sum 72, p. 72.
"Registering:" Shen (23:4) Sum 72, p. 73.

1141 GOUMAS, Yannis
"The Cleopatra, the Semiramis, and the Theodora" (tr. of Alexandros Baras). Mund (5:3) 72, p. 70.
"Early in the Morning" (tr. of Nikos Engonopoulos). Mund (5:3) 72, p. 55.
"Insomnia" (tr. of Alexandros Baras). Mund (5:3) 72, p. 72.
"Morning Song" (tr. of Nikos Engonopoulos). Mund (5:3) 72, p. 52.
"News of the Death of the Spanish Poet Federico García Lorca on August 19, 1936, in a Ditch at Camino de la Fuente" (tr. of Nikos Engonopoulos). Mund (5:3) 72, p. 54.

"Sinbad the Sailor" (tr. of Nikos Engonopoulos). Mund (5:3) 72, p. 48.

1142 GOWER, Herschel
"American Tourists: 1968." Poem (14) Mr 72, p. 46.
"Basic Sermon for a Young Divine." Poem (14) Mr 72, p. 44.
"Duo Ad Infinitum." Poem (14) Mr 72, p. 51.
"The Honors of a Patriarch." Poem (14) Mr 72, p. 52.
"The Jesters Decline a Morning Party." Poem (14) Mr 72, p. 50.
"Me and Uncle Fred was Buddies." Poem (14) Mr 72, p. 45.
"An Old Lie for Helen." Poem (14) Mr 72, p. 43.

1143 GOWER, Ronald
"The Basic Rationale." Folio (8:1) Spr 72, p. 9.
"A Game." Folio (8:1) Spr 72, p. 8.
"Tabula Negra." Folio (8:2) Fall 72, p. 40.

1144 GOWRIE, Grey
"Outside Biba's." Atl (229:5) My 72, p. 42.

1145 GRABER, John
"Pledge." PoetryNW (13:4) Wint 72-73, p. 42.

1146 GRABILL, James
"Moss." PoetryNW (13:2) Sum 72, p. 21.
"The Octave." PoetryNW (13:2) Sum 72, p. 23.
"Short Litany of Greed." PoetryNW (13:4) Wint 72-73, p. 4.
"Trees." PoetryNW (13:4) Wint 72-73, p. 5.
"Wake." PoetryNW (13:4) Wint 72-73, p. 3.
"When We Knew We Were Leaving." PoetryNW (13:2) Sum 72, p. 22.
"Winter Prayer." PoetryNW (13:4) Wint 72-73, p. 6.

1147 GRAFFLIN, Marjorie
"Exit Icarus Solus." MedR (2:2) Wint 72, p. 58.

1148 GRAIS, M.
"Galena and the Kid." AriD (1:3) Spr 72, p. 33.

1149 GRANATA, May
"Updated Overview under Review." EngJ (61:9) D 72, p. 1341.

1150 GRAVELLE, Barbara
"The Fallen Woman." Aphra (3:4) Fall 72, p. 45.

1151 GRAVES, Robert
"The Cupboard." Poetry (121:1) O 72, p. 9.
"The Dilemma." NewYorker (48:23) 29 Jl 72, p. 30.

"A Dream of Frances Speedwell." Cosmo (173:1) Jl 72, p. 38.
"Her Beauty." Playb (19:12) D 72, p. 220.
"The Noose." Playb (19:12) D 72, p. 220.
"The Prepared Statement." Atl (230:4) O 72, p. 119.
"St. Antony of Padua." Atl (230:3) S 72, p. 60.
"Three Times In Love." Esq (78:3) S 72, p. 36.
"The Title of a Poet." Esq (77:3) Mr 72, p. 24.

1152 GRAY, Paul E.
"Bathtub." WindO (9) Spr 72, p. 27.

1153 GREBANIER, Bernard
"Dark Chamber." ChiTM 11 Je 72, p. 4.

1154 GREEAZANIE, Mara
"Love of Country" (tr. by Matthew Kahan, w. Nan Braymer). NewWR (40:4) Aut 72, p. 83.

1155 GREEN, Galen
"For Concha." KanQ (4:3) Sum 72, p. 105.
"January 18, 1919 (Reidenbourg, Germany)." NewYQ (12) Aut 72, p. 72.
"Substar." Zahir (1:4/5) 72, p. 59.
"This corner of the library." RoadAR (3:4) Wint 71-72, p. 20.

1156 GREEN, Lewis W.
"The Dream of Forty-Nine Hells." AbGR Spr-Sum 72, p. 45.

1157 GREENBERG, Alvin
"Agate Hunting at Two Harbors." Epoch (21:2) Wint 71, p. 139.
"Dining Out." PoetryNW (13:4) Wint 72-73, p. 40.
"Directions." PoetryNW (13:4) Wint 72-73, p. 41.
"the house of the would-be gardener: 5." OhioR (13:2) Wint 72, p. 19.
"the house of the would-be gardener: 3." OhioR (13:2) Wint 72, p. 18.
"the inland sea." Qt (5:39/40) Sum-Aut 72, p. 41.
"The Time Machine." LittleM (6:2/3) Sum-Aut 72, p. 66.

1158 GREENBERG, Barbara L.
"I Was Looking." Shen (24:1) Aut 72, p. 59.
"Personae Displaced." PoetryNW (13:3) Aut 72, p. 31.
"Simpson." PoetryNW (13:3) Aut 72, p. 30.
"The Trial of Helena." Qt (5:39/40) Sum-Aut 72, p. 57.

1159 GREENBERG, Judith Anne
"The Day Your Uncle Louie Died." Epoch (22:1) Fall 72, p. 69.

"Melinda." Works (3:3/4) Wint 72-73, p. 130.
"Melinda and the Birds." Works (3:3/4) Wint 72-73, p. 131.
"Melinda in the Mountains." Works (3:3/4) Wint 72-73, p. 131.
"Melinda's Song." Works (3:3/4) Wint 72-73, p. 130.
"the sudden mongoose." Confr (5) Wint-Spr 72, p. 87.

1160 GREENBERG, Uri Zvi
"Poem: Man builds his corner in the universe" (tr. by Dom Moraes). Books (46:2) Spr 72, p. 250.

1161 GREENE, Michael
"A Bed of Roses." Zahir (1:4/5) 72, p. 69.

1162 GREENHOOD, David
"To Know a Mountain." SouthwR (57:4) Aut 72, p. 301.

1163 GREENIA, Steven
"Graylady." Peb (9) Wint 72.

1164 GREGOR, Arthur
"Enough." Esq (78:6) D 72, p. 172.
"History." Comm (95:21) 25 F 72, p. 493.
"I Am Sick of Remembering." St. AR (2:1) Aut-Wint 72, p. 19.
"The Look Back." NewYorker (48:11) 6 My 72, p. 86.
"Oiseau Triste." Nat (215:12) 23 O 72, p. 378.
"Ruined Tracks." Poetry (120:6) S 72, p. 338.
"Wind to Human Voice." Harp (245:1467) Ag 72, p. 113.

1165 GREINKE, L. Eric
"We Drink Another Cup in Silence." StoneD (1:1) Spr 72, p. 33.

1166 GRENELLE, Lisa
"It Was Cold in the House." ChiTM 24 S 72, p. 8.

1167 GRENIER, Mildred
"I Remember May." ChiTM 26 N 72, p. 67.

1168 GREY, Robert Waters
"Driftwood." SouthernPR (13:1) Aut 72, p. 27.
"Home from the Nursery." Folio (8:1) Spr 72, p. 18.

1169 GRIFFEE, Lillian
"Stone Striker." WestR (9:2) Wint 72, p. 56.

1170 GRIFFIN, Jonathan
"A dull day but not cold" (tr. of Fernando Pessoa). Stand (13:3) 72, p. 60.
"In the illbeing I live in" (tr. of Fernando Pessoa). Stand (13:3) 72, p. 59.

1171 GRIFFIN, Walter
"Aunt Ida and Lord Byron." Poem (16) N 72, p. 7.
"Blind." Cord (1:4) 72, p. 9.
"Con Man." Poem (16) N 72, p. 9.
"Dreams." Hiero (7) Ap 72.
"Fat Man." Poem (16) N 72, p. 10.
"Georgia Girl." Confr (5) Wint-Spr 72, p. 17.
"Ladies' Southern Poetry Association." Cim (19) Ap 72, p. 32.
"Lieutenant Manny." Harp (245:1466) Jl 72, p. 71.
"Man on a Motorcycle." Confr (5) Wint-Spr 72, p. 17.
"Man on a Motorcycle." KanQ (4:1) Wint 71-72, p. 46.
"Morning Watch." NYT 30 Ja 72, sec. 4, p. 12.
"My Father." CarolQ (24:1) Wint 72, p. 31.
"My Father." Cord (1:4) 72, p. 8.
"My Father." Harp (245:1466) Jl 72, p. 71.
"Recess: Dementia." NYT 4 Ja 72, p. 32.
"Rough Trade." Poem (16) N 72, p. 8.
"Suicide" (for Stephen Watson, Vassincourt, France, 1956). SouthernPR (12:2) Spr 72, p. 47.
"The Sunbathers." KanQ (4:1) Wint 71-72, p. 46.
"To My Cock." Magazine (5) part 8, 72, p. 23.
"Ulysses Returned." Harp (245:1466) Jl 72, p. 71.
"Ulysses Returned." Zahir (1:4/5) 72, p. 65.

1172 GRIFFITHS, Bryn
"Looking Back." TransR (42/43) Spr-Sum 72, p. 74.
"No Harvest Flower." TransR (42/43) Spr-Sum 72, p. 73.
"War of Love." TransR (41) Wint-Spr 72, p. 105.

1173 GRIGSBY, Gordon
"Looking Up at the Northern Cross During the War." SouthernPR (12:2) Spr 72, p. 43.

1174 GRIGSON, Geoffrey
"After All, White Doves." Poetry (120:6) S 72, p. 337.
"Eleven Poems." Poetry (121:3) O 72, p. 126.

1175 GRIGUOLI, Anne D.
from Dibattito Su Amore: "Skull and Belly" (tr. of Albert Mario Moriconi). MedR (2:4) Sum 72, p. 94.
from Dibattito Su Amore: "The Ballad of Guano" (tr. of Albert Mario Moriconi). MedR (2:4) Sum 72, p. 92.

1176 GRILIKHES, Alexandra
"The Audience to the Dancer." HiramPoR (12) Spr-Sum 72, p. 18.
"Lost At Sea Riding the Drive." HiramPoR (12) Spr-Sum 72, p. 19.
"On March 23, John Ashbery (Reading His Poems)." AmerS (41:3) Sum 72, p. 424.
"Simone Signoret, Talking of Langlois in Truffaut's Film,

'Henri Langlois'." Focus (8:56) 72, p. 35.
"Song, with Foghorns." HiramPoR (12) Spr-Sum 72, p. 20.

1177 GRIMES, Katherine
"Heat" (tr. of Sergio Mondragón, w. Douglas Lawder). Drag (3:2) Sum 72, p. 45.
"Inhabited Clarity" (tr. of Oscar Oliva, w. Douglas Lawder). Drag (3:2) Sum 72, p. 44.
"On the Outside You Are Sleeping and On the Inside You Dream" (tr. of Homero Aridjis, w. Douglas Lawder). Drag (3:2) Sum 72, p. 47.
"Sometimes One Touches a Body" (tr. of Homero Aridjis, w. Douglas Lawder). Drag (3:2) Sum 72, p. 48.

1178 GRIMES, Martha
"Over the River and Through the Woods..." BallSUF (13:1) Wint 72, p. 73.

1179 GRINDAL, Gracia
"Love on the 4th of July." ChrC (89:26) 12 Jl 72, p. 741.
"Second-Day Christmas." ChrC (89:46) 20 D 72, p. 1292.

1180 GROSS, Anton F.
"How to Lower Your Interest Rates." SatEP (244:1) Spr 72, p. 103.
"Way Off Broadway." SatEP (244:1) Spr 72, p. 103.

1181 GROSS, Elizabeth
"Ceremony (for Ray Amorosi who had a "hand" in it)." Meas (2) 72.
"Willow." Meas (2) 72.

1182 GROSS, Suzanne
"Art Lesson." BelPoJ (22:3) Spr 72, p. 34.
"Lycanthropy." BelPoJ (22:3) Spr 72, p. 32.

1183 GROSSMAN, Bruce D.
"Talk." Etc. (29:3) S 72, p. 316.

1184 GROSSMAN, Martin
"The Interview." Drag (3:1) Spr 72, p. 51.

1185 GRUP, T.
"Dublin Song." YaleLit (141:2) 71, p. 32.
"The Tailor to His Son." YaleLit (141:2) 71, p. 32.

1186 GUAJARDO, Arturo Raúl
"Poem: A woman smiles." Iron (1) Spr 72, p. 66.

1187 GUENTHER, John
"Féline." NewYQ (9) Wint 72, p. 57.

1188 GUERNSEY, Bruce H.
"Brendan's Songs." Iron (2) Fall 72, p. 61.
"Crazy!" Drag (3:2) Sum 72, p. 38.
"A Secret Time." Apple (7) Aut 72, p. 33.
"Spring Catch." Apple (7) Aut 72, p. 32.

1189 GUEST, Barbara
"A Map." UnmOx (1:4) Aut 72.
"Poem: I took your dog for a walk." UnmOx (1:4) Aut 72.
"Taxi Poem." UnmOx (1:4) Aut 72.

1190 GUILLEN, Nicolas
"Bars" (tr. by Justin Vitiello). PoetL (67:3) Aut 72, p. 265.
"Cane" (tr. by Justin Vitiello). GreenR (2:3) 72, p. 54.
"Madrigal" (tr. by Justin Vitiello). PoetL (67:3) Aut 72, p. 265.
"The New Woman" (tr. by Justin Vitiello). PoetL (67:3) Aut 72, p. 264.
"Two Children" (tr. by Justin Vitiello). PoetL (67:3) Aut 72, p. 264.
"West Indies, Ltd." (tr. by Justin Vitiello). GreenR (2:3) 72, p. 42.

1191 GUILLEVIC, Eugène
"Bottle" (tr. by Teo Savory). Stand (13:3) 72, p. 67.
"A Hammer" (tr. by James Bertolino). Drag (3:1) Spr 72, p. 78.
"Noises" (tr. by Teo Savory). Iron (1) Spr 72, p. 68.
"Portrait" (tr. by Teo Savory). Stand (13:3) 72, p. 66.
"Winter Tree" (tr. by Teo Savory). Iron (1) Spr 72, p. 69.

1192 GULLANS, Charles
"Metaphysics at the Hog Farm." NYT 9 Jl 72, sec. 4, p. 12.

1193 GUMEDE
"As I Am." JnlOBP (2:16) Sum 72, p. 76.
"I Come Here From Far." JnlOBP (2:16) Sum 72, p. 77.

1194 GUMILIOV, Nicolai
"Genua" (tr. by Leonard Opalov). PoetL (67:1) Spr 72, p. 29.
"Zanzibar Maidens" (tr. by Leonard Opalov). PoetL (67:1) Spr 72, p. 30.

1195 GUNN, James Masson
"Friend." Folio (8:2) Fall 72, p. 38.
"Hip-Zen." Folio (8:2) Fall 73, p. 38.

1196 GUNN, Louise
"Landscape: Vermont." PoetL (67:3) Aut 72, p. 248.

1197 GUNN, Thom
"The Plunge." Isthmus (1) Spr 72, p. 44.

1198 GUPTA, Anupa
"Evening." Meas (3) 72, p. 32.

1199 GUPTA, Rabindra Nath
"All Flesh." Meas (3) 72, p. 33.

1200 GURNEY, John
"Seven Meditations." Stand (14:1) 72, p. 61.

1201 GUSTAFSON, Jim
"Detroit." ParisR (55) Aut 72, p. 151.
"Fat Men (The Attack)." ChiR (23:3) Wint 72, p. 12.
"Fat Men (The Defense)." ChiR (23:3) Wint 72, p. 13.
"Fat Men (The Legends)." ChiR (23:3) Wint 72, p. 12.
"Fat Men (The Myth)." ChiR (23:3) Wint 72, p. 11.
"Fat Men (The Revenge)." ChiR (23:3) Wint 72, p. 14.
"Fat Men (The Ritual)." ChiR (23:3) Wint 72, p. 10.
"Fat Men (The Suicide)." ChiR (23:3) Wint 72, p. 15.
"For Jack." ParisR (55) Aut 72, p. 153.
"Hit the Man Square in the Face with a Board." HangL (18) Fall 72, p. 18.
"january revolution." HangL (16) Wint 71-72, p. 26.
"Justified Fear." Stand (13:4) 72, p. 68.
"Mississippi John Hurt." HangL (17) Sum 72, p. 14.
"The Music." HangL (18) Fall 72, p. 17.
"Rabbit Turds Drip from the Claw of Satan." HangL (18) Fall 72, p. 19.
"(Want)." NewYQ (12) Aut 72, p. 98.

1202 GUSTAFSON, Richard
"The Assignment." MidwQ (14:1) Aut 72, p. 25.
"A Retreat to Buffalo." MidwQ (14:1) Aut 72, p. 10.

1203 GUTHRIE, Ramon
"Diana: In Answer to a Fan Letter." Nat (215:18) 4 D 72, p. 564.
"The Enemy." CarlMis (12:1) Fall-Wint 71-72, p. 9.
"The Poster by the Mailbox." Poetry (120:6) S 72, p. 333.

1204 GUY, Earl
Seven Poems. SoDakR (10:3) Aut 72, p. 12.

1205 HAAG, John
"Calamity Jane: On Pain." Esq (78:1) Jl 72, p. 60.

1206 HACKER, Marilyn
"Alba: March." Stand (13:3) 72, p. 61.
"Aube Provençale." AmerR (15) 72, p. 121.
"Chanson de l'Enfant Prodigue." Poetry (120:5) Ag 72,

p. 276.
"Crépuscule Provençale." AmerR (15) 72, p. 122.
"Iceplants: Army Beach." LittleM (6:1) Spr 72, p. 40.
"Imaginary Translation" (for Tom Disch and for Bill Brodecky). Stand (13:3) 72, p. 62.
"Nimue to Merlin." AmerR (15) 72, p. 120.
"To the Reader." AmerR (15) 72, p. 120.
"Untoward Occurrence at Embassy Poetry Reading." PoetryNW (13:4) Wint 72-73, p. 26.

1207 HADAS, Pamela
"American Girl." AmerR (14) 72, p. 85.
"Hecate." PoetryNW (13:1) Spr 72, p. 13.
"Snapshots of Tokyo Harbour" (for Daisy). SouthernPR (12:2) Spr 72, p. 20.

1208 HADDAD, Joe
"Words to a King." HangL (18) Fall 72, p. 61.

1209 HADLEY, Ruth C.
"Untitled: Part of a faceless crowd." Wind (2:6) Aut 72, p. 12.

1210 HAGAN, John P.
"From Last Songs of the Winter." Wind (2:6) Aut 72, p. 24.

1211 HAGEN, David
"Losing at War." Folio (8:1) Spr 72, p. 8.

1212 HAHN, Hannelore
"Biphabet/Triphabet." NewYQ (9) Wint 72, p. 62.
"The People Said." NewYQ (11) Sum 72, p. 85.

1213 HAHN, Robert
"Concluding." LittleM (6:2/3) Sum-Aut 72, p. 102.
"Self Portrait." Iron (2) Fall 72, p. 10.
"Shoot Out." UnmOx (1:1) N 71, p. 12.
"Transformations on Skiathos after Midnight" (for Phil and Christa Pappas). SouthernPR (12:2) Spr 72, p. 39.

1214 HAIGHT, Barbara
"Two Poems." MichQR (11:3) Sum 72, p. 174.

1215 HAINES, John
"The Ghost Hunter." Antaeus (7) Aut 72, p. 76.
"The Ghost Hunter." Sky (1:1) 71.
"The Ghost Hunter." Sky (1:2) 72, p. 18.
"Leaves and Ashes." Meas (2) 72.
"Meetings." Meas (2) 72.
"The Night the Desert Came." Cafe (4) Fall 72, p. 36.
"Passage." Iron (1) Spr 72, p. 43.
"The Tree That Became a House." MichQR (11:3) Sum

72, p. 158.
"Two Sections from a Dream of New York." Sky (1:1) 71.
"The Weaver (for Blair)." MichQR (11:3) Sum 72, p. 157.
"The Whale in the Blue Washing Machine." Antaeus (7) Aut 72, p. 75.
"The Whistle Column." Antaeus (7) Aut 72, p. 77.
"World of the Hay Mice." Meas (2) 72.

1216 HAINING, James
"Barbara." ExpR (3) Fall-Wint 72-73, p. 38.
"Near Liberty, Illinois." ExpR (3) Fall-Wint 72/73, p. 38.
"Warning." SouthwR (57:3) Sum 72, p. 223.

1217 HALAKI, Theodore
"Ibiza December." Folio (8:2) Fall 72, p. 30.
"In a Circle of Sand." ExpR (3) Fall-Wint 72/73, p. 7.

1218 HALE, Oliver
"Redwood." ChiTM 25 Je 72, p. 14.
"Swallow." ChiTM 10 D 72, p. 8.

1219 HALE, Robert
"And If the Gods Be Dead?" ChrC (89:22) 31 My 72, p. 632.
"Pastoral Relations." ChrC (89:5) 2 F 72, p. 121.

1220 HALL, Carol Turner
"The Absence Flag." PoetryNW (13:4) Wint 72-73, p. 47.
"Dear Girl." Madrona (1:1) Je 71, p. 7.

1221 HALL, Donald
"Back." Iron (1) Spr 72, p. 15.

1222 HALL, Frances
"Descent in a Plane." Qt (5:39/40) Sum-Aut 72, p. 60.
"Hyde Park Corner." Etc. (29:1) Mr 72, p. 20.

1223 HALL, James Baker
"Saturday Night, College Town, South, Young Fellow, Not Much Style, Waits For Score, In Earmuffs." NewYQ (12) Aut 72, p. 67.

1224 HALL, Stephen
"Nestoriah." WormR (47) 72, p. 69.
"Uncle Williams." WormR (47) 72, p. 70.

1225 HALL, Ted
"A Box of Photographs (for my mother)." Peb (7) Aut 71.
"A Family Photograph." Peb (7) Aut 71.

1226 HALL, Wade
"The High Limb." SouthernPR (12:2) Spr 72, p. 12.

1227 HALLA, Robert C.
"Reading the River." RoadAR (3:4) Wint 71-72, p. 39.

1228 HALLIDAY, Mark
"Higher Math." PoetL (67:4) Wint 72, p. 348.
"Monday's Cello." Epos (23:3) Spr 72, p. 22.

1229 HALLMAN, Carol
"Still Life." Wind (2:5) Sum 72, p. 42.

1230 HALMAN, Talat Sait
"And Came the Tailors" (tr. of Targut Uyar). LitR (15:4) Sum 72, p. 496.
"A Butt Cast in the Sea" (tr. of Cemal Süreya). Books (46:2) Spr 72, p. 251.
from Birds of God: Thirty Quatrains (tr. of Fazil Hüsnü Daglarca). LitR (15:4) Sum 72, p. 511.
"Copper Age" (tr. of Melih Cevdet Anday). LitR (15:4) Sum 72, p. 494.
"The Critics" (tr. of Ceyhun Atuf Kansu). LitR (15:4) Sum 72, p. 450.
Four Poems (tr. of Fazil Hüsnü Daglarca). Books (46:2) Spr 72, p. 252.
"November 8, 1945" (tr. of Nazim Hikmet Ran). Books (46:2) Spr 72, p. 252.
"Rose" (tr. of Cemal Süreya). Books (46:2) Spr 72, p. 251.
"That's Blood There..." (tr. of Arif Damar). LitR (15:4) Sum 72, p. 457.
"They" (tr. of Mehmet Çinarli). LitR (15:4) Sum 72, p. 403.

1231 HALPEREN, Max
"Gettysburg." SouthernPR (12: Special Issue) 72, p. 39.

1232 HALPERN, Daniel
"Church in Midsummer." NewYQ (10) Spr 72, p. 51.
"The Ethnic Life." NewYorker (48:13) 20 My 72, p. 36.
"He Loves He Hates" (for Carolyn). Humanist (32:5) S-O 72, p. 44.
"The Hunt." Antaeus (6) Sum 72, p. 69.
"Latin Poem." Antaeus (6) Sum 72, p. 68.
"Note for Mother's Day." Madem (75:1) My 72, p. 148.
"Sale." Esq (78:5) N 72, p. 89.
"Scorpion Hunting." Esq (78:4) O 72, p. 197.
"Snapshots from the Stream." NewYQ (10) Wint 72, p. 52.
"The Spanish School." Shen (23:2) Wint 72, p. 53.

1233 HAMBURGER, Michael
"Afternoon with a Circus and Citadel" (tr. of Paul Celan). QRL (18:1/2) 72, p. 45.
"Alchemical" (tr. of Paul Celan). QRL (18:1/2) 72, p. 47.

"Aphorisms" (tr. of Novalis). QRL (18:1/2) 72, p. 167.
"Crowned Out ..." (tr. of Paul Celan). QRL (18:1/2) 72, p. 44.
"Dumb Autumn Smells" (tr. of Paul Celan). QRL (18:1/2) 72, p. 48.
"From Darkness to Darkness" (tr. of Paul Celan). Nat (215:6) 11 S 72, p. 182.
"In the Daytime" (tr. of Paul Celan). QRL (18:1/2) 72, p. 48.
"Leap-Centuries" (tr. of Paul Celan). QRL (18:1/2) 72, p. 46.
"Love." Stand (13:2) 72, p. 5.
"Plashes the Fountain" (tr. of Paul Celan). QRL (18:1/2) 72, p. 49.
"Story of the Old Wolf" (tr. of G. E. Lessing). QRL (18:1/2) 72, p. 115.
"Tenebrae" (tr. of Paul Celan). Nat (215:6) 11 S 72, p. 182.
"Tiresias" (tr. of G. E. Lessing). QRL (18:1/2) 72, p. 118.
"To My Right" (tr. of Paul Celan). Nat (215:6) 11 S 72, p. 182.
"Travelling V." Poetry (119:5) F 72, p. 287.
"Zeus and the Horse" (tr. of G. E. Lessing). QRL (18:1/2) 72, p. 114.

1234 HAMBY, James A.
"After Vows." WestR (10:1) Spr 73, p. 56.

1235 HAMILL, Sam
"The Search." Spec (14:1/2) My 72, p. 39.
"Seven Faces of Ambiguity" (for Robert Kelly). Spec (14:1/2) My 72, p. 40.

1236 HAMILTON, Alfred Starr
"Cheese-o-grams." NewL (39:1) Aut 72, p. 113.
"Looseleaf." NewL (39:1) Aut 72, p. 113.
"Oxen." NewL (39:1) Aut 72, p. 113.
"Two Moons." NewL (39:1) Aut 72, p. 114.

1237 HAMILTON, Fritz
"For Mommy Who Gave Me a Russian Hat for Christmas." HangL (16) Wint 71-72, p. 27.
"For Patsy." WindO (9) Spr 72, p. 29.
"Good Morning, New Pad." WindO (9) Spr 72, p. 30.
"Goodbye, Janis." WindO (9) Spr 72, p. 29.
"Red Brick In." FreeL (15:1/2) 71-72, p. 65.
"Summer Weekend Evening at the Shore." WindO (9) Spr 72, p. 31.

1238 HAMMER, Adam
"Presence of Steam." Kayak (29) S 72, p. 60.
"The Soft Outfield." Kayak (29) S 72, p. 58.

"Texas." Kayak (29) S 72, p. 60.

1239 HAMORI, Andras
"Ghost Story with Reminiscences of Watteau's Embarquement." Antaeus (5) Spr 72, p. 40.
"Seven Poems" (tr. of Abdallah ibn Al-mu tazz). Literature (15:3) 72, p. 495.

1240 HAMPL, Patricia
"Galena, the Future." Aphra (3:4) Fall 72, p. 56.

1241 HAMPTON, Christopher
"Dante." NYT 5 D 72, p. 46.

1242 HANCOCK, Dorothy
"Words and Laughter." JnlOBP (2:16) Sum 72, p. 35.

1243 HAND, J. C.
"Apre Moi le Deluge (for DBA, WPO & the Gang)." New:ACP (19) Aut 72, p. 43.

1244 HANDEL, Elizabeth Hurd
"Mlle. Gerta." HolCrit (9:1) Ap 72, p. 11.

1245 HANH, Nhat
"The Witness Remains." NYT 31 Mr 72, p. 29.

1246 HANNIGAN, Paul
"Dildo." Granite (2) Wint 71-72, p. 62.
"Elegy." Granite (2) Wint 71-72, back cover.
"The Lash of Reason." Granite (2) Wint 71-72, p. 61.
"The Latest Travel." Granite (2) Wint 71-72, p. 58.
"Ode to Impotence." Granite (2) Wint 71-72, p. 60.
"Talk Show." AriD (1:3) Spr 72, p. 5.
"Wallace Stevens Song." Granite (2) Wint 71-72, p. 59.
"What Are Stars." AriD (1:3) Spr 72, p. 5.

1247 HANSBERGER, Frank O., III.
"To Flora Gardening." SewanR (80:2) Spr 72, p. 265.

1248 HANSEN, Tom
"Poem About Men Named Fred" (for my uncle, dying in a hospital). WindO (11) Aut 72, p. 22.

1249 HANSON, Howard G.
"Despite the Desired Lie." ArizQ (28:4) Wint 72, p. 292.

1250 HANSON, Kenneth O.
"Easter 1969." Nat (214:7) 14 F 72, p. 221.
"Writers Conference." PoetryNW (13:2) Sum 72, p. 43.

1251 HANZLICEK, C. G.
"Evening in Los Angeles." PoetryNW (13:4) Wint 72-73,

p. 30.
"The Life I Have Left." Kayak (29) S 72, p. 48.
"Machinist." Iron (2) Fall 72, p. 11.
"Mirage." NoAmR (257:3) Aut 72, p. 18.
"Nebraska Hotel." SenR (3:1) My 72, p. 34.
"On the Death of John Berryman." SenR (3:1) My 72, p. 33.
"Out of the Oak." Kayak (29) S 72, p. 50.
"Plan for Departure." Kayak (29) S 72, p. 49.

1252 HARD, Lynn
"In the Park." PoetL (67:1) Spr 72, p. 16.

1253 HARDIE, Jack
"The Pallas Murre." ColEng (33:7) Ap 72, p. 801.

1254 HARDING, Donald E.
"that old fly buzzes." WindO (12) Wint 72-73, p. 15.
"To follow no road." WindO (9) Spr 72, p. 6.

1255 HARDING, May D.
"Familial Memory." PoetL (67:3) Aut 72, p. 260.
"View." PoetL (67:1) Spr 72, p. 10.

1256 HARKNESS, Edward
"Drowned Commercial Fishermen." Madrona (1:2) N 71, p. 18.

1257 HARLOW, Michael
"Say Simply a Kind of Perfection (for Robert Lax)." NewYQ (11) Sum 72, p. 63.

1258 HARMER, James B.
"Chiaroscuro" (tr. of Giuseppe Ungaretti). SouthernR (8:2) Spr 72, p. 435.
"I Am a Being" (tr. of Giuseppe Ungaretti). SouthernR (8:2) Spr 72, p. 437.
"Weariness" (tr. of Giuseppe Ungaretti). SouthernR (8:2) Spr 72, p. 434.

1259 HARMON, William
from Book III (William Tecumseh Sherman) of "Looms": "Lt. William & Giviak." AriD (1:3) Spr 72, p. 8.
"Going To." St. AR (1:4) Spr-Sum 72, p. 9.
"Mappa." St. AR (1:4) Spr-Sum 72, p. 9.
"The News." SouthernPR (12:2) Spr 72, p. 25.
poems from "Legion: Civic Choruses." CarolQ (24:2) Spr 72, p. 31.

1260 HARPER, Jean
"The Church Mice." ChiTM 29 O 72, p. 16.

1261 HARPER, Michael S.
"Afterword: A Film." NewL (38:3) Spr 72, p. 86.

"America Calls!" Mund (5:3) 72, p. 20.
"Continuous Visit." NewL (38:3) Spr 72, p. 85.
"Dreams: American." Mund (5:3) 72, p. 22.
"The Drive In." Works (3:3/4) Wint 72-73, p. 7.
"In the Weightroom." Works (3:3/4) Wint 72-73, p. 7.
"Kansas and America." Mund (5:3) 72, p. 23.
"Last Affair: Bessie's Blues Song." Iowa (3:3) Sum 72, p. 21.
"Lathe: Shirl's Tree." PoetryNW (13:2) Sum 72, p. 41.
"The Music of Broadswords." Mund (5:3) 72, p. 23.
"'Rescue Work': Dues." Mund (5:3) 72, p. 23.

1262 HARRIS, Barbara
"Contessa." SouthernR (8:2) Spr 72, p. 394.
"The Fortune Teller." SouthernR (8:2) Spr 72, p. 396.
"When This Ends, And It Will." SouthernR (8:2) Spr 72, p. 393.

1263 HARRIS, Barry
"Thoughts, Number 16 in a Series." Zahir (1:4/5) 72, p. 31.

1264 HARRIS, Jane Gary
Eleven Poems (tr. of Osip Mandelstam). RusLT (2) Wint 72, p. 193.

1265 HARRIS, Lanners L.
"Attica." JnlOBP (2:16) Sum 72, p. 87.

1266 HARRISON, James
"Anthem for Doomed Literature." ColEng (33:7) Ap 72, p. 812.

1267 HARRISON, Janet E.
"No Flowers Please." BallSUF (13:4) Aut 72, p. 2.

1268 HARRISON, Keith
"Anger blasts a white hole in the kitchen." CarlMis (12:2) Spr-Sum 72, p. 94.
"Approaching Minneapolis by Car." NYT 7 N 72, p. 34.
"Fable of the Language Animals." CarlMis (12:2) Spr-Sum 72, p. 91.
"Five Songs from the Dirfting House" (for Tom and Sylvia Rosin). CarlMis (12:2) Spr-Sum 72, p. 88.
"Journal." CarlMis (12:2) Spr-Sum 72, p. 93.

1269 HART, Howard
"Bettina." Isthmus (1) Spr 72, p. 51.
"Spring Song." Isthmus (1) Spr 72, p. 51.

1270 HART, Richard
"One Coyote." Folio (8:1) Spr 72, p. 6.

1271 HARTEN, Lucille B.
"Sweet Sir Walter." Rend (7:1) Spr 72, p. 70.

1272 HARTLEY, Dean Wilson
"Two Guests Come Late to the Poet's Party, But Are Made Welcome Anyway" (for Walt Whitman and Robert Frost). SouthernR (8:2) Spr 72, p. 404.
"When Wanda Landowska Died." SouthernR (8:2) Spr 72, p. 406.

1273 HARTLEY, Lodwick
"Deus Obiit." SouthernPR (12: Special Issue) 72, p. 14.
"Paris: 1928/Quatre Etudes." SouthernPR (12: Special Issue) 72, p. 13.
"Rural Economics." NoCaFo (20:2) My 72, p. 104.
"Song for Lean Years." SouthernPR (12: Special Issue) 72, p. 16.

1274 HARTMAN, Geoffrey
"Spring Offensive." Poetry (120:6) S 72, p. 330.

1275 HARTMANN, Renny
"Alone." Epos (24:1) Fall 72, p. 4.

1276 HARVEY, Gayle
"aftermath of a stroke." Qt (5:39/40) Sum-Aut 72, p. 60.
"8 Mile Run--October." Wind (2:6) Aut 72, p. 9.
"On Not Wanting to Begin Again." Qt (5:38) Spr 72, p. 10.
"Pakastani Mother and Child." Wind (2:6) Aut 72, p. 9.

1277 HARWOOD, Lee
"Blue Enamel Letter J." NewL (38:3) Spr 72, p. 13.
"The First Poem." Iowa (3:2) Spr 72, p. 26.

1278 HASEK, Debbie
"Last Night's Dream." PoetL (67:1) Spr 72, p. 41.
"Spare Time." PoetL (67:1) Spr 72, p. 40.
"Two Faced Life." PoetL (67:1) Spr 72, p. 40.

1279 HASENCLEVER, Walter
"The Campfires at the Coast" (tr. by Reinhold Johannes Kaebitzsch). UTR (1:4) 72.

1280 HASKELL, Philip
"Blind Man." Shen (24:1) Aut 72, p. 69.
"The Islands." PoetryNW (13:1) Spr 72, p. 25.

1281 HASKINS, Lola
"Untitled: And there you were." LittleM (6:2/3) Sum-Aut 72, p. 28.
"Windy Day Wash." Epos (23:4) Sum 72, p. 4.

1282 HASLEY, Louis
"Oh, Lord, Tennyson!" CEACritic (34:2) Ja 72, p. 44.

1283 HASS, Robert
"Concerning the Afterlife the Indians of Central California Had Only the Dimmest Notion." Hudson (25:2) Sum 72, p. 239.
"Politics of a Pornographer." Hudson (25:2) Sum 72, p. 242.
"The Pornographer." Hudson (25:2) Sum 72, p. 240.
"The Pornographer at the End of Winter." Hudson (25:2) Sum 72, p. 241.
"The Pornographer, Melancholy." Hudson (25:2) Sum 72, p. 241.

1284 HATCH, Richard W.
"Kay Ray Mi." SouthernPR (12: Special Issue) 72, p. 46.

1285 HATFIELD, Henry
"Du Hast Diamanten und Perlen" (tr. of Heinrich Heine). BosUJ (20:1/2) 72, p. 61.
"Der König Wiswamitra" (tr. of Heinrich Heine). BosUJ (20:1/2) 72, p. 61.
"Sie Haben Mich Gequälet" (tr. of Heinrich Heine). BosUJ (20:1/2) 72, p. 61.

1286 HATHAWAY, William
"Right Field." NewL (38:3) Spr 72, p. 45.

1287 HAUGAARD, Robert
"Comment on the World Situation." SatEP (244:1) Spr 72, p. 103.

1288 HAVARD, Pauline
"Song of the Flax." LadHJ (89:9) S 72, p. 49.

1289 HAVEN, LeRoy
"For Makeba, Daughter of Sister Queen Sodie." JnlOBP (2:16) Sum 72, p. 14.

1290 HAVIARAS, Stratis
from Apparent Death: "prologue" (tr. by Ruth Whitman). AriD (1:4/5) Sum-Aut 72, p. 46.
"The Clouds" (tr. of Ares Alexandrous). AriD (1:4/5) Sum-Aut 72, p. 17.
"Erosion" (tr. of Nikos Karachalios). AriD (1:4/5) Sum-Aut 72, p. 57.
from Glossary: (II, III) (tr. of Leonidas Zenakos, w. George Economou). AriD (1:4/5) Sum-Aut 72, p. 119.
"Greece, Spring 1967" (tr. by Ruth Whitman). AriD (1:4/5) Sum-Aut 72, p. 47.
"The Gypsy and the Man in the Black Hat" (tr. by Ruth Whitman). AriD (1:4/5) Sum-Aut 72, p. 47.
"My Testament" (tr. of Michael Katsaros). AriD (1:4/5)

Sum-Aut 72, p. 76.
"Paphos" (tr. of Nanas Valaoritis). AriD (1:4/5) Sum-Aut 72, p. 113.
from The Plans for a Journey: "The poet is born mute" (tr. of Th. D. Frangopoulos). AriD (1:4/5) Sum-Aut 72, p. 39.
"Poetry" (tr. by Ruth Whitman). AriD (1:4/5) Sum-Aut 72, p. 49.
"Reincarnation" (tr. by Ruth Whitman). AriD (1:4/5) Sum-Aut 72, p. 48.
"Return" (tr. by Ruth Whitman). AriD (1:4/5) Sum-Aut 72, p. 48.
"Return" (tr. of Ares Alexandrou). AriD (1:4/5) Sum-Aut 72, p. 16.
"Rhythmic Pacing" (tr. of Manolis Anagnostakis). AriD (1:4/5) Sum-Aut 72, p. 20.
"Small Threnody" (tr. of Nanos Valaoritis). AriD (1:4/5) Sum-Aut 72, p. 113.
from The Spikes (tr. of George Thaniel). AriD (1:4/5) Sum-Aut 72, p. 101.
"Supper For the Dead" (tr. of Takis Sinopoulos). AriD (1:4/5) Sum-Aut 72, p. 95.
"Visibility" (tr. of N. D. Karouzos). AriD (1:4/5) Sum-Aut 72, p. 73.

1291 HAWKINS, Bruce
"says the rabbit." HangL (17) Sum 72, p. 17.

1292 HAWKINS, T. Rhodes
"Even When Jesus Was Thirteen, He Was No Idiot: This Surprised Everyone." PoetC (7:1) 72, p. 8.

1293 HAWKS, Jim
"The Eye of the Rose." HangL (18) Fall 72, p. 20.

1294 HAWLEY, Richard A.
"Dialogue." NYT 7 Ja 72, p. 30.

1295 HAWTHORN, Thomas G.
"My Son Laughs." Cim (19) Ap 72, p. 53.

1296 HAY, John
"A Place to Live In." AmerS (41:1) Wint 71-72, p. 133.

1297 al-HAYDARI, Buland
"I Wish You..." (tr. by M. B. Alwan). Books (46:2) Spr 72, p. 249.

1298 HAYDEN, Robert
"Richard Hunt's 'Arachne.'" MichQR (11:1) Wint 72, p. 28.
"Smelt Fishers." MichQR (11:1) Wint 72, p. 29.

1299 HAYES, Charles
"At the Grave Yard." UTR (1:1) 72, p. 14.
"Children of Fantastica." UTR (1:2) 72, p. 16.
"Conversations with Senior Lizards." UTR (1:3) 72, p. 31.
"Mr. Electric Fan." UTR (1:4) 72, p. 16.

1300 HAYMAN, Dick
"Spring Alarm." EngJ (61:2) F 72, p. 229.

1301 HAYN, Annette
"Dollhouse." Zahir (1:4/5) 72, p. 50.
"My Birthday." Zahir (1:4/5) 72, p. 50.

1302 HAYNES, Mary
"Bucolic for Sara English." NewYorker (47:48) 15 Ja 72, p. 30.

1303 HAYS, H. R.
from Portraits in Mixed Media: "The Passion of Saint Theodore." Kayak (30) D 72, p. 48.
"The Old Woman." Iron (1) Spr 72, p. 70.
"Senior Citizen." Iron (1) Spr 72, p. 71.
"Stairway to Winter." Kayak (28) 72, p. 34.

1304 HAYWARD, Max
"How Can You Look at the Neva" (tr. of Anna Akhmatova, w. Stanley Kunitz). Antaeus (6) Sum 72, p. 115.
"I Am Not One of Those Who Left the Land" (tr. of Anna Akhmatova, w. Stanley Kunitz). Antaeus (6) Sum 72, p. 116.
"Pushkin" (tr. of Anna Akhmatova, w. Stanley Kunitz). Antaeus (6) Sum 72, p. 114.
"This Cruel World Has Deflected Me" (tr. of Anna Akhmatova, w. Stanley Kunitz). Antaeus (6) Sum 72, p. 117.

1305 HAZEL, Robert
"Under the Meadow." Esq (78:6) D 72, p. 316.

1306 HAZO, Samuel
"Hunger" (tr. of Adonis). Books (46:2) Spr 72, p. 251.

1307 HEAGY, H. Lee
"Arc-en-Ciel." MinnR (2) Spr 72, p. 83.
"Crystal Turning Point." MinnR (2) Spr 72, p. 84.
"Stationary-Retrograde" (for my daughter, Ligeia). MinnR (2) Spr 72, p. 82.
"Tree-Wolf." MinnR (2) Spr 72, p. 86.

1308 HEANEY, Seamus
"Anahorish." Stand (13:3) 72, p. 4.
"Broagh." Stand (13:3) 72, p. 5.
"Gifts of Rain." Poetry (119:5) F 72, p. 280.

"May." Poetry (119:5) F 72, p. 282.
"Toome." Stand (13:3) 72, p. 5.

1309 HEARST, James
"Cloud Over the Sun." ChiTM 1 O 72, p. 17.
"Come Back, Come Back." WindO (11) Aut 72, p. 38.
"Comfort in an Old Tune." Peb (6) Sum 71.
"Con Man." WormR (46) 72, p. 42.
"A Field You Can Not Own." WormR (46) 72, p. 42.
"Forecast." NYT 2 Ag 72, p. 36.
"Out of Season." Peb (6) Sum 71.
"Textual Matters." MidwQ (14:1) Aut 72, p. 79.
"A Winter Review." WormR (46) 72, p. 43.

1310 HEATON, C. P.
"Symmetry." SouthernPR (12: Special Issue) 72, p. 43.

1311 HEATON, David
"Accidents" (tr. of Jean Follain). Mund (5:1/2) 72, p. 133.
"History" (tr. of Jean Follain). Mund (5:1/2) 72, p. 133.

1312 HEBALD, Carol
"Child Magdalene's Reverie." AntR (31:4) Wint 71-72, p. 564.
"Note from Bellevue." MassR (13:1/2) Wint-Spr 72, p. 284.
"Song." AntR (31:4) Wint 71-72, p. 517.

1313 HECHT, Anthony
"After the Rain." NewYorker (48:29) 9 S 72, p. 111.
"Alceste in the Wilderness." Poetry (121:1) O 72, p. 10.
"A Voice At a Seance." Antaeus (7) Aut 72, p. 132.

1314 HECHT, Roger
"After Kristallnacht." QRL (18:1/2) 72, p. 79.
"Charles." QRL (18:1/2) 72, p. 75.
"An Encounter." QRL (18:1/2) 72, p. 76.

1315 HEDIN, Mary
"Flight." SouthernPR (13:1) Aut 72, p. 48.
"Now." ChiTM 16 Jl 72, p. 12.
"Odyssey: Travelling Home." SoDakR (10:3) Aut 72, p. 33.
"On Rears." Epos (23:3) Spr 72, p. 8.

1316 HEFFERNAN, Michael
"The Apparition." Poetry (119:6) Mr 72, p. 322.
"A Figure of Plain Force." Poetry (119:6) Mr 72, p. 322.
"Lost." Epoch (22:1) Fall 72, p. 33.
"Midwinter Sunday in Orion Township." Epoch (22:1) Fall 72, p. 32.

"Worm's Song." Epoch (22:1) Fall 72, p. 33.

1317 HEFFERNAN, T. C.
"Old Julia." St. AR (2:1) Aut-Wint 72, p. 15.

1318 HEFNER, Robert
"On Record." St. AR (1:4) Spr-Sum 72, p. 39.

1319 HEIDRICK, E.
"Generation Gap." ChrC (89:10) 8 Mr 72, p. 282.

1320 HEIMS, Neil
"Paul Goodman: In Memoriam" (for Sally, Susie, and Daisy). VilV 10 Ag 72, p. 17.

1321 HEINE, Heinrich
"Du Hast Diamanten und Perlen" (tr. by Henry Hatfield). BosUJ (20:1/2) 72, p. 61.
"Der König Wiswamitra" (tr. by Henry Hatfield). BosUJ (20:1/2) 72, p. 61.
"Sie Haben Mich Gequälet" (tr. by Henry Hatfield). BosUJ (20:1/2) 72, p. 61.

1322 HEISE, Hans-Jürgen
"Holidays" (tr. by Ewald Osers). Stand (13:2) 72, p. 58.
"You" (tr. by Ewald Osers). Stand (13:2) 72, p. 58.

1323 HELKENN, Sally Dee
"Teacher's Lounge." EngJ (61:2) F 72, p. 316.

1324 HEMSCHEMEYER, Judith
"My Grandmother Had Bones." SouthwR (57:3) Sum 72, p. 212.
"The Race." TransR (41) Wint-Spr 72, p. 140.

1325 HENDERSON, Archibald
"Church Dinner." Qt (5:39/40) 72, p. 40.
"The Favorite." SouthernHR (6:2) Spr 72, p. 157.
"Malaria." BabyJ (5) N 72, p. 13.
"Moon Throat." AriD (1:3) Spr 72, p. 9.
"No One Spells Out." Epos (23:3) Spr 72, p. 26.

1326 HENDERSON, David
"Black is the home." Magazine (5) part 8, 72, p. 25.
"Fast Movin Man." Works (3:3/4) Wint 72-73, p. 27.
"Harlem Anthropology (for the late Zora Neale Hurston)." SatR (55:37) S 72, p. 40.
"The Mexico City Subway Inaugural Circa 1969 (for Bertha Zapata)." SatR (55:37) S 72, p. 40.
"169 Avenue 'B'" (for Linda & Groovy). Works (3:3/4) Wint 72-73, p. 28.
"Push n Pull." Works (3:3/4) Wint 72-73, p. 26.

1327 HENKIN, Bill
"From an Epistolary Sequence." AmerR (15) 72, p. 209.

1328 HENLEY, Patricia
"Freedom Song." SouthernPR (13:1) Aut 72, p. 18.
"Observation of a Ritual." SouthernPR (13:1) Aut 72, p. 19.

1329 HENNEN, Tom
"Getting Off the Bus." NewL (39:1) Aut 72, p. 122.
"Looking at the Windmill." NewL (39:1) Aut 72, p. 114.
"Woods Night." Cafe (4) Fall 72, p. 24.

1330 HENNESSY, Mark
"Bud" (Part I 1971). Drag (3:2) Sum 72, p. 49.

1331 HENNINGER, Mary
"The Prisoner of Zenda." NewRep (166:13) 25 Mr 72, p. 24.

1332 HENRI, Raymond
"Among the Ruins of the Forum." NYT 27 Ja 72, p. 36.
"The Funeral of My Rich Uncle." ChiTM 25 Je 72, p. 14.
"How God Spent His Summer." Harp (244:1460) Ja 72, p. 87.

1333 HENRY, Gerrit
"Night and Day." Poetry (119:6) Mr 72, p. 335.

1334 HEPWORTH, Rick
"The Sun." Drag (3:1) Spr 72, p. 67.

1335 HERLIHY, Margaret
"A Reed, Though Hollow." PoetL (67:1) Spr 72, p. 47.

1336 HERMAN, Jan
"No Time in Homestead" (w. Jim Brodey). UnmOx (1:3) Sum 72, p. 38.

1337 HERMAN, Shael
"Joe Burns Suits to Order." Iron (2) Fall 72, p. 52.
"Lafe Gurley." SouthernPR (13:1) Aut 72, p. 37.

1338 HERNAN, Owen
"Donavan." MedR (2:2) Wint 72, p. 59.
"Two Lovers in a Windstorm." MedR (2:2) Wint 72, p. 59.

1339 HERNANDEZ, Bob
"I want you to be my nigger." HangL (16) Wint 71-72, p. 60.

1340 HERNTON, Calvin C.
"The Ambiguity of My Imperfection" (to Paul Tillich). GreenR (2:2) 72, p. 14.

1341 HERRICK, Huddee
"At Home." PoetL (67:1) Spr 72, p. 66.
"From Rivers I Have Known." PoetL (67:1) Spr 72, p. 65.
"Sunday Lady." PoetL (67:3) Aut 72, p. 220.
"We Are All Translated." PoetL (67:1) Spr 72, p. 65.

1342 HERRICKSON, Lois March
"Gang Slaying Anniversary." Stand (14:1) 72, p. 16.
"Home." Stand (14:1) 72, p. 16.

1343 HERSCHBERGER, Ruth
"I Went to See a Man in His Decline." ChiTM 30 Ja 72, p. 12.
"Light Snow." CalQ (2) Sum 72, p. 74.
"Stolen Kisses." CalQ (2) Sum 72, p. 75.
"Two for Delmore Schwartz." CalQ (2) Sum 72, p. 76.

1344 HERSCHEL, John
from The Great Way: Eight Poems. MinnR (3) Aut 72, p. 26.

1345 HERSCHEL, Sandi
"Current Events." BeyB (2:2) 72, p. 27.
"With You." Qt (5:38) Spr 72, p. 10.

1346 HERSHEL, Sandi
"The Grammatical Stage of Analysis." WindO (9) Spr 72, p. 16.
"Louie, Feed Me." WindO (9) Spr 72, p. 17.

1347 HERSHON, Michaeleen
"I am a tree." HangL (16) Wint 71-72, p. 28.
"The Lion in the Business Suit." HangL (16) Wint 71-72, p. 30.
"A Short Ride on a Fast Horse." HangL (16) Wint 71-72, p. 29.

1348 HERSHON, Robert
"Pulling Hats Out of Rabbits." ChiR (23:4 & 24:1) 72, p. 79.
"Remarkable." ChiR (23:3) Wint 72, p. 92.
"Salt Flats." PoetryNW (13:2) Sum 72, p. 29.
"The Stanley Brothers." NewL (38:3) Spr 72, p. 64.
"To Kick Him Down the Stairs." ChiR (23:3) Wint 72, p. 90.
"Visit to a Brooklyn Zoo, Not Actually Accompanied by the Woman Who Said 'So What?' About Tigers." ChiR (23:4 & 24:1) 72, p. 78.

1349 HERSKOVITS, Lawrence
"A Recurring Nightmare." Magazine (5) part 8, 72, p. 27.

1350 HERTZ, Alan
"Walking it Off." NewYQ (10) Spr 72, p. 71.

1351 HESSE, Herman
"Lonely Evening" (tr. by Reinhold Johannes Kaebitzsch). UTR (1:4) 72, p. 10.
Ten Lyrics (tr. by John Igo). PoetL (67:2) Sum 72, p. 125.

1352 HEUMANN, Scott
"For My Quieter Classmates..." AAUP (58:3) S 72, p. 321.

1352A HEWITT, Geof
"Star." New:ACP (19) Aut 72, p. 25.
"Trip to the Town of 12 1/2¢ Rubbers" (for Jonathan). NewL (38:4) Sum 72, p. 45.

1353 HEY, Phil
"Gunfighter." Shen (23:4) Sum 72, p. 21.

1354 HEYEN, William
"The Cat." SouthernR (8:1) Wint 72, p. 161.
"Dog Sacrifice at Lake Ronkonkoma." OhioR (14:1) Aut 72, p. 88.
"Four Songs." NewYorker (48:27) 26 Ag 72, p. 26.
"The History of Civilization." WestHR (26:2) Spr 72, p. 145.

1355 HEYNEN, James A.
"Along Lake Michigan." CarolQ (24:2) Spr 72, p. 79.
"Portrait." SouthernPR (13:1) Aut 72, p. 31.

1356 HEYNICKE, Kurt
"In the Middle of the Night" (tr. by Reinhold Johannes Kaebitzsch). UTR (1:4) 72, p. 5.

1357 HICKMAN, Michelle
"Dandelions." WindO (11) Aut 72, p. 41.
"An Excuse for Speaking." HangL (16) Wint 71-72, p. 31.
"From a Tombstone In Co. Longford, Ireland." AriD (1:2) Wint 72, p. 18.
"Reflection." AriD (1:2) Wint 72, p. 19.

1358 HICKS, John V.
"Aubade." MichQR (11:1) Wint 72, p. 39.
"The Dance is Everywhere." MichQR (11:1) Wint 72, p. 41.

1359 HIGGINSON, William J.
"Allen Ginsberg Relaxes at Teaneck, New Jersey, 26 October 1971." Madrona (1:3) My 72, p. 20.
"Two Scenes from My Favorite Movie." Madrona (1:3) My 72, p. 33.

1360 HIKMET, Nâzim
"Poems to Piraye" (tr. by Larry V. Clark). LitR (15:4) Sum 72, p. 440.

1361 HILL, Alberta
"Nommo." JnlOBP (2:16) Sum 72, p. 33.

1362 HILL, Geoffrey
"Copla" (tr. of Sebastian Arrurruz). Stand (14:1) 72, p. 4.

1363 HILL, Hyacinthe
"Orange Miranda." ChiTM 12 Mr 72, p. 12.

1364 HILL, Philip
"Elephants." BabyJ (5) N 72, p. 7.

1365 HILL, Quenton
"Prayer for Black Music." JnlOBP (2:16) Sum 72, p. 58.

1366 HILL, Roberta
"Sleeping with Foxes." PoetryNW (13:4) Wint 72-73, p. 11.
"Star Quilt." PoetryNW (13:4) Wint 72-73, p. 12.

1367 HILL, Tom
"For Paul and Nessa, the Measure." Meas (2) 72.
"The Social Contract." Meas (2) 72.

1368 HILLEBRAND, Robert
"Watch With Me." BelPoJ (22:3) Spr 72, p. 17.

1369 HILTBRUNER, Noreen
"Rainy Morning." SouthernPR (12: Special Issue) 72, p. 41.

1370 HILTON, David
"The Woman Downstairs." NewL (39:1) Aut 72, p. 81.

1371 HIND, Steven
"Adam Let Out of the Cage." KanQ (4:3) Sum 72, p. 117.
"An Ancient Ax-Head Vision." KanQ (4:3) Sum 72, p. 116.
"Bona Dea." KanQ (4:3) Sum 72, p. 117.

1372 HINDLEY, Norman
"Molokai Hunt." GeoR (26:4) Wint 72, p. 510.

1373 HINE, Daryl
"Acre." NewYorker (48:10) 29 Ap 72, p. 42.
"Choubouloute" (An Horatian Ode for Holly Stevens). AmerR (14) 72, p. 162.
"Linear A." Poetry (120:5) Ag 72, p. 287.
"Omega." UnmOx (1:1) N 71, p. 48.

1374 HINER, James
"Staying the Winter." BelPoJ (23:2) Wint 72-73, p. 1.

1375 HIRSCHMAN, Jack
"Kamea" (for Lynn in deerwood brambles). BeyB (2:2) 72, p. 19.
"The Lark." BeyB (2:2) 72, p. 24.
"9." BeyB (2:2) 72, p. 22.
"The Venice Testament." BeyB (2:2) 72, p. 52.

1376 HITZIG, Jean
"Finis." Cosmo (173:1) Jl 72, p. 169.
"Non-Feminist Plea." Cosmo (173:5) N 72, p. 94.
"The Perfect Girl." Cosmo (172:3) Mr 72, p. 118.
"Warning." Cosmo (173:6) D 72, p. 166.

1377 HOBDELL, Roger
"Frontiers of Summer" (Part two). Hudson (25:1) Spr 72, p. 78.

1378 HODGES, Frenchy J.
"I Saw an Old Winter Woman." Phy (33:2) Sum 72, p. 111.

1379 HOEFT, Robert D.
"Fences: The Chicken Wire Fence." Poem (15) Jl 72, p. 23.
"Fences: The Split Rail Fence." Poem (15) Jl 72, p. 19.
"Fences: The Two-Strand Electric Fence." Poem (15) Jl 72, p. 21.
"To My Guru." Folio (8:2) Fall 72, p. 24.
"While Walking." PoetL (67:2) Sum 72, p. 167.

1380 HOFFMAN, Avron
"Goat Lady." LittleM (6:2/3) Sum-Aut 72, p. 108.
"Obvice." LittleM (6:2/3) Sum-Aut 72, p. 109.

1381 HOFFMAN, Cindy
"Home." KanQ (4:1) Wint 71-72, p. 112.

1382 HOFFMAN, Daniel
"Door." Poetry (120:4) Jl 72, p. 199.
"Path." Poetry (120:4) Jl 72, p. 200.
"Runner." SouthernR (8:3) Sum 72, p. 602.
"Shell." Poetry (120:4) Jl 72, p. 200.
"The Translator's Party." SouthernR (8:1) Wint 72, p. 150.

"The Wanderer." Shen (24:1) Aut 72, p. 68.
"The Way." Nat (215:12) 23 O 72, p. 380.
"Window." Poetry (120:4) Jl 72, p. 198.

1383 HOFFMAN, Everett
"Mommsen's Rome." NYT 26 Je 72, p. 32.

1384 HOFFMAN, Jill
"Bagpipes." NewRep (167:17) 4 N 72, p. 25.
Eight Poems. QRL (18:1/2) 72, p. 81.
"Halloween." Antaeus (6) Sum 72, p. 141.
"Helen." Antaeus (6) Sum 72, p. 143.
"Horns." UnmOx (1:1) N 71, p. 10.
"Jack." NewRep (167:18) 11 N 72, p. 27.
"Love." UnmOx (1:1) N 71, p. 11.
"Samson." Antaeus (6) Sum 72, p. 142.

1385 HOFFMAN, Richard C.
"Per Diem." SoDakR (10:4) Wint 72-73, p. 31.
"Shallow Waters." SoDakR (10:4) Wint 72-73, p. 31.

1386 HOFFMAN, Thomas
"Heracles and Alcestis." ColEng (34:3) D 72, p. 453.
"Nursery Rhyme." ColEng (34:3) D 72, p. 451.
"Philip Evergood: American Shrimp Girl (1954)." ColEng (34:3) D 72, p. 452.

1387 HOFMO, Gunvor
"Deep in the Day" (tr. by F. H. König). NoAmR (257:1) Spr 72, p. 69.
"The Last Words" (tr. by F. H. König). NoAmR (257:1) Spr 72, p. 69.
"What Do You Know..." (tr. by F. H. König). NoAmR (257:1) Spr 72, p. 69.

1388 HOGELAND, William Henry, III.
"A Celebration." HangL (18) Fall 72, p. 62.
"we run, hand in hand." HangL (18) Fall 72, p. 62.

1389 HOGGARD, James
"&." BeyB (2:2) 72, p. 43.
"Dilations of Felinity." BeyB (2:2) 72, p. 43.

1390 HOIDA, Peter
"Homage to Guillaume Apollinaire" (tr. of Blaise Cendrars). Stand (13:2) 72, p. 56.

1391 HØJHOLT, Per
"So and So Many Larks" (tr. by Nadia Christensen and Alexander Taylor). WormR (48) 72, p. 122.

1392 HOLDEN, Jonathan
"Breaking In." NoAmR (257:2) Sum 72, p. 27.
"How to Have Fourth of July." NowestR (12:3) Aut 72,

p. 1.
"The Summer of Snakes." NoAmR (257:3) Aut 72, p. 76.
"Taking Rocky's Father to the Hospital." NoAmR (257:4) Wint 72, p. 58.

1393 HOLDERLIN, Friedrich
"Hyperion's Song of Fate" (tr. by H. M. Krohnen). Isthmus (1) Spr 72, p. 66.
"Poet's Courage" (tr. by H. M. Krohnen). Isthmus (1) Spr 72, p. 67.
"To the Fates" (tr. by H. M. Krohnen). Isthmus (1) Spr 72, p. 65.

1394 HOLKEBOER, Robert
"Burning Coal" (tr. of Marc Alyn). Books (46:3) Sum 72, p. 425.
"Daybreak" (tr. of Marc Alyn). Books (46:3) Sum 72, p. 425.

1395 HOLLAHAN, Eugene
"Christmas at Stone Mountain." Shen (23:4) Sum 72, p. 69.
"O Holy Night." GeoR (26:4) Wint 72, p. 505.
"Stone Mountain Escapes: 43. The Figures in the Granite Wall." AriD (1:3) Spr 72, p. 6.
"Stone Mountain Escapes: 37. Lover's Lane." AriD (1:3) Spr 72, p. 6.

1396 HOLLAND, Barbara A.
"Ancestral Vision." Zahir (1:4/5) 72, p. 64.
"A Ceremonial of Wine." Zahir (1:4/5) 72, p. 65.
"Cock Crow in the City." Magazine (5) part 8, 72, p. 28.
"The Daughters of the Twilight." Wind (2:5) Sum 72, p. 49.
"Here More Than Ever Else." NewRena (6) My 72, p. 13.
"The Moment of Truth." NewRena (6) My 72, p. 12.
"Not as the Crippled Tree." NewRena (6) My 72, p. 11.
"Self Sculpture." NewRena (6) My 72, p. 14.
"A Study In Post Office Art." Confr (5) Wint-Spr 72, p. 58.
"A Study in Post Office Art." HangL (17) Sum 72, p. 19.

1397 HOLLAND, Gill
"No Forwarding Address." SouthernPR (12:2) Spr 72, p. 24.

1398 HOLLAND, Joyce
"Oeoeoeoeo." WindO (11) Aut 72, p. 14.

1399 HOLLAND, William
"Waking Up." LittleM (6:2/3) Sum-Aut 72, p. 81.

1400 HOLLANDER, John
"Artesian Well." ColumF (1:2) Spr 72, p. 34.
"Little Tale." NewYorker (48:35) 21 O 72, p. 89.
"Love Is Not a Feeling." Harp (245:1469) O 72, p. 134.
"A Quick Dip in the Darkening Pond." Cim (18) Ja 72, p. 5.
"Rotation of Crops" (for Robert Penn Warren). FourQt (21:4) My 72, p. 18.

1401 HOLLANDER, Robert
"Nomen Enim Verum Dat Definitio Rerum" (for R. A. F.). Cim (18) Ja 72, p. 60.

1402 HOLLO, Anselm
"Empty Kitchen Dinosaur Blues" (for J.). NewL (38:4) Sum 72, p. 11.
"End of Influence" (tr. of Tomaz Salamun). NewL (38:4) Sum 72, p. 110.
"Foggy Night in Newport." NewL (38:4) Sum 72, p. 12.
"Let's Wait" (tr. of Tomaz Salamun). NewL (38:4) Sum 72, p. 109.
"Proverbs" (tr. of Tomaz Salamun). NewL (38:4) Sum 72, p. 108.
"what do you like most in your life" (tr. of Tomaz Salamun). NewL (38:4) Sum 72, p. 110.

1403 HOLLOWAY, Glenna
"Dream Chaser." PoetL (67:2) Sum 72, p. 147.
"Ignis Fatuus." PoetL (67:2) Sum 72, p. 147.
"Swamp Man." PoetL (67:2) Sum 72, p. 147.

1404 HOLLOWAY, John
"Lunar Moment." Stand (13:4) 72, p. 6.
"A Mirror." Hudson (25:1) Spr 72, p. 81.

1405 HOLLOWELL, Grace
"Ecology Becomes Exquisite." Mark (16:2) Sum 72, p. 21.

1406 HOLMAN, Jack C.
"A Case of Absence." TexQ (15:3) Aut 72, p. 90.
"The Days." WestR (9:2) Wint 72, p. 15.
"gentling." TexQ (15:3) Aut 72, p. 91.
"The Other Tourists." ArizQ (28:3) Wint 72, p. 354.
"Renaissance." TexQ (15:3) Aut 72, p. 92.
"sweatdream." TexQ (15:3) Aut 72, p. 91.
"What the Calliope Knows." MedR (2:2) Wint 72, p. 60.
"When I Began Painting." TexQ (15:3) Aut 72, p. 90.

1407 HOLMES, Theodore
"The Master." LitR (16:1) Aut 72, p. 20.
"My Fires." LitR (16:1) Aut 72, p. 21.

1408 HOLMSTRAND, James
"The Canary." Cord (1:3) 72, p. 7.

1409 HOLUB, Miroslav
"Praha Jana Palacha." NewYQ (12) Aut 72, p. 57.

1410 HONIG, Edwin
"Doing Time." NYT 1 Je 72, p. 42.

1411 HOOD, Peter
"Help." Zahir (1:4/5) 72, p. 24.
"Intimate Distance." Zahir (1:4/5) 72, p. 23.
"When Warm Weather Came." EngJ (61:5) My 72, p. 669.

1412 HOOPER, Patricia
"The Children." CarolQ (24:3) Fall 72, p. 88.

1413 HOPE, A. D.
"Parabola." Poetry (120:5) Ag 72, p. 280.

1414 HOPES, David
"Legend of Leaving." HiramPoR (13) Fall-Wint 72, p. 19.

1415 HORNE, Lewis B.
"Into the North." GeoR (26:3) Fall 72, p. 369.

1416 HORNSTEIN, Sally
"The Field and in it are." Spec (14:1/2) My 72, p. 47.
"The dog was curious about something across the road." Spec (14:1/2) My 72, p. 47.

1417 HORVATH, Lou
"Not Here." ParisR (55) Aut 72, p. 126.

1418 HOTHAM, Gary
"Two Haiku." WindO (11) Aut 72, p. 8.

1419 HOUSTON, Julie
"To Iron a Shirt." Epoch (22:1) Fall 72, p. 35.

1420 HOWARD, Ben
"The Departure." MidwQ (14:1) Aut 72, p. 80.

1421 HOWARD, Frances Minturn
"In Memoriam: John Berryman." ChiTM 15 O 72, p. 8.

1422 HOWARD, Richard
"Personal Values." Shen (24:1) Aut 72, p. 3.

1423 HOWARTH, William
"Affluence." KanQ (4:3) Sum 72, p. 129.

1424 HOWE, Fanny
"Mama Knows" (for S. V. S.). Antaeus (6) Sum 72, p. 18.

1425 HOWELL, Anthony
"Animal Lover." Antaeus (7) Aut 72, p. 78.

1426 HOWELL, Mark
"Hitch-hiking." Epoch (21:2) Wint 71, p. 147.

1427 HOWES, Barbara
"Focus." Antaeus (5) Spr 72, p. 105.

1428 HSIN Ch'i-Chi
"To the Tune of Ch'ing Ping Lo" (tr. by David Rafael Wang). Drag (3:1) Spr 72, p. 80.

1429 HSU Chih-mo
"Chance-Meeting" (tr. by Rosa Tsung-yu Kao and Robert Magliola). PoetL (67:4) Wint 72, p. 350.
"Star-Spark of Feeble Flame" (tr. by Rosa Tsung-yu Kao and Robert Magliola). PoetL (67:4) Wint 72, p. 350.

1430 HSUEH T'ao
"The Autumn Brook" (tr. by Kenneth Rexroth and Ling Chung). UnmOx (1:4) Aut 72.
"An Old Poem to Yuan Chen" (tr. by Kenneth Rexroth and Ling Chung). UnmOx (1:4) Aut 72.

1431 HUACO, Enrique
"Consciente de la Brevidad de la Palabra." Mund (5:1/2) 72, p. 30.
"Piel del Tiempo." Mund (5:1/2) 72, p. 24.
"El Tamaño de un Hombre." Mund (5:1/2) 72, p. 28.

1432 HUANG, Po Fei
"Anxiety." Hudson (25:2) Sum 72, p. 245.
"Count One." Hudson (25:2) Sum 72, p. 243.
"Elegy in November." Hudson (25:2) Sum 72, p. 243.
"In the Woods." Hudson (25:2) Sum 72, p. 246.
"June Day." Hudson (25:2) Sum 72, p. 245.
"The Winter Solstice." Hudson (25:2) Sum 72, p. 243.
"Words." Hudson (25:2) Sum 72, p. 244.

1433 HUDDLE, David
"Fish Crazed By Flood." Esq (77:3) Mr 72, p. 194.

1434 HUDZIK, Robert
"The Photograph of Death." PoetryNW (13:1) Spr 72, p. 10.

1435 HUEY, A. D.
"Vignette in a Laundrette." SatEP (244:1) Spr 72, p. 103.

1436 HUGHES, Barbara
"Altadena Foothills." Nat (214:11) 13 Mr 72, p. 343.
"Bamboo." Nat (214:18) 1 My 72, p. 573.
"The Bed." Nat (214:12) 20 Mr 72, p. 382.
"Norwegian Coastline." Nat (214:10) 6 Mr 72, p. 318.
"Visiting Friends Abroad." Nat (214:22) 29 My 72, p. 701.

1437 HUGHES, Beverlee
"Avenue A." WindO (9) Spr 72, p. 10.
"Beyond This Place." MinnR (3) Aut 72, p. 110.
"The Blind Poet Explains." Northeast Sum 72, p. 31.
"Home Movies." Folio (8:1) Spr 72, p. 15.
"Military Manual For Privates." Epos (23:4) Sum 72, p. 19.
"News Report for the Metropolitan Area." Folio (8:1) Spr 72, p. 23.
"Poem to an Old Friend." WindO (12) Wint 72-73, p. 40.

1438 HUGHES, David
"red raspberry picking." Zahir (1:4/5) 72, p. 70.

1439 HUGHES, Dorothy
"Death of a Laundry." Aphra (3:4) Fall 72, p. 37.

1440 HUGHES, Glyn
"The Servant." TransR (41) Wint-Spr 72, p. 103.

1441 HUGHES, Sister Mary Enda
"A Beginning." Cim (19) Ap 72, p. 46.

1442 HUGHES, Ted
"Bawdry Embraced." Poetry (121:1) O 72, p. 12.

1443 HUGO, Richard
"Again, Kapowsin." Iowa (3:1) Wint 72, p. 4.
"Cleggam." Madrona (1:2) N 71, p. 29.
"Driving Montana." PoetryNW (13:3) Aut 72, p. 7.
"Graves at Elkhorn." Madrona (1:2) N 71, p. 30.
"The House on 15th S.W." Iowa (3:1) Wint 72, p. 5.
"In Your Bad Dream." PoetryNW (13:3) Aut 72, p. 6.
"Letter to Peterson from the Pike Place Market." PoetryNW (13:3) Aut 72, p. 3.
"A Letter to Reed from Lolo." Iron (2) Fall 72, p. 12.
"A Night with Cindy at Heitman's." Antaeus (5) Spr 72, p. 38.
"Note to R. H. from Strongsville." Antaeus (5) Spr 72, p. 39.
"On Hearing a New Escalation." Poetry (120:6) S 72, p. 319.
"Plans for Altering the River." PoetryNW (13:3) Aut 72, p. 4.
"Silver Star (for Bill Kittredge)." PoetryNW (13:3) Aut

72, p. 8.
"A Snapshot of 15th S.W." Iron (2) Fall 72, p. 13.
"A Snapshot of the Auxiliary." Iowa (3:1) Wint 72, p. 6.
"Three Stops to Ten Sleep." PoetryNW (13:3) Aut 72, p. 5.
"Why I Think of Dumar Sadly." PoetryNW (13:3) Aut 72, p. 6.

1444 HUI-MING, Wang
Four Woodcuts. NewL (38:3) Spr 72, p. 49.
"10-12-72: Walking with My Daughter When I Knew I Was Half-Blind." NewL (39:2) Wint 72, p. 72.

1445 HULBERT, Debra
"American Dream." PraS (46:3) Aut 72, p. 211.
"Finding." PraS (46:3) Aut 72, p. 210.
"Possession by Foxes." PraS (46:3) Aut 72, p. 209.
"Refrigerator Sex Change No. 1." PraS (46:3) Aut 72, p. 211.

1446 HUMBLE, Christopher
"The Bicycle Race." NYT 27 Ag 72, p. 14.
"Homage to Mexico." NYT 19 Ag 72, p. 22.
"Something Alive." NYT 20 F 72, sec. 4, p. 12.

1447 HUMES, Harry
"Another Dam by Your Army Engineers." WormR (46) 72, p. 32.
"An Answer." WormR (46) 72, p. 33.
"Autumn's Trout." VirQR (48:1) Wint 72, p. 55.
"A Cat Asleep." ChiTM 31 D 72, p. 5.
"The Muskellunge." VirQR (48:1) Wint 72, p. 54.
"Phone Call." WormR (46) 72, p. 32.

1448 HUMMER, Terry
"A Hospital Room, with Fishbowl" (For Wallace Stevens). HiramPoR (13) Fall-Wint 72, p. 22.

1449 HUMPHREY, J.
"For the Licking." Aphra (3:3) Sum 72, p. 17.

1450 HUNT, Thomas Patrick
"The Couple." Epoch (22:1) Fall 72, p. 81.
"Sacred Cow." Epoch (22:1) Fall 72, p. 81.

1451 HUNT, William B.
"Dicke." MinnR (2) Spr 72, p. 115.
"Harvest Birthday." MinnR (2) Spr 72, p. 113.
"How It Might Be." NewYorker (47:53) 19 F 72, p. 48.
"My room labors to be unkempt." PraS (46:1) Spr 72, p. 47.
"Our Lady with Aluminum Hands." MinnR (2) Spr 72, p. 116.

"Wilder Park." MinnR (2) Spr 72, p. 114.

1452 HUNTER, Paul
"Heartwood." PoetryNW (13:2) Sum 72, p. 26.
"Put Your Whole Self In and Shake It All About." NoAmR (257:3) Aut 72, p. 72.
"Song: come midnight some winter." UnmOx (1:1) N 71, p. 63.
"Song: we can be heard a long time coming." UnmOx (1:1) N 71, p. 62.
"Song: what is given you pour." UnmOx (1:1) N 71, p. 63.

1453 HUNTING, Constance
"Charity." ChrC (89:13) 29 Mr 72, p. 354.
"This Person." Qt (5:39/40) Sum-Aut 72, p. 17.

1454 HUOTARI, Robert Heikki
"And Listening." PoetC (7:1) 72, p. 20.

1455 HUSSEY, Anne
"The Apartment Upstairs." SewanR (80:2) Spr 72, p. 285.
"The Chandelier." BelPoJ (23:2) Wint 72-73, p. 9.
"Gypsy Children." BelPoJ (23:2) Wint 72-73, p. 11.
"NasKeag" (for R.W.K.). CarlMis (12:2) Spr-Sum 72, p. 106.
"Practice Rooms." PartR (39:1) Wint 72, p. 57.
"Veteran's Dream." Atl (230:5) N 72, p. 111.
"Women at Forty." Cosmo (173:4) O 72, p. 150.
"Women at Forty." PartR (39:1) Wint 72, p. 56.

1456 HUTCHISON, Joe
"Meditation." ConcPo (5:2) Fall 72, p. 55.
"Poem from my Seventeenth Year." New:ACP (19) Aut 72, p. 40.

1457 HUTTO, Henry Hubert
"Body Count." ChrC (89:22) 31 My 72, p. 630.
"Out Is Where the Black Boots Are." ChrC (89:38) 25 O 72, p. 1068.
"To a Blessed Spinster." Poem (16) N 72, p. 36.
"Yes." ChrC (89:5) 2 F 72, p. 114.

1458 HYDE, Lewis
"The Horse of Dreams" (tr. of Pablo Neruda). Iron (2) Fall 72, p. 21.
"Night time Collection" (tr. of Pablo Neruda). Iron (2) Fall 72, p. 29.
"Unity" (tr. of Pablo Neruda). Iron (2) Fall 72, p. 23.
"We Two Together" (tr. of Pablo Neruda). Iron (2) Fall 72, p. 25.

1459 IGNATOW, David
"The Form Falls In On Itself." NewYQ (9) Wint 72, p. 44.

"From the Observatory." UnmOx (1:4) Aut 72.
"Here I Am." Poetry (120:6) S 72, p. 321.
"I shake my fist at a tree." UnmOx (1:4) Aut 72.
"In a Dream." Etc. (29:1) Mr 72, p. 90.
"A Medical Report." UnmOx (1:4) Aut 72.
"On Poetry." Iron (1) Spr 72, p. 46.
"One World." Iron (1) Spr 72, p. 46.
"Poem." Madrona (1:1) Je 71, p. 7.
"The Question." Madrona (1:2) N 71, p. 3.
"Space Poem." Etc. (29:1) Mr 72, p. 89.
"The trees are stripped bare." UnmOx (1:4) Aut 72.
"Two Poems." Madrona (1:2) N 71, p. 3.
"Winter." Madrona (1:1) Je 71, p. 30.

1460 IGO, John
Ten Lyrics (tr. of Hermann Hesse). PoetL (67:2) Sum 72, p. 125.

1461 IKEMOTO, Takashi
"Zen Poems of China" (tr., w. Lucien Stryk). New:ACP (19) Aut 72, p. 55.

1462 IMANI, Nia Na
"My Man." JnlOBP (2:16) Sum 72, p. 80.

1463 IMMERSI, Richard
"Poem for Kenneth Patchen (1911-1972)." WormR (48) 72, p. 126.
"San Francisco from a Cable Car." WormR (48) 72, p. 125.
"sometimes." WormR (48) 72, p. 125.

1464 INCE, Ozdemir
"Poet." LitR (15:4) Sum 72, p. 500.

1465 INEZ, Colette
"Bells of St. Basil." Confr (5) Wint-Spr 72, p. 18.
"Boarder." Cord (1:3) 72, p. 3.
"Brune." Confr (5) Wint-Spr 72, p. 19.
"Buffalo Sam." Antaeus (5) Spr 72, p. 94.
"Christ, Dove." ChiTM 19 N 72, p. 12.
"Family Life." MinnR (3) Aut 72, p. 94.
"Gorilla Dark." Drag (3:1) Spr 72, p. 56.
"The Helper and the Baker." AriD (1:3) Spr 72, p. 4.
"Karen at the Fork of Darkness." SouthernPR (13:1) Aut 72, p. 13.
"Lakelight Girls." MinnR (3) Aut 72, p. 95.
"Mundugamor." NewYQ (9) Wint 72, p. 60.
"Phenomena, the Oarsman Slides Under my Eyes." NYT 17 Ap 72, p. 32.
"A Rage Inside Her Reticence." AriD (1:3) Spr 72, p. 4.
"Tunnels of Rose." ChiTM 17 S 72, p. 14.
"When Crinkled, Gold Tin Foil." St.AR (2:1) Aut-Wint 72, p. 28.

1466 INGRAM, Forrest
"No Moon No Sun No Shadow." Mund (5:3) 72, p. 32.
"Statued Antinomies." Mund (5:3) 72, p. 33.

1467 INGRAM, Maria
"A Maiden's Small Joy." SouthernPR (13:1) Aut 72, p. 33.

1468 INMAN, Will
"Talk of Crafting." NewYQ (11) Sum 72, p. 52.

1469 INSAN
"Inertia." Zahir (1:4/5) 72, p. 32.
"poem for audrey." Zahir (1:4/5) 72, p. 32.
"Queen Mother of Rythms." Zahir (1:4/5) 72, p. 32.

1470 IOSET, Mark
"Gift." SoDakR (10:1) Spr 72, p. 43.

1471 IRELAND, Alan
"Farewell Poems" (tr. of Yukio Mishima). St.AR (1:4) Spr-Sum 72, p. 11.

1472 IRGAT, Cahit
"Shortcoming" (tr. by Ahmet O. Evin). LitR (15:4) Sum 72, p. 426.

1473 IRION, Mary Jean
"The Coming of Summer." LadHJ (89:7) Jl 72, p. 51.
"In an Empty Cathedral." ChrC (89:12) 22 Mr 72, p. 333.
"On Leaving Frau Freyer's Gasthof." ChrC (89:28) 2 Ag 72, p. 799.

1474 IRWIN, Robert
"Two Poems for Mark Twain." Mark (16:2) Sum 72, p. 21.

1475 ISELY, Helen Sue
"The Fire." Qt (5:39/40) Sum-Aut 72, p. 35.

1476 ITZIN, Charles
"Luz de Corral." NewL (39:2) Wint 72, p. 26.
"Malcolm, Iowa." NewL (39:2) Wint 72, p. 28.

1477 IVANOV, Vyacheslav
"Italian Sonnets" (tr. by Emery E. George). RusLT (4) Aut 72, p. 39.
"Winter Sonnets" (tr. by Emery E. George). RusLT (4) Aut 72, p. 31.

1478 JACKOWSKA, Nicki
"Negative." ChiTM 12 Mr 72, p. 12.

1479 JACKSON, Richard
"Poem with Variable Refrain." Poetry (120:1) Ap 72, p. 38.
"Prologue of a Man Going Blind." Poetry (120:1) Ap 72, p. 37.
"The Room (for Michael Panori)." Poetry (120:1) Ap 72, p. 36.
"Some Haphazard Notes after an Evening Storm (for William Meredith)." Poetry (120:1) Ap 72, p. 36.

1480 JACKSON, Richard X.
"Cities Burning." JnlOBP (2:16) Sum 72, p. 18.

1481 JACKSON, Ron
"A Variation on Seven Questions." NewYQ (12) Aut 72, p. 86.

1482 JACOB, John
"In November, Thought 1890." UTR (1:2) 72, p. 26.
"Then Was." UTR (1:1) 72, p. 21.

1483 JACOB, Max
"Ravignan Street" (tr. by Raymond Federman). Pan (9) 72, p. 10.

1484 JACOBS, A. C.
"I Have Travelled All Day" (tr. of Amir Gilboa). Books (46:2) Spr 72, p. 250.

1485 JACOBS, M. G.
"Suicide." KanQ (4:1) Wint 71-72, p. 110.

1486 JACOBSEN, Josephine
"Conditional Absolution." NewL (38:4) Sum 72, p. 40.
"Future Green." NewL (38:4) Sum 72, p. 66.
"Ghosts at Khe Son." Poetry (120:6) S 72, p. 348.
"The Mexican Peacock" (for Flannery O'Connor). New Yorker (48:18) 24 Je 72, p. 40.

1487 JACOBSEN, Rolf
"The Age of the Great Symphonies" (tr. by Robert Bly). Madrona (1:1) Je 71, p. 19.
"Country Roads" (tr. by Robert Bly). Madrona (1:1) Je 71, p. 32.

1488 JACOBUS, Lee A.
"For Eric Heysteck: Blind and Dead." SouthwR (57:3) Sum 72, p. 216.

1489 JACQUES, Geoffrey
"Epitaph For the Marshall Plan" (for Jimi Hendrix, a dead man). JnlOBP (2:16) Sum 72, p. 61.
"Leaf Poem." StoneD (1:1) Spr 72, p. 57.

"Torn Awning." JnlOBP (2:16) Sum 72, p. 61.

1490 JACQZ, Christian
"Clay Flute." YaleLit (141:2) 71, p. 8.
"Setting Up." YaleLit (141:2) 71, p. 8.

1491 JAFFE, Marie B.
"The Genteel Restaurants." PoetL (67:4) Wint 72, p. 358.

1492 JAFFIN, David
"Birds in a Cage." FreeL (15:1/2) 71-72, p. 80.
"Established." Poem (16) N 72, p. 27.
"Misconceived." FreeL (15:1/2) 71-72, p. 79.
"On the Hanger." Cim (20) Jl 72, p. 51.
"Return." Poem (16) N 72, p. 28.
"The Room." FreeL (15:1/2) 71-72, p. 81.
"Statue in the Park." FreeL (15:1/2) 71-72, p. 81.
"symbols." FreeL (15:1/2) 71-72, p. 77.
"Waiting." FreeL (15:1/2) 71-72, p. 78.

1493 JAKOBOVITS, Leon
"Kinesthetic Conceits." Etc. (29:2) Je 72, p. 144.

1494 JAMALI, Satish
"Annihilation." Meas (3) 72, p. 36.
"Howl." Meas (3) 72, p. 35.
"Through." Meas (3) 72, p. 34.

1495 JAMES, Betty Payne
"Letter from Capernaum." PraS (46:2) Sum 72, p. 150.

1496 JAMES, Eileen M.
"September." Wind (2:6) Aut 72, p. 12.

1497 JAMES, Jamie
"Remaining Possible." BerksR (8:1) Spr 72, p. 36.
"The Sicilian Falcon." BerksR (8:1) Spr 72, p. 35.

1498 JAMES, Thomas
"For Dean." Epoch (21:2) Wint 71, p. 168.
"Laceration." PoetL (67:2) Sum 72, p. 139.
"Longing for Death." PoetL (67:2) Sum 72, p. 140.
"No Music." NoAmR (257:1) Spr 72, p. 33.
"Old Woman Cleaning Silver." PoetL (67:2) Sum 72, p. 140.
"Wine." PoetL (67:2) Sum 72, p. 138.

1499 JANKIEWICZ, Henry
"The Grasshopper and the Cricket." FourQt (21:2) Ja 72, p. 35.

1500 JANOFF, Ron
"The Old Lady's Passion." HangL (16) Wint 71-72, p. 32.

1501 JANOWITZ, Phyllis
"Suite." Nat (215:11) 16 O 72, p. 349.
"Typewriter Without Keys." Nat (215:9) 2 O 72, p. 280.

1502 JARMAN, Mark
"Making Out with the Ghosts of Old Girl Friends." Kayak (30) D 72, p. 22.

1503 JARRELL, Randall
"The Truth." SatR (55:41) O 72, p. 51.
"The Ways and the Peoples." Poetry (121:1) O 72, p. 15.

1504 JARRETT, Dennis
"Summer Night." ParisR (55) Aut 72, p. 22.

1505 JARRETT, Emmett
"Family Scene" (for John and Elaine). Hiero (7) Ap 72.
"For Marge in the Hospital." Hiero (7) Ap 72.
"Presences." Hiero (7) Ap 72.

1506 JAWORSKI, Richard
"U.S. 495, The Beltway around Washington, D.C." UTR (1:2) 72, p. 31.

1507 JEANETTE, Evelyn
"Ladies in Waiting." SatEP (244:2) Sum 72, p. 102.

1508 JEFFERSON, Annetta
"Rain." FreeL (15:1/2) 71-72, p. 68.

1509 JEFFERSON, Todd Davis
"For Father." Folio (8:2) Fall 72, p. 32.

1510 JEFFRIES, Sarah
"Fireplace with a Message." NewRena (6) My 72, p. 46.

1511 JELLEMA, Roderick
"Getting Out: July 21, 1969." LittleM (6:1) Spr 72, p. 7.
"Incarnation." SouthernPR (13:1) Aut 72, p. 32.
"Industrial Park." NewRep (166:4) 22 Ja 72, p. 27.
"Love Note: The Dictionary Says We're Flush." LittleM (6:1) Spr 72, p. 5.
"Walk the Edge." LittleM (6:1) Spr 72, p. 6.

1512 JENKINS, Louis
"Fever." Madrona (1:4) S 72, p. 42.
"Kansas." Madrona (1:4) S 72, p. 40.
"My Father." Madrona (1:4) S 72, p. 41.
"Self Service Laundry." Madrona (1:1) Je 71, p. 10.
"Skillet." Madrona (1:4) S 72, p. 39.
"Snow Storm." Madrona (1:4) S 72, p. 37.
"You Move a Chair." Madrona (1:4) S 72, p. 38.

1513 JENKINSON, J. S.
"Cow Traffic." WindO (10) Sum 72, p. 30.
"Poem: You come to me waving your magic." WindO (10) Sum 72, p. 29.
"The Sea: Poem 1." UTR (1:2) 72, p. 23.
"Springfield Lecture No. 2." WindO (10) Sum 72, p. 30.
"To Richard." WindO (10) Sum 72, p. 29.

1514 JENNINGS, Elizabeth
"Cages and Arenas." NYT 26 F 72, p. 28.
"Not a Mystic." NYT 2 Ja 72, sec. 4, p. 10.
"Two Views." NYT 9 F 72, p. 38.

1515 JENNINGS, Kathleen Ellen
"City Dreams." Shen (23:2) Wint 72, p. 65.
"8." AntR (31:4) Wint 71-72, p. 477.
"The Father, After Long Silence, Speaks." Shen (23:2) Wint 72, p. 66.
"For JRW and MFC." Shen (23:2) Wint 72, p. 68.
"Hayters Gap" (for W. R.). Shen (23:2) Wint 72, p. 69.
"Second Sight: A Departure." Shen (23:2) Wint 72, p. 67.

1516 JENNINGS, Lee Byron
"Mao Tse-Tung." BeyB (2:2) 72, p. 51.

1517 JENSEN, Laura
"A Crow Poem." Madrona (1:3) My 72, p. 7.
"Talking to the Mule." Madrona (1:3) My 72, p. 8.
"Tantrum." PoetryNW (13:3) Aut 72, p. 40.

1518 JHA, Vinay
"Elegy for a School Friend." Meas (3) 72, p. 38.
"A Literary Afternoon." Meas (3) 72, p. 38.

1519 JIRO, Négishi
"Ape." PoetL (67:4) Wint 72, p. 340.
"If Not." PoetL (67:4) Wint 72, p. 338.

1520 JOHNSON, Ann
"Member the night Johnny." WindO (9) Spr 72, p. 39.
"Muriel?" WindO (9) Spr 72, p. 39.

1521 JOHNSON, Elaine
"Advice to Polonius." WindO (10) Sum 72, p. 39.
"Conversation." SouthernPR (12:2) Spr 72, p. 37.
"The Quilt." NoCaFo (20:2) My 72, p. 86.

1522 JOHNSON, F. P.
"Me and Daddy." WindO (10) Sum 72, p. 23.
"?" Cim (19) Ap 72, inside front cover.
"Shared Insulation." WindO (10) Sum 72, p. 23.

1523 JOHNSON, Halvard
"The Answer." LittleM (6:2/3) Sum-Aut 72, p. 80.
"Death Heads." MinnR (3) Aut 72, p. 12.
"Eclipse." MinnR (3) Aut 72, p. 8.
"A Good Place for Burying Strangers." HangL (17) Sum 72, p. 20.
"Greenleaf." MinnR (3) Aut 72, p. 11.
"Heavy Breathing." MinnR (3) Aut 72, p. 10.
"One Good Night." MinnR (3) Aut 72, p. 9.
"Orient Hotel." MinnR (3) Aut 72, p. 5.
"Running Out of Horses." MinnR (3) Aut 72, p. 10.
"Sevens." LittleM (6:1) Spr 72, p. 30.
"Sun Waters." HangL (18) Fall 72, p. 24.

1524 JOHNSON, Jeffrey V.
"In Preparation for Something Great." WestHR (26:3) Sum 72, p. 231.

1525 JOHNSON, Louis
"To a Critic Demanding That Verse Display Social Commitment." ChiTM 20 Ag 72, p. 14.

1526 JOHNSON, Mary
"A Quick Auschwitz Affair." Phoenix (3:4) Aut 72, p. 102.

1527 JOHNSON, Michael L.
"Song of a Summer Night." KanQ (4:3) Sum 72, p. 105.

1528 JOHNSON, R. A.
"The Death of an Aunt" (Alice Hendershot: 1908-1971). Works (3:3/4) Wint 72-73, p. 92.
"The Much It Does Not Take and the Little It Does." HangL (17) Sum 72, p. 21.
"poem: you've got your rabbit look on." HangL (17) Sum 72, p. 21.

1529 JOHNSON, Robin
"Found with Chain." QRL (18:1/2) 72, p. 88.
"Thunder from an Unknown God." QRL (18:1/2) 72, p. 88.

1530 JOHNSON, Ronald
"The Core." Poetry (120:3) Je 72, p. 145.
"Poem: Out from this floor of words." Poetry (120:3) Je 72, p. 144.

1531 JOHNSON, Thomas
"The Apparition." Iron (2) Fall 72, p. 50.
"The Childbearing: A Portrait of Excess." Drag (3:2) Sum 72, p. 32.
"The Cutting Room." St. AR (2:1) Aut-Wint 72, p. 41.
"Disaster Chants." MassR (13:4) Aut 72, p. 657.

"The Founding Family." WindO (12) Wint 72-73, p. 9.
"Giving In At Last." Drag (3:2) Sum 72, p. 33.
"A Grammarian Takes the Morning Air." Poetry (120:3) Je 72, p. 135.
"Indian Creek: Hurricane Weather." Iron (2) Fall 72, p. 48.
"An Inscape for the Afternoon Mail." Drag (3:2) Sum 72, p. 34.
"It Was Not a Time to Retire." SoCaR (5:1) D 72, p. 6.
"Mica." WindO (12) Wint 72-73, p. 8.
"Nearing the Hour of Shiva's Dance" (for Steve Mooney) SouthernPR (12:2) Spr 72, p. 48.
"Night In April With Crickets." Iron (2) Fall 72, p. 47.
"Ooltewah Dusk." GreenR (2:2) 72, p. 17.
"Poem Found Inside an Open Stove Door in Kentucky." Epoch (22:1) Fall 72, p. 80.
"Poem on a Vine Wrestling the Window in Late August." Iron (2) Fall 72, p. 49.
"Rightly, It Would Be Morning." Poetry (120:3) Je 72, p. 136.
"A Word About Form." Epoch (22:1) Fall 72, p. 80.

1532 JOHNSTON, George
"Who Bomb?" Poetry (120:6) S 72, p. 326.

1533 JOHNSTON, J.
"Three Poems." NoAmR (257:2) Sum 72, p. 35.

1534 JONES, Cornelia G.
"Black Adam." JnlOBP (2:16) Sum 72, p. 25.

1535 JONES, Daryl
"Titanic." WestHR (26:2) Spr 72, p. 126.

1536 JONES, Douglas
"and when the spring rain comes." StoneD (1:1) Spr 72, p. 58.

1537 JONES, John Idris
"'The Burden of Englishness.'" TransR (42/43) Spr-Sum 72, p. 75.

1538 JONES, Joseph 63X
"Names Don't Mean a Thing." JnlOBP (2:16) Sum 72, p. 34.

1539 JONES, Paulette
"Reflections In Real Eyes." JnlOBP (2:16) Sum 72, p. 55.

1540 JONES, Robert
"The Need for Martyrs." ChrC (89:45) 13 D 72, p. 1271.

1541 JONES, Rodney G.
"The Aesthetic Parachutists." KanQ (4:1) Wint 71-72, p. 96.

1542 JONES, Tom
"First Words." Cafe (4) Fall 72, p. 25.
"Mussorgsky's 'Pictures'." Cafe (4) Fall 72, p. 25.
"Perfect Sonnets." Cafe (4) Fall 72, p. 25.

1543 JONG, Erica
"Back to Africa." Harp (245:1471) D 72, p. 67.
"The Eggplant Epithalamion (for Grace & David)." NewYQ (10) Spr 72, p. 40.
"The End of the World." ModernPS (3:4) 72, p. 170.
"Hook." Nat (214:18) 1 My 72, p. 568.
"Men." NewYQ (9) Wint 72, p. 53.
"The Send-off" (for Leonard and Patricia). Aphra (3:2) Spr 72, p. 16.
"The Woman Who Loved to Cook." ColumF (1:4) Fall 72, p. 35.

1544 JORDAN, Jim
"Heterosexual Sonnet." HangL (17) Sum 72, p. 22.

1545 JORDAN, June
"On the Murder of Two Human Being Black Men, Denver A. Smith and Leonard Douglas Brown, at Southern University, Baton Rouge, Louisiana, November 16, 1972." VilV 7 D 72, p. 43.

1546 JORGENSEN, Bruce W.
"Incompletions For a Living Father." CarolQ (24:1) Wint 72, p. 76.

1547 JOSEPH, Jenifer S.
"Questions." NegroHB (35:8) D 72, p. 181.

1548 JOUVE
"Lisbe" (tr. by Ed Sanders). UnmOx (1:3) Sum 72, p. 37.

1549 JOYCE, James
"Night Piece." Poetry (121:1) O 72, p. 16.

1550 JOZSEF, Attila
"Bellow, Tower" (tr. by John Batki). SenR (3:1) My 72, p. 17.
"Frost" (tr. by John Batki). SenR (3:1) My 72, p. 21.
"I Did Not Know" (tr. by John Batki). SenR (3:1) My 72, p. 18.
"Medallions 1" (tr. by John Batki). SenR (3:1) My 72, p. 19.
"Medallions 3" (tr. by John Batki). SenR (3:1) My 72, p. 20.

"A Transparent Lion" (tr. by John Batki). SenR (3:1) My 72, p. 16.

1551 JUDSON, John
"Autumn Song." Apple (7) Aut 72, p. 21.
"Before Dawn: Having Risen to Get In a Poem." Hiram-PoR (13) Fall-Wint 72, p. 10.
"Eba Stokes Goes North Under Snow and Trees." KanQ (4:3) Sum 72, p. 88.
"Gary." Shen (23:2) Wint 72, p. 52.
"If You Can't Beat Them." KanQ (4:1) Wint 71-72, p. 97.
"Kyoto--La Crosse." Apple (7) Aut 72, p. 20.
"Lesson Plan Incorporating Theodore Roethke's Film In A Dark Time." Apple (7) Aut 72, p. 22.
"Morning Song." QRL (18:1/2) 72, p. 92.
"My Father's Brown Sweater with the Patched Elbows." QRL (18:1/2) 72, p. 91.
"Once Again Black Orpheus Plays the Sun Up." KanQ (4:3) Sum 72, p. 89.
"Opening Camp: The Second Week." QRL (18:1/2) 72, p. 90.
"The Return: Suite for an Early Spring." QRL (18:1/2) 72, p. 93.
"The Road to Poplar Stream." ColQ (21:2) Aut 72, p. 162.
"September 30th." Apple (7) Aut 72, p. 17.
"Sunday Poem." Apple (7) Aut 72, p. 18.
"Winter Afternoon." Peb (6) Sum 71.

1552 JUERGENSEN, Hans
"Airport." PoetL (67:4) Wint 72, p. 341.
"Blood." UTR (1:1) 72, p. 25.
"Grimm Rationale." PoetL (67:2) Sum 72, p. 146.
"Mysterise." PoetL (67:4) Wint 72, p. 341.

1553 JUERGENSEN, Ilse
"At the Edge of the Carnival." PoetL (67:4) Wint 72, p. 336.
"Words." PoetL (67:4) Wint 72, p. 337.

1554 JUNKINS, Donald
"After the Six a.m. Phone Call About the Fire Headed For Great East Lake, We Drove From Saugus in the '38 Buick." AriD (1:3) Spr 72, p. 22.
"Crossing by Ferry." VirQR (48:4) Aut 72, p. 535.
"Uncle Harry: Shooting Partridge, 1941." Atl (229:1) Ja 72, p. 38.

1555 JUNOD, Joe
"I'm Screaming." St. AR (2:1) Aut-Wint 72, p. 53.
"Watching Men." St. AR (1:4) Spr-Sum 72, p. 30.

1556 JURIS, Prudence
"Trespassing! Public Property." Zahir (1:4/5) 72, p. 71.

1557 JUSSAWALLA, Adil
"The Model." Meas (3) 72, p. 40.
"The Moon and Cloud at Easter." Meas (3) 72, p. 40.

1558 JUSTICE, Donald
"From a Notebook." NoAmR (257:2) Sum 72, p. 32.
"A Letter." Poetry (119:6) Mr 72, p. 326.
"Riddle: White of a blind man's eye." Antaeus (7) Aut 72, p. 24.
"Sonatina in Green (for my students)." Kayak (30) D 72, p. 37.
"White Notes." Poetry (119:6) Mr 72, p. 327.

1559 KABLACK, David
"This Small Bed." PoetL (67:3) Aut 72, p. 225.

1560 KACHUBA, John Barrie
"East Bombay Street." PoetL (67:4) Wint 72, p. 354.

1561 KAEBITZSCH, Reinhold Johannes
"The Accident into Timelessness." UTR (1:1) 72, p. 19.
"And Cute Beast-of-Prey Spots..." (tr. of Ernst Wilhelm Lotz). UTR (1:4) 72, p. 6.
"The Battle Near Saarburg" (tr. of Alfred Lichtenstein). UTR (1:4) 72, p. 8.
"The Campfires at the Coast" (tr. of Walter Hasenclever). UTR (1:4) 72, p. 7.
"Departure" (tr. of Else Lasker-Schueler). UTR (1:4) 72, p. 4.
"Elis" (tr. of Georg Trakl). Wind (2:5) Sum 72, p. 18.
"Eternal Sleep" (tr. of Albert Ehrenstein). UTR (1:4) 72, p. 9.
"First Snow." WindO (10) Sum 72, p. 45.
"Flying into Shannon." BeyB (2:2) 72, p. 44.
"Forest" (tr. of Iwan Goll). UTR (1:1) 72, p. 31.
"The Gardener." Cim (20) Jl 72, p. 32.
"Hunger." UTR (1:4) 72, p. 11.
"In the Middle of the Night" (tr. of Kurt Heynicke). UTR (1:4) 72, p. 5.
"Lonely Evening" (tr. of Herman Hesse). UTR (1:4) 72, p. 10.
"Marsh Lights" (tr. of Rainer Maria Rilke). SenR (3:1) My 72, p. 27.
"Nightmare's Black Eye." Epos (24:1) Fall 72, p. 5.
"Noises." MinnR (3) Aut 72, p. 37.
"Patrol" (tr. of August Stramm). UTR (1:1) 72, p. 32.
"Sun" (tr. of Hugo Ball). WormR (48) 72, p. 118.
"Surrealists Talking." BeyB (2:2) 72, p. 44.
"To Elis" (tr. of Georg Trakl). UTR (1:4) 72, p. 3.
"When Winter Travels Through" (tr. of Christian Morgenstern). Folio (8:1) Spr 72, p. 12.

1562 KAFATOU, Sarah
"The March" (tr. of Titos Patrikios). AriD (1:4/5) Sum-Aut 72, p. 87.
"Northern Spiritual" (tr. of Teos Salapassidis). AriD (1:4/5) Sum-Aut 72, p. 93.

1563 KAFTANTZIS, George
from Twenty-Four Executions: "The Third," "The Eleventh," "The Eighteenth" (tr. by Athan Anagnostopoulos). AriD (1:4/5) Sum-Aut 72, p. 50.

1564 KAHAN, Matthew
"The Burning Steppe" (tr. of Berdynazar Khudainazarov, w. Nan Braymer). NewWR (40:4) Aut 72, p. 13.
"Love of Country" (tr. of Mara Greeazanie, w. Nan Braymer). NewWR (40:4) Aut 72, p. 83.
"Maples in Bloom" (tr. of Yan Sudrabkali, w. Nan Braymer). NewWR (40:4) Aut 72, p. 84.

1565 KAHN, Evelyn
"Old." LittleM (6:2/3) Sum-Aut 72, p. 126.

1566 KAHN, Hannah
"Sky Game." LadHJ (89:5) My 72, p. 116.

1567 KAHN, Irving
"Birdsong." Etc. (29:3) S 72, p. 298.

1568 KAISER, Walter
"Across Gorse" (tr. of George Seferis). AriD (1:2) Wint 72, p. 3.

1569 KAKNAVATOS, Ektor
"Era" (tr. by Stavros Deligiorgis). AriD (1:4/5) Sum-Aut 72, p. 52.
from Scale of the Stone: (25) (tr. by T. K. Scuris). AriD (1:4/5) Sum-Aut 72, p. 54.

1570 KALBFLEISCH, J. B.
"Tumble Weed." Wind (2:5) Sum 72, p. 39.

1571 KALLIO, John
"Immortal Intimation." Zahir (1:4/5) 72, p. 73.

1572 KANE, Thomas S.
"Amo, Amas, Amat." CEACritic (34:3) Mr 72, p. 44.

1573 KANFER, Allen
"Laying On Of Hands." Harp (244:1460) Ja 72, p. 87.
"Sailfish." Esq (78:6) D 72, p. 68.
"Today." Perspec (17:1) Sum 72, p. 12.

1574 KANSU, Ceyhun Atuf
"The Critics" (tr. by Talat Sait Halman). LitR (15:4)

Sum 72, p. 450.

1575 KAO, Rosa Tsung-yu
"Chance-Meeting" (tr. of Hsu Chih-mo, w. Robert Magliola). PoetL (67:4) Wint 72, p. 350.
"Star-Spark of Feeble Flame" (tr. of Hsu Chih-mo, w. Robert Magliola). PoetL (67:4) Wint 72, p. 350.

1576 KAO, Sin-yung
"An Exercise in 三 and 三 三." Literature (15:3) 72, p. 490.

1577 KAPLAN, Milton
"Circe: Afterwards." ColEng (33:4) Ja 72, p. 482.
"Roots." ChiTM 8 O 72, p. 8.

1578 KAPSASKIS, Socrates
"Return from War" (tr. by James Damaskos). AriD (1:4/5) Sum-Aut 72, p. 55.

1579 KAPUTIKIAN, Silva
"Song About Our Stones" (tr. by Bernard Koten, w. Nan Braymer). NewWR (40:4) Aut 72, p. 64.

1580 KARACHALIOS, Nikos
"By Command" (tr. by Ruth Whitman). AriD (1:4/5) Sum-Aut 72, p. 59.
"Episode" (tr. by Stavros Deligiorgis). AriD (1:4/5) Sum-Aut 72, p. 60.
"Erosion" (tr. by Stratis Haviaras). AriD (1:4/5) Sum-Aut 72, p. 57.
"The Last Moment" (tr. by Stavros Deligiorgis). AriD (1:4/5) Sum-Aut 72, p. 58.
"Prophetic" (tr. by Stavros Deligiorgis). AriD (1:4/5) Sum-Aut 72, p. 58.

1581 KARLEN, Arno
"Josh, Away In August." Harp (245:1467) Ag 72, p. 32.
"Polonius Waits Alone Behind the Arras." PoetryNW (13:1) Spr 72, p. 11.

1582 KAROUZOS, N. D.
"Autumn 1953" (tr. by Ruth Whitman). AriD (1:4/5) Sum-Aut 72, p. 72.
"Ikon" (tr. by Ruth Whitman). AriD (1:4/5) Sum-Aut 72, p. 74.
"Vibrations" (tr. by Ruth Whitman). AriD (1:4/5) Sum-Aut 72, p. 71.
"Visibility" (tr. by Stratis Haviaras). AriD (1:4/5) Sum-Aut 72, p. 73.

1583 KARSTEN, Ernie
"Sonnet to an English Class." EngJ (61:7) O 72, p. 1028.

1584 KASHNER, Samuel
"al capone had." HangL (17) Sum 72, p. 67.
"Basketball as a National Anthem." WindO (12) Wint 72-73, p. 13.
"Bounty on Soft Words." WindO (10) Sum 72, p. 4.
"the daily management." WindO (12) Wint 72-73, p. 14.
Eight Poems. WindO (9) Spr 72, p. 37.
"English Class." WindO (11) Aut 72, p. 39.
"i wanted always to." WindO (10) Sum 72, p. 5.
"An Interference." WindO (11) Aut 72, p. 38.
"Kissing you goodbye." HangL (17) Sum 72, p. 66.
"the pain you cause me." WindO (10) Sum 72, p. 5.
"The Poetry of Older Women." WindO (12) Wint 72-73, p. 11.
"Pretending To Be a Poem for Angela Davis." WindO (10) Sum 72, p. 6.
"there was a time when." WindO (10) Sum 72, p. 6.
"we dance." HangL (17) Sum 72, p. 66.
"when evening." WindO (12) Wint 72-73, p. 12.
"when my mother." WindO (10) Sum 72, p. 4.
"you live within." WindO (12) Wint 72-73, p. 14.
"your life is like." HangL (17) Sum 72, p. 67.
"your long legs." WindO (12) Wint 72-73, p. 15.

1585 KASPRZAK, Alan L.
"Year One." EngJ (61:8) N 72, p. 1251.

1586 KASS, Donald
"Limbo." FreeL (15:1/2) 71-72, p. 55.

1587 KAST, Barry
"Remedies." Kayak (30) D 72, p. 45.

1588 KATES, Jim
"The Apologie of John Ketch Esq; July 21, 1683." LittleM (6:1) Spr 72, p. 61.
"The Dying Wolfram Laments His Life." LittleM (6:2/3) Sum-Aut 72, p. 43.
"Stone Rubbing: A Local Graveyard." AriD (1:2) Wint 72, p. 15.
"Week-end." AriD (1:2) Wint 72, p. 14.

1589 KATIBU, Cheo
"Communicate (The Message)." JnlOBP (2:16) Sum 72, p. 57.

1590 KATSAROS, Michael
"In the Dead Forest" (tr. by Thanasis Maskaleris). AriD (1:4/5) Sum-Aut 72, p. 75.
"My Testament" (tr. by Stratis Haviaras). AriD (1:4/5) Sum-Aut 72, p. 76.

1591 KATSELAS, Jane
"Aeroflot." Mund (5:1/2) 72, p. 102.

"Eric." Mund (5:1/2) 72, p. 103.
"Fragment." Mund (5:1/2) 72, p. 102.

1592 KATTERJOHN, Bill
"To an Ending Mist." Wind (2:5) Sum 72, p. 51.

1593 KATZ, David
"Early Spring Editorial." VilV 4 My 72, p. 6.

1594 KATZ, Jonathan
"Christmas Eve 1971." Poem (16) N 72, p. 46.
"Found: Due at the Library." NewYQ (12) Aut 72, p. 97.
"The Lawn." NoAmR (257:4) Wint 72, p. 60.
"Sacred Story." Poem (16) N 72, p. 48.

1595 KATZ, Menke
"Francois Villon (1431-1489)." NYT 26 O 72, p. 42.
"The Message." PoetL (67:4) Wint 72, p. 384.
"My Sister Bloomke." New:ACP (18) Ap 72, p. 19.
"Queens of Autumn." PoetL (67:4) Wint 72, p. 383.
"Swan Song." Epos (24:1) Fall 72, p. 16.
"Waters." PoetL (67:4) Wint 72, p. 383.
"White Little Goat." PoetL (67:1) Spr 72, p. 11.
"Wise Acre." NYT 9 My 72, p. 40.

1596 KATZMAN, Allen
"Confessional." NewYQ (11) Sum 72, p. 53.
"Nothing Succeeds Like." Nat (214:4) 24 Ja 72, p. 125.
"#33." Nat (214:7) 14 F 72, p. 216.

1597 KAUFMAN, Shirley
"Driving on the San Diego Freeway." Nat (215:5) 4 S 72, p. 156.
"Feeding Time in the Lion House." QRL (18:1/2) 72, p. 94.
"Gone with the Popcorn." Field (6) Spr 72, p. 78.
"Michal." QRL (18:1/2) 72, p. 95.
"Signs." MassR (13:4) Aut 72, p. 679.
"Sorrow, Sorrow." MassR (13:4) Aut 72, p. 678.
"Subversion." QRL (18:1/2) 72, p. 99.
"Summer." QRL (18:1/2) 72, p. 96.

1598 KAUFMAN, Wallace
"Research Ship." Granite (2) Wint 71-72, p. 49.

1599 KAVEN, Robert
"Circle (for P. Jostrom)." Nat (214:15) 10 Ap 72, p. 476.
"Idiots, in Apple Creek State Hospital." Nat (214:22) 29 My 72, p. 728.

1600 KAY, John
"Barking at Thunder." WormR (47) 72, p. 101.
"john berryman's unnumbered dream song." WormR (47)

72, p. 102.
"Postmarked in Long Beach." WormR (47) 72, p. 103.

1601 KAYDEN, Eugene M.
"The Cloud in Trousers" (tr. of Vladimir Mayakovsky). ColQ (21:2) Aut 72, p. 233.
"Conversation Between a Bookseller and a Poet" (tr. of Alexander Pushkin). ColQ (21:1) Sum 72, p. 126.
"Eighty-eight poems by Anna Akhmātova" (tr. of Anna Akhmātova). ColQ (20:3) Wint 72, p. 396.
"Emmanuel and other poems" (tr. of Vladimir Solovyóv). ColQ (20:4) Spr 72, p. 546.
"Fantasy and other poems" (tr. of Afanasi Fet). ColQ (20:4) Spr 72, p. 563.
"Fifteen poems by Stepan Shchipachev" (tr. of Stepan Shchipachev). ColQ (21:1) Sum 72, p. 138.
"The March of Man" (tr. of Maxim Gorky). ColQ (20:4) Spr 72, p. 579.
"The Monkey and other poems" (tr. of Vladislav Khodasevich). ColQ (20:4) Spr 72, p. 545.
"Napoleon" (tr. of Alexander Pushkin). ColQ (21:1) Sum 72, p. 119.
"The Nineteenth of October" (tr. of Alexander Pushkin). ColQ (21:1) Sum 72, p. 132.
"Seven poems by Alexander Blok" (tr. of Alexander Blok). ColQ (20:3) Wint 72, p. 443.
"Seven poems by Anna Akhmátova" (tr. of Anna Akhmátova). ColQ (20:4) Spr 72, p. 530.
"Sixteen fables" (tr. of Ivan Krylov). ColQ (21:2) Aut 72, p. 277.
"Sixteen poems by Osip Mandelshtam" (tr. of Osip Mandelshtam). ColQ (20:4) Spr 72, p. 535.
"Songs of Heroic Madness" (tr. of Maxim Gorky). ColQ (21:1) Sum 72, p. 106.
"Thirteen poems by Innokénty Annensky" (tr. of Innokénty Annensky). ColQ (20:3) Wint 72, p. 387.
"Twenty-five poems by Apollon Maikov" (tr. of Apollon Maikov). ColQ (21:2) Aut 72, p. 256.
"Twenty-seven poems by Afanasi Fet" (tr. of Afanasi Fet). ColQ (21:1) Sum 72, p. 90.

1602 KEATS, Eleanor
"Cherry Trees." AntR (31:4) Wint 71-72, p. 478.

1603 KEEFE, Carolyn
"Nativity Play." ChrC (89:46) 20 D 72, p. 1293.

1604 KEELER, Greg
"Manfred's Marlin." Drag (3:2) Sum 72, p. 57.
"To a Poet." Drag (3:2) Sum 72, p. 58.

1605 KEELEY, Edmund
"Antony's Ending" (tr. of C. P. Cavafy, w. Philip

Sherrard). Antaeus (6) Sum 72, p. 39.

"Body, Remember..." (tr. of C. P. Cavafy, w. Philip Sherrard). Nat (215:15) 13 N 72, p. 469.

"Dareios" (tr. of C. P. Cavafy, w. Philip Sherrard). Antaeus (6) Sum 72, p. 42.

"The Distress of Selefkidis" (tr. of C. P. Cavafy, w. Philip Sherrard). Antaeus (6) Sum 72, p. 40.

"An Exiled Byzantine Nobleman Who Composes Verses" (tr. of C. P. Cavafy, w. Philip Sherrard). Antaeus (6) Sum 72, p. 44.

"Exiles" (tr. of C. P. Cavafy, w. Philip Sherrard). NewYorker (48:17) 17 Je 72, p. 31.

"The Footsteps" (tr. of C. P. Cavafy, w. Philip Sherrard). Poetry (120:5) Ag 72, p. 266.

"For Ammonis, Who Died at 29, in 610" (tr. of C. P. Cavafy, w. Philip Sherrard). QRL (18:1/2) 72, p. 42.

"From the School of the Renowned Philosopher" (tr. of C. P. Cavafy, w. Philip Sherrard). NewYorker (48:17) 17 Je 72, p. 31.

"Half an Hour" (tr. of C. P. Cavafy, w. Philip Sherrard). NewYorker (48:17) 17 Je 72, p. 31.

"The Ides of March" (tr. of C. P. Cavafy, w. Philip Sherrard). Poetry (120:5) Ag 72, p. 266.

"In a Large Greek Colony, 200 B.C." (tr. of C. P. Cavafy, w. Philip Sherrard). NewYRB (18:11) 15 Je 72, p. 13.

"Ionic" (tr. of C. P. Cavafy, w. Philip Sherrard). Antaeus (6) Sum 72, p. 47.

"Ithaka" (tr. of C. P. Cavafy, w. Philip Sherrard). QRL (18:1/2) 72, p. 40.

"Julian and the Antiochians" (tr. of C. P. Cavafy, w. Philip Sherrard). NewL (38:3) Spr 72, p. 76.

"Myris: Alexandria, A.D. 340" (tr. of C. P. Cavafy, w. Philip Sherrard). Antaeus (6) Sum 72, p. 45.

"Nero's Respite" (tr. of C. P. Cavafy, w. Philip Sherrard). QRL (18:1/2) 72, p. 42.

"On the Outskirts of Antioch" (tr. of C. P. Cavafy, w. Philip Sherrard). NewL (38:8) Spr 72, p. 77.

"One of Their Gods" (tr. of C. P. Cavafy, w. Philip Sherrard). QRL (18:1/2) 72, p. 41.

"Philhellene" (tr. of C. P. Cavafy, w. Philip Sherrard). Antaeus (6) Sum 72, p. 41.

"A Prince from Western Libya" (tr. of C. P. Cavafy, w. Philip Sherrard). NewYRB (18:11) 15 Je 72, p. 13.

"The Satrapy" (tr. of C. P. Cavafy, w. Philip Sherrard). Nat (215:15) 13 N 72, p. 469.

"Theodotos" (tr. of C. P. Cavafy, w. Philip Sherrard). Poetry (120:5) Ag 72, p. 267.

"Thermopylae" (tr. of C. P. Cavafy, w. Philip Sherrard). QRL (18:1/2) 72, p. 39.

"To Have Taken the Trouble" (tr. of C. P. Cavafy, w. Philip Sherrard). NewYorker (48:17) 17 Je 72, p. 31.

"Very Seldom" (tr. of C. P. Cavafy, w. Philip Sherrard).

QRL (18:1/2) 72, p. 43.
"Waiting for the Barbarians" (tr. of C. P. Cavafy, w. Philip Sherrard). QRL (18:1/2) 72, p. 38.

1606 KEELING, Brian
"Dig." Spec (14:1/2) My 72, p. 48.

1607 KEENAN, John
"Intimations of Mortality." FourQt (21:4) My 72, p. 100.

1608 KEENAN, Terrance
"Phillips Mill." Epoch (21:2) Wint 71, p. 167.

1609 KEEP, William
"A Little Drink and a Drive After a Long Time from Home." CarlMis (12:1) Fall-Wint 71-72, p. 122.

1610 KEFFER, Kenn
"My Wife Works on a Glad Farm." Meas (2) 72.

1611 KEHN, Patrick E.
"Chu Yuan." Zahir (1:4/5) 72, p. 58.
"The Confessions." Shen (23:2) Wint 72, p. 32.
"A Criticism of the Death of the Ball Turret Gunner." SenR (3:1) My 72, p. 55.
"Flying Apart." ChiR (23:4 & 24:1) 72, p. 35.
"From a Letter Home." Peb (9) Wint 72.
"The Night of Fred." ChiR (23:4 & 24:1) 72, p. 34.

1612 KEINONEN, Claudine
"Reflections from a Jet." KanQ (4:1) Wint 71-72, p. 110.

1613 KEITHLEY, George
"The Houses in Hell." NoAmR (257:1) Spr 72, p. 57.
"How Crazy Horse Was Killed." Harp (244:1463) Ap 72, p. 95.

1614 KEIZER, Gary
"Fat Harold." BelPoJ (23:2) Wint 72-73, p. 29.
"A Joyful Noise." BelPoJ (23:2) Wint 72-73, p. 32.

1615 KELLER, David
"A Fragmentary Presence." KanQ (4:3) Sum 72, p. 90.

1616 KELLER, Stephen
"The Appointed." Poem (16) N 72, p. 49.

1617 KELLEY, H. M.
"The Edge of the Jeweled Sword (for Mishima)." St. AR (1:4) Spr-Sum 72, p. 12.

1618 KELLY, David
"The Debt." CalQ (2) Sum 72, p. 78.

"Poem: Ray Godlewski is real." CalQ (2) Sum 72, p. 79.

1619 KELLY, Robert
from Finding the Measure: "Prefix." Spec (14:1/2) My 72, cover.
"The Labyrinth" (for Helen). Spec (14:1/2) My 72, p. 53.
"Love Song." Spec (14:1/2) My 72, p. 52.

1620 KEMP, George Paul
"When I Felt Kicking at the Side of the Mountain." FreeL (15:1/2) 71-72, p. 7.

1621 KEMPHER, Ruth Moon
"The Antennae." WormR (47) 72, p. 78.
"Birthday." SouthernPR (12:2) Spr 72, p. 48.
"Diagnosis of the Robot Girl's Condition." HiramPoR (13) Fall-Wint 72, p. 11.
"Green Tomato." WormR (47) 72, p. 77.
"Lonely Meal, at El Leon Blanco." Drag (3:1) Spr 72, p. 31.
"The Lust Songs and Travel Diary of Sylvia Savage: IV." Epos (23:4) Sum 72, p. 5.
"The Other Side of the Clock." Epos (24:1) Fall 72, p. 20.
"Picture #34" (At the Asylum). GreenR (2:2) 72, p. 29.
"Porch Game." (8:1) Spr 72, p. 21.
"Tradition, As In Sonnets." GreenR (2:2) 72, p. 28.
"Tricks of Light." Folio (8:2) Fall 72, p. 18.

1622 KENISON, Gloria
Eighteen Poems. WormR (46) 72, p. 43.

1623 KENNEDY, Mary
"Lost Hours." Confr (5) Wint-Spr 72, p. 70.

1624 KENNEDY, X. J.
"Ecology." Harp (245:1471) D 72, p. 68.
"Mining Town." Antaeus (5) Spr 72, p. 50.
"Onan's Soliloquy." Antaeus (5) Spr 72, p. 49.
"Robert Frost Discovers Another Road Not Taken." Harp (245:1471) D 72, p. 68.

1625 KENNELLY, Brendan
"Star." NYT 3 Ap 72, p. 36.

1626 KENSETH, Arnold
"Bible Reading." Comm (97:9) 1 D 72, p. 210.
"Variations on a Theme." AmerS (41:2) Spr 72, p. 222.

1627 KENT, H. R.
"Our Lives Which Continue." PraS (46:2) Sum 72, p. 149.

"The Spider Who Lives By Thinking." Poetry (120:3) Je 72, p. 153.

1628 KENYON, Jane
"Grandmother." MichQR (11:3) Sum 72, p. 175.

1629 KEOUGH, W. R.
"coliseum." MedR (2:2) Wint 72, p. 62.
"flowers." MedR (2:2) Wint 72, p. 62.
"the mole." MedR (2:2) Wint 72, p. 62.
"the quince." MedR (2:2) Wint 72, p. 62.

1630 KERN, Gary
"From sunset she appeared" (tr. of Alexander Blok). RusLT (4) Aut 72, p. 20.
"How burdensome to walk among the people" (tr. of Alexander Blok). RusLT (4) Aut 72, p. 19.
"I pass away this life of mine" (tr. of Alexander Blok). RusLT (4) Aut 72, p. 18.

1631 KERSH, Betty
"I Am the Wind." PoetL (67:2) Sum 72, p. 170.

1632 KESSLER, Jascha
"Lines on the Neck of a Crude Amphora which I Dug Up in a Field in Sicily." NYT 22 Jl 72, p. 26.
"Trophies with Canvas in Camp." Kayak (29) S 72, p. 42.

1633 KESSLER, Stephen
"April in Paris." WindO (10) Sum 72, p. 21.
"Drainage." Kayak (30) D 72, p. 29.
"Dusk in Bonny Doon." Kayak (30) D 72, p. 28.
"For Robinson Jeffers." Kayak (30) D 72, p. 31.
"I Was a Teenage Werewolf." WindO (10) Sum 72, p. 20.
"Making These Things." WindO (10) Sum 72, p. 20.
"A Shovel." Kayak (30) D 72, p. 30.

1634 KEVLES, Barbara
"splinters." UTR (1:4) 72, p. 24.
"Unwrapped." UTR (1:1) 72, p. 29.

1635 KEYS, Kerry Shawn
"Round the Tower." Epos (23:3) Spr 72, p. 24.

1636 KEYSER, Gustave
Three Haiku. WindO (10) Sum 72, p. 24.

1637 KGOSITSILE, Keorapetse
"Mirrors, Without Song." Madem (74:6) Ap 72, p. 124.

1638 KHAN, Abdul Majeed
"An Evening in Malnad." Meas (3) 72, p. 41.

1639 KHATTAR, Christopher
"Neither, and Both." HiramPoR (13) Fall-Wint 72, p. 18.

1640 KHERDIAN, David
"For Bill Wehner." Granite (2) Wint 71-72, p. 75.
"It Becomes This for Me." Granite (2) Wint 71-72, p. 76.
"My Mother and the Hummingbird." Apple (7) Aut 72, p. 31.
"A Poem for My Father." MinnR (3) Aut 72, p. 115.

1641 KHODASEVICH, Vladislav
"The Monkey and other poems" (tr. by Eugene M. Kayden). ColQ (20:4) Spr 72, p. 554.

1642 KHUDAINAZAROV, Berdynazar
"The Burning Steppe" (tr. by Matthew Kahan, w. Nan Braymer). NewWR (40:4) Aut 72, p. 13.

1643 KICKNOSWAY, Faye
"Our Gang: Ginger." ParisR (54) Sum 72, p. 136.
"Religious Poem 2: For Robert Bly." MassR (13:4) Aut 72, p. 702.

1644 KILBY, James A.
"Emily Revisiting." SouthernPR (12: Special Issue) 72, p. 50.

1645 KILDARE, D.
"I Could Not Love Thee, Dear, So Much." ColQ (21:1) Sum 72, p. 54.

1646 KILGORE, James
"War in Colorado." FreeL (15:1/2) 71-72, p. 4.
"Your Silence Is Not Clear." FreeL (15:1/2) 71-72, p. 3.

1647 KILINA, Patricia
"Skull of a Horse." SouthwR (57:1) Wint 72, p. 66.

1648 KILLIAN, Chris
"rain covers the icy earth." Folio (8:1) Spr 72, p. 12.

1649 KILLION, Chris
"Mullets." Folio (8:2) Fall 72, p. 17.

1650 KILTY, Sean
"Poem: This world." Spec (14:1/2) My 72, p. 54.

1651 KIMZEY, Ardis
"Between Some Lions..." SouthernPR (12: Special Issue) 72, p. 17.
"Overseen." SouthernPR (12: Special Issue) 72, p. 19.
"Themes on a Variation." SouthernPR (12: Special Issue)

72, p. 18.
"Wintersong." SouthernPR (12: Special Issue) 72, p. 18.

1652 KINCAID, Michael
"Frank Brainard." New:ACP (18) Ap 72, p. 16.
"letter." New:ACP (18) Ap 72, p. 15.

1653 KING, John
"It's Not Going to Stop Raining." PoetL (67:1) Spr 72, p. 16.

1654 KING, Julia Rankin
"The Shipjumpers." PoetC (7:1) 72, p. 18.

1655 KING, Kevin
"Daddy." HolCrit (9:2) Je 72, p. 10.

1656 KINGSTON, Roger P.
"Branches." BosUJ (20:1/2) 72, p. 41.

1657 KINNICK, B. Jo
"Wordsworth at the 'Permanent' Flower Mart--Daffodil Section." EngJ (61:9) D 72, p. 1387.

1658 KINOSHITA, Yuji
"Camping Grounds" (tr. by Robert Epp). PoetL (67:4) Wint 72, p. 351.
"Commuter" (tr. by Robert Epp). PoetL (67:4) Wint 72, p. 352.
"Harbor Festival" (tr. by Robert Epp). PoetL (67:4) Wint 72, p. 353.

1659 KISSICK, Gary
"We were carrying the soul home." Esq (77:4) Ap 72, p. 204.

1660 KIYOKAWA, Shoichi
"nu." NewYQ (11) Sum 72, p. 51.

1661 KLAPPERT, Peter
"The Trapper." Atl (230:6) D 72, p. 87.

1662 KLEIMAN, Charles S.
"Breakdown Lane." UTR (1:1) 72, p. 28.

1663 KLEIN, Elizabeth
"The Wedding Party." LittleM (6:2/3) Sum-Aut 72, p. 76.

1664 KLEIN, Kevin
"Following the Lone Star." Hudson (25:3) Aut 72, p. 449.
"Harlem: November, 1971." Hudson (25:3) Aut 72, p. 447.
"Just Now." Hudson (25:3) Aut 72, p. 450.

"Labor Poem." Hudson (25:3) Aut 72, p. 448.
"When Learning Is an Emergency." Hudson (25:3) Aut 72, p. 448.

1665 KLEIN, Norman
"Sea Dream." Epos (24:1) Fall 72, p. 18.

1666 KLIEWER, Warren
"Summer Stock Theatre: A Handbook." SoDakR (10:4) Wint 72-73, p. 8.
"Why I Should Have Stayed Home." KanQ (4:2) Spr 72, p. 14.

1667 KLIMKOWSKY, Brian
"A Harpsichord Concert." BelPoJ (22:3) Spr 72, p. 6.

1668 KLINE, George L.
"A blindly-flowing sob of Lethe" (tr. of Marina Tsvetaeva). RusLT (2) Wint 72, p. 219.
"Einem alter Architekten in Rom" (tr. of Joseph Brodsky). Antaeus (6) Sum 72, p. 109.
"Evening" (tr. of Joseph Brodsky). Antaeus (6) Spr 72, p. 106.
"Exhaustion now is a more frequent guest" (tr. of Joseph Brodsky). Sum 72, p. 105.
"In Villages God does not live only" (tr. of Joseph Brodsky). Antaeus (6) Sum 72, p. 102.
"The massed magnificence of trumpets" (tr. of Marina Tsvetaeva). RusLT (2) Wint 72, p. 218.
"Nature Morte" (tr. of Joseph Brodsky). SatR (55:33) 12 Ag 72, p. 45.
"The old gods are no longer bountiful" (tr. of Marina Tsvetaeva). RusLT (2) Wint 72, p. 219.
"On empty roads made resonant by winter" (tr. of Marina Tsvetaeva). RusLT (2) Wint 72, p. 217.
"Refusing to catalogue all of one's woes" (tr. of Joseph Brodsky). Antaeus (6) Sum 72, p. 107.
"Sonnet" (tr. of Joseph Brodsky). Antaeus (6) Sum 72, p. 100.
"A soul that knows no moderation" (tr. of Marina Tsvetaeva). RusLT (2) Wint 72, p. 218.
"Spring Season of Muddy Roads" (tr. of Joseph Brodsky). Antaeus (6) Sum 72, p. 103.
"You're coming home again" (tr. of Joseph Brodsky). Antaeus (6) Sum 72, p. 101.

1669 KLOEFKORN, William
Alvin Turner As Farmer. RoadAR (4:2) Sum 72. (Entire issue).
from Alvin Turner as Farmer: (15, 32). Peb (7) Aut 71.
from Alvin Turner as Farmer: (23, 31, 52, 55). PraS (46:2) Sum 72, p. 125.
"Alvin Turner Tells His Wife Goodnight." KanQ (4:1)

Wint 71-72, p. 84.
"The Chinking." PoetC (7:1) 72, p. 10.
from Important Phone Numbers: "786-3165." RoadAR (3:4) Wint 71-72, p. 4.
"The Loon at Night." KanQ (4:3) Sum 72, p. 12.
"Loony." SaltCR (5:1) Wint 72.
"Mrs. Wilma Hunt." SaltCR (5:1) Wint 72.
"Rhodes." SaltCR (5:1) Wint 72.
"Ruby." SaltCR (5:1) Wint 72.

1670 KNAPP, Robert S.
"Spring, on the Way to a Museum." SouthernPR (12:2) Spr 72, p. 42.

1671 KNEIPP, Janet R.
"On reading a student's journal." EngJ (61:6) S 72, p. 858.

1672 KNIGHT, Etheridge
"For Eric Dolphy." NewL (39:1) Aut 72, p. 80.
"feeling fucked/up." NewL (39:1) Aut 72, p. 78.
"My life, the quality of which." NewL (39:1) Aut 72, p. 78.
"No Moon Floods the Memory of That Night." NewL (39:1) Aut 72, p. 77.
"A Poem for Myself, or Blues for a Mississippi Black Boy." NewL (39:1) Aut 72, p. 79.

1673 KNIGHT, Susu
"The Card of False Possession." PoetL (67:3) Aut 72, p. 236.
"The Card of Judgement." PoetL (67:3) Aut 72, p. 237.
"The Card of Partial Loss." PoetL (67:3) Aut 72, p. 236.

1674 KNOEPFLE, John
"the camel." Qt (5:39/40) Sum-Aut 72, p. 38.

1675 KNOTT, Bill
"To Myself" (Carnival). Iowa (3:3) Sum 72, p. 9.
"To Myself: First, cover yourself completely with chameleons." Iowa (3:3) Sum 72, p. 7.
"To Myself: First I loved you." Iowa (3:3) Sum 72, p. 8.
"To Myself" (In September Held). Iowa (3:3) Sum 72, p. 4.
"To Myself: The way the world is not." Iowa (3:3) Sum 72, p. 6.
"To Myself: When we're always alone." Iowa (3:3) Sum 72, p. 6.
"To Myself: Your outer sigh of a body disrobes a snowflake." Iowa (3:3) Sum 72, p. 7.

1676 KOBYLECKY, Jim
"Love Poem IX" (childhood). HangL (18) Fall 72, p. 27.

"The Magician" (Bergman and Auro Lecci). HangL (18) Fall 72, p. 27.
"Remember Diane." HangL (18) Fall 72, p. 28.

1677 KOCH, Claude
"Out." FourQt (21:4) My 72, p. 67.
"Recoveries." FourQt (21:4) My 72, p. 68.
"Shop Talk." SewanR (80:2) Spr 72, p. 292.
"To My Mother Who Will Not Hear." SewanR (80:2) Spr 72, p. 293.
"The Unicorn." SewanR (80:2) Spr 72, p. 291.

1678 KOCH, Kenneth
"Alive for an Instant." NewYRB (19:9) 30 N 72, p. 10.
from The Art of Love: (1, 2). Poetry (121:2) N 72, p. 63.
"First Trip to China." NewYRB (18:5) 23 Mr 72, p. 33.
"Poem for My Twentieth Birthday." Poetry (121:1) O 72, p. 17.

1679 KO Ching-po
"Snow" (tr. of Mao Tse-Tung, w. Willis Barnstone). NewRep (167:12) 30 S 72, p. 30.

1680 KÖNIG, F. H.
"The Birds" (tr. of Halldis Moren Vesaas). NoAmR (257:1) Spr 72, p. 59.
"Bonjour Monsieur Gaugin" (tr. of Astrid Tollefsen). NoAmR (257:1) Spr 72, p. 60.
"Deep in the Day" (tr. of Gunvor Hofmo). NoAmR (257:1) Spr 72, p. 69.
"Fatum" (tr. of Astrid Tollefsen). NoAmR (257:1) Spr 72, p. 60.
"Gustav Vigeland's Woman and Reptile" (tr. of Astrid Hjertenaes). NoAmR (257:1) Spr 72, p. 61.
"If Now Tonight--" (tr. of Halldis Moren Vesaas). NoAmR (257:1) Spr 72, p. 58.
"In the Beginning" (tr. of Astrid Tollefsen). NoAmR (257:1) Spr 72, p. 60.
"The Last Words" (tr. of Gunvor Hofmo). NoAmR (257:1) Spr 72, p. 69.
"The Letter" (tr. of Astrid Tollefsen). NoAmR (257:1) Spr 72, p. 60.
"The Poet Recites His Own Poem" (tr. of Astrid Hjertenaes Andersen). NoAmR (257:1) Spr 72, p. 61.
Ten Poems (tr. of Marie Takvam). NoAmR (257:1) Spr 72, p. 62.
"The Tree" (tr. of Halldis Moren Vesaas). NoAmR (257:1) Spr 72, p. 58.
Twelve Poems (tr. of Kate Naess). NoAmR (257:1) Spr 72, p. 65.
"What Do You Know..." (tr. of Gunvor Hofmo). NoAmR (257:1) Spr 72, p. 69.

1681 KOEPPEL, Fredric
"Potato Sonnet." Epos (23:4) Sum 72, p. 13.
"Short Love Poem Using Fruits and Vegetables." BabyJ (5) N 72, p. 17.

1682 KOERTGE, Ronald
"The Affair." BelPoJ (22:3) Spr 72, p. 5.
"The Babymaker." BelPoJ (22:3) Spr 72, p. 3.
"I Never Touch My Penis." BelPoJ (22:3) Spr 72, p. 5.
"If Other Students." KanQ (4:1) Wint 71-72, p. 41.
"Moving Downstairs." WestHR (26:4) Aut 72, p. 329.
"Opening Day." WestHR (26:4) Aut 72, p. 327.
"The Pied Piper." KanQ (4:1) Wint 71-72, p. 41.

1683 KOETHE, John
"Tiny Figures in the Snow." Poetry (119:4) Ja 72, p. 187.

1684 KOHLER, Dorothea Bell
"Metathesis." Wind (2:6) Aut 72, p. 20.
"Pots." Zahir (1:4/5) 72, p. 63.

1685 KOLUMBAN, Nicholas
"Russian Song" (tr. of Johannes Bobrowski). Folio (8:1) Spr 72, p. 24.

1686 KOLYER, John
"Admiration." PoetL (67:3) Aut 72, p. 263.
"Adulterers." PoetL (67:3) Aut 72, p. 263.

1687 KOOSER, Ted
"Composing at Midnight." PraS (46:4) Wint 72-73, p. 322.
"Country-Western." PraS (46:4) Wint 72-73, p. 322.
"Dream." Meas (2) 72.
"Enough of a Poem for Home." Peb (7) Aut 71.
"Hangover." Meas (2) 72.
"A Memory." Drag (3:1) Spr 72, p. 19.
"The Towncliffe Attitude." SaltCR (5:1) Wint 72.

1688 KOPRINCE, Ralph
"October 19, 1837" (tr. of Wilhelm Küchelbeker). RusLT (3) Spr 72, p. 42.
"Three Meetings" (tr. of Vladimir Solovyov). RusLT (4) Aut 72, p. 21.
"Tsarskoe Selo" (tr. of Wilhelm Küchelbeker). RusLT (3) Spr 72, p. 41.

1689 KORAN, Dennis
"To George Hitchcock." Sky (1:1) 71.

1690 KOSTELANETZ, Richard
"Development." Confr (5) Wint-Spr 72, p. 56.
"Genesis." UnmOx (1:1) N 71, p. 51.

"Me." Confr (5) Wint-Spr 72, p. 37.

1691 KOTEN, Bernard
"Africa" (tr. of James Patterson). NewWR (40:1) Wint 72, p. 58.
"Bombs Against Art" (tr. of Yevgeny Yevtushenko). NewWR (40:1) Wint 72, p. 32.
"The Coming of the Flowers" (tr. of Uigun, w. Nan Braymer). NewWR (40:4) Aut 72, p. 133.
"Invitation to Kirghizstan" (tr. of Kurbanychbek Malikov, w. Nan Braymer). NewWR (40:4) Aut 72, p. 24.
"My Land" (tr. of Eduardo Miezelaitis, w. Nan Braymer). NewWR (40:4) Aut 72, p. 114.
"Song About Our Stones" (tr. of Silva Kaputikian, w. Nan Braymer). NewWR (40:4) Aut 72, p. 64.
from Winter Soldiers: "Introductory Remarks" (tr. of James Patterson). NewWR (40:1) Wint 72, p. 56.
from Winter Soldiers: "The Music of the Black Ghettos" (tr. of James Patterson). NewWR (40:1) Wint 72, p. 56.

1692 KOUSOULAS, Loukas
from Etudes: "If winter flings down snow unstintingly." (tr. by John Fludas and Stuart Silverman). AriD (1: 4/5) Sum-Aut 72, p. 78.

1693 KOVITZ, Alexander
"Basho/1686." ChiR (23:4 & 24:1) 72, p. 83.
"Doe Surprised at the Edge of the Wood." ChiR (23:4 & 24:1) 72, p. 80.
"(1910)." ChiR (23:4 & 24:1) 72, p. 80.
"Sudden Death to a Young Doe." ChiR (23:4 & 24:1) 72, p. 81.
"Yadwigha's Dream." ChiR (23:4 & 24:1) 72, p. 85.

1694 KOWINSKI, William
"Landscapes." AriD (1:3) Spr 72, p. 16.

1695 KRAMER, Aaron
"At Home." ModernPS (3:2) 72, p. 76.
"Combing." MedR (2:3) Spr 72, p. 90.
"Moving Away." NYT 25 Mr 72, p. 30.
"The New Home." FreeL (15:1/2) 71-72, p. 96.
"Quebec." ModernPS (3:2) 72, p. 74.
"When Our Children March." Epos (23:4) Sum 72, p. 6.

1696 KRAMER, Lawrence
"The Capitol of Washing Machines." KanQ (4:3) Sum 72, p. 47.
"The Junkman Dies." QRL (18:1/2) 72, p. 103.
"The Largemouth Black Bass." QRL (18:1/2) 72, p. 104.
"Raw Milk." QRL (18:1/2) 72, p. 100.
"The Rendering Works." QRL (18:1/2) 72, p. 101.

"Scout Knives." QRL (18:1/2) 72, p. 104.
"The Story of My Father and the Great Cave-In." QRL (18:1/2) 72, p. 102.

1697 KRAMER, Lotte
"Lake Galilee." NYT 10 Ap 72, p. 34.
"The Tablecloth." NYT 17 S 72, sec. 4, p. 10.
"Water." NYT 10 F 72, p. 42.

1698 KRAMPF, Thomas
"The Bodhi Tree." Phoenix (3:4) Aut 72, p. 109.
"The Day I Voted for Jesus (to my daughter, Gilda)." Phoenix (3:4) Aut 72, p. 106.
"Gowanus." Phoenix (3:4) Aut 72, p. 110.
"The Medal (to my daughter, Franny)." Phoenix (3:4) Aut 72, p. 104.
"The Sacrifice Flyball." Phoenix (3:4) Aut 72, p. 108.
"To My Daughter, Cecile." Phoenix (3:4) Aut 72, p. 105.

1699 KRAPF, Norbert
"Degree Candidate." EngJ (61:4) Ap 72, p. 594.
"For Bob Dylan." WestHR (26:3) Sum 72, p. 236.
"Minutes for the Meeting." EngJ (61:5) My 72, p. 722.
"Skinning a Rabbit." WestHR (26:3) Sum 72, p. 263.

1700 KRENIS, Linda
"I wanted to tell you about it later." NewYQ (9) Wint 72, p. 37.

1701 KRETZ, Thomas
"A Little Clutch." Folio (8:2) Fall 72, p. 25.
"Modalities." ChrC (89:6) 9 F 72, p. 166.
"Pablo Neruda, Reading." Qt (5:38) Spr 72, p. 12.
"Skiing? Not on Your Life." ChrC (89:4) 26 Ja 72, p. 89.
"So Don't Go Home with a Joe from Work." KanQ (4:1) Wint 71-72, p. 43.

1702 KRIESBERG, Hadea
"The Fall to Heaven a Long Way Up." PoetL (67:2) Sum 72, p. 123.

1703 KRITTER, Ronald
"On Listening to Brandenburg Concerto No. 5." Southern-HR (6:3) Sum 72, p. 244.

1704 KROHN, Herbert
"Trouble with an Angel." NewYQ (11) Sum 72, p. 55.

1705 KROHNEN, H. M.
"Hyperion's Song of Fate" (tr. of Friedrich Holderlin). Isthmus (1) Spr 72, p. 66.
"Poet's Courage" (tr. of Friedrich Holderlin). Isthmus

(1) Spr 72, p. 67.
"To the Fates" (tr. of Friedrich Holderlin). Isthmus (1) Spr 72, p. 65.

1706 KROLL, Ernest
"Appalachia." Cim (20) Jl 72, p. 52.
"Band Organ." WestHR (26:4) Aut 72, p. 368.
"Delaware Valley: Chinese Landscape." ChiTM 27 F 72, p. 12.
"Fall-out." Qt (5:38) Spr 72, p. 22.
"Logorrhea." WestR (9:1) Spr 72, p. 35.
"The Loosened Spirit." PoetC (7:1) 72, p. 16.
"Poet Reading Outdoors (Dunbarton College)." NYT 8 Je 72, p. 46.
"Politician." SouthwR (57:3) Sum 72, p. 189.
"The Sexton's Tale." NYT 22 Je 72, p. 38.
"Words for a Wreath to Be Tossed on the Water." ArizQ (28:1) Spr 72, p. 82.

1707 KROLL, Judith
"India 1969." AntR (31:4) Wint 71-72, p. 494.
"The Penn Central Makes Some Connections." FourQt (21:4) My 72, p. 53.
"A Tree Grows In Israel." AntR (32:1/2) Spr-Sum 72, p. 30.
"Trees." AntR (32:1/2) Spr-Sum 72, p. 58.

1708 KROLOW, Karl
"Deutscher Sommer 1971." Field (6) Spr 72, p. 80.

1709 KROUSE, Charles
"Changing Trains." WindO (9) Spr 72, p. 21.

1710 KROUSE, Ned
"Window Reflection." WindO (10) Sum 72, p. 26.

1711 KRUCHKOW, Diane
"the only one who saw." NewYQ (12) Aut 72, p. 76.

1712 KRUSOE, James
"This is a poem for..." BeyB (2:2) 72, p. 69.
"to the old lady dying in Shanahan's Market, Venice, Calif." BeyB (2:2) 72, p. 72.

1713 KRYLOV, Ivan
"Sixteen fables" (tr. by Eugene M. Kayden). ColQ (21:2) Aut 72, p. 227.

1714 KRYN, Randall
"Life, It Is Green." ChiTM 9 Jl 72, p. 4.

1715 KUAN Han-ch'ing
"Autumn" (tr. by Jerome P. Seaton). Madem (75:6) O 72, p. 136.

1716 KUBACH, David
"P.S. Perhaps I'd better define the term frazil ice, used." Peb (9) Wint 72.
"The Shortest Day of the Year." Epoch (22:1) Fall 72, p. 85.

1717 KU Chih
"Li, on His Way to Chang Chou" (tr. by David Gordon). Literature (15:3) 72, p. 485.

1718 KUCHELBEKER, Wilhelm
"October 19, 1837" (tr. by Ralph Koprince). RusLT (3) Spr 72, p. 42.
"Tsarskoe Selo" (tr. by Ralph Koprince). RusLT (3) Spr 72, p. 41.

1719 KUENSTLER, Frank
"After Montale." Nat (215:8) 25 S 72, p. 250.
"Sophocles (Simmias)." HangL (16) Wint 71-72, p. 33.

1720 KUFA, L. D. M.
"The Beating of the Drums." JnlOBP (2:16) Sum 72, p. 75.

1721 KUGEL, James
"My Life With Eve." Harp (245:1468) S 72, p. 44.

1722 KULIK, William
"Time of the Dungeons" (tr. of Robert Desnos, w. Carole Frankel). Madem (76:2) D 72, p. 104.

1723 KUMAR, Shiv K.
"To a Young Wife." WestHR (26:1) Wint 72, p. 58.

1724 KUMIN, Maxine
"The Bad Trip." AmerR (14) 72, p. 179.
"Beans." Antaeus (5) Spr 72, p. 45.
"Creatures." SatR (55:13) 25 Mr 72, p. 14.
"Cross-Country by County Map." SatR (55:13) 25 Mr 72, p. 15.
"The Dreamer, the Dream." Atl (230:1) Jl 72, p. 61.
"Five Small Deaths in May." BerksR (8:1) Spr 72, p. 23.
"Heaven as Anus." Poetry (120:6) S 72, p. 340.
"The Hermit Wakes to Bird Sounds." NewYorker (48:10) 29 Ap 72, p. 46.
"The Hero." Antaeus (5) Spr 72, p. 43.
"The Horsewoman." MassR (13:1/2) Wint-Spr 72, p. 145.
"Life's Work." MassR (13:1/2) Wint-Spr 72, p. 144.
"Mud." SatR (55:13) 25 Mr 72, p. 14.
"Stones." SatR (55:13) 25 Mr 72, p. 15.
"Turning To." Antaeus (5) Spr 72, p. 41.
"Young Nun at Bread Loaf." Antaeus (5) Spr 72, p. 44.

1725 KUNDIG, Mark
"The Last Migration (after Ts'uei T'u)." NewYQ (12) Aut 72, p. 61.

1726 KUNITZ, Stanley
"How Can You Look at the Neva" (tr. of Anna Akhmatova, w. Max Hayward). Antaeus (6) Sum 72, p. 115.
"I Am Not One of Those Who Left the Land" (tr. of Anna Akhmatova, w. Max Hayward). Antaeus (6) Sum 72, p. 116.
"Pushkin" (tr. of Anna Akhmatova, w. Max Hayward). Antaeus (6) Sum 72, p. 114.
"The Return to the Summer Palace" (tr. of Anna Akhmatova). AriD (1:2) Wint 72, p. 24.
"This Cruel Age Has Deflected Me" (tr. of Anna Akhmatova, w. Max Hayward). Antaeus (6) Sum 72, p. 117.
"Voronezh" (tr. of Anna Akhmatova). AriD (1:2) Wint 72, p. 23.
"When in the Throes of Suicide" (tr. of Anna Akhmatova). AriD (1:2) Wint 72, p. 22.

1727 KUNTZ, R.
"Train Depot at Friant, Calif." Drag (3:1) Spr 72, p. 32.

1728 KUO, Alexander
"Al Sampson Announces a Deer Famine In Northern Wisconsin During a Late Winter Night's Sports Telecast Prepared Especially for Channel 2, WBAY-TV Green Bay." Iron (2) Fall 72, p. 42.

1729 KUPER, Jenny
"you come without music." Isthmus (1) Spr 72, p. 81.

1730 KUPFERBERG, Tuli
"'I Am the Ruler of the CIA.'" VilV 18 My 72, p. 76.
"In Praise of Puerto Ricans." Magazine (5) part 8, 72, p. 29.

1731 KUSCH, Robert
"Islands." Epoch (21:2) Wint 71, p. 164.
"Leaves (November)." Epoch (21:2) Wint 71, p. 165.

1732 KUTZIN, Alice
"Secret Weapon." Cosmo (172:1) Ja 72, p. 70.
"Thoughts in an April Snowstorm." PraS (46:1) Spr 72, p. 61.

1733 KUUMBA
"To Believe." JnlOBP (2:16) Sum 72, p. 43.
"To Black Woman--with love." JnlOBP (2:16) Wint 72, p. 43.

1734 KUZMA, Greg
"After a Day of First Classes" (for David P. Young, whose poem is "August at the Lake"). Cim (21) O 72, p. 11.
"The Age of Carpets." Poetry (120:2) My 72, p. 87.
"Autumn." Works (3:3/4) Wint 72-73, p. 132.
"Beasts." KanQ (4:3) Sum 72, p. 42.
"Borrowing." Meas (2) 72.
"Bunches." Cim (18) Ja 72, p. 61.
"The Children on This Street." SaltCR (5:1) Wint 72.
"The Circus." Sky (1:1) 71.
"The Dancing Bear." SouthernR (8:2) Spr 72, p. 422.
"Dream of the Monday Man." Meas (2) 72.
"The Face." Poetry (120:2) My 72, p. 88.
"Family." Meas (2) 72.
"A Father's Words." Works (3:3/4) Wint 72-73, p. 133.
"For My Wife." Apple (7) Aut 72, p. 11.
"For Now." PraS (46:1) Spr 72, p. 50.
from The Hall of Inventors: (1-17). LittleM (6:2/3) Sum-Aut 72, p. 112.
"House." Poetry (120:2) My 72, p. 87.
"Jeff." Epoch (21:2) Wint 71, p. 146.
"Let There Be an End to Excuses." Sky (1:2) 72, p. 17.
"Loose Ends." OhioR (14:1) Aut 72, p. 39.
"The Mad House." Works (3:3/4) Wint 72-73, p. 133.
"My Brother, Unemployed in His Eighteenth Year." PoetryNW (13:2) Sum 72, p. 45.
"My Father, Divorced." Shen (23:2) Wint 72, p. 38.
"My Life." Iron (1) Spr 72, p. 11.
"Neglect." PraS (46:1) Spr 72, p. 45.
"The New Self." Drag (3:1) Spr 72, p. 42.
"Old Age." Qt (5:37) Wint 72, p. 23.
"The Old People." Cim (21) O 72, p. 10.
"Peace, So That." Poetry (120:6) S 72, p. 329.
"The Petition." Iowa (3:1) Wint 72, p. 10.
"The Phone Call." PoetryNW (13:2) Sum 72, p. 47.
"Poem: I know what you are thinking you." NoAmR (257:3) Aut 72, p. 82.
"Poem from Watching My Son's Hands." PoetryNW (13:2) Sum 72, p. 44.
"The Poor Kids." Drag (3:1) Spr 72, p. 40.
"The Process." Poetry (120:2) My 72, p. 86.
"The Produce Man." OhioR (13:2) Wint 72, p. 53.
"Shoes." PoetryNW (13:2) Sum 72, p. 45.
"Sometimes." Shen (24:1) Aut 72, p. 65.
"Sorrow." Qt (5:39/40) Sum-Aut 72, p. 31.
"Staying Put." Drag (3:1) Spr 72, p. 41.
Ten Poems. PraS (46:4) Wint 72-73, p. 283.
"Today." Iowa (3:1) Wint 72, p. 16.
"Tonight." SaltCR (5:1) Wint 72.
"The Tree." Cim (19) Ap 72, p. 18.
"We." Qt (5:37) Wint 72, p. 23.
"We Are Awakened in the Middle of the Night." Iowa (3:1) Wint 72, p. 10.

"What We Need." OhioR (14:1) Aut 72, p. 39.
"The Wound as Woodsman." SenR (3:1) My 72, p. 7.
"The Zoo." PoetryNW (13:2) Sum 72, p. 46.

1735 KWINT, Kenn
"The Falling Out." Cord (1:4) 72, p. 17.
"The Mad Bomber Is a Poet." Zahir (1:4/5) 72, p. 11.
"Mad-Lux Dolly." Cord (1:4) 72, p. 16.
"More game than." Cord (1:4) 72, p. 16.
"Voices & Hands." WindO (10) Sum 72, p. 27.

1736 KYGER, Joanne
"August 1966." Magazine (5) part 8, 72, p. 30.

1737 KYLE, Jerrie Flesland
"The Solo." BallSUF (13:3) Sum 72, p. 11.

1738 LAATZ, Lenore Ballard
"Anderson the Farmer." ChiTM 23 Ap 72, p. 12.

1739 LaBELLE, Christine
"As a voice." Works (3:3/4) Wint 72-73, p. 94.

1740 LaBOMBARD, Joan
"Sanji's Country." PraS (46:1) Spr 72, p. 46.
"Where Have the Sounds Gone?" ChiTM 18 Je 72, p. 5.

1741 LACHTMAN, Howard
"Fat City." PoetL (67:4) Wint 72, p. 344.
"News from Thermopylae." PoetL (67:4) Wint 72, p. 345.
"The River Merchant to His Wife: A Letter." PoetL (67:4) Wint 72, p. 344.

1742 LACY, Esther
"Repairs to an Airfield Outside Paris." WindO (12) Wint 72-73, p. 4.

1743 LACY, T. R.
"Survey." EngJ (61:8) N 72, p. 1238.

1744 LAGERKVIST, Par
"In the silent river of evening" (tr. by W. H. Auden and Leif Sjöberg). Shen (23:4) Sum 72, p. 76.
"Poem: Everywhere, in all the heavens you will find his footprints" (tr. by W. H. Auden and Leif Sjöberg). WestHR (26:4) Aut 72, p. 350.

1745 LAGOMARSINO, E.
"Composition Eleven." BeyB (2:2) 72, p. 47.

1746 LAINE, William G.
"Coming Out." PoetL (67:2) Sum 72, p. 132.
"December Song." PoetL (67:2) Sum 72, p. 141.

"Trout Lake Prelude." PoetL (67:4) Wint 72, p. 346.

1747 LAING, Alexander
"Candace." CarlMis (12:2) Spr-Sum 72, p. 72.

1748 LAIRD, Antonia B.
"Sore Throat." LadHJ (89:3) Mr 72, p. 141.

1749 LAKIN, R. D.
"Doug." NewRena (6) My 72, p. 28.

1750 LALLY, Michael
"The Buffalo Zoo." GreenR (2:2) 72, p. 12.
"Crazy Curtis & Me." New:ACP (18) Ap 72, p. 13.
"Out In the hall." GreenR (2:2) 72, p. 10.
"Poetry of the Seventies." GreenR (2:2) 72, p. 11.
"Ten Questions to Ask a New Friend by Paul Johnson (age 14)." GreenR (2:2) 72, p. 11.
"We Were Always Afraid of." GreenR (2:2) 72, p. 11.

1751 LAMANTIA, Philip
"Oraibi." Antaeus (6) Sum 72, p. 24.

1752 LAMAR, Paul
"Al's Cow." NYT 27 My 72, p. 28.

1753 LAMB, Helen Keithley
"Allhallows Eve." KanQ (4:3) Sum 72, p. 43.
"The Boys Tramp One behind the Other." KanQ (4:1) Wint 71-72, p. 111.

1754 LANDESS, Thomas H.
"At the Marsalis Park Zoo." SewanR (80:4) Aut 72, p. 614.
"The Day After the Funeral." SewanR (80:4) Aut 72, p. 611.
"Woman Across the Road." SewanR (80:4) Aut 72, p. 612.

1755 LANE, Carmella
"Inertia." MinnR (3) Aut 72, p. 76.
"The Orphan Makes Out." MinnR (3) Aut 72, p. 77.
"This Is a Linear Equation." MinnR (3) Aut 72, p. 76.

1756 LANE, Joy
"Beside a Lion's Grave." SouthwR (57:3) Sum 72, p. 224.

1757 LANE, Mervin
"The Army." SouthernPR (12:2) Spr 72, p. 31.

1758 LANGFORD, Gary R.
"The Warning." Focus (8:56) 72, p. 35.

1759 LANGTON, Daniel J.
"The Fiji Military Band." MinnR (2) Spr 72, p. 99.
"Fresh Air." AmerS (41:1) Wint 71-72, p. 94.
"Inside the Enormous Clockshop." Drag (3:1) Spr 72, p. 58.
"Linda." Drag (3:1) Spr 72, p. 57.
"Reflections: 721." Drag (3:1) Spr 72, p. 58.
"Villanelle." Cim (19) Ap 72, p. 61.

1760 LANN, Richard W.
"'As Flies To ...': Attica." Nat (214:23) 5 Je 72, p. 730.
"Prime Time." Nat (214:25) 19 Je 72, p. 796.

1761 LANTZ, Henry
"Reflections ..." WindO (11) Aut 72, p. 10.
"Work." WindO (11) Aut 72, p. 10.

1762 LAPIDUS, Jacqueline
"Wrong Number." HangL (18) Fall 72, p. 29.

1763 LAPPIN, Linda
"The Murderer's Reflection." Kayak (30) D 72, p. 4.
"Wintering with the Abominable Snowman." Kayak (30) D 72, p. 3.

1764 LaPOINTE, Gatien
"From Earth to the First Branch (for Raymond Jore)" (tr. by A. Poulin, Jr.). Kayak (28) 72, p. 38.

1765 LARA, Omar
"Bad Words for Violeta Parra" (tr. by Edward Oliphant). RoadAR (4:1) Spr 72, p. 27.
"Carpenterings" (tr. by Edward Oliphant). RoadAR (4:1) Spr 72, p. 29.
"Landscape" (tr. by Edward Oliphant). RoadAR (4:1) Spr 72, p. 27.
"Upward" (tr. by Edward Oliphant). RoadAR (4:1) Spr 72, p. 30.
"Without Pretending" (tr. by Edward Oliphant). RoadAR (4:1) Spr 72, p. 31.

1766 LARCOMB, Lee
"The Crazy Lieutenant Talking in Circles." BabyJ (5) N 72, p. 18.

1767 LARDAS, Konstantinos
"Ah! Child." TexQ (15:4) Wint 72, p. 83.
"Angels." TexQ (15:4) Wint 72, p. 84.
"Findings." NYT 28 Ja 72, p. 44.
"Husband." TexQ (15:4) Wint 72, p. 83.
"Wife." TexQ (15:4) Wint 72, p. 83.
"Wife (II)." TexQ (15:4) Wint 72, p. 84.

1768 LARKIN, Joan
"Marizibill" (tr. of Guillaume Apollinaire). SouthernPR (13:1) Aut 72, p. 42.

1769 LARSEN, Carl
"The Color Set." WindO (11) Aut 72, p. 43.
"Red Cross." WormR (47) 72, p. 78.
"Third Rail." WormR (47) 72, p. 79.

1770 LARSEN, R. B. V.
"Arizona Highways." Poem (15) Jl 72, p. 62.
"At Thirty." Poem (15) Jl 72, p. 64.
"My Great Uncle." Poem (15) Jl 72, p. 63.

1771 LARSON, Sheila
"Sometimes." EngJ (61:8) N 72, p. 1247.

1772 LASH, Kenneth
"Hush, Hush." NoAmR (257:2) Sum 72, p. 40.

1773 LASKER-SCHUELER, Else
"Atonement" (tr. by Janine Canan). Isthmus (1) Spr 72, p. 72.
"Departure" (tr. by Reinhold Johannes Kaebitzsch). UTR (1:4) 72, p. 4.
from Hebrew Ballads: "Abel." CalQ (2) Sum 72, p. 60.
from Hebrew Ballads: "Esther." CalQ (2) Sum 72, p. 60.
from Hebrew Ballads: "Moses und Josua." CalQ (2) Sum 72, p. 62.
"Jacob" (tr. by Janine Canan). Isthmus (1) Spr 72, p. 70.
"Pharoh and Joseph" (tr. by Janine Canan). Isthmus (1) Spr 72, p. 69.
"Saul" (tr. by Janine Canan). Isthmus (1) Spr 72, p. 71.

1774 LASSETER, Rollin A., III
"The Krater." SouthernPR (12: Special Issue) 72, p. 41.
"The Permanence of Space" (For St. Joseph of Copertino, Valediction). SewanR (80:4) Aut 72, p. 616.

1775 LATIMER, Dan
"To a Man in the Tramway" (tr. of Hans Magnus Enzensberger). MichQR (11:4) Aut 72, p. 277.

1776 LATTA, Richard
Four Concrete Poems. Peb (9) Wint 72.
"some are just more." St. AR (2:1) Aut-Wint 72, p. 33.
"vase so smooth." BabyJ (5) N 72, p. 23.
"wind kisses my face." BabyJ (5) N 72, p. 23.

1777 LATTA, Ruth
"Fresh rime glistens." WindO (10) Sum 72, p. 43.

1778 LATTIZORI, Debbie
"Parting." EngJ (61:9) D 72, p. 1333.

1779 LATTUADA, Alberto
from Gli Ucceli Indomitabili: "Scherzo" (tr. by Brian Swann and Ruth Feldman). MedR (2:4) Sum 72, p. 100.

1780 LAU, Alan
"Gas Pump Purity." Pan (9) 72, p. 59.

1781 LAUER, Mirko
"Chan Chan" (tr. by David Tipton). Stand (13:3) 72, p. 58.
"Economic Conspiracy" (tr. by David Tipton). Stand (13:4) 72, p. 56.
"J. H. [Javier Heraud]" (tr. by David Tipton). Stand (14:1) 72, p. 32.
"Leit-Motif: Oh Great City of Lima" (tr. by David Tipton). Stand (13:3) 72, p. 56.
"Lynx" (tr. by David Tipton). Stand (14:1) 72, p. 34.
"The Muse Dictates a Sonorous Rhyme: Reported Needed Full-Board Provided" (tr. by David Tipton). Stand (13:3) 72, p. 54.
"Notes on the Moving of a Corpse" (tr. by David Tipton). Stand (13:3) 72, p. 55.
"XVI" (tr. by David Tipton). Stand (14:1) 72, p. 33.

1782 LAUFMAN, Dudley
"Bee Hunt." HangL (16) Wint 71-72, p. 34.
"It's Sunday Again." HangL (16) Wint 71-72, p. 34.
"Notes from a Garden Book." Northeast Sum 72, p. 32.

1783 LAVIN, S. R.
"Harpo Marx & The Last Days of the Warsaw Ghetto." HiramPoR (12) Spr-Sum 72, p. 21.

1784 LAWDER, Donald
"With Amy, Listening to the Forest." BelPoJ (22:3) Spr 72, p. 30.

1785 LAWDER, Douglas
"Heat" (tr. of Sergio Mondragón, w. Katherine Grimes). Drag (3:2) Sum 72, p. 45.
"Inhabited Clarity" (tr. of Oscar Oliva, w. Katherine Grimes). Drag (3:2) Sum 72, p. 44.
"On the Outside You Are Sleeping and On the Inside You Dream" (tr. of Homero Aridjis, w. Katherine Grimes). Drag (3:2) Sum 72, p. 47.
"Sometimes One Touches a Body" (tr. of Homero Aridjis, w. Katherine Grimes). Drag (3:2) Sum 72, p. 48.

1786 LAWRENCE, D. H.
"Birthday." Poetry (121:1) O 72, p. 18.

1787 LAWSON, Paul
"The Knife: An Inscription." Kayak (29) S 72, p. 29.
"System." Kayak (29) S 72, p. 30.
"The Victory." Kayak (29) S 72, p. 28.

1788 LAX, Robert
"Three Chinese Fables: The Dancing Stork, The Rabbit Tree, The Phoenix." MidwQ (13:4) Sum 72, p. 452.

1789 LAYCOCK, Don
"Folk Songs from Papua" (edited by Ulli Beier). UnicornJ (4) 72, p. 85.

1790 LAYTON, Irving
"Magic." UnmOx (1:2) F 72, p. 56.
"Memo to a Suicide." UnmOx (1:4) Aut 72.
"No Exit." UnmOx (1:3) Sum 72, p. 53.

1791 LAZARCHUK, Michael-Sean
"Johnny." ParisR (53) Wint 72, p. 174.
"Johnny 2." ParisR (53) Wint 72, p. 175.

1792 LAZARD, Naomi
"Winter Visit with an Old Friend." NewYorker (47:49) 22 Ja 72, p. 84.

1793 LAZARUS, A. L.
"Song: Rose Pense." Qt (5:39/40) Sum-Aut 72, p. 19.

1794 LEARD, Lonnie
"Game's End." FreeL (15:1/2) 71-72, p. 13.
"Letter from Jesus to His Daddy." FreeL (15:1/2) 71-72, p. 11.
"Man Marks the Earth with Ruin." FreeL (15:1/2) 71-72, p. 9.

1795 LEAVENWORTH, Coman
"The Swimmers." NYT 28 Ap 72, p. 40.

1796 LECHLITNER, Ruth
"Burning Pruned Orchard Boughs." ChiTM 9 Ap 72, p. 12.
"Flight 329: San Francisco-New York." Nat (215:17) 27 N 72, p. 540.
"Persimmon." LitR (16:1) Aut 72, p. 103.
"Told After Breakfast." CarlMis (12:1) Fall-Wint 71-72, p. 108.

1797 LEDBETTER, Jack Tracy
"Chapel Hill" (for Randall Jarrell). BallSUF (13:3) Sum 72, p. 79.
"Lambing Season." BallSUF (13:2) Spr 72, p. 2.
"Maine Coast." BallSUF (13:4) Aut 72, p. 7.

"Night Camp." PoetL (67:2) Sum 72, p. 153.
"Poem: Written for a boy killed just before summer vacation." BallSUF (13:2) Spr 72, p. 38.
"Spider Web." BallSUF (13:1) Spr 72, p. 16.
"Wind River Indian Reservation, Wyoming." Cim (18) Ja 72, p. 27.
"Winter Marsh." PoetL (67:2) Sum 72, p. 153.
"Winter Visitor." PoetL (67:2) Sum 72, p. 154.

1798 LEE, Al
"Miss America Meets Futureman; or The Rape of the Century." Iowa (3:2) Spr 72, p. 12.
"The 250 Years' War." Iowa (3:2) Spr 72, p. 12.

1799 LEE, Lance
"I have seen you strut on the beach." PoetL (67:1) Spr 72, p. 14.

1800 LEFCOWITZ, Barbara F.
"Leaftaking." WindO (9) Spr 72, p. 9.
"Spots of Time." WindO (11) Aut 72, p. 6.

1801 LEGLER, Philip
"Acceptance." QRL (18:1/2) 72, p. 106.
"Cessation of Hostilities: October 15." QRL (18:1/2) 72, p. 107.
"From One Who Has Lost His Balance." QRL (18:1/2) 72, p. 108.
"Play It Again, Sam." Shen (23:2) Wint 72, p. 54.
"Song." QRL (18:1/2) 72, p. 109.
"Winter Warmth." ChrC (89:7) 16 F 72, p. 186.

1802 LEHMAN, David
from Good-Bye Instructions: "1-4 (for Edward W. Said)." Poetry (119:4) Ja 72, p. 197.
"New Year's Day." Poetry (119:4) Ja 72, p. 195.

1803 LEIBY, G. Sterling
"The Bird." SatEP (244:3) Aut 72, p. 88.
"Surprise Package." SatEP (244:3) Aut 72, p. 89.

1804 LEICHLITER, Jo Ann
"Omaha Harbor (aboard the museum ship U.S.S. Hazard)." NYT 4 Jl 72, p. 16.

1805 LEICHNER, Peter
"Unpublished Poem of Albert Einstein." Mark (16:2) Sum 72, p. 20.

1806 LEIGHTON, Lauren
"Dance" (tr. of Denis Davydov). RusLT (3) Spr 72, p. 57.
"To a Pious Charmer" (tr. of Denis Davydov). RusLT

(3) Spr 72, p. 53.
"Song of an Old Hussar" (tr. of Denis Davydov). RusLT (3) Spr 72, p. 55.
"Those Evening Bells" (tr. of Denis Davydov). RusLT (3) Spr 72, p. 56.

1807 LEIPER, Esther M.
"Anne at Midnight" (for Anne Sexton). Zahir (1:4/5) 72, p. 57.
"Fat Alice." Magazine (5) part 8, 72, p. 32.
"The Fox By Hunger." Magazine (5) part 8, 72, p. 34.
"How We Realize." Zahir (1:4/5) 72, p. 57.
"Quarrel in Richmond/Spring 1971." Shen (23:2) Wint 72, p. 34.
"Snow-Watch." Magazine (5) part 8, 72, p. 33.

1808 LEISER, Wayne
"The Bombs Bursting in Air." ChrC (89:39) 1 N 72, p. 1101.
"My Home Is the Sea and Its Marvels." ChrC (89:6) 9 F 72, p. 168.
"On the Morning News, May 3rd." ChrC (89:24) 14 Je 72, p. 683.
"The Spacious Toast to Chou En-Lai." ChrC (89:12) 22 Mr 72, p. 330.

1809 LEIVICK, H.
"Caught" (tr. by Leonard Opalov). PoetL (67:1) Spr 72, p. 33.

1810 LEMASTER, J. R.
"Last Fling of Glory." BallSUF (13:1) Wint 72, p. 80.

1811 LENNON, Florence Becker
"Poetry Festival." LitR (16:1) Aut 72, p. 4.

1812 LENOWITZ, Harris
"El and Anat: The Mourning of Baal" (tr. of Ugaritic tablets). Literature (15:3) 72, p. 492.

1813 LENSON, David R.
"Envoi." Pan (9) 72, p. 32.
"The Grand Quartercentury Tripartite Testamentum." QRL (18:1/2) 72, p. 110.
"The Jade Cameroons." Pan (9) 72, p. 34.
"On Reading the Book of Job." Pan (9) 72, p. 35.
"Seductions." Pan (9) 72, p. 33.
"When the Sun Has Died." QRL (18:1/2) 72, p. 112.

1814 LERMONTOV, Mikhail
"The Dream" (tr. by Walter Arndt). RusLT (3) Spr 72, p. 58.
"Thanksgiving" (tr. by Walter Arndt). RusLT (3) Spr 72,

p. 60.
"We parted--your medallion, though" (tr. by Walter Arndt). RusLT (3) Spr 72, p. 60.
"When I Hear Your Voice" (tr. by Leonard Opalov). PoetL (67:1) Spr 72, p. 32.
"Wherefore" (tr. by Walter Arndt). RusLT (3) Spr 72, p. 60.

1815 LERNER, Arthur
"Inner Journey." Etc. (29:3) S 72, p. 273.

1816 LERNER, Harriet
"The Love Marriage." Aphra (3:4) Fall 72, p. 7.

1817 LESAGE, Paul
"Impressions of Me By My Students/Section 3 8-9 MWF Oct 30, 1970 ISU." Drag (3:1) Spr 72, p. 70.

1818 LESSER, Rika
"Abgesang." YaleLit (141:2) 71, p. 22.
"Elegy for John Curran." YaleLit (141:2) 71, p. 22.
"A Little Myth." YaleLit (141:2) 71, p. 22.
"A Vision." YaleLit (141:2) 71, p. 23.

1819 LESSER, Simon O.
"The Disconnected Telephone." ColEng (33:5) F 72, p. 583.
"The Summer Place." ColEng (33:5) F 72, p. 583.

1820 LESSING, G. E.
"Story of the Old Wolf" (tr. by Michael Hamburger). QRL (18:1/2) 72, p. 115.
"Tiresias" (tr. by Michael Hamburger). QRL (18:1/2) 72, p. 118.
"Zeus and the Horse" (tr. by Michael Hamburger). QRL (18:1/2) 72, p. 114.

1821 LEV, Donald
"Death and Taxes." VilV 30 Mr 72, p. 80.
"The Election." VilV 7 S 72, p. 11.
"Sardine." NewYQ (11) Sum 72, p. 76.

1822 LEVERTOV, Denise
"The Distance." Poetry (120:6) S 72, p. 346.
"February Evening in Boston, 1971." Madrona (1:2) N 71, p. 33.
"The Freeing of the Dust." Field (7) Fall 72, p. 6.
"Obstinate Faith." Nat (215:8) 25 S 72, p. 246.
"A Place of Kindness." Madrona (1:4) S 72, p. 60.
"Scenario." Madrona (1:1) Je 71, p. 25.
"The Woman." Field (7) Fall 72, p. 5.

1823 LEVIN, Arthur
"Leaflets." NewYQ (9) Wint 72, p. 73.

1824 LEVIN, Ruth
"Naked I Go." Wind (2:5) Sum 72, p. 40.
"Untitled: I caught the skillful knife he threw." Wind (2:6) Aut 72, p. 10.

1825 LEVINE, Al
"An Alphabet." NewYorker (48:16) 10 Je 72, p. 33.
"The Bottle." NewYorker (48:11) 6 My 72, p. 36.
"Greeks in Persia." AmerR (15) 72, p. 191.
"The Last Thing." ColumF (1:4) Fall 72, p. 39.
"There Were Certain Kids..." LittleM (6:1) Spr 72, p. 34.
"Your Story." AmerR (15) 72, p. 190.

1826 LEVINE, Philip
"Death Bearing." Poetry (121:2) N 72, p. 84.
"First Love, 1945." Kayak (30) D 72, p. 21.
"Going Home." NewYorker (48:13) 20 My 72, p. 95.
"Grandmother In Heaven." Iron (2) Fall 72, p. 5.
"The Grave of the Kitchen Mouse." Kayak (28) 72, p. 55.
"I've Been Asleep." Poetry (121:2) N 72, p. 85.
"Join Hands." Spec (14:1/2) My 72, p. 60.
"Late Moon." Hudson (25:4) Wint 72-73, p. 593.
"Losing You." Poetry (121:2) N 72, p. 86.
"Nitrate." NoAmR (257:2) Sum 72, p. 39.
"No One Knows the Yellow Grass." OhioR (14:1) Aut 72, p. 40.
"Ruth." NewYorker (48:17) 17 Je 72, p. 93.
"This War." Poetry (120:6) S 72, p. 324.
"War." Hudson (25:4) Wint 72-73, p. 594.

1827 LEVINSON, Fred
"the composure of mr toshiro mifune." Antaeus (5) Spr 72, p. 86.
"Karin, her problems at home." Antaeus (5) Spr 72, p. 84.
"the last sunday of the year." Antaeus (7) Aut 72, p. 99.
"mahogany bust of pliny." Antaeus (7) Aut 72, p. 101.
"richard speck don't go away mad." Antaeus (5) Spr 72, p. 87.
"sharks in shallow water." Antaeus (5) Spr 72, p. 88.
"train to the country." Antaeus (5) Spr 72, p. 85.

1828 LEVIS, Larry
"Hunger." Peb (7) Aut 71.
"L.A., Loiterings." Iowa (3:1) Wint 72, p. 13.
"The Secret." Iowa (3:1) Wint 72, p. 14.

1829 LEVY, John
"Auschwitz." Madrona (1:1) Je 71, p. 26.

"A Road Map." Madrona (1:3) My 72, p. 17.

1830 LEWIS, Harry
"Miles Standish in Heaven (for Cathy Standish)." Lilla (12) Wint 73, p. 52.

1831 LEWIS, James Franklin
"The Search." ArizQ (28:2) Sum 72, p. 150.

1832 LEWIS, Steven
"almost december." RoadAR (3:4) Wint 71-72, p. 14.

1833 LEWIS, Tom J.
"In memorial Landscape" (tr. of Octavio Paz). Books (46:4) Aut 72, p. 547.

1834 LEWIS, Virginia Parker
"Beach Walking in Winter." NYT 12 F 72, p. 28.

1835 LEWISOHN, James
"Letter to John Logan." NewYQ (11) Sum 72, p. 73.
"Poem for Roslyn." NewYQ (11) Sum 72, p. 74.
"Poet" (for Joel Polisner). Shen (23:4) Sum 72, p. 67.
"Reform School." NewYQ (10) Spr 72, p. 36.

1836 LIBBEY, Elizabeth
"The Peninsula Is Open Twenty-Four Hours a Day" (for Norman Dubie). Field (7) Fall 72, p. 68.

1837 LI Ch'ing-chao
"Tune: 'As in a Dream'" (tr. by Eugene Eoyang). Madem (75:6) O 72, p. 136.

1838 LICHTENSTEIN, Alfred
"The Battle Near Saarburg" (tr. by Reinhold Johannes Kaebitzsch). UTR (1:4) 72, p. 8.

1839 LIDDY, James
from Baudelaire's Hell Flowers: "The Debt." Meas (1) 71.
from Baudelaire's Hell Flowers: "The Price." Meas (1) 71.

1840 LIEBERMAN, Laurence
"Increasing Night." QRL (18:1/2) 72, p. 119.
"The Island Drought." QRL (18:1/2) 72, p. 120.
"Lamb and Bear: Jet Landing (for Isaac)." QRL (18:1/2) 72, p. 123.
"Love, the Barber." QRL (18:1/2) 72, p. 124.
"The Osprey Suicides." NewYorker (48:40) 25 N 72, p. 48.
"Rock and Cloud." QRL (18:1/2) 72, p. 122.

1841 LIETZ, Robert
"Poemstudy." Epos (23:4) Sum 72, p. 25.

1842 LIFSHIN, Lyn
"Afterwards." Granite (2) Wint 71-72, p. 43.
"the another, the usual." Magazine (5) part 9, 72, p. 12.
"Because of This We Were Late Everything Got Mixed Up Later I Broke the Door. or, The Leaving." LittleM (6:2/3) Sum-Aut 72, p. 42.
"Blake Etching." WindO (11) Aut 72, p. 21.
"Crows Screeched All Afternoon." WindO (11) Aut 72, p. 19.
"Didn't You." HangL (17) Sum 72, p. 25.
"Doors and Glass." WindO (11) Aut 72, p. 18.
Eight Poems. WindO (10) Sum 72, p. 49.
"Family." BabyJ (5) N 72, p. 25.
"Finger Print" (Twenty Poems). WormR (47) 72, p. 83.
"The Five Places Dream." HangL (17) Sum 72, p. 23.
"For A R." WindO (11) Aut 72, p. 20.
"the glass in." Drag (3:1) Spr 72, p. 43.
"Growing." Granite (2) Wint 71-72, p. 48.
"He Couldn't Tell." Drag (3:2) Sum 72, p. 39.
"the hurt the." Drag (3:1) Spr 72, p. 43.
"I Would Have Except for Black Leaves and the Red in Me Flaking." Granite (2) Wint 71-72, p. 42.
"Late Now." Drag (3:2) Sum 72, p. 36.
"Lately." Northeast Aut-Wint 71-72, p. 18.
"Leaves." LittleM (6:2/3) Sum-Aut 72, p. 39.
"Leaves We Burned That Fall Were Each Other." Granite (2) Wint 71-72, p. 47.
"Like a Carbon Inside." UnmOx (1:2) F 72, p. 39.
"Like An Old Hotel." Northeast Aut-Wint 71-72, p. 19.
"Like Masaccio's." HangL (17) Sum 72, p. 26.
"March: The Missouri." Qt (5:38) Spr 72, p. 21.
"Mooncold and the Fire Escape Is Impossible." Granite (2) Wint 71-72, p. 44.
"Museum." Cord (1:4) 72, p. 1.
Nine Poems. BabyJ (5) N 72, p. 24.
"The No Need For, The Computer Concern Error Letter." Magazine (5) part 9, 72, p. 11.
"No Rose But." WindO (11) Aut 72, p. 20.
"November Poems." OhioR (14:1) Aut 72, p. 87.
"Numbness Falling Off." LittleM (6:2/3) Sum-Aut 72, p. 41.
"The Old House on the Croton." Iron (2) Fall 72, p. 66.
"Photographs." Granite (2) Wint 71-72, p. 46.
"Photographs." Peb (7) Aut 71.
"Picture." Folio (8:1) Spr 72, p. 16.
"Rocky Mountain Come Down." Northeast Aut-Wint 71-72, p. 18.
"snowblindness, circles." Drag (3:2) Sum 72, p. 36.
"snow drifts." New:ACP (18) Ap 72, p. 34.
"So Much About This." WindO (11) Aut 72, p. 19.

"Sometimes." Peb (7) Aut 71.
"Suddenly." HiramPoR (12) Spr-Sum 72, p. 22.
"That Night 3 Deer Running." Peb (7) Aut 71.
"then maybe." SaltCR (5:1) Wint 72.
"then the." Cord (1:3) 72, p. 19.
"This Grey." Folio (8:1) Spr 72, p. 16.
"thoughts of faces on." Qt (5:39/40) Sum-Aut 72, p. 36.
"Timing and the Voices." SaltCR (5:1) Wint 72.
"Truk Lagoon." New:ACP (18) Ap 72, p. 35.
"Trying Not to Think of Cells or Old Animals." Granite (2) Wint 71-72, p. 41.
"We Meet It's The." Cord (1:3) 72, p. 18.
"Why." Cord (1:4) 72, p. 2.
"You'd Think I'd Know About That Water." Cord (1:4) 72, p. 3.

1843 LIGI, Gary E.
"How We Lived and Let Live." SouthernPR (13:1) Aut 72, p. 15.
"Lessons in Loneliness." Poem (16) N 72, p. 30.
"Poem: You were a Sunday morning rain walk." Poem (16) N 72, p. 29.

1844 LIHN, Enrique
"A Roque Dalton." SouthernHR (6:2) Spr 72, p. 160.
"Elegy for Ernesto Che Guevara" (tr. by Edward Oliphant). RoadAR (4:1) Spr 72, p. 69.
"If Poetry Is To Be Written Right" (tr. by Edward Oliphant). RoadAR (4:1) Spr 72, p. 62.
"Jaguar" (tr. by Edward Oliphant). RoadAR (4:1) Spr 72, p. 66.
"News from Babylon" (tr. by Edward Oliphant). RoadAR (4:1) Spr 72, p. 58.
"Revolution" (tr. by Edward Oliphant). RoadAR (4:1) Spr 72, p. 57.
from Written in Cuba: "Thus I see myself in this fragmented world a" (tr. by Edward Oliphant). RoadAR (4:1) Spr 72, p. 64.

1845 LILLY, Octave, Jr.
"I Am Crispus Attacks." NegroHB (35:7) N 72, p. 159.

1846 LIMA, Robert
"Cautious Dampness" (tr. of Vincente Aleixandre). PoetL (67:3) Aut 72, p. 227.
"For a Definition of Mathematics" (tr. of Joseph Tusiani). PoetL (67:3) Aut 72, p. 229.
"Go" (tr. of Manuel Altolaguirre). PoetL (67:3) Aut 72, p. 228.
"If My Hands Could Only Depetal" (tr. of Federico Garcia Lorca). PoetL (67:3) Aut 72, p. 226.
"I'm Tired" (tr. of Luis Cernuda). PoetL (67:3) Aut 72, p. 228.

"The Moon Appears" (tr. of Federico Garcia Lorca). PoetL (67:3) Aut 72, p. 226.
"Nakedness" (tr. of Vincente Aleixandre). PoetL (67:3) Aut 72, p. 228.

1847 LIMAN, Claude G.
"Ping-Pong Opponents: A Round Robin." NowestR (12:3) Aut 72, p. 53.

1848 LINCICOME, David
"Things Come." Epoch (22:1) Fall 72, p. 75.

1849 LINDEGREN, Erik
"The Rain" (tr. by W. H. Auden and Leif Sjöberg). MichQR (11:4) Aut 72, p. 282.
"The Suit K" (tr. by W. H. Auden and Leif Sjöberg). MichQR (11:4) Aut 72, p. 283.

1850 LINDEMAN, Jack
"Civilian Population." ColQ (20:4) Spr 72, p. 470.
"Winding Down." ExpR (2) Wint-Spr 72, p. 34.

1851 LINDH, Howard
"Directions." PraS (46:4) Wint 72-73, p. 341.
"In the Room, We Thought." HolCrit (9:1) Ap 72, p. 11.

1852 LINDH, Stewart
"The Gate at the Throat." AmerR (15) 72, p. 151.
"The Waning of the Middle Ages." Shen (23:4) Sum 72, p. 76.

1853 LINEBARGER, A. Jackson
"White Gold." JnlOBP (2:16) Sum 72, p. 35.

1854 LINER, Amon
from "Marstower." CarolQ (24:2) Spr 72, p. 74.

1855 LING Chung
"Spring Joy" (tr. of Chu Shu-Chen, w. Kenneth Rexroth). NewL (38:4) Sum 72, p. 39.

1856 LINK, Frederick M.
"A View from the Tower." AAUP (58:3) S 72, p. 296.

1857 LINN, Marjorie Lees
"End Result." Folio (8:1) Spr 72, p. 36.
"Lullaby of the Bible Belt." Folio (8:1) Spr 72, p. 58.
"Occasions." Folio (8:2) Fall 72, p. 25.

1858 LINSON, Cornell, Jr.
"To You Nigger On the Murder of Carl Hampton." JnlOBP (2:16) Sum 72, p. 28.

1859 LINTON, Virginia
"The Cold Sky." ChiTM 12 N 72, p. 28.
"The Dusty Shuffle." SoCaR (5:1) D 72, p. 13.

1860 LI Po
"Conversations Among Mountains" (tr. by David Young). Madrona (1:4) S 72, p. 12.
"For Tu Fu" (tr. by David Young). Madrona (1:4) S 72, p. 14.
"A Frontier Song" (tr. by David Gordon). Northeast Aut-Wint 71-72, p. 55.
"Goodbye at the River" (tr. by David Young). Madrona (1:4) S 72, p. 17.
"High in the Mountains, I Fail to Find the Wise Man" (tr. by David Young). Madrona (1:4) S 72, p. 13.
"She Thinks of Him" (tr. by David Young). Madrona (1:4) S 72, p. 16.
"Waking Up Drunk on a Spring Day" (tr. by David Young). Madrona (1:4) S 72, p. 15.

1861 LIPSETT, Chris R.
"Emblem: Bean Game." SoDakR (10:1) Spr 72, p. 90.

1862 LISCOMB, Robie
"Initiation." AriD (1:3) Spr 72, p. 2.

1863 LI Shang-lin
"Letter" (Adapted by Graeme Wilson). NYT 6 S 72, p. 44.

1864 LIU, Stephen Shu-Ning
"My Kite and I." PoetL (67:4) Wint 72, p. 349.
"Ode to Chungking." ExpR (3) Fall-Wint 72/73, p. 12.
"On a Fine September Afternoon." Etc. (29:3) S 72, p. 232.
"Stratocumulus." SoDakR (10:3) Aut 72, p. 81.
"Under Those Banyan Trees." GeoR (26:3) Fall 72, p. 364.
"Vacation." PoetL (67:4) Wint 72, p. 349.

1865 LIU Tsung-yüan
"The Mounds, Early Spring Lifting" (tr. by David Gordon). Literature (15:3) 72, p. 486.
"Snow on the River" (tr. by Arthur Sze). HangL (18) Fall 72, p. 48.

1866 LIVERMORE, Kaye
"Passage." Granite (2) Wint 71-72, p. 67.

1867 LIVINGSTON, Gary
"A Day in Hampstead Heath." ExpR (3) Fall-Wint 72/73, p. 43.
"Hare Krishna." ExpR (3) Fall-Wint 72/73, p. 42.

"Stonehenge IV." LittleM (6:2/3) Sum-Aut 72, p. 103.
"Waiting for the Drummers in Tompkins Square." Works (3:2) Wint-Spr 72, p. 29.

1868 LLOYD, Donald J.
"Rituals." AmerS (41:2) Spr 72, p. 275.

1869 LOCKE, Duane
"Abandoned Farm." Nat (215:6) 11 S 72, p. 184.
"Among Gator Creek Scrub Oaks." UTR (1:2) 72, p. 10.
"The Cloisters." PoetL (67:4) Wint 72, p. 332.
"The Dead Oaks." UTR (1:3) 72, p. 32.
"Scarlet Tanager." PoetL (67:4) Wint 72, p. 332.
"Smoke." UTR (1:4) 72, p. 14.
"The Yellow Flower." UTR (1:1) 72, p. 8.

1870 LOCKLIN, Gerald
"A Beddy-Bye Note to the Princess." WormR (46) 72, p. 62.
"The Drama Student." WormR (46) 72, p. 61.
"the god poem." KanQ (4:1) Wint 71-72, p. 94.
"poop." WormR (47) 72, p. 99.
"roger corbin." WormR (47) 72, p. 97.
"scratch one." WormR (47) 72, p. 98.
"There Are Some Things You Really Get Sick Of." WormR (46) 72, p. 62.
"To Norman Vincent Peale." WormR (46) 72, p. 61.

1871 LOCKWOOD, Sarah
"Royal Incident." PoetL (67:2) Sum 72, p. 145.

1872 LOEWINSOHN, Ron
"All Along the Road." UnmOx (1:4) Aut 72.
"Goat Dance." UnmOx (1:4) Aut 72.
"Heavy." UnmOx (1:4) Aut 72.
"Two Poems." UnmOx (1:4) Aut 72.

1873 LOGAN, Bill
"In Age, in Afternoon." YaleLit (141:1) 71, p. 6.
"Storm Patterns." YaleLit (141:1) 71, p. 6.

1874 LOGAN, Cynthia
"Among the Horses." UnmOx (1:1) N 71, p. 68.

1875 LOGAN, John
"March. The Museum. Buffalo. de Chirico." Cafe (4) Fall 72, p. 17.
"Poem for My Friend Peter at Piihana." Iowa (3:1) Wint 72, p. 19.

1876 LOMAX, Pearl C.
"Compensation." JnlOBP (2:16) Sum 72, p. 60.
"For M." JnlOBP (2:16) Sum 72, p. 60.

1877 LONG, D. S.
"Poem 1224." Kayak (28) 72, p. 36.

1878 LONG, Diane Jolly
"Elegy." ColEng (33:5) F 72, p. 586.

1879 LONG, Julian Oliver
"Fantastics" (eight sonnets). SewanR (80:2) Spr 72, p. 294.

1880 LONG, Pierre
"The Swamp." ColEng (33:6) Mr 72, p. 720.
"Young Man at Piano." ColEng (33:6) Mr 72, p. 719.

1881 LONG, Richard A.
"Paul Laurence Dunbar." Phy (33:4) Wint 72, p. 368.

1882 LONGVILLE, Tim
"Snowman, a Poem Begun the Day Charles Olson Died (for him and for Jack Spicer)." Meas (2) 72.

1883 LOONIN, Al
"Grave." StoneD (1:1) Spr 72, p. 13.
"Imagine walking Rasputin." StoneD (1:1) Spr 72, p. 13.

1884 LORD, Gigi
"It Was Eye Talk." Cafe (4) Fall 72, p. 34.

1885 LORDE, Audre
"As I Grow Up Again." Works (3:3/4) Wint 72-73, p. 29.
"Black Mother Woman." MassR (13:1/2) Wint-Spr 72, p. 222.
Eight Poems. TransR (41) Wint-Spr 72, p. 46.
"Martha." HangL (17) Sum 72, p. 27.

1886 LOTT, Carolyn
"Encounter." SouthernPR (13:1) Aut 72, p. 14.

1887 LOTT, Clarinda Harriss
"Faces." CarolQ (24:1) Wint 72, p. 63.
"Kidney Stew." CarolQ (24:1) Wint 72, p. 62.
"Wolfheart." CarolQ (24:3) Fall 72, p. 80.

1888 LOTT, James
"Oak Hill Retirement Manor." PoetL (67:1) Spr 72, p. 15.

1889 LOTZ, Ernst Wilhelm
"And Cute Beast-of-Prey Spots..." (tr. by Reinhold Johannes Kaebitzsch). UTR (1:4) 72, p. 6.

1890 LOUCHHEIM, Katie
"The People Alps." Esq (78:6) D 72, p. 353.

1891 LOURIE, Dick
"charges." HangL (17) Sum 72, p. 38.
"letter, July 16th." HangL (17) Sum 72, p. 37.
"Toby's song." HangL (17) Sum 72, p. 36.

1892 LOURIE, Iven
"chicago north side poems." HangL (16) Wint 71-72, p. 35.

1893 LOUTSENHIZER, Susan
"Poem for the Artist's Keeper." Peb (7) Aut 71.

1894 LOWENFELS, Walter
"Letters to Aaron Kurtz." Meas (2) 72.
from My Many Lives: "The Paris Years, 1926-1934." ExpR (2) Wint-Spr 72, p. 10.

1895 LOWENSTEIN, Tom
"The Abduction" (from Eskimo). ChiR (24:2) 72, p. 130.
"Dead Man's Song" (from Eskimo). ChiR (24:2) 72, p. 127.
"Dead Man's Song (2)" (from Eskimo). ChiR (24:2) 72, p. 128.
"Greeting to the Women of the Feasting-House" (from Eskimo). ChiR (24:2) 72, p. 129.
"My Breath" (from Eskimo). ChiR (24:2) 72, p. 132.
"Song About the Narwhales" (from Eskimo). ChiR (24:2) 72, p. 126.
"The Sun and the Moon and the Fear of Loneliness" (from Eskimo). ChiR (24:2) 72, p. 131.

1896 LUCAS, John
"Antanacreontics." CarlMis (12:1) Fall-Wint 71-72, p. 109.
"Backside To." CarlMis (12:1) Fall-Wint 71-72, p. 110.
"Nostalgia." CarlMis (12:1) Fall-Wint 71-72, p. 109.
"Sad to Say." CarlMis (12:1) Fall-Wint 71-72, p. 109.
"Seven Lines Sentenced to Salvage." CarlMis (12:1) Fall-Wint 71-72, p. 109.
"Sourcery." CarlMis (12:1) Fall-Wint 71-72, p. 109.

1897 LUCHESSA, Paul
"Hotel Des Invalides." Comm (96:2) 17 Mr 72, p. 35.

1898 LUCINA, Mary R. S. M.
"Sunday Shapes." ChrC (89:8) 23 F 72, p. 223.

1899 LUEDERS, Edward
"Fox." PoetryNW (13:3) Aut 72, p. 39.
"Paradox: Years Later." WestHR (26:4) Aut 72, p. 366.

1900 LUEDERS, Perry H.
"Dinner Time." SoDakR (10:3) Aut 72, p. 83.

1901 LUM, Wing Tek
"On George Jackson." NewYQ (11) Sum 72, p. 75.

1902 LUMMIS, Suzanne
"Audience." Etc. (29:4) D 72, p. 433.

1903 LUMPKIN, Arthur H.
"Camelot." ArizQ (28:4) Wint 72, p. 300.
"Echoes." SewanR (80:2) Spr 72, p. 284.
"Legacy." TexQ (15:4) Wint 72, p. 99.

1904 LUND, Mary Graham
"Great-Grandmother's Mourning Veil." Peb (7) Aut 71.

1905 LUNDE, David
"The House." BabyJ (5) N 72, p. 4.
"Tanka." BabyJ (5) N 72, p. 4.

1906 LUNDQUIST, Robert
"If I Go to the River." Kayak (29) S 72, p. 12.
"On a Darkening Road." Kayak (29) S 72, p. 12.

1907 LUNIA, Jane
"The Lone Ranger and the Neo American Church." CarolQ (24:2) Spr 72, p. 56.
"Taking the Ground." CarolQ (24:2) Spr 72, p. 54.

1908 LUNIN, Jane
"Langley Porter Neuro Psychiatric Institute 3 A. M." MassR (13:3) Sum 72, p. 354.

1909 LURIA, Jack
"Back to the Source (for my children)." NYT 10 Je 72, p. 30.
"Saturday Night in Effingham, Ill. (pop. 9500)." NYT 4 Mr 72, p. 26.

1910 LUSCHEI, Glenna
"Back into My Body." SaltCR (5:1) Wint 72.
"The Feldspar Mine." SaltCR (5:1) Wint 72.
"Wheat Straw." SaltCR (5:1) Wint 72.

1911 LUSK, Charles J.
"Lovequest." Wind (2:5) Sum 72, p. 19.

1912 LUSK, Daniel
"Dakota." SoDakR (10:3) Aut 72, p. 77.
"Horses, Dreams." SoDakR (10:3) Aut 72, p. 77.

1913 LUSTIG, William
"awakening." UTR (1:3) 72, p. 28.
"Fly." UTR (1:1) 72, p. 12.
"he reached out to you." UTR (1:2) 72, p. 15.

1914 LUTZ, Gertrude May
"Incident at the Corner of X." LitR (16:1) Aut 72, p. 135.
"Night Brilliant with Stars." PoetL (67:2) Sum 72, p. 169.

1915 LUX, Thomas
"The Antler Dreams." Stand (13:2) 72, p. 53.
"The Cave or The Mine." Stand (13:2) 72, p. 51.
"The Day of the Lacuna." Field (6) Spr 72, p. 44.
"The 5 Room Apartment." MassR (13:3) Sum 72, p. 450.
"The Gas Station." Stand (13:2) 72, p. 52.
"If You See This Man." MassR (13:3) Sum 72, p. 450.
"The Midnight Tennis Match." MassR (13:3) Sum 72, p. 448.
"My Grandmother's Funeral." Stand (13:2) 72, p. 51.
"The Night Watchman Advertises Himself." Stand (13:2) 72, p. 50.

1916 LUZI, Mario
"Cuma." St. AR (2:1) Aut-Wint 72, p. 54.
from Dal Fonde delle Campagne: "From the Tower" (tr. by I. L. Salomon). MedR (2:4) Sum 72, p. 98.
"L'Immensita dell 'Attimo." St. AR (1:4) Spr-Sum 72, p. 26.
"Natura." St. AR (1:4) Spr-Sum 72, p. 26.
"La Notte Lava la Mente." St. AR (2:1) Aut-Wint 72, p. 54.
from Onore del Vero: "And the Wolf" (tr. by Sonia Raiziss). MedR (2:4) Sum 72, p. 98.
"Somewhere" (tr. by I. L. Salomon). MichQR (11:4) Aut 72, p. 273.
"The Whirlpool of Sickness and Health" (tr. by I. L. Salomon). MassR (13:3) Sum 72, p. 425.
"Within the Year" (tr. by I. L. Salomon). MichQR (11:4) Aut 72, p. 274.

1917 LYLE, K. Curtis
"I Witness." JnlOBP (2:16) Sum 72, p. 45.

1918 LYNCH, Charles
"Biograph #3." JnlOBP (2:16) Sum 72, p. 15.

1919 LYON, George Ella H.
"Sending James Joyce Poster Poem" (for Stephen). LittleM (6:2/3) Sum-Aut 72, p. 7.
"Sunday School." LittleM (6:2/3) Sum-Aut 72, p. 6.
"Untitled: Borrowing your vision, James." LittleM (6:2/3) Sum-Aut 72, p. 5.

1920 LYONS, Richard
"The Picture, 1909." SoDakR (10:3) Aut 72, p. 62.

1921 MacADAMS, Lewis
"English" (to Marty). Isthmus (1) Spr 72, p. 14.

"Gone On." UnmOx (1:1) N 71, p. 7.
"No Controls, No Guidelines." UnmOx (1:2) F 72, p. 26.
"Poem: we didn't ask for a county permit." UnmOx (1:1) N 71, p. 9.
"To the Snoring Blissfully Buddha." UnmOx (1:1) N 71, p. 9.

1922 McALEAVEY, David
"Painted Elk's Dream." Epoch (22:1) Fall 72, p. 76.

1923 McALLASTER, Elva
"A Convention of Archangels." ChiTM 5 N 72, p. 15.

1924 MacARTHUR, Gloria
"Thumbs and Other Camels (from an abortionist's notebook)." BelPoJ (22:3) Spr 72, p. 24.
"Twelve Warm Doves." BelPoJ (22:3) Spr 72, p. 27.

1925 McAULEY, James
"In the Gardens." Poetry (121:2) N 72, p. 89.
"Private Devotions." Poetry (121:2) N 72, p. 88.
"Vision from a Lectern." PoetryNW (13:1) Spr 72, p. 27.
"Winter Drive." Poetry (120:6) S 72, p. 334.
"World on Sunday." Poetry (121:2) N 72, p. 88.

1926 McBAIN, Barbara Mahone
"Sentimental Woman." JnlOBP (2:16) Sum 72, p. 72.

1927 MacBETH, George
"A Prayer to the Clematis, Who Is a Knight of Care." Stand (13:3) 72, p. 50.
"To My Hedgehog, Late Visitor." Stand (13:3) 72, p. 48.
To the Centurion of Wisdom, My Lord Owl." Stand (13:3) 72, p. 49.
"To the Mole, Who Is a Shadow of Nothingness." Stand (13:3) 72, p. 50.
"To the Sister of Twilight, the Mistress Primrose." Stand (13:3) 72, p. 49.

1928 McBRIDE, Roy
"Vietnam: From a Secret Document." Northeast Aut-Wint 71-72, p. 53.

1929 McCAMY, Jean
"A Day of Hatchets." SouthernPR (12:2) Spr 72, p. 36.

1930 McCANN, Richard
"The Creed." KanQ (4:1) Wint 71-72, p. 63.
"O my darling troubles Heaven with her loveliness." Qt (5:37) Wint 72, p. 22.
"Poem for Helen." SouthernPR (13:1) Aut 72, p. 24.

1931 McCAULEY, Carole Spearin
"Memo for my Husband's Birthday." NewRena (6) My 72, p. 41.

1932 Mc CLANE, Kenneth A.
"Cruise." Epoch (21:3) Spr 72, p. 296.
"Perspective." Epoch (21:3) Spr 72, p. 299.

1933 McCLATCHY, J. D.
"On Darwin: A Natural Selection." YaleLit (141:1) 71, p. 24.

1934 McCLOSKEY, Mark
"Chickadees." Iron (2) Fall 72, p. 55.
"Her Musics." Folio (8:2) Fall 72, p. 36.
"I Change on Confirmation Day." St.AR (2:1) Aut-Wint 72, p. 17.
"I Should Know." Peb (7) Aut 71.
"A Map of Kingston Quadrangle, Rhode Island." PoetryNW (13:4) Wint 72-73, p. 9.
"The New Man." PoetryNW (13:4) Wint 72-73, p. 10.
"On the Freeway, as though Nothing Happened." Drag (3:1) Spr 72, p. 50.
"A Riot of Horses." St.AR (1:4) Spr-Sum 72, p. 38.
"The Risk (for Paul Vangelisti)." PoetryNW (13:4) Wint 72-73, p. 8.
"Sea Urchin." St.AR (1:4) Spr-Sum 72, p. 75.
"The Styles." PoetryNW (13:4) Wint 72-73, p. 7.
"Their Blood Shines." St.AR (1:4) Spr-Sum 72, p. 70.
"What Now." Peb (7) Aut 71.
"Woodpeckers." Iron (2) Fall 72, p. 56.

1935 McCLURE, Michael
from the Book of Joanna: "JOANNA, YOU'RE BLACK! YES, YOU'RE ROMANCE!" ParisR (55) Aut 72, p. 101.
"Nineteen Seventytwo." UnmOx (1:4) Aut 72.
"Song Within a Song." UnmOx (1:4) Aut 72.
"Untitled." UnmOx (1:4) Aut 72.
"Written After Finding a Dolphin Skull on the Gulf of California." ParisR (55) Aut 72, p. 98.

1936 McCONNELL, Bonnie
"Red Alert." ArizQ (28:1) Spr 72, p. 26.

1937 McCONNELL, Bruce
"Return." SouthernR (8:1) Wint 72, p. 173.

1938 MacCOOL, Finn
"He sat talking to the other one..." StoneD (1:1) Spr 72, p. 35.
"No. 5 Mechanic St." StoneD (1:1) Spr 72, p. 35.

1939 McCORD, Howard
"Chicago-Albuquerque-Sangre DeCristo." Kayak (29) S 72, p. 61.
"Knowledge." Kayak (29) S 72, p. 62.

1940 McCORMICK, Gary E.
"Singing With Candles." ChiTM 7 My 72, p. 12.

1941 McCOY, D. S.
"Apology for Our Workers." PoetryNW (13:4) Wint 72-73, p. 36.

1942 McCOY, Joan
"Farm Visitor." Comm (97:6) 10 N 72, p. 134.

1943 McCRORIE, Edward
"Dragon Flying." BelPoJ (23:2) Wint 72-73, p. 5.
"Feeding Some Mares." LittleM (6:2/3) Sum-Aut 72, p. 44.
"Stump Ballad." LittleM (6:2/3) Sum-Aut 72, p. 45.
"Sun Story" (for Malcolm). LittleM (6:2/3) Sum-Aut 72, p. 45.

1944 McCURTAIN, Lucile V.
"Forecast." PoetL (67:2) Sum 72, p. 124.

1945 McDONALD, Barry
"Letter from the Hospital." Drag (3:1) Spr 72, p. 1.
"Making a Baby." Apple (7) Aut 72, p. 34.
"My Friends." Drag (3:1) Spr 72, p. 2.
"Your Blues." Peb (7) Aut 71.

1946 MacDONALD, Cynthia
"A Family Question." NewYQ (9) Wint 72, p. 67.
"The Marschallin Gives a Voice Lesson." NewYQ (10) Spr 72, p. 62.
"Mutations." PoetryNW (13:3) Aut 72, p. 29.
"Paintings from the Slaughterhouse: A Slide Show of Hogs." AmerR (14) 72, p. 139.

1947 McDONALD, Roger
"Grasshopper." MinnR (2) Spr 72, p. 12.

1948 McDONALD, Walter
"Faraway Places." BallSUF (13:4) Aut 72, p. 62.

1949 McDUFF, David
"Byzantium" (tr. of Gunnar Ekelöf). Stand (13:4) 72, p. 31.
"Heard in a dream..." (tr. of Gunnar Ekelöf). Stand (13:4) 72, p. 29.
"The Hypnagogue" (tr. of Gunnar Ekelöf). Stand (13:4) 72, p. 32.

"Someone said:" (tr. of Gunnar Ekelöf). Stand (13:4) 72, p. 30.

1950 McELROY, Colleen J.
"News Report." SoDakR (10:4) Wint 72, p. 80.
"Penny-Ante." NowestR (12:2) Spr 72, p. 28.
"Visiting." PoetryNW (13:1) Spr 72, p. 16.

1951 McELROY, David
"Dragging In Winter." Antaeus (7) Aut 72, p. 48.
"Nooksak Reservation." Antaeus (7) Aut 72, p. 50.
"Report from the Correspondent They Fired." Antaeus (7) Aut 72, p. 52.
"Your Great Great..." Antaeus (7) Aut 72, p. 51.

1952 McFARLAND, Myra Mae
"Unpaid Bills." WindO (11) Aut 72, p. 28.

1953 McGOUGH, Roger
"After the Merrymaking, Love?" Madem (74:4) F 72, p. 40.
"P.O.W." Madem (74:4) F 72, p. 40.

1954 McGOVERN, Robert
"Grade One." HiramPoR (12) Spr-Sum 72, p. 23.

1955 McGOWAN, James
"Lessons." CarlMis (12:1) Fall-Wint 71-72, p. 110.

1956 McGRATH, Thomas
"Love Belongs to the North." Cafe (4) Fall 72, p. 5.
Seven Poems. Meas (2) 72.
"Three Poems from a Hospital." UnmOx (1:3) Sum 72, p. 19.

1957 McGREGOR, Jim
"Barbary." Pan (9) 72, p. 47.

1958 McGUINN, Rex
"The Accepted." St. AR (2:1) Aut-Wint 72, p. 28.

1959 MACHADO, Antonio
"'Clouds Torn Open'" (tr. by Robert Bly). MichQR (11:4) Aut 72, p. 279.
"I Go Dreaming Roads" (tr. by William Witherup and Carmen Scholis). Madrona (1:3) My 72, p. 16.

1960 MACHT, Richard
"Poem: out of the woods." Granite (2) Wint 71-72, p. 31.
"Poem: what'd he say he." Granite (2) Wint 71-72, p. 35.

1961 McHUGH, Heather
"Night Hypodermic." Iron (2) Fall 72, p. 38.

1962 MACHVE, Prabhakar
"Demonic" (tr. of Shyam Parmar). Meas (3) 72, p. 52.
"Snake Harvests" (tr. of Shyam Parmar). Meas (3) 72, p. 52.

1963 McINTOSH, Sandy
"The Last Day I Saw You." UnmOx (1:3) Sum 72, p. 12.

1964 McKAUGHAN, Molly
"After Excuses." Works (3:3/4) Wint 72-73, p. 120.
"Bone Dust in Concord California." Works (3:3/4) Wint 72-73, p. 115.
"Grappling." Works (3:3/4) Wint 72-73, p. 117.
"Heading Out." Works (3:2) Wint-Spr 72, p. 51.
"So This Is the Life of a Wife" (for Charlotte). Works (3:3/4) Wint 72-73, p. 121.
"Spaces without Title" (for my mother). Works (3:3/4) Wint 72-73, p. 114.
"That Rabbit, Those Elbows." Works (3:3/4) Wint 72-73, p. 119.

1965 MAC KENZIE, Jean West
"Retired." Epoch (21:3) Spr 72, p. 241.
"Trimming Your Mustache." Epoch (21:3) Spr 72, p. 241.

1966 McKENZIE, Joan
"The Chosen World." ChiTM 23 Ja 72, p. 14.

1967 McKEOWN, Tom
"At the Center of Night." Nat (215:13) 30 O 72, p. 409.
"The City of Salvation." StoneD (1:1) Spr 72, p. 36.
"The Dancer." NYT 11 Jl 72, p. 34.
"The Green Horse that Flies Backwards." Kayak (30) D 72, p. 66.
"The House of Water." Kayak (30) D 72, p. 67.
"The Procession of Ancient Men." Cafe (4) Fall 72, p. 33.

1968 McKERNAN, John
"Reading Weldon Kees in San Francisco." PraS (46:1) Spr 72, p. 56.

1969 McKINLEY, Hugh
"From a Hollowed Reed." WorldO (7:1) Aut 72, p. 31.

1970 McKINLEY, Larry
"Orthodox Wrights." BabyJ (5) N 72, p. 7.

1971 McKINNEY, Irene
"First Warm Day." Epoch (21:2) Wint 71, p. 151.
"Summer Storm in the Animal Graveyard." Epoch (21:2) Wint 71, p. 150.

1972 McLAUGHLIN, Emma S.
"Awakening a Universe from Sleep." PoetL (67:3) Aut 72, p. 277.

1973 McLAUGHLIN, William
"The Anarchist Has Time To Learn His New Math in Sets of Nine." SouthernHR (6:1) Wint 72, p. 44.
"The Orchid Plant." KanQ (4:3) Sum 72, p. 128.
"Our Leader Never Touched Us." SouthernPR (12:2) Spr 72, p. 16.

1974 MacLEISH, Archibald
"Memory Green." NewRep (167:15) 21 O 72, p. 33.
"What She Was Herself.'" NYT 4 My 72, p. 45.

1975 MacLEOD, Norman
"Image Beneath Forests." SouthernPR (12:2) Spr 72, p. 52.

1976 McMICHAEL, James
"The Admiral Benbow." Poetry (120:3) Je 72, p. 141.
"The Inland Lighthouse." Poetry (120:3) Je 72, p. 143.
"Matins." DenQuart (7:1) Spr 72, p. 77.
"Terce." Poetry (120:3) Je 72, p. 142.

1977 McMULLEN, Richard E.
"About Feet." Epoch (21:2) Wint 71, p. 161.
"Bubble Gum." MassR (13:3) Sum 72, p. 358.
"Civic Duty." Cord (1:4) 72, p. 14.
"A Conversation." SouthernPR (13:1) Aut 72, p. 39.
"The Mines at Iron River." Cord (1:4) 72, p. 14.
"Sleepwalking." Folio (8:2) Fall 72, p. 33.

1978 McNAIR, Wesley
"Memory of Kuhre." PraS (46:3) Aut 72, p. 250.
"Thinking about Carnevale's Wife." HangL (17) Sum 72, p. 40.

1979 McNALLY, James
"Lecture." AAUP (58:2) Je 72, p. 159.
"The Meager Magnolia." AAUP (58:2) Je 72, p. 159.

1980 McNALLY, John
"Korea." New:ACP (18) Ap 72, p. 6.
"Nobody But You." New:ACP (18) Ap 72, p. 6.

1981 McNAMARA, Eugene
"Crazy Here, Crazy There" (found poem). BabyJ (5) N 72, p. 32.
"Dillinger's Camera." Poem (15) Jl 72, p. 25.
"The Factory." New:ACP (19) Aut 72, p. 30.
"friend, what country is this." Qt (5:39/40) Sum-Aut 72, p. 42.

"How To Relate in a Meaningful Manner Towards Sensible Objects." Zahir (1:4/5) 72, p. 67.

1982 McNAMEE, Thomas
"Grace." NewYorker (48:41) 2 D 72, p. 54.

1983 McNEIL, Florence
"Burial at Arnans." ConcPo (5:1) Spr 72, p. 64.

1984 McPHERSON, Sandra
"Battlefield." Iowa (3:3) Sum 72, p. 20.
"Collapsars." Field (6) Spr 72, p. 59.
"Holding Pattern." Poetry (119:4) Ja 72, p. 213.
"In the Wake of Darwin's Beagle." Antaeus (6) Sum 72, p. 49.
"Leaves the Color of Library Doors." Field (6) Spr 72, p. 56.
"Letter with a Black Border." Iowa (3:3) Sum 72, p. 19.
"A Little Fire." Poetry (121:2) N 72, p. 96.
"Mishima." Nat (214:10) 6 Mr 72, p. 310.
"Opossum." Shen (24:1) Aut 72, p. 67.
"Seaweeds." Poetry (121:2) N 72, p. 94.
"Selective Letter." Field (6) Spr 72, p. 57.
"Sheep." NYT 14 O 72, p. 32.
"Siberia." Poetry (121:2) N 72, p. 97.
"Some Engravings of Pierré Joseph Redoute." Poetry (121:2) N 72, p. 94.
"Wanting a Mummy." NewRep (166:15) 8 Ap 72, p. 19.
"What He Must Do To Earn Money." NewYorker (48:2) 4 Mr 72, p. 44.

1985 MacQUEEN, James
"Another Incarnation." UTR (1:2) 72, p. 4.
"From Salty Windows." UTR (1:2) 72, p. 5.
"i am silent." UTR (1:4) 72, p. 18.
"India Wharf." UTR (1:3) 72, p. 19.
"Portrait in Reality." UTR (1:2) 72, p. 7.
"Road Poem #6." UTR (1:1) 72, p. 11.
"Road Poem #2." UTR (1:2) 72, p. 8.
"Separation of Wings and Petals." UTR (1:2) 72, p. 6.
"with the season's face hidden." UTR (1:3) 72, p. 20.

1986 McQUILKIN, Frank
"In the Morning the Birds Sing." SouthernHR (6:1) Wint 72, p. 68.
"Moth Poem--Playing with Fire." SouthernHR (6:3) Sum 72, p. 268.
"Two Poems for Crabs in Mating Season." RoadAR (3:4) Wint 71-72, p. 18.

1987 No entry.

1988 McROBERTS, Robert L.
"Poem, Seed." RoadAR (3:4) Wint 71-72, p. 33.
"Trying to Write Before the Last Pro-Football Game of the Year." PoetryNW (13:4) Wint 72-73, p. 37.

1989 MacWILLIAMS, Angelyn
"When I Was Loved." Cosmo (173:4) O 72, p. 142.

1990 MADDEN, David
"Looking at the Dead." MinnR (3) Aut 72, p. 29.
"The Rush, the Pluck, and the Black Helmet." Poem (16) N 72, p. 52.

1991 MADDOX, Donald D.
"Joyce." Qt (5:38) Spr 72, p. 12.

1992 MADDOX, Everette
"Anonymous." Kayak (29) S 72, p. 46.
"Moon Fragment." Shen (23:2) Wint 72, p. 20.
"Quest." SouthernPR (13:1) Aut 72, p. 21.
"To Pogo Possum." KanQ (4:1) Wint 71-72, p. 93.

1993 MADIGAN, Michael
"The Throats of Birds." MichQR (11:3) Sum 72, p. 171.

1994 MADURA, Bernard
"Against Symbolism." CarlMis (12:1) Fall-Wint 71-72, p. 81.

1995 MAGER, Don
"Dublin Crossing (to R.G.)." Peb (7) Aut 71.
"Duccio's Maesta Altarpiece is Borne to Siena Cathedral." Peb (7) Aut 71.
"A Letter." Peb (7) Aut 71.

1996 MAGLIOLA, Robert
"Chance-Meeting" (tr. of Hsu Chih-mo, w. Rosa Tsung-yu Kao). PoetL (67:4) Wint 72, p. 350.
"Star-Spark of Feeble Flame" (tr. of Hsu Chih-mo, w. Rosa Tsung-yu Kao). PoetL (67:4) Wint 72, p. 350.

1997 MAGNER, James Edmund, Jr.
"The Beginning of a Night." HiramPoR (13) Fall-Wint 72, p. 12.
"Hostius Quadra." MedR (2:2) Wint 72, p. 64.
"A Myth for Diane." HiramPoR (13) Fall-Wint 72, p. 13.
"The Women of the Golden Horn." MedR (2:2) Wint 72, p. 64.

1998 MAGORIAN, James
"Canada Lilly." KanQ (4:3) Sum 72, p. 10.
"The Marsh." KanQ (4:3) Sum 72, p. 10.
"The Shovel." KanQ (4:3) Sum 72, p. 11.

1999 MAGOWAN, Robin
"Froggy Bushes, Appenine (Hopscotch Song)." Kayak (29) S 72, p. 25.

2000 MAGRI, Joseph A.
"A Nudge in the Right Direction." Epos (23:3) Spr 72, p. 9.

2001 MAGUIRE, Francis
"For a Dead Entertainer." ChrC (89:36) 11 O 72, p. 1005.
"For an Aging Existentialist." PoetL (67:3) Aut 72, p. 255.
"The Game." ChrC (89:4) 26 Ja 72, p. 87.
"Suomi." Qt (5:37) Wint 72, p. 12.
"Whale Song." Nat (214:8) 21 F 72, p. 248.

2002 MAHAPATRA, Jayanta
"A Dead Boy." St. AR (1:4) Spr-Sum 72, p. 60.
"Hands." ChiR (23:4 & 24:1) 72, p. 77.
"This Stranger, My Daughter." SouthernPR (12:2) Spr 72, p. 32.

2003 MAHNKE, John
"An Old Lady Is Called to the Door." PraS (46:1) Spr 72, p. 59.

2004 MAHONEY, Donal
"Before I Sally Off." Zahir (1:4/5) 72, p. 36.
"Father: Every Morning of his Life." Zahir (1:4/5) 72, p. 36.
"The Free Field." Zahir (1:4/5) 72, p. 37.
"Harvest of Pumpkins." KanQ (4:1) Wint 71-72, p. 94.
"A Song for Ballyheigue." Zahir (1:4/5) 72, p. 37.
"Speech from the Pencil Sharpener." KanQ (4:3) Sum 72, p. 13.
"Straight in his Caneback Chair." KanQ (4:3) Sum 72, p. 14.

2005 MAHONEY, Mary Reeves
"Dear Last Year's Valentine." LadHJ (89:2) F 72, p. 132.

2006 MAIKOV, Apollon
"Twenty-five poems by Apollon Maikov" (tr. by Eugene M. Kayden). ColQ (21:2) Aut 72, p. 256.

2007 MAILMAN, Leo
"alpha beta peach." WormR (48) 72, p. 124.
"captain america incognito." WormR (48) 72, p. 124.
"carpenter's helper." WormR (48) 72, p. 123.

2008 MAINO, Jeannette
"Fishing Boats in Mexico." ChiTM 26 Mr 72, p. 12.

2009 MAIRS, Nancy
"After an Andrew Wyeth Print." AriD (1:3) Spr 72, p. 21.
"Prey." LittleM (6:1) Spr 72, p. 46.

2010 MAISEL, Carolyn
"Flowers." NewYorker (48:27) 26 Ag 72, p. 32.
"Habits of Air." NoAmR (257:4) Wint 72, p. 56.
"They Return Home at Midnight." NoAmR (257:4) Wint 72, p. 55.

2011 MAJOR, Clarence
"Because of Love." Works (3:3/4) Wint 72-73, p. 36.
"Dinner Party." UnmOx (1:4) Aut 72.
"it is this now itself." NewYQ (9) Wint 72, p. 45.
"Poverty & Death." Works (3:3/4) Wint 72-73, p. 37.
"San Miguel Allende." UnmOx (1:4) Aut 72.
"Triangle." UnmOx (1:4) Aut 72.

2012 MAKKAI, Adam
"Falling Upward!" ModernPS (3:3) 72, p. 139.
"How Everything Slowly Petrifies." ModernPS (3:3) 72, p. 139.
"Nocturnal Ships." ModernPS (3:3) 72, p. 140.

2013 MAKUCK, Peter
"Dziadek." SouthernR (8:2) Spr 72, p. 412.
"She." ColEng (33:6) Mr 72, p. 721.
"Something." ColEng (33:6) Mr 72, p. 722.

2014 MALANGA, Gerard
"Don Juan." UnmOx (1:4) Aut 72.
"The Light That Bears with It a Message." UnmOx (1:4) Aut 72.
"My Middle Name." UnmOx (1:3) Sum 72, p. 36.
"Revelation/East Broadway Flashback." UnmOx (1:4) Aut 72.
"R F D 3." UnmOx (1:3) Sum 72, p. 36.
"This Mornings Poem." UnmOx (1:4) Aut 72.
"White Is What You Are." UnmOx (1:4) Aut 72.
"White Light." UnmOx (1:3) Sum 72, p. 36.

2015 MALIK, Keshav
"Fruit of Remembrance." LitR (16:1) Aut 72, p. 52.
"Ideal Summer Sleep." LitR (16:1) Aut 72, p. 53.

2016 MALIKOV, Kurbanychbek
"Invitation to Kirghizstan" (tr. by Bernard Koten, w. Nan Braymer). NewWR (40:4) Aut 72, p. 24.

2017 MALIN, Stephen
"Castaway." SouthwR (57:1) Wint 72, p. 29.

2018 MALLALIEU, H. B.
"Future Shock." Poetry (120:5) Ag 72, p. 274.
"Portrait." Poetry (120:5) Ag 72, p. 273.
"Variation on a Theme of Cavafy." Poetry (120:5) Ag 72, p. 272.

2019 MALLARME, Stephen
"At Baudelaire's Tomb" (tr. by William Doreski). PoetL (67:1) Spr 72, p. 43.
"Prose" (Pour des Esseintes) (tr. by William Doreski). PoetL (67:1) Spr 72, p. 44.
"The Saint" (tr. by William Doreski). PoetL (67:1) Spr 72, p. 46.
"What cloth soaking up time's salve" (tr. by William Doreski). PoetL (67:1) Spr 72, p. 44.

2020 MALLORY, Lee
"Diapos." Spec (14:1/2) My 72, p. 61.
from Diapos: "I am the windmill forever." Hiero (7) Ap 72.
"Ensenada '68." BeyB (2:2) 72, p. 42.
"Montparnasse Handyman." BeyB (2:2) 72, p. 43.

2021 MALONE, Henry
"Flower In My Hand." Iron (1) Spr 72, p. 62.
"Is When." Epoch (21:3) Spr 72, p. 245.
"With This New Poem Comes Fame and My Picture on the Covers of Magazines." NewYQ (11) Sum 72, p. 80.

2022 MALONEY, Frank
"Petrarch." Madrona (1:2) N 71, p. 5.

2023 MALONEY, J. J.
"The Empty Chair." NewL (38:4) Sum 72, p. 106.
"Poems from Prison." NewL (38:3) Spr 72, p. 89.

2024 MALOY, Miriam C.
"Etcetera." Etc. (29:3) S 72, p. 274.

2025 MALTZ, Saul
"Poem of a Workingman" (tr. by Leonard Opalov). PoetL (67:1) Spr 72, p. 32.

2026 MALVEAUX, Julianne
"Too Late." JnlOBP (2:16) Sum 72, p. 62.

2027 MANDELSTAM, Osip
"Armed with the sight of the fine wasps" (tr. by W. S. Merwin and Clarence Brown). Hudson (25:1) Spr 72, p. 73.

Eleven Poems (tr. by Jane Gary Harris). RusLT (2) Wint 72, p. 193.
"Five Poems" (tr. by W. S. Merwin and Clarence Brown). Antaeus (6) Sum 72, p. 92.
Fourteen Poems (tr. by W. S. Merwin and Clarence Brown). QRL (18:1/2) 72, p. 7.
"Hagia Sophia" (tr. by Struven Fehsenfeld). RusLT (2) Wint 72, p. 189.
"I am alone staring into the eye of the ice" (tr. by W. S. Merwin and Clarence Brown). NewYRB (17:12/18:1) 27 Ja 72, p. 35.
"I came upon a lake, a house constructed fresh" (tr. by Struven Fehsenfeld). RusLT (2) Wint 72, p. 192.
"The idol lolls alone inside the mountain's bowels" (tr. by Struven Fehsenfeld). RusLT (2) Wint 72, p. 191.
"Insomnia-Homer. Taut Sails" (tr. by W. S. Merwin and Clarence Brown). Hudson (25:1) Spr 72, p. 71.
"Notre Dame" (tr. by Struven Fehsenfeld). RusLT (2) Wint 72, p. 190.
"Oh the horizon steals my breath and takes it nowhere--" (tr. by W. S. Merwin and Clarence Brown). NewYRB (17:12/18:1) 27 Ja 72, p. 35.
"Sixteen poems by Osip Mandelshtam" (tr. by Eugene M. Kayden). ColQ (20:4) Spr 72, p. 535.
"To the Memory of Andrei Bely" (tr. by Ants Oras). RusLT (4) Aut 72, p. 63.
"Tristia" (tr. by W. S. Merwin and Clarence Brown). Hudson (25:1) Spr 72, p. 71.
"Two Poems" (tr. by Katheryn Szczepanski). Pan (9) 72, p. 55.
"What can we do with the plains' beaten weight?" (tr. by W. S. Merwin and Clarence Brown). NewYRB (17:12/18:1) 27 Ja 72, p. 35.
"We shall meet again, in Petersburg" (tr. by W. S. Merwin and Clarence Brown). Hudson (25:1) Spr 72, p. 72.

2028 MANGINI, Albert
"Work Song." Wind (2:6) Aut 72, p. 29.

2029 MANLEY, Frank
"Advertisement." PartR (39:1) Wint 72, p. 54.
"Faces." PartR (39:1) Wint 72, p. 53.
"Lightning Bugs." PartR (39:1) Wint 72, p. 55.
"Unbuilding." SouthernR (8:4) Aut 72, p. 915.

2030 MANTHOULIS, Rovyros
"How Far to Death" (tr. by Stavros Deligiorgis). AriD (1:4/5) Sum-Aut 72, p. 80.

2031 MANYOSHU
"Waiting" (tr. by Graeme Wilson). NYT 7 Ag 72, p. 26.

2032 MAO Tse-Tung
"The Long March" (tr. by Willis Barnstone). NYT 19 F 72, p. 31.
"Seven Poems" (tr. by Nieh Hua-Ling and Paul Engle). Playb (19:4) Ap 72, p. 163.
"Snow" (tr. by Willis Barnstone and Ko Ching-Po). NewRep (167:12) 30 S 72, p. 30.
"Winter Clouds" (tr. by Willis Barnstone). NYT 19 F 72, p. 31.

2033 MARCUS, Adrianne
"All Our Fantasies" (for Weldon Kees). Works (3:2) Wint-Spr 72, p. 49.
"Being a Woman." Works (3:2) Wint-Spr 72, p. 50.
"La Bruja: The Witch." SouthernPR (13:1) Aut 72, p. 40.
"The Door." SouthernPR (12:2) Spr 72, p. 55.
"It Is Begun Again." ChiTM 9 Ap 72, p. 12.
"A Second Meeting." Qt (5:39/40) Sum-Aut 72, p. 35.
"Youmother." SoDakR (10:1) Spr 72, p. 71.

2034 MARCUS, Mordecai
"Long-Distance." Shen (23:4) Sum 72, p. 70.
"A Quiet Moment in an Age of Confrontation." Peb (6) Sum 71.
"A Religious Upbringing." AriD (1:3) Spr 72, p. 32.
"What's in a Name?" Peb (6) Sum 71.

2035 MARCUS, Morton
"The Bear" (this poem is for Gary Snyder). MinnR (3) Aut 72, p. 39.
"Compost Heap." MinnR (3) Aut 72, p. 38.
"I Am Beginning to Be." MinnR (3) Aut 72, p. 38.
"An Old Man." MinnR (3) Aut 72, p. 39.
"The Quarry." New:ACP (19) Aut 72, p. 31.
"Some Rain." ChiR (23:4 & 24:1) 72, p. 102.
"Spell" (for Norman and Alice Thomas). ChiR (23:4 & 24:1) 72, p. 103.
"Watching Your Gray Eyes." Kayak (29) S 72, p. 51.

2036 MARGOLIS, Gary
"Between the Mountain and the Brook." Epoch (22:1) Fall 72, p. 41.

2037 MARIAH, Paul
"Christmas '62." Confr (5) Wint-Spr 72, p. 74.
"The Count of Numbers." Isthmus (1) Spr 72, p. 40.
"The Holding Companies' Company." Confr (5) Wint-Spr 72, p. 75.
"Mother of Pearl." Isthmus (1) Spr 72, p. 41.
"Near Poetry." MinnR (3) Aut 72, p. 114.

2038 MARIN, Peter
"For Kathryn: The Person Returns in the Shape of the World." Isthmus (1) Spr 72, p. 78.

2039 MARINONI, Rose Azgnoni
"For a First Night in Heaven." Mark (16:2) Sum 72, p. 21.

2040 MARKS, S. J.
"At the State Mental Hospital." NewYorker (48:34) 14 O 72, p. 48.
"Red Grass." PoetryNW (13:1) Spr 72, p. 12.
"Russia." MidwQ (14:1) Aut 72, p. 26.
"What Dreams in the Deepest Sleep." MidwQ (14:1) Aut 72, p. 39.

2041 MARONICK, Gregory
"The Rose Wasp Family: A Fable." PoetryNW (13:1) Spr 72, p. 14.

2042 MARRAFFINO, Elizabeth
"Blue Enamel, Marbles." ExpR (2) Wint-Spr 72, p. 30.
from Leaning Across Rivers, Reaching You: "I go on repeating name after name after name." MinnR (2) Spr 72, p. 95.
from Leaning Across Rivers, Reaching You: "I want to be the opposite of this." MinnR (2) Spr 72, p. 94.
from Leaning Across Rivers, Reaching You: "The stars seem to fly from winter." MinnR (2) Spr 72, p. 95.
from Leaning Across Rivers, Reaching You: "What else is inside me but his voice?" MinnR (2) Spr 72, p. 93.
from The Map of St. Rimbaud: "Light sends down roots." MinnR (2) Spr 72, p. 96.

2043 MARSHALL, Herbert
"Requiem" (tr. of Anna Akhmatova). RusLT (2) Wint 72, p. 201.

2044 MARSHALL, Jack
"Bits of Thirst." Sky (1:1) 71.
"In Your Shoes." Sky (1:2) 72, p. 5.

2045 MARTHEY, Ione U.
"Anesthesia." PoetL (67:4) Wint 72, p. 369.

2046 MARTIN, Charles
"Leaving Buffalo." Poetry (121:3) D 72, p. 138.
"Persistence of Ancestors." Poetry (121:3) D 72, p. 139.
"Scenes Drawn from Life in Buffalo, New York." Poetry (121:3) D 72, p. 137.
"The William Carlos Williams Variations." NewYQ (12) Aut 72, p. 79.

2047 MARTIN, Christopher
"Curious Death." Poetry (119:4) Ja 72, p. 207.
"Georgian Green." Poetry (119:4) Ja 72, p. 208.
"Girls that Swim." Poetry (119:4) Ja 72, p. 207.
"Mock Interview." Poetry (119:4) Ja 72, p. 200.
"News from Guatemala." Poetry (119:4) Ja 72, p. 205.
"Yes or No." Poetry (119:4) Ja 72, p. 206.

2048 MARTIN, F. L.
"You, Henry?" (for John Berryman). Cafe (4) Fall 72, p. 6.

2049 MARTIN, James
"Hitler and Bonhoeffer." AmerR (15) 72, p. 129.
"Pain That Is Delicate, That We Have Saved." ChrC (89:17) 26 Ap 72, p. 483.
"Pastor Bonhoeffer Talks About Hitler." Esq (77:4) Ap 72, p. 29.

2050 MARTIN, Jay
"Wolf House in the Spring." CEACritic (34:4) My 72, p. 22.

2051 MARTIN, Manning
"Numbers." SatEP (244:1) Spr 72, p. 102.

2052 MARTINI, Galen
"There Is a Stranger." New:ACP (19) Aut 72, p. 20.

2053 MARTINSON, David
"General Announcement to All American Poets." NewYQ (12) Aut 72, p. 58.

2054 MARTINSON, Harry
"The Insects" (tr. by W. H. Auden and Leif Sjöberg). MichQR (11:4) Aut 72, p. 284.
from "Li Kan Speaks Beneath the Tree" (tr. by W. H. Auden and Leif Sjöberg). DenQuart (7:3) Aut 72, p. 14.

2055 MARTZ, Murray
"Ginsberg with William Buckley on Educational Television." Peb (6) Sum 71.
"Reading and Approaching Old Crow, or, At middle-age, the professor begins again to write." Peb (7) Aut 71.

2056 MARUYAMA, Kaoru
"Aki." HiramPoR (13) Fall-Wint 72, p. 7.
"Dirge" (tr. by Robert Epp). PoetL (67:4) Wint 72, p. 352.
"Hikari No Michi." HiramPoR (13) Fall-Wint 72, p. 8.
"Night Journey" (tr. by Robert Epp). PoetL (67:4) Wint 72, p. 353.

"The Poetry of Kaoru Maruyama" (tr. by Robert Epp). BelPoJ (22:4) Sum 72 (Entire issue).

2057 MARX, Anne
"After Take-Off." NewYQ (10) Spr 72, p. 47.
"Chillon: Return to Madness." ChiTM 4 Je 72, p. 50.
"Flight Home." PoetL (67:4) Wint 72, p. 366.
"Shift to Low." PoetL (67:4) Wint 72, p. 365.
"Song: For Our Aging Love." PoetL (67:4) Wint 72, p. 365.
"Thesis." NYT 29 Jl 72, p. 24.

2058 MARY ELLEN, Sister, S. S. N. D.
"By Way of Metaphor." LitR (16:1) Aut 72, p. 137.
"Sins of the Just." ArizQ (28:4) Wint 72, p. 318.
"Statement by Indirection." LitR (16:1) Aut 72, p. 136.
"To a Former Student." LitR (16:1) Aut 72, p. 137.
"The Violent Bear It Away." SouthernPR (13:1) Aut 72, p. 20.

2059 MARZAN, Julio
"The Carousel Boy." NewYQ (11) Sum 72, p. 58.

2060 MASARIK, Al
"Not a poem." Cord (1:4) 72, p. 11.
"reunion." Cord (1:4) 72, p. 10.

2061 MASHARIKI, Nyumba (Wayne O. Ross)
"Images." JnlOBP (2:16) Sum 72, p. 81.
"Julia." JnlOBP (2:16) Sum 72, p. 83.
"School Days." JnlOBP (2:16) Sum 72, p. 81.

2062 MASKALERIS, Thanasis
"Bion" (tr. of Ares Alexandrou). AriD (1:4/5) Sum-Aut 72, p. 15.
"The House" (tr. of Nanos Valaoritis). AriD (1:4/5) Sum-Aut 72, p. 114.
"In the Dead Forest" (tr. of Michael Katsaros). AriD (1:4/5) Sum-Aut 72, p. 75.
"Into the Rocks" (tr. of Ares Alexandrou). AriD (1:4/5) Sum-Aut 72, p. 17.
"The Lesson of Dawn" (tr. of Nanos Valaoritis). AriD (1:4/5) Sum-Aut 72, p. 114.
"Troy" (tr. of Nanos Valaoritis). AriD (1:4/5) Sum-Aut 72, p. 112.

2063 MASSA, R. X.
"Evol U." BeyB (2:2) 72, p. 53.
"Mouth." BeyB (2:2) 72, p. 52.

2064 MAST, Vernetta
"Who You Tellin." SouthwR (57:4) Aut 72, p. 310.

2065 MASTERS, Marcia Lee
"Birds." LitR (16:1) Aut 72, p. 92.

"Jealousy." LitR (16:1) Aut 72, p. 93.
"Journey in Switzerland." PoetL (67:1) Spr 72, p. 69.
"The Lake of Nothingness." LitR (16:1) Aut 72, p. 93.
"Song to a Dead Husband." ChiTM 19 N 72, p. 14.
"Worms' Silk." LitR (16:1) Aut 72, p. 95.
"Your Face." LitR (16:1) Aut 72, p. 94.

2066 MATANLE, Stephen
"Poem, for Ellen." Epoch (21:2) Wint 71, p. 135.

2067 MATHIAS, Roland
"They Have Not Survived." TransR (42/43) Spr-Sum 72, p. 77.

2068 MATHIS, Sharon Bell
"My." NegroHB (35:3) Mr 72, p. 67.

2069 MATLOCK, Grace
"He Certainly Did." NoCaFo (20:3) Ag 72, p. 138.

2070 MATROS, Ron
"Oil Spill." Cim (18) Ja 72, p. 38.

2071 MATSON, Clive
"The Haze." HangL (18) Fall 72, p. 30.

2072 MATTESON, Frederic
"Primordial." WestR (9:2) Wint 72, p. 34.

2073 MATTHEWS, Marie
"The Bullfighter's Wife." Epoch (21:2) Wint 72, p. 149.
"My Father's Wife." Epoch (21:2) Wint 71, p. 148.

2074 MATTHEWS, T. S.
"Old Girl." Atl (230:1) Jl 72, p. 55.

2075 MATTHEWS, William
"The Answer." Sky (1:1) 71.
"The Calculus." Peb (6) Sum 71.
"The Cat." Epoch (21:3) Spr 72, p. 238.
"The City of Silence." Drag (3:1) Spr 72, p. 46.
"A common man is walking" (tr. of Jean Follain, w. Mary Feeney). Apple (7) Aut 72, p. 9.
"A crossroads" (tr. of Jean Follain, w. Mary Feeney). Apple (7) Aut 72, p. 7.
"Directions." Kayak (28) 72, p. 48.
"An Egg in the Corner of One Eye." OhioR (13:2) Wint 72, p. 12.
"Holding the Fort." BelPoJ (23:1) Fall 72, p. 1.
"Houses contain so many, many objects" (tr. of Jean Follain, w. Mary Feeney). Apple (7) Aut 72, p. 8.
"In a book dating from the time of Buffon" (tr. of Jean Follain, w. Mary Feeney). Drag (3:2) Sum 72, p. 42.
"It happens" (tr. of Jean Follain, w. Mary Feeney).

Apple (7) Aut 72, p. 5.
"Leaving the Cleveland Airport" (for Robert & Tomas). Iron (1) Spr 72, p. 29.
"Letter to the Dear One." Epoch (21:2) Wint 71, p. 174.
"Marriage." Kayak (28) 72, p. 49.
"Pledge of Allegiance." NewRep (167:2) 8 Jl 72, p. 23.
"Prose poems of Jean Follain" (tr. of Jean Follain, w. Mary Feeney). Iron (1) Spr 72, pp. 23-28.
"Skywriting." Sky (1:2) 72, p. 4.
"Sleeping Alone." Epoch (21:2) Wint 71, p. 173.
"Sticks & Stones." OhioR (13:3) Spr 72, p. 52.
"Store windows start to light up" (tr. of Jean Follain, w. Mary Feeney). Apple (7) Aut 72, p. 8.
"La Tache 1962 (for Michael Cuddihy)." OhioR (13:2) Wint 72, p. 13.
"Two New-Born Pigs." Peb (6) Sum 71.
"The Visionary Picnic." Poetry (119:5) F 72, p. 278.

2076 MATTISON, Alice
"The Landlady's Complaint." AmerR (15) 72, p. 189.

2077 MAUNULA, Allan
"My Heart Is Frost." Epos (23:4) Sum 72, p. 7.

2078 MAURA, Sister, S.S.N.D.
"For the New Occupants." ChiTM 14 My 72, p. 9.
"Former Student." Comm (95:20) 18 F 72, p. 465.
"Tornado Watch." Thought (47:184) Spr 72, p. 101.

2079 MAXSON, Gloria
"Candidate." ChrC (89:30) 30 Ag 72, p. 843.
"Gospel Singer, Mahalia." ChrC (89:18) 3 My 72, p. 574.
"Semanticist." ChrC (89:38) 25 O 72, p. 1060.
"Sensualist." ChrC (89:2) 12 Ja 72, p. 28.
"Warlords." ChrC (89:7) 16 F 72, p. 190.

2080 MAXWELL, Anne
"Overgrowth." FourQt (21:2) Ja 72, p. 8.

2081 MAYAKOVSKY, Vladimir
"The Cloud in Trousers" (tr. by Eugene M. Kayden). ColQ (21:2) Aut 72, p. 233.

2082 MAYER, Gerda
"poems like lace." WindO (10) Sum 72, p. 18.

2083 MAYER, Parm
"Monody, Written on the Eve of Man's Departure." GreenR (2:2) 72, p. 31.

2084 MAYHALL, Jane
"Because I Know So Little." NYT 25 D 72, p. 16.
"On the Meaning of Literary Influence." NYT 1 My 72, p. 32.

2085 MAZZARO, Jerome
"Townscape." Shen (23:4) Sum 72, p. 41.

2086 MBEMBE (Milton Smith)
"African Art." NewL (39:2) Wint 72, p. 43.
"African Art No. 2." NewL (39:2) Wint 72, p. 43.
"High." NewL (39:2) Wint 72, p. 44.
"Survival Poem." NewL (39:2) Wint 72, p. 45.

2087 MEADE, Mary Ann
"Drought." AbGR (3:1) Spr-Sum 72, p. 12.

2088 MEDLEY, Lloyd J.
"Homecoming." JnlOBP (2:16) Sum 72, p. 80.

2089 MEDWICK, Cathleen
"Winnie and the Frog." NewYQ (11) Sum 72, p. 72.

2090 MEDWICK, Lucille
"A century of sand." NewYQ (9) Wint 72, p. 36.
"Requiem." NewYQ (9) Wint 72, p. 35.
"Untitled Life." NewYQ (9) Wint 72, p. 34.

2091 MEE, Suzi
"Song." Stand (13:2) 72, p. 45.

2092 MEEHAN, Brian
"Intransigent She." SouthernR (8:1) Wint 72, p. 187.
"The Sophist in Passion." SouthernR (8:1) Wint 72, p. 186.

2093 MEEK, Jay
"Harold Johnson's Comeback." MassR (13:4) Aut 72, p. 566.
"Hippolyte Géricault." BelPoJ (23:2) Wint 72-73, p. 12.
"In the Running." AntR (32:1/2) Spr-Sum 72, p. 54.
"Letter to Hawthorne." BelPoJ (22:3) Wint 72-73, p. 14.
"More Wonders of the Invisible World." PoetryNW (13:3) Aut 72, p. 37.
"Sonny Liston." Shen (24:1) Aut 72, p. 69.

2094 MEEKER, Don
"Boundary Stakes." KanQ (4:1) Wint 71-72, p. 126.

2095 MEHROTRA, Arvind Krishna
"At Every Step" (tr. of Gajanan Madhav Muktibodh). Mund (5:3) 72, p. 18.
"Between Bricks, Madness." Meas (3) 72, p. 84.
"The Exquisite Corpse." Nat (215:11) 16 O 72, p. 342.
"Fable." Nat (215:11) 16 O 72, p. 342.
"Fantomas." Nat (215:11) 16 O 72, p. 342.

2096 MEINKE, Norman
"One of the Last High-Divers." Qt (5:38) Spr 72, p. 15.

2097 MEINKE, Peter
"Because." NewRep (167:8) 2 S 72, p. 29.
"Each Morning." NewRep (166:21) 20 My 72, p. 32.
"Greta Garbo Poem #41." Cosmo (172:5) My 72, p. 76.
"Lilacs." Cosmo (172:6) Je 72, p. 118.
"Morocco." NewRep (167:21) 2 D 72, p. 24.
"Old Man River." NewRep (166:26) 24 Je 72, p. 25.
"Poem to Old Friends Who Have Never Met." NewRep (166:14) 1 Ap 72, p. 30.

2098 MEIRELES, Cecilia
"Sad" (tr. by D. M. Pettinella). FourQt (21:3) Mr 72, p. 20.
"Solitude" (tr. by D. M. Pettinella). FourQt (21:3) Mr 72, p. 21.

2099 MEISSNER, Bill
"The Blind Man Celebrates His Birthday." NowestR (12:2) Spr 72, p. 17.
"Finding Out Too Many of My Old Friends Have Killed Themselves." NowestR (12:2) Spr 72, p. 15.
"I Feel the Magnet, the Branches Beneath the Woods." Folio (8:1) Spr 72, p. 3.
"Just Passed 23, Looking Wildly for 22." MidwQ (13:3) Spr 72, p. 300.
"The People Dream and Speak of Freedom." MidwQ (13: 3) Spr 72, p. 289.
Promise: Eleven Poems. Northeast Sum 72, p. 17.
"The Test: A Tightrope Walker Can Never Look Down." Shen (24:1) Aut 72, p. 60.
"This Is What the Music Means." NowestR (12:2) Spr 72, p. 18.
"When the Sun Changed and We Left for the North." Folio (8:2) Fall 72, p. 9.

2100 MELLA, John
"Day Comet." LittleM (6:1) Spr 72, p. 12.

2101 MELTZER, David
from The Magic Wound. Meas (1) 71.
"Mouse." Isthmus (1) Spr 72, p. 26.
from State Grant: "Lady socialworker invades our home." Spec (14:1/2) My 72, p. 68.
"Tree." Isthmus (1) Spr 72, p. 5.

2102 MENDELSON, Chaim
"Apollo." Folio (8:1) Spr 72, p. 41.
"Forgive Me For Not Recognizing You." SouthernHR (6:2) Spr 72, p. 155.
"Generation Gap." SouthernHR (6:1) Wint 72, p. 62.
"Lessons." Folio (8:2) Fall 72, p. 41.
"A Reply." Folio (8:1) Spr 72, p. 21.
"Shadowy Recollection." Epos (23:3) Spr 72, p. 15.

2103 MENEBROKER, Ann
"April 25, 1971." Zahir (1:4/5) 72, p. 47.
"The Boy." FourQt (21:2) Ja 72, p. 44.
"The Bright Lie." KanQ (4:1) Wint 71-72, p. 115.
"My Father's Chair" (for C. F. K.). FourQt (21:3) Mr 72, p. 48.
"Nothing But Bones to Bite." Epos (23:4) Sum 72, p. 18.
"Request." Zahir (1:4/5) 72, p. 46.
"Salesman on a Night Out." BabyJ (5) N 72, p. 22.
"Susan's Brown Horse." BabyJ (5) N 72, p. 21.

2104 MENEMENCIOGLU, Nermin
"Arrival" (tr. of Oktay Rifat). LitR (15:4) Sum 72, p. 413.
"The Bedouin" (tr. of Edip Cansever). LitR (15:4) Sum 72, p. 482.
"Guillotine" (tr. of Ulkü Tamer). LitR (15:4) Sum 72, p. 466.
"The Horses" (tr. of Behçet Necatigil). LitR (15:4) Sum 72, p. 463.
"Ill-Fated Youth" (tr. of Necati Cumali). LitR (15:4) Sum 72, p. 464.
"I've Registered for Germany" (tr. of M. Başaran). LitR (15:4) Sum 72, p. 483.

2105 MENESSINI, Orlando Flores
"The Fabulists" (tr. by Gabriel Jiménez Emán). WormR (48) 72, p. 117.

2106 MENKITI, Ifeanyi
"Begun with First Beginnings." SewanR (80:1) Wint 72, p. 122.
"The Hill Beyond Alissa." SewanR (80:1) Wint 72, p. 121.
"The Long Journeys." SouthwR (57:4) Aut 72, p. 281.

2107 MENN, Don
"Poem: fall snow[1]/(slash) slick streets!!!" BeyB (2:2) 72, p. 38.

2108 MENUEZ, Mary Jane
"Evidence." AriD (1:2) Wint 72, p. 38.
"Requiem for Senility." AriD (1:2) Wint 72, p. 39.

2109 MERCHANT, Jane
"Indian Pipe." PoetL (67:3) Aut 72, p. 232.
"Waking at 2 A.M." PoetL (67:3) Aut 72, p. 262.

2110 MERCHANT, Paul
"Geneology" (tr. of Eleni Vakalo). AriD (1:4/5) Sum-Aut 72, p. 111.

2111 MEREDITH, William
"At the Confluence of the Colorado and the Little Colorado." NewYorker (48:10) 29 Ap 72, p. 105.
"At the Natural History Museum." VirQR (48:2) Spr 72, p. 217.
"Hazard, the Painter." Iron (1) Spr 72, p. 74.
"In Loving Memory of the Late Author of the Dream Songs." SatR (55:21) 20 My 72, p. 48.
"Recollection of Bellagio." WorldO (6:3) Spr 72, p. 20.

2112 MERNIT, Susan
"The Gym Teacher Plays Goalie." HangL (16) Wint 71-72, p. 36.

2113 MERRILL, James
"Days of 1971." AmerR (14) 72, p. 34.
"Days of 1935." Hudson (25:1) Spr 72, p. 13.
"Dreams about Clothes" (for John and Anne Hollander). Shen (23:2) Wint 72, p. 3.
"18 West 11th Street." NewYRB (18:12) 29 Je 72, p. 15.
"Electra: A Translation." Perspec (17:1) Sum 72, p. 10.
from Theory of Vision: "The Green Eye." Poetry (121:1) O 72, p. 19.
"Under Libra: Weights and Measures." NewYorker (48:15) 3 Je 72, p. 37.
"Up and Down." NewYorker (48:7) 8 Ap 72, p. 36.
"Yánnina (for Stephen Yenser)." SatR (55:49) D 72, p. 42.

2114 MERWIN, W. S.
"Animals From Mountains." Poetry (120:2) My 72, p. 101.
"Armed with the sight of the fine wasps" (tr. of Osip Mandelstam, w. Clarence Brown). Hudson (25:1) Spr 72, p. 73.
"Ash." QRL (18:1/2) 72, p. 135.
"Ballade of Sayings." NewYorker (48:37) 4 N 72, p. 46.
"Beggars and Kings." Antaeus (6) Sum 72, p. 67.
"Belly-ache" [tr. of Tzotzil (Zanacantán)]. NewYRB (18:7) 20 Ap 72, p. 18.
"The Borrowers." Antaeus (6) Sum 72, p. 66.
"The Chase." Poetry (120:2) My 72, p. 100.
"Clear Lake." Kayak (30) D 72, p. 47.
"The Day." Poetry (120:2) My 72, p. 100.
"The Diggers." QRL (18:1/2) 72, p. 130.
"Dogs." Hudson (25:2) Sum 72, p. 262.
"Elder Brother." QRL (18:1/2) 72, p. 131.
"The Entry." Field (7) Fall 72, p. 76.
"Exercise." Poetry (120:2) My 72, p. 98.
"Eyes of Summer." QRL (18:1/2) 72, p. 135.
"A Fable of the Buyers." NewYorker (47:51) 5 F 72, p. 33.

"Falls." QRL (18:1/2) 72, p. 127.
"Five Poems" (tr. of Osip Mandelstam, w. Clarence Brown). Antaeus (6) Sum 72, p. 92.
"Flies." ColumF (1:3) Sum 72, p. 18.
Fourteen Poems (tr. of Osip Mandelstam, w. Clarence Brown). QRL (18:1/2) 72, p. 7.
"Gift." Nat (215:17) 27 N 72, p. 536.
"Glass." NewYorker (48:35) 21 O 72, p. 44.
"The Good-Bye Shirts." Sky (1:1) 71.
"A Hollow." Iron (2) Fall 72, p. 18.
"I am alone staring into the eye of the ice" (tr. of Osip Mandelstam, w. Clarence Brown). NewYRB (17:12/18:1) 27 Ja 72, p. 35.
"Insomnia. Homer. Taut Sails" (tr. of Osip Mandelstam, w. Clarence Brown). Hudson (25:1) Spr 72, p. 71.
"Malgache" (tr. of Jean Paulhan). Madrona (1:1) Je 71, p. 21.
"A Man" (tr. of Nicanor Parra). Iron (1) Spr 72, p. 36.
"Meeting." Nat (215:17) 27 N 72, p. 536.
"Oh the horizon steals my breath and takes it nowhere--" (tr. of Osip Mandelstam, w. Clarence Brown). NewYRB (17:12/18:1) 27 Ja 72, p. 35.
"Old Flag." Antaeus (6) Sum 72, p. 65.
"A Purgatory." Poetry (120:2) My 72, p. 102.
"The Second Time." Poetry (120:2) My 72, p. 99.
"Song of Man Chipping an Arrowhead." Poetry (120:2) My 72, p. 100.
"Song of the Foreigner" (tr. of Nicanor Parra). Iron (1) Spr 72, p. 37.
"Span." Nat (215:17) 27 N 72, p. 536.
"Speech of a Guide." NewYorker (48:19) 1 Jl 72, p. 35.
"Summits." Hudson (25:2) Sum 72, p. 262.
"The Track." Nat (215:17) 27 N 72, p. 536.
"Travelling." Nat (215:5) 4 S 72, p. 150.
"Tristia" (tr. of Osip Mandelstam, w. Clarence Brown). Hudson (25:1) Spr 72, p. 71.
"We shall meet again, in Petersburg" (tr. of Osip Mandelstam, w. Clarence Brown). Hudson (25:1) Spr 72, p. 72.
"What can we do with the plains' beaten weight?" (tr. of Osip Mandelstam, w. Clarence Brown). NewYRB (17:12/18:1) 27 Ja 72, p. 35.
"When the Horizon Is Gone." BerksR (8:2) Fall-Wint 72, p. 4.
"Who It Is." QRL (18:1/2) 72, p. 126.
"Why Souls Are Lost Now" [tr. of Tzotzil (Zinacantán)]. NewYRB (18:7) 20 Ap 72, p. 18.
"The Writing on a Fallen Leaf." Nat (215:5) 4 S 72, p. 150.

2115 MESSER, Rich
"Hard Candy." Nat (214:17) 24 Ap 72, p. 541.
"Suicide." Nat (214:24) 12 Je 72, p. 765.

"Tourist." DenQuart (7:1) Spr 72, p. 78.

2116 METRULIS, Raymond
"Leo Stonecutter (for Catherine Clay)." Nat (214:19) 8 My 72, p. 602.

2117 MEURER, Marjorie
"Area Code 916." Folio (8:1) Spr 72, p. 10.
"Communion." Folio (8:1) Spr 72, p. 36.

2118 MEWSHAW, Michael
"Mother and the Wheel Chair." YaleR (62:1) Aut 72, p. 80.

2119 MEYER, Thomas
"A Holler for a Tricky Yankee." Lilla (12) Wint 73, p. 51.

2120 MEYERS, Bert
"And Still." Kayak (29) S 72, p. 40.
"The Daughter." Kayak (29) S 72, p. 39.
"Daybreak." Kayak (29) S 72, p. 38.
"Landscapes." Kayak (30) D 72, p. 54.
"The Son." Kayak (29) S 72, p. 38.

2121 MEYERS, William
"The war continues and I want women." NewYQ (12) Aut 72, p. 96.

2122 MEZEY, Robert
"New Poem." Kayak (29) S 72, p. 52.

2123 MICHAELSON, L. W.
"Thoughts on the Grave of William H. Bonney, Ft. Sumner, N.M." Meas (2) 72.

2124 MICHELINE, Jack
"the dead are gone." Magazine (5) part 9, 72, p. 13.

2125 MICHELSON, Peter
"Bestride the Mighty and Heretofore Deemed Endless Missouri: An Essay on the Corps of Discovery." ChiR (23:4 & 24:1) 72, p. 16.

2126 MIDDLETON, Christopher
"The Beautiful Beech" (tr. of Eduard Mörike). BosUJ (20:1/2) 72, p. 19.
"Erinna to Sappho (tr. of Edward Mörike). BosUJ (20:1/2) 72, p. 20.
"In a Park" (tr. of Eduard Mörike). BosUJ (20:1/2) 72, p. 18.
"Offering" (tr. of Eduard Mörike). BosUJ (20:1/2) 72, p. 23.

"On a Lamp" (tr. of Eduard Mörike). BosUJ (20:1/2) 72, p. 21.
"Plague of the Forest" (tr. of Eduard Mörike). BosUJ (20:1/2) 72, p. 22.
"Thoughts Concerning Our German Warriors" (tr. of Eduard Mörike). BosUJ (20:1/2) 72, p. 21.
"Two Lines by Lars Gustafson." BosUJ (20:3) Aut 72, p. 54.

2127 MIEZELAITIS, Eduardo
"My Land" (tr. by Bernard Koten, w. Nan Braymer). NewWR (40:4) Aut 72, p. 114.

2128 MIKOLOWSKI, Ken
"Two Found Porno Poems." Kayak (28) 72, p. 42.

2129 MILBOURN, Lawrence E.
"Funeral." HolCrit (9:1) Ap 72, p. 4.

2130 MILLAN, Gonzalo
"Automobile" (tr. by Edward Oliphant). RoadAR (4:1) Spr 72, p. 36.
"The Iron Hoops of the Tireless Tricycle and the Scrape of a Nail" (tr. by Edward Oliphant). RoadAR (4:1) Spr 72, p. 37.
"A Long Time Already I Have Been" (tr. by Edward Oliphant). RoadAR (4:1) Spr 72, p. 38.
"The Nude Tailor Takes a Break" (tr. by Edward Oliphant). RoadAR (4:1) Spr 72, p. 39.
from Reverses: "I watch myself entering" (tr. by Edward Oliphant). RoadAR (4:1) Spr 72, p. 38.
"Song of Blind Hope" (tr. by Edward Oliphant). RoadAR (4:1) Spr 72, p. 37.

2131 MILLER, E. S.
"Before Retiring." AAUP (58:1) Mr 72, p. 20.
"Plumeria." SoCaR (4:2) Je 72, p. 46.

2132 MILLER, Edmund
"Sioto River." Confr (5) Wint-Spr 72, p. 45.

2133 MILLER, Heather
"The Cremation of R. J." SouthernPR (12:2) Spr 72, p. 13.
"Jenny." NoCaFo (20:2) My 72, p. 97.

2134 MILLER, Hugh
"A Child's Library of Curses" (for Sarah). SatireN (9:2) Spr 72, p. 160.
"Sex in the Apiary." PoetL (67:2) Sum 72, p. 122.

2135 MILLER, Jim W.
"The Shop." SouthernPR (12:2) Spr 72, p. 34.

2136 MILLER, John N.
"The Waiting Room." ChrC (89:11) 15 Mr 72, p. 304.

2137 MILLER, Lanette Bradford
"Two Straight Lions." NYT 24 N 72, p. 36.

2138 MILLER, Marcia Muth
"American Theatre--Nineteenth Century." ArizQ (28:4) Wint 72, p. 366.
"This Place of Living." FreeL (15:1/2) 71-72, p. 48.

2139 MILLER, Naomi
"Coffee." HangL (18) Fall 72, p. 63.
"Every Night." HangL (18) Fall 72, p. 66.
"A woman." HangL (18) Fall 72, p. 65.
"Your top drawer is filled." HangL (18) Fall 72, p. 64.

2140 MILLER, Raeburn
"Advent." KanQ (4:1) Wint 71-72, p. 65.
"For a Lost Picture of My Father." SouthernR (8:2) Spr 72, p. 421.
"An Ode for Defeat." SouthernR (8:2) Spr 72, p. 420.
"The Pornographer Manqué." KanQ (4:1) Wint 71-72, p. 65.

2141 MILLER, Rob
"Union #6." Meas (2) 72.

2142 MILLER, Vassar
"For the Public Library." StoneD (1:1) Spr 72, p. 37.

2143 MILLER, Walter James
"At a Baroque Concert." PoetL (67:2) Sum 72, p. 175.
"The Docking of the Sidney Streeter." PoetL (67:2) Sum 72, p. 176.
"Windy Moment on Brooklyn Heights." PoetL (67:2) Sum 72, p. 175.

2144 MILLIGAN, Thomas
"Eight Jack Dawes Poems." VirQR (48:1) Wint 72, p. 57.

2145 MILLIKEN, Don
"Fourteen Lines from Avignon." LittleM (6:2/3) Sum-Aut 72, p. 121.
"Winter Palace." LittleM (6:1) Spr 72, p. 19.

2146 MILLS, Barriss
"After Winter." ChiTM 7 My 72, p. 12.
"Cliché." ChiTM 3 D 72, p. 30.

2147 MILLS, Ralph J., Jr.
"At the End of the Wars." Kayak (28) 72, p. 31.

"For Natalie." Poem (16) N 72, p. 56.
"For T. S. Eliot in Westminster Abbey." Poem (16) N 72, p. 57.
"For Vallejo." Kayak (28) 72, p. 31.
"Funerals." Kayak (28) 72, p. 30.
"Nerve Gas." Kayak (28) 72, p. 32.
"The Nerve of Feathers." Poem (16) N 72, p. 54.
"The Telephone." Poem (16) N 72, p. 55.

2148 MILNE, Rod
"Dope and the Ninth-Grader." EngJ (61:4) Ap 72, p. 494.

2149 MILOSZ, Oscar V. De Lubicz-
from "cantique de la Connaissance" (tr. by John Peck). QRL (18:1/2) 72, p. 141.
"L'Etrangère" (tr. by John Peck). QRL (18:1/2) 72, p. 139.
"Quand Elle Viendra ..." (tr. by John Peck). QRL (18:1/2) 72, p. 138.
"Le Roi Don Luis ..." (tr. by John Peck). QRL (18:1/2) 72, p. 137.

2150 MINASIAN, Archie
"The Unfortunate." Nat (215:16) 20 N 72, p. 509.

2151 MINER, Virginia Scott
"For Vonda (Who handed me her poems)." KanQ (4:3) Sum 72, p. 45.
"Helen of Troy, Indiana." KanQ (4:3) Sum 72, p. 46.

2152 MINOR, James
"Mission, South Dakota." SoDakR (10:3) Aut 72, p. 85.

2153 MINNIS, John
"Nigger Store." JnlOBP (2:16) Sum 72, p. 20.

2154 MINTZ, Phil
"Climbing." Nat (215:3) 7 Ag 72, p. 94.
"Sometimes, Even in the Snuggest Life, a Poem That Is So True Will Rattle a Cold Draft Under the Windowsill (for Kenneth Patchen)." Nat (214:23) 5 Je 72, p. 738.

2155 MIRANDA, Gary
"For Ann, Sleeping." SouthernPR (12:2) Spr 72, p. 9.
"Inventory." PoetryNW (13:1) Spr 72, p. 28.

2156 MIRON, Gaston
"Dead Leaves and Embers" (tr. by Fred Cogswell). New:ACP (18) Ap 72, p. 33.

2157 MISHIMA, Yukio
"Farewell Poems" (tr. by Alan Ireland). St.AR (1:4) Spr-Sum 72, p. 11.

2158 MITCHELL, Joe
"to you white girl." NewYQ (12) Aut 72, p. 73.

2159 MITCHELL, Roger
from Letters from Siberia: "Sunday Outing." MinnR (2) Spr 72, p. 110.
"Poem: For months I've walked this rocky coast." MinnR (2) Spr 72, p. 5.
"Shirley." ChiTM 23 Jl 72, p. 14.

2160 MITCHELL, Stephen
"The Cave Man Is Not About to Talk" (tr. of Dan Pagis). Humanist (32:1) Ja-F 72, p. 32.
"Song of Red and Blue" (tr. of Amir Gilboa). Humanist (32:1) Ja-F 72, p. 33.
"The Stranger" (tr. of T. Carmi). Humanist (32:1) Ja-F 72, p. 33.

2161 MITCHELL, William R.
"Beyond Relativity." ChrC (89:13) 29 Mr 72, p. 369.
"Meditation on Matthew 5:38-48." ChrC (89:30) 30 Ag 72, p. 846.

2162 MITRA, Tridib
"My Supersonic Life." Meas (3) 72, p. 48.

2163 MITSUI, James
"Layer Five." Madrona (1:3) My 72, p. 4.

2164 MODAYIL, Anna Sujatha
"Loved One." Meas (3) 72, p. 49.
"Waiting." Meas (3) 72, p. 49.

2165 MOEBIUS, Walter
"Making Love in Raga Time." Pan (9) 72, p. 17.

2166 MÖRIKE, Eduard
"The Beautiful Beech" (tr. by Christopher Middleton). BosUJ (20:1/2) 72, p. 19.
"Erinna to Sappho" (tr. by Christopher Middleton). BosUJ (20:1/2) 72, p. 20.
"In a Park" (tr. by Christopher Middleton). BosUJ (20:1/2) 72, p. 18.
"Offering" (tr. by Christopher Middleton). BosUJ (20:1/2) 72, p. 23.
"On a Lamp" (tr. by Christopher Middleton). BosUJ (20:1/2) 72, p. 21.
"Plague of the Forest" (tr. by Christopher Middleton). BosUJ (20:1/2) 72, p. 22.
"Thoughts Concerning Our German Warriors" (tr. by Christopher Middleton). BosUJ (20:1/2) 72, p. 21.

2167 MOFFETT, Judy
"Other Woman." SouthernPR (12:2) Spr 72, p. 23.

2168 MOHR, Howard
"On the Day I Got Tenure." SouthernPR (13:1) Aut 72, p. 38.

2169 MOLESWORTH, Charles
"Driftwood." Nat (215:19) 11 D 72, p. 597.
"Stanzas Occasioned by a View." Poetry (120:2) My 72, p. 71.

2170 MOLTON, Warren Lane
"Myth of a Man." ChrC (89:9) 1 Mr 72, p. 250.
"Nightmare." ChrC (89:43) 29 N 72, p. 1214.

2171 MONDRAGON, Sergio
"Heat" (tr. by Douglas Lawder and Katherine Grimes). Drag (3:2) Sum 72, p. 45.

2172 MONETTE, Paul
"Bathing the Aged." YaleLit (141:1) 71, p. 12.
"Blaze." YaleLit (141:1) 71, p. 13.
"Drifter." YaleLit (141:1) 71, p. 15.
"The Monk's Hours." YaleLit (141:1) 71, p. 14.
"Rebus." YaleLit (141:1) 71, p. 14.
"Thinking of Cindy." YaleLit (141:1) 71, p. 13.

2173 MONROE, Harriet
"Nogi." Poetry (121:1) O 72, p. 21.

2174 MONTAG, Tom
"Winterpoem." RoadAR (3:4) Wint 71-72, p. 10.

2175 MONTAGUE, John
"Courtyard in Winter." Esq (77:6) Je 72, p. 206.
"A Grafted Tongue." UnmOx (1:3) Sum 72, p. 3.
"The Massacre." Nat (215:6) 11 S 72, p. 186.

2176 MONTALE, Eugenio
from Diaro Del '71: "Letter to Bobi" (tr. by G. Singh). MedR (2:4) Sum 72, p. 80.
from Satura: "First January" (tr. by G. Singh). MedR (2:4) Sum 72, p. 79.
from Satura: "Hiding Places" (tr. by G. Singh). MedR (2:4) Sum 72, p. 80.
from Satura: "Late in the Night" (tr. by G. Singh). MedR (2:4) Sum 72, p. 78.
from Two Venetian Pieces: (2) (tr. by G. Singh). MedR (2:4) Sum 72, p. 78.

2177 MONTER, Barbara Heldt
"For Anna Akhmatova" (tr. of Alexander Blok). RusLT (4) Aut 72, p. 19.
"Today I don't want to remember what happened yesterday" (tr. of Alexander Blok). RusLT (4) Aut 72, p. 18.

2178 MONTEZ, Pedro
"La Senora." Folio (8:2) Fall 72, p. 39.

2179 MONTGOMERY, George
from Ask the Grass Why It Grows: "Part Eleven." St. AR (1:4) Spr-Sum 72, p. 76.
"Funeral Fire" (for Paul Blackburn 1926-1971). Zahir (1:4/5) 72, p. 72.
"It Can Be Worn" (for Lyn Lifshin). Zahir (1:4/5) 72, p. 72.

2180 MONTGOMERY, Marion
"I Can See It Both Ways." HolCrit (9:1) Ap 72, p. 11.
"In Nature, Each in His Nature." Poem (16) N 72, p. 39.
"Instructions." Poem (16) N 72, p. 38.
"King Nestor's Palace." CarlMis (12:1) Fall-Wint 71-72, p. 111.
"Robinson Jeffers." GeoR (26:2) Sum 72, p. 225.

2181 MONTGOMERY, Stuart
"blind men." Antaeus (7) Aut 72, p. 105.
"deer tracks." Antaeus (5) Spr 72, p. 92.
"the deserted mosque." Antaeus (7) Aut 72, p. 102.
"Down Wind of Nevada." Antaeus (7) Aut 72, p. 104.
"The eyes of a startled snake are solemn." Antaeus (5) Spr 72, p. 90.
"men blunder." Antaeus (7) Aut 72, p. 106.
"Miriam." Antaeus (7) Aut 72, p. 103.
"the mountain." Antaeus (5) Spr 72, p. 91.
"she listens." MedR (2:2) Wint 72, p. 68.
"turning into a crow." Antaeus (5) Spr 72, p. 89.

2182 MOOD, John J.
"Four Poem Fragments" (tr. of Rainer Maria Rilke). NewYQ (9) Wint 72, p. 64.

2183 MOORE, Audley
"Adam's Song." NYT 28 Ap 72, p. 41.

2184 MOORE, Barbara
"If Time Would Begin." Epos (24:1) Fall 72, p. 6.

2185 MOORE, James
"Attica." GreenR (2:2) 72, p. 13.
"Doors." Iron (2) Fall 72, p. 40.
"When You Embroider." ChiTM 21 My 72, p. 22.

2186 MOORE, John E.
"Gulls." PoetryNW (13:3) Aut 72, p. 24.

2187 MOORE, Marianne
"The Wizard in Words." Poetry (121:1) O 72, p. 22.

2188 MOORE, Mary Louise
"Space Travel." NegroHB (35:4) Ap 72, p. 86.

2189 MOORE, Naomi
"Progeny." Spec (14:1/2) My 72, p. 72.

2190 MOORE, Richard
"Ad Patrem." SouthernR (8:1) Wint 72, p. 153.
"Marriage Blues." Poetry (119:4) Ja 72, p. 209.
"Oddball." HolCrit (9:1) Ap 72, p. 9.
"Pond Thoughts." Poetry (119:4) Ja 72, p. 210.
"Sonnet." Poetry (119:4) Ja 72, p. 212.
"The Tennis Ball." Poetry (119:4) Ja 72, p. 210.

2191 MOORHEAD, Andrea
"Flower Crown and Chill." SewanR (80:1) Wint 72, p. 114.

2192 MORA, Victor Valera
"Quebec" (tr. by Gabriel Jiménez Emán). WormR (48) 72, p. 117.

2193 MORAES, Dom
"Poem: Man builds his corner in the universe" (tr. of Uri Zvi Greenberg). Books (46:2) Spr 72, p. 250.

2194 MORAN, Carol
"The Beating." Works (3:3/4) Wint 72-73, p. 127.
"Connubial." Works (3:3/4) Wint 72-73, p. 127.
"First Question." Works (3:3/4) Wint 72-73, p. 127.
"One Stop in Philadelphia." HangL (18) Fall 72, p. 32.

2195 MORAN, Douglas John
"manuscripts piled about the room." Drag (3:1) Spr 72, p. 68.
"owning you." Drag (3:1) Spr 72, p. 68.

2196 MORAN, Ronald
"After a Question." SouthernR (8:4) Aut 72, p. 902.
"Countries for John." SouthernR (8:4) Aut 72, p. 903.
"Divorcée." SouthernR (8:4) Aut 72, p. 900.
"Incident in a Condemned Building." SouthernR (8:4) Aut 72, p. 899.
"Moving Out." SouthernR (8:4) Aut 72, p. 903.
"Rising toward Birch." SouthernR (8:4) Aut 72, p. 898.
"Taking Out the Nails." SouthernR (8:4) Aut 72, p. 901.

2197 MORAN, Yildiz
from "The Corners of the Round" (tr. of Ozdemir Asaf). LitR (15:4) Sum 72, p. 452.

2198 MORDECHAI, Anny
"Flavors." SouthernPR (12: Special Issue) 72, p. 40.

2199 MOREA, Douglas
"A Cold Husk." NewYorker (48:16) 10 Je 72, p. 40.
"On Fourteenth Street." NewYorker (47:47) 8 Ja 72, p. 32.

2200 MORGAN, Edwin
"Glasgow Sonnets." Stand (13:2) 72, p. 15.

2201 MORGAN, Frederick
"Barbershop Poem." NYT 20 Jl 72, p. 32.
from A Book of Change. Hudson (25:3) Aut 72, p. 361.
"Great Hooks." NewRep (167:14) 14 O 72, p. 25.
from Pages from a Forgotten Book. TexQ (15:3) Aut 72, p. 71.
"Poem of the Self." NewYorker (48:23) 29 Jl 72, p. 75.
"Poems of the Two Worlds." Kayak (30) D 72, p. 5.

2202 MORGAN, Jean
"The Misogynist." NewRep (166:22) 27 My 72, p. 33.
"Summer Place." NewRep (167:13) 7 O 72, p. 23.

2203 MORGAN, John
"Common Sense." PoetryNW (13:1) Spr 72, p. 26.

2204 MORGAN, Phyllis
"Weather of Heaven." PoetryNW (13:1) Spr 72, p. 19.

2205 MORGAN, Robert
"Day Lilies." SouthernPR (12: Special Issue) 72, p. 49.
"Present." Nat (214:4) 24 Ja 72, p. 124.
"Windfall." Nat (214:8) 21 F 72, p. 254.

2206 MORGENSTERN, Christian
"When Winter Travels Through" (tr. by Reinhold Johannes Kaebitzsch). Folio (8:1) Spr 72, p. 12.

2207 MORICONI, Albert Mario
from Dibattito Su Amore: "Skull and Belly" (tr. by Anne D. Griguoli). MedR (2:4) Sum 72, p. 94.
from Dibattito Su Amore: "The Ballad of Guano" (tr. by Anne D. Griguoli). MedR (2:4) Sum 72, p. 92.

2208 MORIN, Edward
"Noblesse." PraS (46:2) Sum 72, p. 143.
"Not Really Knowing the First Day of Spring." ColQ (21:2) Aut 72, p. 161.
"Postcard." Qt (5:37) Wint 72, p. 12.
"The Year of the Vietnam Peace." Focus (9:57) 72, p. 29.

2209 MORLEY, Hilda
"Five Poems." Hudson (25:1) Spr 72, p. 74.
"Leo Nikolayevich Tolstoy." NewL (38:3) Spr 72, p. 87.

2210 MORRIS, Doctor
"1-19-70 (1 Day) The New Day From Atlanta." JnlOBP (2:16) Sum 72, p. 12.
"A Thought Dedicated to an Oasis." JnlOBP (2:16) Sum 72, p. 11.

2211 MORRIS, Harry
"At Loggerheads." SouthernPR (12:2) Spr 72, p. 18.

2212 MORRIS, Herbert
"Above the Midnight Fields." QRL (18:1/2) 72, p. 154.
"Bring Down Darkness on This House Tonight." QRL (18:1/2) 72, p. 148.
"The Casebook of a Man Called Doctor Dratch." Kayak (28) 72, p. 3.
"Darkness Falling on a Bleak Republic." MedR (2:3) Spr 72, p. 92.
"Entrances." AriD (1:3) Spr 72, p. 24.
"The Evening of the Novelist." ModernO (2:1) Wint 72, p. 23.
"Falling Asleep to Music from the Party." QRL (18:1/2) 72, p. 145.
"Moving Deeper." QRL (18:1/2) 72, p. 155.
"Not Answering Your Call Late Some Clear Evening." QRL (18:1/2) 72, p. 147.
"Once in Ahmadabad." Kayak (29) S 72, p. 14.
"One's Youth." Salm (18) Wint 72, p. 105.
"Starting a Life." QRL (18:1/2) 72, p. 154.
"Who I Was with You I Am with No Other." Shen (23:3) Spr 72, p. 71.

2213 MORRIS, John N.
"In the Hamptons." NewYorker (48:24) 5 Ag 72, p. 54.

2214 MORRIS, Richard
"Poetry." Cafe (4) Fall 72, p. 8.

2215 MORRIS, Tudor
"Distances" (tr. of Hilde Domin). DenQuart (6:4) Wint 72, p. 4.
"I Want You" (tr. of Hilde Domin). DenQuart (6:4) Wint 72, p. 1.
"Unicorn" (tr. of Hilde Domin). DenQuart (6:4) Wint 72, p. 3.

2216 MORSE, Robert
"Noche Triste." Poetry (120:5) Ag 72, p. 268.

2217 MOSER, Norm
"Collage No. 11." Magazine (5) part 9, 72, p. 14.
"Start With the Line of the Eye." Meas (2) 72.

2218 MOSES, W. R.
"Another Winter's Tale." KanQ (4:1) Wint 71-72, p. 32.
"As Though." KanQ (4:1) Wint 71-72, p. 32.
"A Small Justice." KanQ (4:1) Wint 71-72, p. 33.

2219 MOSLEY, Walter
"On Edward Brash's 'Black Brother'." ModernPS (3:2) 72, p. 78.
"W. H. Auden." ModernPS (3:2) 72, p. 79.

2220 MOSS, Howard
"Bores" (To a child who asked what a "bore" was). Harp (245:1471) D 72, p. 67.
"Chekhov." NewYorker (48:1) 26 F 72, p. 36.
"Jane Austen." SatR (55:37) S 72, p. 37.
"Johann Sebastian Bach." SatR (55:45) N 72, p. 66.
"Nearing the Lights." NewYorker (48:33) 7 O 72, p. 36.
"The Stairs." NewYorker (47:49) 22 Ja 72, p. 32.
"Venice: A Footnote." Harp (245:1471) D 72, p. 67.
"The Writer at the End of the Bar." AmerR (14) 72, p. 67.

2221 MOTJUWADI, Stanley
"Taken for a Ride." Playb (19:5) My 72, p. 169.

2222 MOTT, Michael
"Past Newfoundland." PraS (46:3) Aut 72, p. 226.
from A Personal Alphabet (A, B, C, E, M, S, W). Poetry (120:1) Ap 72, p. 1.

2223 MOUNDES, Matthaios
"Mannikins" (tr. by Stavros Deligiorgis). AriD (1:4/5) Sum-Aut 72, p. 81.
"Runaway" (tr. by Stavros Deligiorgis). AriD (1:4/5) Sum-Aut 72, p. 82.
"Terminal" (tr. by Stavros Deligiorgis). AriD (1:4/5) Sum-Aut 72, p. 82.

2224 MOUNT, Rena
"Club Manager, Watching." Folio (8:1) Spr 72, p. 31.
"Madhouse Blues." Folio (8:1) Spr 72, p. 27.

2225 MOYER, Donald
"At the Scene of a Motorcycle Accident: A Dream About Gasoline and Rotation." Antaeus (6) Sum 72, p. 138.
"MC: Starting It Up, 2." MinnR (3) Aut 72, p. 104.

2226 MOYO, S. Phaniso C.
"Dear My Kind." JnlOBP (2:16) Sum 72, p. 73.

2227 MTSHALI, Oswald Mbuyiseni
"Pigeons at the Oppenheimer Park." Playb (19:5) My 72, p. 168.

"The Watchman's Blues." Playb (19:5) My 72, p. 168.

2228 MUELLER, Lisel
"Historical Museum, Manitoulin Island." Poetry (120:2) My 72, p. 96.
"Poem: Yes we were happy that Sunday." Cafe (4) Fall 72, p. 12.
"What the Dog Perhaps Hears." ChiTM 5 Mr 72, p. 14.

2229 MUKHERJEE, S.
"Story of an Enterprise" (tr. of Monindra Ray). Meas (3) 72, p. 68.

2230 MUKTIBODH, Gajanan Madhav
"At Every Step" (tr. by Arvind Krishna Mehrotra). Mund (5:3) 72, p. 18.

2231 MULAC, Madeline Wood
"Lost." Poem (15) Jl 72, p. 24.

2232 MULHOLLAND, Kathleen
"Metamorphosis." EngJ (61:9) D 72, p. 1406.

2233 MULLFEATHER
"Mystical Dream." FreeL (15:1/2) 71-72, p. 1.

2234 MULLIGAN, Jerry
"Hubert." Drag (3:2) Sum 72, p. 53.

2235 MULLINS, Helen
"But What of the Eye." Etc. (29:2) Je 72, p. 122.

2236 MULLINS, Sue
"Birth." MassR (13:1/2) Wint-Spr 72, p. 188.
"Female Liberation." MassR (13:1/2) Wint-Spr 72, p. 188.

2237 MULRANE, Scott H.
"Children of the Moon." Wind (2:5) Sum 72, p. 17.
"Music." Esq (78:4) O 72, p. 203.

2238 MUNDELL, William
"Another Garden." PoetL (67:3) Aut 72, p. 216.
"H_2O." PoetL (67:3) Aut 72, p. 233.
"The Kill." NewYQ (12) Aut 72, p. 51.
"Laughter." PoetL (67:3) Aut 72, p. 233.
"Long Distance." PoetL (67:3) Aut 72, p. 234.
"That Path Joy Goes." PoetL (67:3) Aut 72, p. 234.

2239 MURPHEY, Joseph Colin
"Walking Linda to Sleep (for her first birthday)." Qt (5: 39/40) Sum-Aut 72, p. 43.

2240 MURPHY, Richard
"Firebug." NewYRB (19:8) 16 N 72, p. 6.

2241 MURRAY, Donald M.
"After Mary." SouthernPR (13:1) Aut 72, p. 6.

2242 MURRAY, G. E.
"Chicago As the Time of Night" (to Michael Healy, in Cambridge, Massachusetts). Iron (1) Spr 72, p. 19.
"The Plant Rhythms." Iron (1) Spr 72, p. 18.
"Somewhere in Boston There's a Bridge Writing Music." Iron (1) Spr 72, p. 16.
"What the Toads Were Told in Paradise." Iron (1) Spr 72, p. 17.

2243 MURRAY, George
"Seasonal." Epos (23:4) Sum 72, p. 23.

2244 MURRAY, Philip
"American Gothic." GeoR (26:1) Spr 72, p. 89.
"Le Coq Sans Confiance." PoetryNW (13:3) Aut 72, p. 22.
"The Dean of St. Hilary." Poetry (120:4) Jl 72, p. 224.
"Fantasia on a Theme by Mrs. Gaskell." Poetry (120:4) Jl 72, p. 228.
"Lourdes." Poetry (120:4) Jl 72, p. 225.
"Peeping Tom Comes to Realize that Beauty is in the Eyes of Peeping Tom." PoetryNW (13:3) Aut 72, p. 22.

2245 MUSKE, Carol
"Child With Six Fingers." Antaeus (7) Aut 72, p. 97.
"Riddle: I look different in order to look the same." Antaeus (7) Aut 72, p. 30.
"Rite." Antaeus (7) Aut 72, p. 98.

2246 MUTTI, Giuliana
"Blood Signs." MassR (13:1/2) Wint-Spr 72, p. 268.
"In the Season When the Earth" (tr. of La Compiuta Donzella, anonymous 13th century Florentine woman). MassR (13:1/2) Wint-Spr 72, p. 104.

2247 MYERS, J. William
"The Crow." PoetL (67:3) Aut 72, p. 255.
"Ohio Trees in a Village." PoetL (67:3) Aut 72, p. 249.

2248 MYERS, Jack
"Finale." MinnR (2) Spr 72, p. 81.
"Making Do" (to Pat and Pam Hazel). Shen (24:1) Aut 72, p. 47.
"Up." MinnR (2) Spr 72, p. 81.

2249 MYERS, Jack E.
"Farmer." NowestR (12:3) Aut 72, p. 2.

2250 NABHAN, Gary
"long hard times." WestR (9:2) Wint 72, p. 14.

2251 NADIR, Moshe
"Serene" (tr. by Leonard Opalov). PoetL (67:1) Spr 72, p. 34.

2252 NAESS, Kate
Twelve Poems (tr. by F. H. König). NoAmR (257:1) Spr 72, p. 65.

2253 NAHNYBIDA, Simon
"A Scene from Faust" (tr. of Alexander Pushkin, w. Roberta Reeder). RusLT (3) Spr 72, p. 40.

2254 NAKELL, Martin
"Poem in Four Parts." ChiR (24:2) 72, p. 180.

2255 NANDY, Babla
"ALIEN TUNES." Meas (3) 72, p. 50.

2256 NANDY, Pritish
"Eclogue Nine." Meas (3) 72, p. 51.

2257 NAPIER, James J.
"A Slant View." CEACritic (34:2) Ja 72, p. 37.

2258 NASH, Ogden
"The Rejected Portrait." Horizon (14:2) Spr 72, p. 112.
"The Slipshod Scholar Gets Around to Greece." Horizon (14:2) Spr 72, p. 113.

2259 NASH, Valery
"Pas de Folle, 1930." Shen (23:4) Sum 72, p. 75.

2260 NATACHEE, Allan
"Folk Songs from Papua" (edited by Ulli Beier). UnicornJ (4) 72, p. 85.

2261 NATHAN, Leonard
"Breathing Exercises." Shen (23:3) Spr 72, p. 33.
"Confession." QRL (18:1/2) 72, p. 162.
"Expectation." NYT 3 Jl 72, p. 16.
"From the Cold Outside." QRL (18:1/2) 72, p. 160.
"Hay Fever." NewYorker (48:9) 22 Ap 72, p. 48.
"Honorable Mention." NYT 29 Ag 72, p. 32.
"The Hunt." Antaeus (7) Aut 72, p. 64.
"Jane Seagrim's Party." Shen (23:3) Spr 72, p. 35.
"Lull." NYT 26 Mr 72, sec. 4, p. 12.
"Memo." Antaeus (7) Aut 72, p. 63.
"The Penance." NewRep (167:6/7) 19-26 Ag 72, p. 22.
"Pilgrims Down." QRL (18:1/2) 72, p. 161.
"Powers." Antaeus (7) Aut 72, p. 62.
"Pumpernickel." Epoch (22:1) Fall 72, p. 71.

"Revival Meeting for Wheel Chairs and Stretchers." QRL (18:1/2) 72, p. 158.
"Stonecutter's Holiday." Antaeus (7) Aut 72, p. 61.
"To the City." QRL (18:1/2) 72, p. 159.
"Wires." PraS (46:2) Sum 72, p. 173.
"The Word." QRL (18:1/2) 72, p. 161.

2262 NATHAN, Norman
"Blank." SouthernHR (6:3) Sum 72, p. 254.
"Bon Voyage." SouthernHR (6:3) Sum 72, p. 255.
"Closed." SouthernPR (12:2) Spr 72, p. 19.
"Keys." BallSUF (13:1) Spr 72, p. 28.
"Nocturne." Poem (14) Mr 72, p. 39.
"St. Thomas--New York." Qt (5:37) Wint 72, p. 28.
"To Catch the Wind." NYT 9 D 72, p. 34.
"Total." Poem (14) Mr 72, p. 37.
"The Transmigrator Says." Poem (14) Mr 72, p. 38.

2263 NATIONS, Opal L.
"how to use your head to get a living carpet." WormR (48) 72, p. 119.

2264 NAYMAN, Louis
"Frontier Justice." KanQ (4:3) Sum 72, p. 59.

2265 NECATIGIL, Behçet
"The Horses" (tr. by Nermin Menemencioglu). LitR (15:4) Sum 72, p. 463.

2266 NEDELKOFF, Dan
"asking for permission to live." WindO (11) Aut 72, p. 33.
"at your place." WindO (11) Aut 72, p. 33.
"relaxing." WindO (11) Aut 72, p. 33.

2267 NEFF, Allen
"Forty Years of Fall." PoetL (67:3) Aut 72, p. 257.
"Rain on the Road." SouthernHR (6:3) Sum 72, p. 284.
"Storm Windows." Wind (2:5) Sum 72, p. 9.
"To the Last Wolf in Illinois." PoetL (67:3) Aut 72, p. 254.

2268 NELSON, Dale
"Selections from a Work in Progress Based Loosely on the Revised Code of Washington." PoetryNW (13:1) Spr 72, p. 3.

2269 NELSON, H. H.
"Poem Composed Over Several Months." Apple (7) Aut 72, p. 15.

2270 NELSON, Malcolm A.
"Upon the Occasion of the Closing of Another of His Temples, Zeus Speaks:" AAUP (58:4) D 72, p. 398.

2271 NELSON, Nils
"The Night Janitor." Iron (2) Fall 72, p. 9.

2272 NELSON, Paul
"Allergy." QRL (18:1/2) 72, p. 164.
"E. S. P." QRL (18:1/2) 72, p. 166.
"Gorilla." QRL (18:1/2) 72, p. 165.
"The Last Act." Iowa (3:2) Spr 72, p. 14.
"1943." Iowa (3:2) Spr 72, p. 16.
"Putting in Glass." QRL (18:1/2) 72, p. 163.
"Ramses Adamant." Iowa (3:2) Spr 72, p. 14.

2273 NELSON, Peter
"August, Quiet." Iron (2) Fall 72, p. 36.
"Between Lives." Iron (2) Fall 72, p. 34.
"The City In Winter." Iron (2) Fall 72, p. 35.

2274 NELSON, R. S.
"The Shade." SouthernPR (12:2) Spr 72, p. 50.

2275 NELSON, Stanley
"Just For You, Marianne." Confr (5) Wint-Spr 72, p. 22.
"Just for You, Marianne/Moore." Meas (2) 72.
"Scythian Suite." Meas (2) 72.

2276 NEMANIC, Todd
"In the Garden." SoDakR (10:3) Aut 72, p. 84.

2277 NEMEROV, Howard
"The Beautiful Lawn Sprinkler." NewYorker (48:16) 10 Je 72, p. 120.
"The Crossing." NewRep (167:10) 16 S 72, p. 29.
"Questions." NewRep (166:23) 3 Je 72, p. 25.
"Sigmund Freud." Poetry (121:1) O 72, p. 23.
Ten Poems. Poetry (120:4) Jl 72, p. 216.
"To D----, Dead by Her Own Hand." SatR (55:45) N 72, p. 42.
"To The Rulers." NewRep (166:18) 29 Ap 72, p. 27.

2278 NEMET-NEJAT, Murat
"The Address of Turkey" (tr. of Metin Eloğlu). LitR (15:4) Sum 72, p. 404.
"Country" (tr. of Cemal Süreya). LitR (15:4) Sum 72, p. 432.
"Embellishments" (tr. of Sabahattin Kudret Aksal). LitR (15:4) Sum 72, p. 435.
"'Neither Did I See Such Love nor Such Partings'" (tr. of Ilhan Berk). LitR (15:4) Sum 72, p. 439.

2279 NERUDA, Pablo
"Ausencia." NewYQ (12) Aut 72, p. 60.
"Caballo de los Suenos." Iron (2) Fall 72, p. 20.
"Coleccion Nocturna." Iron (2) Fall 72, p. 28.

"El Desvio." NewYQ (12) Aut 72, p. 59.
"V: Manual Metaphysics" (tr. by Ben Belitt). VirQR (48:2) Spr 72, p. 192.
"I Want to Turn to the South: 1941" (tr. by Andrew Glaze). Atl (229:4) Ap 72, p. 46.
"In You the Earth" (tr. by Donald D. Walsh). Atl (229:2) F 72, p. 68.
"Juntos Nosotros." Iron (2) Fall 72, p. 24.
"Lives" (tr. by Donald D. Walsh). Nat (215:14) 6 N 72, p. 438.
"The Mason" (tr. by Donald D. Walsh). Atl (229:2) F 72, p. 69.
"Night on the Island" (tr. by Donald D. Walsh). Atl (229:2) F 72, p. 69.
"The Police" (tr. by Joseph Bruchac and Liliana Goldin). SenR (3:1) My 72, p. 22.
"The Queen" (tr. by Donald D. Walsh). Atl (229:2) F 72, p. 68.
"Sonata and Destructions" (tr. by Robert Bly). AbGR (3:1) Spr-Sum 72, p. 1.
"Unidad." Iron (2) Fall 72, p. 22.

2280 NEUFELDT, Leonard
"The Annunciation." MichQR (11:1) Wint 72, p. 49.
"Cleopatra, Our Cat, Is Recovering." Madrona (1:2) N 71, p. 27.
"The Coat Is Too Thin." MichQR (11:1) Wint 72, p. 48.
"Hands." PoetryNW (13:4) Wint 72-73, p. 36.
"In Retrospect: Thinking for Father." Madrona (1:2) N 71, p. 26.
"Passing Over." Madrona (1:2) N 71, p. 28.
"The Path." KanQ (4:1) Wint 71-72, p. 82.
"Sequel to Silence." WestHR (26:3) Sum 72, p. 212.
"The Touch and Shape of an Elegy." WestHR (26:1) Wint 72, p. 32.

2281 NEUGROSCHEL, Joachim
"I Want to Salute Crudely" (tr. of Jean Arp). DenQuart (6:4) Wint 72, p. 31.
"The Inconceivable That Resounds" (tr. of Jean Arp). DenQuart (6:4) Wint 72, p. 29.
"O Mezzanine" (tr. of Jean Arp). DenQuart (6:4) Wint 72, p. 30.
"What Is That?" (tr. of Jean Arp). DenQuart (6:4) Wint 72, p. 32.

2282 NEUMEYER, Peter F.
"different cases" (for W. M.). SoCaR (5:1) D 72, p. 41.
"Poet Pellets." EngJ (61:8) N 72, p. 1162.
"Rope's End." ColEng (34:3) D 72, p. 445.
"Your Christmas Music" (for friends we make music with). ColEng (34:3) D 72, p. 443.

2283 NEVIUS, Debby
"Cherokee in Tourist Season." SouthernPR (12: Special Issue) 72, p. 50.

2284 NEWBORN, Jud
"Plath." Nat (214:2) 10 Ja 72, p. 62.

2285 NEWHAUSER, Richard G.
"Get and Give." LittleM (6:2/3) Sum-Aut 72, p. 124.
"The Traveler's Epigram." LittleM (6:2/3) Sum-Aut 72, p. 123.

2286 NEWLOVE, Donald
"Bronx Atlas." VilV 7 S 72, p. 14.

2287 NEWMAN, Michael
"Negative Passage." Poetry (119:4) Ja 72, p. 221.
"Red Dogs." NewYQ (9) Wint 72, p. 68.

2288 NEWMAN, Paul Baker
"Forgiveness." SoCaR (5:1) D 72, p. 26.
"Formation." SouthernPR (12:2) Spr 72, p. 22.
"Nineteen." St. AR (1:4) Spr-Sum 72, p. 79.
"Routes." SouthernPR (13:1) Aut 72, p. 11.
"The Soul as Squid." UTR (1:1) 72, p. 20.

2289 NEWTON, Suzanne
"Moses' Staff." SouthernPR (12: Special Issue) 72, p. 52.

2290 NEWTON, Tengemana
"To Kijua: Love Mama." JnlOBP (2:16) Sum 72, p. 36.

2291 NEWTON, Violette
"Dreaming with Father." PoetL (67:4) Wint 72, p. 347.
"General Lee." BallSUF (13:3) Sum 72, p. 44.
"The May When I Grew Up." BallSUF (13:1) Sum 72, p. 80.
"Waiting for Father." PoetL (67:4) Wint 72, p. 347.

2292 NEZVAL, Vitězslav
"Polykač Nožů." Mund (5:1/2) 72, p. 22.
"Rukavice." Mund (5:1/2) 72, p. 18.
"Tento Michelangelův Jinoch." Mund (5:1/2) 72, p. 22.
"Zaječí Kůže." Mund (5:1/2) 72, p. 20.

2293 NIATUM, Duane (McGinnis)
"Black Cherries Moon." NewYQ (9) Wint 72, p. 43.
"Center Moon." NewYQ (9) Wint 72, p. 41.
"Full Leaf Moon." NewYQ (9) Wint 72, p. 40.
"A November Night and Many Streets." Madrona (1:2) N 71, p. 11.
"Our Green Scroll to Full Leaf Moon." Madrona (1:1) Je 71, p. 12.

"Red Berries Moon." NewYQ (9) Wint 72, p. 39.
"Sore Eye Moon." NewYQ (9) Wint 72, p. 42.

2294 NICHOLAS, Michael
"A Song of Water for Water." JnlOBP (2:16) Sum 72, p. 51.

2295 NICHOLSON, Philip
"Be My Pest." SatEP (244:2) Sum 72, p. 102.

2296 NICKERSON, Sheila B.
"Alaska Autumn." Poem (15) Jl 72, p. 11.
"Alaska Welcome." SoDakR (10:4) Wint 72-73, p. 91.
"In the Juneau Cemetery, November." Poem (15) Jl 72, p. 12.
"Letter from Alaska." Poem (15) Jl 72, p. 9.
"Living Among the Totem Carvers." Poem (15) Jl 72, p. 15.
"Sestina." Poem (15) Jl 72, p. 13.

2297 NICKLAUS, Frederick
"Find It by the Gathering of the Gulls." NYT 19 F 72, p. 30.
"Predawn Poem." NYT 24 O 72, p. 42.

2298 NICOLE
"The Death of Things." BallSUF (13:1) Wint 72, p. 2.
"Relationship." BeyB (2:2) 72, p. 42.
"Separate." BeyB (2:2) 72, p. 42.
"So What Do You Look Like, Reality?" NewRena (6) My 72, p. 60.

2299 NIDITCH, Ben Zion
"Joy Street." Poem (16) N 72, p. 33.
"Marblehead." PoetL (67:3) Aut 72, p. 266.

2300 NIECE, Richard
"Sitting in Class." EngJ (61:6) S 72, p. 930.

2301 NIEH Hua-Ling
"Seven Poems" (tr. of Mao Tse-Tung, w. Paul Engle). Playb (19:4) Ap 72, p. 163.

2302 NIEMCZYK, Mike
"Veronica Lake." KanQ (4:2) Spr 72, p. 80.

2303 NIFLIS, Michael
"Blackfoot Chief at a Teacher's College in 1930." DenQuart (7:3) Aut 72, p. 36.
"Gazelle." NYT 11 Mr 72, p. 28.
"Idiosyncrasies." DenQuart (7:3) Aut 72, p. 35.
"My Serpent." DenQuart (7:3) Aut 72, p. 38.
"A Search." Nat (214:5) 31 Ja 72, p. 150.

"Sentimentality." Comm (96:14) 16 Je 72, p. 336.
"The Skull." Nat (214:6) 7 F 72, p. 188.
"Two In Us." NewRep (166:21) 20 My 72, p. 23.

2304 NILSEN, Richard
"Residue." Epoch (22:1) Fall 72, p. 36.
"Trying To Help People." Epoch (22:1) Fall 72, p. 36.

2305 NIMS, John Frederick
"Parting: 1940." Poetry (121:1) O 72, p. 24.

2306 NIST, John
"Telephone Conversation." Qt (5:39/40) Sum-Aut 72, p. 41.

2307 NITCHIE, George W.
"Autumn Letter" (for Judy Anderson). Shen (23:3) Spr 72, p. 84.
"Death by Starvation." PoetryNW (13:4) Wint 72-73, p. 32.
"Stripping an Old Farm House." PoetryNW (13:4) Wint 72-73, p. 32.

2308 NIXON, Colin
"French Cemetery." ChrC (89:36) 11 O 72, p. 1007.

2309 NIXON, John, Jr.
"Bull." SouthernPR (12:2) Spr 72, p. 31.
"A Glitter." GeoR (26:3) Fall 72, p. 369.
"Sweet and Worn Out." GeoR (26:3) Fall 72, p. 368.

2310 NOBLE, J. W.
"Passage." PoetL (67:4) Wint 72, p. 335.
"Recess." PoetL (67:4) Wint 72, p. 333.

2311 NOGUERE, Suzanne
"Poem: When I." Nat (215:1) 10 Jl 72, p. 22.

2312 NOLAN, Pat
"Second Place." Cord (1:4) 72, p. 19.

2313 NOLAN, Tony
"Poem: Looking through venetian blinds." AbGR (3:1) Spr-Sum 72, p. 5.
"Sally's Soul." AbGR (3:1) Spr-Sum 72, p. 6.
"Stanley Oatmeal." AbGR (3:1) Spr-Sum 72, p. 4.

2314 NOLL, Bink
"Fragments." ChiTM 2 Ja 72, p. 4.

2315 NORDFORS, Margaret
"A Death at 55." Madrona (1:2) N 71, p. 32.
"Thanking a Friend." Madrona (1:2) N 71, p. 32.

2316 NORMAN, Albert H.
"Harold You Are My Moon." AntR (31:4) Wint 71-72, p. 518.

2317 NORRIS, Kathleen
"Walking with the Devil, Side by Side." Nat (215:8) 25 S 72, p. 251.

2318 NORRIS, Leslie
"Bridges." Atl (229:6) Je 72, p. 73.
"Burning the Bracken." TransR (42/43) Spr-Sum 72, p. 79.
"His Last Autumn" (for Andrew Young, 1885-1971). Atl (230:5) N 72, p. 73.
"Old Voices." Atl (229:3) Mr 72, p. 61.
"Skulls." NewYorker (47:50) 29 Ja 72, p. 36.

2319 NORSE, Harold
"from all these, you." Kayak (28) 72, p. 12.
"I Am Going to Fly Through Glass (for Anais Nin)." Kayak (28) 72, p. 14.
"Three Parapoems." UnmOx (1:2) F 72, p. 34.

2320 NORTH, Charles
"Another Nice Day for the Race." Poetry (121:3) D 72, p. 142.
"Variation (Overheard)." Poetry (121:3) D 72, p. 141.

2321 NORTH, Mary Hayne
"A Canvas Left Unfinished." VirQR (48:2) Spr 72, p. 220.
"For My Grandmother Mary Hayne." VirQR (48:2) Spr 72, p. 219.

2322 NOTLEY, Alice
"Four Sonnets." ParisR (53) Wint 72, p. 80.

2323 NOVAK, Michael Paul
"At the Prom." FourQt (21:3) Mr 72, p. 22.
"Dawn." KanQ (4:3) Sum 72, p. 14.
"Driving with My Son." Focus (9:57) 72, p. 29.
"Explanation, of Sorts, for Pessimism." FourQt (21:3) Mr 72, p. 22.
"How Deep." Poem (16) N 72, p. 3.
"Huck Comes Back." Poem (16) N 72, p. 6.
"Identifying the Wanderers." Poem (16) N 72, p. 1.
"The Latin Room." KanQ (4:3) Sum 72, p. 15.
"The Night Before the Peace March." WestR (9:1) 72, p. 55.
"Some Tourists." Poem (16) N 72, p. 2.
"A Visit at the Missionary's." Poem (16) N 72, p. 4.

2324 NOVAK, Robert
"tonight children." WindO (11) Aut 72, p. 8.

2325 NOVALIS
"Aphorisms" (tr. by Michael Hamburger). QRL (18:1/2) 72, p. 167.

2326 NOVOTNAK, Paula
"Cheap Apartments." Epos (23:3) Spr 72, p. 12.

2327 NURMI, Earl
"Prayer of the Weeping Multitudes." New:ACP (19) Aut 72, p. 44.

2328 NUSAI, Jude
"Alaska Land Claim." Indian (5:2) Sum 72, p. 31.

2329 NYE, Robert
"Agnus Dei." NowestR (12:3) Aut 72, p. 76.

2330 NYERGES, Anton N.
"Archetypes." Poem (14) Mr 72, p. 5.
"Countercreation." ModernPS (2:6) 72, p. 277.
"Eclogue IV: 1971." Poem (14) Mr 72, p. 3.
"The Intern." Poem (14) Mr 72, p. 4.
"March." ModernPS (2:6) 72, p. 279.
"Nemo." ModernPS (2:6) 72, p. 278.
"Stained Window." ModernPS (2:6) 72, p. 278.

2331 NYHART, Nina
"Seven Dwarf Confessions." AriD (1:2) Wint 72, p. 26.

2332 OAKES, Philip
"Taking a Bath." TransR (41) Wint-Spr 72, p. 107.

2333 OATES, Joyce Carol
"Acceleration Near the Point of Impact." Esq (78:5) N 72, p. 89.
"Firing a Field" (In memory of Flannery O'Connor). MassR (13:3) Sum 72, p. 469.
"Friendly Conversation." SouthernHR (6:1) Wint 72, p. 70.
"Mile-High Monday." Salm (19) Spr 72, p. 66.
"R. D. Laing poses problems." ModernPS (3:3) 72, p. 141.
"Stranded." SouthernHR (6:1) Wint 72, p. 71.
"A Woman Walking in a Man's Sight." SouthernHR (6:1) Wint 72, p. 69.
"A Young Wife." AntR (31:4) Wint 71-72, p. 476.

2334 OBAMOLA
"At a Rally to 'Free' Panther Lonnie McLucas on the New Haven Green--1970." JnlOBP (2:16) Sum 72, p. 22.
"A Black Poem." JnlOBP (2:16) Sum 72, p. 21.

2335 OBERG, Arthur
"After Brunch." UnicornJ (4) 72, p. 47.

"At Thirty, and Looking Back." UnicornJ (4) 72, p. 46.
"Book of the Hours." Madrona (1:3) My 72, p. 39.
"Dancing." QRL (18:1/2) 72, p. 174.
"Eyeing Your World." UnicornJ (4) 72, p. 48.
"Getting the Hang of It." Madrona (1:3) My 72, p. 40.
"Learning American Grace (for Theodore Roethke)." OhioR (14:1) Aut 72, p. 22.
"Lighting Out." NowestR (12:2) Spr 72, p. 46.
"Memory Is Hunger." UnicornJ (4) 72, p. 45.
"Off Range." QRL (18:1/2) 72, p. 173.
"The Smell of Burning." Shen (23:3) Spr 72, p. 79.
"This Christmas." SouthernPR (12:2) Spr 72, p. 40.
"Transparencies." UnicornJ (4) 72, p. 47.
"Walking." QRL (18:1/2) 72, p. 174.

2336 O'BRIEN, Michael
"Berlin 1912" (Else Lasker-Schuler). UnmOx (1:1) N 71, p. 8.
"Rilke's Epitaph." UnmOx (1:1) N 71, p. 7.

2337 OCHESTER, Ed
"Contemplating Suicide." ColQ (21:1) Sum 72, p. 42.
"Dialog." ColQ (21:1) Sum 72, p. 41.
"Morte D'Arthur." WormR (48) 72, p. 137.
"9 Ways to Have a Good Time in Pittsburgh." WormR (48) 72, p. 138.
"A Short Life." ColQ (21:1) Sum 72, p. 42.
"Some Places the Mobil Oil Map Lists as 'Points of Interest in Pittsburgh.'" WormR (48) 72, p. 139.
"Zeno's Arrow." WormR (48) 72, p. 137.

2338 OCHOA, Willie
"Suppertime." WindO (10) Sum 72, p. 41.
"we followed the yellow brick road." WindO (11) Aut 72, p. 24.

2339 O'CONNOR, Philip F.
"The Bends" (for David Ray). GreenR (2:2) 72, p. 39.

2340 O'DALY, Bill
"The Kalahari Bushman." Spec (14:1/2) My 72, p. 73.

2341 ODAM, Joyce
"All I Own of Being Numb." BabyJ (5) N 72, p. 9.
"And Know You Know the Meaning." KanQ (4:3) Sum 72, p. 96.
"As Time in Its Going." WindO (10) Sum 72, p. 38.
"Beneath the Fatal Clock." PraS (46:3) Aut 72, p. 207.
"The Candle." BabyJ (5) N 72, p. 10.
"Flights." PraS (46:3) Aut 72, p. 206.
"He's Got a Very Sad Laugh." SoCaR (5:1) D 72, p. 27.
"Landscape." Epos (23:3) Spr 72, p. 6.
"Leaving Notes on the Kitchen Table." Epos (24:1) Fall

72, p. 24.
"A Letter, Not a Poem." BabyJ (5) N 72, p. 11.
"The Luncheon." BabyJ (5) N 72, p. 11.
"Man Between." KanQ (4:3) Sum 72, p. 96.
"Of Such Safe Green." SoCaR (5:1) D 72, p. 28.
"Sight Seeing At 2:00 A.M." Epos (23:4) Sum 72, p. 24.
"Thanks for The." SoCaR (5:1) D 72, p. 22.
"Under the Snow of Summer." PraS (46:3) Aut 72, p. 208.
"The Visitor." KanQ (4:1) Wint 71-72, p. 11.

2342 ODELL, Clinton
"hexagram for 7 january." SouthernR (8:1) Wint 72, p. 185.

2343 OERKE, Andrew
"The Divine Comedy." Poetry (120:3) Je 72, p. 149.
"The Hippo's Head." NewRep (167:20) 25 N 72, p. 29.

2344 OGAREV, Nikolai
"Fantasia" (tr. by George Genereux). RusLT (3) Spr 72, p. 67.
"Her doorway! Firmly did I pull the bell" (tr. by George Genereux). RusLT (3) Spr 72, p. 66.

2345 OGDEN, Hugh
"The Turning." NoAmR (257:2) Sum 72, p. 46.

2346 OGDEN, John B., Jr.
"Spotted Turtle." PoetL (67:4) Wint 72, p. 375.

2347 OGILVIE, John
"Apocalypse (A University Library)." ArizQ (28:2) Sum 72, p. 100.

2348 O'GORMAN, Ned
"The Drunken Organ Repairman" (Easter, 1968). Horizon (14:2) Spr 72, p. 120.

2349 O'HARA, Frank
"Sleeping on the Wing." NewRep (166:1/2) 1-8 Ja 72, p. 28.

2350 O'HARA, J. D.
"Aristotle Contemplating the Bust of Homer: After Rembrandt." NewYorker (48:42) 9 D 72, p. 40.

2351 OHWOVORIOLE, Morgan
"Another Letter Home." GreenR (2:3) 72, p. 18.
"Good Old Mark." GreenR (2:3) 72, p. 19.
"Home." GreenR (2:3) 72, p. 20.
"my secret prayer." GreenR (2:3) 72, p. 23.
"A Nigerian In America Writes Home." GreenR (2:3) 72, p. 21.

2352 OJAIDE, Tanure
"At the Crossroads." GreenR (2:3) 72, p. 7.
"The Burnt Cowrie." GreenR (2:3) 72, p. 6.
"Map of Time." GreenR (2:3) 72, p. 5.
"Message of Lust." GreenR (2:3) 72, p. 7.
"Possibly Different." GreenR (2:3) 72, p. 10.
"What I Carry Along." GreenR (2:3) 72, p. 3.

2353 O'KEEFE, Richard R.
"Fish." PoetryNW (13:3) Aut 72, p. 14.
"Hawk: In the Manner of a Fugue." PoetryNW (13:3) Aut 72, p. 12.

2354 OLATUNJI, Ade
"Inside for the J. B. 's." JnlOBP (2:16) Sum 72, p. 59.
"One Movement In a Brown Eye." JnlOBP (2:16) Sum 72, p. 60.

2355 OLDER, Julia
"At Full Moon." PoetL (67:3) Aut 72, p. 251.
"A Real Hang-Up." PoetL (67:3) Aut 72, p. 250.
"You Are Always a Voice." PoetL (67:3) Aut 72, p. 250.

2356 OLDKNOW, Anthony
"Lament for the Makers." LittleM (6:2/3) Sum-Aut 72, p. 86.
"Luxe, Calme et Volupte." LittleM (6:2/3) Sum-Aut 72, p. 87.

2357 O'LEARY, Tom
"House on the High Road." MidwQ (14:1) Aut 72, p. 52.

2358 OLIPHANT, Edward
"The Apostate" (tr. of Oliver Welden). RoadAR (4:1) Spr 72, p. 50.
"Automobile" (tr. of Gonzalo Millán). RoadAR (4:1) Spr 72, p. 36.
"Bad Words for Violeta Parra" (tr. of Omar Lara). RoadAR (4:1) Spr 72, p. 27.
"Bitacora" (tr. of Oliver Welden). RoadAR (4:1) Spr 72, p. 48.
"Capitalist Prayer for Che" (tr. of Luis Moreno Pozo). RoadAR (4:1) Spr 72, p. 47.
"Carpenterings" (tr. of Omar Lara). RoadAR (4:1) Spr 72, p. 27.
"Chess" (tr. of Waldo Rojas). RoadAR (4:1) Spr 72, p. 40.
"The Chicken Pieces Are" (tr. of Oliver Welden). RoadAR (4:1) Spr 72, p. 48.
"Copper" (tr. of Andrés Sabella). RoadAR (4:1) Spr 72, p. 9.
"The Difficult Old Man" (tr. of Nicanor Parra). RoadAR (4:1) Spr 72, p. 19.

"Discourse from the Plains" (tr. of Andrés Sabella). RoadAR (4:1) Spr 72, p. 10.

"Elegy for Ernesto Che Guevara" (tr. of Enrique Lihn). RoadAR (4:1) Spr 72, p. 69.

"Elegy for some Miner Boots" (tr. of Andrés Sabella). RoadAR (4:1) Spr 72, p. 9.

"Far North" (tr. of Alicia Galaz). RoadAR (4:1) Spr 72, p. 52.

"Fluctuations" (tr. of Oliver Welden). RoadAR (4:1) Spr 72, p. 50.

"For Roque Dalton" (tr. of Enrique Lihn). SouthernHR (6:2) Spr 72, p. 160.

"For Speaking with the Dead" (tr. of Jorge Teillier). RoadAR (4:1) Spr 72, p. 17.

"Forth Judgment or Ambiguities of the Universe" (tr. of Cecilia Vicuña). RoadAR (4:1) Spr 72, p. 14.

"From the Rescuable Corners" (tr. of Alicia Galaz). RoadAR (4:1) Spr 72, p. 52.

"The Hand of God" (tr. of Hernán Lavín Cerda). RoadAR (4:1) Spr 72, p. 35.

"I Discover Offices and Travelled Passageways" (tr. of Ariel Santibáñez). RoadAR (4:1) Spr 72, p. 56.

"I Don't Believe in the Peaceful Way" (tr. of Nicanor Parra). RoadAR (4:1) Spr 72, p. 19.

"If Poetry Is To Be Written Right" (tr. of Enrique Lihn). RoadAR (4:1) Spr 72, p. 62.

"Inspection of School Supplies Hygiene and Personal Appearance" (tr. of Jaime Quezada). RoadAR (4:1) Spr 72, p. 26.

"The Iron Hoops of the Tireless Tricycle and the Scrape of a Nail" (tr. of Gonzalo Millán). RoadAR (4:1) Spr 72, p. 37.

"Jaguar" (tr. of Enrique Lihn). RoadAR (4:1) Spr 72, p. 66.

"Julian" (tr. of Alicia Galaz). RoadAR (4:1) Spr 72, p. 51.

"Landscape" (tr. of Omar Lara). RoadAR (4:1) Spr 72, p. 27.

"Let It Be Whatever It Is" (tr. of Cecilia Vicuña). RoadAR (4:1) Spr 72, p. 15.

from Letters of the Poet Who Sleeps Sitting Up: (XVI, XVII) (tr. of Nicanor Parra). RoadAR (4:1) Spr 72, p. 21.

"Like a patient Job I bite" (tr. of Armando Uribe). RoadAR (4:1) Spr 72, p. 46.

from The Long Cueca: "I'll sing me a cueca" (tr. of Nicanor Parra). RoadAR (4:1) Spr 72, p. 20.

"A Long Time Already I Have Been" (tr. of Gonzalo Millán). RoadAR (4:1) Spr 72, p. 38.

"Manner in which I Discovered the Two Kinds of Death" (tr. of Cecilia Vicuña). RoadAR (4:1) Spr 72, p. 14.

"Meat Market" (tr. of Waldo Rojas). RoadAR (4:1) Spr 72, p. 42.

"Middle Age" (tr. of Carlos Cortínez). RoadAR (4:1) Spr 72, p. 32.
"Neurotic Art" (tr. of Hernán Lavín Cerda). RoadAR (4:1) Spr 72, p. 34.
"News from Babylon" (tr. of Enrique Lihn). RoadAR (4:1) Spr 72, p. 58.
"Notice of Terminal Illness" (tr. of Guillermo Deisler). RoadAR (4:1) Spr 72, p. 53.
"The Nude Tailor Takes a Break" (tr. of Gonzalo Millán). RoadAR (4:1) Spr 72, p. 39.
"Obscenities of a Sunflower" (tr. of Cecilia Vicuña). RoadAR (4:1) Spr 72, p. 16.
"Public Man" (tr. of Raúl Bruna). RoadAR (4:1) Spr 72, p. 12.
"Result Zero" (tr. of Nicanor Parra). RoadAR (4:1) Spr 72, p. 23.
from Reverses: "I watch myself entering" (tr. of Gonzalo Millán). RoadAR (4:1) Spr 72, p. 38.
"Revolution" (tr. of Enrique Lihn). RoadAR (4:1) Spr 72, p. 57.
"Self Portrait" (tr. of Cecilia Vicuña). RoadAR (4:1) Spr 72, p. 13.
"Song of Blind Hope" (tr. of Gonzalo Millán). RoadAR (4:1) Spr 72, p. 37.
"The Spy Who Came Back from the Cold" (tr. of Federico Schopf). RoadAR (4:1) Spr 72, p. 44.
"Story and Another Story" (tr. of Jaime Quezada). RoadAR (4:1) Spr 72, p. 25.
"Story for the Sleepless" (tr. of Waldo Rojas). RoadAR (4:1) Spr 72, p. 42.
"The Story I Never Found" (tr. of Guillermo Deisler). RoadAR (4:1) Spr 72, p. 54.
"A Street Upon a Time" (tr. of Jaime Quezada). RoadAR (4:1) Spr 72, p. 25.
"Summer Fruit" (tr. of Jorge Teillier). RoadAR (4:1) Spr 72, p. 17.
"Sweet Irish Dreams for Douglas." RoadAR (3:4) Wint 71-72, p. 40.
"A Tale for Cami" (tr. of Miguel Morales Fuentes). RoadAR (4:1) Spr 72, p. 55.
from Telegrams: (III, V) (tr. of Nicanor Parra). RoadAR (4:1) Spr 72, p. 22.
Three Poems (tr. of Armando Uribe). RoadAR (4:1) Spr 72, p. 46.
"To Live (Present Tense)" (tr. of Floridor Perez). RoadAR (4:1) Spr 72, p. 33.
"Triangle" (tr. of Floridor Perez). RoadAR (4:1) Spr 72, p. 33.
"Upward" (tr. of Omar Lara). RoadAR (4:1) Spr 72, p. 30.
"Vigil" (tr. of Jaime Quezada). RoadAR (4:1) Spr 72, p. 26.
"Vital Axiom" (tr. of Oliver Welden). RoadAR (4:1) Spr

72, p. 49.
"Warning" (tr. of Oliver Welden). RoadAR (4:1) Spr 72, p. 49.
"We Knew Nothing" (tr. of Jaime Gómez Rogers). RoadAR (4:1) Spr 72, p. 43.
"Window" (tr. of Waldo Rojas). RoadAR (4:1) Spr 72, p. 41.
"Without Pretending" (tr. of Omar Lara). RoadAR (4:1) Spr 72, p. 31.
from Written in Cuba: "Thus I see myself in this fragmented world a" (tr. of Enrique Lihn). RoadAR (4:1) Spr 72, p. 64.

2359 OLIVA, Oscar
"Inhabited Clarity" (tr. by Douglas Lawder and Katherine Grimes). Drag (3:2) Sum 72, p. 44.

2360 OLIVER, Mary
"Cousin Grace." ChiTM 22 O 72, p. 8.
"Creeks." AmerS (41:2) Spr 72, p. 248.
"Stark County Holidays." ChiTM 24 D 72, p. 5.
"Stone Poem." NYT 16 Mr 72, p. 46.

2361 OLIVER, Raymond
"Lapidary Verses." PraS (46:2) Sum 72, p. 148.
"The Last Judgement." Iowa (3:4) Fall 72, p. 13.
"To Andrei Rublev." PraS (46:3) Aut 72, p. 253.

2362 OLSON, Toby
from Home: "How enter into it: as contract, I'll." Works (3:2) Wint-Spr 72, p. 52.
"The Trouble with This House" (for Diane Wakoski). Works (3:2) Wint-Spr 72, p. 53.

2363 OLU, Niyonu
"When We Are Again One." JnlOBP (2:16) Sum 72, p. 19.

2364 O'MALLEY, Sister Emanuela
"Written in an Abandoned School House." KanQ (4:3) Sum 72, p. 56.

2365 O'NEILL, Laurence
"The Young Girl at the Piano." WestHR (26:4) Aut 72, p. 347.

2366 OPALOV, Leonard
"At Home." PoetL (67:1) Spr 72, p. 23.
"Big and Small" (tr. of Abraham Sutzkever). PoetL (67:1) Spr 72, p. 35.
"Black as the Pupil of the Eye" (tr. of Marina Tsvetaeva). PoetL (67:1) Spr 72, p. 30.
"Caught" (tr. of H. Leivick). PoetL (67:1) Spr 72, p. 34.

"Enticed." Folio (8:1) Spr 72, p. 24.
"Genua" (tr. of Nicolai Gumiliov). PoetL (67:1) Spr 72, p. 29.
"I Came into This World" (tr. of Constantin Balmont). PoetL (67:1) Spr 72, p. 31.
"Myself." PoetL (67:1) Spr 72, p. 26.
"Old Yet Youthful." Folio (8:2) Spr 72, p. 9.
"Poem of a Workingman" (tr. of Saul Maltz). PoetL (67:1) Spr 72, p. 32.
"Question and Answer" (tr. of Abraham Sutzkever). PoetL (67:1) Spr 72, p. 35.
"Rachel Verprinsky." Folio (8:1) Spr 72, p. 13.
"Serene" (tr. by Moshe Nadir). PoetL (67:1) Spr 72, p. 34.
"Sew Me a Green Old Age" (tr. of Shike Driz). PoetL (67:1) Spr 72, p. 35.
"Strange Repository" (tr. of Marina Tsvetaeva). PoetL (67:1) Spr 72, p. 29.
"Symphony in Gray." Folio (8:1) Spr 72, p. 26.
"When I Hear Your Voice" (tr. of Michael Lermontov). PoetL (67:1) Spr 72, p. 32.

2367 OPPEN, George
"A Poem About the Garden." Iron (1) Spr 72, p. 14.
from Some San Francisco Poems: "Combed thru the piers the wind." Iron (1) Spr 72, p. 13.
from Some San Francisco Poems: "O withering seas." Iron (1) Spr 72, p. 12.

2368 OPPENHEIMER, Joel
"April 3 1972." VilV 6 Ap 72, p. 24.
"E.P. 1885-1972." VilV 9 N 72, p. 33.
"a free country." VilV 25 My 72, p. 53.
"July 22: Two Deaths." VilV 3 Ag 72, p. 61.
"Red Star Over China." VilV 24 F 72, p. 10.
"two baseball poems." VilV 4 My 72, p. 89.

2369 OPPENHEIMER, Max, Jr.
"Verlaine" (tr. of Yevgeny Yevtushenko). ColQ (21:1) Aut 72, p. 223.

2370 OPPENHEIMER, Paul
"An Afternoon in Eden." Works (3:3/4) Wint 72-73, p. 99.
"Experience with Saturn." Humanist (32:2) Mr-Ap 72, p. 34.
"Gossip About the Rich Man in Venice." Works (3:3/4) Wint 72-73, p. 98.
"The Killing of Our King." QRL (18:1/2) 72, p. 175.
"Lines for Certain Revolutionaries." QRL (18:1/2) 72, p. 176.
"Mirbeau's Poetic." Works (3:3/4) Wint 72-73, p. 98.

2371 ORAS, Ants
"Imitations of the Koran" (tr. of Alexander Pushkin). SewanR (80:2) Spr 72, p. 276.
"To the Memory of Andrei Bely" (tr. of Osip Mandelstam). RusLT (4) Aut 72, p. 63.

2372 ORLEN, Steven
"The Best Halves of Our Lives." NoAmR (257:3) Aut 72, p. 41.
"Compulsion." Kayak (29) S 72, p. 47.
"The Perfect One." AmerR (14) 72, p. 86.
"The Pig." Iron (1) Spr 72, p. 7.

2373 ORMAND, John
"My Dusty Kinsfolk." TransR (42/43) Spr-Sum 72, p. 80.
"Saying." TransR (41) Wint-Spr 72, p. 105.
"Summer Mist." TransR (42/43) Spr-Sum 72, p. 81.

2374 ORR, Ed
"A Brief Anthology of Kisses." AriD (1:3) Spr 72, p. 1.
"Calculus of Change." Epos (23:3) Spr 72, p. 20.
"Degas' Women." NYT 31 Mr 72, p. 28.
"Excess of Light." Epos (24:1) Fall 72, p. 13.
"Reflections on Cold." Iron (1) Spr 72, p. 35.
"Upon Reading D. H. Lawrence's 'Tourists'." NYT 17 Je 72, p. 28.

2375 ORR, Leonard
"Grasinda" (tr. of Gabrielle D'Annunzio). Wind (2:6) Aut 72, p. 19.

2376 ORTIZ, Elisabeth Lambert
"Kindness and grey days." Folio (8:1) Spr 72, p. 35.
"What you do in a garden to begin your season." Folio (8:1) Spr 72, p. 35.

2377 ORTLEB, Chuck
"Spring Cleaning." ConcPo (5:2) Fall 72, p. 49.

2378 OSAKI, Mark Stephen
"Small Flower" (for Clarice, 16 mo. old). Etc. (29:4) D 72, p. 351.

2379 OSBERG, R. H.
"The Granite Quarry." LittleM (6:2/3) Sum-Aut 72, p. 111.
"Spring Cleaning." LittleM (6:2/3) Sum-Aut 72, p. 110.

2380 OSBORN, Hollis
"The beer can stood before the senate." Drag (3:1) Spr 72, p. 69.
"An old man a young boy went to the zoo." Drag (3:1) Spr 72, p. 69.

2381 OSBORNE, Dorothy S.
"The Visit." SoCaR (5:1) D 72, p. 5.

2382 OSBORNE, J. K.
"Attica State Prison." Madrona (1:2) N 71, p. 34.
"August: North Dakota: Noon." Madrona (1:2) N 71, p. 25.
"Portrait: White Cloud." Madrona (1:2) N 71, p. 24.

2383 OSBORNE, Kenny
"how I live." WindO (9) Spr 72, p. 40.

2384 OSERS, Ewald
"Holidays" (tr. of Hans-Jürgen Heise). Stand (13:2) 72, p. 58.
"You" (tr. of Hans-Jürgen Heise). Stand (13:2) 72, p. 58.

2385 O'SHEEL, Patrick
"What's Half-Apparent." SouthernPR (13:1) Aut 72, p. 49.

2386 OSING, Gordon
"At a Movie." KanQ (4:2) Spr 72, p. 20.
"Bogart and Milton." KanQ (4:2) Spr 72, p. 19.

2387 OSOFSKY, Marcia
"Outside the Glass." SouthernPR (12:2) Spr 72, p. 28.

2388 OSTERLUND, Steven
"The Death of Kenneth Patchen." MassR (13:3) Sum 72, p. 486.

2389 OSTRIKER, Alicia
"Andante." CarlMis (12:1) Fall-Wint 71-72, p. 56.
"The Babe Pome (for Gabriel)." QRL (18:1/2) 72, p. 178.
"Berkshire Hills." CarlMis (12:1) Fall-Wint 71-72, p. 56.
"Chester August 19, 1970." QRL (18:1/2) 72, p. 177.
"Thirst." Shen (23:3) Spr 72, p. 80.

2390 OSTROFF, Anthony
"Suicide Note." Harp (245:1471) D 72, p. 67.

2391 O'SULLIVAN, Garrett
"Variations on a Religious Language" (for Alan Britt who asks for silence). UTR (1:3) 72, p. 14.

2392 OSWALD, Ernest J.
"Soledad (for George Jackson)." NewYQ (9) Wint 72, p. 76.

2393 OURIN, Viktor
"A Friendly Message to Brother Poets." HangL (17) Sum 72, p. 4.

2394 OVERLOOK, Timothy
"Universals." PoetL (67:2) Sum 72, p. 172.

2395 OVERSTREET, David Everett
"Father, to Me." Cim (19) Ap 72, p. 53.
"Reversions in the Car." BeyB (2:2) 72, p. 46.

2396 OVERTON, Ron
"Berne, Indiana." HangL (18) Fall 72, p. 34.
"Compleynte." Peb (9) Wint 72.
"A Confusion." WindO (10) Sum 72, p. 31.
"Landlord." Drag (3:1) Spr 72, p. 36.
"Seville Ghazal." HangL (18) Fall 72, p. 35.
"Sexing the Cat." SaltCR (5:1) Wint 72.
"The Somewhere Else Ghazal." HangL (18) Fall 72, p. 35.
"U.S.A. Ghazal." HangL (18) Fall 72, p. 36.
"Westerns." Peb (9) Wint 72.
"Whim, Without Guilt." WindO (10) Sum 72, p. 31.
"Why the Grades Aren't In." WindO (10) Sum 72, p. 32.

2397 OWEN, Guy
"For James (1926-1965)." SouthernPR (12: Special Issue) 72, p. 45.
"My Father's Curse." SouthernPR (12: Special Issue) 72, p. 45.

2398 OWEN, John Lloyd
"February." NewYorker (47:51) 5 F 72, p. 87.

2399 OWENS, Collie H.
"The Soul in Time" (for Kathy). GeoR (26:4) Wint 72, p. 511.

2400 OWENS, Rochelle
"The Father Song--A Continuation (LXX)." UnmOx (1:4) Aut 72.
"The Marvelous Cat." AriD (1:3) Spr 72, p. 12.
"Telephone Call from a Myth." AriD (1:3) Spr 72, p. 11.
"The Wandering/The Poem for the Father (LXIX)." UnmOx (1:4) Aut 72.
"Within a Prison Within a Prison the Criminal Has an Honest Face." AriD (1:3) Spr 72, p. 10.

2401 OXFORD, Ray B.
"Sandwedge." Broad (61) Jl 72.

2402 PACK, Robert
"At this distance." Antaeus (7) Aut 72, p. 141.

"I Am Rising." AntR (32:1/2) Spr-Sum 72, p. 40.
"Inside My House." NewYQ (11) Sum 72, p. 48.
"Terminal." PoetryNW (13:2) Sum 72, p. 42.

2403 PACKARD, William
"It Rains in My Heart" (tr. of Paul Verlaine). NewYQ (10) Spr 72, p. 94.
"the/happiest/apples." NYT 14 S 72, p. 46.
"Woman in an Asylum." NYT 16 Jl 72, p. 10.

2404 PADDOCK, Joe
"bird light." MidwQ (13:3) Spr 72, p. 333.
"fading trail." MidwQ (13:3) Spr 72, p. 290.

2405 PADGETT, Ron
"Homage to Franz Schubert" (for Alec Bond). ParisR (54) Sum 72, p. 81.
"The Saddest Story." ParisR (54) Sum 72, p. 86.
"Voice." UnmOx (1:3) Sum 72, p. 40.

2406 PADORR, Frances
"Family Christmas in Paris." YaleR (62:1) Aut 72, p. 77.
"Mythic: Daphne." YaleR (62:1) Aut 72, p. 78.
"Sewing." YaleR (62:1) Aut 72, p. 78.

2407 PAGE, William
"Aloha." WindO (12) Wint 72-73, p. 20.
"DNA." WindO (12) Wint 72-73, p. 19.
"The Ventriloquist." WindO (12) Wint 72-73, p. 19.

2408 PAGIS, Dan
"The Cave Man Is Not About to Talk" (tr. by Stephen Mitchell). Humanist (32:1) Ja-F 72, p. 32.

2409 PAIDOUSSI, Eleni
"At the Barracks" (tr. of Yannis Ritsos, w. Dan Georgakas). ChiTM 6 Ag 72, p. 7.

2410 PAINE, Barbara Gordon
"Sea Roses and Blue Shadows (to Miriam and to the Memory of Kenneth Patchen)." NewYQ (11) Sum 72, p. 43.

2411 PALAMAS, Kostes
"Who Knows in Other Stars" (tr. by Rae Dalven). Poetry (120:5) Ag 72, p. 264.

2412 PALMATEER, R.
"The Poem William Carlos Williams Never Wrote But Might Have, Had He Lived on Mangoes for a Year." EngJ (61:6) S 72, p. 891.

2413 PALSSON, Hermann
from Time and Water (1952): Fifteen Poems (tr. of Steinn Steinarr, w. Robin Fulton). MinnR (3) Aut 72, p. 63.

2414 PAPADITSAS, Dimitris
"Freedom 1945" (tr. by Athan Anagnostopoulos). AriD (1:4/5) Sum-Aut 72, p. 83.
"On Patmos" (tr. by Athan Anagnostopoulos). AriD (1:4/5) Sum-Aut 72, p. 84.
"The Passionate Relics" (tr. by Athan Anagnostopoulos). AriD (1:4/5) Sum-Aut 72, p. 84.
"With Soft Voice" (tr. by Athan Anagnostopoulos). AriD (1:4/5) Sum-Aut 72, p. 86.

2415 PARHAM, Robert
"Equanimities." FreeL (15:1/2) 71-72, p. 75.
"Inspector." KanQ (4:1) Wint 71-72, p. 84.

2416 PARKES, Dow
"The Horses of the Sun." Comm (96:15) 30 Je 72, p. 360.

2417 PARLATORE, Anselm
"Apaches Watch from the Hills." Zahir (1:4/5) 72, p. 38.
"Hunger." Iron (1) Spr 72, p. 45.
"I Ferment." Zahir (1:4/5) 72, p. 39.
"In the city of Porsches." Zahir (1:4/5) 72, p. 38.

2418 PARMAR, Shyam
"Demonic" (tr. by Prabhakar Machve). Meas (3) 72, p. 52.
"Snake Harvests" (tr. by Prabhakar Machve). Meas (3) 72, p. 52.

2419 PARR, Michael
"In Windrows of the Hay." NYT 7 O 72, p. 32.

2420 PARRA, Nicanor
"Cancion Para Correr El Sombrero." BerksR (8:1) Spr 72, p. 4.
"The Difficult Old Man" (tr. by Edward Oliphant). RoadAR (4:1) Spr 72, p. 19.
"I Don't Believe in the Peaceful Way" (tr. by Edward Oliphant). RoadAR (4:1) Spr 72, p. 19.
"I Fulfill My Patriotic Duty" (tr. by Miller Williams). Atl (229:3) Mr 72, p. 81.
"Inflation" (tr. by Miller Williams). Atl (229:3) Mr 72, p. 81.
from Letters of the Poet Who Sleeps Sitting Up: (XVI, XVII) (tr. by Edward Oliphant). RoadAR (4:1) Spr 72, p. 21.

from The Long Cueca: "I'll sing me a cueca" (tr. by Edward Oliphant). RoadAR (4:1) Spr 72, p. 20.
"A Man" (tr. by W. S. Merwin). Iron (1) Spr 72, p. 36.
"Result Zero" (tr. by Edward Oliphant). RoadAR (4:1) Spr 72, p. 23.
"The Rule of Three" (tr. by Miller Williams). Atl (229: 3) Mr 72, p. 81.
"Seven" (tr. by Miller Williams). Atl (3) Mr 72, p. 81.
"Song of the Foreigner" (tr. by W. S. Merwin). Iron (1) Spr 72, p. 37.
from Telegrams: (III, V) (tr. by Edward Oliphant). RoadAR (4:1) Spr 72, p. 22.

2421 PARTHASARATHY, R.
"Danger: Poet At Work." Meas (3) 72, p. 54.

2422 PASCHAL, Justin
"Said the Great Theologian." Thought (47:187) Wint 72, p. 536.

2423 PASIKA, Adeline Marcinow
"Summer Daughter." Qt (5:38) Spr 72, p. 11.

2424 PASTAN, Linda
"Algebra." NYT 12 Je 72, p. 34.
"Birds." CarolQ (24:1) Wint 72, p. 77.
"Departures (2)." AriD (1:2) Wint 72, p. 37.
"The Four Steps: For D. S." NYT 22 Ja 72, p. 28.
"The Ides of March." NYT 29 Ap 72, p. 30.
"Killing Time." Antaeus (6) Sum 72, p. 48.
"Morning Afterthoughts." ChiTM 30 Jl 72, p. 11.
"On Going to Sweden for my Fortieth Birthday." NYT 16 S 72, p. 28.
"Poetry Reading." NewYQ (10) Spr 72, p. 43.
"Prunus Mume (for Joan and Peter)." Nat (214:16) 17 Ap 72, p. 506.
"A Sense of Direction." AmerS (41:3) Sum 72, p. 438.
"To Her Lover." Nat (214:15) 10 Ap 72, p. 475.
"Wildflowers" (for Ira). CarolQ (24:1) Wint 72, p. 77.

2425 PASTERNAK, Boris
"Winter Evening" (tr. by Jamie Fuller). RusLT (2) Wint 72, p. 221.

2426 PATCHEN, Kenneth
from "Continuation of The Landscape." Apple (7) Aut 72, frontispiece.

2427 PATEL, M. S.
Ten Poems. Meas (3) 72, p. 43.

2428 PATIGIAN, Lance
"Apologies for the Sleepwalker." Iron (2) Fall 72, p. 53.

2429 PATON, Robert
"Apache Gold." HangL (16) Wint 71-72, p. 37.

2430 PATRICK, Nikki
"A Common Fire at Olduvai." Wind (2:5) Sum 72, p. 43.

2431 PATRIKIOUS, Titos
"Debt" (tr. by T. K. Scuris). AriD (1:4/5) Sum-Aut 72, p. 88.
"Forewarning" (tr. by T. K. Scuris). AriD (1:4/5) Sum-Aut 72, p. 88.
"The March" (tr. by Sarah Kafatou). AriD (1:4/5) Sum-Aut 72, p. 87.

2432 PATTERSON, David
"Untitled: the all-pervading." Wind (2:5) Sum 72, p. 32.

2433 PATTERSON, James
"Africa" (tr. by Bernard Koten). NewWR (40:1) Wint 72, p. 58.
from Winter Soldiers: "Introductory Remarks" (tr. by Bernard Koten). NewWR (40:1) Wint 72, p. 56.
from Winter Soldiers: "The Music of the Black Ghettos" (tr. by Bernard Koten). NewWR (40:1) Wint 72, p. 56.

2434 PATTERSON, Raymond R.
"After the Thousand Day Rebellion." TransR (41) Wint-Spr 72, p. 52.
"Fire at the Negro Institute." TransR (41) Wint-Spr 72, p. 53.

2435 PATTERSON, Rodney L.
"July" (tr. of Innokenty Annensky). RusLT (4) Aut 72, p. 50.
"Nightingale Garden" (tr. of Alexander Blok). RusLT (4) Aut 72, p. 9.
Seventeen Poems (tr. of Konstantin Balmont). RusLT (4) Aut 72, p. 51.
"To Friends" (tr. of Andrei Bely). RusLT (4) Aut 72, p. 61.

2436 PATTON, Elizabeth
"Poetic Instruction." EngJ (61:8) N 72, p. 1158.

2437 PATTON, Patricia F.
"The Old Man." NegroHB (35:8) D 72, p. 181.

2438 PAUKER, John
"Tasty Poem." NewRep (166:6) 5 F 72, p. 25.

2439 PAUL, James
"Wallace Looks So Different From His Photograph." AntR (32:1/2) Spr-Sum 72, p. 180.

2440 PAULHAN, Jean
"Malgache" (tr. by W. S. Merwin). Madrona (1:1) Je 71, p. 21.

2441 PAULI, Kenneth W.
"February Spring." SouthernPR (12:2) Spr 72, p. 33.

2442 PAVIC, Milorad
from Holy Mass for Relja Krilatica: Eight Poems (tr. by Charles Simic). MinnR (2) Spr 72, p. 52.

2443 PAWLOWSKI, Robert
"Dissolution" (for my grandparents). ModernO (2:1) Wint 72, p. 21.

2444 PAYNE, John Burnett
"Tulip Zanzibar" (for Al Levine). BabyJ (5) N 72, p. 19.
"A Witch." Zahir (1:4/5) 72, p. 76.

2445 PAZ, Octavio
"Paisaje Inmemorial." Books (46:4) Aut 72, p. 546.
"Return" (tr. by Eliot Weinberger). Hudson (25:1) Spr 72, p. 9.

2446 PEARCE, Richard
"After the Next Election." Stand (14:1) 72, p. 17.
"Saying No to Our Country." CarlMis (12:2) Spr-Sum 72, p. 2.
"Where You Were Last Seen." ConcPo (5:2) Fall 72, p. 21.
"Winter's Room." ConcPo (5:2) Spr 72, p. 21.

2447 PEARLMAN, Bill
"Fervent Force." Isthmus (1) Spr 72, p. 28.

2448 PECK, John
"Apple." Poetry (119:5) F 72, p. 276.
from "Cantique de la Connaissance" (tr. of Oscar V. De Lubicz-Milosz). QRL (18:1/2) 72, p. 141.
"Cider and Vesalius." Salm (18) Wint 72, p. 101.
"Colophon for Ch'ing-Ming Shang-Ho T'u (The Spring Festival on the River)" (tr. of Chang Tse-Tuan, w. Roderick Whitfield). QRL (18:1/2) 72, p. 194.
"Colophon for Lan-T'ing Hsiu-Hsi (The Gathering at the Orchid Pavilion)" (tr. of Ch'ien Ku). QRL (18:1/2) 72, p. 196.
"Coming Off the Ward." Antaeus (5) Spr 72, p. 116.
"Death of a Stallion." NewYorker (48:4) 18 Mr 72, p. 98.
"L'Etrangère" (tr. of Oscar V. De Lubicz-Milosz). QRL (18:1/2) 72, p. 139.
"Leaving the Coal Cellar." NewYorker (48:25) 12 Ag 72, p. 32.
"The Nautilus." Antaeus (5) Spr 72, p. 117.

"October Cycle." Antaeus (6) Sum 72, p. 70.
"Quand Elle Viendra..." (tr. of Oscar V. De Lubicz-Milosz). QRL (18:1/2) 72, p. 138.
"The Riddle and the Indian Song" (adapted by John Peck). Antaeus (7) Aut 72, p. 8.
"Riddle: Though I light them the face loved, though I bear." Antaeus (7) Aut 72, p. 33.
"Le Roi Don Luis..." (tr. of Oscar V. De Lubicz-Milosz). QRL (18:1/2) 72, p. 137.
"Smoke Around the Bell." Antaeus (5) Spr 72, p. 114.
"Søren." NewYorker (48:14) 27 My 72, p. 42.
"The Spring Festival on the River." NewYorker (48:11) 6 My 72, p. 40.
Thirteen Poems. QRL (18:1/2) 72, p. 182.
"Viaticum." Antaeus (6) Sum 72, p. 71.

2449 PECK, Richard
"Irish Child." ChiTM 17 S 72, p. 14.
"Lincoln Landscape: February." ChiTM 20 F 72, p. 10.

2450 PEDRETTI, Erica
"Dogs are supposed to be walked on a leash" (tr. by Stuart Friebert). Field (7) Fall 72, p. 39.
"Here" (tr. by Stuart Friebert). Field (7) Fall 72, p. 40.
"It's snowing in Plouda" (tr. by Franz Wright). Field (7) Fall 72, p. 41.
"No, That Can't Be" (tr. by Stuart Friebert). Field (7) Fall 72, p. 38.

2451 PEERADINA, Saleem
"III." Meas (3) 72, p. 56.
"You Can't Say He's Not Religious." Meas (3) 72, p. 55.

2452 PELL, Edward
"Raucous." Comm (95:21) 25 F 72, p. 488.

2453 PELLETIER, Gaston
"The Poem as Carcass." Qt (5:39/40) Sum-Aut 72, p. 59.

2454 PENFOLD, Gerda
"the eastern poets visit us." WormR (48) 72, p. 140.
"there is something he doesn't have." WormR (48) 72, p. 139.

2455 PENNINGTON, Lee
"Forgotten Stumps." SouthernPR (12:2) Spr 72, p. 49.

2456 PERCHIK, Simon
"The air is splintered here." Iron (2) Fall 72, p. 63.
"*." Focus (9:57) 72, p. 29.
"Death Leans Left." SouthwR (57:1) Wint 72, p. 53.
"He fondles fruit with branch: his arm." PoetC (7:1)

72, p. 4.
"I aim from turrets." CarolQ (24:3) Fall 72, p. 17.
"I separate in lobbies, each hall." WormR (48) 72, p. 142.
"Outdoors our flower district." GreenR (2:2) 72, p. 21.
"*" (Star). Folio (8:1) Spr 72, p. 8.
"The water lifted :lakes." WormR (48) 72, p. 142.
"Wobbling to the corner." Iron (2) Fall 72, p. 62.

2457 PEREIRA, Sam
"The Collector of Rare Books." Iron (1) Spr 72, p. 53.
"The Marriage of the Portuguese: The Religion." Iron (2) Fall 72, p. 41.
"The Memo on the Senator's Desk." Works (3:3/4) Wint 72-73, p. 124.

2458 PERET, Benjamin
"Hello" (tr. by Michael Benedikt). Kayak (29) S 72, p. 27.
"Twinkling of an Eye" (tr. by Michael Benedikt). Kayak (29) S 72, p. 26.
"Where Are You" (tr. by Michael Benedikt). Field (6) Spr 72, p. 77.

2459 PEREZ, Floridor
"To Live (Present Tense)" (tr. by Edward Oliphant). RoadAR (4:1) Spr 72, p. 33.
"Triangle" (tr. by Edward Oliphant). RoadAR (4:1) Spr 72, p. 33.

2460 PERKINS, James Ashbrook
"The Moment of Truth." AAUP (58:4) D 72, p. 422.

2461 PERKINS, Michael
"And Even If I Tried." NewYQ (11) Sum 72, p. 79.

2462 PERLBERG, Mark
"Early One Morning." Focus (8:56) 72, p. 36.
"A Night Too Hot to Sleep." CarlMis (12:1) Fall-Wint 71-72, p. 54.
"An Officer's Tartar Horse" (tr. of Tu Fu). Focus (8:56) 72, p. 36.
"The Return" (tr. of Tu Fu, w. Lee Feigon). Atl (229:4) Ap 72, p. 103.
"Summer Storm in Wisconsin." CarlMis (12:1) Fall-Wint 71-72, p. 54.

2463 PERLMAN, Jess
"As In Water." Folio (8:2) Fall 72, p. 37.
"The Bridge." PoetL (67:1) Spr 72, p. 13.

2464 PERLMAN, John
"Of Poem." ExpR (3) Fall-Wint 72/73, p. 37.

2465 PERREAULT, John
"Chart for." UnmOx (1:4) Aut 72.
"Permutations." UnmOx (1:4) Aut 72.

2466 PERREAULT, Peter
"Fantasy in Ebony and Ivory." Poem (15) Jl 72, p. 16.

2467 PERRINE, Laurence
"A Burst of Birds." Poem (15) Jl 72, p. 61.
"The Keepsake." Poem (15) Jl 72, p. 60.
"On a Late Schoolboy." EngJ (61:7) O 72, p. 1025.
"The Second Coming (s)--on re-reading his poems--." ColEng (33:4) Ja 72, p. 486.

2468 PERRY, J. D.
"blacksong." Broad (55) Ja 72.

2469 PERRY, Margery-Jean
"I Don't Understand What Kind of a Day It Is." Cord (1:3) 72, p. 4.
"Peep Show." Cord (1:4) 72, p. 3.

2470 PERRY, Thelma D.
"The Possible Dream?" NegroHB (35:4) Ap 72, p. 86.

2471 PESCHEL, Enid Rhodes
"Everyday Song of a Lover" (tr. of Flavien Ranaivo). Confr (5) Wint-Spr 72, p. 85.

2472 PESSOA, Fernando
"A dull day but not cold" (tr. by Jonathan Griffin). Stand (13:3) 72, p. 60.
"In the illbeing I live in" (tr. by Jonathan Griffin). Stand (13:3) 72, p. 59.

2473 PETERFREUND, Stuart
"american night." GreenR (2:2) 72, p. 51.
"First Differences" (for Manna). GreenR (2:2) 72, p. 48.
"The Grammarian." Northeast Aut-Wint, 71-72, p. 13.
"An Hour Past Green River." Shen (24:1) Aut 72, p. 46.
"In the Middle of the Road to Love." LittleM (6:1) Spr 72, p. 11.
"The Midlands." Shen (24:1) Aut 72, p. 47.
"Poem for a Son, Unborn, By a Mother, Unknown." Northeast Aut-Wint 71-72, p. 14.
"simple evensong." GreenR (2:2) 72, p. 50.
"Survival." GreenR (2:2) 72, p. 49.

2474 PETERS, Robert
"absence poem." Meas (2) 72.
"Commercial." Zahir (1:4/5) 72, p. 40.
"Dawn." UnmOx (1:2) F 72, p. 43.
"Dedication for a Book of Poems." LittleM (6:2/3)

Sum-Aut 72, p. 107.
"eastern poem." Meas (2) 72.
"frustration poem." Meas (2) 72.
"In the Mountains." ExpR (2) Wint-Spr 72, p. 32.
"Lesbia's Sparrow." LittleM (6:2/3) Sum-Aut 72, p. 106.
"Memento Mori Poem." ExpR (2) Wint-Spr 72, p. 31.
"My Place In ..." Cafe (4) Fall 72, p. 34.
"Night Trail" (for D. A.). UnmOx (1:1) N 71, p. 6.
"On Cruelty to Animals: A Western Episode." Zahir (1:4/5) 72, p. 41.
"Parable of the Child in the Burnt House." Kayak (29) S 72, p. 9.
"Parable of the Garden." SenR (3:1) My 72, p. 28.
"Parable of the Tree." Kayak (29) S 72, p. 8.
"To Live in the Self." AntR (32:1/2) Spr-Sum 72, p. 102.
"Yet Again." NoAmR (257:2) Sum 72, p. 36.

2475 PETERS, Robert A.
"Division Poem." MinnR (3) Aut 72, p. 101.
"Each Halting Car, Each Carburetor." MinnR (3) Aut 72, p. 100.

2476 PETERSEN, Sister Ingrid
"Grief." SouthwR (57:4) Aut 72, p. 326.

2477 PETERSON, Edith H.
"The Gnomes: For the Spirit of Yukio Mishima." St. AR (1:4) Spr-Sum 72, p. 20.

2478 PETERSON, Eugene H.
"Committee Meeting." ChrC (89:5) 2 F 72, p. 121.

2479 PETERSON, Robert
Five Tankas. PoetryNW (13:2) Sum 72, p. 14.
"Ghazal 1." SenR (3:1) My 72, p. 4.
"Near Ojo Caliente." Kayak (28) 72, p. 53.
"The St. James Hotel (Cimarron, N. M.)." Kayak (28) 72, p. 52.
"Sonnet for Grandpa." Iron (2) Fall 72, p. 46.
"To Teach." SenR (3:1) My 72, p. 5.

2480 PETESCH, Donald A.
"My Mother's Mother in an Iowa Nursing Home." HangL (17) Sum 72, p. 42.

2481 PETRIE, Paul
"Cain." Iowa (3:4) Fall 72, p. 11.
"The Establishment, the Young, the Old, the Blacks, the Whites, the Pinks." CarlMis (12:2) Spr-Sum 72, p. 31.
"Identity." NewYorker (47:51) 5 F 72, p. 38.
"June Bouquet." Peb (6) Sum 71.
"Manhood." Poetry (120:6) S 72, p. 342.

"The Morning News." QRL (18:1/2) 72, p. 199.
"Nixon, Agnew and Jerry Rubin." QRL (18:1/2) 72, p. 201.
"Poem to Bernardine Dohrn." CarlMis (12:2) Spr-Sum 72, p. 32.
"Pollution." QRL (18:1/2) 72, p. 200.
"Recurrent Dream." SouthwR (57:3) Sum 72, p. 234.
"Relevance." NYT 24 Je 72, p. 30.
"The Silent Majority." QRL (18:1/2) 72, p. 200.
"Turner's 'The Burning of the Houses of Parliament'." CarlMis (12:2) Spr-Sum 72, p. 33.

2482 PETROSKI, Catherine
"The Girltree." RoadAR (3:4) Wint 71-72, p. 38.
"Mom, This Music Hurts My Ears. Let's Go." SouthernHR (6:4) Aut 72, p. 356.
"Night Flight." FourQt (21:2) Ja 72, p. 34.

2483 PETROSKI, Henry
"At the Zoo." RoadAR (3:4) Wint 71-72, p. 32.
"A Correspondence." SoCaR (5:1) D 72, p. 14.
"To Make, To Break." Epos (23:3) Spr 72, p. 5.

2484 PETROV, Valeri
"At the Main Entrance." LitR (16:2) Wint 72-73, p. 188.
"Snow." LitR (16:2) Wint 72-73, p. 189.

2485 PETTEYS, D. F.
"Clytemnestra's Urn." NewYQ (12) Aut 72, p. 84.
"Dejection." WestHR (26:1) Wint 72, p. 48.
"The Drum." MedR (2:3) Spr 72, p. 86.
"Entropy Temporarily Defeated." ModernO (2:1) Wint 72, p. 22.
"Entropy Temporarily Defeated." ModernO (2:2) Spr 72, p. 233.
"Kite-poem." WestHR (26:2) Spr 72, p. 146.
"Snow White." Antaeus (7) Aut 72, p. 84.
"The Swans." Shen (24:1) Aut 72, p. 48.

2486 PETTINELLA, D. M.
"Absence" (tr. of Pablo Neruda). NewYQ (12) Aut 72, p. 60.
"Along the Arid Street" (tr. of Camillo Sbarbaro). SenR (3:1) My 72, p. 25.
"Church" (tr. of Carlos Drummond De Andrade). TexQ (15:4) Wint 72, p. 110.
"Deviation" (tr. of Pablo Neruda). NewYQ (12) Aut 72, p. 59.
"The Dream of Two Deer" (tr. of Dámaso Alonso). Mund (5:1/2) 72, p. 117.
"Letter to My Mother in Naples." Qt (5:37) Wint 72, p. 28.
"Life of the Cricket" (tr. of Jorge Carrera Andrade).

Mund (5:3) 72, p. 67.
"Painter's Dream." ChrC (89:23) 7 Je 72, p. 658.
"Pillar in Memory of Leaves" (tr. of Jorge Carrera Andrade). Mund (5:3) 72, p. 69.
from Poesie: "Winter in Luino" (tr. of Vittorio Sereni). MedR (2:4) Sum 72, p. 82.
"Revere Beach in Boston." Qt (5:37) Wint 72, p. 21.
"Sad" (tr. of Cecilia Meireles). FourQt (21:3) Mr 72, p. 20.
"Solitude" (tr. of Cecilia Meireles). FourQt (21:3) Mr 72, p. 21.
"Sunday" (tr. of Jorge Carrera Andrade). Mund (5:3) 72, p. 65.
"Surprise" (tr. of Federico García Lorca). NewRena (6) My 72, p. 43.
"What Was She Like?" (tr. of Dámaso Alonso). Mund (5:1/2) 72, p. 119.
"Words at Sea" (tr. of Carlos Drummond DeAndrade). TexQ (15:4) Wint 72, p. 108.

2487 PETTINGELL, Phoebe
"Fat Tuesday." Poetry (120:3) Je 72, p. 139.
"Frog Prince." Poetry (120:3) Je 72, p. 138.

2488 PEVEAR, Richard
"The Killing of Orpheus." Hudson (25:4) Wint 72-73, p. 568.
"Little Acmeist Elegy." Hudson (25:4) Wint 72-73, p. 570.
"Mnemosyne." Hudson (25:4) Wint 72-73, p. 569.
"Waiting." Hudson (25:4) Wint 72-73, p. 570.

2489 PFINGSTON, Roger
"The Drink." WindO (9) Spr 72, p. 20.
"Insecta: Night Song." BabyJ (5) N 72, p. 3.
"The Men Who Murder Mountains." WindO (9) Spr 72, p. 20.

2490 PFLUM, Richard
"Gravestone." Epos (23:3) Spr 72, p. 10.

2491 PHELPS, Ron
"From the Hotel in Antarctica." MinnR (3) Aut 72, p. 50.

2492 PHILLIPS, Dan K.
"Wanderer." Wind (2:6) Aut 72, p. 27.

2493 PHILLIPS, Douglas
"Bilingual?" TransR (42/43) Spr-Sum 72, p. 82.

2494 PHILLIPS, Homer
"At Ease." SatEP (244:2) Sum 72, p. 102.

2495 PHILLIPS, John R.
"Small Gains." AAUP (58:1) Mr 72, p. 39.

2496 PHILLIPS, Louis
"The Dead Rehearsed." SoDakR (10:1) Spr 72, p. 38.
"The Forward Kingdom." LitR (16:1) Aut 72, p. 107.
"Getting Lost on the IRT." LitR (16:1) Aut 72, p. 106.
"Monopoly." Epoch (21:2) Wint 72, p. 142.
"Number 43." JnlOPC (5:4) Spr 72, p. 835.
"67." Epoch (21:2) Wint 71, p. 143.
"Standing at a Gate in Summer." SoDakR (10:1) Spr 72, p. 38.

2497 PHILLIPS, Michael Joseph
"Harem Poem in Three Parts." WindO (11) Aut 72, p. 12.
"Positive Sonnet." WindO (11) Aut 72, p. 11.

2498 PHILLIPS, Walt
"and at the cemetery." NewRena (6) My 72, p. 52.

2499 PICCOLO, Lucio
"Di soste viviamo; non turbi profondo." MedR (2:2) Wint 72, p. 58.
"Scirocco." MedR (2:2) Wint 72, p. 57.
"The Soul and Sleights of Hand" (tr. by Brian Swann and Ruth Feldman). Antaeus (5) Spr 72, p. 25.
"The Sundial" (tr. by Brian Swann and Ruth Feldman). Antaeus (5) Spr 72, p. 23.
"The Three Figures" (tr. by Brian Swann and Ruth Feldman). Antaeus (5) Spr 72, p. 26.

2500 PICOT, Michele
"The Tenth Song." SouthernPR (12: Special Issue) 72, p. 48.

2501 PIERCE, Edith Lovejoy
"Christmas." ChrC (89:46) 20 D 72, p. 1292.
"The Fifth Horseman." ChrC (89:41) 15 N 72, p. 1146.

2502 PIERCY, Marge
"The Big One." UnmOx (1:2) F 72, p. 38.
"Bloody Kansas in Spring." HangL (17) Sum 72, p. 45.
"Councils." HangL (16) Wint 71-72, p. 39.
"In the Men's Room(s)." Aphra (3:3) Sum 72, p. 15.
"Kneeling here, I feel good." HangL (16) Wint 71-72, p. 38.
"Laying Down the Tower." New:ACP (19) Aut 72, p. 4.
"Three Weeks in the State of Loneliness." HangL (17) Sum 72, p. 43.
"The Visiting Poet Drag." HangL (16) Wint 71-72, p. 40.

2503 PIKE, Lawrence
Cut-up Poems. Kayak (29) S 72, p. 44.
"Radio Pulp Poems." Works (3:3/4) Wint 72-73, p. 74.

2504 PILLIN, William
"Pygmalion." Cafe (4) Fall 72, p. 19.

2505 PINSKER, Sanford
"Last Class." NYT 10 Mr 72, p. 36.
"Look On, Make No Sound." NYT 10 O 72, p. 44.
"My Father, Who Never Owned a Greenhouse (For Theodore Roethke, whose father did)." NYT 21 Je 72, p. 42.
"The Response of Telemachus (with apologies to Tennyson)." NYT 26 N 72, sec. 4, p. 8.

2506 PINSKY, Robert
"Doctor Frolic." Antaeus (7) Aut 72, p. 81.
"The Time of Year, The Time of Day." ModernO (2:2) Spr 72, p. 314.

2507 PIPER, Robert
"Farm Girl." CalQ (2) Sum 72, p. 31.

2508 PIRKLE, Thomas
"Cornfields." Shen (23:3) Spr 72, p. 78.
"Rest Stop." Shen (23:3) Spr 72, p. 77.

2509 PITKIN, Anne
"One for Broken Sea Shells." Madrona (1:2) N 71, p. 8.
"To a Mutual Friend." Madrona (1:1) Je 71, p. 7.
"Words For a Night In August." Epos (23:3) Spr 72, p. 19.

2510 PITRONE, Anne
"At the Defense of Death." HangL (17) Sum 72, p. 52.
"The Earth of the Dead." GreenR (2:2) 72, p. 16.
"The Three Famous Repairmen" (for my grandfather, Sabbatino). HangL (17) Sum 72, p. 47.

2511 PITTS, George
"Scars." ParisR (55) Aut 72, p. 27.

2512 PLANK, Dale
"Before the Funeral" (tr. of Innokenty Annensky). RusLT (4) Aut 72, p. 50.

2513 PLATH, Sylvia
"Metamorphosis." Poetry (121:1) O 72, p. 25.
"Stopped Dead." Madem (74:5) Mr 72, p. 30.
"Winter Trees." Madem (74:5) Mr 72, p. 30.

2514 PLATT, Eugene Robert
"Fly Now, Pay Later." Wind (2:5) Sum 72, p. 31.

2515 PLATT, Kathleen Suzanne
"A Test of Talisman." SoCaR (4:2) Je 72, p. 45.
"Toronto." Wind (2:6) Aut 72, p. 26.

2516 PLEASANTS, Ben
"Goodbye to California." WormR (46) 72, p. 57.

2517 PLIMPTON, Sarah
"the road on the wall." ParisR (53) Wint 72, p. 84.

2518 PLUMB, David
"30 Seconds Over Dakar" (for David Diop). GreenR (2:3) 72, p. 40.

2519 PLUMLEY, William
"Sunday Morning." SouthernPR (12:2) Spr 72, p. 52.

2520 PLUMLY, Stanley
"Buckeye." GreenR (2:2) 72, p. 46.
"Fungo." GreenR (2:2) 72, p. 44.
"How the Plains Indians Got Horses (for Two Skies, a chief of the Humanos, a Texas tribe)." PartR (39:1) Wint 72, p. 60.
"Jarrell." Salm (18) Wint 72, p. 100.
"Like the Man Who Sold Barbwire." PoetryNW (13:1) Spr 72, p. 9.
"Pull of the Earth." Shen (23:3) Spr 72, p. 36.
"Seven or so Handkerchiefs." Salm (18) Wint 72, p. 100.
"So Having Risen Early, This Poem." PoetryNW (13:1) Spr 72, p. 8.
"Under Cows." PoetryNW (13:1) Spr 72, p. 8.
"Walking Out." NewYorker (47:52) 12 F 72, p. 34.
"Woods Lake" (for Wayne). Shen (23:3) Spr 72, p. 37.

2521 PLUMPP, Sterling D.
"A Black Messenger, Stokely Carmichael." JnlOBP (2:16) Sum 72, p. 21.

2522 PLYMELL, Charles
"At a Gas Station in Kansas." ParisR (55) Aut 72, p. 28.
"At a Gas Station in Kansas." WormR (47) 72, p. 82.
"Red Wing." WormR (47) 72, p. 81.

2523 POLAKOW, G.
"Harvest." MidwQ (13:4) Sum 72, p. 364.

2524 POLING, William
"Rena." Epoch (21:2) Wint 71, p. 134.

2525 POLK, Dora
"So the Dirt Is Crumbling." ColEng (33:7) Ap 72, p. 810.
"To a Student Already Poet." ColEng (33:7) Ap 72, p. 811.

2526 POLLAK, Felix
"After the Party." CarlMis (12:1) Fall-Wint 71-72, p. 74.
"Departures." CarlMis (12:1) Fall-Wint 71-72, p. 73.
"Du Musst Dein Leben Aendern." CarlMis (12:1) Fall-Wint 71-72, p. 75.
"Eulogy." Peb (7) Aut 71.
"Evolution." NoAmR (257:3) Aut 72, p. 56.
"Library: Xerox Room." Northeast Aut-Wint 71-72, p. 7.
"Limerick." Peb (7) Aut 71.
"Listening to Joan." Northeast Aut-Wint 71-72, p. 6.
"Maison Rustique or The Countrie Farme." Shen (24:1) Aut 72, p. 61.
"Peripheral Intelligence." Northeast Aut-Wint 71-72, p. 5.
"Sunday Morning View." Northeast Aut-Wint 71-72, p. 4.

2527 POLONITZA, Richard
"a colloque." ChiR (23:4 & 24:1) 72, p. 96.

2528 PONGE, Francis
"The Candle" (tr. by Raymond Federman). Pan (9) 72, p. 11.
"The Pleasures of the Door" (tr. by Raymond Federman). Pan (9) 72, p. 11.

2529 PONSOLDT, Jim
"The Referendum." SouthwR (57:2) Spr 72, p. 117.
"Reliable Information." ColQ (20:4) Spr 72, p. 492.

2530 POOL, Eugene
"In the Sun." AriD Spr 72, p. 3.

2531 PORTER, Peter
"Evolution" (for D. J. Enright). CarlMis (12:1) Fall-Wint 71-72, p. 80.

2532 POSNER, David
"Indian Architecture." QRL (18:1/2) 72, p. 203.
"Riddle: If I were whiter, smoother (this sceptered isle)." Antaeus (7) Aut 72, p. 26.
"The Suicide." NewYorker (48:13) 20 My 72, p. 42.

2533 POSTON, Jane
"Shiva, Nata Raja." NewL (38:3) Spr 72, p. 103.
"Wolf, My Wolf." NewL (38:3) Spr 72, p. 102.

2534 POTAMITIS, Dimitrios
"Decisions" (tr. by Vassilis Zambaras). Madrona (1:1) Je 71, p. 28.
"The New Light" (tr. by Vassilis Zambaras). Madrona (1:1) Je 71, p. 33.

2535 POTMESIL, Milan
"Jan Palach's Prague" (tr. of Miroslav Holub). NewYQ (12) Aut 72, p. 57.

2536 POULIN, A., Jr.
"Beowulf in Ogunquit." ColEng (33:4) Ja 72, p. 478.
"Biddeford Pool." ColEng (33:4) Ja 72, p. 476.
"Buddha and the Pirates." JnlOPC (5:4) Spr 72, p. 831.
"The Coming." Esq (77:5) My 72, p. 137.
"Death and Transfiguration." JnlOPC (5:4) Spr 72, p. 833.
"From Earth to the First Branch (for Raymond Jore)" (tr. of Gatien LaPointe). Kayak (28) 72, p. 38.
"I Woke Up. Revenge." ConcPo (5:1) Spr 72, p. 25.
"The Making of the Day." CarlMis (12:1) Fall-Wint 71-72, p. 83.
"Sailing From Byzantium." ConcPo (5:1) Spr 72, p. 24.
"Snowstorm: Biddeford Pool." ColEng (33:4) Ja 72, p. 475.
"Sons of Witches." ColEng (33:4) Ja 72, p. 477.

2537 POZO, Luis Moreno
"Capitalist Prayer for Che" (tr. by Edward Oliphant). RoadAR (4:1) Spr 72, p. 47.

2538 PRADO, Holly
"Cleaning Out a Room." Apple (7) Aut 72, p. 35.

2539 PRAEGER, Frank
"The Summer of 1953." Folio (8:2) Fall 72, p. 45.

2540 PRASAD, Narmadeshwar
"Two Night Poems." Meas (3) 72, p. 57.

2541 PRATER, Larry C.
"Becoming." KanQ (4:3) Sum 72, p. 127.

2542 PRATT, Charles
"Gestures of Love." Shen (23:2) Wint 72, p. 50.

2543 PRATT, William
"Poems of Rainer Maria Rilke" (tr. of Rainer Maria Rilke). ColQ (21:2) Aut 72, p. 226.

2544 PRAWDZIK, Jo Ann
"The farmer said." Indian (5:2) Sum 72, p. 45.

2545 PRICE, Frances Brown
"A Swedish Tribute to Huck Finn" (tr. of Dan Andersson, w. Marianne Fosselius). Mark (16:2) Sum 72, p. 20.

2546 PRICE, Mauricia
"The Jaunty Lover." WestR (10:1) Spr 73, p. 41.

2547 PRICE, Nancy
"Nassau and Back/Casino, Grand Bahama." KanQ (4:1) Wint 71-72, p. 36.

2548 PRICE, Reynolds
"Seven Poems about Death." Shen (23:4) Sum 72, p. 74.
"To my niece: our photograph, in a hammock." SouthernR (8:4) Aut 72, p. 912.

2549 PRIVETT, Katharine
"A Lullaby." WestR (10:1) Spr 73, p. 60.
"The Song of the Wife." WestR (10:1) Spr 73, p. 42.

2550 PROLA, Diana J.
"Foreshadowing." PoetL (67:1) Spr 72, p. 50.

2551 PRONECHEN, Joseph
"Handball Thoughts." Comm (96:3) 24 Mr 72, p. 62.

2552 PROPPER, Dan
"(A Chagall)." Apple (7) Aut 72, p. 36.

2553 PROSEN, Rose Mary
"The Third Canticle." ColEng (34:3) D 72, p. 454.

2554 PRUNTY, Wyatt
"The Casting." SewanR (80:2) Spr 72, p. 273.
"The Fashion Man." SewanR (80:2) Spr 72, p. 275.
"Passage." SewanR (80:2) Spr 72, p. 272.
"Sleepwalk." SewanR (80:2) Spr 72, p. 271.
"A Song for Ophelia." SewanR (80:2) Spr 72, p. 273.
"The Suitor." SewanR (80:2) Spr 72, p. 275.

2555 PURDY, Al
"Schoolmaster's Song." UnmOx (1:4) Aut 72.
"The Scream." UnmOx (1:3) Sum 72, p. 51.

2556 PURDY, Andrew
"Leopold Bloom." CarolQ (24:1) Wint 72, p. 14.

2557 PURENS, Ilmars
"Curro's Face." Madrona (1:3) My 72, p. 9.
"Fire in the House." SenR (3:1) My 72, p. 36.
"Wallace Stevens (for G. E. M.)." Nat (214:20) 15 My 72, p. 637.

2558 PUSHKIN, Alexander
"Autumn" (tr. by Walter Arndt). RusLT (3) Spr 72, p. 32.
"Conversation Between a Bookseller and a Poet" (tr. by Eugene M. Kayden). ColQ (21:1) Sum 72, p. 126.
"The Godyssey" (tr. by A. D. Briggs). RusLT (3) Spr 72, p. 17.

"Grapes" (tr. by Walter Arndt). RusLT (3) Spr 72, p. 35.
"I loved you--and my love, I think, was stronger" (tr. by Walter Arndt). RusLT (3) Spr 72, p. 36.
"I loved you: love, it very well may be" (tr. by Mark Suino). RusLT (3) Spr 72, p. 36.
"Imitations of the Koran" (tr. by Ants Oras). SewanR (80:2) Spr 72, p. 276.
"A Little House in Kolomna" (tr. by Jamie Fuller). RusLT (3) Spr 72, p. 1.
"Napoleon" (tr. by Eugene M. Kayden). ColQ (21:1) Sum 72, p. 119.
"The Nineteenth of October" (tr. by Eugene M. Kayden). ColQ (21:1) Sum 72, p. 132.
"A Scene from Faust" (tr. by Roberta Reeder and Simon Nahnybida). RusLT (3) Spr 72, p. 40.
"You're the kind that always loses" (tr. by Walter Arndt). RusLT (3) Spr 72, p. 35.

2559 PYBUS, Rodney
"Summer's Lease." Stand (13:2) 72, p. 12.

2560 QABBANI, Nizar
"Interrogation" (tr. by M. Bakir Alwan). ConcPo (5:2) Fall 72, p. 39.

2561 QUAGLIANO, Tony
"I Read This Poem About Geometry." WestR (10:1) Spr 73, p. 46.
"Oldenburg, Heisenberg and Oscar 'Shotgun' Albarado." WestR (10:1) Spr 73, p. 40.

2562 QUASIMODO, Salvatore
"I Have Lost Nothing" (tr. by Livio Fragiacomo). SenR (3:1) My 72, p. 26.

2563 QUEZADA, Jaime
"Inspection of School Supplies Hygiene and Personal Appearance" (tr. by Edward Oliphant). RoadAR (4:1) Spr 72, p. 26.
"Story and Another Story" (tr. by Edward Oliphant). RoadAR (4:1) Spr 72, p. 25.
"A Street Upon a Time" (tr. by Edward Oliphant). RoadAR (4:1) Spr 72, p. 25.
"Vigil" (tr. by Edward Oliphant). RoadAR (4:1) Spr 72, p. 26.

2564 QUINN, John
"Above Walton Store." NowestR (12:2) Spr 72, p. 42.
"The Trout in Zigzag Creek (for Judith Root)." NowestR (12:2) Spr 72, p. 41.

2565 QUINN, John Robert
"Pigeons." ChrC (89:28) 2 Ag 72, p. 793.

2566 RAAB, Lawrence
"At Evening: One Way and Then Another." AntR (31:4) Wint 71-72, p. 576.
"The Dream of Rousseau." Atl (229:2) F 72, p. 62.
"Lessons in Magic: The Egg Bag." Peb (9) Wint 72.
"Magritte: The Song of the Glass Keys and the Cape of Storms." AmerS (41:1) Wint 71-72, p. 111.
"Riddle." Kayak (30) D 72, p. 11.
"The Summer Vacation." SouthernPR (12:2) Spr 72, p. 41.
"The Survivors." NewYQ (10) Spr 72, p. 54.
"Water." Shen (24:1) Aut 72, p. 36.
"The Wolf's Journey." Shen (24:1) Aut 72, p. 35.

2567 RADHUBER, Stanley
"Crossing." ChiR (24:2) 72, p. 58.
"Learning About Pipers." ChiR (24:2) 72, p. 57.
"Learning About Yodellers." ChiR (24:2) 72, p. 56.
"Leaving Chartres." NowestR (12:2) Spr 72, p. 44.
"A Neighbor Robbed and Knifed." Northeast Sum 72, p. 11.
"The Swimming Hole." Northeast Sum 72, p. 12.
"The Winter After the Assassinations." Northeast Sum 72, p. 13.

2568 RADIN, Doris
"The Aunt." Peb (9) Wint 72.
"Captiva Key." MinnR (3) Aut 72, p. 106.
"The Rite." MinnR (3) Aut 72, p. 108.
"Song of the Jequirity Beads." MinnR (3) Aut 72, p. 107.

2569 RAGAN, James
"Bloom Falling Awake." MidwQ (13:2) Wint 72, p. 133.
"Cancelling My Twenty-Sixth Year." Mund (5:1/2) 72, p. 139.
"Ether Room." Mund (5:1/2) 72, p. 138.
"Fire Near Dead-Stream Road." NowestR (12:3) Aut 72, p. 75.
"Gerasim" [for Ján Ragan (1901-1971)]. Mund (5:1/2) 72, p. 140.
"Insomnia: Gathering Bones." LittleM (6:1) Spr 72, p. 35.
"Sisyphus Blind." MidwQ (13:2) Wint 72, p. 168.
"The Wounds." SouthernPR (12:2) Spr 72, p. 28.

2570 RAGAN, Sam
"Markings." SouthernPR (12: Special Issue) 72, p. 21.
"A Poet Is Somebody Who Feels." SouthernPR (12: Special Issue) 72, p. 23.
"'The Prophet.'" SouthernPR (12: Special Issue) 72,

p. 20.
"That Summer." SouthernPR (12: Special Issue) 72, p. 22.
"They Drive by Night." SouthernPR (12: Special Issue) 72, p. 21.

2571 RAI, Alok
"Poem I." Meas (3) 72, p. 60.
"Poem II." Meas (3) 72, p. 60.

2572 RAI, Amit
"Kasauli--1960." Meas (3) 72, p. 58.
"A Paratrooper's Dream." Meas (3) 72, p. 59.
"Poem: behind the brothel i met a man who cut his fist." Meas (3) 72, p. 58.

2573 RAICHOWDHRY, Samir
"Amaar Vietnam." Meas (3) 72, p. 69.
"Citizen of Hajipeer." Meas (3) 72, p. 73.
"Draft Outline WW III." Meas (3) 72, p. 71.
"Dressdecency." Meas (3) 72, p. 73.
"Needle Shunting." Meas (3) 72, p. 72.
"Purgatorio" (tr. of Jibanananda Das). Meas (3) 72, p. 19.
"Revolt Against Poetry." Meas (3) 72, p. 70.

2574 RAINE, Kathleen
"Oreads." NewYorker (48:45) 30 D 72, p. 36.

2575 RAINE, Nancy
"Lana Would." MassR (13:1/2) Wint-Spr 72, p. 187.

2576 RAINER, Wolf
"Easter 1971." Pan (9) 72, p. 26.

2577 RAIZISS, Sonia
from Il Mio Male: (4, 5, 11, 14, 16, 19, 21, 27) (tr. of Alfredo De Palchi). MedR (2:4) Sum 72, p. 89.
from Onore del Vero: "And the Wolf" (tr. of Mario Luzi). MedR (2:4) Sum 72, p. 98.
"Pig Farm." Epoch (21:2) Wint 71, p. 132.
from Gli Strumenti Umani: "Six in the Morning" (tr. of Vittorio Sereni). MedR (2:4) Sum 72, p. 81.
"Visit of a Schizoid." Drag (3:1) Spr 72, p. 26.

2578 RAMKE, Bin
"Chauntecleer and the Favorite Wife." QRL (18:1/2) 72, p. 206.
"To Grow Hydrangeas in the Rain." QRL (18:1/2) 72, p. 205.
"Nursery Rhyme." OhioR (13:3) Spr 72, p. 27.

2579 RAMSEY, Jarold
"After the Epidemic." QRL (18:1/2) 72, p. 209.
"Dreaming of Cannons." Atl (229:4) Ap 72, p. 105.
"For an Amazingly Dermographic Girl Whose Manuscript of Poems I Lost in College." QRL (18:1/2) 72, p. 208.
"In the Thicket." Atl (229:4) Ap 72, p. 104.
"Intimations." QRL (18:1/2) 72, p. 209.
"The Lighter Side." PraS (46:3) Aut 72, p. 236.
"Looking Out of the Album." QRL (18:1/2) 72, p. 208.
"Love in an Earthquake." QRL (18:1/2) 72, p. 207.
"Poem for Jean Tinguely." Atl (230:3) S 72, p. 65.
"Words from a Voyage." QRL (18:1/2) 72, p. 211.

2580 RAMSEY, Paul
"About Gods." SouthernPR (13:1) Aut 72, p. 50.
"The Advance." Shen (24:1) Aut 72, p. 32.
"Consolations." Shen (24:1) Aut 72, p. 32.
"On TV Football: New Year's Weekend." Shen (24:1) Aut 72, p. 32.
"Proposals." CarlMis (12:1) Fall-Wint 71-72, p. 40.

2581 RAN, Nazim Hikmet
"November 8, 1945" (tr. by Talat S. Halman). Books (46:2) Spr 72, p. 252.

2582 RANAIVO, Flavien
"Everyday Song of a Lover" (tr. by Enid Rhodes Peschel). Confr (5) Wint-Spr 72, p. 85.

2583 RANDALL, Dudley
"Green Apples." Broad (62) Ag 72.

2584 RANDALL, James PoSamm
"The Arms Race." Broad (61) Jl 72.
"Therapy Plea for Status-Quo Anxiety Frustration." Broad (61) Jl 72.

2585 RANDOLPH, Robert M.
"The Purer Part." CarlMis (12:2) Spr-Sum 72, p. 55.

2586 RANKIN, Paula
"The Entertainers." WindO (12) Wint 72-73, p. 36.
"Goodwill." WindO (12) Wint 72-73, p. 39.
"Helping the Vampire." WindO (12) Wint 72-73, p. 38.
"Nag's Head, October." RoadAR (3:4) Wint 71-72, p. 37.
"Reservoir, Late October." WindO (12) Wint 72-73, p. 37.
"The Star." WindO (12) Wint 72-73, p. 37.

2587 RANKIN, Rush
"The Fastest Gun in the West." NewYQ (9) Wint 72, p. 77.

"The Movie of Horse Hunting." BelPoJ (22:3) Spr 72, p. 7.
"A Teetotaler Attends the Party." SouthernPR (13:1) Aut 72, p. 19.

2588 RANSMEIER, J. C.
"Artificial Tulips." Folio (8:1) Spr 72, p. 30.
"At the Concert." Folio (8:1) Spr 72, p. 30.
"Couplet." Folio (8:1) Spr 72, p. 30.
"For Crista, After Paralysis." Folio (8:2) Fall 72, p. 36.
"The Girl I Love." Folio (8:2) Fall 72, p. 36.

2589 RASUL, Sha'ir
"Directions." JnlOBP (2:16) Sum 72, p. 27.
"Directions--Change Two" (Same checks, same poems). JnlOBP (2:16) Sum 72, p. 27.

2590 RATNER, Rochelle
"Because You Ask Me Not to Worship Fires." Nat (214:14) 3 Ap 72, p. 446.
"Borges." Salm (19) Spr 72, p. 72.
"The Bucket." Drag (3:1) Spr 72, p. 25.
"Bullpond." LittleM (6:1) Spr 72, p. 62.
"Camping, I Suddenly Realize It's November." Epoch (21:3) Spr 72, p. 284.
"Dry Leaves." Epoch (21:3) Spr 72, p. 285.
"The Echo of Plant Life." Shen (23:2) Wint 72, p. 21.
"Explanation." Northeast Sum 72, p. 35.
"Farmhouse." Northeast Aut-Wint 71-72, p. 44.
"If Stars Could Settle Down and Watch the Waves Fall." Nat (214:21) 22 My 72, p. 663.
"The Last Ghost." Shen (23:4) Sum 72, p. 66.
"The Most Secret Secret I Can Tell You." LittleM (6:1) Spr 72, p. 64.
from Pirate's Song: "Closing his stone eyes a moment." Shen (23:4) Sum 72, p. 67.
from Pirate's Song: "How should I try to get outside this city?" Iron (2) Fall 72, p. 37.
"Sailboat." Epoch (21:3) Spr 72, p. 284.
"School Drawing." Epoch (21:3) Spr 72, p. 284.
"Unpicked Grapes." Epoch (21:3) Spr 72, p. 285.
"A Welcome Mat Outside, Not Inside, Inside out." HangL (18) Fall 72, p. 38.

2591 RATTI, John
"Helen." Salm (18) Wint 72, p. 95.
"King Ludwig to His Brother Otto." Salm (18) Wint 72, p. 94.

2592 RAWORTH, Tom
"Births of Images and Deaths" (for Stan and Jane Brakhage). Iowa (3:2) Spr 72, p. 8.

"Future Models May Have Infra-red Sensors." Iowa (3:2) Spr 72, p. 4.
"In the Beginning Was the Word, and the Word Was With God, and the Word Was God." Iowa (3:2) Spr 72, p. 6.
"Poetry Now" (for Andrew Carrigan). Iowa (3:2) Spr 72, p. 6.
"Rather a Few Mistakes Than Fucking Boredom." Iowa (3:2) Spr 72, p. 7.
"Two Together." Iowa (3:2) Spr 72, p. 5.

2593 RAY, David
"Archeology." Iowa (3:4) Fall 72, p. 6.
"Aunt Ruth & Uncle Mac." Meas (2) 72.
"Drinking." QRL (18:1/2) 72, p. 212.
"Driving Through the Winnebago Reservation." QRL (18:1/2) 72, p. 213.
"The House." Meas (2) 72.
"My Place on the Tapestry" (after William Morris). Iowa (3:4) Fall 72, p. 7.
"The Washing Machine." QRL (18:1/2) 72, p. 214.
"The Way We Were." Iowa (3:4) Sum 72, p. 6.

2594 RAY, Debi
"Criminal, As I Am" (tr. by the poet and Jagdish Chakrabaty). Meas (3) 72, p. 63.
"Hunger, I'm." Meas (3) 72, p. 61.

2595 RAY, Monindra
"Story of an Enterprise" (tr. by S. Mukherjee). Meas (3) 72, p. 68.

2596 RAY, Tarapada
"Because I Thought That" (tr. by the poet and Michael Aldrich). Meas (3) 72, p. 76.
"Car Going Far (A Long Distance Car)" (tr. of Shokti Chattopadhyay, w. Michael Aldrich). Meas (3) 72, p. 11.
"Kush-Kush" (tr. by the poet and Michael Aldrich). Meas (3) 72, p. 75.

2597 RAYMOND, Richard C.
"Crow Country." WorldO (6:4) Sum 72, p. 62.

2598 REA, Steven
"the summer of yogurt." NewYQ (12) Aut 72, p. 92.

2599 REA, Susan
"The Chipmunk." Confr (5) Wint-Spr 72, p. 49.

2600 REALL, Genevieve
"Faith." ChrC (89:9) 1 Mr 72, p. 243.

2601 REATH, Gary
"Not Quite Monday Morning." SouthernPR (12: Special Issue) 72, p. 48.

2602 RECHTER, Judith
"Weeds." Focus (8:56) 72, p. 35.

2603 RED CLOUD, Fred
"Thanksgiving." PoetL (67:3) Aut 72, p. 241.
"Your Face." PoetL (67:3) Aut 72, p. 241.

2604 REDDY, T. J.
"The Axil of the Axis." St. AR (2:1) Aut-Wint 72, p. 19.

2605 REDGROVE, Peter
"Intimate Supper." TransR (41) Wint-Spr 72, p. 139.

2606 REDSHAW, Thomas Dillon
"pillow talk." Humanist (32:2) Mr-Ap 72, p. 35.

2607 REED, F. G.
"On the Beach." Stand (13:2) 72, p. 43.
"The Reject." Stand (13:2) 72, p. 43.

2608 REED, Ishmael
"Kali's Galaxy." Works (3:3/4) Wint 72-73, p. 23.
"Poison Light" (for J. Overstreet). Works (3:3/4) Wint 72-73, p. 22.

2609 REED, J. D.
"'Just a Prisoner of Your Love' Ode." BerksR (8:1) Spr 72, p. 12.
"'Just a Prisoner of Your Love' Ode." MassR (13:4) Aut 72, p. 581.
"Ode on Insomnia." NewYorker (48:25) 12 Ag 72, p. 49.
"Ode on Roundheads." Iron (1) Spr 72, p. 42.
"Ode on the Gothic Novel." Iron (1) Spr 72, p. 42.
"Ode to Bill Knott (1940-1966)." UnmOx (1:3) Sum 72, p. 14.
"Om Almost Ode." Iron (1) Spr 72, p. 41.
"Spring Song." MassR (13:4) Aut 72, p. 582.
"Your Complimentary River Ode." NewYorker (48:24) 5 Ag 72, p. 28.

2610 REED, John R.
"Burg Rheinfels." Works (3:3/4) Wint 72-73, p. 122.
"I Used to Think." Works (3:3/4) Wint 72-73, p. 123.

2611 REED, Lou
"The Murder Mystery." ParisR (53) Wint 72, p. 20.

2612 REED, Philip
"A Difficult Man Meets His Supper." WestR (9:2) Wint 72, p. 9.

2613 REED, R. A.
"Letter to a Friend." WindO (9) Spr 72, p. 8.

2614 REEDER, Roberta
"A Scene from Faust" (tr. of Alexander Pushkin, w. Simon Nahnybida). RusLT (3) Spr 72, p. 40.

2615 REES, Gomer
"On Being Invited and Then Uninvited to Marianne Moore's Eighty-third Birthday Party." MinnR (3) Aut 72, p. 20.
"Our Museum." MinnR (3) Aut 72, p. 21.

2616 REEVE, F. D.
"The Blue Cat Rumble." LittleM (6:1) Spr 72, p. 36.
"The Blue Cat's Daughter." LittleM (6:1) Spr 72, p. 39.
"The Revenant of Red Square." UnmOx (1:1) N 71, p. 47.
"Rubbings." UnmOx (1:1) N 71, p. 46.

2617 REEVES, Campbell
"'And Speaking of the Taniwha...'" NoCaFo (20:2) My 72, p. 80.
"The Dappled Ponies." SouthernPR (12: Special Issue) 72, p. 25.
"The Goose-Girl." SouthernPR (12: Special Issue) 72, p. 25.
"A Little Salt." SouthernPR (12: Special Issue) 72, p. 27.
"Pilgrim in the Andes." SouthernPR (12: Special Issue) 72, p. 24.

2618 REIGSTAD, Thomas J.
"One Year Ago" (to Ogden Nash). EngJ (61:8) N 72, p. 1263.

2619 REILLY, Edward J.
"No Love Poem." Epos (23:4) Sum 72, p. 9.

2620 REIN, David M.
"A Baseball Player Looks at a Poet." EngJ (61:6) S 72, p. 922.

2621 REISS, James
"Everything But." VirQR (48:2) Spr 72, p. 223.
"The Green Tree." AmerR (15) 72, p. 152.
"The Real Truth about Aunt Bibs and Me." PraS (46:1) Spr 72, p. 46.
"The Snake Man." VirQR (48:2) Spr 72, p. 221.
"Tell Me a Story." VirQR (48:2) Spr 72, p. 222.

2622 REITER, Thomas
"Cold Orchard." KanQ (4:1) Wint 71-72, p. 123.

2623 REMLEY, David
"Acoma Poem for Stasia." SoDakR (10:4) Wint 72-73, p. 83.

2624 RENDLEMAN, Danny L.
"The Drowned Darling." Drag (3:1) Spr 72, p. 39.
"F Stop." Iron (2) Fall 72, p. 39.
"The Fixed and the Movable Festivals." HangL (16) Wint 71-72, p. 41.
"Forgive Us Then." NowestR (12:3) Aut 72, p. 26.
"Gate." Epoch (22:1) Fall 72, p. 49.
"The Girl Who Sweeps the Porch." Field (6) Spr 72, p. 95.
"Grimace." Zahir (1:4/5) 72, p. 11.
"Grimace." Zahir (1:4/5) 72, p. 30.
"Guile." Field (6) Spr 72, p. 93.
"Here in the Ear." Field (7) Fall 72, p. 67.
"Hotel Calico" (for my father). Field (6) Spr 72, p. 94.
"Illuminations." Epoch (21:2) Wint 71, p. 144.
"The Insomnolent." CarolQ (24:3) Fall 72, p. 44.
"Loving Against the Grain." CarolQ (24:3) Fall 72, p. 45.
"Memorial Day." Sky (1:1) 71.
"The Metaphor." Field (7) Fall 72, p. 62.
"Milk & Honey." Field (7) Fall 72, p. 64.
"Needing Binoculars." Field (7) Fall 72, p. 66.
"Open Door." Sky (1:1) 71.
"Poem Begun." Epoch (22:1) Fall 72, p. 48.
"The Secret of the Camera." Epoch (22:1) Fall 72, p. 48.
"Tongue." Field (7) Fall 72, p. 63.
"Trout." CarolQ (24:3) Fall 72, p. 46.

2625 RENSCHEN, Denice
"Stepping bank-to-bank." HiramPoR (13) Fall-Wint 72, p. 15.

2626 RESZLER, André
"Delphes." Mund (5:3) 72, p. 14.

2627 RETTMANN, Bruce R.
"Dog barked when I went by." Magazine (5) part 9, 72, p. 15.
"My soul is black." Magazine (5) part 9, 72, p. 17.
"Rocket Attack." Magazine (5) part 9, 72, p. 20.

2628 REVERDY, Pierre
"Flower-Market Quay" (tr. by Michael Benedikt). Drag (3:1) Spr 72, p. 79.

2629 REXROTH, Kenneth
"The Autumn Brook" (tr. of Hsueh T'ao, w. Ling Chung). UnmOx (1:4) Aut 72.

"For the Courtesan Ch'ing Lin, To the Tune 'The Love of the Immortals'" (tr. of Wu Tsao, w. Ling Chung). NewYQ (12) Aut 72, p. 43.
"An Old Poem to Yuan Chen" (tr. of Hsueh T'ao, w. Ling Chung). UnmOx (1:4) Aut 72.
"Playing All a Summer's Day by the Lake (to the Tune 'Clear Bright Joy')" (tr. of Chu Shu-chen, w. Ling Chung). Kayak (30) D 72, p. 18.
"Plum Blossoms" (tr. of Chu Shu-chen, w. Ling Chung). Kayak (30) D 72, p. 20.
"Spring Joy" (tr. of Chu-Shu-chen, w. Ling Chung). NewL (38:4) Sum 72, p. 39.
"Spring Night (to the Tune 'Panning Gold')" (tr. of Chu Shu-chen, w. Ling Chung). Kayak (30) D 72, p. 19.

2630 REYES, Carlos
"For a Student." Meas (2) 72.
"In Three Frames." MinnR (3) Aut 72, p. 113.
"Love at First Sight." MinnR (3) Aut 72, p. 112.
"The Mythical Animal Known as the Unicorn." Meas (2) 72.
"Rocks" (for Richard Johnson). MinnR (3) Aut 72, p. 112.

2631 REYNOLDS, Michael S.
"All the Young Pilots." SouthernPR (12: Special Issue) 72, p. 30.
"For a Young Pilot Who Once Ejected above the Sierras without a Parachute and Lived." SouthernPR (12: Special Issue) 72, p. 32.
"The Outer Banks: Death's Other Promises." SouthernPR (12: Special Issue) 72, p. 29.
"Traffic Directions for My Daughter in Spring Time." SouthernPR (12: Special Issue) 72, p. 31.

2632 REZENDES, Michael
"Afternoon." HangL (17) Sum 72, p. 68.

2633 REZMERSKI, John Calvin
"Heyoka Ceremony." SoDakR (10:3) Aut 72, p. 3.

2634 RHAMAN, Yusef
"Cosmic--Black lady." JnlOBP (2:16) Sum 72, p. 24.

2635 RHOADES, Priscilla
"The Fisherman's Lady." Iowa (3:4) Fall 72, p. 5.

2636 RHODEN, Kerney
"Platforms." Poetry (120:1) Ap 72, p. 22.
"The Scenario." Poetry (120:1) Ap 72, p. 21.

2637 RICAPITO, Joseph V.
from Florentine Streets: "Each Day Trains." TexQ

(15:4) Wint 72, p. 57.
from Florentine Streets: "I Shall Not Bury Myself." TexQ (15:4) Wint 72, p. 56.
from Florentine Streets: "Now That We Are Gone." TexQ (15:4) Wint 72, p. 56.
from Florentine Streets: "On a Florentine Autumn Morning." TexQ (15:4) Wint 72, p. 55.

2638 RICCIO, Ottone M.
"Morning Picnic." New:ACP (19) Aut 72, p. 28.
"Our Last Word." Magazine (5) part 9, 72, p. 21.
"The Single Moment." Qt (5:39/40) Sum-Aut 72, p. 19.

2639 RICE, Nancy
"Deprivation." MassR (13:1/2) Wint-Spr 72, p. 280.

2640 RICH, Adrienne
"Dialogue." UnmOx (1:4) Aut 72.
"Diving Into the Wreck." SatR (55:17) 22 Ap 72, p. 59.
"Ghazal XXXIV" (tr. of Mirza Ghalib). Madem (74:3) Ja 72, p. 50.
"Song." Aphra (3:2) Spr 72, p. 2.
"Waking in the Dark." PartR (39:4) Aut 72, p. 531.

2641 RICHARDS, George
"Down East (for Barry)." Peb (7) Aut 71.

2642 RICHARDS, Tad
"The Marsupials of the Mind." Etc. (29:3) S 72, p. 250.

2643 RICHARDSON, Dorothy Lee
"Establishment." ChiTM 16 Ja 72, p. 14.
"Husbandman." PoetL (67:1) Spr 72, p. 39.

2644 RICHARDSON, James
"The Condemned." Shen (24:1) Aut 72, p. 50.
"The Crime." Shen (24:1) Aut 72, p. 49.
"Somebody Else." PraS (46:4) Wint 72-73, p. 341.

2645 RICHIE, Gene
"Weeding and Watering." HiramPoR (13) Fall-Wint 72, p. 23.

2646 RICHMAN, Daniel
"Blast-off." Confr (5) Wint-Spr 72, p. 83.

2647 RICKERT, Robert
"Salesman." SouthernPR (13:1) Aut 72, p. 18.

2648 RIDDLE, Barbara
"Cheese Sandwich Poem." Kayak (30) D 72, p. 24.

2649 RIDLAND, John
"Late Sunlight in Certain Treetops." NYT 3 Ja 72, p. 26.
"Riddle: You are a handicap." Antaeus (7) Aut 72, p. 32.

2650 RIESE, M. L.
"Squirrels." PoetL (67:2) Sum 72, p. 142.

2651 RIETH, John
from Love Quintet: (Ceremony of Tea). BallSUF (13:1) Wint 72, p. 13.

2652 RIFAT, Oktay
"Arrival" (tr. by Nermin Menemencioglu). LitR (15:4) Sum 72, p. 413.

2653 RIGGS, Dionis Coffin
"Misunderstanding." ChiTM 23 Jl 72, p. 14.

2654 RIGSBEE, David
"Among the Finnish Islands." St.AR (1:4) Spr-Sum 72, p. 74.

2655 RILKE, Rainer Maria
"Evening in Skane" (tr. by Robert Bly). Madrona (1:2) N 71, p. 12.
"Fifth Elegy" (tr. by David Young). Field (7) Fall 72, p. 24.
"Four Poem Fragments" (tr. by John J. Mood). NewYQ (9) Wint 72, p. 64.
"Marsh Lights" (tr. by Reinhold Johannes Kaebitzsch). SenR (3:1) My 72, p. 27.
"Poems of Rainer Maria Rilke" (tr. by William Pratt). ColQ (21:2) Aut 72, p. 226.
"Sixth Elegy" (tr. by David Young). Field (7) Fall 72, p. 33.
"Third Elegy" (tr. by David Young). Field (6) Spr 72, p. 63.

2656 RIMBAUD, Arthur
"Marine" (tr. by William Doreski). PoetL (67:1) Spr 72, p. 43.
"Sleeper in the Vale" (tr. by Lora Dunetz). PoetL (67:1) Spr 72, p. 20.

2657 RINALDI, Nicholas
"Consumer." PraS (46:1) Spr 72, p. 51.
"Gambler." SouthernPR (12:2) Spr 72, p. 36.

2658 RIND, Sherry
"Bloom." GeoR (26:4) Wint 72, p. 508.
"Kite." Madrona (1:1) Je 71, p. 10.

2659 RISI, Nelo
from Dentro la Sostanza: "The Garden of Europe" (tr. by Brian Swann and Ruth Feldman). MedR (2:4) Sum 72, p. 99.

2660 RISTAU, Harland
"Collage #12." WindO (12) Wint 72-73, p. 30.

2661 RITCHEY, Barbara
"Question." EngJ (61:9) D 72, p. 1318.

2662 RITCHIE, Elisavietta
"Eclipse: Washington D C." NYT 22 Mr 72, p. 46.
"Family Album." ChiTM 19 N 72, p. 10.
"A Gift of Peaches." PoetL (67:2) Sum 72, p. 168.
"Ocean." PoetL (67:2) Sum 72, p. 170.
"Oriental Paysagists: Indochina." NYT 13 My 72, p. 30.
"The Puffball Offering." DenQuart (7:1) Spr 72, p. 80.

2663 RITSOS, Yannis
"At the Barracks" (tr. by Eleni Paidoussi and Dan Georgakas). ChiTM 6 Ag 72, p. 7.
"Injustice" (tr. by Rae Dalven). Poetry (120:5) Ag 72, p. 260.
"Security" (tr. by Rae Dalven). Poetry (120:5) Ag 72, p. 261.
"Without Position" (tr. by Rae Dalven). Poetry (120:5) Ag 72, p. 260.

2664 RIZZA, Peggy
"Summer Landscape." Madem (75:4) Ag 72, p. 384.

2665 ROBBINS, Chris
"Recipe." RoadAR (3:4) Wint 71-72, p. 21.

2666 ROBBINS, Martin
"The Cortege Passed." St. AR (1:4) Spr-Sum 72, p. 54.
"Farewell, Moon." NYT 27 F 72, sec. 4, p. 12.
"Memo: On the Exiles." ColQ (21:1) Sum 72, p. 67.
"Of an Evening." NYT 25 Je 72, sec. 4, p. 14.
"Three Case Histories (With Closing Hymn)." ColQ (20:4) Spr 72, p. 478.

2667 ROBERTS, Jim
"The Beach." Spec (14:1/2) My 72, p. 77.

2668 ROBERTSON, Joe
"seated in the sunshine today." WindO (10) Sum 72, p. 7.

2669 ROBERTSON, Kell
"Black and White Christmas." Cafe (4) Fall 72, p. 13.

2670 ROBIN, Ralph
"In the Secret File." NewRep (167:4) 22 Jl 72, p. 24.

2671 ROBINS, Carl A.
from The Wind Is Rising: "Bereavement." Magazine (5) part 9, 72, p. 22.
"Young America." Magazine (5) part 7, 72.

2672 ROBINSON, Lillian S.
"Miss America." MassR (13:1/2) Wint-Spr 72, p. 176.

2673 ROBINSON, Sandy
"I Had To Be Told." JnlOBP (2:16) Sum 72, p. 34.

2674 ROBINSON, Sondra
"Desert Poem." SoDakR (10:1) Spr 72, p. 73.
"Moth." SoDakR (10:1) Spr 72, p. 73.
"Mushrooms Are Still Mysterious." SoDakR (10:4) Wint 72-73, p. 4.

2675 ROCHE, Paul
"The American Dream." NewYQ (11) Sum 72, p. 49.
"The Strong Can Keep the Transient Young." ChiTM 11 Je 72, p. 4.

2676 RODAX, Yvonne
"Wool-Worker." PoetL (67:3) Aut 72, p. 223.

2677 RODEIRO, Jose Manuel
"Life." Cord (1:3) 72, p. 2.

2678 RODIERO, Joseph
"Arctic Wind in a Sunny Day" (tr. of Nico Suarez). UTR (1:4) 72, p. 27.
"Country Life" (for my father and mother) (tr. of Nico Suarez). UTR (1:4) 72, p. 30.
Eight Poems (tr. of Nico Suarez). UTR (1:3) 72, p. 3.
"The Lips of the Sky" (tr. of Nico Suarez). UTR (1:4) 72, p. 32.

2679 RODITI, Edouard
"The Lethargic Muse." ExpR (3) Fall-Wint 72/73, p. 6.

2680 ROECKER, W. A.
"Friends." Meas (2) 72.
"Idaho Marsh." Drag (3:1) Spr 72, p. 71.
"Kicking the Horse." Drag (3:1) Spr 72, p. 71.
"Knives: Bonner, Montana." Iron (1) Spr 72, p. 73.
"Song." Drag (3:1) Spr 72, p. 72.
"Walking into Kentucky Robie's Drunk." Meas (2) 72.
"You Know Me." Meas (2) 72.

2681 ROETHKE, Theodore
"The Beautiful Disorder" (arr. from the Notebooks,

1954-1963, by David Wagoner). Peb (8) Spr 72, p. 26.

2682 ROGERS, Del Marie
"Apex." SouthernPR (12: Special Issue) 72, p. 42.
"Home." Folio (8:1) Spr 72, p. 14.
"Morning Ceremony." Meas (2) 72.

2683 ROGERS, Jaime Gómez
"We Knew Nothing" (tr. by Edward Oliphant). RoadAR (4:1) Spr 72, p. 43.

2684 ROGERS, Patrick
"Breaking the Circle." ConcPo (5:1) Spr 72, p. 69.
"Post Sitting." ConcPo (5:1) Spr 72, p. 68.

2685 ROJAS, Waldo
"Chess" (tr. by Edward Oliphant). RoadAR (4:1) Spr 72, p. 40.
"Meat Market" (tr. by Edward Oliphant). RoadAR (4:1) Spr 72, p. 42.
"Story for the Sleepless" (tr. by Edward Oliphant). RoadAR (4:1) Spr 72, p. 42.
"Window" (tr. by Edward Oliphant). RoadAR (4:1) Spr 72, p. 41.

2686 ROM, Ronnie
"To Sylvia Plath after reading The Bell Jar." HangL (18) Fall 72, p. 67.

2687 ROMANO, Liboria
"En Passage." PoetL (67:2) Sum 72, p. 185.

2688 ROOT, Judith
"Man In Brown." NowestR (12:3) Aut 72, p. 29.

2689 ROPER, Renee
"Listen to the Self." JnlOBP (2:16) Sum 72, p. 71.

2690 RORTY, Amelie Oksenberg
"Let Chaos Be Our Rain." QRL (18:1/2) 72, p. 215.

2691 ROSBERG, Rose
"Mr. Blake's Tiger." SouthernHR (6:1) Wint 72, p. 68.

2692 ROSE, Harriet
"The Saint Working in the World" (for St. John of the Cross). UTR (1:1) 72, p. 27.

2693 ROSELIEP, Raymond
"Carol, This Year." ChrC (89:46) 20 D 72, p. 1292.
"A Floral Note." EngJ (61:1) Ja 72, p. 91.
"Mississippi." NewL (39:1) Aut 72, p. 89.
"My Homily, August Derleth." ChiTM 6 Ag 72, p. 7.
"La Nuit Nuptiale." NewL (39:1) Aut 72, p. 89.

"Variation on a Theme." NewL (39:1) Aut 72, p. 90.
"Wading." NewL (39:1) Aut 72, p. 88.
"Who's Afraid?" NewL (39:1) Aut 72, p. 89.
"Young Shepherd." ChrC (89:46) 20 D 72, p. 1291.

2694 ROSEMAN, Sabina Jacyna
"The Black Bag." Magazine (5) part 9, 72, p. 24.

2695 ROSEN, Aaron
"On the Frontier." Epoch (21:2) Wint 71, p. 154.
"Staying Home." Epoch (21:2) Wint 71, p. 155.

2696 ROSEN, Kenneth
"F. Scott Fitzgerald." BerksR (8:2) Fall-Wint 72, p. 32.
"Gorham, Maine." AntR (31:4) Wint 71-72, p. 552.
"Old Times." HangL (16) Wint 71-72, p. 45.
"Robberies." HangL (16) Wint 71-72, p. 43.

2697 ROSENBERG, David
"Afternoon." ParisR (53) Wint 72, p. 74.

2698 ROSENBERG, Robert
"Walk At Four Oaks." Epoch (21:2) Wint 71, p. 131.

2699 ROSENBLATT, Herta
"Too Long." Epos (23:3) Spr 72, p. 27.

2700 ROSENBLATT, Jon
"Four Days Ago." CarolQ (24:1) Wint 72, p. 80.

2701 ROSENBLUM, Martin J.
"Summer/Fall: 1971." RoadAR (3:4) Wint 71-72, p. 6.
"Two Day Place" (after David Kherdian's Homage to Adana). HangL (18) Fall 72, p. 39.

2702 ROSENTHAL, Abby
"Larkin and Chestnut: An Automobile Accident" (for Jeanne Lance). ChiR (23:4 & 24:1) 72, p. 33.
"Old Man with Shears Among Roses." ChiR (23:4 & 24:1) 72, p. 32.

2703 ROSENTHAL, David
"For Lynn." QRL (18:1/2) 72, p. 217.
"Frost." QRL (18:1/2) 72, p. 218.
"This It Is." Humanist (32:2) Mr-Ap 72, p. 34.
"Vicious Dog." NYT 3 F 72, p. 32.
"Winter in the Imperial City (Peking, 1971)." Nat (214:2) 10 Ja 72, p. 56.

2704 ROSENTHAL, M. L.
"Deaths of the Poets." Nat (214:26) 26 Je 72, p. 825.
"Intermission." Antaeus (7) Aut 72, p. 143.
"Like Morning Light" (An inscription for Eva E.,

1918-1936, whom I knew as a child in Passaic, N.J.). Salm (19) Spr 72, p. 70.
"My Friend's Anger." Humanist (32:3) My-Je 72, p. 42.
"Sparrow." NewYQ (10) Spr 72, p. 42.

2705 ROSENTHAL, Melinda
"Three Poems" (tr. of Claude Vigée, w. Manfred Wolf). SouthernR (8:2) Spr 72, p. 429.

2706 ROSKOLENKO, Harry
"Images of Disorder." NYT 21 D 72, p. 34.
"Manhattan." NYT 5 Jl 72, p. 38.

2707 ROSNER, Martin C.
"In Flight." NYT 25 S 72, p. 36.

2708 ROSS, Geraldine
"Typist Appli-can't." SatEP (244:3) Aut 72, p. 89.

2709 ROTH, Paul
"Another Darkness." UTR (1:2) 72, p. 12.
"On My Way." UTR (1:1) 72, p. 16.
"To a Dead Wren." UTR (1:4) 72, p. 20.

2710 ROTHENBERG, Jerome
"Ancestral Scenes: 'The Student'." UnmOx (1:4) Aut 72.

2711 ROULSTON, Robert
"A Grunt My Word." ColEng (33:7) Ap 72, p. 812.

2712 ROWLEY, Harold
"So We Did It." SatEP (244:3) Aut 72, p. 89.

2713 ROYSTER, Philip M.
"Mythic Dreams." JnlOBP (2:16) Sum 72, p. 18.

2714 RUARK, Gibbons
"The Deer Who Never Comes." PoetryNW (13:1) Spr 72, p. 21.

2715 RUBALD, Tim
"Yoga Exercises Prove Fatal." BabyJ (5) N 72, p. 22.

2716 RUBENSTEIN, Roberta
"Spilled from a Grecian Urn." Poem (14) Mr 72, p. 10.
"Variations on a Euclidean Theme." ColQ (20:4) Spr 72, p. 500.

2717 RUBIN, Larry
"After the Summer Tour." Peb (6) Sum 71.
"The Bachelor, at Sea." SewanR (80:4) Aut 72, p. 624.
"The Bachelor: First Routine Checkup." Esq (78:6) D 72, p. 356.

"Breakdown (II)." SouthernHR (6:1) Sum 72, p. 52.
"Curtains of the Sea." Poetry (119:6) Mr 72, p. 338.
"Evening in the Lounge." Cim (20) Jl 72, p. 53.
"From Miami, with Love" (for Liv). CarlMis (12:1) Fall-Wint 71-72, p. 77.
"Lines for a Dean of Men, Once a Preacher, Going into Retirement" (to E. H. R.). SouthernPR (12:2) Spr 72, p. 46.
"The Metamorphosis" (for V. H.). Etc. (29:4) D 72, p. 385.
"The Old Jew." Shen (24:1) Aut 72, p. 43.
"Pygmalion." Peb (6) Sum 71.
"The Subjectivist, Musing Over Some Old Letters." SouthernHR (6:1) Wint 72, p. 52.
"Total Recall." SewanR (80:4) Aut 72, p. 623.
"The Voyager, to a Former Friend, A Lifeguard." Peb (6) Sum 71.

2718 RUDMAN, Mark
"Down in Dixie." NowestR (12:3) Aut 72, p. 41.
"Scrapings." CalQ (3) Aut 72, p. 50.

2719 RUDNIK, Charles
Eight Poems. QRL (18:1/2) 72, p. 219.

2720 RUDNIK, Raphael
"Aria." QRL (18:1/2) 72, p. 223.
"Elements of Immortality." QRL (18:1/2) 72, p. 224.
"The End of a Day." QRL (18:1/2) 72, p. 223.
"Going On." Nat (215:10) 9 O 72, p. 312.
"Lachiman Gurung, Gurka from Nepal." Nat (215:13) 30 O 72, p. 408.
"Talking to the Sky." Nat (214:8) 21 F 72, p. 252.
"The Story of Troy." QRL (18:1/2) 72, p. 223.

2721 RUDOLPH, Lee
"Appeal to the Governor." QRL (18:1/2) 72, p. 225.
"The Glassbottomed House." Kayak (30) D 72, p. 62.
"The Hands." QRL (18:1/2) 72, p. 226.
"Hard Times." QRL (18:1/2) 72, p. 226.
"Noon." QRL (18:1/2) 72, p. 227.

2722 RUDOLPH, Lillian
"Ten Dreams." LadHJ (89:2) F 72, p. 133.

2723 RUGGLES, Eugene
"Evening Begins Near the Pacific." Isthmus (1) Spr 72, p. 52.
"Looking for Warmth Among Men." Isthmus (1) Spr 72, p. 4.
"Our Pages." Isthmus (1) Spr 72, p. 13.

2724 RUKEYSER, Muriel
"Searching/Not Searching." NewYQ (12) Aut 72, p. 37.

"A Simple Experiment." AmerR (15) 72, p. 174.

2725 RULISON, Helen
"Words." SouthernPR (12: Special Issue) 72, p. 47.

2726 RUMAKER, Michael
"Four Months After the Breakdown." EverR (16:95) Fall 72, p. 46.

2727 RUPPELL, Peter
"Poem: Enough." Pan (9) 72, p. 22.
"Poem: Faint flowers I had found when the wheat was cut." Pan (9) 72, p. 24.

2728 RUSH, Michael
"Grape Creek." PoetryNW (13:1) Spr 72, p. 22.
"The Pimp Gets Religion." Madrona (1:3) My 72, p. 37.
"The Whore." Madrona (1:3) My 72, p. 36.

2729 RUSS, J. J.
"Sunday Drive." Cim (19) Ap 72, p. 68.

2730 RUSS, Lawrence
"Morning." Iowa (3:3) Sum 72, p. 13.
"October Rain." Epoch (21:2) Wint 71, p. 138.
"Spells." Iowa (3:3) Sum 72, p. 13.

2731 RUSS, Peyton
"Composition II." Etc. (29:1) Mr 72, p. 46.

2732 RUSSELL, Herb
"Arboreal Apartments." FreeL (15:1/2) 71-72, p. 74.
"Life in Lacuna." FreeL (15:1/2) 71-72, p. 72.
"Raintrees of New Harmony." FreeL (15:1/2) 71-72, p. 73.

2733 RUSSELL, Norman H.
"after the night of sweats." SoDakR (10:4) Wint 72-73, p. 89.
"all my dreams." SoDakR (10:4) Wint 72-73, p. 89.
"all the white night." PraS (46:1) Spr 72, p. 35.
"and saw strange things." MidwQ (13:3) Spr 72, p. 269.
"the beetle." UTR (1:1) 72, p. 4.
"the dust settles from the day." MidwQ (13:2) Wint 72, p. 145.
"each day i am stronger." PoetryNW (13:2) Sum 72, p. 37.
"the gods like light." UTR (1:2) 72, p. 20.
"great owl great eagle of the night." Northeast Aut-Wint 71-72, p. 12.
"he becomes older." PoetryNW (13:2) Sum 72, p. 36.
"how many days?" PraS (46:1) Spr 72, p. 37.
"i am afraid of the old man." PoetryNW (13:2) Sum 72, p. 36.

"i laughed i listen." PraS (46:1) Spr 72, p. 36.
"if I kill a man." MidwQ (13:3) Spr 72, p. 299.
"the lives of the people." MidwQ (13:2) Wint 72, p. 144.
"message from a warrior." Hiero (7) Ap 72.
"moons and suns have spun beyond counting." Northeast Aut-Wint 71-72, p. 9.
"a music or a message." MidwQ (13:4) Sum 72, p. 454.
"my own voice." Northeast Aut-Wint 71-72, p. 11.
"our medicine man." MidwQ (13:2) Wint 72, p. 146.
"the singing of the gods." MidwQ (13:4) Sum 72, p. 386.
"the sky of the leaves." Hiero (7) Ap 72.
"snow likely." PraS (46:1) Spr 72, p. 35.
"speaking to the child." Hiero (7) Ap 72.
"the strength of my horse." Northeast Aut-Wint 71-72, p. 10.
"when the woods stop speaking." UTR (1:1) 72, p. 5.
"the wind." MidwQ (13:3) Spr 72, p. 308.

2734 RUSSELL, Richard
"Dog Canyon." SouthwR (57:2) Spr 72, p. 124.

2735 RUSSELL, William
"Going Back." Zahir (1:4/5) 72, p. 25.

2736 RUSSO, A. P.
"Thing (to be destroyed)." Zahir (1:4/5) 72, p. 61.

2737 RUTSALA, Vern
"Boxing Day." Poetry (119:4) Ja 72, p. 193.
"Heroes!" Peb (7) Aut 71.
"Lament for Receptions." Peb (7) Aut 71.
"Mesh." Poetry (119:4) Ja 72, p. 194.
"A Secret Army." Poetry (119:4) Ja 72, p. 192.
"They." Peb (7) Aut 71.

2738 RYAN, Florence Holmes
"The Naked Self with Clothes On, Yet." Folio (8:2) Spr 72, p. 21.

2739 RYAN, Michael R.
"Drowning." Nat (214:24) 12 Je 72, p. 763.
"Flight." Nat (214:26) 26 Je 72, p. 823.
"Letter from an Institution." CarlMis (12:1) Fall-Wint 71-72, p. 87.
"One Stop in the Snake House." NoAmR (257:2) Sum 72, p. 31.

2740 RYAN, Richard
"Galaxy." Humanist (32:2) Mr-Ap 72, p. 35.
"Return." Nat (215:15) 13 N 72, p. 472.

2741 RYAN, W. E.
"Funeral." SoDakR (10:3) Aut 72, p. 82.

2742 RYAN, William M.
"Catharsis for David & Me." Cord (1:4) 72, p. 24.
"Sunday Mass." Cord (1:4) 72, p. 26.

2743 RYDER, Barbara
"Burning Off." QRL (18:1/2) 72, p. 228.
"The Discipline." QRL (18:1/2) 72, p. 229.
"Encounter." Salm (19) Spr 72, p. 69.
"Goat Rocks." QRL (18:1/2) 72, p. 228.
"Independence Day." Salm (19) Wint 72, p. 68.
"Late Frost." Salm (19) Spr 72, p. 70.

2744 RYERSON, Alice
"A Chance of Dreaming." Epos (23:3) Spr 72, p. 23.

2745 RYUICHI, Tamura
"Chestnut Tree" (tr. by Harold P. Wright). NewYQ (10) Spr 72, p. 70.

2746 SAARI, Anil
"Bicycle." Meas (3) 72, p. 77.
"Poem: listen." Meas (3) 72, p. 78.

2747 SAAVEDRA, Carlos Castro
"Cine Gratis." MinnR (3) Aut 72, p. 74.

2748 SABA, Umberto
from Mediterranea: "Mediterranean" (tr. by Brian Swann and Ruth Feldman). MedR (2:4) Sum 72, p. 99.

2749 SABELLA, Andrés
"Copper" (tr. by Edward Oliphant). RoadAR (4:1) Spr 72, p. 9.
"Elegy for some Miner Boots" (tr. by Edward Oliphant). RoadAR (4:1) Spr 72, p. 9.
"Discourse from the Plains" (tr. by Edward Oliphant). RoadAR (4:1) Spr 72, p. 10.

2750 SABOTKA, Edward F.
"Modulo 7." BeyB (2:2) 72, p. 50.
"Renewal." BeyB (2:2) 72, p. 48.

2751 SABUKEWICZ, Charles
"Clock Song." Epos (24:1) Fall 72, p. 12.

2752 as-SABUR, Salah Abd
"Silence and the Wind" (tr. by M. Bakir Alwan). Books (46:2) Spr 72, p. 248.

2753 SACHTOURIS, Miltos
"The Cafe" (tr. by Ruth Whitman). AriD (1:4/5) Sum-Aut 72, p. 91.
"Chronicle" (tr. by Ruth Whitman). AriD (1:4/5)

Sum-Aut 72, p. 89.
"The Drowned Man" (tr. by Ruth Whitman). AriD (1:4/5) Sum-Aut 72, p. 90.
"I Live Close" (tr. by Ruth Whitman). AriD (1:4/5) Sum-Aut 72, p. 91.
"The Mouse" (tr. by Ruth Whitman). AriD (1:4/5) Sum-Aut 72, p. 92.
"She Who Was Coming" (tr. by Ruth Whitman). AriD (1:4/5) Sum-Aut 72, p. 92.
"Sparrows" (tr. by Ruth Whitman). AriD (1:4/5) Sum-Aut 72, p. 90.

2754 SADOFF, Ira
"Another Country." MinnR (2) Spr 72, p. 49.
"The City." MinnR (2) Spr 72, p. 51.
Eleven Poems. AntR (32:1/2) Spr-Sum 72, p. 196.
"It's So Late." CarolQ (24:2) Spr 72, p. 59.
"Journey to the East." MinnR (2) Spr 72, p. 51.
"Our Leaving." CarolQ (24:2) Spr 72, p. 59.
"The Return to Mysticism." MinnR (2) Spr 72, p. 50.
"The Shape of Content." Shen (23:2) Wint 72, p. 50.
"Take One." CarolQ (24:2) Spr 72, p. 58.

2755 SADOWSKI, Lois
"Migration." PoetL (67:3) Aut 72, p. 256.
"Proud Turtle." WestHR (26:2) Spr 72, p. 156.
"Transfer Point." PoetL (67:3) Aut 72, p. 262.

2756 St. FRANCIS, Carol Herring
"Sorrow." Wind (2:5) Sum 72, p. 27.

2757 St. JOHN, Primus
"After the Truckers Restaurant." PoetryNW (13:2) Sum 72, p. 39.
"Benign Neglect/Mississippi, 1970." Works (3:3/4) Wint 72-73, p. 9.
"Field." PoetryNW (13:2) Sum 72, p. 40.
"A Poem to My Notebook, Across Winter." Works (3:3/4) Wint 72-73, p. 10.

2758 SAJKOVIC, Olivera
"Departure." NewRena (6) My 72, p. 22.
"Encounter." NewRena (6) My 72, p. 23.

2759 SAKURAI, Emiko
"Banquet at the Tso Villa" (tr. of Tu Fu). Literature (15:3) 72, p. 488.
"The Winding River II" (tr. of Tu Fu). Literature (15:3) 72, p. 488.

2760 SAKUTARO, Hagiwara
"Bottles" (tr. by Graeme Wilson). DenQuart (6:4) Wint 72, p. 35.

"Corpse and Bamboo" (tr. by Graeme Wilson). DenQuart (6:4) Wint 72, p. 35.
"Penitentiary" (tr. by Graeme Wilson). AmerS (41:3) Sum 72, p. 363.
"Toy Box: Evening" (tr. by Graeme Wilson). DenQuart (6:4) Wint 72, p. 36.
"Useless Book" (tr. by Graeme Wilson). DenQuart (6:4) Wint 72, p. 36.
"White Night" (tr. by Graeme Wilson). AmerS (41:3) Sum 72, p. 364.

2761 SALAAM, Kalamu ya (Val Ferdinand)
"Colored boys Eighty years old (& Other Peoples)." JnlOBP (2:16) Sum 72, p. 83.
"Looking" (sitting on the dock of the bay--for Otis). JnlOBP (2:16) Sum 72, p. 82.

2762 SALAMUN, Tomaz
"End of Influence" (tr. by Anselm Hollo). NewL (38:4) Sum 72, p. 110.
"Let's Wait" (tr. by Anselm Hollo). NewL (38:4) Sum 72, p. 109.
"Proverbs" (tr. by Anselm Hollo). NewL (38:4) Sum 72, p. 108.
Three Poems (tr. by Elliott Anderson). NewL (38:4) Sum 72, p. 108.
"what do you like most in your life" (tr. by Anselm Hollo). NewL (38:4) Sum 72, p. 110.

2763 SALAPASSIDIS, Teos
"Northern Spiritual" (tr. by Sarah Kafatou). AriD (1:4/5) Sum-Aut 72, p. 93.
"O-24" (tr. by Athan Anagnostopoulos). AriD (1:4/5) Sum-Aut 72, p. 94.

2764 SALEH, Dennis
"Desert." Poetry (120:3) Je 72, p. 162.

2765 SALES, Richard
"The Angel." ConcPo (5:1) Spr 72, p. 60.

2766 SALOMON, I. L.
"Corso Lodi" (tr. of Vittorio Sereni). MichQR (11:4) Aut 72, p. 273.
from Dal Fonde delle Campagne: "From the Tower" (tr. of Mario Luzi). MedR (2:4) Sum 72, p. 98.
from Origine: (1) (tr. of Alfredo De Palchi). MedR (2:4) Sum 72, p. 88.
"Portrait on a Tombstone" (tr. of Vittorio Sereni). MichQR (11:4) Aut 72, p. 272.
"Somewhere" (tr. of Mario Luzi). MichQR (11:4) Aut 72, p. 273.
"The Whirlpool of Sickness and Health" (tr. of Mario

Luzi). MassR (13:3) Sum 72, p. 425.
"With My Brother at Settignano, 1959" (tr. of Carlo Betocchi). MichQR (11:4) Aut 72, p. 275.
"Within the Year" (tr. of Mario Luzi). MichQR (11:4) Aut 72, p. 273.

2767 SALSICH, Albert
"Goodbye, Berlin." Confr (5) Wint-Spr 72, p. 61.
"Incident." NowestR (12:3) Aut 72, p. 27.
"Moving the Beach." Confr (5) Wint-Spr 72, p. 60.
"The Problem." Perspec (17:1) Sum 72, p. 31.

2768 SALTMAN, Benjamin
"The Death of Ruben Salazar." Cafe (4) Fall 72, p. 12.
"The Fathers." NoAmR (257:2) Sum 72, p. 30.
"Fog in the Neighborhood." Madrona (1:2) N 71, p. 13.
"I Think of My Daughter's Birth." Iowa (3:1) Wint 72, p. 18.

2769 SALTZMAN, Paul
"Take It." St. AR (1:4) Spr-Sum 72, p. 53.
"Yes." St. AR (1:4) Spr-Sum 72, p. 39.

2770 SALYERS, Paul
"Sharecroppers." Wind (2:6) Aut 72, p. 20.

2771 SAMPLEY, Arthur M.
"The Playhouse." SouthwR (57:2) Spr 72, p. 149.

2772 SAMPSON, Dennis N.
"Autumn: From Shoals of Wind to January." SoDakR (10:3) Aut 72, p. 68.
"The Farmhouse." SoDakR (10:3) Aut 72, p. 68.
"Noon." SoDakR (10:3) Aut 72, p. 68.

2773 SAMPSON, Judith F.
"Revealing the Future of the Waters." WestHR (26:2) Spr 72, p. 139.

2774 SAMSON, Ann
"Biopsy." Cafe (4) Fall 72, p. 26.
"Eye of a Needle." Cafe (4) Fall 72, p. 27.

2775 SANCHEZ, Ricardo
"Two Years Ago." Conrad (4:1) 72, p. 33.

2776 SANCHEZ, Sonia
"right on: wite america." StoneD (1:1) Spr 72, p. 52.
"summer words of a sistuh addict." StoneD (1:1) Spr 72, p. 53.
"Three X Three." MassR (13:1/2) Wint-Spr 72, p. 106.

2777 SANDBERG, Karl
"Night Watch." CarlMis (12:2) Spr-Sum 72, p. 57.

2778 SANDERS, Ed
"Lisbe" (tr. of Jouve). UnmOx (1:3) Sum 72, p. 37.

2779 SANDERS, Ralph
"The Machine." Cord (1:3) 72, p. 6.

2780 SANDERS, Scott
"We Find the Beginning." WestR (10:1) Spr 73, p. 2.

2781 SANDRICH, Nina
"Bon Appetit." FourQt (21:3) Mr 72, p. 35.
"The Difference." FourQt (21:3) Mr 72, p. 34.
"A Game of Hop Scotch." FourQt (21:3) Mr 72, p. 34.
"Mother-May-I." FourQt (21:2) Ja 72, p. 19.

2782 SANDY, Stephen
"Farm." QRL (18:1/2) 72, p. 231.
"A Frame." QRL (18:1/2) 72, p. 230.
"Halves." QRL (18:1/2) 72, p. 232.
"Landing." OhioR (14:1) Aut 72, p. 20.
"Northway Tanka." Hudson (25:4) Wint 72-73, p. 539.
"Spider." Hudson (25:4) Wint 72-73, p. 242.
"Watching." AntR (31:4) Wint 71-72, p. 556.

2783 SANER, Reg
"Breathing a Fine Wilderness in the Air." OhioR (13:2) Wint 72, p. 36.
"Learning the Possibilities." KanQ (4:3) Sum 72, p. 40.
"Listening for Indians." OhioR (13:2) Wint 72, p. 37.
"Voices at the Edge of the Mirror." PraS (46:1) Spr 72, p. 57.
"The Wolf Under the Skin." Works (3:3/4) Wint 72-73, p. 103.

2784 SANESI, Roberto
"April." MedR (2:4) Sum 72, p. 86.
from Un Lavoro Difficile: "In Consequence" (tr. by William Alexander). MedR (2:4) Sum 72, p. 86.
"Park Hotel" (tr by William Alexander). MichQR (11:4) Aut 72, p. 276.
from Viaggio Verso il Nord: "Journey Toward the North" (tr. by William Alexander). MedR (2:4) Sum 72, p. 84.
from Viaggio Verso il Nord: "Vaucluse" (tr. by William Alexander). MedR (2:4) Sum 72, p. 83.

2785 SANGE, Gary
"Long After the Accident." QRL (18:1/2) 72, p. 236.
"Not Missing." CarolQ (24:2) Spr 72, p. 27.
"Separation." QRL (18:1/2) 72, p. 234.
"Truckdriver." QRL (18:1/2) 72, p. 235.

2786 SANJULO
"If You Would Just Stop." JnlOBP (2:16) Sum 72, p. 13.

2787 SANSOM, Vivian
"In the Early Morning Sunlight." ChiR (23:4 & 24:1) 72, p. 101.

2788 SANTIBANEZ, Ariel
"I Discover Offices and Travelled Passageways" (tr. by Edward Oliphant). RoadAR (4:1) Spr 72, p. 56.

2789 SAPP, Dennis H.
"What." Etc. (29:3) S 72, Inside Front Cover.

2790 SARGENT, Elizabeth
"Jazzmen." Cosmo (173:1) Jl 72, p. 149.
"The Old Jockey." Cosmo (173:1) Jl 72, p. 149.
"Waiting." Cosmo (173:1) Jl 72, p. 149.

2791 SAROT, Ellin
"3 Too Young." LittleM (6:2/3) Sum-Aut 73, p. 83.

2792 SAROYAN, Aram
Poems. ParisR (53) Wint 72, p. 28.

2793 SARTON, May
"Prisoner at a Desk." Poetry (119:5) F 72, p. 269.

2794 SASLOW, Helen
"Caged." HangL (18) Fall 72, p. 41.
"How Can I Keep It from Ending?" HangL (18) Fall 72, p. 40.

2795 SASSO, Laurence J., Jr.
"Renting a Room." Confr (5) Wint-Spr 72, p. 71.

2796 SASSO, Louis
"The Man in the Blue Shirt." AriD (1:2) Wint 72, p. 35.
"Two Poems for Diane Wakoski." AriD (1:2) Wint 72, p. 34.

2797 SASSOONIAN, Manuchehr
Concrete poem. NewYQ (12) Aut 72, p. 56.

2798 SATHOFF, Craig E.
"Skeletons in the Classroom." EngJ (61:1) Ja 72, p. 58.

2799 SATO, Hiroaki
"Handmade Proverbs" (for Joan Miro) (tr. of Shuzo Takiguchi). Iron (2) Fall 72, p. 45.
"Shadow's Path" (tr. of Shuzo Takiguchi). Iron (2) Fall 72, p. 44.
Twenty-one Modern Japanese Poems (tr. by Hiroaki Sato). Granite (2) Wint 71-72, pp. 3-30.

2800 SAULAITIS, Marija
Eleven Poems. LitR (16:1) Aut 72, p. 140.

2801 SAUNDERS, Sally
"Set Off." Mark (16:2) Sum 72, p. 20.

2802 SAVAGE, Emmy
"For Sam." AriD (1:2) Wint 72, p. 30.
"Leaving Mountains." AriD (1:2) Wint 72, p. 30.
"La Noche Buena." AriD (1:2) Wint 72, p. 31.
"Roofs, Mexico 1971." CarolQ (24:1) Wint 72, p. 81.

2803 SAVINO, R.
"it." EverR (16:95) Fall 72, p. 125.

2804 SAVORY, Teo
"Bottle" (tr. of Guillevic). Stand (13:3) 72, p. 67.
"Noises" (tr. of Guillevic). Iron (1) Spr 72, p. 68.
"Portrait" (tr. of Guillevic). Stand (13:3) 72, p. 66.
"Winter Tree" (tr. of Guillevic). Iron (1) Spr 72, p. 69.

2805 SAWYER, Kathleen
"Because I am the tell-tale." Pan (9) 72, p. 62.

2806 SAX, Boria
"City Boy in the Country." HangL (17) Sum 72, p. 54.

2807 SAYRES, William
"Bertha Wiggems." Works (3:3/4) Wint 72-73, p. 128.
"Chancay, Peru." Cim (18) Ja 72, p. 11.
"Conversation." MedR (2:2) Wint 72, p. 63.
"The Cranial Courtship of W. Fits (the Cold Cream King)." Works (3:3/4) Wint 72-73, p. 129.
"Neighbor in Ward Six." WestR (10:1) Spr 73, p. 56.
"Omar Jones Says." Qt (5:38) Spr 72, p. 22.
"Randolph Ingraham (Author of This Side of Beyond)." KanQ (4:1) Wint 71-72, p. 12.

2808 SBARBARO, Camillo
"Along the Arid Street" (tr. by D. M. Pettinella). SenR (3:1) My 72, p. 25.

2809 SCARBROUGH, George
"April Reunion." SewanR (80:4) Aut 72, p. 625.

2810 SCHAAF, Richard
"Collision of Continents." AriD (1:3) Spr 72, p. 14.
"My Daddy's Tattoo." AriD (1:3) Spr 72, p. 14.

2811 SCHAEFFER, Susan Fromberg
"Ancestress, First Generation." Shen (23:2) Wint 72, p. 36.
"Counting Sheep." Humanist (32:4) Jl-Ag 72, p. 43.
"Delusion #16." HangL (18) Fall 72, p. 42.
"Elegy for Sylvia Plath." MedR (2:3) Spr 72, p. 80.
"Famine Days." AriD (1:3) Spr 72, p. 37.
"First Love." ChiTM 14 My 72, p. 9.

"Footstool Toad." GreenR (2:2) 72, p. 43.
"For Judy Garland." CarolQ (24:3) Fall 72, p. 84.
"The Hills." MedR (2:3) Spr 72, p. 85.
"Late Afternoon." AriD (1:3) Spr 72, p. 39.
"Love Story." Madrona (1:3) My 72, p. 30.
"Mad Child." CarlMis (12:1) Fall-Wint 71-72, p. 106.
"Medean." ChiR (23:4 & 24:1) 72, p. 94.
"Night with Stars." Iowa (3:2) Spr 72, p. 23.
"Now We Are Poor." GreenR (2:2) 72, p. 42.
"Poem: Godless, we lead." Hiero (7) Ap 72.
"Post Mortem." Salm (19) Spr 72, p. 67.
"Prospectus." ColEng (33:6) Mr 72, p. 712.
"Proverbs." Poetry (120:1) Ap 72, p. 6.
"Proverbs (I-V)." MedR (2:3) Spr 72, p. 82.
"Reading the Signs." ColEng (33:6) Mr 72, p. 716.
"Recovery." GreenR (2:2) 72, p. 41.
"Sale." Confr (5) Wint-Spr 72, p. 73.
"Saturday Noon in the Yard." GreenR (2:2) 72, p. 40.
"Seashore." ChiTM 22 O 72, p. 8.
"She Undergoes Testing." Granite (2) Wint 71-72, p. 78.
"She Writes a Letter Home." Iowa (3:2) Spr 72, p. 22.
"Sleep." Kayak (28) 72, p. 50.
"Sleeping In the Country." Epoch (21:3) Spr 72, p. 274.
"Song for You." SouthernHR (6:2) Spr 72, p. 156.
"Stained Glass Window." Shen (23:2) Wint 72, p. 35.
"A Suicide." AriD (1:3) Spr 72, p. 35.
"Suicide." Poetry (120:1) Ap 72, p. 11.
"A Suicide." SouthernHR (6:3) Sum 72, p. 242.
"Sun Song." Salm (19) Spr 72, p. 67.
"The Teachers." MedR (2:3) Spr 72, p. 85.
"Tides." AriD (1:3) Spr 72, p. 34.
"To Someone Who Was Never Unhappy, or Afraid." ColEng (33:6) Mr 72, p. 714.
"Valentine's Day: Some Sun, Some Storm." Hiero (7) Ap 72.
"The Wait." NoAmR (257:3) Aut 72, p. 38.
"The Watch." Works (3:2) Wint-Spr 72, p. 44.
"Winter Wood." Madem (76:2) D 72, p. 104.
"Wyoming." AriD (1:3) Spr 72, p. 38.

2812 SCHAURIEN, Judith
"She Dreams..." ChiR (23:3) Wint 72, p. 83.

2813 SCHAUT, Milton
"Fragment from the Horofitz Dream Book." Drag (3:2) Sum 72, p. 60.
"The New Sacrifice." Drag (3:2) Sum 72, p. 59.

2814 SCHECHTER, Avra
"High Holiday." New:ACP (19) Aut 72, p. 32.

2815 SCHECHTER, Ruth Lisa
"In the Beginning." NewYQ (9) Wint 72, p. 54.

2816 SCHEIBLI, Silvia
"a cactus is like a pet." UTR (1:3) 72, p. 23.
"Daily Reminders." UTR (1:3) 72, p. 26.
"First Call of the Cicada." UTR (1:3) 72, p. 24.
"the murder of mustang." UTR (1:3) 72, p. 22.
"My Feet Tangled in Yucca Fibers." UTR (1:3) 72, p. 25.
"Old Pelican." UTR (1:1) 72, p. 10.
"A Transformation." UTR (1:3) 72, p. 27.
"transplanting a cactus." UTR (1:4) 72, p. 15.
"Vision of Raphael Alberti." UTR (1:2) 72, p. 14.
"Yellow." UTR (1:2) 72, p. 13.

2817 SCHEIRMAN, Marian Thomson
"Inside Dope." SatEP (244:1) Spr 72, p. 102.

2818 SCHELL, Jessie
"In the Village Cemetery, Lincoln, Massachusetts." GeoR (26:3) Fall 72, p. 365.
"Letter from a Far City." GeoR (26:3) Fall 72, p. 367.
"Waking." GeoR (26:3) Fall 72, p. 366.

2819 SCHENKER, Donald
"Here I Am Again, Folks." HangL (17) Sum 72, p. 58.

2820 SCHEVILL, James
"The Dramatic Poet Argues With the Lyric Poet." Antaeus (6) Sum 72, p. 75.
"The Game-Master Explains the Rules of the Game for Bombs." PraS (46:1) Spr 72, p. 58.
"A Screamer Discusses Methods of Screaming." Antaeus (6) Sum 72, p. 76.

2821 SCHIFF, Linda
"Impaled." PoetL (67:3) Aut 72, p. 268.
"Last Visit." PoetL (67:3) Aut 72, p. 261.

2822 SCHIFFMAN, Paul
"At Morning Light." VilV 19 O 72, p. 36.
"The Day Comes In." VilV 23 N 72, p. 42.

2823 SCHIMMEL, Harold
"End of Summer Evening" (tr. of Yehuda Amichai). Humanist (32:1) Ja-F 72, p. 32.

2824 SCHLOSS, David
"Atlantis." HiramPoR (12) Spr-Sum 72, p. 25.
"The Clarity of Flight." PoetryNW (13:2) Sum 72, p. 33.
"Notes from the Interior." Poetry (120:3) Je 72, p. 140.
"Objects." HiramPoR (12) Spr-Sum 72, p. 24.
"The Passionate Friendship." PoetryNW (13:2) Sum 72, p. 33.
"A Suicide Pact." ChiR (23:3) Wint 72, p. 87.

2825 SCHMID, Vernon
"Dust Swirls." Wind (2:5) Sum 72, p. 41.

2826 SCHMIDT, Michael
"Cave Pool." Poetry (120:3) Je 72, p. 154.
"Scorpion." Poetry (119:5) F 72, p. 267.
"Thrush Stone." Poetry (120:3) Je 72, p. 156.
"Trap." Poetry (119:5) F 72, p. 266.
"The Winter Bird." Poetry (120:3) Je 72, p. 155.

2827 SCHMIDT, Tom V.
"Butcherboy." Sky (1:1) 71.
"The Common Cold." New:ACP (18) Ap 72, p. 10.
"The Dream." New:ACP (18) Ap 72, p. 9.
"From New Zealand." HangL (17) Sum 72, p. 62.
"Standing on the Old Fair Oaks Bridge over the American River." HangL (17) Sum 72, p. 60.

2828 SCHMITZ, Dennis
"Bathing in Dead Man Creek" (for George Keithley). Field (6) Spr 72, p. 15.
from The California Phrasebook. Iron (1) Spr 72, p. 30.
"Chicago: Star & Garter Theater." Field (6) Spr 72, p. 13.
"Chicago: Queen of Heaven Mausoleum." Field (6) Spr 72, p. 14.
"D. E. W. Line." Epoch (21:3) Spr 72, p. 283.

2829 SCHOEBERLEIN, Marion
"Ballet." NYT 13 Ja 72, p. 40.
"For the Last Time a Poet." Confr (5) Wint-Spr 72, p. 73.

2830 SCHOENER, Wilhelmina Laird
"Thesis to the Archives." KanQ (4:1) Wint 71-72, p. 95.

2831 SCHOLIS, Carmen
"I Go Dreaming Roads" (tr. of Antonio Machado, w. William Witherup). Madrona (1:3) My 72, p. 16.

2832 SCHOLTEN, Martin
"The Dove Descending." Epos (23:4) Sum 72, p. 26.

2833 SCHOPF, Federico
"The Spy Who Came Back from the Cold" (tr. by Edward Oliphant). RoadAR (4:1) Spr 72, p. 44.

2834 SCHOR, Sandra
"The Leopard" (for Phyllis Bolton). Confr (5) Wint-Spr 72, p. 49.

2835 SCHRAM, Irene
"Single-Stroke." Confr (5) Wint-Spr 72, p. 90.

2836 SCHRAMM, Richard
"Birthright." Iowa (3:2) Spr 72, p. 18.
"The Calamity." Poetry (120:2) My 72, p. 93.
"Departures." NewYorker (47:53) 19 F 72, p. 88.
"Dolmen." Antaeus (5) Spr 72, p. 51.
"Escape." Poetry (120:2) My 72, p. 89.
"The Inheritors." Poetry (120:2) My 72, p. 95.
"Messageries Maritimes." Poetry (120:2) My 72, p. 94.
"Penitence." Poetry (120:2) My 72, p. 92.
"Stray." WestHR (26:1) Wint 72, p. 34.
"Tremor." WestHR (26:1) Wint 72, p. 31.

2837 SCHREIBER, Jan
"Digression before a Painter." SouthernR (8:1) Wint 72, p. 166.
"From Baudelaire." SouthernR (8:1) Wint 72, p. 167.
"Now Winter Nights Enlarge." SouthernR (8:1) Wint 72, p. 168.

2838 SCHREIBER, Ron
"Brave New World." Perspec (17:1) Sum 72, p. 63.
"Gathering Blueberries." MinnR (2) Spr 72, p. 97.
"Odds: 17%." Perspec (17:1) Sum 72, p. 63.
"Tracking Me Down." MinnR (2) Spr 72, p. 98.
"western land, 1971." SouthernPR (12:2) Spr 72, p. 54.

2839 SCHRÖER, Rolf-Rafael
"Was Dann." Field (7) Fall 72, p. 74.

2840 SCHULMAN, Grace
"In the Country of Urgency, There Is a Language (to Marianne Moore)." Nat (214:12) 20 Mr 72, p. 374.
"To Julia de Burgos" (tr. of Julia de Burgos). Nat (215:10) 9 O 72, p. 314.

2841 SCHULTZ, Philip
"Lines to a Jewish Cossack" (for Isaac Babel). CarolQ (24:1) Wint 72, p. 74.
"Song for a Sheerbeaver." CarolQ (24:1) Wint 72, p. 75.
"What I Don't Want to Do." NewYQ (12) Aut 72, p. 82.

2842 SCHUYLER, James
"Blue." NewYorker (48:26) 19 Ag 72, p. 32.
"The Crystal Lithium" (for R. J.). ParisR (53) Wint 72, p. 103.
"Deep Winter." Poetry (121:3) D 72, p. 150.
"The Dog Wants His Dinner" (for Clark Coolidge). ParisR (53) Wint 72, p. 99.
"In earliest morning." ParisR (53) Wint 72, p. 95.
"In Wiry Winter." Poetry (121:3) D 72, p. 152.
"May, 1972." Poetry (120:6) S 72, p. 327.
"A Penis Moon." ParisR (53) Wint 72, p. 98.
"Poem: This beauty that I see." Poetry (121:3) D 72,

p. 150.
"Running Footsteps." ParisR (53) Wint 72, p. 101.
"So Good." Poetry (121:3) D 72, p. 153.
"A Stone Knife." ParisR (53) Wint 72, p. 93.
"The Trash Book" (for Joe Brainard). ParisR (53) Wint 72, p. 97.

2843 SCHWARTZ, Delmore
"A Poet's Notebooks" (Selections arr. by Lila Lee Valenti). NewYQ (10) Spr 72, p. 111.
"Syracuse Campus." Hiero (7) Ap 72.

2844 SCHWARTZ, Howard
"A Bamboo Flute" (for Richard Wortman). Folio (8:2) Fall 72, p. 37.

2845 SCOTT, Herbert
"The Madman." Iowa (3:3) Sum 72, p. 18.

2846 SCOTT, Louise
"Heron Bird." Wind (2:6) Aut 72, p. 27.

2847 SCOTT, Merial
"EKG." SoDakR (10:3) Aut 72, p. 74.

2848 SCOTT, Vera Austen
"About the Land." PoetL (67:3) Aut 72, p. 244.

2848A SCOTTY
"and i look at roger." WindO (9) Spr 72, p. 11.
"mr. jones wakes up." WindO (9) Spr 72, p. 11.
"your eyes like a doughnut." WindO (9) Spr 72, p. 12.

2849 SCRIABINE, Raisa
"I Am at the Bottom" (tr. of Innokenty Annensky, w. Harvey Feinberg). RusLT (4) Aut 72, p. 49.
"It Happened at Vallen Koski" (tr. of Innokenty Annensky, w. Harvey Feinberg). RusLT (4) Aut 72, p. 48.
"Waiting at the Station" (tr. of Innokenty Annensky, w. Harvey Feinberg). RusLT (4) Aut 72, p. 47.

2850 SCULLY, James
"Avenue of the Americas." MassR (13:3) Sum 72, p. 401.
"'Splendid-Throned, Deathless Aphrodite.'" MassR (13:3) Sum 72, p. 406.
"Walking with Dierdre." MassR (13:3) Sum 72, p. 405.

2851 SCURIS, T. K.
"Debt." (tr. of Titos Patrikious). AriD (1:4/5) Sum-Aut 72, p. 88.
"Forewarning" (tr. of Titos Patrikious). AriD (1:4/5) Sum-Aut 72, p. 88.
from Scale of the Stone: (25) (tr. of Ektor Kaknavatos). AriD (1:4/5) Sum-Aut 72, p. 54.

2852 SEARS, Donald A.
"Marina di Carrara." SouthernPR (12:2) Spr 72, p. 14.

2853 SEARS, Peter
"Bargain." HangL (18) Fall 72, p. 44.
"Before the Stray Dogs Start Following." 5 F 72, p. 28.
"Bike Run." NYT 20 Ja 72, p. 42.
"Findings." Cord (1:4) 72, p. 6.
"Icehouse Beach." Field (7) Fall 72, p. 9.
"Postcard." Madem (75:1) My 72, p. 148.
"Skylight of the Well Lit Brain." Cord (1:4) 72, p. 6.
"Switch." HangL (18) Fall 72, p. 45.
"Turning to Women." Field (7) Fall 72, p. 7.
"Without Me/Frost Stuns Precision Grinding/Sweeps to City Softball Title." HangL (18) Fall 72, p. 43.

2854 SEATON, Jerome P.
"Autumn" (tr. of Kuan Han-ch'ing). Madem (75:6) O 72, p. 136.

2855 SEBENTHALL, R. E.
"The Atavists." St. AR (1:4) Spr-Sum 72, p. 70.
"Main Street." Perspec (17:1) Sum 72, p. 29.
"Nativities." Perspec (17:1) Sum 72, p. 30.
"The Prophets." Perspec (17:1) Sum 72, p. 28.

2856 SECRIST, Margaret
"Goldenrod." PoetL (67:2) Sum 72, p. 152.
"Nothing Is Ever Lost." PoetL (67:1) Spr 72, p. 57.
"Picture Window." PoetL (67:1) Spr 72, p. 57.

2857 SEDRIKS, Andre
"Farewell." NewYQ (10) Spr 72, p. 72.
"The Last Hangover." NewYQ (9) Wint 72, p. 61.

2858 SEELYE, John
"Garbage." NewRep (166:19) 6 My 72, p. 30.

2859 SEESE, Ethel Gray
"Dimensions." Wind (2:5) Sum 72, p. 43.

2860 SEFERIS, George
"Across Gorse" (tr. by Walter Kaiser). AriD (1:2) Wint 72, p. 2.
"Against Woodwaxen" (tr. by John Chioles). Atl (229:5) My 72, p. 58.
"Sur Les Aspalathes." AriD (1:2) Wint 72, p. 4.

2861 SEGOVIA, Thomas
from Cancionero de Abajo: "5: Song of the Rain" (tr. by Nathaniel Tarn). QRL (18:1/2) 72, p. 238.
from Cancionero del Claro Palacio: "1: The Radiant Palace" (tr. by Nathaniel Tarn). QRL (18:1/2) 72, p. 238.

from Canciones sin Su Musica: (1, 2, 11) (tr. by Nathaniel Tarn). QRL (18:1/2) 72, p. 239.
from Interludio Idilico: "Coda" (tr. by Nathaniel Tarn). QRL (18:1/2) 72, p. 237.

2862 SEIDEL, Frederick
"What One Must Contend With." NewYRB (19:8) 16 N 72, p. 38.

2863 SEIDMAN, Hugh
"At Edge" (for Clayton). UnmOx (1:1) N 71, p. 59.
"Auto Eighty Six." NewYQ (9) Wint 72, p. 48.
"Beginnings." Poetry (120:4) Jl 72, p. 204.
"Bonamo." NewYQ (9) Wint 72, p. 47.
"Greene Street" (for D. A.). UnmOx (1:1) N 71, p. 60.
"It's Sunday." UnmOx (1:2) F 72, p. 37.
"Untowards." NewYQ (9) Wint 72, p. 46.

2864 SEIFERT, Edward
"Nightly News." ChrC (89:39) 1 N 72, p. 1098.

2865 SEILER, Barry
"Casting Bread." NowestR (12:3) Aut 72, p. 14.
"The Day II." NowestR (12:3) Aut 72, p. 15.
"An Essay on Strangers." Peb (9) Wint 72.
"Keep Talking." Peb (9) Wint 72.

2866 SEITZ, Ron
"Age." Wind (2:6) Aut 72, p. 27.
"8:30 PM." Wind (2:5) Sum 72, p. 20.

2867 SELLERY, J'Nan
"Corrida de Toros." ColEng (33:7) Ap 72, p. 803.
"Glued Fast." ColEng (33:7) Ap 72, p. 804.

2868 SEMONES, Charles
"Outer Dark, Inner Dark." Wind (2:5) Sum 72, p. 29.

2869 SEPAMLA, Sydney
"To Whom It May Concern." Playb (19:5) My 72, p. 169.

2870 SEPEHRI, Sohrab
"The Sound of Water's Footsteps" (tr. by Massud Farzan). Mund (5:1/2) 72, p. 13.

2871 SERENI, Vittorio
"Corso Lodi" (tr. by I. L. Salomon). MichQR (11:4) Aut 72, p. 273.
from Poesie: "Winter in Luino" (tr. by Dora M. Pettinella). MedR (2:4) Sum 72, p. 82.
"Portrait on a Tombstone" (tr. by I. L. Salomon). MichQR (11:4) Aut 72, p. 272.
from Gli Strumenti Umani: "Saba" (tr. by Brian Swann

and Ruth Feldman). MedR (2:4) Sum 72, p. 81.
from Gli Strumenti Umani: "Six in the Morning" (tr. by Sonia Raiziss). MedR (2:4) Sum 72, p. 81.

2872 SEROTE, Mongane Wally
"The Clothes." Playb (19:5) My 72, p. 169.

2873 SESSIONS, David
"Coast." Sky (1:1) 71.
"The Dismembered Man." Peb (9) Wint 72.
"Joy." Sky (1:1) 71.

2874 SETIAN
"Santa Maria Sopra Minerva." Folio (8:1) Spr 72, p. 34.

2875 SEUBERT, Millie
"The Kitchen Is Waiting." Cim (19) Ap 72, p. 54.

2876 SEVERY, Bruce
"Baudelaire." Cafe (4) Fall 72, p. 11.

2877 SEXTON, Anne
"Angel of Beachhouses and Picnics." AmerR (15) 72, p. 73.
"Angel of Blizzards and Blackouts." AmerR (15) 72, p. 74.
"Angel of Clean Sheets." NewRep (166:7) 12 F 72, p. 26.
"Angel of Fire and Genitals." NewRep (166:7) 12 F 72, p. 26.
"Angel of Little Neck Clams." NewRep (166:7) 12 F 72, p. 26.
"Baby Picture." Kayak (30) D 72, p. 15.
"Clothes." Kayak (30) D 72, p. 16.
"Going Gone." ModernO (2:2) Spr 72, p. 228.
"Grandfather, Your Wound." NewYorker (48:32) 30 S 72, p. 40.
"The Hoarder." NewRep (166:9) 26 F 72, p. 23.
"Jesus Unborn." ModernO (2:2) Spr 72, p. 230.
"The One-Legged Man." NewYorker (48:30) 16 S 72, p. 34.
"Praying On a 707." Atl (230:6) D 72, p. 115.
"Santa." Madem (76:1) N 72, p. 120.

2878 SEXTON, Tom
"Buffalo Hunter." KanQ (4:3) Sum 72, p. 41.
"Driving Through Astoria." KanQ (4:3) Sum 72, p. 41.
Thirteen Poems. UnicornJ (4) 72, p. 59.

2879 SHABAD, Theodore
"Be a Good Beaver" (tr. of Andrei Voznesensky). NYT 31 D 72, sec. 4, p. 9.

2880 SHACKELFORD, Rudy
"An Autograph Manuscript of Von Dittersdorf." PraS (46:3) Aut 72, p. 205.
"Entreaties." NewRep (166:5) 29 Ja 72, p. 25.
"The Hawk." NYT 8 Ap 72, p. 28.
"Nocturne." PraS (46:3) Aut 72, p. 204.
"The Red Metronome (after Matisse)." NYT 30 My 72, p. 36.

2881 SHACKLEFORD, Ruby P.
"Autumn." ArizQ (28:3) Aut 72, p. 242.

2882 SHAIN, Rick
"Glimmer." ChiTM 23 Ja 72, p. 14.

2883 SHAMBAUGH, Joan
"How Great It Was..." Folio (8:2) Fall 72, p. 30.

2884 SHANGO, Chaka (Horace Coleman)
"Black Gifts for a Black Child." Broad (56) F 72.

2885 SHAPCOTT, Thomas W.
"The Gift." NYT 17 Ja 72, p. 30.
"In the Park." NYT 14 Ag 72, p. 26.
"Lesbians." NewYQ (11) Sum 72, p. 65.
"A Reconciliation with Johannes Brahms." NewYQ (11) Sum 72, p. 64.
"Waking." NYT 23 Ap 72, sec. 4, p. 14.

2886 SHAPER, James P.
"Night Before the Last Day." PoetL (67:3) Aut 72, p. 261.
"Watergate." PoetL (67:2) Sum 72, p. 168.

2887 SHAPIRO, David
"About This Course." Poetry (121:2) N 72, p. 101.
"Cosmografia e Geografia." Pan (9) 72, p. 3.
"18 Ode." Pan (9) 72, p. 5.
"John Chagy at the Piano." UnmOx (1:1) N 71, p. 20.
"Master of Seedboxes." UnmOx (1:1) N 71, p. 19.
"Ode." ParisR (53) Wint 72, p. 75.
"Ode to Timaeus." Pan (9) 72, p. 2.
"The Old Bride." Pan (9) 72, p. 4.
"The Page-Turner." NewYorker (48:43) 16 D 72, p. 36.
"Taking a Look." UnmOx (1:1) N 71, p. 18.
"Zappas at the Zappeion." Pan (9) 72, p. 6.

2888 SHAPIRO, Harvey
"City Portrait." Hudson (25:4) Wint 72-73, p. 615.
"A Day." Atl (229:5) My 72, p. 62.
"Easy." Hudson (25:4) Wint 72-73, p. 615.
"Every Day." Hudson (25:4) Wint 72-73, p. 615.
"For the Sparrows on New Year's Morning." Hudson

(25:4) Wint 72-73, p. 614.
"In the Room." Hudson (25:4) Wint 72-73, p. 613.
"'Jesus, Mary I Love You Save Souls'." Hudson (25:4) Wint 72-73, p. 614.
"Like a Beach." Nat (215:8) 25 S 72, p. 247.

2889 SHAPIRO, Karl
"Flying First Class." NewRep (167:5) 5-12 Ag 72, p. 30.
"Girls Working in Banks." Esq (77:6) Je 72, p. 198.

2890 SHARPE, Philip
"The Shepherd Eyes Death." Stand (14:1) 72, p. 60.
"The Shepherd on Work." Stand (14:1) 72, p. 59.

2891 SHATRAW, Harriet
"Death." Wind (2:6) Aut 72, p. 25.

2892 SHAW, Robert B.
"Another Day." Poetry (119:6) Mr 72, p. 339.
"Grass Widows." Poetry (119:6) Mr 72, p. 340.
"Tagalong." Poetry (119:6) Mr 72, p. 340.

2893 SHAWN, Susan
"i have seen the open eyes of the enemy." NewYQ (10) Spr 72, p. 56.

2894 SHCHIPACHEV, Stepan
"Fifteen poems by Stepan Shchipachev" (tr. by Eugene M. Kayden). ColQ (21:1) Sum 72, p. 138.

2895 SHEARS
"To pray I kiss the limpid fingers." UTR (1:2) 72, p. 22.

2896 SHEARS, Dirk
"Prayer-song." KanQ (4:1) Wint 71-72, p. 42.

2897 SHELTON, Richard
"Choose One from Among Them." NewYorker (48:23) 29 Jl 72, p. 26.
"Coda." Iron (1) Spr 72, p. 34.
"Fathers and Sons." Iron (1) Spr 72, p. 32.
"The Fourteenth Anniversary." Poetry (121:2) N 72, p. 90.
"The Great Gulf." NewYorker (48:19) 1 Jl 72, p. 30.
"The Gypsies." ChiTM 20 F 72, p. 10.
"The Heroes of Our Time." Peb (7) Aut 71.
"My Love." SenR (3:1) My 72, p. 1.
"Poem Completed by St. John Perse." SenR (3:1) My 72, p. 2.
"San Juan's Day." NewYorker (48:17) 24 Je 72, p. 91.
"The Seven Ages of Man." Field (6) Spr 72, p. 20.
"Seven Preludes to Silence." NewYorker (48:2) 4 Mr 72,

p. 36.
"What We Love." Iron (1) Spr 72, p. 33.

2898 SHEPHERD, J. Barrie
"Ash Wednesday." NewRep (166:8) 19 F 72, p. 25.
"Highway Safety Trends." ChrC (89:14) 5 Ap 72, p. 393.
"Lent Inc." ChrC (89:7) 16 F 72, p. 186.
"The Shepherd's Question." ChrC (89:46) 20 D 72, p. 1293.

2899 SHEPPS, Judy
"Atomic Limbo." Zahir (1:4/5) 72, p. 62.
"Calculations." Zahir (1:4/5) 72, p. 74.
"Fantasizing Concrete." Zahir (1:4/5) 72, p. 62.
"Galilee Sunset." Zahir (1:4/5) 72, p. 62.
"Ladies Home Journal." Zahir (1:4/5) 72, p. 63.
"Nightwings." Wind (2:5) Sum 72, p. 20.

2900 SHERRARD, Philip
"Antony's Ending" (tr. of C. P. Cavafy, w. Edmund Keeley). Antaeus (6) Sum 72, p. 39.
"Body, Remember..." (tr. of C. P. Cavafy, w. Edmund Keeley). Nat (215:15) 13 N 72, p. 469.
"Dareios" (tr. of C. P. Cavafy, w. Edmund Keeley). Antaeus (6) Sum 72, p. 42.
"The Distress of Selefkidis" (tr. of C. P. Cavafy, w. Edmund Keeley). Antaeus (6) Sum 72, p. 40.
"An Exiled Byzantine Nobleman Who Composes Verses" (tr. of C. P. Cavafy, w. Edmund Keeley). Antaeus (6) Sum 72, p. 44.
"Exiles" (tr. of C. P. Cavafy, w. Edmund Keeley). NewYorker (48:17) 17 Je 72, p. 31.
"The Footsteps" (tr. of C. P. Cavafy, w. Edmund Keeley). Poetry (120:5) Ag 72, p. 266.
"For Ammonis, Who Died at 29, in 610" (tr. of C. P. Cavafy, w. Edmund Keeley). QRL (18:1/2) 72, p. 42.
"From the School of the Renowned Philosopher" (tr. of C. P. Cavafy, w. Edmund Keeley). NewYorker (48:17) 17 Je 72, p. 31.
"Half an Hour" (tr. of C. P. Cavafy, w. Edmund Keeley). NewYorker (48:17) 17 Je 72, p. 31.
"The Ides of March" (tr. of C. P. Cavafy, w. Edmund Keeley). Poetry (120:5) Ag 72, p. 266.
"In a Large Greek Colony, 200 B.C." (tr. of C. P. Cavafy, w. Edmund Keeley). NewYRB (18:11) 15 Je 72, p. 13.
"Ionic" (tr. of C. P. Cavafy, w. Edmund Keeley). Antaeus (6) Sum 72, p. 47.
"Ithaka" (tr. of C. P. Cavafy, w. Edmund Keeley). QRL (18:1/2) 72, p. 40.
"Julian and the Antiochians" (tr. of C. P. Cavafy, w. Edmund Keeley). NewL (38:3) Spr 72, p. 76.
"Myris: Alexandria, A.D. 340" (tr. of C. P. Cavafy, w.

Edmund Keeley). Antaeus (6) Sum 72, p. 45.
"Nero's Respite" (tr. of C. P. Cavafy, w. Edmund Keeley). QRL (18:1/2) 72, p. 42.
"On the Outskirts of Antioch" (tr. of C. P. Cavafy, w. Edmund Keeley). NewL (38:3) Spr 72, p. 77.
"One of Their Gods" (tr. of C. P. Cavafy, w. Edmund Keeley). QRL (18:1/2) 72, p. 41.
"Philhellene" (tr. of C. P. Cavafy, w. Edmund Keeley). Antaeus (6) Sum 72, p. 41.
"A Prince from Western Libya" (tr. of C. P. Cavafy, w. Edmund Keeley). NewYRB (18:11) 15 Je 72, p. 13.
"The Satrapy" (tr. of C. P. Cavafy, w. Edmund Keeley). Nat (215:15) 13 N 72, p. 469.
"Theodotos" (tr. of C. P. Cavafy, w. Edmund Keeley). Poetry (120:5) Ag 72, p. 267.
"Thermopylae" (tr. of C. P. Cavafy, w. Edmund Keeley). QRL (18:1/2) 72, p. 39.
"To Have Taken the Trouble" (tr. of C. P. Cavafy, w. Edmund Keeley). NewYorker (48:17) 17 Je 72, p. 31.
"Very Seldom" (tr. of C. P. Cavafy, w. Edmund Keeley). QRL (18:1/2) 72, p. 43.
"Waiting for the Barbarians" (tr. of C. P. Cavafy, w. Edmund Keeley). QRL (18:1/2) 72, p. 38.

2901 SHERWIN, Judith Johnson
"Arrangement for Voices." ColumF (1:3) Sum 72, p. 35.
"A Denial." SewanR (80:2) Spr 72, p. 287.
"Garden." Shen (23:3) Spr 72, p. 81.
"No Place I've Been." SouthwR (57:4) Aut 72, p. 300.
"Say Friend." AmerS (41:2) Spr 72, p. 283.
"Sorry, Sweetheart, Here's." BelPoJ (22:3) Spr 72, p. 1.

2902 SHIFFERT, Edith
"Storks." MidwQ (13:4) Sum 72, p. 350.

2903 SHIHAB, Naomi
"An Unobscure Wise Poem for William Blake." ModernPS (3:2) 72, p. 77.
"We Have Traveled, We Have Been To Other Countries." ModernPS (3:2) 72, p. 77.

2904 SHINDLER, Beverly
"Watch It: They're Watching You." VilV 24 F 72, p. 81.

2905 SHOEMAKER, Jack
from Exocycloida. Meas (1) 71.
"The Voyage." Meas (2) 72.

2906 SHOEMAKER, Lynn
"Black Elk Speaks." SoDakR (10:3) Aut 72, p. 70.
"Coming Home." Field (7) Fall 72, p. 22.
"Familiar." Epoch (21:3) Spr 72, p. 244.
"The Feeding." WormR (48) 72, p. 140.

"The Hanging Tree." SoDakR (10:3) Aut 72, p. 70.
"Icicles at the Top of a Cliff." Epoch (22:1) Fall 72, p. 86.
"The Left Side of the Mural." WormR (48) 72, p. 141.
"The road thins at its edges." BeyB (2:2) 72, p. 58.
"Sending Your Tongue to Another Country." BeyB (2:2) 72, p. 59.
"Sizes." WormR (48) 72, p. 141.
"Transplanting a True Clown's Nose." BeyB (2:2) 72, p. 59.

2907 SHOOK, Margaret
"Complaint" (for Ken Kesey, Philip Roth, Leslie Fiedler, and all the boys at the old Bar X). MassR (13:1/2) Wint-Spr 72, p. 219.

2908 SHORE, Jane
"Doors." Iowa (3:3) Sum 72, p. 16.
"Epigram of the Smothering Lover." AntR (31:4) Wint 71-72, p. 518.
"Noon." Iowa (3:3) Sum 72, p. 16.
"Poem: When you drop like an angel from the half-light." Iowa (3:3) Sum 72, p. 14.
"What the Trees Said." Iowa (3:3) Sum 72, p. 14.

2909 SHOSTAK, Robert
"The Campus Sages." EngJ (61:2) F 72, p. 260.

2910 SHRIVER, Peggy
"Airplane Landing" (a poem for children). SouthernPR (12: Special Issue) 72, p. 55.

2911 SHUNTARO, Tanikawa
"Night Jazz" (tr. by Harold P. Wright). NewYQ (9) Wint 72, p. 59.

2912 SHUTTLEWORTH, Paul
"Strawberry Oil." ChiTM 3 D 72, p. 30.

2913 SIEGEL, Marcella
"Dark Interruption." PoetL (67:2) Sum 72, p. 143.
"Prayer in a Space Age." PoetL (67:2) Sum 72, p. 137.
"The Spider." PoetL (67:2) Sum 72, p. 144.

2914 SIEGEL, Robert
"Apocalypse." BosUJ (20:1/2) 72, p. 66.
"Approaching Dover." Granite (2) Wint 71-72, p. 65.
"Ego." Poetry (119:6) Mr 72, p. 320.
"Fall." Granite (2) Wint 71-72, p. 64.
"For the Wind." ColQ (20:3) Wint 72, p. 374.
"Great Murderers." Humanist (32:6) N-D 72, p. 34.
"Mulberry Tree." Granite (2) Wint 71-72, p. 63.
"Shoveling Snow Off the Roof." Granite (2) Wint 71-72,

p. 66.
"A Visit to the Farm." Poetry (119:6) Mr 72, p. 319.

2915 SIEGEL, Rochelle Ann
"The Murderers." SenR (3:1) My 72, p. 35.

2916 SIKAKANE, Joyce Nomafa
"An Agony." Playb (19:5) My 72, p. 168.

2917 SIKELIANUS, Angelos
"Free Dodecanese" (tr. by Rae Dalven). Poetry (120:5) Ag 72, p. 261.
"Supper" (tr. by Rae Dalven). Poetry (120:5) Ag 72, p. 263.

2918 SILBERMAN, Alex
"The Man Who Wants." Epoch (21:2) Wint 71, p. 157.

2919 SILKIN, Jon
"Air That Pricks Earth with Life and Turns." Poetry (119:5) F 72, p. 249.
"Poem: As each of you sits, neither facing." Poetry (120:6) S 72, p. 349.

2920 SILLITOE, Alan
"Alchemist." NewYorker (48:3) 11 Mr 72, p. 42.

2921 SILVERMAN, Stuart
"Blake Saw God." Confr (5) Wint-Spr 72, p. 21.
from Etudes: "If winter flings down snow unstintingly" (tr. of Loukas Kousoulas, w. John Fludas). AriD (1: 4/5) Sum-Aut 72, p. 78.
"For Anna Akhmatova." Confr (5) Wint-Spr 72, p. 20.
"Horses Riding Astride the People" (tr. of George Gavalas, w. John Fludas). AriD (1:4/5) Sum-Aut 72, p. 43.
"It's One Thing to Move." AriD (1:2) Wint 72, p. 10.
"On the Edge of a Bridge" (tr. of Nikos Vranas, w. John Fludas). AriD (1:4/5) Sum-Aut 72, p. 116.
"Portrait of a Dean." AriD (1:2) Wint 72, p. 13.
"Roethke's Muse." Confr (5) Wint-Spr 72, p. 20.
"Seven Brief Poems and an Epilogue." AriD (1:2) Wint 72, p. 11.
"This Day." Focus (8:56) 72, p. 37.

2922 SILVERSTEIN, Zona
"On the Way Home." Shen (23:3) Spr 72, p. 83.
"To a Man Who Said He Wanted to Know." Shen (23:3) Spr 72, p. 83.

2923 SILVERTON, Michael
"Poems." Harp (245:1471) D 72, p. 68.

2924 SIMIC, Charles
"Breasts." Field (6) Spr 72, p. 29.
"Charles Simic." Epoch (21:3) Spr 72, p. 236.
"Elegy for Isaac Newton." Iron (1) Spr 72, p. 8.
from Holy Mass for Relja Krilatica: Eight Poems (tr. of Milorad Pavic). MinnR (2) Spr 72, p. 52.
"Home." NewYorker (48:12) 13 My 72, p. 44.
"The Last." Kayak (28) 72, p. 63.
"Nothing." Epoch (21:3) Spr 72, p. 237.
"Poem: About this time, each day." Epoch (21:3) Spr 72, p. 237.
"Poems from White." Iron (1) Spr 72, p. 10.
"The Riddle." Cafe (4) Fall 72, p. 35.
"Solitude." Nat (215:10) 9 O 72, p. 315.
"Soul-catching" (for George Quasha). Antaeus (5) Spr 72, p. 96.
"The Soup." Antaeus (5) Spr 72, p. 95.
"That Straightlaced Christian Thing Between Her Legs." OhioR (13:3) Spr 72, p. 30.

2925 SIMMONS, Judy D.
"Generations." PoetL (67:1) Spr 72, p. 70.

2926 SIMMS, Preston
"Have You." SouthernPR (12: Special Issue) 72, p. 56.

2927 SIMON, Greg
"Center." NewYorker (48:9) 22 Ap 72, p. 122.

2928 SIMON, Jane
"Niños." WindO (10) Sum 72, p. 48.

2929 SIMON, John Oliver
"come from the deepnightroad." HangL (18) Fall 72, p. 47.
"How There Come To Be So Many Joshua Trees at Lee Flat." HangL (18) Fall 72, p. 46.
Two Poems. New:ACP (18) Ap 72, p. 8.

2930 SIMPSON, Grace P.
"After the Hurricanes." ChrC (89:35) 4 O 72, p. 978.

2931 SIMPSON, Louis
"Before Poetry Reading." ColumF (1:4) Fall 72, p. 16.
"Big Dream, Little Dream." ColumF (1:2) Spr 72, p. 43.

2932 SINCLAIR, Bennie Lee
"The Arrowhead Scholar." SoCaR (4:2) Je 72, p. 5.
"Peritonitis and Sweet Dreams." SoCaR (5:1) D 72, p. 24.

2933 SINGH, G.
from Diaro del '71: "Letter to Bobi" (tr. of Eugenio

Montale). MedR (2:4) Sum 72, p. 80.
from Satura: "First January" (tr. of Eugenio Montale). MedR (2:4) Sum 72, p. 79.
from Satura: "Hiding Places" (tr. of Eugenio Montale). MedR (2:4) Sum 72, p. 80.
from Satura: "Late in the Night" (tr. of Eugenio Montale). MedR (2:4) Sum 72, p. 78.
from Two Venetian Pieces: (2) (tr. of Eugenio Montale). MedR (2:4) Sum 72, p. 78.

2934 SINOPOULOS, Takis
"Supper for the Dead" (tr. by Stratis Haviaras). AriD (1:4/5) Sum-Aut 72, p. 95.

2935 SISSMAN, L. E.
"Memento Mory's." Harp (245:1471) D 72, p. 67.

2936 SISSON, Jonathan
"Hearts Played by Three and These Are Their Hands." LittleM (6:2/3) Sum-Aut 72, p. 97.

2937 SJOBERG, Leif
"In the silent river of evening" (tr. of Par Lagerkvist, w. W. H. Auden). Shen (23:4) Sum 72, p. 76.
"The Insects" (tr. of Harry Martinson, w. W. H. Auden). MichQR (11:4) Aut 72, p. 284.
from "Li Kan Speaks Beneath the Tree" (tr. of Harry Martinson, w. W. H. Auden). DenQuart (7:3) Aut 72, p. 14.
"Poem: Everywhere, in all the heavens you will find his footprints" (tr. of Par Lagerkvist, w. W. H. Auden). WestHR (26:4) 72, p. 350.
"The Rain" (tr. of Erik Lindegren, w. W. H. Auden). MichQR (11:4) Aut 72, p. 282.
"The Suit K" (tr. of Erik Lindegren, w. W. H. Auden). MichQR (11:4) Aut 72, p. 283.

2938 SJOSTRAND, Osten
"Each Particle Has the Whole Universe for Its Field of Activity" (tr. by Robin Fulton). DenQuart (7:3) Aut 72, p. 19.
"In the Beginning" (tr. by Robin Fulton). DenQuart (7:3) Aut 72, p. 20.
"Thoughts Before a Papal Galley" (tr. by Robin Fulton). DenQuart (7:3) Aut 72, p. 17.

2939 SKEETER, Sharyn-Jeanne
"laughing past my own pain." Works (3:3/4) Wint 72-73, p. 8.
"Mother Goose was." Works (3:3/4) Wint 72-73, p. 8.

2940 SKILES, D. K.
"A Heron at Dawn." NewYQ (12) Aut 72, p. 63.

2941 SKINNER, Knute
"Last Line for a Limerick Contest." SatireN (9:2) Spr 72, p. 172.

2942 SKLAR, Morty
"Rape." NewYQ (11) Sum 72, p. 86.

2943 SKLAREW, Myra
"Birth." NYT 24 My 72, p. 46.
"Cabala." CarolQ (24:1) Wint 72, p. 108.
"Companion." AriD (1:2) Wint 72, p. 17.
"Hydrangea." CarolQ (24:1) Wint 72, p. 109.
"My Daughter's Dream." AriD (1:2) Wint 72, p. 16.
"Yes and his Heart was Going Like Mad and Yes I said Yes I Will Yes." NYT 27 Ap 72, p. 42.

2944 SKLOOT, Floyd
"Blackberry Brandy." ConcPo (5:1) Spr 72, p. 74.

2945 SKRAINKA, Robert L.
"A Break." Focus (9:57) 72, p. 29.
"Romance, Winter Exposure." Comm (96:2) 17 Mr 72, p. 39.

2946 SKRATZ, G. P.
"Tortoise Poem." WindO (11) Aut 72, p. 45.

2947 SLADE, Leon
"Indian Summer." CarlMis (12:1) Fall-Wint 71-72, p. 89.

2948 SLATER, Cathy
"Loss Poem." Isthmus (1) Spr 72, p. 73.

2949 SLATER, Robert
"Morning Raga." NewL (38:4) Sum 72, p. 65.
"Rag/Time." NewL (38:4) Sum 72, p. 64.

2950 SLAVIN, Stephen L.
"No Place." PoetL (67:3) Aut 72, p. 252.

2951 SLAVITT, David R.
"Georgica: Book I." GeoR (26:1) Spr 72, p. 5.

2952 SLUTERBECK, Kay
"The Endless Purr." WindO (12) Wint 72-73, p. 28.
"A God Poem." WindO (10) Sum 72, p. 54.
"Lunch Time." WindO (10) Sum 72, p. 54.
"Message Found by a Phone." WindO (10) Sum 72, p. 54.
"My Father." WindO (9) Spr 72, p. 28.
"Old Fish." WindO (11) Aut 72, p. 44.
"The only time I ever." WindO (10) Sum 72, p. 54.
"Some Thoughts on Mirrors." WindO (11) Aut 72, p. 44.
"Starlings in Autumn." WindO (12) Wint 72-73, p. 28.

2953 SMITH, A. J. M.
"Lines Written on the Occasion of President Nixon's Address to the Nation, May 8, 1972." Poetry (120:6) S 72, p. 335.

2954 SMITH, Anita Speer
"Now That I've Convinced You." ChrC (89:4) 26 Ja 72, p. 86.

2955 SMITH, Arthur E.
"The Calf." Epoch (21:3) Spr 72, p. 289.
"The Lake Valley Indian Camp." Epoch (21:3) Spr 72, p. 289.
"The Patio Is Screened." Epoch (21:3) Spr 72, p. 288.
"Today Is Spring, Today Is." SoDakR (10:1) Spr 72, p. 4.

2956 SMITH, Barbara
"Juvenile Fiction." WestR (10:1) Spr 73, p. 55.

2957 SMITH, Carole Anne
"The Strip." SouthernPR (12: Special Issue) 72, p. 40.

2958 SMITH, Craig
"creed." St. AR (1:4) Spr-Sum 72, p. 34.
"Monday Morning 10 A. M." Qt (5:37) Wint 72, p. 11.
"There Are These Winters." Qt (5:37) Wint 72, p. 11.

2959 SMITH, D. V.
"Nike." St. AR (1:4) Spr-Sum 72, p. 59.
"Stopping Over in Rudy, Arkansas." PoetL (67:4) Wint 72, p. 338.

2960 SMITH, David
from Trilce: "XX-XXV." (tr. of César Vallejo). Field (6) Spr 72, p. 87.

2961 SMITH, David Jeddie
"Bad Man's Lament (after Lee Marvin)." MidwQ (13:3) Spr 72, p. 334.
"The Buffalo Stamp." Drag (3:1) Spr 72, p. 55.
"Flood." St. AR (1:4) Spr-Sum 72, p. 59.
"Head Feint, Forearm, and Glory." LittleM (6:1) Spr 72, p. 54.
"Listen You Guys." MidwQ (13:3) Spr 72, p. 270.
"On the Water." SouthwR (57:2) Spr 72, p. 125.
"The Powerless House" (for Gilbert Page). LittleM (6: 2/3) Sum-Aut 72, p. 38.
"The Tattooed Man." KanQ (4:3) Sum 72, p. 28.
"Those Who Are Left." PraS (46:3) Aut 72, p. 254.

2962 SMITH, Eugene J.
"Thoroughbreds." Comm (95:18) 4 F 72, p. 427.

2963 SMITH, Harry
"3/Day of the Earth." UTR (1:2) 72, p. 32.

2964 SMITH, Isiah
"From the Window of the Barber Shop." Magazine (5) part 9, 72, p. 25.

2965 SMITH, Ken
"The Blinding." Iron (2) Fall 72, p. 59.
"Bowl." Stand (13:2) 72, p. 30.
from Calling the Wild Turkey: (4, 6, 7, 9, 10, 11, 12, 13). QRL (18:1/2) 72, p. 241.
"eight nowhere." Kayak (28) 72, p. 19.
"First Day in the City." NewL (39:2) Wint 72, p. 42.
from Ghetto Songs: "Belmont" (for Jon Silkin). Stand (14:1) 72, p. 7.
from Ghetto Songs: "Maria the Thief" (for Jon Silkin). Stand (14:1) 72, p. 6.
from Ghetto Songs: "The Tivoli Bar" (for Jon Silkin). Stand (14:1) 72, p. 7.
"The Island." Iron (2) Fall 72, p. 60.
"Passing Bell." NewL (39:2) Wint 72, p. 42.
"SS." Stand (13:2) 72, p. 32.
"The Sioux Cleared from Minnesota." TransR (41) Wint-Spr 72, p. 138.
"The Third Month." NewYQ (10) Spr 72, p. 60.
"To Survive." Stand (13:2) 72, p. 30.
"Two Poems." Peb (7) Aut 71.
"Wants." Stand (13:2) 72, p. 31.
"The Wedding." Stand (13:2) 72, p. 31.

2966 SMITH, Lawrence R.
"The Dream." Folio (8:2) Fall 72, p. 30.

2967 SMITH, LeRoy, Jr.
"The Prisoner." NYT 18 Je 72, sec. 4, p. 14.

2968 SMITH, Lisa
"Mutant." PoetL (67:4) Wint 72, p. 339.
"Surfer's Sonnet." PoetL (67:3) Aut 72, p. 249.

2969 SMITH, Marcel
"Man with Chainsaw." SoCaR (4:2) Je 72, p. 33.

2970 SMITH, Merissa
"Luna." Spec (14:1/2) My 72, p. 83.
"Black Jade" (for Sylvia Plath). Spec (14:1/2) My 72, p. 84.

2971 SMITH, Patricia Clark
"Travelling with Friends." SoDakR (10:4) Wint 72-73, p. 33.

2972 SMITH, R. B.
"To the Muse Affectionately." ColEng (33:4) Ja 72, p. 487.

2973 SMITH, Ray
"Note for Henry James." SouthernHR (6:2) Spr 72, p. 190.
"Robinson in Tilbury Town." SouthernHR (6:2) Spr 72, p. 190.

2974 SMITH, Robert
"Fading." Confr (5) Wint-Spr 72, p. 82.
"A Vision of Yellow Buses." SoCaR (4:2) Je 72, p. 34.

2975 SMITH, Robin
"Like lives of silent peoples." FreeL (15:1/2) 71-72, p. 54.

2976 SMITH, Sister Pam
"Two Women" (for C. O. H.). BelPoJ (23:2) Wint 72-73, p. 23.
"The Young Woman Explains Why She Has Become a Nun" (for Sister M. Paul). BelPoJ (23:2) Wint 72-73, p. 26.

2977 SMITH, Terry
"Chance Meeting Old Friends." Epos (23:3) Spr 72, p. 21.
"Comic Book Morning." WindO (11) Aut 72, p. 48.
"UPI #5: Connecticut Boy Grows Tree from Stomach." WindO (11) Aut 72, p. 47.

2978 SMITH, Tom
"Supermarket." BeyB (3:1) 72, p. 10.
"Traffic." BeyB (2:2) 72, p. 9.

2979 SMITH, William Jay
"An Ironical Elegy Born in Those Most Distressing Moments When ... One Cannot Write" (tr. of Andrei Voznesensky, w. Nicholas Fersen). NewRep (167:19) 18 N 72, p. 31.

2980 SMYTH, Paul
"The First Alter." AmerS (41:1) Wint 71-72, p. 50.
"Matins." Shen (23:3) Spr 72, p. 40.
from Native Grass: "Two Thoughts." Wind (2:6) Aut 72, p. 16.
"Of His Affliction." Poetry (120:1) Ap 72, p. 28.

2981 SNEYD, Steve
"Last Wasp of Summer." Zahir (1:4/5) 72, p. 8.
"Space Program." Zahir (1:4/5) 72, p. 7.
"Unicorn Export-Import Entertains a Prospective Customer." Zahir (1:4/5) 72, p. 9.
"The Wrecker." Zahir (1:4/5) 72, p. 5.

2982 SNOW, Walter
"Bound in Shallows (Ben Jonson recalls an obscure playwright)." WormR (46) 72, p. 45.

2983 SNYDER, Bob
"Agony in Akron." Wind (2:6) Aut 72, p. 15.
"The Refounding of Saint Mary's West Virginia." CarolQ (24:1) Wint 72, p. 73.
"Route Fifty." Wind (2:6) Aut 72, p. 15.
"These." Wind (2:6) Aut 72, p. 16.

2984 SNYDER, Gary
"As for Poets." AmerR (15) 72, p. 99.
"Black Mesa Mine No. 1." Kayak (30) D 72, p. 56.
"The Egg." Kayak (30) D 72, p. 57.
"Mother Earth." NYT 13 Jl 72, p. 35.
"Smokey the Bear Sutra." WindO (9) Spr 72, p. 41.
"Source." UnmOx (1:1) N 71, p. 67.

2985 SNYDER, Jane
"Poem: Please send." NewYQ (10) Spr 72, p. 69.

2986 SNYDER, Richard
"Countess Tessie Takes Off." BeyB (2:2) 72, p. 40.
"Gravity Experiment." BeyB (2:2) 72, p. 41.
"In the Case of X vs. Y." BeyB (2:2) 72, p. 41.
"Wage, Strike, Freeze, POW." Cord (1:4) 72, p. 15.

2987 SOBIN, A. G.
"Animus." KanQ (4:1) Wint 71-72, p. 96.
"Concerning Archeology: A Report, A Photograph, A Painting" (for Arthur Vogelsang). BelPoJ (23:2) Wint 72-73, p. 42.
"Found Poem: A Song For Your Child." Drag (3:1) Spr 72, p. 35.
"Iowa Autumnal No. 2." KanQ (4:3) Sum 72, p. 57.
"Song." NewYQ (12) Aut 72, p. 91.
"Song: 16. i. 70." UTR (1:1) 72, p. 30.
"Working at Night Going Off." UTR (1:2) 72, p. 25.

2988 SOHN, Charles
"Regulations for Fall." PoetC (7:1) 72, p. 12.
"What Is the Half-Life of an Adam on the Eve of Paradise?" CarolQ (24:3) Fall 72, p. 79.

2989 SOLAN, Miriam
"Nonstop Props and Continental Breakfast." NewYQ (10) Spr 72, p. 65.

2990 SOLDOFSKY, Alan
"The Bends." Sky (1:1) 71.
"The Old Ones." Sky (1:1) 71.

2991 SOLLID, John
"Going Home: 1970." FreeL (15:1/2) 71-72, p. 56.
"Little Lyric #2." FreeL (15:1/2) 71-72, p. 59.
"Sea Known." FreeL (15:1/2) 71-72, p. 57.

2992 SOLOGUB, Fyodor
Three Unpublished Poems. RusLT (4) Aut 72, p. 365.

2993 SOLOMON, Oliva
"Fig Preserves." BallSUF (13:3) Sum 72, p. 21.

2994 SOLOMON, Rob
"Unfinished Poem." HangL (16) Wint 71-72, p. 55.

2995 SOLOVYOV, Vladimir
"Dearest friend, do you not see" (tr. by Samuel D. Cioran). RusLT (4) Aut 72, p. 30.
"Emmanuel and other poems" (tr. by Eugene M. Kayden). ColQ (20:4) Spr 72, p. 546.
"Three Meetings" (tr. by Ralph Koprince). RusLT (4) Aut 72, p. 21.

2996 SOLVIN, Lois C.
"Daughter-in-law." Wind (2:6) Aut 72, p. 23.
"Shut Out." Wind (2:5) Sum 72, p. 19.

2997 SOLZHENITSYN, Aleksandr
"Lament for Tvardovsky." NYT 12 F 72, p. 29.

2998 SOMMER, Piotr
Two Poems. Shen (23:2) Wint 72, p. 33.

2999 SORRELLS, Helen
"After Grass." NoAmR (257:1) Spr 72, p. 7.
"The Breaking." CarlMis (12:2) Spr-Sum 72, p. 130.
"The Hypnotist." SouthernPR (13:1) Aut 72, p. 44.
"Migraine." PraS (46:3) Aut 72, p. 237.

3000 SORRENTINO, Gilbert
"The Assumption of Black Sambo." UnmOx (1:3) Sum 72, p. 18.
"Cynical." UnmOx (1:3) Sum 72, p. 17.

3001 SOSKIS, David A.
"Anniversary" (for Emmy). ConcPo (5:2) Fall 72, p. 27.
"The Confessions of Dr. Cone." ConcPo (5:2) Fall 72, p. 27.

3002 SOUCEK, Judith
"Primordial Guesser." SouthernPR (12:2) Spr 72, p. 29.

3003 SOULE, Jean Conder
"Best Solution." SatEP (244:3) Aut 72, p. 88.

"The Wet Look." SatEP (244:2) Sum 72, p. 102.

3004 SOUTHERLAND, Ellease
"The Retelling." PoetL (67:2) Sum 72, p. 145.

3005 SOUTHWICK, Marcia
"Travelling from Washington to Franklin." AriD (1:2) Wint 72, p. 7.

3006 SPACKS, Barry
"Ballade of the Surfers." MassR (13:3) Sum 72, p. 328.
"Malediction." Poetry (120:2) My 72, p. 82.
"The Pale Ones." Atl (230:3) S 72, p. 87.
"A Quiet Day." Poetry (120:2) My 72, p. 82.
"Recalling Mr. Frost (for Nick and Eva Linfield)." NYT 29 D 72, p. 24.
"The Slow Year." Poetry (120:2) My 72, p. 83.
"To a Lady." NYT 17 My 72, p. 46.

3007 SPANBAUER, Tom
"the barracks is empty because." Drag (3:2) Sum 72, p. 51.

3008 SPANK
"Do You Remember." JnlOBP (2:16) Sum 72, p. 18.

3009 SPEAR, Terry G.
"Lyric." Comm (96:7) 21 Ap 72, p. 166.

3010 SPENDER, Stephen
"Late Stravinsky Listening to Late Beethoven" (to Robert Craft). NewYRB (18:9) 18 My 72, p. 14.

3011 SPIELBERG, Peter
"Carpe Diem." ConcPo (5:1) Spr 72, p. 73.

3012 SPIRE, André
"Retour des Martinets" (tr. by Stanley Burnshaw). MassR (13:3) Sum 72, p. 325.

3013 SPIVACK, Kathleen
"Blurring." Atl (229:1) Ja 72, p. 80.
"Dido: Swarming." Poetry (120:4) Jl 72, p. 195.
"Smoke." Esq (77:6) Je 72, p. 45.

3014 SPIVEY, Kregg
"I Swing the Axe." SoCaR (5:1) D 72, p. 23.

3015 SPRACKLEN, Myrtle
"Rejection." Phy (33:1) Spr 72, p. 32.

3016 SPRUNT, William
"The Magician" (for A.D.). SouthernPR (12: Special Issue) 72, p. 53.

3017 SQUIRES, Bonnie
"Former Student." EngJ (61:1) Ja 72, p. 35.
"Poetry Workshop." EngJ (61:8) N 72, p. 1188.

3018 SQUIRES, Radcliffe
"Waiting in the Bone." MichQR (11:3) Sum 72, p. 163.

3019 STAAL, Doris
"Crust." Nat (215:20) 18 D 72, p. 634.
"The Garden." Madrona (1:2) N 71, p. 7.

3020 STAFF, Susan
"Response-ability." ChrC (89:40) 8 N 72, p. 1125.

3021 STAFFORD, Kim
"The pilgrim martyred" (from Jung). Drag (3:1) Spr 72, p. 33.

3022 STAFFORD, William
"At Dawn." StoneD (1:1) Spr 72, p. 33.
"At the Coast." MichQR (11:2) Spr 72, p. 103.
"Converts." Drag (3:1) Spr 72, p. 65.
"The Escape." Hudson (25:2) Sum 72, p. 221.
"Father and Son." Atl (229:5) My 72, p. 75.
"For a Child Gone to Live in a Commune." AmerS (41:4) Aut 72, p. 519.
"Friend." Hudson (25:2) Sum 72, p. 220.
"From a Historian." Drag (3:1) Spr 72, p. 64.
"Ghazal XXXIV" (tr. of Mirza Ghalib). Madem (74:3) Ja 72, p. 50.
"Gifts from a Train." StoneD (1:1) Spr 72, p. 32.
"Hero." ChiTM 27 F 72, p. 12.
"In the White Sky." Hudson (25:2) Sum 72, p. 219.
"Incident In Fortran." Esq (78:5) N 72, p. 89.
"Room 000." NewRep (166:4) 22 Ja 72, p. 25.
"Sleeping on the Sisters Land." Hudson (25:2) Sum 72, p. 219.
"So Clear, So Cold." OhioR (13:3) Spr 72, p. 69.
"'Story of a Piebald Horse.'" StoneD (1:1) Spr 72, p. 32.
".38." OhioR (13:3) Spr 72, p. 70.
"Those Others." NewRep (167:15) 21 O 72, p. 40.
"Two Cold Rivers." AmerS (41:1) Wint 71-72, p. 120.
"Walking Away an Undeclared War." Poetry (120:6) S 72, p. 323.
"Weeds." Hudson (25:2) Sum 72, p. 220.
"What You Do Is Important." MichQR (11:2) Spr 72, p. 103.
"Yucca Flowers." NewYorker (48:13) 20 My 72, p. 134.

3023 STAGE, Stephen
"Robert Bly Speaks as a Young Man." Spec (14:1/2) My 72, p. 85.

3024 STAHL, Jane Lyn
"hand, incorporated." FreeL (15:1/2) 71-72, p. 90.
"Telegram." FreeL (15:1/2) 71-72, p. 92.

3025 STANFORD, Ann
"The Artist Underground." VirQR (48:3) Sum 72, p. 399.
"The Burning of Ilium." Poetry (120:6) S 72, p. 357.
"The Covenant of Grace." SouthernR (8:2) Spr 72, p. 381.
"Down, Down." VirQR (48:3) Sum 72, p. 398.
"Dreaming of Foxes." VirQR (48:3) Sum 72, p. 400.
"Overlappings." CalQ (3) Aut 72, p. 52.

3026 STANFORD, Frank
"The Actresses of Night." Iowa (3:3) Sum 72, p. 24.
"The Buried Sword." Iowa (3:3) Sum 72, p. 22.
"Chimera." HolCrit (9:1) Ap 72, p. 12.
"Keeping the Lord's Night Watch." Iowa (3:3) Sum 72, p. 23.
"The Paramour." Iowa (3:3) Sum 72, p. 24.
"Tapsticks." MassR (13:4) Aut 72, p. 583.

3027 STANISHEV, Krustyo
"In Memory of Bogdan Borov." LitR (16:2) Wint 72-73, p. 239.

3028 STANKIEWICZ, Marketa Goetz
"The Bizarre Town, Nr. 38" (tr. of Vitězslav Nezval). Mund (5:1/2) 72, p. 21.
"The Gloves" (tr. of Vitězslav Nezval). Mund (5:1/2) 72, p. 19.
"In the Louvre, Nr. 4" (tr. of Vitězslav Nezval). Mund (5:1/2) 72, p. 23.
"The Sword Swallower" (tr. of Vitězslav Nezval). Mund (5:1/2) 72, p. 23.

3029 STANSBERGER, Rick
"A Prodigious Bust." HiramPoR (13) Fall-Wint 72, p. 24.

3030 STANTON, Maura
"The New Sergeant's Wife." CarlMis (12:1) Fall-Wint 71-72, p. 90.

3031 STAPLETON, Wilson
"winosong." Wind (2:5) Sum 72, p. 8.

3032 STARBUCK, George
"Dear Fellow Teacher." SatR (55:41) O 72, p. 51.
"Sonnet with a Different Letter at the End of Every Line." NewYorker (48:22) 22 Jl 72, p. 26.

3033 STARZYNSKI, David
"A Canyon." WestR (10:1) Spr 73, p. 42.

"That's Not an Everything." Wind (2:6) Aut 72, p. 18.

3034 STATHATOS, John Constantine
"The Meaning of the Blind" (tr. of Eleni Vakalo). Mund (5:1/2) 72, p. 134.

3035 STAWSKI, Robert
"Cinquains." St. AR (1:4) Spr-Sum 72, p. 33.
"Tired." St. AR (2:1) Aut-Wint 72, p. 15.

3036 STEDINGH, R. W.
"High Noon." LittleM (6:2/3) Sum-Aut 72, p. 88.

3037 STEEL, Danielle F.
"did you mean." Cosmo (173:6) D 72, p. 72.
"i sat and watched." Cosmo (173:6) D 72, p. 72.
"What is it like for you right now?" Cosmo (173:2) Ag 72, p. 169.

3038 STEELE, Richard
"Under Capricorn." KanQ (4:3) Sum 72, p. 126.

3039 STEELE, Timothy
"Coda in Wind." SouthernR (8:1) Wint 72, p. 170.
"Cowboy." ModernO (2:1) Wint 72, p. 26.
"Homecoming in Late March." Poetry (119:6) Mr 72, p. 329.
"October Dusk." SouthernR (8:1) Wint 72, p. 171.
"Reading Habits." ModernO (2:1) Wint 72, p. 25.
"September Noon" (for My Wife). SouthernR (8:1) Wint 72, p. 172.
"Wait." Poetry (119:6) Mr 72, p. 329.

3040 STEFANILE, Felix
"American Legend." VirQR (48:3) Sum 72, p. 394.
"Riding the Storm." VirQR (48:3) Sum 72, p. 397.
"The Weather Didn't Do Us Any Good." VirQR (48:3) Sum 72, p. 393.

3041 STEFLIK, Mary Anne
"TV." UTR (1:2) 72, p. 18.
"Somewhere." UTR (1:1) 72, p. 17.

3042 STEILING, David
"The Hymn of the Clan of the Coyote." SouthernPR (13:1) Aut 72, p. 16.

3043 STEIN, Gertrude
"Stanzas in Meditation." Poetry (121:1) O 72, p. 26.

3044 STEINARR, Steinn
from Time and Water (1952): Fifteen Poems (tr. by Robin Fulton and Hermann Palsson). MinnR (3) Aut 72, p. 63.

3045 STEINGASS, David
"Blizzard." NewL (39:2) Wint 72, p. 20.
"From 'Six Days In July'." NoAmR (257:4) Wint 72, p. 34.

3046 STEINGESSER, Martin
"Babyhip." EverR (16:95) Fall 72, p. 106.
"The Bus Like a Toy Seems to Be." Confr (5) Wint-Spr 72, p. 46.
"In Dangerous Times One Must Resort to Extravagant Measures." ExpR (3) Fall-Wint 72/73, p. 8.
"Machismo." NYT 13 O 72, p. 38.

3047 STEINKE, Russell
"Neap Tide." Epoch (21:2) Wint 71, p. 166.

3048 STEINMAN, Lisa M.
"Note." Cafe (4) Fall 72, p. 21.

3049 STEPANCHEV, Stephen
"A Fever in Flushing." NYT 5 Ap 72, p. 44.
"John Berryman." NewYQ (11) Sum 72, p. 56.
"Tears Drop in My Heart" (tr. of Paul Verlaine). NewYQ (10) Spr 72, p. 93.
"V. I. P." Nat (214:21) 22 My 72, p. 669.
"The Vacation Ends." Confr (5) Wint-Spr 72, p. 69.
"The White Lilacs." ChiTM 30 Ap 72, p. 14.

3050 STEPHENS, James
"Doven the Puffed Grouse." Northeast Aut-Wint 71-72, p. 51.
"Scissors Cuts Paper, Paper Covers Stone, Stone Dulls Scissors." Northeast Aut-Wint 71-72, p. 52.

3051 STEPHENS, Meic
"Elegy for Llewelyn Humphries." TransR (42/43) Spr-Sum 72, p. 83.

3052 STEPHENS, Rosemary
"Mermaid Waiting." Poem (16) N 72, p. 23.
"A New Odysseus." Poem (16) N 72, p. 25.
"The Nightingale." Poem (16) N 72, p. 26.
"The Swim." Poem (16) N 72, p. 24.

3053 STERN, Richard
"Above the Snow." CarlMis (12:1) Fall-Wint 71-72, p. 78.

3054 STERN, Robert
"Opus II." UTR (1:2) 72, p. 35.
"tonight." UTR (1:3) 72, p. 12.

3055 STERNBERG, Ricardo da Silveira Lobo
"Darkness in America." Drag (3:1) Spr 72, p. 29.

"In light of the latest news" (tr. of Carlos Drummond De Andrade, w. Duane Ackerson). Drag (3:1) Spr 72, p. 82.
"Insomnia." Drag (3:2) Sum 72, p. 56.
"Literary Politics" (to Manuel Bandeira) (tr. of Carlos Drummond De Andrade, w. Duane Ackerson). Mund (5:3) 72, p. 59.
"Lorca." Drag (3:1) Spr 72, p. 30.
"Moonlight in Any City..." (tr. of Carlos Drummond De Andrade, w. Duane Ackerson). Mund (5:3) 72, p. 59.
"News Poem" (tr. of Carlos Drummond De Andrade, w. Duane Ackerson). Drag (3:1) Spr 72, p. 84.
"Our Time" (to Osvaldo Alves) (tr. of Carlos Drummond De Andrade, w. Duane Ackerson). Mund (5:3) 72, p. 57.
"Poem of Seven Facets" (tr. of Carlos Drummond De Andrade, w. Duane Ackerson). Drag (3:1) Spr 72, p. 83.
"The Survivor" (tr. of Carlos Drummond De Andrade, w. Duane Ackerson). Drag (3:1) Spr 72, p. 81.
"Treblinka." Drag (3:1) Spr 72, p. 30.

3056 STERNLICHT, Sanford
"Panic in Pompeii." SouthwR (57:3) Sum 72, p. 187.

3057 STETLER, Charles
"Jeep." KanQ (4:3) Sum 72, p. 115.
"Shane." WormR (46) 72, p. 35.
"Spirit of the 49-ers" (Thirteen Poems). WormR (48) 72, p. 127.

3058 STETSON, Catherine
"F.S." Nat (214:22) 29 My 72, p. 700.
"Masculine/Feminine (for Ted Hughes)." Nat (214:25) 19 Je 72, p. 798.
"One Plus Action." Nat (214:26) 26 Je 72, p. 825.

3059 STEVENS, Wallace
"Phases." Poetry (121:1) O 72, p. 31.

3060 STEVENSON, Anne
"The Sirens Are Virtuous." MichQR (11:1) Wint 72, p. 38.
"Siskin." MichQR (11:1) Wint 72, p. 36.
"Two Women." MichQR (11:1) Wint 72, p. 37.

3061 STEWART, Dolores
"Eva Braun." Peb (7) Aut 71.

3062 STEWART, Jimmy
"Poem I." JnlOBP (2:16) Sum 72, p. 10.

3063 STEWART, Jody
"Eastern United States (I)." AriD (1:3) Spr 72, p. 18.

"Poem: Crow calls." AriD (1:3) Spr 72, p. 18.

3064 STILES, Ward
"After the Ambush." PoetryNW (13:2) Sum 72, p. 13.
"Midnight on the Highway." NowestR (12:2) Spr 72, p. 30.

3065 STILLINGER, Jack
"The Articulators." KanQ (4:1) Wint 71-72, p. 64.
"Promises." KanQ (4:1) Wint 71-72, p. 64.

3066 STOCK, Ely
"Fat Professor Without Snowshoes Describes March Vacation." ColEng (33:5) F 72, p. 579.

3067 STOCK, Norman
"Wallace Stevens in an Airplane." NewYQ (9) Wint 72, p. 58.
"Wallace Stevens Makes Love on Sunday Morning." NewYQ (9) Wint 72, p. 58.
"Wallace Stevens Smokes a Cigar." NewYQ (9) Wint 72, p. 58.

3068 STOCK, Robert
"Blissoming: Naming It As It Is." (1:1) N 71, p. 61.
"The Hound Without Plumes" (to Joaquin Cardozo) (tr. of João Cabral De Melo Neto). Works (3:2) Wint-Spr 72, p. 4.
"Promised Landfall." ExpR (3) Fall-Wint 72/73, p. 33.
"Riddle: I sit secreted in the dark." Antaeus (7) Aut 72, p. 28.
"Sigismondo Malatesta Brings His Favorite Philosopher's Bones to Italy." Works (3:3/4) Wint 72-73, p. 80.
"Mayapán" (tr. of Ernesto Cardenal). Works (3:3/4) Wint 72-73, p. 82.

3069 STOKES, Terry
"Breakfast Song." Cafe (4) Fall 72, p. 32.
"Gold, the Peace of Space." Sky (1:2) 72, p. 7.
"I Won't Explain." Nat (214:3) 17 Ja 72, p. 88.
"A Man All Grown Up Is Supposed To." Antaeus (7) Sum 72, p. 83.
"Pouring Yourself." Iron (2) Fall 72, p. 51.
"Rules." Nat (214:3) 17 Ja 72, p. 88.
"Spending Your Life Killing Yourself." Nat (214:2) 10 Ja 72, p. 58.
"Stone Dream." Sky (1:2) 72, p. 6.
"Straightening Up." Esq (78:6) D 72, p. 126.
"The Sun Stiffened." Drag (3:1) Spr 72, p. 22.
"Thursday." NewYorker (48:34) 14 O 72, p. 151.
"Travis, The Kid Was All Heart." Antaeus (7) Aut 72, p. 82.

3070 STOKESBURY, Leon
"To All Those Considering Coming to Fayetteville." SouthernPR (13:1) Aut 72, p. 45.

3071 STOLOFF, Carolyn
"Again and Again." PraS (46:3) Aut 72, p. 255.
"Arrival at St. George." UnicornJ (4) 72, p. 39.
"Bearing It." UnicornJ (4) 72, p. 44.
"Bermuda Notebook." UnicornJ (4) 72, p. 40.
"Brick by Brick." UTR (1:1) 72, p. 6.
"The Image." Drag (3:1) Spr 72, p. 23.
"I Will Not Go to Mikonos." UnicornJ (4) 72, p. 43.
"Mornings and Evenings." UnicornJ (4) 72, p. 38.
"Odyssey of the Hair." Epoch (21:3) Spr 72, p. 300.
"Pictures." CarlMis (12:1) Fall-Wint 71-72, p. 35.
"The Poet." CarlMis (12:1) Fall-Wint 71-72, p. 37.
"September Night." UTR (1:1) 72, p. 7.
"This Spain." UnicornJ (4) 72, p. 42.
"Under the Sun." CarlMis (12:1) Fall-Wint 71-72, p. 36.

3072 STONE, Arlene
"Luv Sing: chaw thet." BeyB (2:2) 72, p. 45.
"Luv Sing: dream crutch." BeyB (2:2) 72, p. 44.

3073 STONE, Carolyn Rose
"The Inheritance." WindO (11) Aut 72, p. 39.

3074 STONE, Joan
"Amanita." Madrona (1:1) Je 71, p. 11.
"A Different View." KanQ (4:1) Wint 71-72, p. 109.
"Sounding." Madrona (1:2) N 71, p. 9.

3075 STONE, John H.
"Lines for a Last Class." SouthernHR (6:1) Wint 72, p. 62.

3076 STONE, Larry
"Alba." Madrona (1:1) Je 71, p. 28.

3077 STOOP, Norma McLain
"Country Song." LadHJ (89:9) S 72, p. 194.

3078 STOREY, Edward
"The Day's Hope." NYT 3 Mr 72, p. 38.
"Genesis." NYT 5 Je 72, p. 32.
"Sacrament." NYT 21 O 72, p. 32.

3079 STOTT, William
"Insinuating the world of noon." FourQt (21:2) Ja 72, p. 7.
"Punctured by light." FourQt (21:2) Ja 72, p. 7.

3080 STOUT, Robert Joe
"Abbie Hoffman Makes the Cover of 'Time'." AriD (1:3) Spr 72, p. 7.
"Before Integration." Focus (8:56) 72, p. 37.
"The Creative Writing Center." Folio (8:2) Fall 72, p. 20.
"The End of the Establishment." Comm (97:3) 20 O 72, p. 56.
"In the House of Pioneers." Poem (16) N 72, p. 12.
"Inheritance." BabyJ (5) N 72, p. 3.
"Native Texan." Folio (8:1) Spr 72, p. 39.
"The Planter's French Mistress." ExpR (3) Fall-Wint 72/73, p. 46.

3081 STOUTENBURG, Adrien
"Cellar." PoetryNW (13:3) Aut 72, p. 18.
"The Fashion Model At Home." Kayak (29) S 72, p. 36.
"Landscape." Epoch (21:2) Wint 71, p. 152.
"Plaything." Kayak (29) S 72, p. 37.
"The Sleep of Animals." Epoch (21:2) Wint 71, p. 153.
"The Watch." PoetryNW (13:3) Aut 72, p. 17.
"A Winter View." PoetryNW (13:3) Aut 72, p. 16.

3082 STRAMM, August
"Patrol" (tr. by Reinhold Johannes Kaebitzsch). UTR (1:1) 72, p. 32.

3083 STRAND, Mark
"Away." NewYorker (48:22) 22 Jl 72, p. 36.
"Buster Keaton Looks in the Woods For His Love Who Is a Real Cow" (tr. of Rafael Alberti). Antaeus (7) Aut 72, p. 153.
"The Butterfly Messenger" (tr. of Peruvian Indian Folksong). Madrona (1:1) Je 71, p. 31.
"Charlie's Sad Date" (tr. of Rafael Alberti). Antaeus (7) Aut 72, p. 149.
"Crystalline River" (tr. of Peruvian Indian Folksong). Madrona (1:1) Je 71, p. 32.
"Days." OhioR (13:2) Wint 72, p. 73.
"Elegy for My Father" (Robert Strand 1908-68). Field (6) Spr 72, p. 5.
"From a Notebook." FourQt (21:4) My 72, p. 91.
"Harold Lloyd, Student" (tr. of Rafael Alberti). Antaeus (7) Aut 72, p. 151.
"In Celebration." OhioR (13:2) Wint 72, p. 72.
"The Moldy Angel" (tr. of Rafael Alberti). Peb (6) Sum 71.
"On the Day of His Death By an Armed Hand" (tr. of Rafael Alberti). Antaeus (7) Aut 72, p. 155.
"Song of the Angel Without Luck" (tr. of Rafael Alberti). Peb (6) Sum 71.
"The Story of Our Lives." NewYorker (48:37) 4 N 72, p. 55.

"War Song" (tr. from the Quechua). Madrona (1:1) Je 71, p. 20.

3084 STRAUS, Leonard K.
"For Isaac Babel 1894-1941?" LitR (16:1) Aut 72, p. 51.

3085 STRELLEC, David
"Merle's a Spy for Our Side." Peb (6) Sum 71.
"The Sky Diver Has a Dream." Peb (6) Sum 71.

3086 STRONGIN, Lynn
"Emily Dickinson Postage Stamp." Aphra (3:3) Sum 72, p. 55.
"A Lovely Kind of Land." Confr (5) Wint-Spr 72, p. 33.
"On the Head of a Coin (Sappho)." NewYQ (12) Aut 72, p. 62.

3087 STROUD, Drew McCord
"On Hearing the News, In Advance, Of the Death of Jorge Luis Borges." MedR (2:2) Wint 72, p. 67.
"La Raza." MedR (2:2) Wint 72, p. 67.
"To the Dark Lady in Autumn." ExpR (2) Wint-Spr 72, p. 35.
"Visit." MedR (2:2) Wint 72, p. 67.

3088 STROZIER, Robert
"My Cousin." KanQ (4:3) Sum 72, p. 44.

3089 STRUNK, Orlo, Jr.
"Next Time." ChrC (89:31) 6 S 72, p. 870.

3090 STRUTHERS, Ann
"Bethany Beach, Delaware." GreenR (2:2) 72, p. 34.
"From the Library Windows." GreenR (2:2) 72, p. 35.

3091 STRYK, Lucien
"The Lesson." MidwQ (13:2) Wint 72, p. 184.
"The Loser." SouthernPR (12:2) Spr 72, p. 26.
"Map." ChiTM 30 Ja 72, p. 12.
"Thoroughbred Country." NYT 3 S 72, sec. 4, p. 12.
"To Roger Blin." NYT 16 Ag 72, p. 36.
"The Writer's Wife." LitR (16:1) Aut 72, p. 138.
"Zen Poems of China" (tr., w. Takashi Ikemoto). New:ACP (19) Aut 72, p. 55.

3092 STUART, Dabney
"Deer." MedR (2:3) Spr 72, p. 88.
"Fun House." SouthwR (57:2) Spr 72, p. 134.
"Making Love." PoetryNW (13:3) Aut 72, p. 34.
"Mirrors." SouthwR (57:2) Spr 72, p. 134.
"New Year's." MedR (2:3) Spr 72, p. 88.
"Nomad." NewYorker (47:47) 8 Ja 72, p. 72.
"Pregnancy." OhioR (13:3) Spr 72, p. 83.

"The Refugee." OhioR (13:3) Spr 72, p. 82.
"St. David's Church: Radnor, Pennsylvania." Antaeus (7) Aut 72, p. 133.
"The Snake Charmer." SouthwR (57:1) Wint 72, p. 41.
"The Whore's Dream." Humanist (32:5) S-O 72, p. 45.

3093 STUART, Jane
"Angelus." ArizQ (28:2) Sum 72, p. 159.
"Aviary." Poem (14) Mr 72, p. 62.
"Composition." SouthernPR (13:1) Aut 72, p. 43.

3094 STUART, Jesse
"Five Sonnets on Death." Wind (2:6) Aut 72, p. 54.
"From the Jasmine Room." ArizQ (28:1) Spr 72, p. 54.

3095 STUBBINGS, Shirley Beavis
"The Glass-Blower Spins an Hour Glass." Epos (24:1) Fall 72, p. 19.

3096 STUCKEY, Elma
"Preacher Man." JnlOBP (2:16) Sum 72, p. 63.
"Rebel." JnlOBP (2:16) Sum 72, p. 63.
"Sally." JnlOBP (2:16) Sum 72, p. 63.
"Talkin It Over." JnlOBP (2:16) Sum 72, p. 63.

3097 STUDEBAKER, William
"Sunday Park." Drag (3:2) Sum 72, p. 50.

3098 STYRON, Rose
"Nomen." YaleR (62:2) Wint 73, p. 266.
"Train Across America." YaleR (62:2) Wint 73, p. 264.

3099 SUAREZ, Nico
Eight Poems. UTR (1:3) 72, p. 3.
"Los Labios del Cielo." UTR (1:4) 72, p. 32.
"Vida de Campo" (para mi padre y mi madre). UTR (1:4) 72, p. 28.
"Viento Artico en un Dĭa de Sol." UTR (1:4) 72, p. 27.

3100 SUBRAMANIAN, Sujatha Bala
"Poem I." Meas (3) 72, p. 79.

3101 SUDERMAN, Elmer F.
"The First Crop." Cim (20) Jl 72, p. 43.
"A Trot into the Past." Wind (2:5) Sum 72, p. 27.

3102 SUDRABKALI, Yan
"Maples in Bloom" (tr. by Matthew Kahan, w. Nan Braymer). NewWR (40:4) Aut 72, p. 84.

3103 SÜREYA, Cemal
"A Butt Cast in the Sea" (tr. by Talat S. Halman). Books (46:2) Spr 72, p. 251.

"Country" (tr. by Murat Nemet-Nejat). LitR (15:4) Sum 72, p. 432.
"Rose" (tr. by Talat S. Halman). Books (46:2) Spr 72, p. 251.

3104 SUHL, Yuri
"Survivor." NYT 13 Ap 72, p. 42.

3105 SUINO, Mark
"I loved you: love, it very well may be" (tr. of Alexander Pushkin). RusLT (3) Spr 72, p. 36.

3106 SUK, Julie
"Cataloguing the Pre-Columbian." Qt (5:37) Wint 72, p. 30.
"Watching the Day Go." SouthernPR (12:2) Spr 72, p. 14.

3107 SUKENICK, Lynn
"Eggs." GreenR (2:2) 72, p. 36.
"Let's Begin with Something Light." HangL (16) Wint 71-72, p. 46.
"The Poster" (for S. P.). HangL (16) Wint 71-72, p. 48.
"Self-Consciousness." Epoch (22:1) Fall 72, p. 31.
"You Leave." GreenR (2:2) 72, p. 38.

3108 SULKIN, Sidney
"Advertisement Advertisement Advertisement Advertisement Advertisement." KanQ (4:3) Sum 72, p. 108.
"Pigeon Bones." CarolQ (24:1) Wint 72, p. 58.

3109 SULLIVAN, Francis
"Ballad of a Raggedy Monk." LittleM (6:2/3) Sum-Aut 72, p. 68.

3110 SULLIVAN, Frank
"Greetings, Friends!" NewYorker (48:44) 23 D 72, p. 31.

3111 SULLIVAN, James
"Eremesis." Comm (96:9) 5 My 72, p. 217.

3112 SULLIVAN, John
"mad dog has cleaved cold." KanQ (4:3) Sum 72, p. 110.

3113 SULLIVAN, Nancy
"At Yaddo, Thinking About the War." Poetry (120:6) S 72, p. 343.

3114 SULLIVAN, Rob
"Poem for Gary." Folio (8:1) Spr 72, p. 18.

3115 SULLIVAN, Sister M. Paulinus I. H. M.
"Laudate In Lindisfarne" (for St. Cuthbert). Comm (96:10) 12 My 72, p. 239.

3116 SULLIVAN, William
"December 11." Qt (5:38) Spr 72, p. 22.

3117 SUMMERS, David
"A Letter." AmerS (41:2) Spr 72, p. 249.

3118 SUNDT, Harold
"Stillmotion." NewYQ (12) Aut 72, p. 83.

3119 SUNWALL, James
"To a Poet of Small Success." SouthernHR (6:4) Aut 72, p. 317.

3120 SUPERVIELLE, Jules
"God Remembers His First Tree" (tr. by Neil Curry). Stand (13:2) 72, p. 57.

3121 SUT-NAHSI
"II. Wise One." JnlOBP (2:16) Sum 72, p. 54.

3122 SUTTER, Barton
"What the Country Man Knows By Heart." PoetryNW (13:3) Aut 72, p. 26.

3123 SUTZKEVER, Abraham
"Big and Small" (tr. by Leonard Opalov). PoetL (67:1) Spr 72, p. 35.
"Question and Answer" (tr. by Leonard Opalov). PoetL (67:1) Spr 72, p. 35.

3124 SWAN, Jan
"Omen." NewYorker (48:31) 23 S 72, p. 36.

3125 SWANGER, David
"Rejection Slip #14 from The New Yorker." PoetryNW (13:4) Wint 72-73, p. 38.

3126 SWANN, Brian
"Anglo-Saxon Riddles" (tr. by Brian Swann). Antaeus (7) Aut 72, p. 12.
"August Maine." YaleR (62:2) Wint 73, p. 264.
"Bargain." Antaeus (5) Spr 72, p. 47.
"The Birds." ColEng (33:4) Ja 72, p. 484.
"buttons." TexQ (15:2) Sum 72, p. 62.
from Dentro la Sostanza: "The Garden of Europe" (tr. of Nelo Risi, w. Ruth Feldman). MedR (2:4) Sum 72, p. 99.
"The Dying Gaul (to Desmond O'Grady)." MichQR (11:1) Wint 72, p. 46.
"The Edge." ExpR (3) Fall-Wint 72/73, p. 34.
"Fairytale." ExpR (3) Fall-Wint 72/73, p. 31.
"Full Blue Moon in Provence." ColEng (33:4) Ja 72, p. 485.

"Klasik Turk Musigi." ExpR (3) Fall-Wint 72/73, p. 35.
"Landscape with Tree." Focus (8:56) 72, p. 37.
"Marriage." Shen (23:4) Sum 72, p. 80.
from Mediterranea: "Mediterranean" (tr. of Umberto Saba, w. Ruth Feldman). MedR (2:4) Sum 72, p. 99.
"Mystics to the Sea." BallSUF (13:3) Sum 72, p. 66.
"Owls." Antaeus (5) Spr 72, p. 46.
"Poems from Il Limone Lunare" (tr. of Danilo Dolci, w. Ruth Feldman). MedR (2:4) Sum 72, p. 39.
"Preparing." NewYQ (10) Spr 72, p. 48.
"Princeton. May Day." Salm (18) Wint 72, p. 99.
"Quiet" (for Angela). Antaeus (5) Spr 72, p. 48.
"Riddle: I can stare a large pore." Antaeus (7) Aut 72, p. 29.
"Riddles of Heithrek" (tr. by Brian Swann). Antaeus (7) Aut 72, p. 18.
"River Tiber." MedR (2:3) Spr 72, p. 78.
"Sirocco" (tr. of Lucio Piccolo, w. Ruth Feldman). MedR (2:2) Wint 72, p. 57.
"The Soul and Sleights of Hand" (tr. of Lucio Piccolo, w. Ruth Feldman). Antaeus (5) Spr 72, p. 25.
from Gli Strumenti Umani: "Saba" (tr. of Vittorio Sereni, w. Ruth Feldman). MedR (2:4) Sum 72, p. 81.
"The Sundial" (tr. of Lucio Piccolo, w. Ruth Feldman). Antaeus (5) Spr 72, p. 23.
"Textures" (for Angela). TexQ (15:2) Sum 72, p. 63.
"The Three Figures" (tr. of Lucio Piccolo, w. Ruth Feldman). Antaeus (5) Spr 72, p. 26.
from Gli Uccelli Indomitabili: "Scherzo" (tr. of Alberto Lattuada, w. Ruth Feldman). MedR (2:4) Sum 72, p. 100.
"Unknowing." Poetry (121:3) D 72, p. 145.
"Waiting." NYT 14 Je 72, p. 46.
"We live by pauses; don't let deep searching" (tr. of Lucio Piccolo, w. Ruth Feldman). MedR (2:2) Wint 72, p. 58.
"The Wife's Lament." MichQR (11:1) Wint 72, p. 47.

3127 SWARD, Robert
"Dr. Soft on Marriage." Iowa (3:4) Fall 72, p. 8.
"The Next Poem You Write." Iowa (3:4) Fall 72, p. 10.
"Solipsist." Iowa (3:4) Fall 72, p. 10.
"Voices." SenR (3:1) My 72, p. 6.

3128 SWEARINGEN, Scott
"they bed the field, utter and careless." Cim (19) Ap 72, p. 54.

3129 SWEET, Robert Burdette
"The Seal." PoetL (67:3) Aut 72, p. 253.
"The Whale." PoetL (67:3) Aut 72, p. 253.

3130 SWENSON, Karen
"Moon Walk." Epos (24:1) Fall 72, p. 23.
"The Phosphorescent Man." SatR (55:29) 15 Jl 72, p. 39.
"Spring Walk." Humanist (32:6) N-D 72, p. 32.

3131 SWENSON, May
"July 4th." Poetry (120:6) S 72, p. 353.
"The Pure Suit of Happiness." NewYorker (48:5) 25 Mr 72, p. 38.
"Running on the Shore." NewYorker (48:25) 12 Ag 72, p. 28.
"September Things." NewYorker (48:32) 30 S 72, p. 118.
"This Morning." ChiTM 19 Mr 72, p. 14.
"Today." Qt (5:39/40) Sum-Aut 72, p. 3.
"The Willets." ModernO (2:2) Spr 72, p. 315.

3132 SWIFT, Joan
"The Midway Sails for Vietnam: April 10, 1972." Field (7) Fall 72, p. 10.
"Seastars." NowestR (12:3) Aut 72, p. 78.
"Ultra Violet." NYT 12 Mr 72, sec. 4, p. 10.

3133 SWIGART, Rob
"Galactophilia: According to Hoyle." BelPoJ (22-3) Spr 72, p. 20.
"King Demetrius" (tr. of C. P. Cavafy). Antaeus (7) Aut 72, p. 145.
"Nero's Term" (tr. of C. P. Cavafy). Antaeus (7) Aut 72, p. 144.
"Orophernes" (tr. of C. P. Cavafy). Antaeus (7) Aut 72, p. 147.
"The Retinue of Dionysus" (tr. of C. P. Cavafy). Antaeus (7) Aut 72, p. 146.
"Uncle Toby's Garlic Armchair Diesel." BelPoJ (22-3) Spr 72, p. 19.
"The Wind Tunnel." PoetryNW (13:4) Wint 72-73, p. 39.

3134 SWINTON, John R.
"Explanation." HolCrit (9:4) D 72, p. 4.
"A Spider and its Web." NYT 10 My 72, p. 46.

3135 SYKES, Velma West
"Ulysses, Would-Be Draft-Evader." KanQ (4:3) Sum 72, p. 69.

3136 SYLVESTER, Janet
from Woman Seated with Three Apples in Her Lap: "And there is the question of the plant." Works (3:3/4) Wint 72-73, p. 125.

3137 SZCZEPANSKI, Katheryn
"Two Poems" (tr. of Osip Mandelstam). Pan (9) 72, p. 55.

3138 SZE, Arthur
"Anchored at Ching Huai River" (tr. of Tu Mu). HangL (18) Fall 72, p. 49.
"Snow on the River" (tr. of Liu Tsung-yuan). HangL (18) Fall 72, p. 48.

3139 TAGLIABUE, John
"Medieval and Modern Synthesis." Qt (5:39/40) Sum-Aut 72, p. 34.
"Three Poems." Kayak (30) D 72, p. 61.
"Waiting Room." Qt (5:39/40) Sum-Aut 72, p. 34.

3140 TAGLIARINO, Salvatore
"Jeannette." UTR (1:2) 72, p. 30.

3141 TAKAMURA, Kotaro
"A Bladesmith" (tr. by Michiko Widigen). Madrona (1:1) Je 71, p. 18.

3142 TAKIGUCHI, Shuzo
"Handmade Proverbs" (for Joan Miro) (tr. by Hiroaki Satô). Iron (2) Fall 72, p. 45.
"Shadow's Path" (tr. by Hiroaki Sato). Iron (2) Fall 72, p. 44.

3143 TAKVAM, Marie
Ten Poems (tr. by F. H. König). NoAmR (257:1) Spr 72, p. 62.

3144 TALARICO, Ross
"The Balancing." PoetryNW (13:2) Sum 72, p. 24.
"Breaking Ground." Iowa (3:1) Wint 72, p. 16.
"The House." Iowa (3:1) Wint 72, p. 17.
"Night Prayer." Iowa (3:1) Wint 72, p. 18.
"Observations of a Fugitive." SouthernPR (13:1) Aut 72, p. 35.
"Sunday/Central Park, 1971." Shen (23:4) Sum 72, p. 47.

3145 TALCOTT, William
"Beautiful Wonderful--an ecological solution." Zahir (1:4/5) 72, p. 10.
"Clinging Thunder" (for c.). Isthmus (1) Spr 72, p. 77.
"Equinox." CalQ (2) Sum 72, p. 73.
"Mucha Woman." Isthmus (1) Spr 72, p. 74.
"Ring Around the Drain" (for Andrei Codrescu). CalQ (3) Aut 72, p. 37.
"Saeculum Matris." Isthmus (1) Spr 72, p. 76.
"Saturn." Isthmus (1) Spr 72, p. 75.
"She lay there like a movie." Zahir (1:4/5) 72, p. 10.
"Two Trees In Red Air." Isthmus (1) Spr 72, p. 103.

3146 TALL, Deborah
"Accident." Iron (1) Spr 72, p. 54.
"The Blue Forest." Nat (215:18) 4 D 72, p. 572.
"Rivals." Nat (215:14) 6 N 72, p. 442.

3147 TAMER, Ulkü
"Guillotine" (tr. by Nermin Menemencioglu). LitR (15:4) Sum 72, p. 466.

3148 TANDAN, Mohini
"The Awakenings." Meas (3) 72, p. 80.

3149 TANNENBAUM, Philip
"Family Night at S & S." New:ACP (19) Aut 72, p. 24.
"Song of the Open Road." New:ACP (19) Aut 72, p. 23.

3150 TANNENBAUM, Sheldon
"Charity." Iron (1) Spr 72, p. 44.

3151 TAPSCOTT, Steven
"Dedications (for Rory Holscher)." Peb (9) Wint 72.

3152 TARAJIA, Omari Kenyatta
"Mama." JnlOBP (2:16) Sum 72, p. 44.

3153 TARGAN, Barry
"Machine." Drag (3:1) Spr 72, p. 21.
"Newer Fictions." Drag (3:1) Spr 72, p. 20.

3154 TARN, Nathaniel
from Cancionero de Abajo: "5: Song of the Rain" (tr. of Thomas Segovia). QRL (18:1/2) 72, p. 238.
from Cancionero del Claro Palacio: "1: The Radiant Palace" (tr. of Thomas Segovia). QRL (18:1/2) 72, p. 238.
from Canciones sin Su Musica: (1, 2, 11) (tr. of Thomas Segovia). QRL (18:1/2) 72, p. 239.
from Interludio Idilico: "Coda" (tr. of Thomas Segovia). QRL (18:1/2) 72, p. 237.
"Lyrics for the Bride of God: Section: The Artemision (2)." UnmOx (1:4) Aut 72.
"Lyrics for the Bride of God, the Jubilation." ChiR (23:3) Wint 72, p. 7.
"Olvido Inolvidable" (for Octavio Paz). Books (46:4) Aut 72, p. 609.

3155 TASHOFF, Gene
"Stoic, 1936." EverR (16:95) Fall 72, p. 114.

3156 TATE, Allen
from Sonnets of the Blood: "vii." Poetry (121:1) O 72, p. 34.

3157 TATE, James
from Absences. PartR (39:2) Spr 72, p. 188.
"A Friend Told Me." Atl (229:3) Mr 72, p. 90.
"I Speak No Language, I Play No Instrument." Epoch (21:3) Spr 72, p. 242.
"Listen, Stupid Toy." Epoch (21:3) Spr 72, p. 243.
"Numb Poem." Drag (3:1) Spr 72, p. 14.
"The Red Laugh." ChiTM 4 Je 72, p. 50.
"Snuffing Out a Candle." AriD (1:2) Wint 72, p. 1.
"When It Has Done With Us." AriD (1:2) Wint 72, p. 1.

3158 TATE, James O.
"Death in Baltimore, With Beauty." MedR (2:3) Spr 72, p. 93.
"You Know Who." MedR (2:3) Spr 72, p. 93.

3159 TATE, Judith
"What an Arrival That Would Be." Comm (96:11) 19 My 72, p. 266.

3160 TAUGHER, Stephan
"Nearer the Moose's Shadow" (for John). Drag (3:1) Spr 72, p. 15.

3161 TAYLOR, Alexander
"So and So Many Larks" (tr. of Per Højholt, w. Nadia Christensen). WormR (48) 72, p. 122.
"Zadar." MedR (2:2) Wint 72, p. 61.

3162 TAYLOR, Charles B.
"A Freshman Views the Heart of Darkness." Conrad (3:2) 71-72, p. 35.

3163 TAYLOR, Davis
"My Hands." CarlMis (12:2) Spr-Sum 72, p. 86.
"The Paratrooper." CarlMis (12:2) Spr-Sum 72, p. 85.
"We Too Have Bicycles." CarlMis (12:2) Spr-Sum 72, p. 87.

3164 TAYLOR, Denise
"ours is suitcases." Zahir (1:4/5) 72, p. 46.

3165 TAYLOR, John
"Poem with Sharks." PoetryNW (13:3) Aut 72, p. 20.
"Z." ConcPo (5:1) Spr 72, p. 72.

3166 TAYLOR, Kenneth Lee
"Weight and Light." BelPoJ (22:3) Spr 72, p. 39.

3167 TAYLOR, Prentiss
"Tony." JnlOBP (2:16) Sum 72, p. 49.

3168 TAYLOR, Richard
"The Buffalo Near Simpsonville, Ky." Wind (2:5) Sum 72, p. 32.
"Our Unfaithful Wife." Iron (1) Spr 72, p. 61.

3169 TAYLOR, Rod
"Our Electric Train." SouthernR (8:1) Wint 72, p. 188.

3170 TAYLOR, Rossmé
"Leaf." PoetL (67:4) Wint 72, p. 343.

3171 TAYLOR, William E.
"The Jolly Rapist." SouthernPR (12:2) Spr 72, p. 3.
"Lessons of the Skin." Peb (7) Aut 71.
"Nature Tends Toward Chaos." Epos (24:1) Fall 72, p. 7.
"Prolegomena to Any Future Book of Pornographic Poems." SouthernPR (12:2) Spr 72, p. 3.

3172 TAYLOR, William J.
"The Waiting." PoetL (67:1) Spr 72, p. 19.

3173 TEILLIER, Jorge
"For Speaking with the Dead" (tr. by Edward Oliphant). RoadAR (4:1) Spr 72, p. 17.
"Summer Fruit" (tr. by Edward Oliphant). RoadAR (4:1) Spr 72, p. 17.

3174 TEMPLE, Jacques
"Central Park" (tr. by Raymond Federman). Pan (9) 72, p. 12.
"Justine (for Lawrence Durrell)" (tr. by Raymond Federman). Pan (9) 72, p. 12.

3175 TERR, Leonard B.
"Possibility." SouthwR (57:2) Spr 72, p. 107.

3176 TERRIS, Virginia R.
"Black Fire." LitR (15:3) Spr 72, p. 364.
"Cricket Song." LitR (15:3) Spr 72, p. 363.
"The Dying Body Shrouds the Infant Mind." LitR (15:3) Spr 72, p. 362.

3177 TEWARI, Sachin
"On Life." Meas (3) 72, p. 82.
"Untitled." Meas (3) 72, p. 82.

3178 THALLAS, Yannis
from Anatomy: (4, 8, 9) (tr. by Stavros Deligiorgis). AriD (1:4/5) Sum-Aut 72, p. 99.

3179 THANIEL, George
"The Bruise" (tr. of Dinos Christianopoulos). AriD

(1:4/5) Sum-Aut 72, p. 27.
"Love in the Field" (tr. of Dinos Christianopoulos). AriD (1:4/5) Sum-Aut 72, p. 27.
"On the Road to Damascus" (tr. of Dinos Christianopoulos). AriD (1:4/5) Sum-Aut 72, p. 27.
"Prelude" (tr. by Athan Anagnostopoulos). AriD (1:4/5) Sum-Aut 72, p. 103.
"Rock Gardens." AriD (1:4/5) Sum-Aut 72, p. 103.
"The Sea" (tr. of Dinos Christianopoulos). AriD (1:4/5) Sum-Aut 72, p. 26.
from The Spikes (tr. by Stratis Haviaras). AriD (1:4/5) Sum-Aut 72, p. 101.
"Verses of St. Agnes for St. Sebastian" (tr. of Dinos Christianopoulos). AriD (1:4/5) Sum-Aut 72, p. 28.

3180 THASSITIS, Panos K.
"Karaghiozes" (tr. by James Damaskos). AriD (1:4/5) Sum-Aut 72, p. 105.
"Servants" (tr. by James Damaskos). AriD (1:4/5) Sum-Aut 72, p. 104.

3181 THATCHER, Hale
"Boxcars." Isthmus (1) Spr 72, p. 12.
"Homecoming." Isthmus (1) Spr 72, p. 11.
"The Snake charmer." Isthmus (1) Spr 72, p. 10.

3182 THAYER, Ernest L.
"Casey at the Bat." SatEP (244:2) Sum 72, p. 87.

3183 THEODORAKOPOULOS, Loukas
"The House 2" (tr. by Athan Anagnostopoulos). AriD (1:4/5) Sum-Aut 72, p. 108.
"Like a Worn Out Shoe" (tr. by Athan Anagnostopoulos). AriD (1:4/5) Sum-Aut 72, p. 107.
"The Night and the Barracks" (tr. by Athan Anagnostopoulos). AriD (1:4/5) Sum-Aut 72, p. 106.
"The Slug" (tr. by Athan Anagnostopoulos). AriD (1:4/5) Sum-Aut 72, p. 107.

3184 THEOTOKA, Coralia
"Stones" (tr. by Theodora Vasils). ChiR (23:3) Wint 72, p. 85.

3185 THIBAUDEAU, Colleen
"My Granddaughters Are Combing Out Their Long Hair." Poetry (120:2) My 72, p. 85.

3186 THOMAS, D. M.
"Friday Evening." NewL (39:1) Aut 72, p. 111.
"Kerenza on Sand Dunes." Poetry (119:5) F 72, p. 260.
"Rest-Home, Visiting Hour." NewL (39:1) Aut 72, p. 110.
"The Sea-King to Kerenza." Poetry (119:5) F 72, p. 259.

3187 THOMAS, Dylan
"We Lying by Seasand." Poetry (121:1) O 72, p. 33.

3188 THOMAS, F. Richard
"We Are Forcing Forsythia." WindO (10) Sum 72, p. 19.

3189 THOMAS, Jack Wilson
"Arntson at Twenty-three." WormR (47) 72, p. 95.
"Assassin." WormR (47) 72, p. 95.
"Blessing." Peb (6) Sum 71.
"Camping Near Stoney Creek." Peb (6) Sum 71.
"One Night Stand." WormR (47) 72, p. 96.
"Stoney Creek Canyon." Peb (6) Sum 71.
"Sunflowers." WormR (47) 72, p. 95.
"The Turkish Hotel, the Bedroom in Denver." WormR (47) 72, p. 96.
"What the Buck and Doe Dreamed." WormR (47) 72, p. 95.

3190 THOMAS, Joanne
"Attention: Coke Machine." SatEP (244:1) Spr 72, p. 102.

3191 THOMAS, Lorenzo
"Displacement." ParisR (55) Aut 72, p. 23.
"Guerilla Girls." ParisR (55) Aut 72, p. 26.

3192 THOMAS, Ned
"Supermarket." TransR (42/43) Spr-Sum 72, p. 84.

3193 THOMAS, Peter
"The Lascars." TransR (42/43) Spr-Sum 72, p. 85.
"Sold Out." ChiTM 29 O 72, p. 16.

3194 THOMAS, Warren
"A Man in the Clouds." BelPoJ (22:3) Spr 72, p. 18.

3195 THOMPSON, Bill
"Moon thru my window." Cafe (4) Fall 72, inside back cover, back cover.

3196 THOMPSON, Don
"Evening" (for Manuel Durán). Works (3:2) Wint-Spr 72, p. 47.
"Medusa." Works (3:2) Wint-Spr 72, p. 46.
"Sunflower." Works (3:2) Wint-Spr 72, p. 47.
"The Translator." GreenR (2:2) 72, p. 18.

3197 THOMPSON, Gary
"in the new life i will allow." Iron (1) Spr 72, p. 20.

3198 THOMPSON, James W.
"High Priestess and the Penitents" (an aside to Simone).

TransR (41) Wint-Spr 72, p. 58.
"Jester to Jet Set or Tang Dynasty Toad." TransR (41) Wint-Spr 72, p. 59.
"Ritual Games." AntR (32:1/2) Spr-Sum 72, p. 56.

3199 THOMPSON, Marilyn
"A Day." NowestR (12:2) Spr 72, p. 79.
"A Morning." NowestR (12:2) Spr 72, p. 80.

3200 THONG, Huynh Sanh
"Three poems by Nguyen Trai" (tr. of Nguyen Trai). ColQ (21:1) Sum 72, p. 89.

3201 THORNBURG, Thomas R.
"Poem in the Summer Solstice" (for Joseph Satterwhite). BallSUF (13:3) Sum 72, p. 50.
"To S. T. of Dyeing Her Hair." BallSUF (13:1) Wint 72, p. 72.

3202 THORNE, Evelyn
"Act V." Epos (24:1) Fall 72, p. 26.
"good citizens." St. AR (1:4) Spr-Sum 72, p. 74.
"Metamorphosis." UTR (1:2) 72, p. 29.
"Such a Pleasant Chat." Folio (8:2) Fall 72, p. 22.

3203 THORPE, Dwayne
"Kansas Deserted." Epoch (21:2) Wint 71, p. 163.
"Macaroni." SenR (3:1) My 72, p. 56.

3204 THRIFT, Carol
"My Brother Has Come Home." Folio (8:1) Spr 72, p. 15.

3205 THURSTON, Norman
"1 April, 1972." SouthernPR (13:1) Aut 72, p. 7.

3206 TIDLER, Charles
"Bingo, Nevada." WormR (48) 72, p. 113.
"Dam Flat Tire First Snow & Walked Home." WormR (48) 72, p. 114.
"The Day the Baby Smiled." WormR (48) 72, p. 114.
"A William Carlos Williams Poem" (for Peter Wellman). WormR (48) 72, p. 114.

3207 TIMMERMAN, John
"First Guard: Hill 569." PoetL (67:4) Wint 72, p. 356.
"The Prison in Dordrecht." ArizQ (28:1) Spr 72, p. 73.

3208 TIMMONS, Wayne
"Chart of Place." FreeL (15:1/2) 71-72, p. 50.

3209 TIPTON, David
"Chan Chan" (tr. of Mirko Lauer). Stand (13:3) 72, p. 58.

"Economic Conspiracy" (tr. of Mirko Lauer). Stand (13:4) 72, p. 56.
"J. H. [Javier Heraud]" (tr. of Mirko Lauer). Stand (14:1) 72, p. 33.
"Leit-Motif: Oh Great City of Lima" (tr. of Mirko Lauer). Stand (13:3) 72, p. 56.
"Lynx" (tr. of Mirko Lauer). Stand (14:1) 72, p. 34.
"The Muse Dictates a Sonorous Rhyme: Reported Needed Full-Board Provided" (tr. of Mirko Lauer). Stand (13:3) 72, p. 54.
"Notes on the Moving of a Corpse" (tr. of Mirko Lauer). Stand (13:3) 72, p. 55.
"XVI" (tr. of Mirko Lauer). Stand (14:1) 72, p. 33.

3210 TIPTON, James
"Love Poem." MedR (2:3) Spr 72, p. 79.
"O Carib Isle." MedR (2:3) Spr 72, p. 79.
"Open Letter." SoDakR (10:4) Wint 72-73, p. 32.
"Poem: She is sitting on a basket of guitars, waiting for fingers." MedR (2:3) Spr 72, p. 79.
"River Poem." Esq (78:6) D 72, p. 126.

3211 TJALSMA, H. W.
"Conversation with an Angel" (tr. of Joseph Brodsky, w. Harvey Feinberg). New:ACP (18) Ap 72, p. 22.

3212 TODD, Albert C.
"Smog" (tr. of Yevgeny Yevtushenko, w. John Updike). NewYQ (10) Spr 72, p. 75.

3213 TOLLEFSEN, Astrid
"Bonjour Monsieur Gaugin" (tr. by F. H. König). NoAmR (257:1) Spr 72, p. 60.
"Fatum" (tr. by F. H. König). NoAmR (257:1) Spr 72, p. 60.
"In the Beginning" (tr. by F. H. König). NoAmR (257:1) Spr 72, p. 60.
"The Letter" (tr. by F. H. König). NoAmR (257:1) Spr 72, p. 60.

3214 TOMIKEL, John
"Russians in Belgrade." SoCaR (5:1) D 72, p. 49.

3215 TOMLINSON, Charles
"Against Portraits." Stand (13:4) 72, p. 16.
"Hawks." Hudson (25:2) Sum 72, p. 224.
"In October." Stand (13:4) 72, p. 17.
"The Lighthouse." Poetry (120:3) Je 72, p. 150.
"MacKinnon's Boat." Antaeus (6) Sum 72, p. 52.
"On Water." Poetry (120:3) Je 72, p. 151.
"La Promenade de Protée." Hudson (25:2) Sum 72, p. 224.
"Le Rendez-vous des Paysages." Hudson (25:2) Sum 72,

p. 223.
"Rower." Hudson (25:2) Sum 72, p. 222.
"The Sea Is Open to the Light." Poetry (120:3) Je 72, p. 150.
"The Thief's Journal." Stand (13:4) 72, p. 17.

3216 TOMLINSON, Randy
"Found Drug Store Display." WormR (46) 72, p. 65.
"Poem: All the secrets." WormR (46) 72, p. 64.
"Today." Folio (8:1) Spr 72, p. 23.

3217 TOPRAK, Omer Faruk
"After One O'Clock at Night" (tr. by Manfred Bormann). LitR (15:4) Sum 72, p. 414.

3218 TOOTELL, Jack
"Last Hour." Focus (8:56) 72, p. 36.

3219 TOROK, Lou
"After Attica: A New World Prayer." Etc. (29:3) S 72, p. 255.

3220 TOUSTER, Alison
"Embittered Frost." CEACritic (35:1) N 72, p. 38.
"To W. C. Williams." CEACritic (34:4) My 72, p. 19.

3221 TOWLE, Tony
"The Works of Li Po." NewYorker (48:33) 7 O 72, p. 40.

3222 TOWNLEY, Rod
"Bestiary." StoneD (1:1) Spr 72, p. 50.

3223 TRAI, Nguyen
"Three poems by Nguyen Trai" (tr. by Huynh Sanh Thong). ColQ (21:1) Sum 72, p. 89.

3224 TRAKL, Georg
"Anif." Mund (5:3) 72, p. 28.
"Elis" (tr. by Reinhold Johannes Kaebitzsch). Wind (2:5) Sum 72, p. 18.
"To Elis" (tr. by Reinhold Johannes Kaebitzsch). UTR (1:4) 72, p. 3.
"Verklärung." Mund (5:3) 72, p. 30.
"Verwandlung des Bösen." Mund (5:3) 72, p. 24.

3225 TRAMMELL, Robert
"American Idealism." SouthwR (57:3) Sum 72, p. 180.

3226 TRANBARGER, Ossie E.
"The Puritan." KanQ (4:1) Wint 71-72, p. 36.

3227 TRANSTROMER, Tomas
"The Journey" (tr. by Thomas and Vera Vance). Granite (2) Wint 71-72, p. 56.
"The Name" (tr. by Robert Bly). Books (46:1) Wint 72, p. 48.
"The Open Window" (tr. by Robert Bly). Books (46:1) Wint 72, p. 48.

3228 TRAXLER, Patricia
"On Dissolving Bonds" (Postcard to a former spouse). HangL (18) Fall 72, p. 50.

3229 TREE, Lysa
"her." St. AR (1:4) Spr-Sum 72, p. 18.
"image." St. AR (2:1) Aut-Wint 72, p. 28.

3230 TREITEL, Margot
"Institutional Tennis." HangL (17) Sum 72, p. 63.
"The last straw." HangL (17) Sum 72, p. 63.
"Pink Lanterns, Triangles, or Octagon Cages." RoadAR (3:4) Wint 71-72, p. 9.

3231 TRIAS, Peter
"Olympus." NYT 18 F 72, p. 34.

3232 TRIEM, Eve
"The Bed." PoetryNW (13:2) Sum 72, p. 38.
"The Farewell Moon." ChiTM 20 Ag 73, p. 14.
"The Ghost of My Lai." Madrona (1:1) Je 71, p. 24.
"One Memory of Rose." St. AR (1:4) Spr-Sum 72, p. 75.
"A View of Queen Anne Hill." Madrona (1:1) Je 71, p. 11.

3233 TRIPP, John
"Anglo-Welsh Testimony." TransR (42/43) Spr-Sum 72, p. 89.
"Roots." TransR (42/43) Spr-Sum 72, p. 86.
"Welcome to Wales." TransR (42/43) Spr-Sum 72, p. 87.

3234 TRIVELPIECE, Laurel
"Knowing the Dusk." NowestR (12:2) Spr 72, p. 65.
"Niobe." Works (3:2) Wint-Spr 72, p. 48.

3235 TROUPE, Quincy
"Midtown Traffic." NewYQ (11) Sum 72, p. 61.

3236 TROWBRIDGE, William
"Ma Barker Bagged." SouthernPR (12:2) Spr 72, p. 44.

3237 TROWER, Peter
"Grease for the Wheels of Winter." Poetry (121:3) D 72, p. 125.

3238 TRUDELL, Dennis
"Louisville Slugger." PoetryNW (13:2) Sum 72, p. 17.

3239 TRUEMAN, Terry
"A Poem For Walt Whitman Written at Charles Krafft's Cabin." Meas (2) 72.

3240 TRUESCHLER, Josephine
"Remedy for Headache." ColEng (33:5) F 72, p. 585.

3241 TRUESDALE, C. W.
"Pater Familias" (for Tony Oursler). LittleM (6:2/3) Sum-Aut 72, p. 73.

3242 TRUSCOTT, Robert Blake
"From the South." St. AR (1:4) Spr-Sum 72, p. 25.
"Ulysses." PoetL (67:4) Wint 72, p. 357.

3243 TSATSOS, Jeanne
"Confrontation." SouthernHR (6:4) Aut 72, p. 404.

3244 TS'UI Hao
"On Jo Yeh Stream" (tr. by David Gordon). Literature (15:3) 72, p. 487.

3245 TSVETAEVA, Marina
"Black as the Pupil of the Eye" (tr. by Leonard Opalov). PoetL (67:1) Spr 72, p. 30.
"A blindly-flowing sob of Lethe" (tr. by George L. Kline). RusLT (2) Wint 72, p. 219.
"The bond between your soul and mine was quite" (tr. by Jamie Fuller). RusLT (2) Wint 72, p. 214.
"The House" (tr. by Jamie Fuller). RusLT (2) Wint 72, p. 215.
"I--a spotless page beneath your pen" (tr. by Jamie Fuller). RusLT (2) Wint 72, p. 214.
"Just like the hour of the Moon" (tr. by Jamie Fuller). RusLT (2) Wint 72, p. 216.
"The massed magnificence of trumpets" (tr. by George L. Kline). RusLT (2) Wint 72, p. 218.
"The old gods are no longer bountiful" (tr. by George L. Kline). RusLT (2) Wint 72, p. 219.
"On empty roads made resonant by winter" (tr. by George L. Kline). RusLT (2) Wint 72, p. 217.
"A soul that knows no moderation" (tr. by George L. Kline). RusLT (2) Wint 72, p. 218.
"Strange Repository" (tr. by Leonard Opalov). PoetL (67:1) Spr 72, p. 29.

3246 TUCKER, David
"Report on the Fire Raid." SenR (3:1) My 72, p. 59.

3247 TUCKER, T.
"Professor Emeritus." PoetC (7:1) 72, p. 26.
"Social Scientist." PoetC (7:1) 72, p. 24.

3248 TU FU
"Banquet at the Tso Villa" (tr. by Emiko Sakurai). Literature (15:3) 72, p. 488.
"In the City on Business I Meet One Friend and We Spend the Night Eating and Drinking at the House of Another" (tr. by David Young). NewL (38:3) Spr 72, p. 46.
"An Officer's Tartar Horse" (tr. by Mark Perlberg & Lee Feigon). Focus (8:56) 72, p. 36.
"The Return" (tr. by Mark Perlberg and Lee Feigon). Atl (229:4) Ap 72, p. 103.
"Thinking of My Brothers on a Moonlit Night" (tr. by David Young). NewL (38:3) Spr 72, p. 48.
"The Winding River II" (tr. by Emiko Sakurai). Literature (15:3) 72, p. 488.

3249 TURKAY, Osman
"The Mediterranean Light." LitR (15:4) Sum 72, p. 480.

3250 TUMPOSKY, Dan
"Assassin." ExpR (2) Wint-Spr 72, p. 38.

3251 TU MU
"Anchored at Ching Huai River" (tr. by Arthur Sze). HangL (18) Fall 72, p. 49.

3252 TURCO, Lewis
"Death: Tarot Key XIII." Poetry (120:4) Jl 72, p. 209.
"The Devil: Tarot Key XV." Poetry (120:4) Jl 72, p. 210.
"Epistles: The Tarot IX of Swords." Poetry (120:4) Jl 72, p. 211.
"Foxfire: Tarot Queen of Pentacles." Poetry (120:4) Jl 72, p. 208.
"The Hanged Man: Tarot Key XII." Iowa (3:4) Fall 72, p. 25.
"Landscape." PoetryNW (13:4) Wint 72-73, p. 25.
"The Last Schooner." LittleM (6:2/3) Sum-Aut 72, p. 24.
"The Lovers: Tarot Key VI." Poetry (120:4) Jl 72, p. 208.
from Seasons of the Blood: Poems on the Tarot: "Toad: The Tarot King of Pentacles." Salm (19) Spr 72, p. 71.
"The Tower: Tarot Key XVI." Poetry (120:4) Jl 72, p. 211.
"Turberson." Cim (18) Ja 72, p. 37.

3253 TURNER, Aquadene
"How Wonderful a Gift." JnlOBP (2:16) Sum 72, p. 16.

"This Flowered River." JnlOBP (2:16) Sum 72, p. 16.

3254 TURNER, Frederick
"The Journal of Ernest Polycarpe Bougainville." Spec (14:1/2) My 72, p. 97.
"Kindertotenlied." Spec (14:1/2) My 72, p. 95.

3255 TURNER, Katharine C.
"Hallie." PoetL (67:3) Aut 72, p. 217.
"Wonderland." Comm (96:3) 24 Mr 72, p. 65.

3256 TURNER, Myron
"At the Door." PoetryNW (13:4) Wint 72-73, p. 34.

3257 TURNER, Tamu
"The Soil." JnlOBP (2:16) Sum 72, p. 81.

3258 TUSIANI, Joseph
"For a Definition of Mathematics" (tr. by Robert Lima). PoetL (67:3) Aut 72, p. 229.

3259 TWEGBE, Billoh-Gma
"Come Home." JnlOBP (2:16) Sum 72, p. 64.

3260 TYLER, Robert L.
"The Afflatus in the Tropics." WindO (9) Spr 72, p. 36.
"Afternoon in Narragansett." WindO (9) Spr 72, p. 35.
"Blackballed." Folio (8:2) Fall 72, p. 29.
"Calypso I: A Kind of a Symbol." ExpR (3) Fall-Wint 72/73, p. 44.
"Calypso II: A Kind of Disillusion." ExpR (3) Fall-Wint 72/73, p. 45.
"For the Record." Wind (2:5) Sum 72, p. 48.
"I. D. Card." Folio (8:2) Fall 72, p. 35.
"Insomnia." ArizQ (28:3) Aut 72, p. 224.
"Lesson." Peb (7) Aut 71.
"Name Dropping." Folio (8:2) Fall 72, p. 35.
"To A. M.: 1863-1947." BallSUF (13:2) Spr 72, p. 80.

3261 TYLER, Wayne
"Show Business or No Business." CEACritic (34:3) Mr 72, p. 44.

3262 TYUTCHEV, Fyodor
"About What, Night Wind, Do You Cry?" (tr. by Jamie Fuller). RusLT (3) Spr 72, p. 63.
"Autumn Evening" (tr. by Jamie Fuller). RusLT (3) Spr 72, p. 63.
"Day and Night" (tr. by Jamie Fuller). RusLT (3) Spr 72, p. 64.
"Dream on the Sea" (tr. by Jamie Fuller). RusLT (3) Spr 72, p. 61.
"Huddled hamlets, scanty granges" (tr. by Walter Arndt).

RusLT (3) Spr 72, p. 65.
"Silentium" (tr. by Walter Arndt). RusLT (3) Spr 72, p. 65.

3263 TZOTZIL (Zinacantán)
"Belly-ache" (tr. by W. S. Merwin). NewYRB (18:7) 20 Ap 72, p. 18.
"Why Souls Are Lost Now" (tr. by W. S. Merwin). NewYRB (18:7) 20 Ap 72, p. 18.

3264 UBERMAN, Leonard
"The Newspaper Notes the Anniversary of Bleriot's Flight." FreeL (15:1/2) 71-72, p. 51.

3265 ÜSTUN, Nezvat
"The Gate of the Lost" (tr. by Mina Urgan). LitR (15:4) Sum 72, p. 416.

3266 UGARITIC
"El and Anat: The Mourning of Baal" (tr. by Harris Lenowitz). Literature (15:3) 72, p. 492.

3267 UHLICH, Richard
"Commuter." ColEng (34:3) D 72, p. 448.
"Early Gothic." ColEng (34:3) D 72, p. 449.
"Feedback." ColEng (34:3) D 72, p. 450.
"San Francisco." ColEng (34:3) D 72, p. 447.
"Six O'Clock News Round-Up." ColEng (34:3) D 72, p. 446.

3268 UIGUN
"The Coming of the Flowers" (tr. by Bernard Koten, w. Nan Braymer). NewWR (40:4) Aut 72, p. 133.

3269 UKA, Kalu
"Earth to Earth." GreenR (2:3) 72, p. 16.
"New Order." GreenR (2:3) 72, p. 17.

3270 ULIN, Howard L.
"Retreat." ChiTM 16 Jl 72, p. 12.

3271 UMPHREY, Robert E.
"What Awareness Stirs You, Cypress?" UTR (1:1) 72, p. 23.

3272 UNAMUNO, Miguel de
"Me Destierro..." (tr. by Stanley Burnshaw). MassR (13:3) Sum 72, p. 327.
"Throw Yourself Like Seed" (tr. by Robert Bly). MichQR (11:4) Aut 72, p. 280.

3273 UNGARETTI, Giuseppe
"Chiaroscuro." SouthernR (8:2) Spr 72, p. 434.

"Noia." SouthernR (8:2) Spr 72, p. 434.
"Sono una creatura." SouthernR (8:2) Spr 72, p. 436.

3274 UNGERER, Kathy
"Barnegat." AntR (31:4) Wint 71-72, p. 547.
"Good Crumbs." AntR (31:4) Wint 71-72, p. 545.
"An Interdiction Is Addressed to the Hero." Iowa (3:4) Fall 72, p. 26.
"The Interdiction Is Violated." Iowa (3:4) Fall 72, p. 26.
"Moll on the Moon." AntR (31:4) Wint 71-72, p. 549.
"Moll Pitcher Comes to Dinner." AntR (31:4) Wint 71-72, p. 548.
"Moll Pitcher In British Honduras." AntR (31:4) Wint 71-72, p. 549.
"Moll Pitcher In East Calais." AntR (31:4) Wint 71-72, p. 548.
"Pretending to Die With My Grandmother." AntR (31:4) Wint 71-72, p. 546.

3275 UNICORN
"Last Laugh." ExpR (3) Fall-Wint 72/73, p. 40.

3276 UNTERECKER, John
"Brisk Afternoons." Drag (3:1) Spr 72, p. 49.
"Carrowkeel" (w. Roger Conover). UnmOx (1:4) Aut 72.
"The Kitchen, 1926-1939." NewYorker (48:5) 25 Mr 72, p. 42.
"Political Poem." SouthernPR (13:1) Aut 72, p. 15.
"Ragged Autumn." SouthernPR (13:1) Aut 72, p. 34.
"Thief." Shen (23:2) Wint 72, p. 23.
"Towards Morning." UnmOx (1:1) N 71, p. 21.
"The Washington Scene." UnmOx (1:2) F 72, p. 30.

3277 UPDIKE, John
"A Bicycle Chain." NewYorker (48:8) 15 Ap 72, p. 48.
"The Cars in Caracas." NewYorker (48:45) 30 D 72, p. 27.
"Insomnia the Gem of the Ocean." NewYorker (48:30) 16 S 72, p. 40.
"Sand Dollar." Atl (229:3) Mr 72, p. 43.
"Smog" (tr. of Yevgeny Yevtushenko, w. Albert C. Todd). NewYQ (10) Spr 72, p. 75.
"Sunday." AmerS (41:3) Sum 72, p. 389.
"Wind." Comm (95:16) 21 Ja 72, p. 373.
"Young Matrons Dancing." SatR (55:5) 29 Ja 72, p. 6.

3278 URBAN, John Robert
"Diogenes." MedR (2:3) Spr 72, p. 85.

3279 URDANG, Constance
"The Fruit." Peb (9) Wint 72.
"Riddle: Out it comes." Antaeus (7) Aut 72, p. 27.

3280 URGAN, Mina
"The Gate of the Lost" (tr. of Nezvat Ustün). LitR (15:4) Sum 72, p. 416.

3281 URIBE, Armando
"Like a patient Job I bite" (tr. by Edward Oliphant). RoadAR (4:1) Spr 72, p. 46.
Three Poems (tr. by Edward Oliphant). RoadAR (4:1) Spr 72, p. 46.

3282 UYAR, Turgut
"And Came the Tailors" (tr. by Talat Sait Halman). LitR (15:4) Sum 72, p. 496.

3283 VACHON, Doug
"Just like the movies, again." WindO (10) Sum 72, p. 8.
"Rare, like love." WindO (10) Sum 72, p. 8.
"You wouldn't believe the kind of people that." WindO (10) Sum 72, p. 9.

3284 VAKALO, Eleni
"Dirge" (tr. by James Damaskos). AriD (1:4/5) Sum-Aut 72, p. 110.
"Geneology" (tr. by Paul Merchant). AriD (1:4/5) Sum-Aut 72, p. 111.
"The Meaning of the Blind" (tr. by John Constantine Stathatos). Mund (5:1/2) 72, p. 134.
"Song of the Hanged" (tr. by James Damaskos). AriD (1:4/5) Sum-Aut 71, p. 109.

3285 VALAORITIS, Nanos
"Great Zodiac Water-Clock." Kayak (28) 72, p. 16.
"The House" (tr. by Thanasis Maskaleris). AriD (1:4/5) Sum-Aut 72, p. 114.
"The Lesson of Dawn" (tr. by Thanasis Maskaleris). AriD (1:4/5) Sum-Aut 72, p. 114.
"Life in the Suburbs." Kayak (28) 72, p. 17.
"Paphos" (tr. by Stratis Haviaras). AriD (1:4/5) Sum-Aut 72, p. 113.
"Small Threnody" (tr. by Stratis Haviaras). AriD (1:4/5) Sum-Aut 72, p. 113.
"They ordered me to take off my clothes." AriD (1:4/5) Sum-Aut 72, p. 115.
"Troy" (tr. by Thanasis Maskaleris). AriD (1:4/5) Sum-Aut 72, p. 112.

3286 VALENTI, Lila Lee
"A Poet's Notebooks" (Selections from notes of Delmore Schwartz). NewYQ (10) Spr 72, p. 111.

3287 VALENTINE, Jean
"Elegy." Antaeus (7) Aut 72, p. 72.
"He Said." UnmOx (1:4) Aut 72.

"Kin." Harp (245:1468) S 72, p. 44.
"The Knife." Field (7) Fall 72, p. 20.
"Letter." UnmOx (1:4) Aut 72.
"Scopolamine." Antaeus (7) Aut 72, p. 73.
"A Suicide." Antaeus (7) Aut 72, p. 74.
"Three Voices." Field (7) Fall 72, p. 19.

3288 VALLEJO, César
from Trilce: "XX-XXV" (tr. by David Smith). Field (6) Spr 72, p. 87.

3289 VANCE, Thomas
"The Journey" (tr. of Tomas Tranströmer). Granite (2) Wint 71-72, p. 56.

3290 VANCE, Vera
"The Journey" (tr. of Tomas Tranströmer). Granite (2) Wint 71-72, p. 56.

3291 Van DEMARR, Lee
"The Dream of the Aged Ted Williams." PoetryNW (13:2) Sum 72, p. 12.
"Grapefruit Sonnet." PoetryNW (13:2) Sum 72, p. 13.
"The Official Report on the Drowning of Li Po." PoetryNW (13:2) Sum 72, p. 10.

3292 Van DOREN, Mark
"And All the While." Hudson (25:2) Sum 72, p. 184.
"The Garden of My Own Mind." Hudson (25:2) Sum 72, p. 184.
"Good Riddance." NewYorker (48:39) 18 N 72, p. 52.
"The Possessed." Hudson (25:2) Sum 72, p. 185.

3293 Van DUYN, Mona
"End of May." NewYorker (48:14) 27 My 72, p. 36.
"Since You Asked Me..." Poetry (120:2) My 72, p. 105.
"A Small Excursion." Poetry (120:2) My 72, p. 103.
"Walking the Dog: A Diatribe." NewYorker (48:26) 19 Ag 72, p. 26.

3294 Van EGMOND, Peter
"'Bearded Oaks.'" SouthernPR (12:2) Spr 72, p. 45.

3295 VANGELISTI, Paul
"Poem for the Wind Poem" (for Margaret). Spec (14:1/2) My 72, p. 101.

3296 Van HOUTEN, Lois
"Journey Through the Door." Epos (23:3) Spr 72, p. 25.

3297 Van RIPER, Anthony
"Enough!" CEACritic (34:4) My 72, p. 16.

3298 Van TILBURG, Mark
"The Common Body." OhioR (13:2) Wint 72, p. 94.

3299 VARGO, George
"Personal Poem No. 1 to Ted Berrigan." StoneD (1:1) Spr 72, p. 11.
"Scorpio." StoneD (1:1) Spr 72, p. 11.

3300 VARMA, Monika
"An Answer." Meas (3) 72, p. 83.

3301 VAS DIAS, Robert
"Adversaries." PartR (39:3) Sum 72, p. 377.
"Passage." PartR (39:3) Sum 72, p. 376.
"Text for the Fall Appearance Opera." PartR (39:3) Sum 72, p. 376.

3302 VASILS, Theodora
"Stones" (tr. of Coralia Theotoka). ChiR (23:3) Wint 72, p. 85.

3303 VAUGHN, Jeff
"ocean." AbGR (3:1) Spr-Sum 72, p. 14.
"the old men people." AbGR (3:1) Spr-Sum 72, p. 13.
"Poem: Noise is the sound of people." AbGR (3:1) Spr-Sum 72, p. 21.
"tropical topic." AbGR (3:1) Spr-Sum 72, p. 15.

3304 VAZAKAS, Byron
"Multiple Dishonor on the Rive Gauche." NYT 4 F 72, p. 30.
"The Paris Move." NYT 17 N 72, p. 46.
"Praise Be, Chartres." Comm (96:13) 2 Je 72, p. 312.
"Tableaux for M. Daguerre." Nat (214:13) 27 Mr 72, p. 410.

3305 VEBLEN, Peter
"Salmon." Isthmus (1) Spr 72, p. 46.

3306 VEGA, Janine Pommy
"Poem to the Viking Warrior Angel." Magazine (5) part 9, 72, p. 28.

3307 VEITCH, Tom
"Three Poems." UnmOx (1:3) Sum 72, p. 35.

3308 VELA, Richard R.
"Blue Animals." Epos (23:3) Spr 72, p. 14.
"Elegy: For a Son." St. AR (1:4) Spr-Sum 72, p. 39.
"To That Man Who Thought He Saw a Vision of the Virgin Mary Naked in the Rio Grande." SouthernPR (12:2) Spr 72, p. 5.

3309 VELDE, William
"Barnum & Co." NoAmR (257:2) Sum 72, p. 37.

3310 VELLA, Michael
"Exorcism." Isthmus (1) Spr 72, p. 53.

3311 VELTRI, George
"I've Got a Fan in my Closet." NewYQ (12) Aut 72, p. 95.

3312 VENTADOUR, Fanny
"Carved by Loss." UTR (1:1) 72, p. 26.
"No Need to Wail." Epos (24:1) Fall 72, p. 10.
"They Are Opening Hearts Like Almonds." Epos (23:3) Spr 72, p. 4.

3313 VENTERS, Travis
"The Traveler's Arrival (for Stephie)." Pan (9) 72, p. 39.

3314 VERLAINE, Paul
"Il Pleure dans Mon Coeur." NewYQ (10) Spr 72, p. 91.

3315 VERMONT, Charlie
"my muse wears contact lenses." ParisR (55) Aut 72, p. 69.

3316 VERNON, John
"The Bodies Under Poems." PoetryNW (13:1) Spr 72, p. 37.
"The Green Children." PoetryNW (13:1) Spr 72, p. 38.
"We Are All One." PoetryNW (13:1) Spr 72, p. 38.
"Winter Morning." Cafe (4) Fall 72, p. 32.

3317 VERRET, Cathy
"i want out so bad." Drag (3:1) Spr 72, p. 76.

3318 VESAAS, Halldis Moren
"The Birds" (tr. by F. H. König). NoAmR (257:1) Spr 72, p. 59.
"If Now Tonight--" (tr. by F. H. König). NoAmR (257:1) Spr 72, p. 58.
"The Tree" (tr. by F. H. König). NoAmR (257:1) Spr 72, p. 58.

3319 VICUÑA, Cecilia
"Forth Judgment or Ambiguities of the Universe" (tr. by Edward Oliphant). RoadAR (4:1) Spr 72, p. 13.
"Let It Be Whatever It Is" (tr. by Edward Oliphant). RoadAR (4:1) Spr 72, p. 15.
"Manner in which I Discovered the Two Kinds of Death" (tr. by Edward Oliphant). RoadAR (4:1) Spr 72, p. 14.
"Obscenities of a Sunflower" (tr. by Edward Oliphant).

RoadAR (4:1) Spr 72, p. 16.
"Self-Portrait" (tr. by Edward Oliphant). RoadAR (4:1) Spr 72, p. 13.

3320 VIDAVER, Doris
from Manuscripts & Tapestries: "Before a Drawing by the Young Buonarrotti." LitR (16:1) Aut 72, p. 19.
from Manuscripts & Tapestries: "Renoir Etching, Presented." LitR (16:1) Aut 72, p. 18.
from Vita Brevis: "Old Chess Players, Seated." LitR (16:1) Aut 72, p. 16.
from Vita Brevis: "On Separation." LitR (16:1) Aut 72, p. 17.
from Vita Brevis: "Prophecy." LitR (16:1) Aut 72, p. 14.
from Vita Brevis: "The Reaper." LitR (16:1) Aut 72, p. 15.

3321 VIEIRA, John
"A Dream That Knows No Waking." AriD (1:3) Spr 72, p. 27.
"Poem: On a frozen." AriD (1:3) Spr 72, p. 26.

3322 VIERECK, Alexis
"Accident (for Bill Mullen)." Poetry (119:6) Mr 72, p. 330.

3323 VIERECK, Peter
"The Applewood Ballad." NewYQ (11) Sum 72, p. 45.

3324 VIGEE, Claude
"Three Poems." SouthernR (8:2) Spr 72, p. 428.

3325 VILHJALMSSON, Thor
"The Blue Horses" (tr. by Frederic Will). AriD (1:3) Spr 72, p. 31.

3326 VILLANO, Bob
"dreams." Cord (1:3) 72, p. 14.
"The 5th at Aqueduct" ($2 to win on Gross Deception). Cord (1:3) 72, p. 10.
"the plan." Cord (1:3) 72, p. 12.
"the steel ball (was not alive in 1935)." Cord (1:3) 72, p. 16.

3327 VILLASEÑOR, Laura
"Adam" (tr. of José Gorostiza). Mund (5:3) 72, p. 11.
"At Sea Level" (tr. of Marco Antonio Montes De Oca). Mund (5:3) 72, p. 61.
"From the Thwarted Poem" (tr. of José Gorostiza). Mund (5:3) 72, p. 7.
"Light in Readiness" (tr. of Marco Antonio Montes De Oca). Mund (5:3) 72, p. 63.

"Mirror No" (tr. of José Gorostiza). Mund (5:3) 72, p. 13.

3328 VINCENT, Stephen
from Elevator Landscapes: "Fifteen." HangL (16) Wint 71-72, p. 50.
from Elevator Landscapes: "Five." HangL (16) Wint 71-72, p. 49.
from Elevator Landscapes: "Twelve." HangL (16) Wint 71-72, p. 49.
from Elevator Landscapes: "0." HangL (16) Wint 71-72, p. 51.
from The Movie Poems: "In the movie I'm as old." Isthmus (1) Spr 72, p. 43.
from The Movie Poems: "In the movie in hell there are no acts." Isthmus (1) Spr 72, p. 43.

3329 VINZ, Mark
"Detour: North Dakota, Heading East." Nat (214:1) 3 Ja 72, p. 23.
"If There Were Something There." SoDakR (10:3) Aut 72, p. 86.
"Love Poem: The Way Back." SoDakR (10:3) Aut 72, p. 86.
"September Poem." SoDakR (10:3) Aut 72, p. 86.

3330 VITIELLO, Justin
"Bars" (tr. of Nicholas Guillen). PoetL (67:3) Aut 72, p. 265.
"Cane" (tr. of Nicholas Guillen). GreenR (2:3) 72, p. 54.
"Madrigal" (tr. of Nicholas Guillen). PoetL (67:3) Aut 72, p. 265.
"The New Woman" (tr. of Nicholas Guillen). PoetL (67:3) Aut 72, p. 264.
"Two Children" (tr. of Nicholas Guillen). PoetL (67:3) Aut 72, p. 264.
"West Indies Ltd." (tr. of Nicholas Guillen). GreenR (2:3) 72, p. 42.

3331 VLIET, R. G.
"Dogs Countless as Stars." Kayak (30) D 72, p. 32.
"The Shade." Kayak (30) D 72, p. 32.
"Sometimes I Think I Am an Elemental Angel." Field (7) Fall 72, p. 23.

3332 VOELKER, David
"5 Overs." WindO (10) Sum 72, p. 36.

3333 VOGELSANG, Arthur
"Dolly Out." KanQ (4:2) Spr 72, p. 71.

3334 VOIGT, Ellen Bryant
"American at Auschwitz." ColQ (21:1) Sum 72, p. 18.

"Animal Study." SewanR (80:2) Spr 72, p. 269.
"Claiming Kin." Iowa (3:4) Fall 72, p. 29.
"Delilah." SewanR (80:2) Spr 72, p. 270.
"Farm Wife." Iowa (3:4) Fall 72, p. 28.
"There Is Something I Should Say Before You Go." ColQ (21:1) Sum 72, p. 20.

3335 VONASCH, Patricia
"Days." NowestR (12:2) Spr 72, p. 82.

3336 Von ENDE, Frederick
"Creative Writing Assignment #3: The Shakespearean Sonnet." SatireN (9:2) Spr 72, p. 146.

3337 VOSE, Julia
"this woman looks familiar." Isthmus (1) Spr 72, p. 38.
"Unmoney My Love." Isthmus (1) Spr 72, p. 39.

3338 VOSIK, Tom
"To Someone Nameless." Poetry (121:1) O 72, p. 35.

3339 VOZNESENSKY, Andrei
"Be a Good Beaver" (tr. by Theodore Shabad). NYT 31 D 72, sec. 4, p. 9.
"An Ironical Elegy Born in Those Most Distressing Moments When ... One Cannot Write" (tr. by William Jay Smith and Nicholas Fersen). NewRep (167:19) 18 N 72, p. 31.
"It Doesn't Get Written" (tr. by Robin Fulton). Stand (13:2) 72, p. 49.

3340 VRANAS, Nikos
"On the Edge of a Bridge" (tr. by John Fludas and Stuart Silverman). AriD (1:4/5) Sum-Aut 72, p. 116.

3341 WADE, Grace
"Storms." HiramPoR (13) Fall-Wint 72, p. 16.

3342 WADE, John
"Narrower." SoDakR (10:4) Wint 72-73, p. 6.
"November Blues." SoDakR (10:4) Wint 72-73, p. 6.
"Report." SoDakR (10:4) Wint 72-73, p. 6.
"Ringmore." ExpR (2) Wint-Spr 72, p. 39.
"Up North." WindO (11) Aut 72, p. 46.
"View." SoDakR (10:4) Wint 72-73, p. 6.

3343 WADE, Seth
"The Boa" (tr. of Andres Eloy Blanco). Drag (3:1) Spr 72, p. 77.

3344 WAGNER, D. R.
"Always the light, always." Meas (2) 72.
"It Always Sounds Different to Me." Meas (2) 72.

"A Sonata for Bears." Cord (1:3) 72, p. 1.

3345 WAGNER, Mary
"The city of my dreams." Isthmus (1) Spr 72, p. 16.
"Iris love is blue love." Isthmus (1) Spr 72, p. 16.

3346 WAGONER, David
"The Beautiful Disorder" (arr. from the Notebooks of Theodore Roethke, 1954-1963). Peb (8) Spr 72, p. 26.
"The Burning Bush." Poetry (120:4) Jl 72, p. 196.
"Dust Devil." Poetry (120:4) Jl 72, p. 194.
"Elegy for a Woman Who Remembered Everything." NewRep (166:24) 10 Je 72, p. 23.
"Muse." Poetry (120:4) Jl 72, p. 196.
"Prayer." Poetry (120:4) Jl 72, p. 197.
"Raging." OhioR (13:3) Spr 72, p. 55.
"Tachycardia at the Foot of the Fifth Green." OhioR (13:3) Spr 72, p. 54.
"A Touch of the Mother." Peb (6) Sum 71.
"Worms." Poetry (120:4) Jl 72, p. 196.

3347 WAHLE, F. Keith
"First Snow in Cedar Rapids, Iowa." WindO (10) Sum 72, p. 37.
"Portrait." WindO (9) Spr 72, p. 22.
"A Small Town." WindO (10) Sum 72, p. 37.

3348 WAINWRIGHT, Jeffrey
"The Migrant from England." Stand (13:4) 72, p. 4.

3349 WAITKINS, Ray
"Sad Writer." UnmOx (1:1) N 71, p. 47.

3350 WAKOSKI, Diane
"Beyond the Wall Covered With Morning Glories." Nat (215:15) 13 N 72, p. 476.
"Her Throat." Iron (1) Spr 72, p. 39.
"I Am the Daughter of the Sun--" Cim (21) O 72, p. 8.
"I Have Had to Learn to Live With My Face." Cosmo (172:2) F 72, p. 104.
"Love Letter Postmarked Van Beethoven." Cosmo (173:4) O 72, p. 217.
"The Marshall." UnmOx (1:1) N 71, p. 13.
"Offering to Trade Lives With the Clam." Cim (21) O 72, p. 9.
"Poem Dressed In a White Baggy Suit." Iron (1) Spr 72, p. 40.
from Smudging: "Anger at the Weather." UnmOx (1:2) F 72, p. 52.
from Smudging: "Ladies, Listen to Me." UnmOx (1:2) F 72, p. 49.
from Smudging: "The Empress No. 8" (to DDP). UnmOx (1:2) F 72, p. 46.

from Smudging: "Without Desolation" (to Jerome Rothenberg). UnmOx (1:2) F 72, p. 47.
"Thanking My Mother For Piano Lessons." Cosmo (172:2) F 72, p. 106.
"Transformations (for All the Imaginary Men)." Kayak (28) 72, p. 28.
"What I Want in a Husband Besides a Mustache." Cosmo (172:4) Ap 72, p. 108.
"What the Struggle Is All About." Cim (21) O 72, p. 6.
"When the Shoe Fits." Iron (1) Spr 72, p. 38.

3351 WALCOTT, Derek
"The Muse of History at Rampanalgas." NewYorker (48:36) 28 O 72, p. 36.

3352 WALD, Eva
"Littering Highways Is Unlawful." Kayak (30) D 72, p. 52.

3353 WALDEN, William
"The Signs." NYT 17 Mr 72, p. 40.

3354 WALDMAN, Anne
"Curt Flood." ParisR (53) Wint 72, p. 171.
"Holy City." Iowa (3:4) Fall 72, p. 27.

3355 WALDROP, Keith
"Business Hours" (for Austin Warren). NewYorker (48:28) 2 S 72, p. 32.

3356 WALKER, Alice
"Burial." Harp (244:1462) Mr 72, p. 73.
"For My Sister Molly." Harp (244:1462) Mr 72, p. 72.
"The Girl Who Died #1." Broad (60) Je 72.
"He Said Come." Broad (60) Je 72.
"J, My Good Friend." Broad (60) Je 72.
"Lost My Voice? of Course" (for Beanie). Broad (60) Je 72.
"Revolutionary Petunias." Broad (60) Je 72.

3357 WALKER, Biron
"The End of the Affair." Comm (95:15) 14 Ja 72, p. 352.
"Misgivings." Comm (96:18) 11 Ag 72, p. 430.
"Motel Lounge, With Blue." SewanR (80:1) Wint 72, p. 113.
"O Sancta Simplicitas." Comm (96:1) 10 Mr 72, p. 9.

3358 WALKER, David
"Ancestral Photograph (1860)." SenR (3:1) My 72, p. 61.
"The Lover: Paris, 1830." SenR (3:1) My 72, p. 60.
"Memoranda Upon War and Its Operations." Madrona (1:2) N 71, p. 14.

"Two Fragments from a Last Letter Home (September 1944)." NowestR (12:3) Aut 72, p. 39.

3359 WALKER, Kathleen D.
"Idyll IV (Vae Victis!)" SewanR (80:2) Spr 72, p. 288.

3360 WALKER, Ted
"Afterward." NewYorker (48:33) 7 O 72, p. 140.
"August." NewYorker (48:27) 26 Ag 72, p. 57.
"Letter to Barbados." NewYorker (48:8) 15 Ap 72, p. 44.
"Pig Pig." Stand (13:3) 72, p. 22.

3361 WALLACE, Robert
"The Angry Swallow." SaltCR (5:1) Wint 72.
"The Bomb." SaltCR (5:1) Wint 72.
"How Not to Write a Poem: Don't." VirQR (48:3) Sum 72, p. 402.
"Night of December 25th." SaltCR (5:1) Wint 72.
"Steps." SaltCR (5:1) Wint 72.

3362 WALLACE, Ronald
"Dream Foes." PoetL (67:3) Aut 72, p. 235.
"Exit." Qt (5:39/40) Sum-Aut 72, p. 61.
"Grannie, With Churchyard." SoDakR (10:4) Wint 72-73, p. 90.
"'The Hills Are Alive with the Sound of.'" PoetL (67:3) Aut 72, p. 257.
"In Tal-y-bont Mill." PoetL (67:3) Aut 72, p. 306.

3363 WALLACE-CRABBE, Chris
"Mark Antony." CarlMis (12:1) Fall-Wint 71-72, p. 85.

3364 WALLEGHEN, Michael Van
"Where She Lives." Iowa (3:2) Spr 72, p. 17.

3365 WALLENSTEIN, Barry
"Dream of Awaking." Humanist (32:2) Mr-Ap 72, p. 34.
"I Have Wandered Through Similar Solitudes." NYT 5 S 72, p. 36.
"A Wonderful Change." NYT 13 Ja 72, p. 30.

3366 WALSH, Chad
"The Crossroads Where the Amnesty Is Nailed." ChrC (89:13) 29 Mr 72, p. 354.
"Sapphics." NYT 19 My 72, p. 36.

3367 WALSH, Donald D.
"In You the Earth" (tr. of Pablo Neruda). Atl (229:2) F 72, p. 68.
"The Mason" (tr. of Pablo Neruda). Atl (229:2) F 72, p. 69.
"Lives" (tr. of Pablo Neruda). Nat (215:14) 6 N 72, p. 438.

"Night on the Island" (tr. of Pablo Neruda). Atl (229:2) F 72, p. 69.
"The Queen" (tr. of Pablo Neruda). Atl (229:2) F 72, p. 68.

3368 WALSH, F. O.
"One Good Out-of-Turn Deserves Another." SatEP (244:1) Spr 72, p. 102.
"Planned Husbandhood." SatEP (244:1) Spr 72, p. 102.

3369 WALSH, Michael
"XIX." Meas (2) 72.

3370 WALSH, Tom
"Bellevue." ParisR (54) Sum 72, p. 135.
"Ersatz Amour." ParisR (54) Sum 72, p. 134.

3371 WALTERS, Robert
"After the Party." GeoR (26:3) Fall 72, p. 373.
"Immortal Africanus." GeoR (26:3) Fall 72, p. 375.
"Metamorphosis." GeoR (26:3) Fall 72, p. 373.
"Old Sailor." GeoR (26:3) Fall 72, p. 374.
"Rain" (for Karen). GeoR (26:3) Fall 72, p. 376.

3372 WALTERS, Thomas N.
"After the Party." SouthernPR (12: Special Issue) 72, p. 33.
"Red River." SouthernPR (12: Special Issue) 72, p. 36.
"Viva Zapata." SouthernPR (12: Special Issue) 72, p. 34.
"William Shakespeare Hart." SouthernPR (13:1) Aut 72, p. 38.
"Wind across the Everglades." SouthernPR (12: Special Issue) 72, p. 37.
"Zorba the Greek." SouthernPR (12: Special Issue) 72, p. 35.

3373 WALTERS, Winifred Fields
"Navajo Sighs." SoDakR (10:4) Wint 72-73, p. 82.

3374 WAN Kin-lau
"Lion and Sand." Poetry (120:2) My 72, p. 75.

3375 WANG Ch'i
"Plum Flowers Are" (tr. by David Gordon). Northeast Aut-Wint 71-72, p. 3.

3376 WANG, David Rafael
"To the Tune of Ch'ing Ping Lo" (tr. of Hsin Ch'i-Chi). Drag (3:1) Spr 72, p. 80.

3377 WANGBERG, Mark
"Night." Folio (8:1) Spr 72, p. 26.
"Out of Hand." GreenR (2:2) 72, p. 23.

"Poem: Lying on a pontoon raft." GreenR (2:2) 72, p. 22.
"Sandy." GreenR (2:2) 72, p. 22.
"Smoke Fingers." Cim (19) Ap 72, p. 75.

3378 WANTLING, Wm
"there are a few things to note." Peb (9) Wint 72.

3379 WARD, Herman M.
"The Frog." NYT 5 Ja 72, p. 36.
"The Murder." NYT 16 O 72, p. 36.
"The Professional Poet." EngJ (61:4) Ap 72, p. 549.

3380 WARD, Joanne
"Poem for Women's Liberation." PoetryNW (13:2) Sum 72, p. 19.

3381 WARREN, F. Eugene
"I Am the Fierce & Drunken Father." KanQ (4:1) Wint 71-72, p. 77.
"The Prisoner's Wife." RoadAR (3:4) Wint 71-72, p. 8.

3382 WARREN, James E., Jr.
"Ego to Id" (The Secret Sharer). Conrad (3:3) 71-72, p. 36.

3383 WARREN, Robert Penn
"Natural History." NewYorker (48:6) 1 Ap 72, p. 38.
"Solipsism and Theology." NewYorker (47:50) 29 Ja 72, p. 44.

3384 WARSH, Lewis
"I Put On My Clothes." UnmOx (1:4) Aut 72.
"On Running." UnmOx (1:4) Aut 72.

3385 WARTTS, Eddie
"It Ain't Worth the Price You Pay." JnlOBP (2:16) Sum 72, p. 48.

3386 WASHINGTON, Raymond
"She." EverR (16:95) Fall 72, p. 139.

3387 WATERMAN, Andrew
"Death in the Valley." Stand (13:2) 72, p. 44.
"Man Cycling Home in Donegal." TransR (41) Wint-Spr 72, p. 141.
"The Song." Stand (13:2) 72, p. 44.

3388 WATERS, Michael
"The Chauffeur." ModernPS (3:3) 72, p. 138.

3389 WATTERLOND, Michael
"Breaking Out." SouthernR (8:1) Wint 72, p. 183.

"Summer Nights." SouthernR (8:1) Wint 72, p. 184.

3390 WATTS, Frederick David
"Amanteca." YaleLit (141:2) 71, p. 20.
"Aubade" (for Naomi S.). YaleLit (141:2) 71, p. 21.
"L'Esthetique de Deux." YaleLit (141:2) 71, p. 21.
"Forest" (for Wallace Stevens). YaleLit (141:2) 71, p. 20.

3391 WAX, Judith
"Playboy's Christmas Cards." Playb (19:12) D 72, p. 150.
"That Was the Year That Was." Playb (19:1) Ja 72, p. 101.

3392 WAYMAN, Tom
"The Axis." MassR (13:4) Aut 72, p. 539.
"The Ecology of Place" (for Paul Bryant and Benton MacKay). LittleM (6:1) Spr 72, p. 59.
"The Man With the Wrong Dreams." PoetryNW (13:2) Sum 72, p. 8.
"Night Song on Lac Simon." KanQ (4:1) Wint 71-72, p. 113.
"Unemployment." New:ACP (18) Ap 72, p. 14.
"The Uses of Love." KanQ (4:1) Wint 71-72, p. 112.
"Wayman in the Workforce: Teacher's Aide." LittleM (6:1) Spr 72, p. 58.

3393 WEALES, Gerald
"Animal Rhymes." Harp (244:1461) F 72, p. 60.

3394 WEATHERBY, Gregg
"Living In." New:ACP (18) Ap 72, p. 17.
"Terminal." Epoch (21:2) Wint 71, p. 178.

3395 WEATHERLY, Tom
"th closer to the centre." StoneD (1:1) Spr 72, p. 30.
"Maumau American Cantos" (for diane baum & gregory corso & all th poets at th fest). StoneD (1:1) Spr 72, p. 59.

3396 WEAVER, Marvin
"The Hunt." HolCrit (9:2) Je 72, p. 4.

3397 WEAVER, Roger
"The Hole in the Wind." ColEng (33:4) Ja 72, p. 480.
"The Judgement." ColEng (33:4) Ja 72, p. 480.
"Troilist Song." ColEng (33:4) Ja 72, p. 481.

3398 WEBB, Charles, Jr.
"Ego." ColQ (21:2) Aut 72, p. 186.
"End of a Flamenco Concert." Madrona (1:1) Je 71, p. 13.

"Learning to Live With It." Madrona (1:3) My 72, p. 2.
"The Swindle." SouthernPR (13:1) Aut 72, p. 51.

3399 WEBB, Harri
"Israel." TransR (42/43) Spr-Sum 72, p. 93.
"The Stone Face." TransR (42/43) Spr-Sum 72, p. 91.
"Synopsis of the Great Welsh Novel." TransR (42/43) Spr-Sum 72, p. 90.

3400 WEBB, Igor
"Marx's Grave." Stand (13:3) 72, p. 64.
"Sugar Is." Stand (13:3) 72, p. 65.

3401 WEEKS, Ramona
"The Actor." WestR (10:1) Spr 73, p. 54.
"Antarctic Farewell." WestR (10:1) Spr 73, p. 71.
"The Hairdresser." ChiTM 16 Ja 72, p. 14.

3402 WEEKS, Robert Lewis
"On Rand McNally's Shoulders." CarlMis (12:2) Spr-Sum 72, p. 131.
"On the Difficulty of Writing Poetry in Park Hill." CarlMis (12:2) Spr-Sum 72, p. 132.
"The Wind That Blows Through Me" (for Jack Beckett). CarlMis (12:2) Spr-Sum 72, p. 136.

3403 WEGELA, F.
"Windy Night." PoetL (67:1) Spr 72, p. 22.

3404 WEICK, George
"Prelude to Isis." Folio (8:1) Spr 72, p. 25.

3405 WEIDMAN, Phil
Fifteen Poems. WormR (46) 72, p. 29.

3406 WEIGEL, John A.
"I Have Heard Computers Clicking Each to Each." AAUP (58:1) Mr 72, p. 29.

3407 WEIL, Simone
"Prometheus" (tr. by William Burford). Phoenix (3:4) Aut 72, p. 92.

3408 WEINBERG, Susan A.
"Strangers in Afternoons." MedR (2:2) Wint 72, p. 63.

3409 WEINBERGER, Eliot
"Return" (tr. of Octavio Paz). Hudson (25:1) Spr 72, p. 9.

3410 WEINER, Arthur
"Apparition." Zahir (1:4/5) 72, p. 53.
"Dirge for JL." Zahir (1:4/5) 72, p. 53.

"Nightmare." Zahir (1:4/5) 72, p. 52.

3411 WEINFIELD, Henry
"The Fisherman and His Soul (after Oscar Wilde)." Poetry (119:5) F 72, p. 261.

3412 WEINGARTEN, Ann
"Day-Taste." WindO (12) Wint 72-73, p. 30.

3413 WEINGARTEN, Roger
"The Dance of Queen Elizabeth." ChiR (24:2) 72, p. 141.
"Litany." Iowa (3:2) Spr 72, p. 19.
"Norman's Tragic Encounter." ChiR (24:2) 72, p. 140.
"A Song of Youth." Iowa (3:2) Spr 72, p. 21.
"Study for the Figure of Poetry on the Ceiling of the Segnatura." Iowa (3:2) Spr 72, p. 20.
"To My Mare Harnessed to Pharoh's Chariot I Compare You, My Love." AmerR (14) 72, p. 213.
"Veni Vidi Piccolomini." Iowa (3:1) Wint 72, p. 12.
"What Are Birds Worth" (for L.D.). Iowa (3:1) Wint 72, p. 12.

3414 WEINIG, Sister Mary Anthony, SHCJ
"Of Fear and What It Is Cast Out By." SouthernHR (6:1) Wint 72, p. 72.

3415 WEINMAN, Paul
"She Walked Through the Swamp." New:ACP (19) Aut 72, p. 42.
"The Source of Cheese." New:ACP (19) Aut 72, p. 42.
"Talking." Northeast Aut-Wint 71-72, p. 42.
"Time to Take." Peb (6) Sum 71.

3416 WEISENTHAL, Morris
"Ocean." NYT 29 F 72, p. 34.

3417 WEISMAN, Richard
"Inside the Cylinder of Tribulations" (tr. of Paul Eluard). SenR (3:1) My 72, p. 13.
"Nil" (tr. of Paul Eluard). SenR (3:1) My 72, p. 14.
"The Unequalled" (tr. of Paul Eluard). SenR (3:1) My 72, p. 15.

3418 WEISMILLER, Edward
"A Common Enough Story: Featuring the Muse." AmerS (41:1) Wint 71-72, p. 63.

3419 WEISS, Theodore
"And Then." Antaeus (7) Aut 72, p. 136.
"Before the Night." Esq (78:3) S 72, p. 20.
"An Everlasting Once." Antaeus (7) Aut 72, p. 138.
"Good Luck." Antaeus (7) Aut 72, p. 140.
"Off to Patagonia." Antaeus (7) Aut 72, p. 134.

"Touchstone." Nat (214:13) 27 Mr 72, p. 406.
"Your Father's Sunday Baths." Humanist (32:3) My-Je 72, p. 43.

3420 WEISSLITZ, E. F.
"Canada Geese." BallSUF (13:1) Aut 72, p. 17.

3421 WEISSMAN, David
"Killing Time." CarolQ (24:3) Fall 72, p. 81.

3422 WEITZEL, Allen F.
"September 5." ChiTM 6 F 72, p. 12.

3423 WELBURN, Ron
"Baliophone." Works (3:3/4) Wint 72-73, p. 25.
"Capricorn Orange." Works (3:3/4) Wint 72-73, p. 25.
"Lords Taylored." JnlOBP (2:16) Sum 72, p. 79.
"A Theory of Nature." Works (3:3/4) Wint 72-73, p. 24.

3424 WELCH, Don
"Rural Winters." SaltCR (5:1) Wint 72.
"To a Student in a Psychiatric Hospital." PoetL (67:3) Aut 72, p. 219.

3425 WELCH, James
"Directions to the Nomad." AmerR (14) 72, p. 114.
"Dreaming with Others." UnicornJ (4) 72, p. 34.
"Laughing in the Belly." UnicornJ (4) 72, p. 36.
"Talking Night Again up the Rattlesnake" (for Lois). UnicornJ (4) 72, p. 35.
"Weekend Trip to the Big Hole Country." UnicornJ (4) 72, p. 37.

3426 WELDEN, Oliver
"The Apostate" (tr. by Edward Oliphant). RoadAR (4:1) Spr 72, p. 50.
"Bitacora" (tr. by Edward Oliphant). RoadAR (4:1) Spr 72, p. 48.
"The Chicken Pieces Are" (tr. by Edward Oliphant). RoadAR (4:1) Spr 72, p. 48.
"Fluctuations" (tr. by Edward Oliphant). RoadAR (4:1) Spr 72, p. 50.
"Vital Axiom" (tr. by Edward Oliphant). RoadAR (4:1) Spr 72, p. 49.
"Warning" (tr. by Edward Oliphant). RoadAR (4:1) Spr 72, p. 49.

3427 WELLES, Lauri
"The moon tugs at the skin of night." Drag (3:1) Spr 72, p. 24.

3428 WEST, John Foster
"Hill Hunger." NoCaFo (20:4) N 72, p. 158.

"Totem." <u>SouthernPR</u> (12:2) Spr 72, p. 26.

3429 WEST, Thomas
"A Diagnosis." <u>Zahir</u> (1:4/5) 72, p. 59.

3430 WEST, Thomas A., Jr.
"Ant Farm." <u>Works</u> (3:3/4) Wint 72-73, p. 126.
"Stamp Collection." <u>PoetL</u> (67:2) Sum 72, p. 163.
"To the Rifle Range." <u>PoetL</u> (67:2) Sum 72, p. 163.
"We Lean Against Night Trees." <u>PoetL</u> (67:2) Sum 72, p. 164.
"The Woodcock's Call." <u>PoetL</u> (67:2) Sum 72, p. 144.

3431 WESTBROOK, N. A.
"Poem: a haze has fallen." <u>SouthernPR</u> (12:2) Spr 72, p. 47.

3432 WESTBURG, Barry
"In Des Moines." <u>Epoch</u> (21:2) Wint 71, p. 141.
"Yes and No." <u>Epoch</u> (21:2) Wint 71, p. 140.

3433 WESTERFIELD, Nancy G.
"A Novice Raped in the Convent Orchards of Mary Reparatrix." <u>PoetL</u> (67:2) Sum 72, p. 115.
"Recovery Room." <u>ColEng</u> (33:7) Ap 72, p. 807.
"Shopping for Seaweed in an Inland City." <u>ColEng</u> (33:7) Ap 72, p. 806.

3434 WHALEN, Philip
"In the Night." <u>Spec</u> (14:1/2) My 72, p. 102.
"Minuscule Threnody." <u>Spec</u> (14:1/2) My 72, p. 102.
"The Morning in Albuquerque." <u>StoneD</u> (1:1) Spr 72, p. 36.

3435 WHEATCROFT, John
"Beauty and the Beast." <u>CarolQ</u> (24:3) Fall 72, p. 86.
"Campus Affair." <u>AAUP</u> (58:3) S 72, p. 266.
"Rut." <u>BallSUF</u> (13:1) Wint 72, p. 59.

3436 WHEELER, Raymond
"Now That You're Dead." <u>PoetL</u> (67:1) Spr 72, p. 37.
"Though We May Never Know." <u>PoetL</u> (67:1) Spr 72, p. 37.

3437 WHEELER, Richard L.
"Communication." <u>LadHJ</u> (89:7) Jl 72, p. 160.

3438 WHELTON, Clark
"On Learning That Joel Oppenheimer's Favorite World War II Fighter Plane Was the Bell P-39 Airacobra." <u>VilV</u> 21 D 72, p. 19.

3439 WHISNANT, Charleen
"When I Saw That Bald Head, I Knew I Was Innocent." St. AR (1:4) Spr-Sum 72, p. 34.

3440 WHITE, Fred D.
"The Moon Is Not the Same as NYC." NewRena (6) My 72, p. 51.

3441 WHITE, Gail Brockett
"The Brownstone Mansion Goes Down." WindO (12) Wint 72-73, p. 16.
"Camelot." St. AR (2:1) Aut-Wint 72, p. 17.
"For Karla." SoCaR (4:2) Je 72, p. 28.
"For Tom." WindO (12) Wint 72-73, p. 17.
"The Gift." PoetL (67:1) Spr 72, p. 17.
"The Historian." WindO (12) Wint 72-73, p. 17.
"The Hunt." Folio (8:1) Spr 72, p. 34.
"Intimations of Immorality." SouthernPR (12:2) Spr 72, p. 9.
"The Last Days of Sappho." St. AR (1:4) Spr-Sum 72, p. 44.
"Living with One Person." Zahir (1:4/5) 72, p. 55.
"The Manx Method." Zahir (1:4/5) 72, p. 56.
"The Marriage." Epos (24:1) Fall 72, p. 11.
"Mary of Magdala." PoetL (67:1) Spr 72, p. 18.
"May Walk." WindO (12) Wint 72-73, p. 16.
"Three Haiku." WindO (9) Spr 72, p. 5.
"Will the poem I thought of." Zahir (1:4/5) 72, p. 55.
"Written in Mississippi." ChiTM 19 N 72, p. 8.

3442 WHITE, J. P.
"At That Time." Nat (214:23) 5 Je 72, p. 734.
"Beggar." Nat (214:12) 20 Mr 72, p. 381.
"One Way." Nat (214:16) 17 Ap 72, p. 504.

3443 WHITE, James L.
"Frisbee" (for Mr. James Purdy). PraS (46:2) Sum 72, p. 142.
"Maria Conception's Child." PraS (46:3) Aut 72, p. 224.

3444 WHITE, Patrick
"Anniversary I." SouthernPR (13:1) Aut 72, p. 8.

3445 WHITE, Saundra
"Colors." JnlOBP (2:16) Sum 72, p. 36.

3446 WHITE, William M.
"Eulogy." Folio (8:1) Spr 72, p. 22.

3447 WHITEHEAD, Arlette Lees
"Caravan." PoetL (67:1) Spr 72, p. 14.

3448 WHITEHEAD, James
"After Reading Beowulf Again." HolCrit (9:2) Je 72, p. 7.

3449 WHITEHEAD, Lorita
"Divinest Syzygy." Atl (229:6) Je 72, p. 41.

3450 WHITEURS, Sandra
"It looked so good." JnlOBP (2:16) Sum 72, p. 56.
"Remember the times." JnlOBP (2:16) Sum 72, p. 56.

3451 WHITMAN, Ruth
from Apparent Death: "prologue" (tr. of Stratis Haviaras). AriD (1:4/5) Sum-Aut 72, p. 46.
"Autumn 1953" (tr. of N. D. Karouzos). AriD (1:4/5) Sum-Aut 72, p. 72.
"By Command" (tr. of Nikos Karachalios). AriD (1:4/5) Sum-Aut 72, p. 59.
"The Cafe" (tr. of Miltos Sachtouris). AriD (1:4/5) Sum-Aut 72, p. 91.
"Chronicle" (tr. of Miltos Sachtouris). AriD (1:4/5) Sum-Aut 72, p. 89.
"The Crippled Dog" (tr. of Dimitris Doukaris). AriD (1:4/5) Sum-Aut 72, p. 38.
"The Drowned Man" (tr. of Miltos Sachtouris). AriD (1: 4/5) Sum-Aut 72, p. 90.
"Greece, Spring 1967" (tr. of Stratis Haviaras). AriD (1:4/5) Sum-Aut 72, p. 47.
"The Gypsy and the Man in the Black Hat" (tr. of Stratis Haviaras). AriD (1:4/5) Sum-Aut 72, p. 47.
"Laying a Fire." NewRep (167:11) 23 S 72, p. 25.
"The Little Tree" (tr. of Jacob Glatstein). Nat (215:13) 30 O 72, p. 411.
"I Live Close" (tr. of Miltos Sachtouris). AriD (1:4/5) Sum-Aut 72, p. 91.
"Ikon" (tr. of N. D. Karouzos). AriD (1:4/5) Sum-Aut 72, p. 74.
"Krypteria" (tr. of Dimitris Doukaris). AriD (1:4/5) Sum-Aut 72, p. 38.
"The Mouse" (tr. of Miltos Sachtouris). AriD (1:4/5) Sum-Aut 72, p. 92.
"A Pantoum for Chamber Music in Early December." ChiTM 13 F 72, p. 12.
"The Passion of Lizzie Borden." MassR (13:1/2) Wint-Spr 72, p. 151.
"Photographs" (tr. of Dimitris Doukaris). AriD (1:4/5) Sum-Aut 72, p. 36.
"Poetry" (tr. of Stratis Haviaras). AriD (1:4/5) Sum-Aut 72, p. 49.
"Reincarnation" (tr. of Stratis Haviaras). AriD (1:4/5) Sum-Aut 72, p. 48.
"Return" (tr. of Stratis Haviaras). AriD (1:4/5) Sum-Aut 72, p. 48.

"She Who Was Coming" (tr. of Miltos Sachtouris). AriD (1:4/5) Sum-Aut 72, p. 92.
"Sparrows" (tr. of Miltos Sachtouris). AriD (1:4/5) Sum-Aut 72, p. 90.
"Translating (for Jacob Glatstein)." NewYQ (10) Spr 72, p. 95.
"Vibrations" (tr. of N. D. Karouzos). AriD (1:4/5) Sum-Aut 72, p. 71.

3452 WHITMAN, William
"Births and Deaths." Shen (24:1) Aut 72, p. 66.
"Homage to Point Reyes." BelPoJ (23:1) Fall 72, p. 6.
"The Spruce at Buzzard's Bay." BelPoJ (22:3) Spr 72, p. 21.
"That Night in My Office in a Sleeping Bag on My Desk." MassR (13:3) Sum 72, p. 408.

3453 WHITMER, Martin Linwood
"May 8, 1972." ChrC (89:21) 24 My 72, p. 596.

3454 WHITNER, Banta
"Forest." CarolQ (24:1) Wint 72, p. 57.

3455 WHITTEMORE, Reed
"Money." NewRep (166:3) 15 Ja 72, p. 26.
"Ode to New York." NewRep (166:11) 11 Mr 72, p. 20.
"Oh There You Are!" NewRep (166:25) 17 Je 72, p. 30.
"The Washington Rag-Time After-Election Gloom-Doom Stomp." NewRep (167:19) 18 N 72, p. 34.

3456 WHITWORTH, Tom
"She the Wall." Drag (3:1) Spr 72, p. 75.
"Stately Ant." Drag (3:1) Spr 72, p. 75.

3457 WHYATT, Frances
"Path (for Toni in memoriam ... 'Why?')." Nat (214:17) 24 Ap 72, p. 534.
"Seeding the Thunder or I Dream of Cowboys" (for Diane Wakoski). SouthernPR (13:1) Aut 72, p. 36.

3458 WIATER, Michael
"For Joanne." Meas (2) 72.
"'M. F. W. '--1." Meas (2) 72.
"Sleep Walker." Meas (2) 72.

3459 WIBKING, Gladys
"Song to the Mountain." PoetL (67:3) Aut 72, p. 246.

3460 WICHERN, Angie
"Balloon." WindO (9) Spr 72, p. 40.

3461 WICHERN, Dana
"Love Poem." WindO (10) Sum 72, p. 13.

3462 WICKERT, Max
"Aubade." Poetry (119:4) Ja 72, p. 219.
"Nocturne." Poetry (119:4) Ja 72, p. 218.

3463 WICKLUND, Millie Mae
"The Set." Cafe (4) Fall 72, p. 20.

3464 WIDIGEN, Michiko
"A Bladesmith" (tr. of Kotaro Takamura). Madrona (1:1) Je 71, p. 18.

3465 WIDMER, Kingsley
"Drumming Above (after Corbière's Toit)." Meas (2) 72.

3466 WIEBE, Dallas
"The Loneliness of the German Barber." SouthernPR (12:2) Spr 72, p. 42.

3467 WIEGNER, Kathleen
"Summer Night." MinnR (3) Aut 72, p. 99.
Ten Poems. Northeast Aut-Wint 71-72, p. 23.

3468 WIKKRAMASINHA, Lakdhas
"Discarded Tins." Madrona (1:1) Je 71, p. 23.
"Hanging Man." Madrona (1:1) Je 71, p. 27.
"News." Madrona (1:1) Je 71, p. 22.
"The Poet." Madrona (1:1) Je 71, p. 22.

3469 WILBUR, Frederick
"Susan's Window." Shen (23:4) Sum 72, p. 78.

3470 WILBUR, Richard
"The Mind-Reader." NewYRB (19:1) 20 Jl 72, p. 29.
"A Wedding Toast." AmerS (41:4) Aut 72, p. 558.

3471 WILCHINS, Howard M.
"Dirge for Jimmy." PoetL (67:4) Wint 72, p. 367.

3472 WILD, Peter
"Angel." Peb (7) Aut 71.
"The Biographer." Wind (2:6) Aut 72, p. 57.
"Bonifacio." Meas (1) 71.
"The Buffalo." NoAmR (257:3) Aut 72, p. 45.
"The Buffalo." Poetry (120:4) Jl 71, p. 202.
"Cities." Peb (7) Aut 71.
"The Cobbler." PraS (46:4) Wint 72-73, p. 320.
"Displacement." FreeL (15:1/2) 71-72, p. 99.
"A Drought for the New Pilots." PraS (46:1) Spr 72, p. 18.
"The Eskimo Mask." MinnR (2) Spr 72, p. 78.
"The Fathers." GreenR (2:2) 72, p. 27.
"For Judy Jukowski." Epoch (21:2) Wint 71, p. 136.
"Going to Sleep With Your Rings On." Cord (1:3) 72,

p. 28.
"In China." MinnR (2) Spr 72, p. 77.
"Invasion." MinnR (2) Spr 72, p. 76.
"The Martyrs." LittleM (6:2/3) Sum-Aut 72, p. 125.
"Monologue." PraS (46:1) Spr 72, p. 17.
"Nalgas Paradas." Wind (2:6) Aut 72, p. 57.
Nine Poems. Cord (1:3) 72, p. 27.
"Outlaws in North America." WormR (48) 72, p. 121.
"Outposts." GreenR (2:2) 72, p. 27.
"Peluca." WormR (48) 72, p. 120.
"Pescuezo." UnmOx (1:1) N 71, p. 4.
"Poem: There are no medals for loneliness." Poetry (120:4) Jl 72, p. 201.
"Pollen." ChiR (23:4 & 24:1) 72, p. 31.
"The Prince." PraS (46:4) Wint 72-73, p. 321.
"The Princess and the Frog." LittleM (6:1) Spr 72, p. 8.
"Quotient." Qt (5:37) Wint 72, p. 21.
"Ranch." UnmOx (1:2) F 72, p. 32.
"Recrimination." Epoch (21:2) Wint 71, p. 137.
"Relationship." FreeL (15:1/2) 71-72, p. 98.
"Relief." Folio (8:2) Fall 72, p. 14.
"Salvation." MinnR (2) Spr 72, p. 75.
"Santa Teresas." Iron (1) Spr 72, p. 65.
"Saturday Night." HiramPoR (12) Spr-Sum 72, p. 26.
"The Season." PraS (46:1) Spr 72, p. 19.
"Sleeping." Qt (5:39/40) Sum-Aut 72, p. 40.
"Soap." Qt (5:39/40) Sum-Aut 72, p. 39.
"The Stamp." LittleM (6:2/3) Sum-Aut 72, p. 125.
"Status." UnmOx (1:1) N 71, p. 5.
"Sun." PraS (46:4) Wint 72-73, p. 319.
"Telephone Man." UnmOx (1:2) F 72, p. 33.
Ten Poems. Zahir (1:4/5) 72, p. 17.
"The Tortured Man." ChiR (23:4 & 24:1) 72, p. 30.

3473 WILDE, Heather
"how do i/we know where we/i started. where." NewL (39:1) Aut 72, p. 108.
"I Know From Experience..." NewL (39:1) Aut 72, p. 109.
"I Told You So." NewL (39:1) Aut 72, p. 109.
"Loving Mother." NewL (39:1) Aut 72, p. 110.
"Making a Pair of Scissors." NewL (39:1) Aut 72, p. 109.
"Silent Day for Rocks." NewL (39:1) Aut 72, p. 108.
"Tuesday." NewL (39:1) Aut 72, p. 109.

3474 WILDER, Amos N.
"Aquarius--Christian Style." ChrC (89:46) 20 D 72, p. 1292.

3475 WILDMAN, John Hazard
"Precisely Imprecise." NYT 19 Mr 72, sec. 4, p. 14.

3476 WILKINSON, Constance Elena
"Margarita, La Infanta." Aphra (3:1) Wint 71-72, p. 27.

3477 WILKINSON, R. T.
"for a moment." Drag (3:2) Sum 72, p. 37.
"I know the names of all the stars." Drag (3:2) Sum 72, p. 37.

3478 WILL, Frederic
"The Blue Horses" (tr. of Thor Vilhjálmsson). AriD (1:3) Spr 72, p. 31.
"Catechism." ChiR (24:2) 72, p. 134.
"Dawn." ChiR (24:2) 72, p. 134.
"Frozen Foods." MinnR (2) Spr 72, p. 79.
"Hands." ChiR (24:2) 72, p. 135.
"In Slovakia." SouthwR (57:3) Sum 72, p. 188.
"A Little Brandy." MinnR (2) Spr 72, p. 80.
"O Pioneers." MinnR (2) Spr 72, p. 80.
"Summer." KanQ (4:1) Wint 71-72, p. 66.
"Swimming." CarlMis (12:1) Fall-Wint 71-72, p. 84.
"Two Flowing Away Poems." AntR (32:1/2) Spr-Sum 72, p. 92.

3479 WILLARD, Nancy
"Angels Shade Vida." Kayak (30) D 72, p. 34.
"A Speech for the Unborn." AntR (31:4) Wint 71-72, p. 493.
"Tigers Shake Up Pitchers Again." Kayak (30) D 72, p. 35.

3480 WILLEMS, J. Rutherford
"Notes on a Poem from Missouri." Isthmus (1) Spr 72, p. 29.

3481 WILLEY, Wilbur
"Color." EngJ (61:1) Ja 72, p. 27.

3482 WILLIAMS, C. K.
"Claws (from the Sanskrit of MAYURA)." Poetry (120:6) S 72, p. 354.
"The Little Shirt." Iron (1) Spr 72, p. 5.
"Then the Brother of the Wind." Iron (1) Spr 72, p. 6.

3483 WILLIAMS, Charles W.
"Persons." EngJ (61:4) Ap 72, p. 507.

3484 WILLIAMS, Dennis
"A Riddle: What Am I." Madrona (1:2) N 71, p. 2.

3485 WILLIAMS, Evan Gwyn
"Submerged Tree Stumps: Ynys Las." TransR (42/43) Spr-Sum 72, p. 94.
"Swansea Valley 1971." Stand (14:1) 72, p. 5.

3486 WILLIAMS, Helen
"Alpine Meadow." DenQuart (7:3) Aut 72, p. 41.
"For My Father." DenQuart (7:3) Aut 72, p. 40.

3487 WILLIAMS, Herbert
"Depopulation." TransR (42/43) Spr-Sum 72, p. 95.

3488 WILLIAMS, John Stuart
"Break." TransR (42/43) Spr-Sum 72, p. 96.

3489 WILLIAMS, Liz
"Why I Stay." Cosmo (172:6) Je 72, p. 62.

3490 WILLIAMS, Michael
"A Mad King Weeps the Loss of His Son." SouthernPR (13:1) Aut 72, p. 8.

3491 WILLIAMS, Miller
"I Fulfill My Patriotic Duty" (tr. of Nicanor Parra). Atl (229:3) Mr 72, p. 81.
"I Go Out of the House for the First Time." MedR (2:3) Spr 72, p. 89.
"Inflation" (tr. of Nicanor Parra). Atl (229:3) Mr 72, p. 81.
"The Rule of Three" (tr. of Nicanor Parra). Atl (229:3) Mr 72, p. 81.
"Seven" (tr. of Nicanor Parra). Atl (229:3) Mr 72, p. 81.
"Song To Pass Around the Hat" (tr. of Nicanor Parra). BerksR (8:1) Spr 72, p. 5.
"A Toast to Floyd Collins." PoetryNW (13:3) Aut 72, p. 40.

3492 WILLIAMS, O. S.
"Paw Paw Woman." Folio (8:2) Fall 72, p. 38.
"The Pottery." Folio (8:2) Fall 72, p. 38.

3493 WILLIAMS, Paul
"A Favorite Honey Locust." KanQ (4:3) Sum 72, p. 73.
"Hip Scotch." Phoenix (3:4) Aut 72, p. 101.
"It Used to be Simple." KanQ (4:3) Sum 72, p. 74.

3494 WILLIAMS, Thomas
"Giraffe." Harp (245:1469) O 72, p. 135.
"The Ice Fisherman." Harp (245:1469) O 72, p. 135.
"Twentieth Anniversary Love Poem." AmerR (14) 72, p. 95.

3495 WILLIAMS, Ursula Vaughan
"'Ainsi Le Bon Temps Regrettons...'." Antaeus (5) Spr 72, p. 111.
"Geriatric Ward." Antaeus (5) Spr 72, p. 112.
"Man Without Myth." Antaeus (5) Spr 72, p. 109.

"The Prisoner." Antaeus (5) Spr 72, p. 110.
"What was the kingdom?" Antaeus (5) Spr 72, p. 113.

3496 WILLIAMS, William Carlos
"Proof of Immortality." Poetry (121:1) O 72, p. 38.

3497 WILLIAMSON, Alan
"C., Again." NewYorker (47:48) 15 Ja 72, p. 27.
"The First Spring Nights." Poetry (119:5) F 72, p. 252.
"Temporary Earth." Poetry (119:5) F 72, p. 253.
"Two Faces." PoetryNW (13:3) Aut 72, p. 34.
"War in the Valley of Vision: Christmas 1967." VirQR (48:1) Wint 72, p. 52.

3498 WILLIAMSON, Peter
"The Condor." NYT 29 S 72, p. 42.
"Shrunken River, with Owls." NYT 30 D 72, p. 20.

3499 WILLIS, B. Tolson
"A Drowning." BallSUF (13:3) Sum 72, p. 31.

3500 WILSON, Emily Herring
"Blue Ridge and Louisiana." SouthernPR (13:1) Aut 72, p. 46.

3501 WILSON, Graeme
"Approach to Haneda." NYT 9 Ja 72, sec. 4, p. 16.
"At a Malaysian Wedding." DenQuart (6:4) Wint 72, p. 33.
"Bottles" (tr. of Hagiwara Sakatarō). DenQuart (6:4) Wint 72, p. 35.
"Corpse and Bamboo" (tr. of Hagiwara Sakutarō). DenQuart (6:4) Wint 72, p. 35.
"Joke for Ghosts." DenQuart (6:4) Wint 72, p. 34.
"Letter" (After Li Shang-lin, 813-858). NYT 6 S 72, p. 44.
"Loneliness" (tr. of Guchi Daigaku). DenQuart (7:3) Aut 72, p. 48.
"Penitentiary" (tr. of Hagiwara Sakutarō). AmerS (41:3) Sum 72, p. 363.
"Rainer Maria Rilke." NYT 24 Mr 72, p. 40.
"A Small Anthology of Modern Japanese Poetry" (tr. by Graeme Wilson). DenQuart (7:2) Sum 72, pp. 46-54.
"Snowdrop." NYT 26 My 72, p. 34.
"Toy Box: Evening" (tr. of Hagiwara Sakutarō). DenQuart (6:4) Wint 72, p. 36.
"Useless Book" (tr. of Hagiwara Sakutarō). DenQuart (6:4) Wint 72, p. 36.
"Waiting" (tr. from the Manyoshu). NYT 7 Ag 72, p. 26.
"White Night" (tr. of Hagiwara Sakutarō). AmerS (41:3) Sum 72, p. 364.
"Yeats." DenQuart (6:4) Wint 72, p. 33.
"Yeats." NYT 23 F 72, p. 40.

3502 WILSON, Keith
"Ashore." Meas (2) 72.
"Blue Star on the Horizon." Meas (2) 72.
"viii." Drag (3:1) Spr 72, p. 48.
"The Evokation." ExpR (3) Fall-Wint 72/73, p. 28.
"In Silence, In Corewood Holiness." ExpR (2) Wint-Spr 72, p. 4.
"Lincoln County, New Mexico." EverR (16:95) Fall 72, p. 96.
"Memory of a Victory." Peb (9) Wint 72.
"Mexico: By the Train Station " ExpR (3) Fall-Wint 72/73, p. 29.
"New Mexico II." ExpR (2) Wint-Spr 72, p. 6.
"The Ring of Annapolis." ExpR (2) Wint-Spr 72, p. 7.
"vi." Drag (3:1) Spr 72, p. 47.

3503 WILSON, Robley, Jr.
"War." NewYorker (48:4) 18 Mr 72, p. 44.

3504 WILSON, William J.
"The Sunshine State." Folio (8:1) Spr 72, p. 59.

3505 WINKLER, David
"Athens to Memphis--and Back Again." Wind (2:5) Sum 72, p. 30.
"Evil." Wind (2:6) Aut 72, p. 37.

3506 WINKLER, J. S.
"On the Eastern Front." SouthernPR (13:1) Aut 72, p. 49.

3507 WINN, O. Howard
"A Child's Garden." WindO (10) Sum 72, p. 25.
"I Was Sitting on a Mountain." Epoch (22:1) Fall 72, p. 34.
"Metamorphosis." Etc. (29:2) Je 72, p. 188.
"Song to the Best of the Hydrogen Bomb." FreeL (15: 1/2) 71-72, p. 67.

3508 WINSLOW, Pete
"Burning Submarines." Sky (1:1) 71.
from A Daisy in the Memory of a Shark: "The earth is playing the role of nursemaid of young owls." New:ACP (18) Ap 72, p. 7.
from A Daisy in the Memory of a Shark: "Three poems." HangL (18) Fall 72, p. 51.
"Doors Clanging Shut in the Cells of the Body." HangL (16) Wint 71-72, p. 52.
"Emergency Kisses." St. AR (2:1) Aut-Wint 72, p. 27.
"How Like a Whore." St. AR (1:4) Spr-Sum 72, p. 28.
"Insomnia." Sky (1:1) 71.
"Kicking Against the Pricks." St. AR (1:4) Spr-Sum 72, p. 79.

"Medical Dental Poem." HangL (16) Wint 71-72, p. 53.

3509 WITHERUP, William
"Fort Ord: My Lai: Wounded Knee." Madrona (1:1) Je 71, p. 21.
"I Go Dreaming Roads" (tr. of Antonio Machado, w. Carmen Scholis). Madrona (1:3) My 72, p. 16.
"Upstairs in the Education Wing." Madrona (1:1) Je 71, p. 19.
"Soledad: 9/12/70." GreenR (2:2) 72, p. 30.

3510 WITT, Harold
"Barbie." NewL (39:1) Aut 72, p. 84.
"Brand X." SouthernPR (13:1) Aut 72, p. 41.
"Bubbles." PoetryNW (13:1) Sum 72, p. 16.
"Catalina." PoetL (67:4) Wint 72, p. 364.
"Dr. Earl Blood, the Painless Dentist." Peb (6) Sum 71.
"Dressed for an Occasion." PoetL (67:3) Aut 72, p. 224.
"Elementary Education." Peb (6) Sum 71.
"Golden Gloves." PoetryNW (13:4) Wint 72-73, p. 35.
"The Harpsichord." NYT 11 N 72, p. 32.
"Helen Payne, Spotter." PoetryNW (13:2) Sum 72, p. 15.
"Henna Vinal, Birdwatcher." PoetryNW (13:2) Sum 72, p. 15.
"House." NYT 6 Mr 72, p. 32.
"Margo Martine, Studio of the Dance." WindO (10) Sum 72, p. 28.
"Miss Dancey." Northeast Aut-Wint 71-72, p. 49.
"Moment in a Garden." PoetL (67:4) Wint 72, p. 363.
"Next Door." Drag (3:1) Spr 72, p. 38.
"Point Lobos." PoetL (67:4) Wint 72, p. 362.
"Stellar's Jay." NYT 19 Ap 72, p. 46.
"Uncles in the Orchard." Peb (6) Sum 71.
from Winesburg by the Sea: "Chest 46", Waist 32", Biceps 18"." WindO (12) Wint 72-73, p. 18.
from Winesburg by the Sea: "Later." Drag (3:1) Spr 72, p. 37.
from Winesburg by the Sea: "Mrs. Nice at the Talkies." ConcPo (5:1) Spr 72, p. 34.
from Winesburg by the Sea: "Out of a Seasleep." Wind (2:6) Aut 72, p. 13.
from Winesburg by the Sea: "Percy Tilg, Mortician." Northeast Sum 72, p. 14.
from Winesburg by the Sea: "Those Times When Richard Bathelmess Went Up." Wind (2:6) Aut 72, p. 13.

3511 WITTENBERG, Rudolf
"Last Night I Hated the Smell." Nat (215:3) 7 Ag 72, p. 90.

3512 WITTIG, Monique
"From Les Guérillères." Aphra (3:1) Wint 71-72, p. 41.

3513 WOESSNER, Warren
"The Butterflies Return." HangL (17) Sum 72, p. 64.
"A Gesture." Meas (2) 72.
"Heard in Galena, Illinois." New:ACP (19) Aut 72, p. 21.

3514 WOIWODE, L.
"Watch the Wind." Atl (230:4) O 72, p. 85.

3515 WOLF, H. R.
"To a Mountain Girl 3 (for M.S.: 1940-1962). Pan (9) 72, p. 49.
"To a Mountain Girl 2 (for E.)." Pan (9) 72, p. 48.

3516 WOLF, Manfred
"Three Poems" (tr. of Claude Vigée, w. Melinda Rosenthal). SouthernR (8:2) Spr 72, p. 429.

3517 WOLFE, Marianne
"Before Image Lake." Spec (14:1/2) My 72, p. 106.
"From the Inside." Spec (14:1/2) My 72, p. 104.
"Waiting." Spec (14:1/2) My 72, p. 103.

3518 WOLFERT, Adrienne
"Saga of the Slothful Soul." PoetL (67:4) Wint 72, p. 325.

3519 WOLFERT, Helen
"The Design." QRL (18:1/2) 72, p. 250.

3520 WOLPIN, Jeff
"To Nancy." Cim (19) Ap 72, p. 55.

3521 WOLTER, Richard
"A Formless Cloud in a Windless Sky." HangL (16) Wint 71-72, p. 54.

3522 WOLVEN, Fred
"After the Death of Theodore Roethke." UTR (1:2) 72, p. 24.
"Of Death's Skull." UTR (1:1) 72, p. 22.
"The Silence of Stone." UTR (1:3) 72, p. 16.
"the young tree." UTR (1:4) 72, p. 21.

3523 WONDER, S. P.
"Carrying Cattails." Epoch (21:3) Spr 72, p. 292.

3524 WOOD, George Roland
"Juvenescence." AbGR (3:1) Spr-Sum 72, p. 2.

3525 WOODARD, Charles R.
"Twelve Poems." Poem (15) Jl 72, p. 39.

3526 WOODS, Barbara Gullo
"The Senior Citizen's Night In." Cim (20) Jl 72, p. 53.

3527 WOODS, Bruce
"For a Woman I Call 'Fox'." PoetC (7:1) 72, p. 14.

3528 WOODS, Carl
"Juana." Poem (16) N 72, p. 37.
"New Beatitudes." Epos (24:1) Fall 72, p. 9.

3529 WOODS, John
from Affection for Machinery: "How clearly a spoon must think of its duties." PoetryNW (13:3) Aut 72, p. 45.
"Getting Out of Public Office." PoetryNW (13:3) Aut 72, p. 45.
"The Minutes of the Faculty Senate Meeting." PoetryNW (13:3) Aut 72, p. 44.
"Outburst from a Little Face." Field (7) Fall 72, p. 44.
"Signing Up for 1944." Field (7) Fall 72, p. 45.
"The Uncles." PoetryNW (13:3) Aut 72, p. 46.
"Werther Nights." Field (7) Fall 72, p. 42.
"Where an Old Hand Has Touched." Field (7) Fall 72, p. 43.
"You Can't Eat Poetry." PoetryNW (13:3) Aut 72, p. 44.

3530 WOODS, John A.
"Bees." Antaeus (6) Sum 72, p. 127.

3531 WOODS, Margherita
"Astronomer." Epos (24:1) Fall 72, p. 15.
"Hunger." Rend (7:1) Spr 72, p. 12.
"The Nursing Home." Rend (7:1) Spr 72, p. 52.

3532 WOODWARD, Jeff
"Lonely Hearts." WindO (11) Aut 72, p. 27.
"Nadine." WindO (11) Aut 72, p. 27.
"Poem: the morning rice boils in the flat of." WindO (10) Sum 72, back cover.

3533 WOOTEN, Anna
"Photograph." AbGR (3:1) Spr-Sum 72, p. 58.
"Stroke." AbGR (3:1) Spr-Sum 72, p. 59.

3534 WORLEY, James
"Memo from a 20th Century Truce Team." ChrC (89:41) 15 N 72, p. 1152.
"On Christmas Eve." ChrC (89:46) 20 D 72, p. 1298.
"Sweet Are the Uses." ChrC (89:16) 19 Ap 72, p. 442.

3535 WORSLEY, Alice F.
"Classroom Encounter." EngJ (61:6) S 72, p. 838.
"Taos." WestR (9:1) Spr 72, p. 22.

3536 WORTHINGTON, T. J.
"Wanderers." SouthernPR (13:1) Aut 72, p. 5.

3537 WORTMAN, Edith Powell
"Campaign in the Neck." SatEP (244:3) Aut 72, p. 89.

3538 WRIGHT, Celeste Turner
"The House That Isn't There." ArizQ (28:2) Sum 72, p. 141.

3539 WRIGHT, Charles
"Blackwater Mountain." Poetry (119:4) Ja 72, p. 215.
"Dog Creek Mainline." Poetry (120:4) Jl 72, p. 212.
"Emblems." Iowa (3:2) Spr 72, p. 11.
"The Fever Toy." Poetry (120:4) Jl 72, p. 215.
"The Grave of the Right Hand." Poetry (121:1) O 72, p. 39.
"Negatives." Poetry (120:4) Jl 72, p. 214.
"Nouns." Poetry (119:4) Ja 72, p. 216.
"The Other Side." Iowa (3:2) Spr 72, p. 10.
"Portrait of the Poet in Abraham von Werdt's Dream." Poetry (119:4) Ja 72, p. 216.
"Victory Garden." Poetry (120:6) S 72, p. 360.

3540 WRIGHT, Franz
"It's snowing in Plouda" (tr. of Erica Pedretti). Field (7) Fall 72, p. 41.

3541 WRIGHT, Harold P.
"Chestnut Tree" (tr. of Tamura Ryuichi). NewYQ (10) Spr 72, p. 70.
"Night Jazz" (tr. of Tanikawa Shuntaro). NewYQ (9) Wint 72, p. 59.

3542 WRIGHT, James
"Bologna: A Poem About Gold." Esq (78:6) D 72, p. 50.
"Prayer to the Good Poet." NewYorker (48:34) 14 O 72, p. 42.
"Well, What Are You Going to Do?" Nat (215:20) 18 D 72, p. 630.

3543 WRIGHT, Jay
"The Appearance of a Lost Goddess." Works (3:3/4) Wint 72-73, p. 20.
"The Desert Revival." JnlOBP (2:16) Sum 72, p. 50.
"Jason Visits His Gypsy." Works (3:3/4) Wint 72-73, p. 19.
"Sources" (5). HangL (18) Fall 72, p. 57.
"Sources" (4). HangL (18) Fall 72, p. 56.
"Sources" (6). HangL (18) Fall 72, p. 57.
"Sources" (3). HangL (18) Fall 72, p. 55.
"Sources" (2). HangL (18) Fall 72, p. 53.

3544 WRIGHT, Richard
Ten Haiku. NewL (39:1) Aut 72, p. 82.

3545 WU Tsao
"For the Courtesan Ch'ing Lin, To the Tune 'The Love of the Immortals'" (tr. by Ling Chung and Kenneth Rexroth). NewYQ (12) Aut 72, p. 43.

3546 WYATT, Charles
"The Fish's Head." UTR (1:3) 72, p. 13.
"I Heard Again Words." UTR (1:2) 72, p. 28.

3547 WYLIE, Robert
"Brenda." PoetL (67:2) Sum 72, p. 143.

3548 WYNDHAM, Harald
"The Anarchist's Letter." Drag (3:2) Sum 72, p. 55.
"In Memory of HPW." Drag (3:2) Sum 72, p. 55.
"Upon Seeing Two Pictures of Dorothy Pound." Drag (3:2) Sum 72, p. 55.

3549 WYSE, Lois
"But the Motor's Still Good." Cosmo (172:1) Ja 72, p. 137.
"I Still Love You." LadHJ (89:8) Ag 72, p. 50.
"Just Because I Share Your Name Does Not Mean I Share Your Opinion." LadHJ (89:7) Jl 72, p. 96.
"Talkative." Cosmo (172:1) Ja 72, p. 72.
"The Thing About Southern Women." LadHJ (89:5) My 72, p. 80.
"Under False Lashes." LadHJ (89:10) O 72, p. 94.
"With a Twist of Truth." LadHJ (89:9) S 72, p. 182.

3550 X, Carlin
"The Last Days." JnlOBP (2:16) Sum 72, p. 9.

3551 XABA, Nomusa
"In the Time To Come." JnlOBP (2:16) Sum 72, p. 26.

3552 YAKUBU, Yakie
"If." JnlOBP (2:16) Sum 72, p. 17.
"Let Yo Spirit Go." JnlOBP (2:16) Sum 72, p. 77.
"On May 19, 1971." JnlOBP (2:16) Sum 72, p. 78.

3553 YANG Wan-li
"Going to Hsieh's Lake by Boat" (tr. by Jonathan Chaves). Madem (75:6) O 72, p. 136.
"Poems of Yang Wan-li" (tr. by Jonathan Chaves). Hudson (25:3) Aut 72, p. 403.

3554 YATES, Peter
"In the Fourth Year of Nixon." AS (9:2) Sum-Fall 72, p. 275.

3555 YETMAN, Lesley
"your strength." LitR (15:3) Spr 72, p. 252.

3556 YEVTUSHENKO, Yevgeny
"Bombs Against Art" (tr. by Bernard Koten). NewWR (40:1) Wint 72, p. 32.
"Smog" (tr. by John Updike, w. Albert C. Todd). NewYQ (10) Spr 72, p. 75.
"Verlaine" (tr. by Max Oppenheimer, Jr.). ColQ (21:2) Aut 72, p. 223.

3557 YOUNG, Al
"Not Her, She Aint No Gypsy." Works (3:3/4) Wint 72-73, p. 30.

3558 YOUNG, Clemewell
"Dream." PoetL (67:2) Sum 72, p. 142.
"Last Refuge." PoetL (67:2) Sum 72, p. 176.
"My Father's Hands." PoetL (67:4) Wint 72, p. 404.
"Newspaper Assignment." PoetL (67:2) Sum 72, p. 179.
"Out a New Hampshire Window." PoetL (67:2) Sum 72, p. 174.

3559 YOUNG, D. R.
"Going Back to New York for R and R." AbGR (3:1) Spr-Sum 72, p. 23.
"Ultramarine Sleep." AbGR (3:1) Spr-Sum 72, p. 22.

3560 YOUNG, David
"A Calendar: The Beautiful Names of the Months." Madrona (1:4) S 72, p. 21.
"Chromos." Antaeus (6) Sum 72, p. 86.
"Conversations Among Mountains" (tr. of Li Po). Madrona (1:4) S 72, p. 12.
"February." Madrona (1:1) Je 71, p. 30.
"Fifth Elegy" (tr. of Rainer Maria Rilke). Field (7) Fall 72, p. 24.
"For Tu Fu" (tr. of Li Po). Madrona (1:4) S 72, p. 14.
"Goodbye at the River" (tr. of Li Po). Madrona (1:4) S 72, p. 17.
"Hearing You Read." Madrona (1:4) S 72, p. 18.
"High in the Mountains, I Fail to Find the Wise Man" (tr. of Li Po). Madrona (1:4) S 72, p. 13.
"Homing." OhioR (13:2) Wint 72, p. 38.
"In the City on Business I Meet One Friend and We Spend the Night Eating and Drinking at the House of Another" (tr. of Tu Fu). NewL (38:3) Spr 72, p. 46.
"In the Middle of December." Madrona (1:4) S 72, p. 19.
"Mandelstam." Antaeus (6) Sum 72, p. 89.
"Many" (tr. of Hilde Domin). Field (6) Spr 72, p. 19.
"Ohio." PoetryNW (13:2) Sum 72, p. 18.
"A Project for Freight Trains." AmerR (15) 72, p. 100.
"She Thinks of Him" (tr. of Li Po). Madrona (1:4) S 72,

p. 16.
"Sixth Elegy" (tr. of Rainer Maria Rilke). Field (7) Fall 72, p. 33.
"Teddy Roosevelt." Madrona (1:4) S 72, p. 20.
"Thinking of My Brothers on a Moonlit Night" (tr. of Tu Fu). NewL (38:3) Spr 72, p. 48.
"Third Elegy" (tr. of Rainer Maria Rilke). Field (6) Spr 72, p. 63.
"Waking Up Drunk on a Spring Day" (tr. of Li Po). Madrona (1:4) S 72, p. 15.

3561 YOUNG, Geoffrey
"Grandmother Young." Meas (1) 71.
"Martin Luther King, April 5, 1968: apologies to Frank O'Hara." Cord (1:3) 72, p. 5.
"28. XI. 68." Meas (1) 71.

3562 YOUNG, George M., Jr.
"Three Lectures on the Skeleton." Granite (2) Wint 71-72, p. 39.

3563 YOUNG, Karl
"the red road." RoadAR (3:4) Wint 71-72, p. 17.

3564 YOUNG, Shellie
"A Mutual Understanding." Drag (3:1) Spr 72, p. 73.

3565 YOUNG, Steven C.
"Clapping Song." Kayak (29) S 72, p. 24.
"Skip-Rope Rhyme." Kayak (29) S 72, p. 24.

3566 YOUNG, Virginia Brady
"Anachronism." KanQ (4:2) Spr 72, p. 58.
"A Couple of Facts." HiramPoR (12) Spr-Sum 72, p. 29.
"January Tree." HiramPoR (12) Spr-Sum 72, p. 27.
"Kailua, Hawaii." Qt (5:37) Wint 72, p. 27.
"Present Perfect." HiramPoR (12) Spr-Sum 72, p. 28.
"To the Man in Charge of Cablegrams." SouthernHR (6:3) Sum 72, p. 286.
"Two Haiku." Northeast Sum 72, p. 30.

3567 YVONNE
"Poems." Aphra (3:3) Sum 72, p. 29.
"2 A.M." Aphra (3:3) Sum 72, p. 28.

3568 ZACH, Nathan
"I Sit at the Edge of the Street" (tr. by Adam Gillon). Books (46:2) Spr 72, p. 249.

3569 ZADE, Wayne
"The Flying Dutchman." Poetry (121:3) D 72, p. 148.
"House." Peb (7) Aut 71.
"The Hunter." Poetry (121:3) D 72, p. 147.

"My Brother Comes Home From School on His Birthday." Peb (7) Aut 71.
"Trade Expectations." Poetry (121:3) D 72, p. 147.

3570 ZAGOREN, Ruby
"Sing to Me." LadHJ (89:6) Je 72, p. 58.

3571 ZAHLER, Leah
"Collective." Aphra (3:4) Fall 72, p. 29.

3572 ZAISS, David
"A Figment of Fire-Breathing." PoetryNW (13:4) Wint 72-73, p. 13.
"The Syllabus." PoetryNW (13:4) Wint 72-73, p. 15.
"Word Labeling." PoetryNW (13:4) Wint 72-73, p. 14.

3573 ZALESKI, Jan
"Father." PoetryNW (13:4) Wint 72-73, p. 38.

3574 ZAMBARAS, Vassilis
"Decisions" (tr. of Dimitrios Potamitis). Madrona (1:1) Je 71, p. 28.
"The New Light" (tr. of Dimitrios Potamitis). Madrona (1:1) Je 71, p. 33.

3575 ZANDER, William
"Chinese Restaurant." Madrona (1:3) My 72, p. 31.
"Darkroom." Madrona (1:3) My 72, p. 29.
"May 16, 1971." RoadAR (3:4) Wint 71-72, p. 34.
"Passed My Hearing Test." RoadAR (3:4) Wint 71-72, p. 35.
"The Storm." Kayak (28) 72, p. 47.

3576 ZANZOTTO, Andrea
from La Belta: "In a Foolish History of Vampires" (tr. by Patrick Creagh). MedR (2:4) Sum 72, p. 97.
from IX Ecloghe: "Through the New Window" (tr. by Patrick Creagh). MedR (2:4) Sum 72, p. 95.

3577 ZARANKA, William
"Auden's Quicksands." DenQuart (7:2) Sum 72, p. 17.
"Berryman's Ode." DenQuart (7:2) Sum 72, p. 16.
"The Cropdusting of James Dickey." DenQuart (7:2) Sum 72, p. 14.
"Memories of Robert Lowell's Aunt Maria-Martha." DenQuart (7:2) Sum 72, p. 16.
"Richard Wilbur's Conceit Upon the Feet." DenQuart (7:2) Sum 72, p. 18.
"Robert Creeley in the Ladies' Room at the Bus Terminal." DenQuart (7:2) Sum 72, p. 19.

3578 ZAWADIWSKY, Christine
"Bringing in the Sheep (for Christian)." PoetC (7:1) 72,

p. 6.
"Christmas." Epoch (21:2) Wint 71, p. 159.
"Flying." WindO (11) Aut 72, p. 30.
"In grade school there were boys with thick." Folio (8:1) Spr 72, p. 38.
"Innuendos." StoneD (1:1) Spr 72, p. 56.
"Not This." Epoch (21:2) Wint 71, p. 158.
"Then We'll All Come Out." StoneD (1:1) Spr 72, p. 56.

3579 ZEGERS, Kip
"I am stuck to a kitchen chair." New:ACP (19) Aut 72, p. 38.

3580 ZEISER, Keith
"Papa." WestR (9:2) Wint 72, p. 34.

3581 ZEITZ, Gray
"Life Songs." Wind (2:6) Aut 72, p. 56.
"Moon Song" (for Richard). Wind (2:5) Sum 72, p. 49.

3582 ZELLIKOFF, Louis
Three Poems (tr. of Rasul Gamzatov). NewWR (40:4) Aut 72, p. 151.

3583 ZENAKOS, Leonidas
"Amulet" (tr. by James Damaskos). AriD (1:4/5) Sum-Aut 72, p. 118.
"Anunciation" (tr. by James Damaskos). AriD (1:4/5) Sum-Aut 72, p. 121.
"Eternal" (tr. by James Damaskos). AriD (1:4/5) Sum-Aut 72, p. 121.
from Glossary: (II, III) (tr. by George Economou and Stratis Haviaras). AriD (1:4/5) Sum-Aut 72, p. 119.

3584 ZIMMER, Paul
"Sonnet: Organic Form and Final Meaning in the Plumèd Zimmer." PoetryNW (13:1) Spr 72, p. 36.
"Zimmer Imagines His Ancestors." PoetryNW (13:1) Spr 72, p. 35.

3585 ZIMMERMAN, Eleanor B.
"Civilized Countries Do Not Continuously Make Music." BeyB (3:1) 72, p. 39.

3586 ZIMMERMAN, Toni
"Courage Is Like Perhaps." KanQ (4:1) Wint 71-72, p. 68.

3587 ZINNES, Harriet
"Rose Window." Nat (214:20) 15 My 72, p. 631.

3588 ZIVKOVIC, Peter D.
"After So Many Years." CarlMis (12:2) Spr-Sum 72,

p. 117.
"An Animal Note to the Middle Aged." Epos (24:1) Fall 72, p. 8.
"Cinder Street Love in Hammerville (for John Carr)." Poem (16) N 72, p. 40.
"Death Came in Tucson at 8:50." Poem (16) N 72, p. 43.
"Grecian Lady." ChiR (23:3) Wint 72, p. 84.
"Midwest." Poem (15) Jl 72, p. 36.
"Missionary." ChiTM 26 N 72, p. 67.
"Singing Sisters (for Ilene Newcomer)." ChiTM 30 Jl 72, p. 11.
"Swear That You'll Always Despise Me." LitR (16:1) Aut 72, p. 126.
"Wallenda." SoCaR (4:2) Je 72, p. 2.
"Warrior Son." Poem (16) N 72, p. 44.

3589 ZOHN, Ann E.
"Regret." WestR (9:2) Wint 72, p. 80.

3590 ZOLYNAS, Al
"The Pacific Slides Up the Beaches of the West Coast." WestR (9:1) Spr 72, p. 22.

3591 ZOUMBOULAKIS, Nikos
"Give Me a Place to Stand" (tr. by Athan Anagnostopoulos). AriD (1:4/5) Sum-Aut 72, p. 123.
"Root" (tr. by Athan Anagnostopoulos). AriD (1:4/5) Sum-Aut 72, p. 124.
"Unknown Words" (tr. by Athan Anagnostopoulos). AriD (1:4/5) Sum-Aut 72, p. 122.

3592 ZU-BOLTON, Ahmos II
"Of Berryman." Cafe (4) Fall 72, p. 9.

3593 ZUCKER, David H.
"March." Pan (9) 72, p. 54.
"Origin Obscure." Pan (9) 72, p. 52.
"Thunderbolt." Shen (23:4) Sum 72, p. 46.

3594 ZUCKER, J.
"Searching Through the Sink or The Last Dead Animal Poem." Folio (8:1) Spr 72, p. 20.

3595 ZUCKER, Jack
"Beginnings (for my mother)." SouthernPR (12:2) Spr 72, p. 10.

3596 ZWEIG, Martha MacNeal
"Counting Colors." LitR (16:1) Aut 72, p. 50.
"Gregor Samsa." BeyB (2:2) 72, p. 39.
"The Hill." Epoch (22:1) Fall 72, p. 47.
"Scraps." LitR (16:1) Aut 72, p. 48.
"Watch." BeyB (2:2) 72, p. 39.

"You Get Up Too." BelPoJ (22:3) Spr 72, p. 2.

3597 ZWEIG, Paul
"Liberation Manual." Iowa (3:4) Fall 72, p. 4.
"Night Song." Poetry (120:3) Je 72, p. 152.

3598 ZWINGER, Susan
"Deckers." Poetry (119:6) Mr 72, p. 324.
"Driving It West (for Richard Hugo)." Poetry (119:6) Mr 72, p. 323.
"To Drown Here (To B. B.)." NoAmR (257:3) Aut 72, p. 25.
"To the Mad Gardener of Solon." NoAmR (257:3) Aut 72, p. 27.

3599 ZYDEK, Fredrick
"When You Run Away In Words." Etc. (29:4) D 72, p. 386.

INDEX OF POEMS